IMMERSIVE VIDEO TECHNOLOGIES

IMMERSIVE VIDEO TECHNOLOGIES

Edited by

GIUSEPPE VALENZISE
Université Paris-Saclay, CNRS, CentraleSupélec
Laboratoire des signaux et systèmes
Gif-sur-Yvette, France

MARTIN ALAIN
Huawei Ireland Research Centre
Dublin, Ireland

EMIN ZERMAN
STC Research Center
Mid Sweden University
Sundsvall, Sweden

CAGRI OZCINAR
Samsung R&D UK
London, United Kingdom

ACADEMIC PRESS
An imprint of Elsevier

ELSEVIER

Academic Press is an imprint of Elsevier
125 London Wall, London EC2Y 5AS, United Kingdom
525 B Street, Suite 1650, San Diego, CA 92101, United States
50 Hampshire Street, 5th Floor, Cambridge, MA 02139, United States
The Boulevard, Langford Lane, Kidlington, Oxford OX5 1GB, United Kingdom

Notices

ISBN: 978-0-323-91755-1

For information on all Academic Press publications
visit our website at https://www.elsevier.com/books-and-journals

Publisher: Mara Conner
Acquisitions Editor: Tim Pitts
Editorial Project Manager: Howi M. De Ramos
Production Project Manager: Prem Kumar Kaliamoorthi
Cover Designer: Vicky Pearson Esser

Typeset by VTeX

Working together
to grow libraries in
developing countries

www.elsevier.com • www.bookaid.org

Contents

PART 4 Volumetric video

List of contributors

Ali Ak
Nantes Université, École Centrale Nantes, CNRS, LS2N, UMR 6004, Nantes, France
IPI, LS2N, Nantes University, Nantes, France

Martin Alain
Huawei Ireland Research Centre, Dublin, Ireland

Faouzi Alaya Cheikh
The Department of Computer Science, The Norwegian University of Science and Technology, Gjøvik, Norway

Evangelos Alexiou
DIS, Centrum Wiskunde en Informatica, Amsterdam, the Netherlands

Federica Battisti
Department of Information Engineering, University of Padova, Padova, Italy

Michel Bätz
Fraunhofer Institute for Integrated Circuits IIS, Erlangen, Germany

Marco Cagnazzo
LTCI, Télécom Paris, Institut polytechnique de Paris, Palaiseau, France
Department of Information Engineering, University of Padua, Padua, Italy

Pablo Cesar
Centrum Wiskunde en Informatica, Amsterdam, the Netherlands
DIS, Centrum Wiskunde en Informatica, Amsterdam, the Netherlands
Multimedia Computing, TU Delft, Delft, the Netherlands
Delft University of Technology, Delft, the Netherlands

Fang-Yi Chao
V-SENSE, Trinity College, The University of Dublin, Dublin, Ireland

Kelvin Chelli
Saarland Informatics Campus, Saarbruecken, Germany

Siheng Chen
Shanghai Jiao Tong University, Shanghai, China

Simone Croci
Trinity College, The University of Dublin, Dublin, Ireland

Frédéric Dufaux
Université Paris-Saclay, CNRS, CentraleSupélec, Laboratoire des signaux et systèmes, Gif-sur-Yvette, France

Peter Eisert
Fraunhofer HHI, Berlin, Germany
Humboldt University Berlin, Berlin, Germany

Ingo Feldmann
Fraunhofer HHI, Berlin, Germany

Laura Fink
Fraunhofer Institute for Integrated Circuits IIS, Erlangen, Germany

Siegfried Fößel
Fraunhofer Institute for Integrated Circuits IIS, Erlangen, Germany

Søren Forchhammer
Technical University of Denmark, Kgs. Lyngby, Denmark

Stephan Fremerey
Ilmenau University of Technology, Ilmenau, Germany

Patrick Garus
Orange Labs, Guyancourt, France

Florian Goldmann
Fraunhofer Institute for Integrated Circuits IIS, Erlangen, Germany

Danillo Graziosi
Sony Corporation of America, San Jose, CA, United States

Alan Guedes
Department of Electrical & Electrical Engineering, UCL, London, United Kingdom

Muhammad Shahzeb Khan Gul
Fraunhofer Institute for Integrated Circuits IIS, Erlangen, Germany

Cornelius Hellge
Fraunhofer HHI, Berlin, Germany

Volker Helzle
Filmakademie Baden-Württemberg, Ludwigsburg, Germany

Thorsten Herfet
Saarland Informatics Campus, Saarbruecken, Germany

Anna Hilsmann
Fraunhofer HHI, Berlin, Germany

Tobias Jaschke
Fraunhofer Institute for Integrated Circuits IIS, Erlangen, Germany

Joël Jung
Tencent Media Lab, Palo Alto, CA, United States

Joachim Keinert
Fraunhofer Institute for Integrated Circuits IIS, Erlangen, Germany

Maja Krivokuća
InterDigital INC, Cesson-Sévigné, France

Guillaume Lavoué
Origami, LIRIS, Lyon University, Lyon, France

Pierre Lebreton
NTT Network Service Systems Laboratories, Tokyo, Japan

Patrick Le Callet
Nantes Université, École Centrale Nantes, CNRS, LS2N, UMR 6004, Nantes, France
IPI, LS2N, Nantes University, Nantes, France

Mikael Le Pendu
Inria, Rennes, France

Jie Li
EPAM Systems, Hoofddrop, the Netherlands
Centrum Wiskunde en Informatica, Amsterdam, the Netherlands

Jingyu Liu
Technical University of Denmark, Kgs. Lyngby, Denmark

Claire Mantel
Technical University of Denmark, Kgs. Lyngby, Denmark

Rafał K. Mantiuk
University of Cambridge, Cambridge, United Kingdom

Jean-Eudes Marvie
InterDigital INC, Cesson-Sévigné, France

Thomas Maugey
Inria, Rennes, France

Marta Milovanović

Orange Labs, Guyancourt, France

LTCI, Télécom Paris, Institut polytechnique de Paris, Palaiseau, France

Yana Nehmé

Origami, LIRIS, Lyon University, Lyon, France

Néill O'Dwyer

V-SENSE, School of Computer Science and Statistics, Trinity College Dublin, Dublin, Ireland

Cagri Ozcinar

Samsung UK, London, United Kingdom

Rafael Palomar

The Department of Computer Science, The Norwegian University of Science and Technology, Gjøvik, Norway

The Intervention Centre, Oslo University Hospital, Oslo, Norway

Jiahao Pang

InterDigital, New York, NY, United States

Egidijus Pelanis

The Intervention Centre, Oslo University Hospital, Oslo, Norway

Institute of Clinical Medicine, University of Oslo, Oslo, Norway

Nico Prappacher

Fraunhofer Institute for Integrated Circuits IIS, Erlangen, Germany

Rahul Prasanna Kumar

The Intervention Centre, Oslo University Hospital, Oslo, Norway

Maurice Quach

Université Paris-Saclay, CNRS, CentraleSupélec, Laboratoire des signaux et systèmes, Gif-sur-Yvette, France

Alexander Raake

Ilmenau University of Technology, Ilmenau, Germany

Audiovisual Technology Group, Ilmenau University of Technology, Ilmenau, Germany

Silvia Rossi

Department of Electrical & Electrical Engineering, UCL, London, United Kingdom

Oliver Schreer

Fraunhofer HHI, Berlin, Germany

Ashutosh Singla

Ilmenau University of Technology, Ilmenau, Germany

Aljosa Smolic
Trinity College, The University of Dublin, Dublin, Ireland
V-SENSE, School of Computer Science and Statistics, Trinity College Dublin, Dublin, Ireland

Milan Stepanov
Université Paris-Saclay, CNRS, CentraleSupélec, Laboratoire des signaux et systèmes, Gif-sur-Yvette, France

Dong Tian
InterDigital, New York, NY, United States

Laura Toni
Department of Electrical & Electrical Engineering, UCL, London, United Kingdom

Giuseppe Valenzise
Université Paris-Saclay, CNRS, CentraleSupélec, Laboratoire des signaux et systèmes, Gif-sur-Yvette, France

Irene Viola
Centrum Wiskunde en Informatica, Amsterdam, the Netherlands
DIS, Centrum Wiskunde en Informatica, Amsterdam, the Netherlands

Congcong Wang
The Engineering Research Center of Learning-Based Intelligent System, Ministry of Education, and the School of Computer Science and Engineering, Tianjin University of Technology, Tianjin, China

Gareth W. Young
V-SENSE, School of Computer Science and Statistics, Trinity College Dublin, Dublin, Ireland

Jin Zeng
Tongji University, Shanghai, China

Emin Zerman
STC Research Center, Mid Sweden University, Sundsvall, Sweden

Fangcheng Zhong
University of Cambridge, Cambridge, United Kingdom

Matthias Ziegler
Fraunhofer Institute for Integrated Circuits IIS, Erlangen, Germany

Preface

In the past decades, digital video experiences have been continuously evolving towards a higher degree of immersion and realism. This development has been possible thanks to a number of technological advances. New acquisition and display devices enable capturing and rendering of video with unprecedented realism, through technologies such as Ultra High Definition (UHD), High Frame Rate (HFR), High Dynamic Range (HDR), and Wide Color Gamut (WCG). Wireless networks such as 5G and future 6G promise to deliver broadband communications and ultra low-latency (1 ms) to support telepresence in future applications such as *tactile Internet*. On the processing side, the advent of powerful graphic processing units (GPU) with massive parallelization have facilitated the surge of sophisticated image processing, computer vision and machine learning methods. Thanks to these new tools, it is possible to capture the content of a scene beyond the capabilities of the acquisition sensor, leading to computational photography and new rendering techniques. Visualization and interaction devices such as head-mounted displays (HMD), glasses-free multiview (or light field) displays, and haptic interfaces start to hit the market. At the same time, video formats such as volumetric video that provide six-degrees-of-freedom interaction are being standardized. All together, these technologies will contribute to the development of the *metaverse*, a set of perpetual and concurrent virtual spaces implementing various forms of *extended reality* (XR).

In this context, immersive video technologies enable new ways of visual communication and storytelling. The applications of immersive video are numerous and go beyond entertainment: they include interactions with objects and robots, tele-surgery, collaborative working, virtual driving, serious games, remote assistance and therapy, and many other examples. Immersive video technologies represent a major step forward in video technology, and are attracting a growing interest from manufacturers and service providers, with the goal to enhance the quality of experience of users.

This book aims to provide an overview and introduction to these new immersive video technologies. Specifically, we address different stages in the content production and delivery chain from acquisition and representation, to coding, streaming, visualization and quality monitoring. The book focuses on three main immersive modalities: omnidirectional video, light fields, and volumetric video. While not necessarily covering all the possible immersive video formats, these modalities are representative of the main commercially available (or viable) solutions nowadays. Furthermore, they pave the way to future immersive technologies where the boundaries between modalities fade away and vanish. We have intentionally left out other traditional immersive video formats, such as stereo and multiview video which have been thoroughly studied before and for which we provide references to previous books and surveys whenever needed. We also do not examine holography. While holography is perhaps the ultimate form of immersive video, its deployment is still far from the consumer market, mainly due to optical and physical limitations. The interested reader can easily find dedicated books covering holography both from the optical and signal processing perspectives.

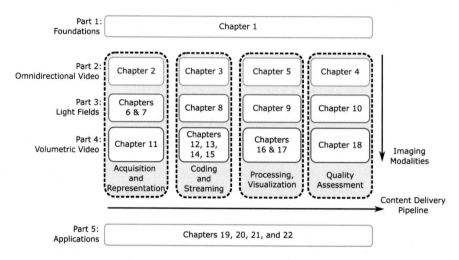

Figure 0.1 The organization of the book and the two main axes.

The organization of the book follows the two axes introduced above, as illustrated in Fig. 0.1: immersive video modalities on one hand, and stages of the content delivery pipeline on the other hand. There are three main immersive imaging modalities, which are reflected in the main book parts: Part 2 discusses the omnidirectional video (ODV) technologies; Part 3 focuses on light fields (LF); and Part 4 scrutinizes techniques for volumetric video (VV). The different stages of the content delivery pipeline are reflected in the different chapters for each part, and cover image acquisition and representation, coding and streaming, processing, visualization, and quality assessment. Part 1 and Part 5 are transversal, as they provide a general introduction and discuss different applications of immersive video, respectively. We describe the structure of the book in further detail in the following.

The foundational definitions regarding immersion and presence, which define immersive video, are discussed in Part 1. Chapter 1 is the only chapter in this part and provides the theoretical background for the modalities discussed in the book and definitions for the relevant terms that are necessary to understand the needs and the concepts of different immersive video technologies. The main stages of video content delivery chain are briefly explained, also laying out the limitations and challenges for immersive video.

Omnidirectional video and how it is captured, processed, transmitted, and used are discussed in Part 2. In Chapter 2, Maugey discusses existing omnidirectional video acquisition techniques including how ODVs are represented and rendered after acquisition. A multi-view ODV dataset capture is also discussed in the same chapter. Rossi, Guedes and Toni focus in Chapter 3 on the user behavior in consuming ODVs and the implications on ODV streaming systems. They also provide a comprehensive overview of the research efforts in this field. Croci, Singla, Fremeret, Raake, and Smolic deal with subjective and objective quality assessment for ODV in Chapter 4, discussing different methodologies. Finally, in Chapter 5, Chao, Battisti, Lebreton, and Raake discuss how to estimate visual saliency for ODVs, and how to collect visual attention data from observers.

Light fields are discussed in Part 3. This part starts with two chapters by Herfet, Chelli, and Le Pendu: Chapter 6 explains LF image and video acquisition; Chapter 7 presents different LF representations. Stepanov, Valenzise, and Dufaux discuss compression and transmission for LFs and describe the advances in JPEG Pleno standardization in Chapter 8. In Chapter 9, Keinert et al. discuss how LF can be captured, processed, and rendered for media applications, and how they can be integrated into a VR environment, as well as their quality enhancement through neural networks. Lastly, Ak and Le Callet present an overview of various subjective and objective factors affecting the Quality of Experience for LFs in Chapter 10.

Volumetric video (VV) is among the most compelling immersive technologies as it enables a full interaction between users and the scene. Part 4 regroups several volumetric video representations. This part starts with Chapter 11, where Eisert, Schreer, Feldmann, Hellge, and Hilsmann focus on various stages of VV acquisition, interaction, streaming and rendering, including interesting discussions on how to animate and make transformations on the volumetric content. In Chapter 12, Garus, Milovanović, Jung, and Cagnazzo present the MPEG Immersive Video (MPEG-I) coding standard, which is the successor of 3D-HEVC and implements a 2D-based texture-plus-depth scene representation for free viewpoint video. A native 3D representation is point clouds. The state-of-the-art techniques for point cloud compression, including available standards and recent learning-based approaches, are presented in Chapter 13 by Valenzise, Quach, Tian, Pang, and Dufaux. In Chapter 14, Marvie, Krivokuća, and Graziosi discuss another representation for VV that is more common in computer graphics, i.e., 3D dynamic meshes, and they provide a review of state-of-the-art dynamic mesh compression. In Chapter 15, Viola and Cesar offer an overview of the current approaches and implementations for VV streaming, focusing on both theoretical approaches and their adaptation to networks and users. In Chapter 16, Chen and Zheng discuss various processing methods that can be used to analyze, modify, and synthesize VVs for different tasks. Liu, Zhong, Mantel, Forchhammer, and Mantiuk describe the concept of computational 3D displays, underlying key performance factors from a visual perception point of view. Lastly, in Chapter 18, Alexiou and others present an overview of subjective and objective quality methods used for VVs in point cloud and 3D mesh formats.

Finally, Part 5 focuses on various applications that can benefit from immersive video technologies. In Chapter 19, Palomar, Kumar, Wang, Pelanis, and Cheikh describe how 3D organs models are used in mixed reality, after their digital twins are obtained by magnetic resonance and computed tomography scans. Helzle describes the use of light fields and immersive LED walls for visual effects in immersive media productions in Chapter 20. Young, O'Dwyer and Smolic discuss how volumetric video can be used as a novel medium for creative storytelling by describing some of the experiments conducted within the V-SENSE project in Chapter 21. In the last Chapter 22, Li and Cesar describe various social VR applications using immersive video technologies.

By covering the essential immersive video technologies in use today, this book has the ambition to become a reference for those interested in the fundamentals of immersive video, the various stages of the content lifespan, as well as the potential practical applications. Assuming basic knowledge on image and video processing, the book should be of interest to a broad audience with different backgrounds and expectations, including engineers, practitioners, researchers, as well as professors, graduate and undergraduate students, and managers making technological decisions about immersive video.

The Editors

Giuseppe Valenzise, Martin Alain, Emin Zerman, and Cagri Ozcinar

PART 1

Foundations

CHAPTER 1

Introduction to immersive video technologies

Martin Alain[a,e], **Emin Zerman**[b,e], **Cagri Ozcinar**[c], **and Giuseppe Valenzise**[d]
[a]Huawei Ireland Research Centre, Dublin, Ireland
[b]STC Research Center, Mid Sweden University, Sundsvall, Sweden
[c]Samsung UK, London, United Kingdom
[d]Université Paris-Saclay, CNRS, CentraleSupélec, Laboratoire des signaux et systèmes, Gif-sur-Yvette, France

Chapter points

- What is immersion
- Degrees of freedom
- The plenoptic function
- Immersive imaging modalities
- Immersive video content delivery pipeline

1.1. Introduction

Imaging technologies enable humankind to capture and store the visual information from real world scenes. Although traditionally images have been stored on physical media (e.g., photographic film), with the advent of digital image processing, we can capture, store, compress, and transmit images and videos digitally and in real time. This enabled *telepresence* by delivering the visual information to distant locations. The term telepresence refers to the "sense of being physically present at a remote location through interaction with the system's human interface" [1], a phenomenon that a human operator develops. The term *presence* is also coined for "being there" for other virtual environments [2], as well as *immersion*, for "concentration to the virtual environment instead of real world" [3]. Immersion is considered as one of the factors which are necessary for presence [4]. Therefore the technologies which try to provide a virtual presence are called *immersive* imaging technologies.

The state-of-the-art immersive video technologies extend the visual sensation, augment the viewer's "presence," and provide the viewer with a higher degree of freedom (DoF) than what traditional displays offer (see Fig. 1.1). The traditional imaging systems record the scene from only a single viewpoint selected by the content creator, which

---

[e] Martin Alain and Emin Zerman were with V-SENSE, Trinity College Dublin, Dublin, Ireland at the time of writing this chapter.

Immersive Video Technologies
https://doi.org/10.1016/B978-0-32-391755-1.00007-9
3

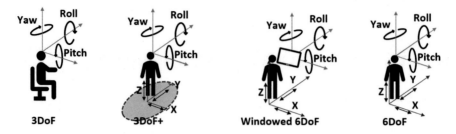

Figure 1.1 Increasing degrees of freedom (DoF) provides a more immersive experience.

provides essentially zero DoF, as the viewer does not have any freedom over the viewpoint selection. Instead, the immersive imaging systems can provide more than three DoF. 3DoF generally refers to the rotational movement (i.e., changes in yaw, roll, pitch angles), whereas 6DoF refers to both rotational and translational (e.g., changes in the location in 3D space) movement. 3DoF+ denotes a system that enables limited spatial movement in addition to unrestricted 3DoF rotational movement. Different imaging modalities make use of one or more of these DoF categories.

Recently, these imaging technologies gained a lot of interest in academia and industry, including standardization bodies (e.g., JPEG [5] and MPEG [6,7]), and it became a hot research topic. In this chapter, we introduce the main concepts underlying the two main axes of this book for immersive video technologies: three different imaging modalities and the stage in the content delivery pipeline. We also discuss the current challenges for immersive video technologies. Please note that we focus in this chapter and this book in general on imaging systems aiming at capturing and reproducing real-world scene, rather than computer generated content.

1.2. What is immersion?

This book focuses on how we capture, process, transmit, use, and perceive various immersive video technologies. However, before advancing any further, we should answer the first question our readers might have: *"What is immersion?"*. One can also ask another question in a different format: *"What makes a video immersive?"*.

To answer this question, we need to understand how immersion and other related terms are defined in the scientific literature by the cognition and virtual reality experts. The subsection that follows focuses on description and discussion of these definitions. We then define what immersion means in the context of immersive video, and we discuss which aspects are important to *make a video immersive*. In the next subsection, we also discuss how immersive video technologies relate to extended reality concepts.

1.2.1 Definitions

The concepts of presence and immersion are discussed in great detail by many scholars, including the ones working on human cognition, robotics, and virtual reality. In this section, we will describe the mainly used four terms that are relevant for the scope of this book: telepresence, presence, embodiment, and immersion.

Telepresence: *Telepresence* is the first term to be coined that is relevant to presence and other relevant terms. The term was coined as a response to the needs of the robotics community. The term describes the relationship between the human operator and the environment in which a remote machine is located, where the human operator would get a "sense of being physically present at a remote location through interaction with the system's human interface" [1]. The term was then adopted by the virtual reality community as well.

Presence: The term *presence* was initially referring to the "experience in natural surroundings," whereas telepresence was used for the experience in mediated environments [8]. In time, this distinction based on mediation of the environment was viewed unnecessary [2], and the term *presence* started to be used for both natural and mediated environments. It is defined as "being there" [8] or "perceptual illusion of nonmediation" [4] (i.e., as if the virtual environment was "real"). As one of the loaded terms among others, presence can have many different lenses to look from. Lombard & Ditton [4] identified six different viewpoints and aspects that define and affect presence. Immersion is described as one of these aspects. Presence is considered an essential element for immersive technologies [9].

Embodiment: Since it is used in virtual reality terminology, the term *embodiment* seems related to presence and immersion concepts. Nevertheless, the term embodiment relates to an avatar that represents the users' body in a virtual environment. This avatar can be either a photorealistic one or not. If the users of a virtual environment (or a virtual reality application) "embodies" the virtual avatar they are given, they can use the body for physical and social needs in the said virtual environment and do not experience any discomfort during their activities [10]. Currently, most of the applications for the considered immersive video modalities do not employ a virtual avatar, and there is little need to consider embodiment in most of the applications.

Immersion: The term *immersion* comes from the English word "immerse," meaning "to become completely involved in something" or "to put something or someone completely under the surface of a liquid" [11]. One of the earliest descriptions in the virtual reality literature describes it as "a term that refers to the degree to which a virtual environment submerges the perceptual system of the user in computer-generated stimuli" [8]. This is similar to covering over (or blocking) the users' senses (both physical and psychological; discussed more in the next subsection) with the virtual environment or virtual reality application. It is also mentioned that immersion can be measured; physical immersion can be measured by identifying number of senses that are covered by the environment and psychological immersion needs to be reported by the user [4].

1.2.2 Immersion

Immersion can be perceptual (i.e., physical or sensory) or psychological [4]. The sensory immersion is achieved by "shutting off" as many senses as possible, including sight (with head-mounted displays), hearing (with audio), touch (with haptics), smell and taste (with olfactory devices). On the other hand, psychological immersion can happen on the cognition level if the user is involved with the material enough and feels lost in the environment. Since immersion has both physical and psychological aspects, any number of interesting activities can achieve user immersion, including daydreaming, reading a book, and cinema (i.e., traditional video). Nevertheless, in this book, we only consider the video technologies that attempt at both physical and psychological immersion. That is, the users should see a different (or augmented) visual and feel present in the prepared environment.

We identified two aspects that are crucial in defining the immersive video technologies: realism and interactivity.

It is hard to define realism in one way since it is our brains that define what "real" is. Lombard & Ditton argue that there are two types of realism: social realism and perceptual realism [4]. Social realism is the type of realism that focuses on the conceptual relationships in the environment, especially between people or agents. Therefore a video game can be compelling or feel "real" to players, even though the avatars or objects in the game do not look as they do in real life. Perceptual realism, on the other hand, focuses on recreating the actual 3D world with highest fidelity, and the perceptual realism for visuals is sometimes called photorealism. Since the users can believe the environment is "real" with social realism, we understand and acknowledge that photorealism (or perceptual realism) is not necessary for immersion in video technologies. Nevertheless, since realism is a very important part of video technologies, the immersive video modalities in this book put a much heavier focus on perceptual realism.

The second aspect, interactivity, is also key in how video technologies become immersive. It is argued that interaction is a crucial element in perceiving a technological system as a social agent instead of hardware [4], which can be very important in achieving immersion. Recent immersive imaging systems enable and promote interaction in a far greater degree than traditional video, and this is also supported by new lightweight wearables, haptics controllers, and headsets. Furthermore, the low latency between users, which come with increased connection speeds, promotes much smoother user-to-user interaction.

1.2.3 Extended reality

With the help of advanced imaging and display technologies, humankind now can create alternative distinct realities, different from the actual real life we are living in. The early developments for "virtual" realities began after the displays could be made small enough so that an individual can use it to create a different environment. The concept of "suspension of disbelief" was already known to humankind for centuries in literary works, such as novels or drama. That is, the audience deliberately chooses to forget that the literary piece they are experiencing is not real and is fiction. The term was coined by an English poet, Samuel Taylor Coleridge, in 1817 [12], and its use (or re-use) in computer graphics and imaging systems were only possible after the medium was ready to create such virtual environments.

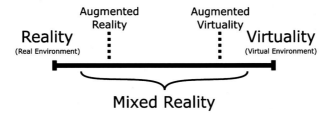

Figure 1.2 The reality-virtuality continuum suggested by Milgram et al. [13].

In 1995, Milgram et al. [13] suggested that the changes in reality can be shown on a spectrum (or a continuum), as shown on Fig. 1.2. On one end, our actual real environment is situated, and on the other hand the virtual environment is situated. With small changes and additions, the relationship between reality and virtuality can be changed. Adding virtual elements to reality, we obtain *"augmented reality"* systems, which augments (or improves) our reality with virtual elements. By adding real elements to virtuality, we can obtain *"augmented virtuality"* systems, which amend the virtual environment with elements from real world. Everything in between was described as mixed reality, as the systems lying on this part of the spectrum can have elements from both reality and virtuality.

The virtual reality term was popularized around the 1980s, even though the first attempts for virtual reality precede that time. Since the aim of creating the first virtual reality systems was to create an alternative reality to our own, the concept of presence was very important. So, the virtual reality community continued on developing the terminology that is discussed above. VR mainly focuses on creating new virtual environments for users to feel "presence" in by cutting their senses off the actual world.

Augmented reality, on the other hand, aims to build on top of the actual world and light from the real world to augment (or enhance) our experience in reality. These enhancements can be any form of modality, and for video technologies, it generally includes either a computer-generated imagery, text, or shapes with or without colors.

Extended reality is generally used as an umbrella term that refers to whole continuity spectrum (including augmented, virtual, and mixed realities) used in conjunction with equipment that allows capture & display of and interaction with the aspects of the said realities. The immersive video technologies can sometimes cover the real world (e.g., in the case of omnidirectional video; see Part 2), can be used to augment the reality with volumetric 3D media (e.g., volumetric video; see Part 4), or can be versatile and be used for all extended reality applications (e.g., light fields; see Part 3).

Metaverse is also a popular concept and term that attracts a lot of attention nowadays. Although there are different viewpoints and definitions, one definition of metaverse can be considered as "an immersive Internet as a gigantic, unified, persistent, and shared realm" [14]. As this concept aims to bring all digital assets under a united umbrella, immersive video technologies will be important as much as other extended reality technologies. Nevertheless, metaverse is not discussed further in the book.

In the next section, we discuss how immersion is used for video technologies and different imaging modalities covered in this book.

1.3. Immersive video

In this section, we first start with the description of a foundational technical concept: the plenoptic function, which describes the light rays in space. We then briefly mention the historical perspective and evaluation of how video has been becoming immersive. Finally, we describe which imaging modalities are discussed within the scope of this book.

1.3.1 Foundations: the plenoptic function

Traditional imaging technologies focus on projecting the 3D world onto a 2D plane, and they are designed to acquire and display visual media from a fixed viewpoint. Immersive video technologies, on the other hand, aim to allow users to immerse themselves in the presented visual media by providing a more thorough reconstruction of the 3D world. The new immersive technologies vastly change the view-scape compared to traditional video displays, as illustrated in Fig. 1.3.

To formulate the acquisition processes, we can consider light as a field and assume that the 7-dimensional plenoptic function $P(\theta, \phi, \lambda, t, x, y, z)$ describes all possible visible light [15], considering every location x, y, z, every angle θ, ϕ, each wavelength λ, and each time instant t, as shown in Fig. 1.4. The plenoptic function remains a theoretical concept, which immersive imaging modalities aim to replicate or approximate, based on some assumptions, for example, the radiance of a light ray remains constant along its path through empty space. Though remaining a theoretical concept, its study has led to the development of the broad image-based rendering (IBR) field, whose goal is to capture images of the real world such that they can then be used to render novel images

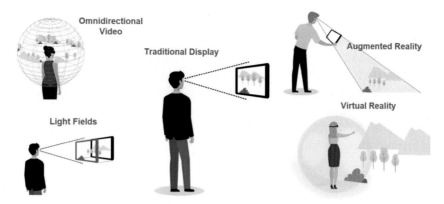

Figure 1.3 The immersive imaging modalities provide additional degrees of freedom compared to traditional display.

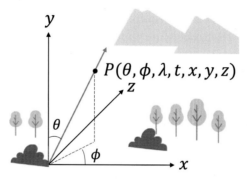

Figure 1.4 The 7D plenoptic function measures the intensity of light seen from any point in space (x, y, z), any angular viewing direction (θ, ϕ), over time (t), for each wavelength (λ).

corresponding to different viewpoints, hence achieving 6DoF in a virtual reproduction of a real world scene. Note that taking into account the viewing direction allows capturing and reproducing subtle lighting effects, such as reflections and non-specularities. As discussed above, increasing the DoF is a key feature of immersive imaging systems. Thus, to some extent, we can consider that all imaging modalities discussed are subsampling the plenoptic function.

1.3.2 Historical perspective and evolution

During the evolution of digital imaging technologies, how images and video are represented always changed. This started with improving the acquisition and display frame rate, at first for the black-and-white (or rather grayscale) images. Following this, introduction of sound to videos and introduction of color always increased the power of video on "suspending the disbelief."

In our search to increase the immersiveness, stereo 3D was developed, which created an intense hype during the 1950s. At first anaglyph projection systems (which is not ideal for color representations) and light polarization were used at cinemas. Around the 1970s, the active shutter systems were developed. Advances in display technologies in the 1980s and 1990s also made glasses-free 3D perception by a technique called autostereoscopy possible in consumer electronics and household TV sets.

It can be noticed that the public's interest in these technologies follows a wave pattern that is similar to the Gartner hype cycle. Whenever there is a new technology, a very prominent expectation wave comes. However, this wave then fades until the technology advances enough to produce capable devices to realize what was imagined. Then, this creates a new expectation wave for more advanced technologies. The above history of stereoscopic 3D shows an example of this. Similarly, the first virtual reality headsets were developed in the 1980s, and virtual reality (or at least the idea of alternative/virtual realities) became popular. Until recently, virtual reality was not prominent in the public eye since there were no equipment affordable by the consumers. With the new affordable headsets, VR has become popular again as people can now buy and keep a headset at their homes.

Similarly, other immersive technologies came to fruition recently. Light fields were first discussed in the 1990s, but until now there were not many applications possible due to physical and computational limitations. Similarly the idea of volumetric video was around since the 70s, which was popularized by R2D2's projection of Princess Leia on Star Wars. Recent advances in image acquisition, processing capabilities, deep learning techniques, and display technologies make realization of immersive video technologies possible for 3DoF, 3DoF+, and 6DoF applications.

On the other hand, computer graphics has been exploring virtual visual content creation and 6DoF rendering since its beginning. This was possible, thanks to having no physical limitations that forbade capturing light (or simulated light) going towards any direction. Though originally designed to represent computer-generated objects and scene, typically using polygons to represent the geometry and texture map images to represent the appearance, the tools developed in the computer graphics field can be useful for representing immersive imaging content. Indeed, such tools have been optimized for years for efficiency and visual quality. Once the scene geometry and objects are known, efficient rendering algorithms can be used (which include hardware acceleration) to render images corresponding to the desired viewport direction and orientation. Though particularly relevant for volumetric videos, which relies on geometric representations such as point clouds or textured meshes, omnidirectional videos and light fields have also benefited from rendering tools first developed in the computer graphics field. Furthermore, when considering immersive video technologies, geometry and appearance are not computer-generated, but rather estimated from images of a real-world scene.

1.3.3 Imaging modalities

Considering what is discussed above for the immersiveness of video technologies, one can identify many imaging (which includes display as well) modalities. The following modalities can be considered among immersive video technologies, as they enrich the traditional video and provide a more realistic or immersive experience: high dynamic range (HDR) video, high frame rate (HFR) video, stereoscopic (or multiview) video, hologram technology, omnidirectional video, light fields, and volumetric video.

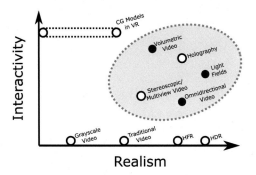

Figure 1.5 A comparison of interactivity and realism aspects of various modalities of video technologies.

These modalities do increase the realism or sense of presence through their unique ways. Nevertheless, referring to our discussion on realism and interactivity in Section 1.2.2, we can consider the interactivity vs. realism graph, as shown in Fig. 1.5. Some of the modalities mentioned above have high realism, but they might not have high interactivity, for example, HDR and HFR technologies. On the other hand, the low-polygon computer graphics models in virtual reality applications are very interactive, but they lack realism. Taking only the modalities with high interactivity and high realism, we end up with five main imaging modalities: multiview video, holography, omnidirectional video, light fields, and volumetric video.

Since both multiview video and holography have been thoroughly studied in the past in many scientific articles and books, this book only focuses on three main imaging modalities: omnidirectional video, light fields, and volumetric video. Each of these imaging modalities are briefly discussed below, and each have a part of several chapters in this book.

1.3.4 Omnidirectional imaging

Omnidirectional imaging systems [16,17] capture different viewing angles over time. Typically, the 360-degree camera is fixed in space, and it captures the world around the camera. Therefore the 7D plenoptic function becomes 2D: $P(\theta, \phi)$ (3D for omnidirectional video). Ideally, all the rays coming from different parts from the sphere are captured. However, in practice, there are physical limitations, such as parts that cannot be captured well (e.g., north and south poles of the sphere, as either of the poles are generally used for the handle that keeps the cameras together) or the need to stitch visual from various cameras placed.

1.3.5 Light field imaging

Light field has the broadest definition of all these imaging modalities as it aims to consider the light as a field, much similar to electromagnetic fields [18,19]. However, for practical reasons, it is mostly simplified. The most commonly used simplification is the two parallel planes parameterization of the 4D light field. In this context, the light rays are parameterized by their intersection with two parallel planes (a, b) and (x, y),[1] i.e., there is a one-to-one mapping between (a, b, x, y) and (x, y, θ, ϕ), and the 7D plenoptic function can be reduced to the 4D light field $L(a, b, x, y)$ for static scenes, as illustrated in Fig. 1.6. The time dimension t needs to be added when considering light field videos. Once captured, the original scene can be rendered for the user with realistic parallax, increasing the immersion, by giving the depth information to the viewer. Developments in the recent light field capturing systems [20] use spherical light field parametrization and show that the light field imaging systems can be utilized to capture and render panoramic scenes with 3DoF+. This illustrates that the different modalities presented in this chapter are part of a continuum rather than isolated concepts.

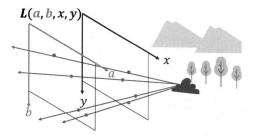

Figure 1.6 Light field imaging aims to consider the light as a field, much similar to electro-magnetic fields. However, for practical reasons, it is mostly simplified. The most commonly used simplification is the two parallel planes parameterization of the 4D light field. In this context, the light rays are parameterized by their intersection with two parallel planes (a, b) and (x, y).

1.3.6 Volumetric 3D imaging

Volumetric 3D imaging systems [21–23] retain most of the variables from the original 7D plenoptic function as the capture systems for this imaging modality needs capturing

---

[1] Note that the notations in this book differ from tradition light field notations (s, t, u, v), see Chapter 7.

from various angles around the object in focus. For this purpose, dedicated studios are built and cameras are placed around the edges of these studios to capture what is placed in the center. Although these dedicated studios are required for high-quality capture and content creation, it is also possible to make use of handheld cameras to capture volumetric content [23]. The static 3D contents and scenes can be captured casually using a single handheld camera, and multiple handheld cameras can be used for the capture of dynamic volumetric content outside dedicated studios.

A recent and fast growing trend is to use neural networks to represent a scene, called neural representation [24,25]. In such representation, the neural network typically serves as a continuous estimate of a function taking the position and orientation as input, and evaluating the corresponding scene color and transparency as output. Such representations enable high-quality 6DoF rendering. By using a differentiable rendering process, the neural network representing the scene can be trained from a set of calibrated input views.

1.4. Challenges in the processing and content delivery pipeline

Similar to traditional imaging pipelines, the immersive imaging pipeline starts with the image acquisition of the real-world objects. After the image acquisition, a processing step is generally required to transform the raw images into a desired representation. The content can then be compressed for storage or streaming. Unlike traditional 2D images, immersive video content is not meant to be visualized all at once by the user. This requires the design of specific rendering algorithms, streaming strategies, and/or dedicated visualization hardware. Finally, the quality of the novel immersive video content needs to be evaluated, knowing that this can be impacted by any of the previous steps.

1.4.1 Acquisition and representations

We saw in the previous section that the ability to provide an immersive imaging experience comes from the ability to sample the plenoptic function, in particular sampling light rays coming from multiple angles or directions. For this purpose, multiple acquisition devices and systems have been designed, which we review in this section.

1.4.1.1 Acquisition of 2D images and videos

As some of these systems rely on traditional 2D cameras, we first give here a reminder about traditional 2D cameras. As illustrated in Fig. 1.7, a 2D camera can be modeled by a main lens and an image sensor. Light rays emitted from objects in multiple directions are thus re-converged through the lens on the image sensor, which is similar to having one single ray combining the intensity of all rays going through the lens optical center. For this reason, 2D camera cannot directly capture immersive imaging content, as the angular information is lost. The pinhole camera model [26] is usually adopted for 2D

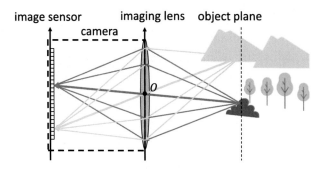

Figure 1.7 2D lens camera model. Light rays arriving from different angles are all integrated on the same pixel of the image sensor, as if a single ray was going through the optical center of the lens.

cameras. Such model is essential to make a connection between pixels and world coordinates. Precise calibration procedures are required to obtain accurate model parameters.

1.4.1.2 Acquisition of immersive imaging data

There are two main categories of systems designed to capture immersive imaging content with regular 2D cameras: either use a single camera, which is moved to capture different viewpoints of the scene or object of interests, or use multiple cameras rigged together and pointing in different directions. The first solution is usually simpler to implement, and allows for dense sampling of the plenoptic functions, as very close viewpoint images can be captured. However, it is by design limited to static scenes. To capture video contents, camera rigs have to be used, which are technically more challenging to implement and more expensive. It is also limited to a sparse sampling of the plenoptic function, as the camera casings mechanically prevent close viewpoints to be captured.

Existing systems adopt different camera geometries depending on the targeted immersive imaging modality: arranging outward looking cameras on a sphere can be used to capture omnidirectional videos or spherical light fields. Using inward looking cameras on a sphere can also be used to capture spherical light fields, and, in theory, volumetric videos. The most popular light field representation is based on the two parallel plane parameterization, which can be captured by arranging the cameras on a plane. Note that volumetric video usually does not impose any specific geometry on the camera positions, but does require the knowledge of the camera model parameters, i.e., for the pinhole camera model, intrinsics, and extrinsics parameters.

Some specific camera designs beyond the traditional 2D cameras have also been proposed. Early works on curved mirror-based cameras or using fisheye lenses have been proposed to capture omnidirectional videos. More recently, lenslet arrays have been added to regular cameras to capture light fields. Note that specific models have to be derived for such cameras. Ongoing research is being carried out which combines multiple of the specific camera designs presented above to increase the immersion and provide full 6DoF content, e.g., use an array of omnidirectional camera [27], or multiple plenoptic cameras [28]. One of the challenges of such systems is their calibration to obtain an accurate estimate of their model parameters, which is more difficult than for the 2D pinhole camera model.

1.4.1.3 *From raw data to content creation*

Following acquisition, the captured raw images need to be processed to create the target immersive content and fit the target modality representation. Different processing methods are needed depending on the immersive imaging modality.

Several low-level image processing steps are common to most modalities and extend the traditional 2D image processing techniques. This can include, debayering the raw image to obtain color RGB images, de-noising, or super-resolution. When creating immersive imaging content, additional care has to be taken to enforce the consistency of the processing among the different viewpoints. Furthermore, as mentioned in the previous section, a calibration step is often required to estimate the parameters of the model associated with the camera used for acquisition. Typically, parameters of the pinhole camera model for data captured with regular 2D cameras can be estimated using structure-from-motion (SfM) [26]. Calibration is also required for other processing methods, such as depth estimation. Depth estimation is an essential step of volumetric video content creation, but can also provide additional data for further post-production and processing tasks, especially for light fields or stereo omnidirectional imaging. The estimated depth can be useful for various computer vision tasks, such as segmentation, scene understanding, and view synthesis.

The different modalities discussed in this book may also require more specific processing. This typically includes stitching for omnidirectional imaging, rectifying the viewpoints images for light fields, and 3D reconstruction for volumetric imaging, as mentioned above.

As part of content generation stage, recent learning-based approaches allow to create novel neural representations for enhanced rendering operations.

1.4.2 Compression and transmission
1.4.2.1 *Compression of immersive videos*

Due to their massive data size, cost-efficient coding solutions are required to store and deliver immersive videos. The majority of existing immersive video coding solutions are based on the video coding standards: high-efficiency video coding (HEVC) [29] and versatile video coding (VVC). Each coding standard aims to achieve approximately 50% bitrate reduction over its predecessor coding standard. For instance, VVC has achieved up to 50% bitrate reduction compared to HEVC by implementing new improvements for hybrid prediction/transform coding scheme and a set of new tools [30].

Omnidirectional video (ODV) is stored and transmitted with its 2D planar representations, containing redundant pixels. Several cost-efficient viewport-based coding techniques exist to exploit these redundant pixels, which VR devices do not use [31]. For instance, coding-friendly representations, such as cube map projections (CMP) and truncated square pyramid (TSP), achieve a cost-efficient coding performance.

Light fields consist in a collection of images, which exhibit a lot of self-similarities. These redundancies can be used to design cost-efficient compression algorithms to help reduce the light field substantial volume of data. For instance, sparse subset coding techniques select only a subset of the light field views for encoding, and they reconstruct the remaining views at the decoder.

Volumetric video coding standard solutions is typically divided into two parts based on the used representations, namely, mesh-based and point-cloud-based compression techniques. For point cloud compression, two different point cloud coding techniques are commonly used for volumetric video compression: geometry-based PCC (G-PCC) and video-based PCC (V-PCC) [32].

Immersive video standardization activities have recently been started with ISO/IEC MPEG immersive video (MIV) standard [7]. The upcoming MIV standardization aims to provide the capability to compress a given 3D scene representation captured by multiple real or virtual cameras. The MIV coding framework is designed to utilize multiview video plus depth representation of immersive video data to enable 3D reconstruction with 6DoF capability. A test model framework, which consists of reference software encoder, decoder, and renderer, was developed for immersive video during this standardization activity.

1.4.2.2 Streaming of immersive videos

State-of-the-art video communication technologies are adaptive bitrate (ABR) streaming system, which is designed to deliver a given captured video to the users in the most cost-efficient way possible and with the highest quality. In the ABR streaming, a given captured video is prepared in several representations, encoded at different bitrates, resolution, and frame-rate. Each video representation is divided into a number of equal duration segments. Different segments are aligned such that the client device can request an appropriate segment of video representation based on the network bandwidth. Fig. 1.8 illustrates a schematic diagram for adaptive video delivery system.

In omnidirectional video streaming, only a small portion of a given content, called viewport, is used by the HMDs. Therefore a very high resolution of the omnidirectional video is needed to deliver a perceptually acceptable quality level. To deploy omnidirectional video in adaptive streaming frameworks, the MPEG created the omnidirectional media format (OMAF) [33], which has two editions.

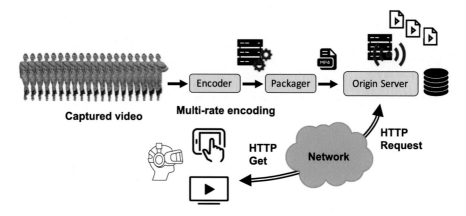

Figure 1.8 Schematic diagram of adaptive video delivery system.

Due to its interactive use cases, cost-efficient streaming and transmission delay play important roles in light field streaming. To achieve cost-efficient transmission, most of the studies use approaches similar to sparse subset light field coding, wherein only a subset of the views can be transmitted to clients. In particular, transmission delay is an essential aspect that should be taken into account in light field streaming due to its interactive use cases, as studied in [34].

The volumetric video introduces additional challenges in streaming frameworks as real-time interaction with the content becomes crucial. Adaptive streaming strategies for point cloud representations have been investigated to optimize volumetric video streaming systems. For instance, in [35], various point cloud density levels were generated using spatial sub-sampling algorithms per given 3D point cloud content. The experimental results show that sub-sampling-based rate adaptation can significantly save point cloud streaming bandwidth.

1.4.2.3 Challenges for immersive video

To enable content delivery over the Internet (i.e., online) or any other medium (e.g., offline, stored media), compression and transmission techniques are needed to be developed. The presentation of the content itself at the receiver side requires specific rendering algorithms. Moreover, special display devices are used to present the visual output of these immersive imaging systems. Although there are lossless alternatives, most of the compression and transmission techniques introduce some form of perceptual or non-perceptual losses, and the rendering algorithm can also introduce visual artifacts. To ensure the highest quality of experience for the viewers, several quality assessment and visual attention mechanisms are used both during the compression and transmission and during the presentation of the media afterwards.

1.4.3 Rendering and display

As described above, digital imaging technologies rely on tightly packed and very structured grid of pixels. The pixel values that are already processed are passed to the rendering and display step, and converted into light at the display device. The pixel values are already given to the display driver, and there is little in terms of rendering for traditional video.

Since most of the rendering is already done prior to video distribution, rendering in traditional images and video usually refers to the techniques that determines the location within the screen, the spatial resolution, and the temporal resolution of the video. This includes solving problems such as subsampling and anti-aliasing.

Similarly, display is rather straightforward compared to other techniques that are used in immersive imaging technologies. There are different display technologies, including liquid crystal display (LCD), plasma display panel (PDP), and organic light-emitting diode (OLED) displays. Although technologies differ in terms of the presence of backlight, light leakage from different angles, and the contrast ratios, essentially, all display technologies for traditional video rely on using the pixel grid with minimal change in the location or spatial resolution of the pixels, as mentioned above. Except for a small number of curved and/or foldable displays, all of them are essentially 2D planes.

Due to their unique requirements and different representation structures, immersive video technologies need specialized rendering methods to either render the spherical view onto the planar display, find the corresponding viewpoint for the light fields by image-based rendering, or render and rasterize the 3D models of the volumetric video. The techniques for renderings and novel display technologies are discussed in the following chapters, in each part for the three different display modalities.

1.4.4 Quality assessment

Images and video are versatile and can be used for many different tasks in addition to human consumption. Since immersive imaging technologies target recreation of the real world through digital imaging systems [36], end-users for immersive video technologies are human viewers. In this context, quality is described as "the outcome of an individual's comparison and judgment process. It includes perception, reflection about the perception, and the description of the outcome" [37]. Moreover, the term quality of experience (QoE) is defined as "the degree of delight or annoyance of the user of an application or service" both in general sense [37] and for immersive media technologies [36].

Numerical quality scores can be obtained via psychophysical user studies (also known as subjective quality experiments) or quality estimation algorithms (also known as objective quality metrics). Briefly, the subjective quality assessment provides ground truth ratings of visual quality, while being time and cost expensive. The latter, objective quality metrics, are easy to execute, but they only offer computational predictions of visual quality.

1.4.4.1 Subjective quality assessment

As per its definition, quality is subjective. In subjective quality experiments, viewers (i.e., participants) are presented with visual stimuli and asked to provide their response to the experiment question. The collected data can be treated as ground truth in many cases; however, if not carefully planned, the tests may result in misleading and noisy data due to various psychological effects [38]. To minimize the noise in these tests, throughout years, there have been many efforts to create standards and recommendations by standardization committees (e.g., International Telecommunications Union (ITU)) or groups formed by scientific experts (e.g., Moving Picture Experts Group (MPEG)) [39–42].

The subjective tests mainly fall into one of two categories: rating and ranking. Rating tests ask participants to "rate" (i.e., determine the quality of) the visual stimulus presented to them. Ranking tests ask participants to provide an order of preference. In rating tests, the participants can be presented with either a single stimulus, double stimuli, or multiple stimuli. The single stimulus (SS) methodologies generally ask to determine the inherent quality of the presented visual. Absolute category rating (ACR) [40], ACR with hidden reference (ACR-HR) [40], and single stimulus continuous quality evaluation (SSCQE) [39,41] are three commonly used SS rating methodologies. The double stimulus (DS) methodologies present two visuals at the same time. Degradation category rating (DCR) [40], double stimulus impairment scale (DSIS) [41], double-stimulus continuous quality evaluation (DSCQE) [39,41] are three commonly used DS methodologies. There can be also multiple stimulus presented to the viewer at the same time, of which subjective assessment methodology for video quality (SAMVIQ) [42] is an example. In ranking tests, the most simple methodology is simply ranking multiple visuals, followed by statistical analysis. A very popular ranking method in signal processing and computer graphics communities is pairwise comparisons (PWC) methodology [40], in which the viewer is asked which option they prefer from two simultaneously presented stimuli. But, in some cases, a psychometric scaling may be necessary, which has its own challenges [43].

After data collection, to remove noisy data or to understand whether the results have meaningful difference, statistical analysis methods are used in most cases. These include outlier detection and removal [41], analysis of variance (ANOVA), pooling individual subjective quality scores, finding mean and standard deviation, and finding confidence intervals. These steps ensure that the collected data are cleaned and any bias or erroneous data are removed before their use.

1.4.4.2 Objective quality metrics

As mentioned above, subjective quality tests require meticulous effort in planning, execution, and analysis of results of the psychophysical user studies. Conducting such studies are not feasible for many applications, including compression, transmission, and other tasks that need to be completed in real-time. For this purpose, objective quality metrics are used to estimate the visual quality of a given video.

Quality metrics work on the pixel values of video frames. Metrics can have different approaches for traditional video. Mean squared error (MSE) and peak signal-to-noise ratio (PSNR) focus on the pixel error values. Structural similarity index measure (SSIM [44]) and other structural similarity-based metrics (e.g., MS-SSIM [45], FSIM [46], etc.) leverage human visual system principles, which mainly focus on identifying similarities between luminance and contrast of the two images. Information fidelity criterion (IFC) [47] and visual information fidelity (VIF) [48] rely on the statistical characteristics of the image extracted using information theory principles. Some hybrid metrics, such as video quality metric (VQM) [49] and video multi-assessment fusion (VMAF) [50] combine various features to create a single estimation measure for video. Other recent methods use neural network approaches [51].

The estimated quality values generally have numerical values that may be arbitrarily different from metric to metric. Therefore when using these metrics in real applications or when bench-marking their performances, a fitting can be done to the subjective quality scores' range (e.g., from 0.8–1 to 0–100). This fitting can be done either using polynomial functions or nonlinear functions [52]. For performance comparisons, a set of statistical performance metrics (which were recommended by ITU [53]) are widely used in the literature. These metrics are: Pearson correlation coefficient (PCC), Spearman's rank order correlation coefficient (SROCC), root mean squared error (RMSE), and outlier ratio (OR). Recently, other methods to evaluate objective metrics were proposed [52,54,55], based on reformulating the task from correlation to classification.

1.4.4.3 Challenges and limitations for immersive video technologies

In immersive video technologies, although the foundational data structures rely on legacy imaging systems and pixel-based grid structures, the new representations and perceptual limitations dictate a different set of challenges and limitations. For example, the spherical nature of omnidirectional video, combined with the characteristics of human visual perception, makes ODV quality assessment very different from traditional video quality assessment.

1.5. Discussion and perspectives

Immersive imaging systems aim at capturing and reproducing the plenoptic function. We presented, in this chapter, the theoretic background of the immersive video technologies, technologies that affect all modalities, and a brief overview of the content delivery pipeline, from image acquisition to display and quality assessment. This book, and therefore this chapter, focuses on three current prominent modalities: omnidirectional imaging, light field imaging, and volumetric imaging, i.e., point cloud and textured meshes. One of the fundamental components of all these systems and modalities is to capture light from different angles. These systems thus capture a lot of visual data, which require specific acquisition systems and more efficient compression methods for storage and streaming purposes. Furthermore, the visual information captured is not intended to be visualized all at once, but rather needs dedicated rendering algorithms, which can be displayed on traditional 2D screens or more advanced immersive display systems, such as head-mounted displays or light field displays.

One of the key technologies enabling rapid improvement of immersive imaging systems is deep learning, either as a tool to improve processing of classical immersive imaging modalities, or as a novel immersive imaging representation.

As discussed in the following chapters, there have been significant advances in immersive imaging technologies in recent years. Nevertheless, several challenges still lie ahead. These challenges include the popularization of immersive imaging systems, improving the reproduction fidelity of the captured real-world content by developing better display and rendering systems, increasing the speed of 3D reconstruction for volumetric imaging systems to enable real-time 3D content creation, understanding and leveraging user behavior to increase the efficiency in adaptive streaming and compression, and more efficient compression and transmission systems to deal with the increasing amount of information captured by the immersive imaging systems.

References

[1] M. Minsky, Telepresence, Omni (1980) 45–51.

[2] W.A. IJsselsteijn, H. De Ridder, J. Freeman, S.E. Avons, Presence: concept, determinants, and measurement, in: Human Vision and Electronic Imaging V, vol. 3959, International Society for Optics and Photonics, 2000, pp. 520–529.

[3] J. Takatalo, G. Nyman, L. Laaksonen, Components of human experience in virtual environments, Computers in Human Behavior 24 (1) (2008) 1–15.

[4] M. Lombard, T. Ditton, At the heart of it all: The concept of presence, Journal of Computer-Mediated Communication 3 (2) (1997).

[5] P. Schelkens, T. Ebrahimi, A. Gilles, P. Gioia, K.-J. Oh, F. Pereira, C. Perra, A.M.G. Pinheiro, JPEG Pleno: Providing representation interoperability for holographic applications and devices, ETRI Journal 41 (1) (2019) 93–108, https://doi.org/10.4218/etrij.2018-0509.

[6] M. Domański, O. Stankiewicz, K. Wegner, T. Grajek, Immersive visual media - MPEG-I: 360 video, virtual navigation and beyond, in: International Conference on Systems, Signals and Image Processing (IWSSIP), 2017.

[7] J.M. Boyce, R. Doré, A. Dziembowski, J. Fleureau, J. Jung, B. Kroon, B. Salahieh, V.K.M. Vadakital, L. Yu, MPEG immersive video coding standard, Proceedings of the IEEE 109 (9) (2021) 1521–1536, https://doi.org/10.1109/JPROC.2021.3062590.

[8] F. Biocca, B. Delaney, Immersive virtual reality technology, in: F. Biocca, M.R. Levy (Eds.), Communication in the Age of Virtual Reality, Lawrence Erlbaum Associates, Inc., 1995, pp. 57–124.

[9] H.G. Hoffman, J. Prothero, M.J. Wells, J. Groen, Virtual chess: Meaning enhances users' sense of presence in virtual environments, International Journal of Human-Computer Interaction 10 (3) (1998) 251–263.

[10] U. Schultze, Embodiment and presence in virtual worlds: a review, Journal of Information Technology 25 (4) (2010) 434–449.

[11] Cambridge English Dictionary, immerse, https://dictionary.cambridge.org/dictionary/english/immerse, 2022.

[12] S.T. Coleridge, Biographia Literaria, chapter xiv, Littlehampton Book Services, West Sussex, England, 1975 (1817).

[13] P. Milgram, H. Takemura, A. Utsumi, F. Kishino, Augmented reality: A class of displays on the reality-virtuality continuum, in: Telemanipulator and Telepresence Technologies, vol. 2351, International Society for Optics and Photonics, 1995, pp. 282–292.

[14] L.-H. Lee, T. Braud, P. Zhou, L. Wang, D. Xu, Z. Lin, A. Kumar, C. Bermejo, P. Hui, All one needs to know about metaverse: A complete survey on technological singularity, virtual ecosystem, and research agenda, arXiv preprint, arXiv:2110.05352, 2021.

[15] E.H. Adelson, J.R. Bergen, The plenoptic function and the elements of early vision, in: Computational Models of Visual Processing, MIT Press, 1991, pp. 3–20.

[16] Y. Yagi, Omnidirectional sensing and its applications, IEICE Transactions on Information and Systems 82 (3) (1999) 568–579.

[17] K.K. Sreedhar, I.D.D. Curcio, A. Hourunranta, M. Lepistö, Immersive media experience with MPEG OMAF multi-viewpoints and overlays, in: Proceedings of the 11th ACM Multimedia Systems Conference, 2020, pp. 333–336.

[18] I. Ihrke, J. Restrepo, L. Mignard-Debise, Principles of light field imaging: Briefly revisiting 25 years of research, IEEE Signal Processing Magazine 33 (5) (2016) 59–69.

[19] G. Wu, B. Masia, A. Jarabo, Y. Zhang, L. Wang, Q. Dai, T. Chai, Y. Liu, Light field image processing: An overview, IEEE Journal of Selected Topics in Signal Processing 11 (7) (2017) 926–954.

[20] M. Broxton, J. Flynn, R. Overbeck, D. Erickson, P. Hedman, M. Duvall, J. Dourgarian, J. Busch, M. Whalen, P. Debevec, Immersive light field video with a layered mesh representation, ACM Transactions on Graphics 39 (4) (Jul. 2020), https://doi.org/10.1145/3386569.3392485.

[21] A. Smolic, 3D video and free viewpoint video—from capture to display, Pattern Recognition 44 (9) (2011) 1958–1968.

[22] A. Collet, M. Chuang, P. Sweeney, D. Gillett, D. Evseev, D. Calabrese, H. Hoppe, A. Kirk, S. Sullivan, High-quality streamable free-viewpoint video, ACM Transactions on Graphics 34 (4) (Jul. 2015), https://doi.org/10.1145/2766945.

[23] R. Pagés, K. Amplianitis, D. Monaghan, J. Ondřej, A. Smolić, Affordable content creation for free-viewpoint video and VR/AR applications, Journal of Visual Communication and Image Representation 53 (2018) 192–201, https://doi.org/10.1016/j.jvcir.2018.03.012.

[24] S. Lombardi, T. Simon, J. Saragih, G. Schwartz, A. Lehrmann, Y. Sheikh, Neural volumes: Learning dynamic renderable volumes from images, ACM Transactions on Graphics 38 (4) (2019) 65, 14pp.

[25] B. Mildenhall, P.P. Srinivasan, M. Tancik, J.T. Barron, R. Ramamoorthi, R. Ng, NeRF: Representing scenes as neural radiance fields for view synthesis, in: Proceedings of the European Conference on Computer Vision, 2020.

[26] R. Hartley, A. Zisserman, Multiple View Geometry in Computer Vision, Cambridge University Press, 2003.

[27] T. Maugey, L. Guillo, C.L. Cam, FTV360: a multiview 360° video dataset with calibration parameters, in: Proceedings of the 10th ACM Multimedia Systems Conference, 2019, pp. 291–295.

[28] O. Johannsen, A. Sulc, B. Goldluecke, On linear structure from motion for light field cameras, in: Proceedings of the IEEE International Conference on Computer Vision, 2015, pp. 720–728.

[29] M. Wien, J.M. Boyce, T. Stockhammer, W.-H. Peng, Standardization status of immersive video coding, IEEE Journal on Emerging and Selected Topics in Circuits and Systems 9 (1) (2019) 5–17.

[30] N. Sidaty, W. Hamidouche, O. Déforges, P. Philippe, J. Fournier, Compression performance of the versatile video coding: HD and UHD visual quality monitoring, in: 2019 Picture Coding Symposium (PCS), IEEE, 2019, pp. 1–5.

[31] R. Shafi, W. Shuai, M.U. Younus, 360-degree video streaming: A survey of the state of the art, Symmetry 12 (9) (2020) 1491.

[32] D.B. Graziosi, O. Nakagami, S. Kuma, A. Zaghetto, T. Suzuki, A. Tabatabai, An overview of ongoing point cloud compression standardization activities: video-based (V-PCC) and geometry-based (G-PCC), APSIPA Transactions on Signal and Information Processing 9 (2020).

[33] ISO/IEC, Information Technology — Coded Representation of Immersive Media — Part 2: Omni-directional Media Format, Standard, International Organization for Standardization, Jan. 2019.

[34] M. Alain, C. Ozcinar, A. Smolic, A study of light field streaming for an interactive refocusing application, in: 2019 IEEE International Conference on Image Processing (ICIP), IEEE, 2019, pp. 3761–3765.

[35] M. Hosseini, C. Timmerer, Dynamic adaptive point cloud streaming, in: Proceedings of the 23rd Packet Video Workshop, 2018, pp. 25–30.

[36] A. Perkis, C. Timmerer, S. Baraković, J. Baraković Husić, S. Bech, S. Bosse, J. Botev, K. Brunnström, L. Cruz, K. De Moor, A. de Polo Saibanti, W. Durnez, S. Egger-Lampl, U. Engelke, T.H. Falk, J. Gutiérrez, A. Hameed, A. Hines, T. Kojic, D. Kukolj, E. Liotou, D. Milovanovic, S. Möller, N. Murray, B. Naderi, M. Pereira, S. Perry, A. Pinheiro, A. Pinilla, A. Raake, S.R. Agrawal, U. Reiter, R. Rodrigues, R. Schatz, P. Schelkens, S. Schmidt, S.S. Sabet, A. Singla, L. Skorin-Kapov, M. Suznjevic, S. Uhrig, S. Vlahović, J.-N. Voigt-Antons, S. Zadtootaghaj, QUALINET white paper, on definitions of immersive media experience (IMEx), European Network on Quality of Experience in Multimedia, Systems and Services, 14th QUALINET meeting (online), https://arxiv.org/abs/2007.07032, May 2020.

[37] P. Le Callet, S. Möller, A. Perkis, Qualinet white paper on definitions of quality of experience, European Network on Quality of Experience in Multimedia Systems and Services (COST Action IC 1003), Lausanne, Switzerland, Version 1.2 (Mar 2013).

[38] F. De Simone, Selected contributions on multimedia quality evaluation, Ph.D. thesis, École Polytechnique Fédérale de Lausanne, 2012.

[39] T. Alpert, J. Evain, Subjective quality evaluation: the SSCQE and DSCQE methodologies, EBU Technical Review, 1997.

[40] ITU-T, Subjective video quality assessment methods for multimedia applications, ITU-T Recommendation P.910, Apr 2008.

[41] ITU-R, Methodology for the subjective assessment of the quality of television pictures, ITU-R Recommendation BT.500-13, Jan 2012.

[42] F. Kozamernik, V. Steinmann, P. Sunna, E. Wyckens, SAMVIQ—A new EBU methodology for video quality evaluations in multimedia, SMPTE Motion Imaging Journal 114 (4) (2005) 152–160.

[43] E. Zerman, V. Hulusic, G. Valenzise, R.K. Mantiuk, F. Dufaux, The relation between MOS and pairwise comparisons and the importance of cross-content comparisons, in: IS&T Electronic Imaging, Human Vision and Electronic Imaging XXII, 2018.

[44] Z. Wang, A.C. Bovik, H.R. Sheikh, E.P. Simoncelli, Image quality assessment: From error visibility to structural similarity, IEEE Transactions on Image Processing 13 (4) (2004) 600–612.

[45] Z. Wang, E.P. Simoncelli, A.C. Bovik, Multiscale structural similarity for image quality assessment, in: 37th Asilomar Conference on Signals, Systems Computers, vol. 2, IEEE, 2003, pp. 1398–1402.

[46] L. Zhang, L. Zhang, X. Mou, D. Zhang, FSIM: A feature similarity index for image quality assessment, IEEE Transactions on Image Processing 20 (8) (2011) 2378–2386, https://doi.org/10.1109/TIP.2011.2109730.

[47] H.R. Sheikh, A.C. Bovik, G. De Veciana, An information fidelity criterion for image quality assessment using natural scene statistics, IEEE Transactions on Image Processing 14 (12) (2005) 2117–2128.

[48] H.R. Sheikh, A.C. Bovik, Image information and visual quality, IEEE Transactions on Image Processing 15 (2) (2006) 430–444.

[49] M.H. Pinson, S. Wolf, A new standardized method for objectively measuring video quality, IEEE Transactions on Broadcasting 50 (3) (2004) 312–322, https://doi.org/10.1109/TBC.2004.834028.

[50] Z. Li, A. Aaron, I. Katsavounidis, A. Moorthy, M. Manohara, Toward a practical perceptual video quality metric, https://medium.com/netflix-techblog/toward-a-practical-perceptual-video-quality-metric-653f208b9652, Jan 2019.

[51] M. Xu, J. Chen, H. Wang, S. Liu, G. Li, Z. Bai, C3DVQA: Full-reference video quality assessment with 3D convolutional neural network, in: IEEE International Conference on Acoustics, Speech and Signal Processing (ICASSP), 2020, pp. 4447–4451.

[52] ITU-T, Method for specifying accuracy and cross-calibration of video quality metrics (VQM), ITU-T Recommendation J.149, Mar 2004.

[53] ITU-T, Methods, metrics and procedures for statistical evaluation, qualification and comparison of objective quality prediction models, ITU-T Recommendation P.1401, Jul 2012.

[54] L. Krasula, K. Fliegel, P. Le Callet, M. Klíma, On the accuracy of objective image and video quality models: New methodology for performance evaluation, in: 8th International Conference on Quality of Multimedia Experience (QoMEX), IEEE, 2016.

[55] E. Zerman, G. Valenzise, F. Dufaux, An extensive performance evaluation of full-reference HDR image quality metrics, Quality and User Experience 2 (5) (2017), https://doi.org/10.1007/s41233-017-0007-4.

PART 2

Omnidirectional video

CHAPTER 2

Acquisition, representation, and rendering of omnidirectional videos

Thomas Maugey
Inria, Rennes, France

2.1. Introduction

A *spherical image* is an image O depicting the visual information converging to a point $\mathbf{o}$. More concretely, this visual information is represented on a unitary sphere centered at $\mathbf{o}$. A value $O(\mathbf{p}_s)$, *i.e.*, the visual information at position $\mathbf{p}_s$, corresponds to the color of a point positioned on the line spanned by $\mathbf{o}$ and $\mathbf{p}_s$. Conversely, the color of a given point $\mathbf{p}$ in the 3D space is described at position $\mathbf{p}_s$, *i.e.*, the projection of $\mathbf{p}$ on the sphere. If $\mathbf{p}$ and $\mathbf{p}_s$ are expressed in the coordinate system centered at $\mathbf{o}$ (see Fig. 2.1), the following relationship holds:

$$\mathbf{p}_s = \frac{\mathbf{p}}{\|\mathbf{p}\|}. \tag{2.1}$$

As shown in Fig. 2.1, the points lying on the sphere can be parameterized by two angles, as in the physics convention specified by ISO standard 80000-2:2019:

- the *polar* angle $\theta \in [0, \pi]$, which gives the angle between $\mathbf{p}_s$ and the polar axis, *i.e.*, the z-axis. This angle is analog to the geographic latitude.

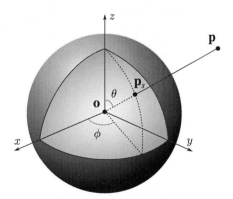

Figure 2.1 A spherical image O captures the light activity converging to a point $\mathbf{o}$. The point $\mathbf{p}_s$, that is the projection of $\mathbf{p}$ on the unitary sphere of center $\mathbf{o}$, is parameterized by the polar and azimuth angles (θ, ϕ).

Immersive Video Technologies
https://doi.org/10.1016/B978-0-32-391755-1.00008-0
27

- the *azimuth* angle $\phi \in \left]-\pi, \pi\right]$, which gives the angle between $\mathbf{p}_s$ and the x-axis. This angle is analog to the geographic longitude.

If we denote

$$\mathbf{p}_s = \begin{pmatrix} x_s \\ y_s \\ z_s \end{pmatrix}, \tag{2.2}$$

we have

$$\theta = \arccos z_s = \arctan \frac{\sqrt{x_s^2 + y_s^2}}{z_s} \tag{2.3}$$

$$\phi = \begin{cases} \arctan \frac{y_s}{x_s} & \text{if } x_s > 0 \\ \arctan \frac{y_s}{x_s} + \pi & \text{if } x_s < 0 \\ \pi & \text{if } x_s = 0 \end{cases} \tag{2.4}$$

And conversely, we have

$$x_s = \cos \phi \sin \theta \tag{2.5}$$

$$y_s = \sin \phi \sin \theta \tag{2.6}$$

$$z_s = \cos \theta. \tag{2.7}$$

By construction, a spherical image captures the light coming from all directions. This is the reason why it is also called an *omnidirectional image* or *360° image*.[1]

Many technologies (such as robotics, augmented/virtual reality, vehicle driving assistance, arts, etc.) clearly benefit from an omnidirectional vision. In the particular case of immersive multimedia, it enables a user to observe a scene with 3 degrees of freedom, corresponding to the three rotations of the head, giving him/her the sensation of being inside the scene. Capturing and displaying an image with 360° of field of view is however not an easy task. On top of that, processing the information that is lying on a unitary sphere cannot be done with the conventional 2D tools because of the peculiar sphere topology. In other words, omnidirectional imaging is much more complex to handle than the classical 2D format. On the one hand, for 2D images, *we watch and process what we capture* (if we neglect demosaicking and other small preprocessing steps), leading to a processing pipeline that is really simple (see Fig. 2.2). On the other hand, for omnidirectional imaging, *we don't directly capture, process and watch the spherical image*, leading to a much more complex processing pipeline (see Fig. 2.3). In particular, the merging of different captures is necessary to build the spherical image O. Moreover, a mapping operation is usually necessary before the development of processing tools.

---

[1] All terms will be used equivalently in what follows.

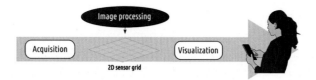

Figure 2.2 2D image processing pipeline.

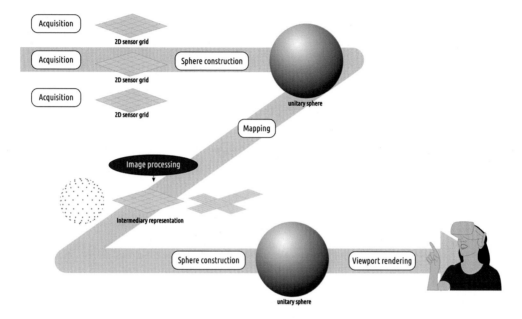

Figure 2.3 360° image processing pipeline.

Finally, the sphere is only partly watched, and a projection on a so-called viewport is necessary.

The aim of this chapter is to detail this processing pipeline and answer the following questions: how is the spherical image built from different captures (Section 2.2)? How is the spherical image represented to enable efficient processing (Section 2.3)? How the spherical image is displayed to the users (Section 2.4)? We finally end the chapter by a discussion of the potentials of multi-view omnidirectional capture systems (Section 2.5).

2.2. Acquisition and projection model

2.2.1 Acquisition general principles

In practice, it is impossible to capture, with a single camera, the light ray coming from *every* direction, *i.e.*, covering the entire sphere. Omnidirectional cameras thus combine the information coming from several cameras. There exist mostly two approaches to do such combination. The first one is to rely on regular perspective cameras, whose projection model is well-known and calibrated with conventional tools [1–4]. This however requires a great number of cameras and a significant processing effort before obtaining the spherical image. This type of device is thus heavy and expensive, which penalizes the generalization of its usage. To be able to use less cameras for the acquisition, these ones need to cover the widest angle possible. In the following, we detail two types of acquisition devices enabling to cover a whole hemisphere: the catadioptric and the fish-eye-based systems.

2.2.2 Catadioptric capture

Catadioptric capture consists in acquiring the scene reflected on a curved mirror [5–9]. The type and position of the camera should be set as a function of the mirror's shape. There exist different types of systems that depends on the mirror's type. In the following, we only focus on two illustrative capture systems: the hyper-catadioptric and para-catadioptric ones.

2.2.2.1 Hyper-catadioptric

As illustrated in Fig. 2.4, the hyper-catadioptric system is the coupling of a hyperboloidal mirror and a perspective camera. The perspective camera is placed such that its center lies at the second focus of the hyperboloid spanned by the mirror. The first focus is inside the mirror. Its shape follows the following equation:

$$\rho = \frac{\alpha}{1 + e \cos \gamma},\tag{2.8}$$

where α is the distance between the hyperboloid summit and its center, and e is the hyperboloid eccentricity. The reason why placing the perspective camera at this exact place is that all the rays directing to the first focus reflect on the mirror and converge to the second focus, which coincides with the camera center. Said differently, doing so guarantees that each pixel on the sensor array corresponds to a direction of convergence towards the first focus (which will be the sphere center). We can easily write the equations modeling this projection. Let us consider a point in the 3D world expressed in the 3D coordinate system, centered at the first focus of the hyperboloid:

$$\mathbf{p} = \begin{pmatrix} x \\ y \\ z \end{pmatrix}.\tag{2.9}$$

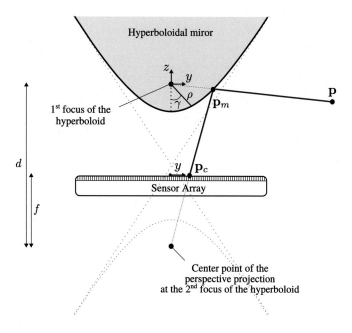

Figure 2.4 Hyper-catadioptric capture.

The projection of $\mathbf{p}$ on the mirror is denoted by $\mathbf{p}_m$ and we have

$$\mathbf{p}_m = \frac{\rho}{\|\mathbf{p}\|} \cdot \mathbf{p} \quad \Leftrightarrow \quad \begin{pmatrix} x_m \\ y_m \\ z_m \end{pmatrix} = \frac{\rho}{\sqrt{x^2 + y^2 + z^2}} \begin{pmatrix} x \\ y \\ z \end{pmatrix}. \tag{2.10}$$

Then, the perspective projection of $\mathbf{p}_m$ on the sensor array (at position $\mathbf{p}_c$) can be written:

$$\mathbf{p}_c = f \begin{pmatrix} \frac{x_m}{z_m + d} \\ \frac{y_m}{z_m + d} \end{pmatrix}, \tag{2.11}$$

where f is the focal length of the perspective camera, and d is the distance between the two hyperboloid focuses. Based on the following relationship that holds for an hyperboloid:

$$d = \frac{2\alpha e}{1 - e^2}, \tag{2.12}$$

and on the fact that

$$\cos(\gamma) = \frac{z}{\|\mathbf{p}\|}, \tag{2.13}$$

we can combine Eqs. (2.10) and (2.11) and we obtain

$$\mathbf{p}_c = \left(\frac{\frac{1-e^2}{1+e^2}fx}{\frac{2e}{1+e^2}\sqrt{x^2+y^2+z^2}+z}, \frac{\frac{1-e^2}{1+e^2}fy}{\frac{2e}{1+e^2}\sqrt{x^2+y^2+z^2}+z} \right)^\top. \qquad (2.14)$$

Constructing the spherical image is then possible since every pixel $\mathbf{p}_c$ corresponds to a different direction converging to the first hyperboloid focus. The hyper-catadioptric capture is a fine and controllable acquisition process. Indeed, Eq. (2.14) only depends on two known values: the eccentricity e and camera focal length f. Being able to rely on a precise projection model is indeed a great advantage for many computer vision or image processing tasks (calibration, camera pose, and depth estimation, etc.). This system has however two drawbacks. First it covers only an hemisphere, and it is impossible to capture the second hemisphere, because the perspective camera takes too much space for having a second symmetric mirror. Second, the setting of such device is sensitive since the camera center should be placed exactly at the second focus. This system is thus costly and not really relevant for the public market.

2.2.2.2 Para-catadioptric

Para-catadioptric system's principle also consists in filming the reflexion of the scene on a curved mirror. However, the shape of the mirror is now paraboloidal. A paraboloid can be seen as a hyperboloid, whose eccentricity e is 1, and whose second focus is at the infinite (*i.e.*, its polar equation is $\rho = \frac{\alpha}{1+\cos\theta}$). For such mirror's shape, the perspective camera is thus replaced by an orthogonal camera (the captured rays are orthogonal to the camera plane), as shown in Fig. 2.5. The advantage of such system is that the relative position of the camera and the mirror is not important, as every ray converging to the paraboloidal center reflects parallelly to the z-axis.

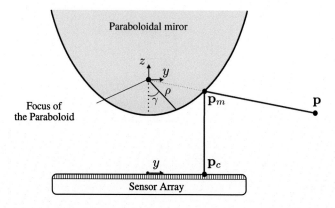

Figure 2.5 Para-catadioptric capture.

As for the hyper-catadioptric system, we can write the relationship between the coordinate of a point **p** and its projection on the camera plane $\mathbf{p}_c$. First, the projection of **p** on the mirror can be written as

$$\mathbf{p}_m = \frac{\rho}{\|\mathbf{p}\|} \cdot \mathbf{p} \quad \Leftrightarrow \quad \begin{pmatrix} x_m \\ y_m \\ z_m \end{pmatrix} = \frac{\rho}{\sqrt{x^2 + y^2 + z^2}} \begin{pmatrix} x \\ y \\ z \end{pmatrix}. \tag{2.15}$$

The equation of the orthogonal projection on the sensor array is simply

$$\mathbf{p}_c = \begin{pmatrix} x_m \\ y_m \end{pmatrix}. \tag{2.16}$$

Knowing that $\cos(\theta) = \frac{z}{\|\mathbf{p}\|}$, we can finally write that

$$\mathbf{p}_c = \left(\frac{\alpha x}{\sqrt{x^2 + y^2 + z^2} + z}, \frac{\alpha y}{\sqrt{x^2 + y^2 + z^2} + z} \right)^\top. \tag{2.17}$$

We can directly see that Eqs. (2.14) and (2.17) have the same shape. Hence, similar to hyper-catadioptric system, the para-catadioptric one can be precisely calibrated and can be very useful for high-precision technology. However, as the hyper-catadioptric system, the para-catadioptric one has the drawback of capturing only an hemisphere without the possibility of doing multi-camera acquisition.

2.2.3 Fish-eye capture

In the recent years, omnidirectional cameras have appeared on the public market. This would not have been possible if those cameras were relying on the aforementioned capture's principles (too fine and costly to produce). Low-cost cameras all rely on multi-view wide angle capture. The wide angle is obtained with the usage of fish-eye lenses. A fish-eye lens is an easily-built lens, whose shape brings a radial distortion enabling to deviate the light rays such that a wide angle is covered. The radial distortion is brought by the fact that the refraction depends on the incidence angle (as depicted in Fig. 2.6). More concretely, let us consider a point **p**, whose light ray hits the center of the lens with an angle γ (i.e., the incidence angle). If the lens is not distorted, the projection $\mathbf{p}_c$ on the sensor array is at position

$$r' = f \tan \gamma. \tag{2.18}$$

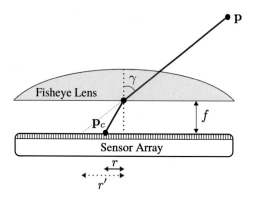

Figure 2.6 Fish-eye lens capture.

The radial distortion is present when the true position of $\mathbf{p}_c$ is at $r = g(\theta) < r'$. Contrary to the catadioptric systems that are finely designed and modeled very accurately, finding the true relationship g between r and γ is impossible, and only empirical estimation can be made. For that purpose, several models have been proposed in the literature [10]. Here is a list of the most well-known ones:

$$\text{Equidistant:} \qquad r = f\gamma \qquad (2.19)$$

$$\text{Equi-solid:} \qquad r = 2f \sin\frac{\gamma}{2} \qquad (2.20)$$

$$\text{Orthographic:} \qquad r = f \sin\gamma \qquad (2.21)$$

$$\text{Stereographic:} \qquad r = f \tan\frac{\gamma}{2} \qquad (2.22)$$

$$\text{Polynomial:} \qquad r = f(k_1\theta + k_2\theta^3 + \ldots + k_n\theta^{2n-1}) \qquad (2.23)$$

For each fish-eye to calibrate, there is a compromise between the complexity of the model and the accuracy of the approximation. Despite this need for model fitting, fish-eye-based systems have known a great success in the recent years, and now equip all the low-cost cameras available on the public market, and also more professional equipment.

2.2.4 Unified spherical model

As explained in the previous sections, acquiring spherical data can be done in different manners, and each of them relies on a specific model. This leads to major issues, because the type of device that is used for capture is sometimes not known when dealing with a spherical image. In that case, retrieving the spherical image from the acquired 2D image is difficult. For that reason, authors in [5,11] have proposed a method that enables to

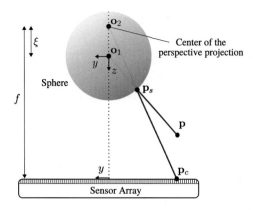

Figure 2.7 Unified spherical model.

model all capture systems at the same time. For that purpose, they construct a fake capture process and model it. This so-called *unified spherical model* is depicted in Fig. 2.7. First the color of a point at position **p** is projected on the unitary sphere of center $\mathbf{o}_1$ (the spherical image that we aim to capture). This projection can be written as

$$\mathbf{p}_s = \frac{\mathbf{p}}{\|\mathbf{p}\|} \quad \Leftrightarrow \quad \begin{pmatrix} x_s \\ y_s \\ z_s \end{pmatrix} = \frac{1}{\sqrt{x^2 + y^2 + z^2}} \begin{pmatrix} x \\ y \\ z \end{pmatrix}. \tag{2.24}$$

Then, the point at position $\mathbf{p}_s$ is captured by a perspective camera of focal length f that is centered at the point $\mathbf{o}_2$, that is, the translation of $\mathbf{o}_1$ along the z-axis with a value ξ. This perspective projection can be written as

$$\mathbf{p}_c = f \begin{pmatrix} \frac{x_s}{z_s + \xi} \\ \frac{y_s}{z_s + \xi} \end{pmatrix}. \tag{2.25}$$

If we combine (2.24) and (2.25), we obtain

$$\mathbf{p}_c = \left(\frac{fx}{\xi\sqrt{x^2 + y^2 + z^2} + z}, \frac{fy}{\xi\sqrt{x^2 + y^2 + z^2} + z} \right)^{\top}. \tag{2.26}$$

We can see that by adjusting f and ξ properly, this unified spherical model can fit both catadioptric project rules in (2.14) and (2.17). Moreover, the same authors have shown in [12] that this model well approximates most of the fish-eye lenses too.

2.2.5 Stitching for sphere construction

We recall that each of the acquisition systems introduced above only corresponds to a partial sphere capture. To build an image that covers the whole sphere surface, one generally needs to combine several acquisitions. This is done in general with multiple fish-eye acquisitions, as it is hardly conceivable to combine multiple catadioptric systems. An example of dual fish-eye capture is shown in Fig. 2.12(a). The problem is not entirely solved at this stage. Indeed, each fish-eye image has its own spherical model (*e.g.*, the unified spherical model introduced in Section 2.2.4), and thus the spherical image lying on a unique sphere is not built yet. The *stitching* operation exactly corresponds to this operation, *i.e.*, merging all captured image into a single spherical image. In practice, the different spheres corresponding to each fish-eye sensor are not overlapped, which makes the stitching task difficult. The different spherical images should be blended and warped such that their overlapping image content is aligned: *e.g.*, an object should appear only once and not be cut, luminosity should be consistent. In the case of video stitching, an additional difficulty is that the different sensors may not be finely synchronized. Interested readers may refer, for example, to [13–15] for more details on how stitching methods work.

In this chapter, we emphasize two important points when dealing with stitching. First, they are error prone, with important visual artifact. As discussed in [16], stitching errors are really salient, and hence seriously decrease the user experience quality. Second, the stitching operation annihilates any model parameterization performed on each sensor. If, for example, each fish-eye lens is calibrated with Eq. (2.26), it means that one is able to retrieve the direction corresponding to each pixel value. After the stitching operation, since the different images are blended and warped, errors may be introduced between the true orientation of an object and its representation on the sphere [17].

2.3. Sphere representation

By definition, the acquired omnidirectional image or video lies on the sphere that is not an Euclidean space, on which the conventional image processing tools are well-defined. To move to a more friendly topology, mapping is usually made, as explained in Fig. 2.3. As tons of different mapping have been conceived, we only review the most meaningful and adopted ones in this section, namely the equirectangular, the cubemap, and the pyramidal. We finally end this section by describing how some authors have proposed to work directly on the sphere.

2.3.1 Equirectangular projection

Without any doubts, *equirectangular* or *panorama* projection is the most widely used. It basically consists in sampling with a uniform step the polar and azimuth angles θ

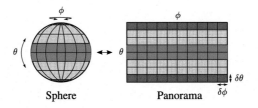

Figure 2.8 Equirectangular projection.

and ϕ, as illustrated in Fig. 2.8. The simplicity of its construction makes its usage and visualization straightforward. The reason why this representation seems very familiar to all of us is also because it is how the earth is mapped on a planisphere. An example of such image is shown in Fig. 2.12(b).

Despite the uniformity of the steps used to sample the polar and azimuth angles, the obtained distribution of the pixels on the sphere is not at all uniform. As can be seen in Fig. 2.8, two regions of equal area in the panorama (the blue at the equator and the red at the poles) actually correspond to two regions of strongly different sizes on the sphere. This naturally causes huge visual distortion and can limit the performance of image processing algorithms. Moreover, as seen in Fig. 2.12(b), such a mapping also leads to radial distortion, and thus to the curvature of lines. Finally, the equirectangular mapping creates artificial loss of continuities that are not present on the sphere. Therefore two neighboring points on the sphere can be mapped at extreme positions on the panorama. All these mapping artifacts have to be taken into account in the image processing algorithms, and such a task is not always straightforward.

2.3.2 CubeMap projection

To avoid the spherical distortion brought by equirectangular projection, another mapping has been proposed and widely used by researchers and companies. As depicted in Fig. 2.9, the so-called *cubemap* projection consists in projecting the spherical image onto the six faces of a cube centered around the sphere center **o**. The cube is then unfolded, and can even be re-arranged to form an image with a 2D shape. It is worth noting that the projection on each individual face mimics a perspective camera capture with a field of view of $\frac{\pi}{2} \times \frac{\pi}{2}$. The resulting images have thus a natural image statistics, in which the standard image processing algorithms are well performing. This can be observed in the cubemap image example of Fig. 2.12(c). However, such representation creates numerous discontinuities in the image, which can create misleading artifacts: some fake corners appear, some objects are cut and are described on several faces, etc. Moreover, the distribution of the pixels on the sphere remains quite nonregular.

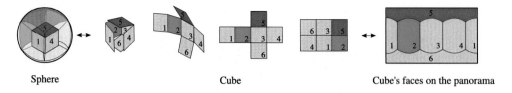

Figure 2.9 CubeMap projection.

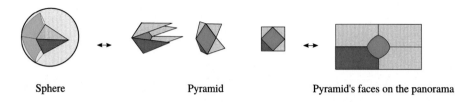

Figure 2.10 Pyramidal projection.

2.3.3 Other mapping

Naturally, many other mappings exist or can be conceived.[2] Basically, many of them consists in projecting the sphere on a polyhedron. An example of rhombic dodeca-hedron mapping is shown in Fig. 2.12(d). Increasing the number of faces leads to a more uniform sampling of the sphere, while it increases the number of artificial discontinuities. One of these mappings deserves our attention, since the particular shape of the polyhedron that is used enables interesting applications. In the so-called *pyramidal* projection, the sphere is projected on a pyramid with a square basis. Each face of the pyramid is then unfolded and the triangular faces are used to complete the square, as illustrated in Fig. 2.10. Obviously, this type of projection does not give the same importance to the different sphere subparts. Indeed, the basis (in blue) is represented with a much denser pixel resolution than the other parts. This nice property is used in particular for streaming application. Watching a video in a given direction, a user is sent the pyramidal representation, where the basis is pointing towards the users field of vision. If he/she moves the head, then a new pyramidal representation suited to the new vision orientation is sent, and during the time the new representation is received the user is able to watch the desired content with the low-resolution face. Typically, several pyramidal versions of each omnidirectional video are stored to serve any desired viewing direction. An example of pyramidal projection is shown in Fig. 2.12(e).

---

[2] https://map-projections.net/.

2.3.4 On-the-sphere representation

As discussed in the former sections, mapping the sphere on one or several 2D plane(s) leads to severe issues that have to be circumvented by major change in the traditional image processing algorithms. To avoid facing those problems, some researchers have proposed to process the omnidirectional image directly on the sphere (see Fig. 2.12(f)). Though it is clear that avoiding the mapping operation enables to get rid of the mapping artifacts, other major problems may occur when processing visual data lying on the sphere, because of the non-Euclidean nature of its topology.

The interest of handling the visual data on the sphere resides in the fact that the definition domain is *continuous* and *regular*. Regularity implies that the pixels are uniformly distributed. In practice, it means that each pixel of the sphere should have a constant number of direct neighbors, and that everywhere on the sphere the distance between two neighbors is constant. Finding such a uniform sampling of the sphere is an open mathematical problem (see the Thomson problem [18]). However, many pseudo-optimal solutions exist. Here is a non-exhaustive list: Gauss–Legendre [19], icosahedron-based [20–22], spiral [23], igloo [24], triangular [25], HEALPix [26], etc. Each of these methods offer specific properties about pixel area equality, uniformity of the distribution, hierarchical arrangement, etc.

Though offering nice pseudo-uniform pixel distributions, the aforementioned sampling algorithm leads to unstructured topologies, in which even the most basic image processing operations are not defined, *e.g.*, translation, transform, filtering, convolution, sampling. Intensive research efforts have been conducted recently to find good definitions for those tools. Presenting those methods in depth goes far beyond the scope of this chapter. We only review three main families: the continuous, the graph, and the sampling-dependent approaches.

The continuous approach: though being non-Euclidean, the sphere is a well-known manifold with an easy parameterization. For example, it is possible to formalize mathematically the notion of frequencies on the sphere, namely the *spherical harmonics* defined as solutions of the Laplace equation. Based on those definitions, it is possible to define convolution, transform, and filter operations in the frequency domain, enabling interesting processing [27,28]. These methods are however very complex [29,30]. Some methods have been proposed to reduce the complexity, but often at the price of less processing capabilities (*i.e.*, isotropic kernel filter [31] or restricted displacement on the sphere [32]).

The graph approach: first, a graph $\mathcal{G} = (\mathcal{V}, \mathcal{E}, \mathcal{W})$ is defined on the sphere such that the vertices $\mathcal{V}$ are the pixels, the edges $\mathcal{E}$ link direct neighboring pixels, and the weights $\mathcal{W}$ assigned to each edge are built with a decreasing function of the geodesic distance between the corresponding nodes. With the recent major advances in the *graph signal*

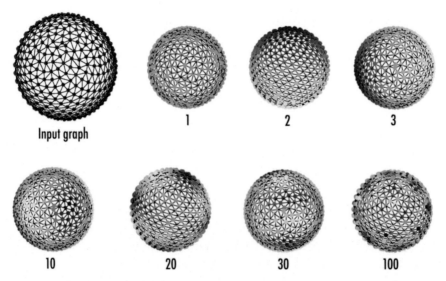

Figure 2.11 Different transform basis obtained with the graph-based transform defined on a graph lying on the sphere. The amount of variation (analogous to spatial frequencies) is growing when the index of the basis is increasing.

processing field [33,34], it has become possible to process a signal (here the spherical image) defined on a graph. In particular, the so-called graph Fourier transform (GFT) basis has been defined as the eigenvectors of the Laplacian operator:

$$\mathbf{L} = \mathbf{D} - \mathbf{A}, \tag{2.27}$$

where $\mathbf{A}$ is the weighted adjacency matrix ($\mathbf{A}_{i,j}$ is equal to $w_{i,j}$ if node i and j are linked and 0 otherwise), and $\mathbf{D}$ is the degree matrix (that is a diagonal matrix giving for each node the sum of incoming weights). This GFT is one natural extension of the discrete cosine transform on graphs [35]. In Fig. 2.11, we show the input graph and a sample of the GFT basis. Many other tools such as filters [36], sampling [37], translation [38,39], or even deep learning architectures [40,41] have been studied leading to interesting results.

The sampling-dependent approach: though being non-Euclidean, some sampling methods offer a certain regularity in the inherent pixel organization over the sphere. For example, spherical wavelet, as defined in [42], benefits from the hierarchical structure of the polyhedron recursive sampling. The HEALPix sampling offers nice properties that the authors in [43] have exploited to define translation and convolution operations that is consistent, directional, and much more expressive than the graph-based ones.

(a) Captured image with double fish-eye

(b) Equirectangular

(c) CubeMap

Figure 2.12 Different spherical image formats.

(d) Rhombic dodecahedron

(e) Pyramid

(f) On-the-Sphere

Figure 2.12 (*continued*)

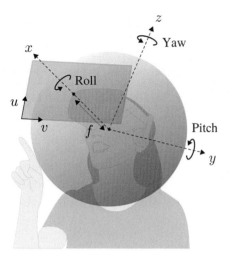

Figure 2.13 Viewport is represented in blue and the spherical image in red. Yaw, pitch, and roll parameters are embedded in a rotation matrix **R**.

2.4. Rendering

As stated in the introduction of this chapter, spherical images cannot be watched directly by humans. Because of the limited field of view in human vision, only a subpart of the sphere has to be displayed. This means that, contrary to 2D images, the portion of the image that is watched depends on the user will. The visualization thus requires an *interaction* from the user (and this is actually what creates the sensation of immersion). This interaction, done by head movement or mouse/keyboard control, drives three rotation angles parameters: yaw, pitch and roll angles, depicted in Fig. 2.13. These angles are embedded in a rotation matrix **R** [44]. This rotation matrix enables in practice to point the x-axis towards the direction of the user sight.[3] The user then only sees the part of the sphere that is pointed by the rotated x-axis. However, the user does not watch the spherical data directly since it is not suited for the human visual system. Instead, the spherical data is projected onto a so-called *viewport*, that is, simply an image tangent to the sphere. It is centered around the x-axis, and its width, height, and resolution set the field of view rendered to the user.

---

[3] In the literature, the usual axis pointing towards the user's vision direction is the z-axis. We have chosen to adapt the axis name here for sake of consistency in regards to over all coordinate systems used in this chapter.

If we denote by $\mathbf{p}_s = (x, y, z)^\top$ one pixel on the spherical image, its projection on the viewport $(u, v)^\top$ is given by

$$\begin{pmatrix} u \\ v \\ 1 \end{pmatrix} \equiv \begin{pmatrix} k_u c_u & 0 & k_u f \\ k_v c_v & k_v f & 0 \\ 1 & 0 & 0 \end{pmatrix} \mathbf{R} \begin{pmatrix} x \\ y \\ z \end{pmatrix}, \tag{2.28}$$

where the center of the viewport is at (c_u, c_v), and (k_u, k_v) are the vertical and horizontal resolutions. In (2.28), the pixels u and v are expressed in homogeneous coordinates. It means that the vector $(u, v, 1)^\top$ is homogeneous to the matrix product at the right of the sign $\equiv$ (i.e., a further division by the 3rd element is needed).

2.5. Towards multi-view acquisition

We have seen in the previous section, that 360° data enables a user to change his angle of view, interacting with 3 degrees of freedom: yaw, roll, and pitch, embedded in a rotation matrix $\mathbf{R}$. Clearly providing the sensation of being inside the scene, spherical imaging has thus been seen as the cornerstone of immersive multimedia. However, ultimate free navigation in a scene is achieved when a translation $\mathbf{t}$ over x, y, and z is additionally possible, which is not the case with a simple omnidirectional capture. This is the reason why several researches have investigated the possibility of performing multi-view 360° capture. As it is illustrated in Fig. 2.14, such system enables the user to do translations at sampled positions, i.e.,

$$\mathbf{t} \in \{\delta_i\}_{0 \leq i \leq N}, \tag{2.29}$$

where the δ_i are the position of the N cameras. In that case, 6 degrees of freedom are given to the users, in which 3 of them are discrete. If the number of camera N is sufficiently large or the distance between the δ_i is small, a quite good level of immersion sensation can be given to the users.

Such an approach has been widely popularized by the Google street view system [45], in which it is possible to visit numerous cities and roads in the world. The user is allowed to translate at predefined position, and at each of them, a 360° vision is provided. Similar systems have been investigated at smaller scale to perform, for example, event detection [46], or 3D reconstruction [47]. In [48,49], a dataset of multi-view omnidirectional captures is available publicly. The shared sequences consist of indoor and outdoor scenes captured with 40 omnidirectional cameras. The relative positions of the cameras are also provided. This is indeed the challenge of such camera system, not only the internal camera model needs to be estimated, but additionally their external parameters, i.e., their position in the world environment. For that purpose, the epipolar geometry theory can be extended to omnidirectional vision [50–53].

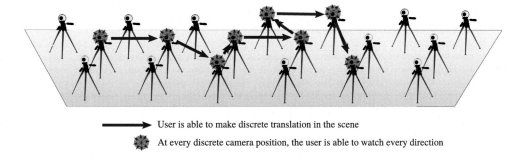

→ User is able to make discrete translation in the scene

✳ At every discrete camera position, the user is able to watch every direction

Figure 2.14 User navigation possibility in a multi-view 360° capture system.

Such new acquisition system opens exciting research challenges. The most obvious and impacting one is the virtual view synthesis. Indeed, having the possibility of generating virtual spherical images between the positions δ_i would enable to reach a smooth free navigation around the 6 degrees of freedom, and thus a total immersion in the scene. First works are going into that directions [54], but a lot of improvement are still necessary to be able to render virtual viewpoint in, for example, a system such as [48,49]. A second research challenge deals with the compression and streaming of such huge data. As it will be explained in a dedicated chapter of this book, the compression of a single omnidirectional video is already not straightforward since the user interactions have to be taken into account. But when it deals with several viewpoints, the difficulty is at a higher level, along with the need of competitive compression solutions due to gigantic data size [55,56].

Acknowledgment

The author would like to thank Aline Roumy, Navid Mahmoudian Bidgoli, and Kai Gu for their help during the writing of this chapter.

References

[1] H. Afshari, L. Jacques, L. Bagnato, A. Schmid, P. Vandergheynst, Y. Leblebici, Hardware implementation of an omnidirectional camera with real-time 3D imaging capability, in: 2011 3DTV Conference: The True Vision-Capture, Transmission and Display of 3D Video (3DTV-CON), IEEE, 2011, pp. 1–4.

[2] H. Afshari, L. Jacques, L. Bagnato, A. Schmid, P. Vandergheynst, Y. Leblebici, The PANOPTIC camera: a plenoptic sensor with real-time omnidirectional capability, Journal of Signal Processing Systems 70 (3) (2013) 305–328.

[3] D. Scaramuzza, K. Ikeuchi, Omnidirectional Camera, 2014.

[4] S. Kasahara, S. Nagai, J. Rekimoto, First person omnidirectional video: System design and implications for immersive experience, in: Proceedings of the ACM International Conference on Interactive Experiences for TV and Online Video, 2015, pp. 33–42.

[5] C. Geyer, K. Daniilidis, Catadioptric projective geometry, International Journal of Computer Vision 45 (3) (2001) 223–243.

[6] S.K. Nayar, Catadioptric omnidirectional camera, in: Proceedings of IEEE Computer Society Conference on Computer Vision and Pattern Recognition, IEEE, 1997, pp. 482–488.

[7] S. Baker, S.K. Nayar, A theory of catadioptric image formation, in: Sixth International Conference on Computer Vision (IEEE Cat. No. 98CH36271), IEEE, 1998, pp. 35–42.

[8] S. Baker, S.K. Nayar, A theory of single-viewpoint catadioptric image formation, International Journal of Computer Vision 35 (2) (1999) 175–196.

[9] X. Ying, Z. Hu, Can we consider central catadioptric cameras and fisheye cameras within a unified imaging model, in: European Conference on Computer Vision, Springer, 2004, pp. 442–455.

[10] F. Bettonvil, Fisheye lenses, WGN, Journal of the International Meteor Organization 33 (2005) 9–14.

[11] J. Courbon, Y. Mezouar, L. Eckt, P. Martinet, A generic fisheye camera model for robotic applications, in: 2007 IEEE/RSJ International Conference on Intelligent Robots and Systems, IEEE, 2007, pp. 1683–1688.

[12] J. Courbon, Y. Mezouar, P. Martinet, Evaluation of the unified model of the sphere for fisheye cameras in robotic applications, Advanced Robotics 26 (8–9) (2012) 947–967.

[13] R. Szeliski, Image alignment and stitching: A tutorial, Foundations and Trends® in Computer Graphics and Vision 2 (1) (2006) 1–104.

[14] W. Xu, Panoramic video stitching, Ph.D. thesis, University of Colorado at Boulder, 2012.

[15] L. Wei, Z. Zhong, C. Lang, Z. Yi, A survey on image and video stitching, Virtual Reality & Intelligent Hardware 1 (1) (2019) 55–83.

[16] R.G. de A. Azevedo, N. Birkbeck, F. De Simone, I. Janatra, B. Adsumilli, P. Frossard, Visual distortions in 360-degree videos, arXiv preprint, arXiv:1901.01848, 2019.

[17] F. Hawary, T. Maugey, C. Guillemot, Sphere mapping for feature extraction from 360° fish-eye captures, in: 2020 IEEE 22nd International Workshop on Multimedia Signal Processing (MMSP), IEEE, 2020, pp. 1–6.

[18] J.J. Thomson, XXIV. On the structure of the atom: an investigation of the stability and periods of oscillation of a number of corpuscles arranged at equal intervals around the circumference of a circle; with application of the results to the theory of atomic structure, The London, Edinburgh, and Dublin Philosophical Magazine and Journal of Science 7 (39) (1904) 237–265.

[19] A. Doroshkevich, P. Naselsky, O.V. Verkhodanov, D. Novikov, V. Turchaninov, I. Novikov, P. Christensen, L.-Y. Chiang, Gauss–Legendre Sky Pixelization (GLESP) for CMB maps, International Journal of Modern Physics D 14 (02) (2005) 275–290.

[20] J.R. Baumgardner, P.O. Frederickson, Icosahedral discretization of the two-sphere, SIAM Journal on Numerical Analysis 22 (6) (1985) 1107–1115.

[21] M. Tegmark, An icosahedron-based method for pixelizing the celestial sphere, arXiv preprint, arXiv:astro-ph/9610094, 1996.

[22] D.A. Randall, T.D. Ringler, R.P. Heikes, P. Jones, J. Baumgardner, Climate modeling with spherical geodesic grids, Computing in Science & Engineering 4 (5) (2002) 32–41.

[23] E.B. Saff, A.B. Kuijlaars, Distributing many points on a sphere, The Mathematical Intelligencer 19 (1) (1997) 5–11.

[24] R.G. Crittenden, N.G. Turok, Exactly azimuthal pixelizations of the sky, arXiv preprint, arXiv:astro-ph/9806374, 1998.

[25] A.S. Szalay, R.J. Brunner, Astronomical archives of the future: a virtual observatory, Future Generation Computer Systems 16 (1) (1999) 63–72.

[26] K.M. Gorski, E. Hivon, A.J. Banday, B.D. Wandelt, F.K. Hansen, M. Reinecke, M. Bartelmann, HEALPix: A framework for high-resolution discretization and fast analysis of data distributed on the sphere, The Astrophysical Journal 622 (2) (2005) 759.

[27] J.R. Driscoll, D.M. Healy, Computing Fourier transforms and convolutions on the 2-sphere, Advances in Applied Mathematics 15 (2) (1994) 202–250.

[28] J.-P. Antoine, P. Vandergheynst, Wavelets on the 2-sphere: A group-theoretical approach, Applied and Computational Harmonic Analysis 7 (3) (1999) 262–291.

[29] T.S. Cohen, M. Geiger, J. Köhler, M. Welling, Spherical CNNs, arXiv preprint, arXiv:1801.10130, 2018.

[30] C. Esteves, A. Makadia, K. Daniilidis, Spin-weighted spherical CNNs, arXiv preprint, arXiv:2006.10731, 2020.

[31] C. Esteves, C. Allen-Blanchette, A. Makadia, K. Daniilidis, Learning SO(3) equivariant representations with spherical CNNs, in: Proceedings of the European Conference on Computer Vision (ECCV), 2018, pp. 52–68.

[32] P.J. Roddy, J.D. McEwen, Sifting convolution on the sphere, IEEE Signal Processing Letters 28 (2021) 304–308.

[33] D.I. Shuman, S.K. Narang, P. Frossard, A. Ortega, P. Vandergheynst, The emerging field of signal processing on graphs: Extending high-dimensional data analysis to networks and other irregular domains, IEEE Signal Processing Magazine 30 (3) (2013) 83–98.

[34] A. Ortega, P. Frossard, J. Kovačević, J.M. Moura, P. Vandergheynst, Graph signal processing: Overview, challenges, and applications, Proceedings of the IEEE 106 (5) (2018) 808–828.

[35] A. Sandryhaila, J.M. Moura, Discrete signal processing on graphs: Frequency analysis, IEEE Transactions on Signal Processing 62 (12) (2014) 3042–3054.

[36] A. Sandryhaila, J.M. Moura, Discrete signal processing on graphs: Graph filters, in: 2013 IEEE International Conference on Acoustics, Speech and Signal Processing, IEEE, 2013, pp. 6163–6166.

[37] S. Chen, R. Varma, A. Sandryhaila, J. Kovačević, Discrete signal processing on graphs: Sampling theory, IEEE Transactions on Signal Processing 63 (24) (2015) 6510–6523, https://doi.org/10.1109/TSP.2015.2469645.

[38] B. Girault, P. Gonçalves, É. Fleury, Translation on graphs: An isometric shift operator, IEEE Signal Processing Letters 22 (12) (2015) 2416–2420.

[39] D.I. Shuman, B. Ricaud, P. Vandergheynst, Vertex-frequency analysis on graphs, Applied and Computational Harmonic Analysis 40 (2) (2016) 260–291.

[40] M.M. Bronstein, J. Bruna, Y. LeCun, A. Szlam, P. Vandergheynst, Geometric deep learning: going beyond Euclidean data, IEEE Signal Processing Magazine 34 (4) (2017) 18–42.

[41] M. Cheung, J. Shi, O. Wright, L.Y. Jiang, X. Liu, J.M. Moura, Graph signal processing and deep learning: Convolution, pooling, and topology, IEEE Signal Processing Magazine 37 (6) (2020) 139–149.

[42] P. Schröder, W. Sweldens, Spherical wavelets: Efficiently representing functions on the sphere, in: Proceedings of the 22nd Annual Conference on Computer Graphics and Interactive Techniques, 1995, pp. 161–172.

[43] N. Mahmoudian Bidgoli, R.G. de A. Azevedo, T. Maugey, A. Roumy, P. Frossard, OSLO: On-the-Sphere Learning for Omnidirectional images and its application to 360-degree image compression, arXiv e-prints, arXiv:2107.09179, 2021.

[44] M. Yu, H. Lakshman, B. Girod, A framework to evaluate omnidirectional video coding schemes, in: 2015 IEEE International Symposium on Mixed and Augmented Reality, IEEE, 2015, pp. 31–36.

[45] D. Anguelov, C. Dulong, D. Filip, C. Frueh, S. Lafon, R. Lyon, A. Ogale, L. Vincent, J. Weaver, Google street view: Capturing the world at street level, Computer 43 (6) (2010) 32–38.

[46] H. Cho, J. Jeong, K.-J. Yoon, EOMVS: Event-based omnidirectional multi-view stereo, IEEE Robotics and Automation Letters 6 (4) (2021) 6709–6716.

[47] C. Won, J. Ryu, J. Lim, OmniMVS: End-to-end learning for omnidirectional stereo matching, in: Proceedings of the IEEE/CVF International Conference on Computer Vision, 2019, pp. 8987–8996.

[48] T. Maugey, L. Guillo, C.L. Cam, FTV360: a multiview 360° video dataset with calibration parameters, in: Proceedings of the 10th ACM Multimedia Systems Conference, 2019, pp. 291–295.

[49] https://project.inria.fr/ftv360/.

[50] P. Sturm, Multi-view geometry for general camera models, in: 2005 IEEE Computer Society Conference on Computer Vision and Pattern Recognition (CVPR'05), vol. 1, IEEE, 2005, pp. 206–212.

[51] P. Sturm, S. Ramalingam, S. Lodha, On calibration, structure from motion and multi-view geometry for generic camera models, in: Imaging Beyond the Pinhole Camera, Springer, 2006, pp. 87–105.

[52] I. Tošić, P. Frossard, Spherical imaging in omni-directional camera networks, in: Multi-Camera Networks, Principles and Applications, 2009.

[53] J. Schneider, W. Förstner, Bundle adjustment and system calibration with points at infinity for omnidirectional camera systems, Photogrammetrie–Fernerkundung–Geoinformation (PFG) 4 (2013) 309–321.

[54] Kai Gu, Thomas Maugey, Sebastian Knorr, Christine Guillemot, Omni-nerf: neural radiance field from 360° image captures, in: ICME 2022-IEEE International Conference on Multimedia and Expo, 2022.

[55] X. Corbillon, F. De Simone, G. Simon, P. Frossard, Dynamic adaptive streaming for multi-viewpoint omnidirectional videos, in: Proceedings of the 9th ACM Multimedia Systems Conference, 2018, pp. 237–249.

[56] H. Pang, C. Zhang, F. Wang, J. Liu, L. Sun, Towards low latency multi-viewpoint 360° interactive video: A multimodal deep reinforcement learning approach, in: IEEE INFOCOM 2019-IEEE Conference on Computer Communications, IEEE, 2019, pp. 991–999.

CHAPTER 3

Streaming and user behavior in omnidirectional videos

Silvia Rossi, Alan Guedes, and Laura Toni
Department of Electrical & Electrical Engineering, UCL, London, United Kingdom

3.1. Introduction

Over the past few years, the synergistic development of new mobile communication services (*i.e.*, 5G mobile networks) and new cutting-edge portable devices (*i.e.*, smartphones) have helped for a breakthrough in video streaming services. In this context, the concept of *immersive and interactive communication* is spreading, identifying a completely novel way of communicating with other people and displaying multimedia content. Traditional remote communications (*e.g.*, television, radio, video calling) are no more sufficient tools for our society: humans are inherently social, in need of realistic experiences, and traditional remote communications do not offer such full sense of immersion and a natural experience/interactions [1]. The impact of realistic experience in remote communications would interest society on wide levels as it addresses a compelling need in reducing environmental impact, in enabling remote working, answering also natural emergencies needs (*e.g.*, reduced travel in pandemic, tornadoes, etc.). In this context, virtual reality (VR) is an example of immersive technology, which has already landed in our everyday life, with an impact ($21.83 billion in 2021, with a projection of growth to $69.6 billion by 2028 [2]) across major economic sectors beyond entertainment, *e.g.*, e-healthcare, e-education, and cultural heritage [3].

VR technology refers to a fully digital environment that replaces the real world, and in which the user is **immersed**, allowing the user to experience a completely new reality. The revolutionary novelty introduced by VR and immersive technology at large is indeed to provide viewers with the possibility to interact with the digital surrounding environment, and with feelings of engagement and presence in a virtual space, even if they are not physically there [4,5]. Specifically, **presence** refers to the illusory feeling experienced by the user of being in a virtual environment different from the physical one, where they are actually located [4]. A condition necessary for presence is the immersion that refers more to technical properties of the system that are needed to simulate a realistic virtual environment [6]. **Interactivity** is, on the other hand, the possibility for users to change the virtual environment with their movements [7]. Thus the role of user interaction is crucial to "be present" in the virtual world: being able to move naturally helps the illusion of being in a different place. Novel types of multimedia content are

Immersive Video Technologies
https://doi.org/10.1016/B978-0-32-391755-1.00009-2

49

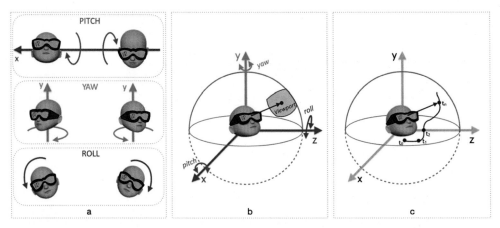

Figure 3.1 Navigation in immersive content: a) rotational head movements (pitch, yaw, and roll); b) navigation system on viewing sphere at generic time instant; c) navigation trajectory over time.

therefore needed to ensure a sufficient level of immersion, presence, and interactivity, which are the three crucial factors to guarantee high quality of experience (QoE) in a VR system [8,9]. In particular, *omnidirectional videos* (ODVs) (also named 360° or spherical videos), which capture a 360° scene instantaneously, are emerged as a new type of media content that promises an immersive and interactive experience. The viewer is placed at the center of the virtual space (*i.e.*, viewing sphere) and provided with a VR device—typically a head-mounted display (HMD)—which facilitates he/she experiencing a 3-degree of freedom (DoF) interaction with the content, by looking up/down (pitch) or left/right (view) or by tilting their head from side to side (roll), as shown in Fig. 3.1a. These head rotations enable free navigation within the immersive scene as the user displays *only* a restricted field of view (FoV) of the environment around themselves, named the *viewport*, identified by the viewing direction at any given time (Fig. 3.1b). Hence, the sequence of the user viewing direction over time can be approximated by projecting the viewport center on the viewing sphere (Fig. 3.1c), and it can be used to identify the user behavior in an immersive experience. The new type of navigation within the video content shows a clear evolution of the user's role from merely passive in traditional video applications into interactive consumers in VR systems.

The new format as well as the new way of consuming the content open the gate to many promising VR applications, but also pose completely new challenges. One key challenge raised from the interactivity level is the high resolution and low-latency required to ensure a full sense of presence. The user needs to have ultra-low switching delays when changing the displayed viewport to avoid discomfort. This can be ensured by sending to all users the entire content at high-quality, assuming that the desired viewport will be then exported during rendering. This solution is the first one

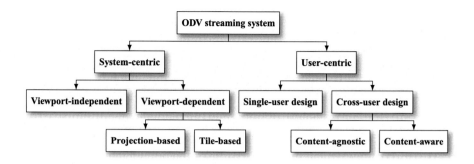

Figure 3.2 Proposed taxonomy of researches related with ODV streaming systems.

that has been proposed, extending the well-established and optimized methods for 2D videos to spherical content. These methodologies are usually user-agnostic and aimed at improving the overall performance through enhancements in the system. The main drawback of these solutions is that they are extremely bandwidth-consuming (up to 43 MB/s for 8K spherical video [10]) since the entire ODV content is delivered to final clients, pushing the available bandwidth to the limit, with a negative impact on the final quality. In practice, only a small portion (typically around 15% of the entire video [11]) of the overall content is displayed by the user, making these solutions extremely inefficient. Recently, more attention has been put on the final users, leading to personalized systems, which put the user at the center of the system and tailor every aspect of the coding–delivery–rendering chain to the viewer interaction. For example, only the predicted content of interest for the final user is pushed into the delivery network [11]. The main aim of these personalized systems is not only to optimize the user's QoE, but also to overcome ODV streaming limitations, such as reducing bandwidth and storage usage. However, this comes at the price of requiring the knowledge of user interactivity patterns in advance. Therefore inspired by recommender system and 5G network communities [12–14], we propose to name the first line of improvements as *system-centric streaming*, whereas the second one as *user-centric streaming*. Fig. 3.2 shows this proposed taxonomy for ODV streaming solutions and all subcategories that will be under examination in the following.

In this chapter, we provide an overview of the research efforts that have been dedicated to advance ODV streaming strategies, with a specific attention to the more recent user-centric systems. Due to this popularity, many survey papers [15–24] have been published already to summarize the main contributions to ODV streaming systems. Table 3.1 depicts these works visualizing their main topics of interest, highlighting also the level of investigation across the end-to-end pipeline.

As it is evident from Table 3.1, the majority of existing surveys are deeply focused on compression, delivery, and quality assessment aspects. For instance, Zink et al. [18] have

Table 3.1 Surveys related with ODV streaming systems. Level of investigation per each topic: ▨ mentioned; ▨ sufficient; ▨ deep.

Survey	Acquisition	Compression	Delivery	Rendering	Quality Assessment	Prediction	Behavioral Analysis
Chen et al. [15]		deep	sufficient		deep		
He et al. [16]	sufficient	sufficient	deep			sufficient	
Fan et al. [17]	mentioned	sufficient	mentioned	mentioned	sufficient		
Zink et al. [18]	deep	mentioned		mentioned	mentioned		
Azevedo et al. [19]		sufficient	deep	deep	sufficient		
Yaqoob et al. [20]		deep	deep		sufficient	sufficient	
Shafi et al. [21]		deep	sufficient	sufficient	deep		
Xu et al. [22]		sufficient	sufficient	mentioned	deep	sufficient	mentioned
Ruan et al. [23]	mentioned		mentioned				
Chiarotti [24]		sufficient	deep		deep	deep	mentioned
Our chapter		sufficient	deep			deep	deep

provided a general overview of the main challenges and the first attempts of solution per each step of the ODV streaming pipeline, from acquisition to the final user rendering experience. Chen et al. [15] have mainly explored the most recent projections methods aimed at improving video coding and transmissions, and reducing video quality distortions. More insights on system design and implementations have been described in [17,20,23]. In particular, both Fan et al. [17] and Yaqoob et al. [20] have examined existing protocols and standards together with optimal ODV streaming solutions. Ruan et al. [23] have instead investigated solutions for VR systems, but mainly from a network services perspective. Visual quality artifacts have been deeply investigated by Azevedo et al. [19]; they describe their sources and features at each step of the system; authors have also presented an overview of existing tools for quality assessment (objective and subjective). Similarly, a deep focus on visual quality assessment, together with attention models and compression, is given by Xu et al. [22]. Authors have highlighted the importance of predicting where viewers mainly put their attention during immersive navigation (*i.e.*, saliency maps) to benefit the entire system since users are the final consumers. They have also partially addressed the need of understanding behavioral features to help in modeling user attention, presenting the main outcomes from existing navigation dataset analysis. Following this direction, the recent work presented by Chiarotti [24] has showed the importance of estimating navigation path also for quality evaluation, neglecting however the behavioral analysis. To the best of our knowledge, these are the only existing surveys which explicitly bring out the importance of the new role of users in ODV streaming applications, and thus the need of understanding their behavior. As shown in Table 3.1, behavioral analysis has been highly overlooked. One of the main contributions of this chapter is to fill in this gap by discussing in-depth the role of the user in ODV streaming strategies.

The remaining of this chapter is structured as follows: Section 3.2 describes recent advances in video streaming towards supporting ODV, from services popularization to standardizing. Section 3.3 provides an overview of coding and delivery strategies for the system-centric streaming, especially introducing differences between viewport-independent and viewport-dependent methods. Section 3.4 highlights the role of the user behavior in ODV streaming and lists datasets for ODV user analyses. Section 3.5 describes how such novel interactivity can drastically improve the status quo using user-centric streaming. To conclude, we present final remarks and highlight new directions in Section 3.6.

3.2. Streaming pipeline: evolution towards ODV

In this section, we provide an overview of the ODV streaming pipeline. We start with an historical overview of ODV to contextualize the first steps that opened the gate to ODV streaming research, which is the main focus of this current chapter, we then

Table 3.2 ODV streaming historical timeline.

2007	Google launches Street View [25]
2011	*ISO publishes MPEG-DASH* [26]
2014	Google launches Cardboard and Facebook acquired Oculus. [27,28]
2015	YouTube and Facebook social platforms allow ODV upload [29,30]
	MPEG standardized MPEG-DASH SRD to support tiled streaming [31]
2016	BBC and ARTE begin sharing ODV content [32,33]
	Facebook proposes Pyramid projection [34]
	MPEG standardized HEVC encoding with Motion Constrained Tile Set [35]
	First viewport prediction algorithms
2017	Vimeo platform allows ODV upload [36]
	YouTube proposes equiangular cubemap projection [37]
	First user navigation datasets for User Behavioral Analyses
2019	*MPEG standardized OMAF* [38]
2021	Facebook promotes VR towards metaverse applications [39]

conclude by explaining how key components of the streaming pipeline, from acquisition to rendering, have evolved and have been standardized to enable ODV services.

Table 3.2 depicts the historical evolution that led to current technology used on ODV systems. This evolution has been characterized by three key components: 1) large-scale utilization of ODV applications; 2) ODV displaying technology; 3) technological advances in the streaming pipeline. The first service that appeared in 2007 based on omnidirectional content was the Google maps street view, which allows users to virtually navigate on a street using a sequence of omnidirectional images [25]. After this, the ODV market has grown significantly mainly when YouTube and Facebook (and Vimeo) allowed the upload and share of 360-degree content on their platforms in 2015 (in 2017) [29,30,36]. The interest in ODV systems then has been grown exponentially: for example, BBC and the French cultural network ARTE used 360-video for immersive documentaries. Now, 360-degree content is widely used across multiple sectors (*e.g.*, e-culture, entertainment, retail, live sports) amplified even further from recent attention to metaverse applications. This widespread of ODV service was further pushed by the advances on HMDs: in 2014 Google proposed an affordable mobile-based HMD, called Cardboard, and Facebook made a two-billion-dollar acquisition of the HMD company Oculus. This has led to an ever-growing desire for the users to experience ODV systems, highlighting the compelling need for research advances, and even standardizing steps on ODV streaming pipeline. The well-known MPEG-dynamic adaptive streaming over HTTP (DASH)—de-facto streaming solutions standardized in 2011 [26]—has been improved to enable ODV systems (italic and blue text in Table 3.2). Moreover, new sphere-to-plane projections were proposed from Facebook and YouTube, namely, pyramid (2016) and equiangular cubemap (2017), to map the spherical content into 2D domain.

In parallel, DASH streaming was extended to the tile-based encoding that has played a key role in viewport dependent streaming. The video content is spatially cropped in different bitstreams, named tiles, each of those independently coded from the other tiles, allowing for unequal quality levels [40]. This is possible, thanks to the *HEVC motion-constrained tile set* (MCTS) technology [35], which eliminates dependencies between tiles, restricting the encoding of visual objects motion, also called motion vectors (MV), at tile boundaries. Tiles from different encoding quality can therefore be combined in a single HEVC bitstream, and the reconstructed bitstream is HEVC compliant and requires only a single decoder for the playback. The other key aspect of tile-based streaming is the DASH *spatial relationship description* (SRD) [31], which enables the transmission of only a portion of the video to display devices. This, in combination with multi-quality tile-based coding, allows us to send at high quality only the portion of interest to the VR user. This will be a key advance in viewport-dependent streaming technologies (discussed in Section 3.3.2).

These above DASH extensions were then consolidated on *omnidirectional media format (OMAF)* [38], the first international standard for storage and distribution of ODVs, a result of the efforts of MPEG, 3GPP, and VR industry forum (VRIF) [41]. OMAF specifies tile-based streaming, ensuring that the OMAF player rewrites the encoded tiles syntax structures to merge them and decode them as one single bitstream [38,42]. Several tools have been proposed to experiment with OMAF: as encoding tools, the Kavazaar [43] that easily supports tile sets; as players, the Fraunhofer OMAF.js[1] and Nokia.[2] OMAF allowed the inclusion of other media types beyond ODVs, such as still images, spatial audio, associated timed text, multiple viewpoints, and even a 2D video overlayed on the ODV [44]. These technological advances and standardization pushed research efforts to improve even further the ODV pipeline to achieve better services in terms of bandwidth, storage, networking caching, and perceived user quality. In what follows, we describe the entire pipeline from acquisition to rendering to show how this has been adapted from classical 2D video to ODV streaming. Then, in the subsequent sections, we provide an overview of the main technological advances, mainly from the coding and streaming perspective. Initial efforts were mainly focused on system-centric streaming, see Section 3.3. At the same time, some researchers focused their studies on understanding how users navigate within VR content (bold and green text in Table 3.2). By analyzing users' trajectories, these studies were able to develop viewport prediction algorithms (2016) and make them available to the community with datasets of user navigation patterns (2017). These datasets are briefly described in Section 3.4. These

---

[1] https://github.com/fraunhoferhhi/omaf.js.
[2] https://github.com/nokiatech/omaf.

initial works opened the gate to user-centric system research, described in depth in Section 3.5.

3.2.1 Adaptive ODV streaming pipeline

We now describe each processing step of the ODV streaming pipeline, focusing mainly on MPEG-DASH [26],[3] and highlighting the main novelties from classical video streaming pipeline to ODV. Fig. 3.3 depicts the adaptive ODV streaming pipeline, with dash dotted green boxes characterizing the system-centric streaming (on what we are going to focus on at the moment) and solid line blue boxes identifying further evolution of ODV streaming toward user-centric ones, described in Section 3.5.

As already discussed in Chapter 2 of this book [46], the first step is the *Acquisition*, which is different from the 2D video counterpart due to the spherical nature of the media format. Most ODV cameras currently capture an entire 360-degree field of view using multi-sensor systems, in which the final picture is generated from multiple inputs signals. These signals are then processed by a stitching algorithm, where the overlapping regions between the camera views are aligned, and then warped in sphere surface. To be processed by existing 2D media processing tools, the spherical content is projected into a planar representation, which is usually called *Panorama*. This is the *Projection* step. The most commonly employed sphere-to-plane projections are the equirectangular projection (ERP) (Fig. 3.4b) and cubemap projection (CMP) (Fig. 3.4c) [47], which are supported by the OMAF standard. The ERP is the simplest and the most popular projection format, which maps the viewing sphere onto the panorama through the longitude and the latitude values. However, it is well known that this project suffers from an unequal sampling of points introduced in the pole areas, leading to more artifacts and less efficient compression and rendering tasks at the poles [19]. The other well-known projection is the Cubemap, which has been introduced by the industrial sector initially for the gaming community. In this projection, the sphere is first mapped to a cube, which is then unfolded, and each face is arranged into the panorama frame. Though a lower distortion is achieved with CMP than with ERP, the project still suffers from unequal distribution of pixels (higher distribution towards the corners of the cube), which still affects the overall quality during rendering phase.

Once the content is projected into a 2D plane, it can be processed by the *Encoding* step, using the state-of-the-art codec from classical 2D media compression, such as High-Efficiency Video Coding (HEVC/H.265) [48]. Typically, in DASH, clients *pull* the content from the server, instead of being the server *pushing* it to clients. Specifically,

---

[3] It is worth mentioning that other ODV streaming protocols (not purely DASH based) have been proposed [45], however we mainly focus on DASH advances as this conceptually covers the majority of the works.

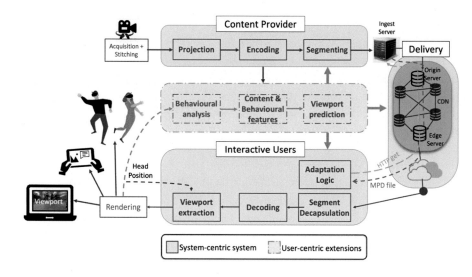

Figure 3.3 System-centric and User-centric ODV streaming pipeline.

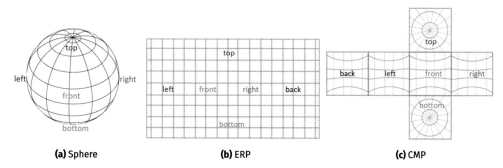

(a) Sphere   **(b)** ERP   **(c)** CMP

Figure 3.4 Widely adopted projections from a) spherical domain to plane: b) ERP and c) CMP.

each content is encoded into multiple resolutions and quality levels (*representations*), and each client dynamically selects the best representations when fetching video segments using HTTP requests. Hence, the encoding step produces multiple quality levels (representations). Each encoded representation is then segmented: the *Segmenting* step breaks the video into *temporal* chunks (usually 2 s long) and stored at the server side. The different available representations of these chunks are described at the server, which, in the case of DASH, is done on the DASH Media Presentation Description (DASH-MPD). The client then selects the most appropriate chunk representation to request, as explained later. DASH streaming was extended to the tile-based encoding that has played a key role in viewport-dependent streaming. The video content is *spatially* cropped into different bitstreams, named tiles, each of those encoded at a different coding rates and resolutions independently from the other tiles. This enables per-tile representations that are stored at the server [40], providing the client with the freedom to select unequal quality in the ODV.

The chunks created by the encoder are then ingested in a HTTP origin server that will process clients requests, *Delivery* step. This origin server is usually inside a content delivery network (CDN), which is an optimized infrastructure that redistributes chunks on multiple servers, ultimately reaching clients locations. At the client site, the chunks are processed by *Segment Decapsulation* to extract HEVC bitstream, which is then decoded in the *Decoding* step and fed into the playout buffer. In parallel, still at the decoder side, the *Adaptation Logic* dynamically decides the best representations to request for the upcoming chunk. This selection is based on the client connection and buffer condition as well as the device capabilities. The pipeline ends with *Rendering*, which back-projects the decoded planar representation in the spherical geometry and displays the content of interest to the final user. This content of interest (viewport) is evaluated in the prior step, *Viewport extraction*, in which the current user viewing direction is translated into the displayed viewport.

3.3. System-centric streaming

Advances in the streaming pipeline were initially aimed at improving the overall system performance in terms of consumed bandwidth, storage cost, and networking reliability metrics. These streaming solutions are defined in this chapter as system-centric ones as they usually optimize systems design, being usually user-agnostic (neglecting user behavior analyses and prediction). In the following, we further categorize system-centric solutions in viewport-independent and viewport-dependent streaming. *Viewport-independent* solutions are the most similar to traditional adaptive 2D video streaming, in which the entire panorama is encoded and treated equally. Specifically, each representation available at the server side is encoded with a uniform quality and resolution across the entire panorama. As a consequence, for any final client to be able to display VR content at high-quality, the entire panorama will be downloaded at high quality. This ensures low latency for viewport-switching, but it is extremely costly in terms of storage and bandwidth usage [49]. Moreover, it assumes that the whole panorama is equally important, which is clearly not the case in VR systems. To strike the optimal balance between bandwidth waste and switching latency, ODV user interactivity needs to be taken into account, leading to streaming strategies adapting not only to the content, but also to users, *viewport-dependent* streaming. The key assumption is that not the entire panorama is equally important since during the navigation users focus more on some areas than others. In 2012, Alface et al. [50] were the first ones to show that an ideal knowledge of the user interaction could lead to saving bandwidth, when transmitting only the viewport (region of interest to the user). In the following, we present in details advances on both viewport-dependent and viewport-independent streaming solutions.

3.3.1 Viewport-independent streaming

Beyond initial works that applied classical DASH streaming to ODVs [29], recent works that fall under the viewport-independent framework are mainly focused on improving the encoding step, overcoming issues related to sphere-to-plane projection. One goal is to encode the ODV in the spherical domain with no need to project the content into a bi-dimensional space. For instance, Vishwanath et al. [51] propose to encode the inter-frame motion vector (MV) directly on the sphere instead of the planar domain, avoiding distortions during the sphere-to-plane conversion. The MV is expressed as rotation on the sphere (rotational motion vector), and results demonstrate good gains compared to standard HEVC 2D video encoding. Also working on the sphere, Bidgoli et al. [52] propose a representation learning approach for spherical data. To avoid distortion from planar projection and yet exploit the benefit of deep learning for features extraction, the authors propose a new sphere convolution operation to keep the high expressiveness of 2D convolution, while having the advantage of uniform sampling on the sphere. This can lead to better coding efficiency, as shown in the paper. These aforementioned approaches show promising use of an on-the-sphere encoding strategy for omnidirectional images.

3.3.2 Viewport-dependent streaming

Viewport-dependent solutions are based on the assumption that the content is not equally important (*spatially*), since users require to display only a portion of it. Therefore it is clear that a non-uniform streaming should be considered to ensure higher quality to the areas more likely to be displayed. The adaptation to the viewport has been implemented in both the projection and the (tile-based) encoding step of the streaming pipeline. The former (*projection-based approach*) adapts the bitrate allocation during projection, making this an unequal allocation that prioritizes areas of interest for the final users. The latter (*tile-based approach*) has emerged when tiled-based coding was proposed by HEVC encoding MCTS, and most of the ODV works have focused afterwards on tile-based streaming for ODV. We detail these two approaches in what follow.

Projection-based approach

Projection-based approaches (also called viewport-dependent projections [20]) aim at projecting the spherical content in such a way that the most important areas (most likely to be displayed) are the least distorted during the projection step of the pipeline. Selecting unequal levels of encoding rates across the panorama offers better QoE, but at a price of generating multiple versions of the same panorama (each version with a different area at high-quality). This impacts the storage cost (higher than the viewport-independent case) and the caching hit ratio (lower since users might prefer different versions, depending on their focus of attention). Examples of viewport-dependent projections are the pyramid projection (Fig. 3.5a) and [34], the truncated square pyramid

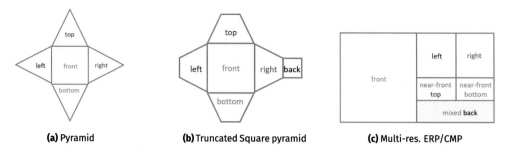

(a) Pyramid   **(b)** Truncated Square pyramid   **(c)** Multi-res. ERP/CMP

Figure 3.5 Viewport-dependent projections.

projection (TSP) (Fig. 3.5b) [53]. The first one projects the sphere onto a pyramid, with an intentional unequal allocation of points: more data points to the pyramid base. The pyramid is then unwrapped and resized into 2D space (see figure) and encoded with classical 2D codec tools. The novelty is that this projection encodes at the higher quality the area corresponding to the bottom face of the pyramid, which will be matched with the viewing direction of the users. The projection however suffers from a rapid quality degradation when moving from the bottom face to the lateral ones. This is obviated in the TSP, a truncated version of the pyramid projection. Compared to a viewport-independent ERP, Facebook estimated that CMP has 25% improvement compression efficiency, whereas Pyramid has a 80% gain [34]. With the ultimate goal of leaning toward more viewport-dependent projections, variations of the classical ERP and CMP have been proposed. Multi-resolution variants of ERP and CMP have been presented in [53], in which the content is first projected into the plane (or the cube), and then re-sized and scaled to fit the rectangular plane, as shown in the Fig. 3.5c. In the final arrangement, some areas have a much larger scale and sampling, and this should cover ideally the viewport of interest to final users.

Tiled-based approach

Corbillon et al. [54] proposed an unequal encoding bitrates for ODVs, such that within the panorama one region of attention is encoded at higher quality. Each user would then select the version with the high-quality region overlapping with their viewport. This pillar work has introduced the concept that the content is not spatially equally important, opening the gate to tile-based approach. Today, it has been improved by current standardized tiled streaming using the HEVC MCTS, which encodes tiles at different bitrates and resolutions, creating per-tile representations that are stored at the server. The key novelty of a tile-based system is that tiles can be independently fetched by the client at the desired quality level. This creates a more flexible transmission strategy able to compose the user viewport with higher quality tiles. This higher level of flexibility however comes at the price of server processing and storage costs (a large number of representations encoded and made available at the main server), and larger computational costs for the final user to select the representation to request (larger search space in the adaptation logic). To overcome these limitations and profit the most from tile-based strategies, researchers have focused their studies on 1) optimal design of the tiles at the encoder side; or 2) optimized tiles distribution in the network delivery (*e.g.*, client adaptation, multi-path and caching).

The tile-based encoding strategy directly impacts the server-side storage costs, hence the compelling need to optimize it for omnidirectional content. Graf et al. [55] published one of the first works in this direction, showing that different tiling patterns have a different impact on the server-side costs, with the final result being that a 6×4 pattern shows most improvements. Researchers evolved then the studies toward viewport-dependent tile-based design [56,57]. Ozcinar et al. [56] design an optimal tiling scheme and the required encoding bitrate levels based on a probabilistic model that reflects the users interactivity, showing the gain in terms of users' QoE. Still optimizing the tiles at the server side, but with more focus on the storage costs, Rossi et al. [57] propose an optimization problem at the server side aimed at selecting the optimal bitrate per tile to be stored at the main server to minimize the quality distortion at the user side, while respecting the storage cost constraint. This optimization has been done considering non-rectangular and 6-tiles configuration and including users viewing direction probability in the optimization model.

Instead of optimizing the tile design at the server side, many other works have been focused on optimizing designs at the user side, studying optimal adaptation logic in viewport-dependent tile-based solutions. Ashan et al. [58] propose a buffer-based algorithm to optimize the bitrate of area in the panorama overlapping the users' viewport. The main challenge is that this does not simply imply selecting the optimal representation from the MPD, but it rather needs a mapping from tile's bitrate to viewport quality. Other efforts instead focused on adapting the strategy to users' interaction, exploiting either the knowledge of the viewing direction [59] or probabilistic/average models, such as the heatmap [60]. Fu et al. [59] propose an adaptation logic based on sequential reinforcement learning (RL), with the agent reward being the quality experienced by the users. The RL agent implicitly learns the interaction model and refines the adaptation logic based on the users' behavior, showing a gain of 12% QoE improvement with respect to nonviewport-dependent strategies. Rossi et al. [60] propose a navigation-aware adaptation logic using a probabilistic heatmap model. Other parallel researches have improved network aspects, such as multi-path, pre-fetching, decoding offloading, and caching strategies. Duanmu et al. [61] developed a multi-path video streaming in heterogeneous WiFi and 5G networks. To efficiently utilize the high bandwidth available in 5G and maximize the rendered video quality, their client fetches videos from two networks. The 5G network was used to pre-fetch high-quality video chunks and re-transmit chunks that cannot be delivered in time through WiFi. Nguyen et al. [62] also address pre-fetching, but using the new package prioritization feature from HTTP/2 to deliver high-quality tiles. Then, in a new direction, Nguyen et al. [63] investigated multi-path streaming, but for decoding offloading. They consider a mobile VR device and a PC with access to the stream server and connected using a millimeter-wave (mmWave) network in the 60 GHz band. At the same time, tiles are fetched and decoded by devices, and the PC shares the decoded frames via mmWave to the mobile. Such collaborative decoding offloaded processing costs by 25%, speeding up of the decoding of all tiles. Finally, Maniotis et al. [64] improves the server cache hit ratio by using a RL framework based on tiles heatmap, showing an improvement of the proposed viewport-dependent caching mechanism against other caching schemes, such as least frequently used (LFU) and least recently used (LRU).

The works mentioned so far have shown the gain of proposing viewport-dependent tile-based streaming and its impact across different steps of the pipeline. However, limitations still remain in the intrinsic definition of tile-based streaming. For example, the MCTS restricts the inter-frame prediction of visual objects between tiles, reducing the encoding efficiency. To obviate this limitation, Son et al. [65] propose new HEVC extensions to enable inter-frame prediction, when an encoded object has dependency from outside the tile using the HEVC scalability extension and extracting the object from an up-sampled version of the base layer. Another limitation of tile-based coding is the intra-frame redundancy, which is not minimized across tiles. Bidgoli et al. [66] address this limitation by allowing the encoder to detect reference regions outside the current fetched tiles. Then, they propose an encoding in which the intra-frame reference region is at the center of a requested tile to improve client intra-frame decoding.

Despite these last limitations, viewport-dependent tile-based streaming has been widely adopted for ODV streaming. A key aspect across all these works is the user's information, expressed, for example, either via viewport trajectory or heatmap. The advances made so far have motivated researchers to dig deeper into the study of user's behavior, as discussed in the following section.

3.4. The role of the user in ODV

In the following, we provide an overview on the recent ODV multimedia datasets made recently available to our community and the tool developed to perform behavioral data analysis from these datasets.

3.4.1 ODV navigation datasets

We provide an overview of the datasets collecting user's navigation data during immersive experiences. We summarize these datasets in Table 3.3, and highlight that they are limited to i) *publicly* available dataset, with data related to ii) ODV content (no images), and iii) navigation trajectories (i.e., head and/or eye movements). To mimic a real-life

Table 3.3 ODV navigation datasets publicly available. Link to each dataset can be found in the Bibliography.

Y	Reference	Test Preparation			Subj.	Available Data	
		ODVs	Len.	Category		Format	Others
2017	Corbillon [67]	5	70 s	Content Genres	59	Quaternion	Open source software.
	Lo [68]	10	60 s		50	Euler angles	Saliency and motion maps.
	Wu [69]	18	164–655 s	Content Genres	48	Quaternion	Free-task and Task experiments.
	Xu [70]	48	20–60 s	Content Genres	40	Spherical coord.	VQA task.
2018	Ozcinar [71]	6	10 s	Content Genres	17	Spherical coord.	Open source software.
	Fremerey [72]	20	30 s	-	48	Euler angles	Open source software.
	Xu [73]	58	10–80 s	Content Genres	76	Spherical coord.	HM and EM data.
	David [74]	19	20 s	Content Features	57	Spherical coord.	HM and EM data, saliency maps.
	Zhang [75]	104	20–60 s	Content Genres	20★	Spherical coord.	HM and EM data and heatmaps.
	Xu [76]	208	20–60 s	Content Genres and Feat., Camera Motion	31★	Spherical coord.	HM and EM data.
2019	Nasrabadi [77]	28	60 s	Camera Motion	60	Quaternion	Questionnaire on attention.
2020	Rossi [57]	15	20 s	Content Genres	31▲	Spherical coord.	Data also from Laptop and Tablet, code ODV storage optimization.
	Rondón [78]	306	20–655 s	-	~42★	Spherical coord.	Aggregation datasets [67–69,73,74,76].
2021	Dharmasiri [79]	88	30–655 s	-	~45★	Euler angles♦	Aggregation datasets [67–69,77,80,81], code video segment categorization.
	Chakareski [82]	15	36 s	Content Genres	5–12	Euler angles	RD characteristics of full UHD ODVs.

★ per video.
▲ per video and device.
♦ roll angle was ignored.

condition, VR users cannot display the entire environment around themselves, but only a restricted portion (*i.e.*, viewport). Specifically, the sequence of spatio-temporal points representing the user's viewing direction over time identifies users' attention within an immersive experience. Based on VR device technology, the user's viewing direction can be represented either by head or eye movements. The head movement determines the field of view (FoV) as the pixel area of ODV, which is displayed by a given user over time, whereas the eye movement datasets contain the specific area within the FoV that captures the user attention and can be classified as salient.

The navigation trajectories are collected via a three-steps collection procedure: *1)* Test Preparation, *2)* Subjective Test, and *3)* Data Formatting and Storage. The selection of video content to be used during subjective experiments is one of the first steps. During *test preparation*, ODVs are selected based on several criteria: video length, number of video, content category, features, and attributes. Considering the video sequence length, Ozcinar et al. present [71] the shortest group of videos (*i.e.*, 10 s) whereas Duanmu et al. [83] have the longest one with sequence in the range of 60–120 seconds. The widest range of ODVs is instead proposed by Xu et al. [76] with videos of variable length, from 10 up to 80 seconds. Also, in terms of number of video contents, there are various choices: only 5 videos (with 2 more ODVs used during the training phase) in [67] as opposed to 208 ODVs in [76]. Interestingly, two of the most recent datasets presented [78,79] integrate previous databases, such as [67–69,73,74,76] and [67,68,77,80,81], respectively. Therefore they become among the largest and most heterogeneous ODV datasets currently publicly available. Another criteria to select ODVs is the one based on three main categories: *Content Genres*, *Content Features*, and *Camera Motion*. For instance, authors in [75] select their video only based on the content genres, offering mainly sport activities related videos. A wider range of genres (*e.g.*, music shows, documentaries, short movies, computer animation and gaming) can be found in most of the publicly available datasets [57,69,70,73]. Other authors choose their content based on attributes such as camera motion [77], outdoor/indoor scene [74] or a mix of all the aforementioned video categories (*i.e.*, indoor/outdoor scene, fixed/moving camera, and different content genres) [76]. It is worth mentioning that the most recent dataset presented by Chakareski et al. [82] is the only one which presents full UHD ODVs.

The second step of the data collection campaign is the *subjective test*, which represents the core data collection step. Most of the datasets collect navigation data during free-task experiments, which means that viewers could move inside the video content as they wished. There are, however, a few examples where users were asked to take some specific actions. For instance, the work presented in [69] proposes two different experiments: a first set of ODVs are used to identify the natural behavior in a free-navigation experiment, whereas a second set is more specific to VR live streaming applications. In fact, in the second experiment live recorded ODV have been used to mimic the case of live-streaming data-tracking, and beyond objective head-movements trajectories, also subjective perception of the video content was captured. Similarly, authors [77] study participant's attention, presence, and discomfort levels by a questionnaire at the end of the vision session. Auxiliary subjective quality scores were collected also in [70], in which the dataset is used for visual quality assessment (VQA) tasks. Looking more specifically at the capturing of the objective data (*i.e.*, trajectories), there are different types of VR devices that can be used, such as laptop, tablet, and smartphone. Under the assumption that it provides to most immersive experience, the most widely adopted device is the head-mounted display (HMD): a helmet with a display and movement sensor able to adapt the rendered image to user's viewing direction. Other datasets however do exist with data collected by other devices. Duanmu et al. [83] propose navigation trajectories experienced only on laptop, whereas Rossi et al. [57] collect users trajectories across multiple devices (tablet and laptop, in addition to HMD), with the main purpose of studying the effect of the displaying device in the user's navigation. Moreover, most of the presented ODV datasets provide the viewers navigation trajectories as a sequence of head movements over time [67–73]. Even if the head position is a valuable proxy of the user viewing direction, people can still move their eyes and focus on a specific area of the displayed viewport keeping the head fixed. Thus for specific applications, such as visual attention modeling or quality assessment, recording eye gaze movements during the navigation is equally valuable. Hence, there are also dataset containing both information [74–76].

The last part of the creation of an ODV dataset is the *data formatting and storage* of the collected navigation trajectories in an immersive scenario. Since the navigation within ODV is restricted to 3-DoF movements (Fig. 3.1), only rotational movements are captured neglecting potential translational movements. These rotational movements can be represented based on several conventions within a spherical system: Euler angles (*i.e.*, yaw, pitch, and roll); spherical coordinates (*i.e.*, latitude and longitude), and quaternion. The first two formats are the most common, as shown in Table 3.3, whereas quaternion is employed only by [67,77], highlighting the higher accuracy and robustness of the quaternion in representing rotational movements. Finally, some of the current publicly available dataset provide also some other data: software that have been used to record users' attention during subjective experiments to encourage the community to extend their collected data [67,71,72]; saliency [74] and motion maps [68]; other algorithms, such as server storage optimization and video segment categorization in [57] and [79], respectively; rate-distortion (RD) characteristics of UHD ODV to correlate with user navigation in [82].

3.4.2 Behavioral analysis within ODVs

Most of the above papers present, along with the dataset, a general statistical characterization of users' behavior. This has opened the gate to a new research area aimed at capturing key features that characterize users' interaction while experiencing ODV. In what follow, we depict the main findings of this prominent area of research on behavioral analysis. In particular, we distinguish two strands of investigation: a more traditional one aimed at identifying general behavioral features of users while navigating; and a second one focused on identifying more specific and representative users features of the users' behavior, such as users' similarity based on trajectory-based data analysis.

Traditional data analysis

The way in which users typically interact with ODVs has been analyzed mainly in terms of general metrics, such as angular velocity, frequency of fixation, and mean exploration angles. Other than these quantitative metrics, a visual (and qualitative) tool used to study user's behavior in VR is the heatmap, which identifies areas of the content mostly attended by viewers within a time interval. The investigations based on these aforementioned metrics have given intuitions to answer some key-questions. Finding an answer for these issues is indeed a first step towards the design of user-centric solutions for ODV system. We now summarize the most relevant questions (from a more generic to a more specific behavioral perspective) and the works that aimed at answering them.

Where do users usually look at (on average)? Understanding the areas on which users focus the most within the spherical content is key to optimize the streaming pipeline via viewport-dependent coding techniques or adaptation logic, as described in Section 3.3.2, and thus ensuring a good final quality. For this reason, many different researchers at first focused on showing through statistical analysis that users prefer to look at the equatorial area of ODVs, rather than at the poles [67,71,74–76]. For instance, some [67,71] use heatmaps averaged across users per each content to show that the users head is densely distributed over time in the equatorial region and in particular, above 100° in terms of latitude. A similar behavior has been confirmed by Xu et al. [76] analyzing eye movements: the distribution of gaze fixations shows indeed an equatorial tendency, and, moreover, users move more frequently on the left and right directions than up and down. Deeper investigations on the equatorial bias have highlighted that viewers spend more time towards the front center area of ODVs, where typically the main relevant scene is located [70,72,73,83]. Finally, Fremerey et al. [72] illustrate in their behavioral analysis that users change their viewing direction only for a short period of time, and, in general, prefer to display the video from a more central and comfortable position.

How do users actually move over time? The average spatial distribution of users' attention might not be enough to characterize their behavior. For example, a deeper understanding on how viewers actually navigate over time within the video content would allow us to distinguish behaviors that can be predicted or not. In detail, erratic and random navigation within the spherical content is usually challenging to predict. This is the case of the beginning of the navigation within new ODV, in which a predominance of exploratory movements has been pointed out, highlighting their randomness, and therefore their difficulty to be anticipated [67,69,79]. However, after a period in the range of 10–20 seconds, viewers tend to converge to common (and more predictable) directions, which typically correspond to the main focus of attentions (FoAs) in the scene. Once users find their main point of interest, they tend to not move too much [79]. Corbillon et al. [67] show that in a window of 2 seconds, the 95% of analyzed subjects stay within a ray of $\pi/2$ from the initial position. This more static and understandable (FoA driven) behavior make the users' interaction much more predictable than the initial explorative phase.

How is the user behavior affected by VR devices? Since ODVs can be experienced by different apparatus, a consequent rising question is on the influence of the selected VR devices on the users interactivity. Focusing on the spatial average distribution, the device seems to have a small impact on the overall visitation density: a central and equatorial bias is preserved when navigating via a desktop [83]. Looking at the users' attention over time, however, a dependency on the device has been observed. After a highly-exploratory behavior at the beginning of the immersive experience (which remains despite the adopted viewing device [84]), a more dynamic navigation has been observed for users displaying ODVs with a laptop than with HMD or tablet [57]. For example, this can be related to a lower sense of immersion and engagement that leads to more explorative movements. Thus taking into account different VR devices is relevant and fruitful to understand the difference in terms of user interactivity. Furthermore, analysis has been presented by Broeck et al. [84], focusing on user experience with heterogeneous VR devices, such as HMD, tablet, and smartphones. In particular, two kinds of omnidirectional video sequences were analyzed: video with a static scene (*e.g.*, recorded with a fixed camera) and moving scene. The results show that users explore more in the latter type of content. As expected, the immersion sensation is higher with HMD than other devices, whereas the tablet offers less immersion. Beyond traditional objective (implicit) metrics, such as statistical tool, VR experience can be analyzed through subjective (explicit) metrics, such as users' feedback, and interesting observations can be deduced by comparing implicit and explicit feedback. In [84], authors interviewed participants querying about their sense of immersion during the experience. This explicit data matches the more implicit ones based on users movements since subjects felt more immersed with HMD, despite being less comfortable than with smartphones.

How is the user behavior affected by content genres? Similarly to the previous question, the correlation between users movements and video content has been analyzed from different perspectives. Xu M. et al. [70] show that when the main objects in the scene are not located in the central area of the video, users are not focused in the central area of the content, but they instead follow the FoA. Ozcinar et al. [71] show a direct correlation between the distribution of fixation points and the video complexity, in terms of spatial information (SI) and temporal information (TI). In particular, the lower is the TI, the greater is the number of fixations located in the same region. Moreover, the way in which users navigate inside ODVs change for different video categories [57,85]. For instance, Almquist et al. [85] highlight that viewers tend to be more uniformly distributed for videos without moving objects, whereas Rossi et al. observe that ODVs without a main object in the scene bring users to have highly exploratory interaction, especially with HMD. On the contrary, the level of interactivity is not correlated with the viewing device if there is a main focus of attention in the video which capture user attention [57]. Finally, the correlation between navigation patterns and the video content is significantly relevant such that Dharmasiri et al. [79] use the fixation distribution as a proxy for their video categorization algorithm.

Are users consistent in their navigation? A final and yet important question is if users tend to navigate in a consistent way. In other words, researchers have studied the average behavior of users, but also their variance and deviation. Small variance means that heatmaps can be representative enough of the users' behavior, leading to reliable prediction of the user interaction. A general high consistency among users in terms of spatial distribution has been identified by general statistical analysis for head movements. For instance, Xu et al. [70] evaluate a high linear correlation between heatmaps generated by two random sets of users. A similar outcome has been shown in [73] where in particular, it has been highlighted that almost 50% of users focus on the same viewing area among 8 quantized regions of the ODV. These works mainly focused on summary statistics, such as mean and variance, of users' behavior averaged across users. Looking at deeper analysis focused on pairwise comparison, authors in [76] have evaluated the average intersection angle of eye-gaze direction per each pair of participants across each content. This analysis highlights heterogeneity in users' behavior, in contrast with the observations carried out from the other studies. This inconsistency suggests the need to go beyond traditional statistical analysis to better understand the user behavior within immersive content. Moreover, beyond the inconsistency just highlighted, it is worth mentioning that most of the above studies are focused on behaviors averaged over time, for example, heatmaps and eye fixation. These metrics are highly informative about the spatial behavior (where do users tend to look at), but only partially informative about at the temporal behavior (we can deduce how much erratic users tend to be, but not really if two users are interacting similarly). However, deeper temporal analysis is essential to develop reliable users prediction algorithm, deeper behavioral analysis, and enable user-centric systems. In what follow, we review this second strand of research focused on trajectory-based data analysis and highlight the key outcomes and novelty that emerge and how this can lead to user-centric systems.

Trajectory-based data analysis

As emerged in the previous discussion, behavioral analysis based on statistical tools or heatmap provides a general understanding of user's behavior in ODV content failing in detecting deep insights into users' attention dynamics, such as how much viewers interact in harmony among themselves. Specifically, there are still crucial questions that need to be addressed: "*Are users interacting in a similar way? Can human behavior be predicted?*" Answering these questions is indeed essential for many and not trivial tasks. In this context, detecting viewers who are navigating in a similar way would help to improve the accuracy and robustness of predictive algorithm, and thus to personalize the delivery strategy. This information could also be exploited for identifying key navigation trajectories, which can be used either to optimize video coding or QoE assessment. Beyond immersive video streaming system applications, being able to detect users who are interacting in a similar way from those who are not, might be essential for medical purposes, such as studying psychiatric disorders [86,87]. Equipped with this motivation, a new direction of behavioral analysis has started aimed at identifying behavior similarities among users, across video content and/or devices. This has led to the development of new metrics and tools built in the space-time trajectory domain.

Clustering is one of the most popular and robust techniques to infer data structure, it has been therefore employed in the context of VR applications. Based on intuitions from vehicle trajectory prediction, Petrangeli et al. [88] model each user navigation as independent trajectories in terms of roll, pitch, and yaw angles, and apply a spectral clustering [89,90] to identify trajectories with similar behavior over time. The dominant trajectories, identified by the main clusters, are eventually used to predict new viewers. Though this method is efficient in discovering general trends of users' attention, it is not focused on identifying clusters that are consistent in terms of displayed content; meaning that users in the same group do not necessarily consume the same portion of ODV. Clustering to perform long-term trajectory predictions is presented in [91], where authors first adopt a well-known spectral clustering algorithm, density-based spatial clustering of applications with noise (DBSCAN), to identify key clusters and trajectories from a set of training samples. Then, when new (test) users start an ODV streaming session, they are assigned to a specific cluster, and future trajectories are predicted accordingly. This association step is based on viewing direction comparison measured in the equirectangular plane, neglecting the actual spherical geometry. Therefore the clusters identified by both algorithms suffer of two major shortcomings: 1) not identifying group of users necessarily consuming the same portion of the ODV; 2) not necessarily considering the spherical geometry into account. To overcome these limitations, a novel spherical clustering tool specific for ODV users has been proposed in [92]. This is a graph-based algorithm that is able to identify groups of viewers based on their consistency in the navigation. In practice, authors first define a metric to quantify the commonly displayed portion of the content (*i.e.*, overlapped viewport) among users; based on this metric, they build a graph, whose nodes are associated to different viewers, and finally, a clustering method based on Bron–Kerbosh algorithm is applied to build clusters as cliques (*i.e.*, sub-graph of inter-connected nodes). Thus the algorithm detects and groups users *only if* they consistently display similar viewports over time, while consuming the same ODV content, and this viewport comparison is done taking into account also the spherical geometry of the content. Due to its robustness and specificity for VR content, this tool has been used to analyze navigation patterns in some publicly available datasets, such as [57,77]. The number of total clusters and users per cluster is a proxy of users' similarity in exploring ODVs: the fewer the clusters, the more users are focused on a similar area of the video content, highlighting a similar behavior. Both [57,77] have showed that videos characterized by a dominant focus of attention (*i.e.*, moving objects) are explored in a similar way by users, except few exceptions due to camera motion [77]. For instance, videos that have a vertical camera motion bring viewers not to be focused on a specific area, but to be distributed on the landscape.

With the idea of developing an objective metric able to assess users' similarity in a spatio-temporal domain, Rossi et al. [57] propose a novel *affinity metric* to quantify the detected similarities among viewers via the spherical clustering. This is evaluated as the normalized weighted average of cluster popularity (*i.e.*, how many users per cluster): 0 when users are not clustered together because of being highly dispersed in the navigation; 1 when users share a strong similarity in their trajectories. Equipped with this tool, they noticed that the affinity between users is highly correlated to the selected VR device: HMD leads to higher *affinity metric* than other devices. A similar outcome has been also identified by authors [93], which directly compare different prediction models for navigation trajectories collected by different devices, such as HMD, PC, and smartphone. Other than showing that exploration done via desktop is more static than the other devices, a higher prediction accuracy for HMD users has also been verified, especially in the near future. Following this research direction, a novel viewport clustering algorithm as a tool for behavioral analysis and video categorization has been proposed recently [79]. The main novelty is to consider multimodal clustering analysis, in which the spherical location of each viewer is augmented by other modalities as input such as head movement speed and the percentage of the sphere explored in a given time window. In this way, users in the same clusters are similar not only in terms of displayed viewport, but also for the style of exploration.

Beyond clustering, other tools have been proposed to understand similarities and study user predictability. In [94], authors propose to base their behavioral analysis on tools from information theory, such as actual entropy, transfer entropy, and mutual information, which quantify randomness and uncertainty in the trajectories of users. For example, the actual entropy is low for users that experience "repetitive" behavior (trajectories) over time, leading to highly predictable users. From a first intra-behavior analysis, aimed at studying the behavior of one single user across diverse contents, profiling behaviors have been identified: some viewers conserve similar navigation independently by the video content. Moreover, they also quantify more randomness in navigation trajectories within ODVs lacking specific FoA. As second line of investigation, an inter-user behavior analysis has also been conducted, measuring how informative other users' behavior is for a current user. In other words, the study quantifies how much information about the predictability within a specific content can be extracted by the navigation of a given group of users. This analysis is similar to the previous one based on clusters and users' similarity. However, the information theory tools capture a more meaningful behavior and better quantify viewers similarity during their navigation than metrics based only on the spatial location of users, such as the spherical clustering proposed in [92].

3.5. User-centric ODV streaming

The tools and metrics discussed in Section 3.4.2 enable a deeper understanding and prediction level of the users' interaction, opening the gate to personalized and user-centric systems, Fig. 3.3 (light blue and green boxes), where the different steps of the pipeline are tuned based on single user's behavior. In the following, we review the main contributions that have been proposed toward user-centric systems, distinguishing the work based on the type of behavioral information: i) extracted from a single user (*single-user design*), ii) extracted from multiple users (*cross-user design*).

3.5.1 Single-user designs

A key step in user-centric systems is the prediction of the users' head movement. The first and among the simplest technique (and most widely adopted) is based on the past and current trajectory of a single user, neglecting other viewers and video content information. Qian et al. [95] have experimentally shown how three simple logistic regression models, such as average, linear regression (LR) and weighted LR (WLR) with a moving window of 1 second are able to successfully anticipate the user behavior in the next short time window (*i.e.*, 0.5, 1, and 2 seconds). For the first time, authors are able to prove the potentiality of the prediction. Specifically, giving higher fetching priority to tiles that most likely will be displayed can reduce the bandwidth usage up to 80%. Multiple works have followed all adopting such simple predictive algorithms for user-centric adaptation logic, showing the gain in terms of bandwidth, re-buffering, and final quality experience by the user. Experimental validation has been proposed in [96], in which the user-centric adaptation logic has been tested on real-world 4G bandwidth. Results have shown that the proposed strategy maintains a good displayed quality (the same achieved when sending the entire panorama), but with a reduction of bandwidth overload up to 35%. Logistic regression based on historical data has been used also in [97], in which the adaptation logic for ODV streaming optimizes the optimal representation per tile to request according to network bandwidth and predicted users' head movements. Their analysis emphasized the need of accurately predicting future viewport position for ODV streaming. A WLR algorithm is considered in a similar framework, but in the case of scalable video coding [98]. Specifically, high-quality representations of tiles within the predicted viewport are prefetched shortly before being visualized to ensure high quality in the displayed content and at the same time to reduce storage costs at the server-side, which has been an open challenge especially for ODV that is highly data intensive.

Most of these works have shown the potentiality of user-centric systems, but suffer from poor prediction accuracy in the long-term (mainly due to the lack of other users and content information). At the same time, the behavioral studies highlighted in Section 3.4.2 have shown a strong consistency and similarity in the way in which users navigate ODVs, motivating cross-users designs described in the following subsection.

3.5.2 Cross-user designs

To breakthrough the limitation of single-user frameworks, a new research direction has been carried out aimed at exploiting behavioral information from *multiple* users to identify and predict the most popular trends in navigating ODVs and develop user-centric systems accordingly. In the following, we review these efforts, first describing the work that are *content-agnostic*, mainly based on user cross-users information. Then, we introduce the *content-based* works, in which users' information is augmented by content information.

Content-agnostic designs

At first, linear model (LR) and classical clustering have been widely used to infer single user behavior from cross-user information [88,91,99,100]. For example, with the main intent to improve the long-term users' viewport prediction, Ban et al. [99] propose a viewport prediction approach based on k-nearest-neighbors (KNN) algorithm and aimed at combining both behavioral characteristics of the single-user and those extracted by benchmark viewers. Specifically, the algorithm is composed of two main steps: *i)* the user head position is predicted via LR model based on the historical movements of only the single user under investigation; *ii)* this prediction is then used to form the K nearest users set, as the users with the closest viewport centers previously collected. The K-NN set is used to compute the viewing probability per tiles. This is one of the proposed methods by Xie et al. [91], aimed at using cross-user information to identify main clusters of users, and then predict new users mimicking the behavior of the closest cluster. Per each detected group, the viewing probability of tiles is then computed and applied to support the viewport prediction during video playback of new viewers. Even if the prediction is more accurate in a time window of 3 seconds and longer, viewers are clustered based on Euclidean distance, neglecting the actual spherical geometry, resulting in not fully representative clusters. With the idea of exploiting the spherical geometry, other white-box models have been proposed. For instance, Hu et al.

in [101] use a graph–based approach to improve the accuracy of viewport prediction in a QoE-optimized ODV streaming system. The authors first predict tiles in the FoV by a tile-view graph learned from historical users' navigation trajectories: a weighted graph is constructed, in which each vertex corresponds to a tile, whereas the weight is given by users' behavior. From the constructed graph, a tile view probability is finally evaluated and used to optimize the downloading bitrate per tile in a limited bandwidth system, but maximizing the users' quality of experience. The authors deeply compare their proposed system with other algorithms (both navigation predictive and streaming) reaching 20% improvement in terms of users' QoE.

Beyond the models discussed above, cross-users data analysis have opened the gate to deep learning frameworks aimed at inferring non–linear interactivity models from a training dataset of collected trajectories based. These models have been augmented also by auxiliary losses [80] or by probabilistic models [102,103] or state-of-the-art transformers [104] aimed at inferring the prediction error. For example, a Gaussian distribution based on previous immersive navigation experiences is used to model the distribution of short-term prediction error for new viewers in the system. This prediction approach is used to improve a viewport-dependent streaming system following a tile-based streaming approach in [102] and an improved coding technique (*i.e.*, pyramid projection) to adapt quality distribution based on users' behavior in [103]. Instead, Chao et al. [104] propose a viewport prediction transformer method for ODV, named 360° viewport prediction transformer (VPT360), taking advantage of transformer architecture [105].

Content-aware designs

In the previous sections, we have described the advances made toward user-centric systems, where user behavioral analysis was carried out by looking only at users data. However, the studies in Section 3.4.2 have shown that users' attention is steered by the content as well. Therefore, in what follow, we review user-centric designs in which researchers have used both users trajectories and content features to infer user behavior.

A very well known metric that maps content features into user attention is the *saliency map*, which estimates the eye fixation for a given omnidirectional content. Since a correlation between saliency map and user trajectory has been empirically proved in [106], many efforts have been dedicated to study, infer, and exploit saliency in ODV streaming. Specifically, deep learning frameworks aimed at predicting users trajectories were augmented by using saliency maps as further input [73,107,108]. Different learning architectures and paradigms were considered in these studies: reinforcement learning-based (RL-based) approach looking at the user's behavior as sequential actions taken over time [73]; and recurrent learning approach, exploiting the temporal correlation of users trajectories [107,108]. Xu et al. [73] proposed an RL-based workflow that first estimates the saliency map for each frame, and then predicts the viewport direction based on historical data and predicted saliency. This prediction is cast as a RL agent that aims at minimizing the prediction loss (dissimilarity between the predicted and ground-truth trajectories). Its viewport prediction is however short-term, being limited to the next frame only (*i.e.*, about 30 ms prediction ahead). In the case of recurrent neural networks, Nguyen et al. [107] feed a long short-term memory (LSTM) network with both saliency (inferred by a CNN model) and historical head orientation from users. The learning framework was able to overcome main limitations, such as central saliency bias and single object focus (*i.e.*, ODV users quickly scan through all objects in a single viewport). Interestingly, Rondón et al. [108] show that the historical data points (in terms of past trajectories) and content features may influence the future trajectories differently based on the prediction horizon. They observe that users trajectory is affected by the content mainly if toward the end of the trajectory. This is explained by the fact that at the initial phase of the trajectory users tend to have more erratic (and less content driven) behavior. As a consequence, they propose a prediction model that initially prioritizes user trajectory inertia, counting more the visual content at a later stage. As a consequence, they consider both positional features and saliency as two time series to feed to the LSTM, as opposed to other works that only consider the former ones. In this way, Rondón et al. sequence-to-sequence method showed better results compared to other LSTM ones, such as Nguyen et al. [107], which do not consider time-dependency in the saliency maps. These deep learning frameworks have strong potentiality, but it is well known that they are data-hungry, with a tendency of poor training accuracy or lack of generalization in the case of the limited datasets. Hence, works have been also presented in a parallel direction of "shallow" learning frameworks, such as the one from Zhang et al. [109]. The authors designed their trajectory prediction as a sparse directed graph problem inferred by past users' positions, saliency map data, and the biological human head model (which defines transition constraints on the graph given the physiological constraints, such as impossible head movements).

Beyond saliency maps, other content features have been considered. In the case of dynamic scenes, for example, saliency might not be representative enough, and *content motion* can be preferred as a feature. Such motion can be captured from either optical video flow [110–112] or from individually detected objects' movements [113,114]. The optimal flow can be extracted by the well-known differential method Lucas–Kanade algorithm, as well as by Gaussian mixture models [112]. In [110], the optical flow as well as the saliency and the past trajectory are input to a LSTM-based prediction model. User-centric systems that exploit the proposed fixation prediction network achieve a reduction of both bandwidth consumption and initial buffering time. Deep learning frameworks have also been considered to extract content features and favor the temporal prediction of users viewing trajectories. Park et al. [115] implement a 3D-CNN to extract spatio-temporal features from both saliency and optical flow to predict future viewing directions. The predicted trajectory is then exploited in a RL model that determines the downloading order and the downloading bitrate for tile-based streaming. Xu et al. [111] also exploit the CNN architecture, but for predicting users' gaze. With this goal in mind, authors created an eye-tracking dataset captured from dynamic scenes. The computed saliency maps and the content motion maps are in two spatial scales: at the entire panorama image; and at a sub-image centered at the current gaze point. Both saliency and motion maps feed a CNN for feature extraction, and then a LSTM predicts gaze direction using the current time and gaze point. Moreover, other works use individually detected objects' movements, mostly following the success of YOLO (you only look once) [116] for objection recognition. Chopra et al. [113] propose an online regression model based on trajectories of both users and the main objects, which are extracted online from the detection model. They claim that the user's head movement highly depends on objects trajectories. Their experiments highlight 34% model weighted given the object's trajectories. Park et al. [114] argued that the semantic video information of motion objects (*e.g.*, people, cars) is also useful to predict the users' behavior. Given that extracting video semantic information is a high-computing task, something not common in mobile devices or HMD, they proposed a server-side analysis shared with clients in DASH MPD files. The shared information contains objects presented in tiles and the probabilities of each object being seen given other users viewing them. In other words, objects that were of interest to most of the users will have higher probability to be followed by a new user.

3.6. Conclusions and perspectives

Omnidirectional videos (ODVs) have become widely spread since 2007 with their first commercial application (*i.e.*, Google street view) and have attracted a growing attention in the multimedia community. This novel multimedia format has revolutionized how users engage and interact with media content, going beyond the passive paradigm of traditional video technology, and offering higher degrees of presence and interaction. Thus many new challenges have risen over the entire end-to-end communication chain due to the novel role of the user and the new geometry. For example, the spherical content need to be efficiently delivered to the viewer, taking into account also the aspect of user-content interaction and bandwidth limitation. In this context, this chapter presents a summary of research advances in ODV adaptive streaming, clearly distinguishing works in terms of *system-centric* and *user-centric* streaming solutions. System-centric approaches come from a quite straightforward extension of well-established solutions for the 2D video pipeline, adding value in the streaming strategy, making it user-aware (*i.e.*, tile-based viewport-dependent streaming). Given the key role of the users, behavioral investigations on how viewers navigate within ODV have attracted a lot of interest, showing the benefit of understanding users' behavior, and enable personalized ODV streaming solutions (*i.e.*, user-centric streaming system).

Despite the intense efforts, there are still several potential research directions in this area. Looking at the streaming pipeline, advances can be done in making ODV processing steps even more geometry- and user-aware. In the first direction, for instance, on-sphere encoding methods instead of plane ones have shown promising results for omnidirectional images [52], and many future works could be done also on ODVs. Coding efficiency can be improved further, thereby also advancing tile-based design. To the best of our knowledge, user-behavior, spherical geometry, and content motion are not simultaneously taken into account when optimizing the design of the tiles. On a parallel direction, viewport prediction research has been experiencing still many open challenges. Novel approaches are now emerging to improve the prediction accuracy, considering different information, such as spatial audio and user emotion. For instance, authors in [117] propose to improve prediction incorporating spatial audio characteristics of the video content. However, there is a lack of public ODV dataset with spatial audio information to enable such direction [118]. Regarding emotion, there are efforts to enable labeling emoting during VR presentation [119] to create ground truth for user emotion during immersion in ODV. However, a trained model with such data can automatically detect emotion from recorded pupils to perform predictions [120].

As emerged in Section 3.4.2, an increasing interest in modeling and understanding users' behavior in ODV systems has been shown recently. Even if some key questions have been addressed, there are still open issues. For instance, a better understanding of common behavioral information among users is still missing and could be eventually exploited in a proper tool that identifies *ODV viewers' profiling*. A user profile is a collection of information that describes the behavioral features of a user and that is used to identify key behaviors. In the ODV context, users' profiles can be utilized for different purposes, such as enabling new modalities for *viewport prediction* and *streaming services optimized for users' profiles*. Of strong interest for industry would be the live-streaming scenarios (*e.g.*, live sports), in which users' profile might have a high impact, especially in reducing the cold-start problem in online prediction models. Even if user profiling can benefit for providing better services, it raises significant concerns toward user *privacy*. Some very recent works have been focused on this specific issue, aiming at developing user-centric solutions that are privacy-compliant. For instance, Wei et al. point out two directions to protect user viewport [121]. First, by using the federated learning method during training, only the model parameters are sent to the prediction server. Another way is obfuscating the real user position by performing a normalized number of camouflaged tile requests. Their experiments have shown that the scale of camouflaged requests is determinant in achieving better prediction, and users might decide such scale of data sharing (trade off between privacy and service personalization).

Finally, it is also worth mentioning the growing interest for *volumetric video*. This content, also known as holograms, will completely revolutionize the way we communicate. Moving from 3-DoF to 6-DoF systems, the user is not more limited to head movements (as in omnidirectional content), but can perform body movements freely among holograms, dynamically changing the both perspective and proximity from which he/she sees them. Research challenges linked to volumetric visual data are still numerous and in their infant phase, as discussed in part IV of this book [122]. Volumetric signals are typically represented as dynamic polygon meshes or point clouds. Therefore the regular pixel-grids (frames in traditional multimedia content) or the sphere-based acquisition pattern (typical of 360° contents) are left to more abstract data structure. With volumetric videos, a collection of color points information evolving over time is acquired, with no hard constraints on the preservation of geometry over time. Even if the signal has a completely different structure, volumetric videos share some common challenges with omnidirectional content, such as a large volume of data, ultra-low delay application, and the uncertainty of user requests. Thus all the studies done for the user-centric system in ODV and presented in this work can be exploited in a new solution for a more immersive system with volumetric representation.

References

[1] J.G. Apostolopoulos, P.A. Chou, B. Culbertson, T. Kalker, M.D. Trott, S. Wee, The road to immersive communication, Proceedings of the IEEE 100 (4) (2012) 974–990.

[2] I. Grand View Research, Virtual Reality Market Size, Share & Trends Analysis Report by Technology (Semi & Fully Immersive, Non-immersive), by Device (HMD, GTD), by Component (Hardware, Software), by Application, and Segment Forecasts, 2021–2028, https://www.grandviewresearch.com/industry-analysis/virtual-reality-vr-market, 2021.

[3] C. Flavián, S. Ibáñez-Sánchez, C. Orús, The impact of virtual, augmented and mixed reality technologies on the customer experience, Journal of Business Research 100 (2019) 547–560.

[4] M. Slater, M.V. Sanchez-Vives, Enhancing our lives with immersive virtual reality, Frontiers in Robotics and AI 3 (2016) 74.

[5] J.L. Rubio-Tamayo, M. Gertrudix Barrio, F. García García, Immersive environments and virtual reality: Systematic review and advances in communication, interaction and simulation, Multimodal Technologies and Interaction 1 (4) (2017) 21.

[6] M.V. Sanchez-Vives, M. Slater, From presence to consciousness through virtual reality, Nature Reviews. Neuroscience 6 (4) (2005) 332–339.

[7] M.-L. Ryan, Immersion vs. interactivity: Virtual reality and literary theory, SubStance 28 (1999) 110–137.

[8] J. Mütterlein, The three pillars of virtual reality? Investigating the roles of immersion, presence, and interactivity, in: Proceedings of the 51st Hawaii International Conference on System Sciences, 2018.

[9] A. Perkis, C. Timmerer, S. Baraković, J.B. Husić, S. Bech, S. Bosse, J. Botev, K. Brunnström, L. Cruz, K. De Moor, et al., QUALINET white paper on definitions of immersive media experience (IMEx), in: European Network on Quality of Experience in Multimedia Systems and Services, 14th QUALINET Meeting (online), 2020.

[10] M.T. Vega, J. van der Hooft, J. Heyse, F. De Backere, T. Wauters, F. De Turck, S. Petrangeli, Exploring New York in 8K: an adaptive tile-based virtual reality video streaming experience, in: Proceedings of the 10th Multimedia Systems Conference, ACM, 2019, pp. 330–333.

[11] B. Han, Mobile immersive computing: Research challenges and the road ahead, Communications Magazine 57 (10) (2019) 112–118.

[12] P. Cremonesi, F. Garzotto, R. Turrin, User-centric vs. system-centric evaluation of recommender systems, in: IFIP Conference on Human-Computer Interaction, Springer, 2013, pp. 334–351.

[13] R. Stankiewicz, P. Cholda, A. Jajszczyk, QoX: What is it really?, Communications Magazine 49 (4) (2011) 148–158.

[14] M. Agiwal, A. Roy, N. Saxena, Next generation 5G wireless networks: A comprehensive survey, IEEE Communications Surveys & Tutorials 18 (3) (2016) 1617–1655.

[15] Z. Chen, Y. Li, Y. Zhang, Recent advances in omnidirectional video coding for virtual reality: Projection and evaluation, Signal Processing 146 (2018) 66–78.

[16] D. He, C. Westphal, J.J. Garcia-Luna-Aceves, Network support for AR/VR and immersive video application: A survey, in: Proceedings of the 15th International Joint Conference on e-Business and Telecommunications, Science and Technology Publications, 2018, pp. 359–369.

[17] C.-L. Fan, W.-C. Lo, Y.-T. Pai, C.-H. Hsu, A survey on 360° video streaming: Acquisition, transmission, and display, ACM Computing Surveys 52 (4) (2019) 1–36.

[18] M. Zink, R. Sitaraman, K. Nahrstedt, Scalable 360° video stream delivery: Challenges, solutions, and opportunities, Proceedings of the IEEE 107 (4) (2019) 639–650.

[19] R.G.d.A. Azevedo, N. Birkbeck, F. De Simone, I. Janatra, B. Adsumilli, P. Frossard, Visual distortions in 360° videos, IEEE Transactions on Circuits and Systems for Video Technology 30 (8) (2020) 2524–2537.

[20] A. Yaqoob, T. Bi, G.-M. Muntean, A survey on adaptive 360° video streaming: Solutions, challenges and opportunities, IEEE Communications Surveys & Tutorials 22 (4) (2020) 2801–2838.

[21] R. Shafi, W. Shuai, M.U. Younus, 360° video streaming: A survey of the state of the art, Symmetry 12 (9) (2020) 1491.

[22] M. Xu, C. Li, S. Zhang, P. Le Callet, State-of-the-art in 360° video/image processing: Perception, assessment and compression, IEEE Journal of Selected Topics in Signal Processing 14 (1) (2020) 5–26.

[23] J. Ruan, D. Xie, Networked VR: state of the art, solutions, and challenges, Electronics 10 (2) (2021) 166.

[24] F. Chiariotti, A survey on 360-degree video: Coding, quality of experience and streaming, Computer Communications 177 (2021) 133–155.

[25] Google, Street view's 15 favorite street views, https://blog.google/products/maps/street-views-15-favorite-street-views/, 2020.

[26] I. Sodagar, The MPEG-DASH standard for multimedia streaming over the Internet, IEEE Multi-Media 18 (4) (2011) 62–67.

[27] Meta, Facebook to acquire Oculus, https://about.fb.com/news/2014/03/facebook-to-acquire-oculus/, 2014.

[28] Google, Open sourcing Google cardboard, https://developers.googleblog.com/2019/11/open-sourcing-google-cardboard.html, 2019.

[29] Google, A new way to see and share your world with 360-degree video, https://blog.youtube/news-and-events/a-new-way-to-see-and-share-your-world/, 2015.

[30] Meta, Insights from a year of 360 videos on Facebook, https://facebook360.fb.com/2017/02/16/insights-from-a-year-of-360-videos-on-facebook/, 2017.

[31] ISO Central Secretary, Spatial relationship description, generalized URL parameters and other extensions, Standard Tech. Rep., ISO/IEC 23009-1:2014/Amd 2, International Organization for Standardization, Geneva, CH, 2015.

[32] BBC, Click: How we made BBC's first fully 360-degree show, https://www.bbc.com/news/technology-35752662, 2016.

[33] DigitalTV Europe, Arte launches virtual reality TV app, https://www.digitaltveurope.com/2016/01/14/arte-launches-virtual-reality-tv-app/, 2016.

[34] E. Kuzyakov, D. Pio, Next-generation video encoding techniques for 360° video and VR, https://engineering.fb.com/2016/01/21/virtual-reality/next-generation-video-encoding-techniques-for-360-video-and-vr/, 2016.

[35] Y.-K. Wang, M.K. Hendry, Viewport dependent processing in VR: partial video decoding, in: Proceedings of the 116th MPEG Meeting of ISO/IEC JTC1/SC29/WG11, MPEG, vol. 116, 2016, https://mpeg.chiariglione.org/meetings/116.

[36] Vimeo, Vimeo 360: A home for immersive storytelling, https://vimeo.com/blog/post/introducing-vimeo-360/, 2017.

[37] Google, Improving VR videos, https://youtube-eng.googleblog.com/2017/03/improving-vr-videos.html, 2017.

[38] M.M. Hannuksela, Y.-K. Wang, An overview of Omnidirectional MediA Format (OMAF), Proceedings of the IEEE 109 (9) (2021) 1590–1606.

[39] Facebook, Introducing meta: A social technology company, https://about.fb.com/news/2021/10/facebook-company-is-now-meta/, 2021.

[40] J. Le Feuvre, C. Concolato, Tiled-based adaptive streaming using MPEG-DASH, in: Proceedings of the 7th International Conference on Multimedia Systems, MMSys '16, Association for Computing Machinery, 2016.

[41] ISO Central Secretary, Information technology — Coding of audio-visual objects — Part 12: ISO base media file format, 2020.

[42] T. Le Thanh, J.-B. Jeong, S. Lee, J. Kim, E.-S. Ryu, An efficient viewport-dependent 360 VR system based on adaptive tiled streaming, in: Computers, Materials and Continua, vol. 66, Tech Science Press, 2021, pp. 2627–2643.

[43] M. Viitanen, A. Koivula, A. Lemmetti, A. Ylä-Outinen, J. Vanne, T.D. Hämäläinen, Kvazaar: Open-source HEVC/H.265 encoder, in: Proceedings of the 24th ACM International Conference on Multimedia, 2016, http://doi.acm.org/10.1145/2964284.2973796.

[44] K.K. Sreedhar, I.D.D. Curcio, A. Hourunranta, M. Lepistö, Immersive media experience with MPEG OMAF multi-viewpoints and overlays, in: Proceedings of the 11th Multimedia Systems Conference, ACM, 2020, pp. 333–336.

[45] H.S. Kim, S.B. Nam, S.G. Choi, C.H. Kim, T.T.K. Sung, C.-B. Sohn, HLS-based 360 VR using spatial segmented adaptive streaming, in: IEEE International Conference on Consumer Electronics, 2018, pp. 1–4.

[46] T. Maugey, Acquisition, representation, and rendering of omnidirectional videos, in: Immersive Video Technologies, Elsevier, 2022, Chapter 2.

[47] D. Pio, E. Kuzyakov, Under the hood: Building 360 video, https://engineering.fb.com/2015/10/15/video-engineering/under-the-hood-building-360-video/, 2015.

[48] G.J. Sullivan, J.-R. Ohm, W.-J. Han, T. Wiegand, Overview of the High Efficiency Video Coding (HEVC) standard, IEEE Transactions on Circuits and Systems for Video Technology 22 (12) (2012) 1649–1668.

[49] S. Afzal, J. Chen, K.K. Ramakrishnan, Characterization of 360-degree videos, in: Proceedings of the Workshop on Virtual Reality and Augmented Reality Network, ACM, 2017, pp. 1–6.

[50] P.R. Alface, J.-F. Macq, N. Verzijp, Interactive omnidirectional video delivery: A bandwidth-effective approach, Bell Labs Technical Journal 16 (4) (2012) 135–147.

[51] B. Vishwanath, T. Nanjundaswamy, K. Rose, Rotational motion model for temporal prediction in 360° video coding, in: 19th International Workshop on Multimedia Signal Processing, IEEE, 2017.

[52] N.M. Bidgoli, R.G.d.A. Azevedo, T. Maugey, A. Roumy, P. Frossard, OSLO: On-the-Sphere Learning for Omnidirectional images and its application to 360-degree image compression, arXiv preprint, arXiv:2107.09179, 2021.

[53] K.K. Sreedhar, A. Aminlou, M.M. Hannuksela, M. Gabbouj, Viewport-adaptive encoding and streaming of 360-degree video for virtual reality applications, in: International Symposium on Multimedia, IEEE, 2016, pp. 583–586.

[54] X. Corbillon, A. Devlic, G. Simon, J. Chakareski, Optimal set of 360-degree videos for viewport-adaptive streaming, in: Proceedings of the 25th International Conference on Multimedia, ACM, 2017, pp. 943–951.

[55] M. Graf, C. Timmerer, C. Mueller, Towards bandwidth efficient adaptive streaming of omnidirectional video over HTTP: Design, implementation, and evaluation, in: Proceedings of the 8th ACM on Multimedia Systems Conference, ACM, 2017.

[56] C. Ozcinar, J. Cabrera, A. Smolic, Visual attention-aware omnidirectional video streaming using optimal tiles for virtual reality, IEEE Journal on Emerging and Selected Topics in Circuits and Systems 9 (1) (2019) 217–230.

[57] S. Rossi, C. Ozcinar, A. Smolic, L. Toni, Do users behave similarly in VR? Investigation of the user influence on the system design, ACM Transactions on Multimedia Computing, Communications, and Applications 16 (2) (2020) 1–26, https://github.com/V-Sense/VR_user_behaviour.

[58] S. Ahsan, A. Hourunranta, I.D.D. Curcio, E. Aksu, FriSBE: adaptive bit rate streaming of immersive tiled video, in: Proceedings of the 25th Workshop on Packet Video, ACM, 2020, pp. 28–34.

[59] J. Fu, X. Chen, Z. Zhang, S. Wu, Z. Chen, 360SRL: A sequential reinforcement learning approach for ABR tile-based 360 video streaming, in: International Conference on Multimedia and Expo, IEEE, 2019, pp. 290–295.

[60] S. Rossi, L. Toni, Navigation-aware adaptive streaming strategies for omnidirectional video, in: 19th International Workshop on Multimedia Signal Processing, IEEE, 2017, pp. 1–6.

[61] F. Duanmu, E. Kurdoglu, Y. Liu, Y. Wang, View direction and bandwidth adaptive 360 degree video streaming using a two-tier system, in: International Symposium on Circuits and Systems, IEEE, 2017, pp. 1–4.

[62] M. Nguyen, D.H. Nguyen, C.T. Pham, N.P. Ngoc, D.V. Nguyen, T.C. Thang, An adaptive streaming method of 360 videos over HTTP/2 protocol, in: 4th NAFOSTED Conference on Information and Computer Science, IEEE, 2017, pp. 302–307.

[63] D.V. Nguyen, T.T. Le, S. Lee, E.-S. Ryu, SHVC tile-based 360-degree video streaming for mobile VR: PC offloading over mmWave, Sensors 18 (11) (2018) 3728.

[64] P. Maniotis, N. Thomos, Viewport-aware deep reinforcement learning approach for 360° video caching, IEEE Transactions on Multimedia 24 (2022) 386–399.

[65] J. Son, D. Jang, E.-S. Ryu, Implementing motion-constrained tile and viewport extraction for VR streaming, in: Proceedings of the 28th SIGMM Workshop on Network and Operating Systems Support for Digital Audio and Video, ACM, 2018, pp. 61–66.

[66] N.M. Bidgoli, T. Maugey, A. Roumy, Fine granularity access in interactive compression of 360-degree images based on rate-adaptive channel codes, IEEE Transactions on Multimedia 23 (2020) 2868–2882.

[67] X. Corbillon, F. De Simone, G. Simon, 360-degree video head movement dataset, in: Proceedings of the 8th on Multimedia Systems Conference, ACM, 2017, pp. 199–204, https://doi.org/10.1145/3193701.

[68] W.-C. Lo, C.-L. Fan, J. Lee, C.-Y. Huang, K.-T. Chen, C.-H. Hsu, 360° video viewing dataset in head-mounted virtual reality, in: Proceedings of the 8th on Multimedia Systems Conference, ACM, 2017, pp. 211–216, https://doi.org/10.1145/3192927.

[69] C. Wu, Z. Tan, Z. Wang, S. Yang, A dataset for exploring user behaviors in VR spherical video streaming, in: Proceedings of the 8th on Multimedia Systems Conference, ACM, 2017, pp. 193–198, https://doi.org/10.1145/3192423.

[70] M. Xu, C. Li, Y. Liu, X. Deng, J. Lu, A subjective visual quality assessment method of panoramic videos, in: International Conference on Multimedia and Expo, IEEE, 2017, pp. 517–522, https://github.com/Archer-Tatsu/head-tracking.

[71] C. Ozcinar, A. Smolic, Visual attention in omnidirectional video for virtual reality applications, in: 2018 Tenth International Conference on Quality of Multimedia Experience, IEEE, 2018, pp. 1–6, https://github.com/cozcinar/omniAttention.

[72] S. Fremerey, A. Singla, K. Meseberg, A. Raake, AVtrack360: An open dataset and software recording people's head rotations watching 360° videos on an HMD, in: Proceedings of the 9th Multimedia Systems Conference, ACM, 2018, pp. 403–408, https://github.com/acmmmsys/2018-AVTrack360.

[73] M. Xu, Y. Song, J. Wang, M. Qiao, L. Huo, Z. Wang, Predicting head movement in panoramic video: A deep reinforcement learning approach, IEEE Transactions on Pattern Analysis and Machine Intelligence 41 (11) (2018) 2693–2708, https://github.com/YuhangSong/DHP.

[74] E.J. David, J. Gutiérrez, A. Coutrot, M.P. Da Silva, P.L. Callet, A dataset of head and eye movements for 360° videos, in: Proceedings of the 9th Multimedia Systems Conference, ACM, 2018, pp. 432–437, https://salient360.ls2n.fr/datasets/.

[75] Z. Zhang, Y. Xu, J. Yu, S. Gao, Saliency detection in 360° videos, in: Proceedings of the European Conference on Computer Vision, 2018, pp. 488–503, https://github.com/xuyanyu-shh/Saliency-detection-in-360-video.

[76] Y. Xu, Y. Dong, J. Wu, Z. Sun, Z. Shi, J. Yu, S. Gao, Gaze prediction in dynamic 360 immersive videos, in: Proceedings of the Conference on Computer Vision and Pattern Recognition, IEEE, 2018, pp. 5333–5342, https://github.com/xuyanyu-shh/VR-EyeTracking.

[77] A.T. Nasrabadi, A. Samiei, A. Mahzari, R.P. McMahan, R. Prakash, M.C. Farias, M.M. Carvalho, A taxonomy and dataset for 360° videos, in: Proceedings of the 10th Multimedia Systems Conference, ACM, 2019, pp. 273–278, https://github.com/acmmmsys/2019-360dataset.

[78] M.F.R. Rondón, L. Sassatelli, R. Aparicio-Pardo, F. Precioso, A unified evaluation framework for head motion prediction methods in 360° videos, in: Proceedings of the 11th Multimedia Systems Conference, ACM, 2020, pp. 279–284, https://gitlab.com/miguelfromeror/head-motion-prediction/tree/master.

[79] A. Dharmasiri, C. Kattadige, V. Zhang, K. Thilakarathna, Viewport-aware dynamic 360° video segment categorization, in: Proceedings of the 31st Workshop on Network and Operating Systems Support for Digital Audio and Video, ACM, 2021, pp. 114–121, https://github.com/theamaya/Viewport-Aware-Dynamic-360-Video-Segment-Categorization.

[80] Y. Bao, H. Wu, T. Zhang, A.A. Ramli, X. Liu, Shooting a moving target: Motion-prediction-based transmission for 360-degree videos, in: International Conference on Big Data, IEEE, 2016.

[81] Y. Guan, C. Zheng, X. Zhang, Z. Guo, J. Jiang, Pano: Optimizing 360° video streaming with a better understanding of quality perception, in: Proceedings of the ACM Special Interest Group on Data Communication, 2019, pp. 394–407.

[82] J. Chakareski, R. Aksu, V. Swaminathan, M. Zink, Full UHD 360-degree video dataset and modeling of rate-distortion characteristics and head movement navigation, in: Proceedings of the 12th Multimedia Systems Conference, ACM, 2021, pp. 267–273, https://alabama.app.box.com/v/8k-360-dataset.

[83] F. Duanmu, Y. Mao, S. Liu, S. Srinivasan, Y. Wang, A subjective study of viewer navigation behaviors when watching 360-degree videos on computers, in: International Conference on Multimedia and Expo, IEEE, 2018, pp. 1–6.

[84] M.V.d. Broeck, F. Kawsar, J. Schöning, It's all around you: Exploring 360° video viewing experiences on mobile devices, in: Proceedings of the 25th International Conference on Multimedia, ACM, 2017, pp. 762–768.

[85] M. Almquist, V. Almquist, V. Krishnamoorthi, N. Carlsson, D. Eager, The prefetch aggressiveness tradeoff in 360° video streaming, in: Proceedings of the 9th Multimedia Systems Conference, ACM, 2018, pp. 258–269.

[86] K. Srivastava, R.C. Das, S. Chaudhury, Virtual Reality Applications in Mental Health: Challenges and Perspectives, vol. 23, Wolters Kluwer–Medknow Publications, 2014.

[87] R.F. Martin, P. Leppink-Shands, M. Tlachac, M. DuBois, C. Conelea, S. Jacob, V. Morellas, T. Morris, N. Papanikolopoulos, The use of immersive environments for the early detection and treatment of neuropsychiatric disorders, Frontiers in Digital Health 2 (2021) 40.

[88] S. Petrangeli, G. Simon, V. Swaminathan, Trajectory-based viewport prediction for 360-degree virtual reality videos, in: International Conference on Artificial Intelligence and Virtual Reality, IEEE, 2018, pp. 157–160.

[89] S. Atev, G. Miller, N.P. Papanikolopoulos, Clustering of vehicle trajectories, IEEE Transactions on Intelligent Transportation Systems 11 (3) (2010) 647–657.

[90] A.Y. Ng, M.I. Jordan, Y. Weiss, On spectral clustering: Analysis and an algorithm, in: Advances in Neural Information Processing Systems, 2002, pp. 849–856.

[91] L. Xie, X. Zhang, Z. Guo, CLS: A cross-user learning based system for improving QoE in 360-degree video adaptive streaming, in: Proceedings of the 26th International Conference on Multimedia, ACM, 2018, pp. 564–572.

[92] S. Rossi, F. De Simone, P. Frossard, L. Toni, Spherical clustering of users navigating 360° content, in: International Conference on Acoustics, Speech and Signal Processing, IEEE, 2019, pp. 4020–4024.

[93] T. Xu, B. Han, F. Qian, Analyzing viewport prediction under different VR interactions, in: Proceedings of the 15th International Conference on Emerging Networking Experiments and Technologies, ACM, 2019, pp. 165–171.

[94] S. Rossi, L. Toni, Understanding user navigation in immersive experience: an information-theoretic analysis, in: Proceedings of the 12th International Workshop on Immersive Mixed and Virtual Environment Systems, ACM, 2020, pp. 19–24.

[95] F. Qian, L. Ji, B. Han, V. Gopalakrishnan, Optimizing 360° video delivery over cellular networks, in: Proceedings of the 5th Workshop on All Things Cellular: Operations, Applications and Challenges, ACM, 2016, pp. 1–6.

[96] S. Petrangeli, V. Swaminathan, M. Hosseini, F. De Turck, An HTTP/2-based adaptive streaming framework for 360° virtual reality videos, in: Proceedings of the 25th International Conference on Multimedia, ACM, 2017, pp. 306–314.

[97] D.V. Nguyen, H.T. Tran, A.T. Pham, T.C. Thang, An optimal tile-based approach for viewport-adaptive 360-degree video streaming, IEEE Journal on Emerging and Selected Topics in Circuits and Systems 9 (1) (2019) 29–42.

[98] A.T. Nasrabadi, A. Mahzari, J.D. Beshay, R. Prakash, Adaptive 360-degree video streaming using scalable video coding, in: Proceedings of the 25th International Conference on Multimedia, ACM, 2017, pp. 1689–1697.

[99] Y. Ban, L. Xie, Z. Xu, X. Zhang, Z. Guo, Y. Wang, Cub360: Exploiting cross-users behaviors for viewport prediction in 360 video adaptive streaming, in: International Conference on Multimedia and Expo, IEEE, 2018, pp. 1–6.

[100] A.T. Nasrabadi, A. Samiei, R. Prakash, Viewport prediction for 360° videos: a clustering approach, in: Proceedings of the 30th Workshop on Network and Operating Systems Support for Digital Audio and Video, ACM, 2020, pp. 34–39.

[101] M. Hu, J. Chen, D. Wu, Y. Zhou, Y. Wang, H.-N. Dai, TVG-Streaming: Learning User Behaviors for QoE-Optimized 360-Degree Video Streaming, IEEE Transactions on Circuits and Systems for Video Technology 31 (10) (2021) 4107–4120.

[102] L. Xie, Z. Xu, Y. Ban, X. Zhang, Z. Guo, 360ProbDASH: improving QoE of 360 video streaming using tile-based HTTP adaptive streaming, in: Proceedings of the 25th International Conference on Multimedia, ACM, 2017, pp. 315–323.

[103] Z. Xu, X. Zhang, K. Zhang, Z. Guo, Probabilistic viewport adaptive streaming for 360-degree videos, in: International Symposium on Circuits and Systems, IEEE, 2018, pp. 1–5.

[104] F.-Y. Chao, C. Ozcinar, A. Smolic, Transformer-based long-term viewport prediction in 360° video: scanpath is all you need, in: 23th International Workshop on Multimedia Signal Processing, IEEE, 2021.

[105] T. Wolf, J. Chaumond, L. Debut, V. Sanh, C. Delangue, A. Moi, P. Cistac, M. Funtowicz, J. Davison, S. Shleifer, et al., Transformers: State-of-the-art natural language processing, in: Proceedings of the Conference on Empirical Methods in Natural Language Processing: System Demonstrations, ACL, 2020, pp. 38–45.

[106] A.D. Aladagli, E. Ekmekcioglu, D. Jarnikov, A. Kondoz, Predicting head trajectories in 360° virtual reality videos, in: International Conference on 3D Immersion, IEEE, 2017, pp. 1–6.

[107] A. Nguyen, Z. Yan, K. Nahrstedt, Your attention is unique: detecting 360-degree video saliency in head-mounted display for head movement prediction, in: Proceedings of the 26th International Conference on Multimedia, ACM, 2018, pp. 1190–1198.

[108] M.F.R. Rondon, L. Sassatelli, R. Aparicio-Pardo, F. Precioso, Track: A new method from a re-examination of deep architectures for head motion prediction in 360-degree videos, IEEE Transactions on Pattern Analysis and Machine Intelligence (2021).

[109] X. Zhang, G. Cheung, Y. Zhao, P. Le Callet, C. Lin, J.Z.G. Tan, Graph learning based head movement prediction for interactive 360 video streaming, IEEE Transactions on Image Processing 30 (2021) 4622–4636.

[110] C.-L. Fan, J. Lee, W.-C. Lo, C.-Y. Huang, K.-T. Chen, C.-H. Hsu, Fixation prediction for 360° video streaming in head-mounted virtual reality, in: Proceedings of the 27th Workshop on Network and Operating Systems Support for Digital Audio and Video, Association for Computing Machinery, New York, NY, USA, 2017, pp. 67–72.

[111] Y. Xu, Y. Dong, J. Wu, Z. Sun, Z. Shi, J. Yu, S. Gao, Gaze prediction in dynamic 360° immersive videos, in: 2018 IEEE/CVF Conference on Computer Vision and Pattern Recognition, 2018, pp. 5333–5342.

[112] X. Feng, V. Swaminathan, S. Wei, Viewport prediction for live 360-degree mobile video streaming using user-content hybrid motion tracking, Proceedings of the ACM on Interactive, Mobile, Wearable and Ubiquitous Technologies 3 (2019) 1–22.

[113] L. Chopra, S. Chakraborty, A. Mondal, S. Chakraborty, PARIMA: viewport adaptive 360-degree video streaming, in: Proceedings of the Web Conference, ACM, 2021, pp. 2379–2391.

[114] J. Park, M. Wu, K.-Y. Lee, B. Chen, K. Nahrstedt, M. Zink, R. Sitaraman, SEAWARE: semantic aware view prediction system for 360-degree video streaming, in: International Symposium on Multimedia, IEEE, 2020, pp. 57–64.

[115] S. Park, M. Hoai, A. Bhattacharya, S.R. Das, Adaptive streaming of 360-degree videos with reinforcement learning, in: Proceedings of the IEEE/CVF Winter Conference on Applications of Computer Vision, 2021, pp. 1839–1848.

[116] A. Farhadi, J. Redmon, YOLOv3: An incremental improvement, in: Computer Vision and Pattern Recognition, Springer Berlin/Heidelberg, Germany, 2018, pp. 1804–2767.

[117] F.-Y. Chao, C. Ozcinar, L. Zhang, W. Hamidouche, O. Deforges, A. Smolic, Towards audio-visual saliency prediction for omnidirectional video with spatial audio, in: International Conference on Visual Communications and Image Processing, IEEE, 2020, pp. 355–358.

[118] T.L. Pedro Morgado, Nuno Vasconcelos, O. Wang, Self-supervised generation of spatial audio for 360° video, in: Proceedings of the 32nd International Conference on Neural Information Processing Systems, ACM, 2018, pp. 360–370.

[119] T. Xue, A.E. Ali, T. Zhang, G. Ding, P. Cesar, RCEA-360VR: real-time, continuous emotion annotation in 360° VR videos for collecting precise viewport-dependent ground truth labels, in: Proceedings of the International Conference on Human Factors in Computing Systems 2021, ACM, 2021, pp. 1–15.

[120] L.J. Zheng, J. Mountstephens, J. Teo, Four-class emotion classification in virtual reality using pupillometry, Journal of Big Data 7 (1) (2020) 1–9.

[121] X. Wei, C. Yang, FoV privacy-aware VR streaming, arXiv:2110.10417, 2021.

[122] M. Quach, G. Valenzise, D. Tian, F. Dufaux, Geometry-based pcc + video-based pcc, in: Immersive Video Technologies, Elsevier, 2022.

CHAPTER 4

Subjective and objective quality assessment for omnidirectional video

Simone Croci[a], Ashutosh Singla[b], Stephan Fremerey[b], Alexander Raake[b], and Aljosa Smolic[a]

[a]Trinity College, The University of Dublin, Dublin, Ireland
[b]Ilmenau University of Technology, Ilmenau, Germany

4.1. Introduction

Video quality is a perceptual event that happens in the mind of the viewer. Accordingly, video quality assessment can validly and reliably only be performed with human viewers, for example, in dedicated video quality tests, often referred to as "subjective tests." Subjective testing is time- and resource-consuming and cannot be applied at scale for media technology assessment, for example, as part of video encoding optimization, or for large-scale video quality monitoring of a running service. Hence, a variety of approaches have been developed in the past to replace or at least complement subjective tests by instrumental, algorithmic video quality metrics or models. In the literature, these are mostly referred to as "objective" models,[1] as it is done in this chapter, too.

For traditional video, subjective tests are typically conducted using standardized methods, such as ITU-T Rec. P.910, P.912, P.913, or P.915 (for 3D video), including the widely used absolute category rating (ACR) with ratings on a 5-point scale and subsequent averaging yielding the so-called mean opinion score (MOS). Additional test methods, such as the double-stimulus continuous quality-scale (DSCQS) and double-stimulus impairment scale (DSIS) methods are described in ITU-R BT.500 [1]. Moreover, BT.500 contains information such as test room and screen specifications, recommended screen-size-dependent viewing distances and statistical analysis methods for test results. Further examples of subjective test methods are given in Section 4.3 of this chapter. Regarding objective video quality models for 2D video, different overviews and performance analysis results for various algorithms have been provided, for example, in [2–7], as well as in the more recent works [8,9]. The latest standardized methods for as-

---

[1] It is noted that the term "objective" may wrongly imply superiority over "subjective" tests. With subjective tests, objectivity can be obtained by an appropriate choice of test subjects and statistical analysis methods. Hence, no assessment method is subjective or objective per se, and also an "objective" model may be used in a subjective and even a wrong manner for applications or video formats that it has not been developed for.

Immersive Video Technologies
https://doi.org/10.1016/B978-0-32-391755-1.00010-9

85

sessing 2D video quality are the three different types of video quality models described in ITU-T Rec. P.1204 [10–13]. Further examples are given in Section 4.6.2.1.

In the case of immersive, audiovisual media applications and services, video quality is one of several constituents of a more holistic experience, that is, quality of experience (QoE) of the user. According to its most widely accepted definition, QoE is "the degree of delight or annoyance of the user of an application or service" [14–16]. Besides visual quality, further constituents of immersive media QoE are, for example, audio quality, presence, and cybersickness, see, e.g., [17–20]. For further considerations regarding immersive media QoE definitions, see, for example, [21].

When assessing omnidirectional video (ODV), both subjective and objective methods have to fulfill the special requirements of the immersive media format: video is captured with a 360° field of view using a multi-lens and/or –sensor camera set-up, represented in a spherical projection format, encoded in a dedicated manner, transmitted on a per-frame or in a tile-based manner, and presented using a head mounted display (HMD) or some screen- or projector-based omnidirectional playback approach. In the current chapter, the focus is on HMD-type playback. Wearing an HMD, users can explore ODV content with head- and eye-movements, similar to how they perceive their real-life environment from a fixed vantage point. In this case, ODV enables three degrees of freedom (3-DoF) for the visual exploration, in the angular coordinates pitch (up-down), yaw (left-right), and roll (movement in the frontal plane).

Accordingly, adequately exploring ODV content during a subjective video quality test may take more time than the typically short viewing of traditional 2D video of around 5 to 10 seconds during short-term video quality tests [2–9]. For ODV, 30 to 60 seconds viewing time may be more appropriate so that users may have time to look around. Another alternative may be to show a reference version of a given content and subsequently its processed versions under test (e.g., video-coding related) multiple times. The presentation approach and viewing time may be chosen in light of the specific ODV contents, and of whether there are interesting and/or quality-relevant visual parts shown in other than the initial frontal direction. Furthermore, the specific goals of the test are decisive for choosing a suitable video presentation method.

Another important topic is the capturing process of behavioral data. Already for 2D video quality assessment, eyetracking has been used to assess how viewers perceive videos, for tasks such as free exploration or video quality assessment [22]. Based on the eyetracking data, visual attention can be analyzed. As discussed in more detail in Chapter 5 on ODV saliency, attention is typically analyzed in terms of overt and covert components, and in terms of top-down and bottom-up contributions. Here, overt refers to the part of visual attention that can directly be assessed using head- and eyetracking, whereas covert refers to aspects of attention that cannot be discerned directly from eyetracking (e.g., mentally focusing on visual information in the periphery of the eye). Top-down visual attention refers to the steering of attention by intentional focusing. In turn, bottom-up visual attention corresponds to visual saliency, that is, the signal- and content-related information provided by the image, video or more holistically visual-scene that attracts and steers visual attention.

Visual saliency and, hence, information about the viewing behavior of viewers were shown to provide complementary information about video quality, too (see, e.g., [22]). Also, image or video quality degradations, or simply the task of rating video quality were shown to influence the viewers' exploration behavior (see, e.g., [23–26]). For ODV, research on capturing, analyzing and/or modeling head- and possibly eyetracking data has been presented, e.g., in [24,27–31]. Knowledge of visual saliency can help to develop attention-aware objective quality models. In addition, such information can be used in tile-based ODV delivery approaches, where important regions, such as the current and especially the expected following viewports are predicted and correspondingly higher-quality/higher-bitrate versions thereof are streamed dynamically, see Section 4.5 and Chapter 5 on ODV saliency. Hence, most recent tests on omnidirectional quality assessment included the capture and analysis of head-rotation and partly also of eyetracking data. Head-tracking and, increasingly, also eyetracking are integrated features of today's HMDs, so that this kind of information can be obtained more readily than in case of classical 2D video, where an additional tracking equipment is required. More details on capturing head-rotation data in subjective tests are provided in Section 4.3.3 and from a more holistic standpoint in Chapter 5 on ODV saliency. How viewing behavior can be included in objective quality models to improve predictions is described in Section 4.6. In a content-aware ODV quality model, aspects such as the relevance of specific regions of the spherical video representation can be reflected in terms of a viewing-direction- and, hence, content-dependent weighting. For objective model development, the input information and relevant features need to reflect the fact that ODV relies on a specific projection format that is employed for a given content.

There are a number of contributions of this chapter. It provides a systematic overview of subjective test methods applicable to ODV quality assessment as well as a summary of various subjective tests investigating specific aspects of ODV technology. Here, different influence factors that may affect ODV quality are considered [32]. In the second part, corresponding objective metrics are summarized, spanning from traditional video metrics, ODV metrics based on traditional visual computing techniques, and ODV metrics based on deep learning. The remainder of the chapter is organized as follows: Section 4.2 indicates how subjective quality assessment can be conducted, considering aspects such as the test method, test environment, and voting techniques. In Section 4.3, a number of publications on short-term video quality assessment are summarized, considering tests for which the video duration is considered to be less than or equal to 30 s. These tests investigate the impact of factors such as the video resolution, framerate, and encoding, for example, in terms of the quantization parameter (QP), motion interpolation, and bitrate. Besides encoding-related factors, the impact of effects such as judder and the employed projection format are included. Furthermore, papers are considered that compare different subjective test methods. Section 4.4 provides an overview of research using long-term video quality assessment for ODV, considering videos with a duration more than 30 s, with similar factors considered as for the short sequences. In Section 4.5, research on subjective video quality assessment for tile-based streaming is briefly surveyed.

The second part addresses objective video quality assessment. Here, Section 4.6 gives an introduction and an overview of the quality metrics that can be applied to ODV. The quality metrics overview is organized in three parts: a) metrics for traditional video that can be applied to ODV stored in planar formats (Section 4.6.2.1), b) metrics for ODV based on traditional visual computing techniques (Section 4.6.2.2), and c) metrics for ODV based on deep learning (Section 4.6.2.3). Section 4.7 introduces a recent ODV metric called VIVA-Q and a comparison study with common metrics for ODV. The chapter is concluded in Section 4.8.

4.2. Subjective quality assessment

This section presents detailed information on the test methods used for the assessment of video quality for short and long-term ODVs with and without audio. Watching an ODV with an HMD can provide an immersive experience to the users, because of the large field of view and the freedom to explore the scene. As discussed in Section 4.1, the ODV experience with an HMD is characterized by different QoE-constituents, such as media quality (audio and video), presence, and cybersickness. In this chapter, subjective quality assessment for ODV only addresses video quality as the key QoE constituent with regard to immersive visual technology.

For the assessment of 2D video quality, there are different standardized test methods, such as absolute category rating (ACR), double stimulus impairment scale (DSIS), and pair comparison (PC), standardized in ITU-T Rec. P.910 [33]. Based on work that is reviewed in this chapter, these test methods are now recommended for the evaluation of ODV quality; see ITU-T Rec. P.919 [19]. Besides these conventional test methods, newly developed or adapted test methods have been proposed for ODV quality assessment. Examples are modified paired comparison (M-PC) [34], modified-ACR (M-ACR) [35], and subjective assessment of multimedia panoramic video quality (SAMPVIQ) [36]. In what follows, general aspects of subjective test set-ups for ODV quality assessment are outlined and a number of test methods described.

4.2.1 Test environment

A controlled environment is desired to conduct the ODV subjective test, as is the case also for other types of media quality assessment. In the current chapter, ODV viewing with HMDs is addressed. Here, inside-out tracking technology is used that enables precise measurement of head-position and, if needed for the test task, of corresponding controllers' positions. Inside-out tracking means that the HMD is equipped with sensors to determine its position in the room by its own, so that for most inside-out tracked HMDs no additional hardware is needed, such as, e.g., base stations. With an HMD and the typical VR-type viewing of ODV, see-through is not enabled, and hence the visual impact of the test environment is rather low. As a consequence, there is no need for a dedicated lighting or wall paint as is recommended for on-screen 2D or 3D video quality tests (e.g., D65 light of 6500K and light-gray curtains; see ITU-R BT.500 [1]). As audio is typically presented in an acoustically open manner, that is, without the usage of closed headphones, the background noise in the room should adhere to similar settings as used in typical 2D video quality assessment. To avoid effects of sunlight on the tracking system of an HMD, closed curtains or blinds should be employed. The base stations should be kept in the opposite corners and their height should be set to approximately 2 m to get an unobstructed view of each other. When a viewer wears the HMD, the interpupillary distance (IPD), focus, and head-band straps of the HMD are adjusted according to the viewer's requirements.

A user can explore scenes with an HMD while sitting on a swivel chair or standing. As translational motion can typically not be converted into appropriate changes of the user's viewport for ODV, only three degrees of freedom (3-DoF) are usually provided.

To collect quality ratings and possibly further data, different approaches are conceivable, as outlined in Section 4.2.3. Note that the experimenter should always be present in the room or be visually monitoring the user from an adjacent room, to pause or stop the subjective test in case that viewer experiences strong symptoms of simulator sickness. Further details about the test environment, equipment, and the minimum number of subjects for the test are given in ITU-T Rec. P.919 [19].

4.2.2 Descriptions of test methods

Generally, before starting the test, pre-screening of the subjects is performed for color blindness (e.g., using Ishihara plates, cf. [19]) and visual acuity (e.g., using Snellen charts, cf. [19]). For subjective video quality evaluation, the following scaling methods were shown to be suitable for ODV: absolute category rating (ACR), modified ACR (M-ACR), double-stimulus impairment scale (DSIS), paired comparison (PC), and modified paired comparison (M-PC).

In the ACR test method (Fig. 4.1a), subjects view the test video only once and are asked to rate the absolute quality of the video on a five-point scale (English labels: 5≡Excellent, 4≡Good, 3≡Fair, 2≡Poor, 1≡Bad), as shown in Fig. 4.2a.

In the M-ACR test method (Fig. 4.1b), subjects watch the same video twice and are asked to rate the quality of the video using the ACR scale. With the repeated viewing, also short video sequences of below 30 s can be used (such as the rather common 8 to

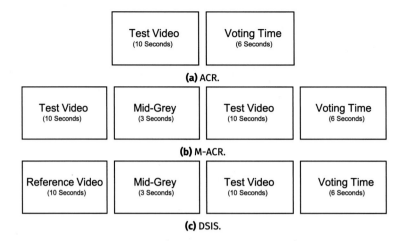

Figure 4.1 Presentation of one stimulus for different test methods.

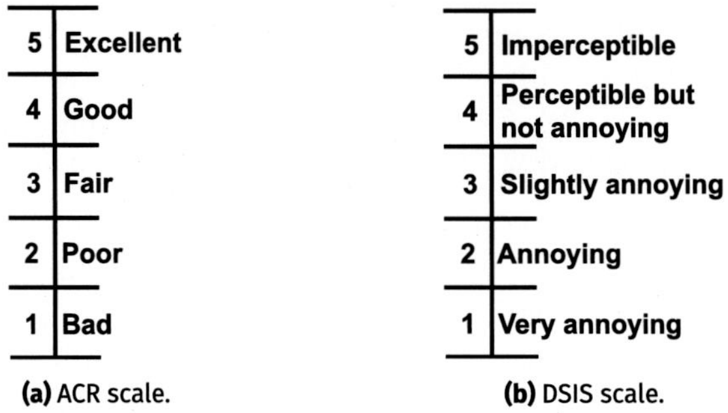

Figure 4.2 Scales used in ACR and DSIS.

10 s video sequences). Here, the repetition is sought to ensure a thorough exploration of the content by the viewer, even if the individual ODV presentation time is short.

In the DSIS test method (Fig. 4.1c), first the pristine reference video is presented to the subjects, and then the impaired test video. Subjects are then asked to rate the impairments on a 5-point scale (English labels: 5≡Imperceptible, 4≡Perceptible but not annoying, 3≡Slightly annoying, 2≡Annoying, 1≡Very annoying). An example of the DSIS scale is shown in Fig. 4.2b.

4.2.3 Collection of users' ratings

To capture participants' ratings during the test, different scoring methods, such as verbal rating, controller-based, and traditional (paper-based) scoring methods could be used. In the verbal voting method, the scale is displayed on the HMD screen and the participant has to say the number aloud so that the test supervisor could note down the rating [35, 37]. In the controller-based rating, the voting interface is integrated into the video player, and the participant's response is recorded with the help of a controller [38]. In both of these methods, users do not have to take off their HMDs to provide their responses. However, a conventional paper-based rating method can be used to collect the ratings for the case of long video duration (60 s or more) or after the test session, where for example the user needs to fill in questionnaires related to simulator sickness and presence. In [20], Gutierrez et al. found that verbal and controller-based voting methods have similar performance. Hence, in ITU-T Rec. P.919, both of these voting methods have been recommended.

4.3. Short-term video assessment

There are manifold studies in the state-of-the-art that evaluated the subjective video quality using different test methods, such as ACR [20,34,39–50], M-ACR [35,48,51], PC [45,52], M-PC [34], DSIS [20,37,48,53], subjective assessment of multimedia video quality (SAMVIQ) [36], and SAMPVIQ [36]. For short-term video quality evaluation, the duration of the processed video sequences (PVS) is considered to be less than or equal to 30 s. Table 4.1 lists the subjective tests, the test method used to assess the quality, and what was assessed in the subjective test. The following studies were conducted without audio: [20,34,35,37,40–42,44,45,48,51–53], whereas two studies used audio in their subjective tests [20,50]. For some of the studies, it is not clear if they used audio or not [39,46]. In the following, different studies on ODV quality are surveyed in relation to the factors that were addressed.

4.3.1 Video-related factors

Typical video processing and encoding settings were investigated with regard to their impact on video quality, such as video resolution, framerate, quantization parameter (QP), motion interpolation algorithms, and bitrate, see, e.g., [35,37,39,40,42,45,48,51, 52]

Tran et al. [39] investigated the impact of different QP values and resolutions on the perceptual quality of ODV using the ACR test method. They found that 4K (3840×1920) and 2.5K (2560×1440) provide better perceptual quality as compared to lower resolutions (FHD and HD). With regard to QP, no significant difference was found between videos that are encoded with QP values of 22 and 28. Furthermore, they noticed that the resulting subjective quality scores are about 0.5 MOS higher when watching ODVs on a mobile 2D screen than on an HMD, irrespective of the resolution and used video sequence.

In [40], Duan et al. compared the effect of different resolutions (4096×2048, 2048×1024, and 1024×512), framerates (30, 15, and 5), and bitrates (70, 10, and 2;

Table 4.1 Summary of the subjective tests for short-term ODVs.

Author	Test Method	Video Duration	What have been assessed?
Croci et al. [51]	M-ACR	10 s	Video quality
Tran et al. [39]	ACR	30 s	Video quality, simulator sickness, and presence
Duan et al. [40]	ACR	15 s	Video quality
Xu et al. [41]	SSCQS (ACR)	12 s	Video quality
Lopes et al. [42]	ACR and ACR-HR	10 s	Video quality
Zhang et al. [44]	ACR-HR	10 s	Video quality
Hofmeyer et al. [45]	ACR	20 s	Video quality
Mahmoudpour et al. [46,54]	SSCQS (ACR)	6–12 s	Video quality
Singla et al. [35]	M-ACR	10 s	Video quality and simulator sickness
Singla et al. [37]	DSIS	10 s	Video quality and simulator sickness
Singla et al. [48]	ACR, M-ACR, and DSIS	10	Video quality and simulator sickness
Fremerey et al. [34,52]	ACR, M-PC	20 s	Video quality
Hanhart et al. [53]	DSIS	10 s	Video quality
Gutierrez et al. [20]	ACR and DCR	10–30 s	Video quality and simulator sickness
Zhang et al. [36]	SSCQS, SAMVIQ, and SAMPVIQ	10 s	Video quality
Li et al. [23]	SSCQS	10–23 s	Video quality

all in MBit/s) on the video quality. From the study, it is noticeable that higher resolution, framerate, and bitrate lead to a better subjective video quality. However, the difference between 70 MBit/s and 10 MBit/s is minimal, irrespective of resolution. Additionally, from the results, it can be observed that framerate and resolution have more impact on quality scores than bitrate.

The optimal bitrate for FHD up to 8K resolution was found in [35,37,48,51] using different test methods (ACR, M-ACR, and DSIS). The selection of the optimal encoding parameters (bitrate and resolution) is useful for HTTP-based adaptive streaming to efficiently transmit ODV without any significant loss in quality.

The impact of temporal resolution (framerate), spatial resolution, and QP on visual quality was evaluated by Lopes et al. in [42]. They observed that the MOS value remains constant when the framerate increased from 30 fps to 60 fps, and also when the spatial resolution increased from 3840×1920 to 7680×3840. Furthermore, Singla et al. [48] compared three different resolutions (4K, 6K, and 8K) using three different test methods (ACR, M-ACR, and DSIS). The advantage of 6K over 4K can be noticed; however, the advantage of 8K over 6K cannot be noticed irrespective of the test methods. One should note that the advantage of using a higher resolution was not seen in [42], probably because of the resolution limitation of Oculus Rift (resolution: 2160×1200) used in this study.

A study by Hofmeyer et al. [45] also investigated the influence of framerate on ODV quality. It showed that content should be played out at the refresh rate of the HMD, in this study, an HTC Vive Pro. That should be done to avoid black frame insertion, resulting in characteristic motion artifacts, such as stuttering of the video, also called motion judder. Furthermore, it should be avoided to play out contents of lower framerates, especially 25 and 50 fps. In a subjective test with 12 expert subjects, the authors found out that the 90 fps versions of two computer-generated contents are clearly preferred over their lower framerate variants (25, 30, 50, and 60 fps). In addition, three different motion interpolation algorithms were applied on the 30 fps source videos to increase the framerate to 90 fps. For most of the ODV contents, the application of motion interpolation from 30 to 90 fps can increase the perceived video quality. Hence, it was concluded that motion interpolation is a tool to increase the video quality of ODVs, especially if the contents are only available at a relatively low framerate and should be played out on an HMD. A subsequent study conducted by Fremerey et al. [52] showed that the simple blending between two frames should not be used for motion interpolation, because it does not increase the perceived quality. Furthermore, it was shown that motion interpolation is more suitable for high and medium motion ODVs.

In a study by Fremerey et al. [34], the authors investigated the performance of three different motion interpolation algorithms applied on 15 ODVs with a duration of 20 s. All videos had an original framerate of 30 fps and were interpolated to their respective 90 fps versions. To assess QoE, two subjective tests were conducted with 24 and 27 naive participants, while the modified paired comparison (M-PC) and the ACR test methods were used. The test results showed that motion interpolation algorithms principally can increase the overall ODV quality as they can reduce effects such as motion judder. Furthermore, it was proven that motion judder has a worse impact on the overall video quality than artifacts such as mosquito noise or others introduced by motion interpolation algorithms. In general, subjects seem to prefer a smooth playout of the contents. If there is enough GPU computing power and time available, from all three motion interpolation algorithms, Super-SloMo, which was published in a study by Jiang et al. [55], seems to be the most suitable. If there are fewer resources available, FFmpeg motion compensated interpolation (MCI) should be used for frame interpolation.

4.3.2 Test methods

There are some studies reported in the state–of–the–art that compare different subjective test methods for the visual quality assessment of ODV [20,36,37,41,48].

Zhang et al. [36] assessed the performance of three different subjective test methods: SSCQS, SAMVIQ, and SAMPVIQ with respect to video quality metric (VQM). They used the correlation between VQM and the test methods to compare which of the test methodologies has the best performance. Their results suggested that the SAMPVIQ subjective data is best correlated with VQM. Hence, the SAMPVIQ test method performed better compared to the other two test methods. In [48], Singla et al. compared the performance of three different test methods: ACR, M–ACR, and DSIS. Based on the statistical reliability computed using the method described in [56], the DSIS test method is found to be more reliable compared to ACR and M–ACR test methods.

Xu et al. [41] proposed two different ODV quality assessment methods, called overall-different MOS (O-DMOS) and vectorized-different MOS (V-DMOS). O-DMOS is used to evaluate the overall quality of a video sequence, and V-DMOS is used to evaluate the quality of the different regions of an ODV based on the viewing direction data and raw quality scores. Their results suggested that both of these test methods are efficient for the evaluation of video quality. However, in our opinion, they are not proposing a test method, but methods to calculate the regional and overall quality using the 100-point ACR test method.

In [20], different subjective tests were conducted by several labs across Europe and China. Their main aim was to evaluate the difference between test methods (ACR vs DCR) and the impact of sequence duration on the quality ratings. Their experimental results showed that for 10 s and 20 s sequences, the test method has an impact on the quality ratings. For 30 s sequences, no impact of the methodology was found.

4.3.3 Head-rotation data

When conducting a subjective test with HMDs, it is advisable to record the head-rotation data of the viewers while exploring the test contents. For example, for the case of ODV, this knowledge can inform film makers about which parts of the video are typically explored by a person and which not. This knowledge is especially relevant for the process of production, and very important to enable a good way of storytelling. With the help of this information, up to a specific extent viewers can also be "guided" to specific parts of the video. Moreover, head-rotation data can also be used to develop saliency models, which are discussed in more detail in Chapter 5 on ODV saliency. Additionally, head-rotation data can help to understand how people rate the audiovisual quality of ODV. In a study by Fremerey et al. [24], it was noticed that different encoded versions of a video sequence were explored in the same way by the subjects in a task-related scenario, where the participants had to rate the audiovisual quality of each stimulus using a 5-point ACR scale.

Head-rotation data can be obtained quite easily as typical HMD software development kits provide access to them. In a study by Fremerey et al. [31], a framework to capture and analyze head-rotation data of people watching ODV was made publicly available.[2] It also contains a dataset of head-rotation data gathered from 48 people watching 20 different ODVs in a task-free scenario and an analysis of this captured data. There are a few datasets where the head-rotation data of viewers is available. In [57], Wu et al. published a dataset containing the head-rotation data of 48 people watching 18 different ODVs on an HMD. In a study by David et al. [58], head and eye tracking data was collected from 57 subjects while viewing 19 videos on an HMD in a task-free scenario. Duanmu et al. [59] published a dataset gathered from over 50 viewers watching 12 different ODVs with a 2D screen under free-viewing conditions. The dataset includes trajectory data collected while the participants were using the mouse to navigate and explore the ODVs. In a study by Almquist et al. [60], head rotation data from 32 viewers watching 30 different ODVs were recorded. Ozcinar et al. [28] published a dataset where 17 participants watched 6 different ODVs. In a paper by Xu et al. [61], a dataset from 58 subjects watching 76 different ODVs was published.

4.3.4 Other factors

Some researchers compared the effect of judder [46] and encoding algorithms, finding the best video resolution on an HMD [44] and the best projection formats [23].

Mahmoudpour et al. [46] studied the effect of motion judder on the visual quality. They found that at high quality levels, the impact of judder on visual quality is significant, especially at high object velocity in videos. In another study [54], the authors conducted a subjective test, where 20 participants watched 15 different ODVs at a framerate of 30 fps. Motion judder was found to have a major impact on the perceived video quality, especially when participants were tracking the moving objects of the ODV scene.

Zhang et al. [44] proposed a display protocol for ODV with an HMD. They suggested to re-sample ODVs before coding to an optimal resolution based on the HMD resolution. They found 3600×1800 to be the optimal video resolution for HTC Vive. However, the authors did not derive a generic formula that is based on the resolution and FOV of the HMD.

Hanhart et al. [53] evaluated the performance of two different encoders (H.265 and H.266) on the visual quality of ODV using a 2D display. Their results showed that H.266 outplayed H.265 at low and intermediate bitrates. At higher bitrates, the performances of H.265 and H.266 are comparable.

Li et al. [23] compared three different projection schemes: ERP, reshaped cubemap projection (RCMP), and truncated square pyramid projection (TSP). Their results

---

[2] https://github.com/Telecommunication-Telemedia-Assessment/AVTrack360.

showed that TSP provides better subjective quality compared to the other projection schemes. However, at high bitrates, the impact of the projection schemes on video quality is minimal.

The visual quality was assessed with and without audio by Gutierrez et al. [20]. Their results supported that visual quality can be assessed in the presence and absence of audio. However, they did not use spatial audio. So, it could be possible, if spatial audio is used with ODV, that the presence of audio may have an impact on visual quality.

4.4. Long-term video assessment

In this section about long-term video quality assessment, only the research papers are considered that used video sequences whose duration is greater than 30 s. There are very few studies reported in the state-of-the-art that used the sequences of such duration [17, 49,62,63], which are listed in Table 4.2. The following studies are conducted with audio [17,62,63], whereas Anwar et al. [49] discarded the audio in their subjective tests.

Table 4.2 Summary of the subjective tests for long-term ODVs.

Author	Test Method	Video Duration	What have been assessed?
Singla et al. [17]	ACR	60–65 s	Video quality and simulator sickness
Covaci et al. [62]	ACR	60 s	Video quality
Singla et al. [63]	ACR	60–65 s	Video quality, simulator sickness, and presence
Anwar et al. [49]	ACR	60 s	Video quality and cybersickness

Singla et al. [17] evaluated the impact of HMDs and video resolution on the subjective quality using two different HMDs: HTC Vive and Oculus Rift. Their results showed that 4K provides better quality than FHD irrespective of the HMD. The same effect was observed in [63]. In [63], the same video sequences were used, but videos were displayed using HTC Vive Pro. It was further noticed that the users provided lower ratings to those contents that have higher motion in them, and vice-versa. Furthermore, it was observed that HTC Vive provides slightly better quality than Oculus Rift. However, the refresh rate, resolution, and FOV are the same for both of these devices.

Covaci et al. [62] created a multi-sensory experience while watching ODV. They simulated the effect of wind and scent while watching roller coaster and coffee shop/lavender field videos. Their experimental results show that when users watched ODVs with multi-sensory effects, they provided higher ratings irrespective of resolution. This shows that multi-sensory effects help in enhancing the perceived video quality. Anwar et al. [49] investigated the impact of resolution, QP, rendering device, gender, user's interest, and familiarity with VR on the perceptual quality of ODVs. With the increase in QP and decrease in resolution, the perceptual quality decreases, which is obvious. Furthermore, they found that users' interest has an impact on the quality scores. Users rated interesting content a bit higher as compared with the non-interesting ones. It was also noticed that when a user is watching interesting content, lower quality is acceptable too.

4.4.1 Review papers

There are two review papers found in the state-of-the-art that summarize several subjective evaluation methodologies [18,64] for the visual quality assessment of ODV. In [18], Li et al. reviewed studies related to ODIs and ODV. They arranged the reviewed studies based on test material display, test method, processing of the subjective scores, and datasets. However, they did not provide any recommendations, or guidelines for selecting the appropriate test methods. Singla et al. [64] reviewed studies related to video only. In their paper, recommendations were provided on how to improve users' experience.

4.5. Tile-based streaming

In viewport-adaptive tile-based streaming, only the current viewport is streamed in a high resolution, and the rest in a low resolution [70]. There are different solutions available for tile-based streaming of ODV in the state-of-the-art [70–77]. This viewport adaptive streaming technique has shown advantages over the classical approaches, where the whole frame is sent at one quality level, because of the significant reduction in the bandwidth requirements. To investigate the impact of tile-based streaming on users' perceived quality, subjective tests need to be conducted. There are a few works reported in the state-of-the-art that conducted subjective tests to evaluate the impact of different influencing factors, such as delay [67,68] and streaming strategies [65,66], on subjective video quality. Table 4.3 lists the subjective tests, the test methods used to assess the quality, and what have been assessed in the subjective test.

Table 4.3 Summary of the subjective tests for tile-based streaming of ODV.

Author	Test Method	What have been assessed?
Curcio et al. [65]	ACR–HR	Video quality
Schatz et al. [66]	ACR	Video quality
Singla et al. [67]	ACR	Video quality and simulator sickness
Cortes et al. [68]	DCR	Video quality, simulator sickness, and presence
Anwar et al. [69]	ACR	Video quality, immersion, and presence

The first subjective quality assessment on tile-based streaming was conducted by Curcio et al. [65]. They compared two different delivery configurations: 1) background tiles were streamed at high resolution, but with low signal-to-noise ratio (SNR), 2) background tiles were streamed at low resolution. It was found in their study that streaming the background tiles at the same resolution of the foreground tiles, but at lower SNR, is preferred over the other configuration. Furthermore, Schatz et al. [66] also compared two different strategies for tile-based streaming: full and partial delivery. Full delivery is regarded as the user receiving a full ODV. The tiles belonging to the user's FOV are obtained in high quality and the rest in low quality. Partial delivery means that only the tiles belonging to the user's FOV are transmitted, and the rest area is blank. Their results indicated that users clearly preferred full delivery over partial delivery. Moreover, they found a suitable QP to encode the background tiles equal to 32. It is worth noting that the authors conducted the subjective test on a 2D screen.

In [67], the impact of video resolution and motion-to-high-resolution latency[3] was assessed on video quality and simulator sickness for different latency values. Their results showed that delay (motion-to-high-resolution latency) values greater than 47 ms have a visible impact on the quality ratings. Furthermore, it was found that the delay value does not have an impact on the scores of simulator sickness, because the background is always visible in low resolution. The impact of stalling was investigated by Anwar et al. in [69] for different bitrates at 4K resolution. They considered four different cases of stalling: no stalling, initial stalling, middle stalling, and multiple stallings. It is obvious that users provided the highest ratings for the case of no stalling, and the lowest ratings for the case of the multiple stallings, irrespective of the bitrate. It is also noticed that the subjects are more tolerant when stalling occurs once than multiple times. Furthermore, immersion and presence scores decrease with the increase of stalling events.

Cortés et al. [68] investigated to what extent the video delay often occurring in viewport adaptive immersive streaming has an influence on quality, presence, and simulator sickness. Results showed that the length of video delay or the choice of a particular adaptation scheme (foveated imaging, tile-based 360° video, pan tilt zoom (PTZ) video delivery, PTZ video delivery over preregistered background) do not have any significant influence on the perceived level of simulator sickness and presence. In addition, it was concluded that the delay condition in combination with the adaptation scheme has a significant effect on the perceived quality.

4.6. Objective quality assessment

4.6.1 Introduction

For objective quality assessment, quality metrics are used, which compute objective quality scores that should be correlated with subjective quality scores gathered from hu-

---

[3] The time it takes to update the FOV in a higher resolution when a user turns the head.

man viewers during subjective quality tests. In general, it is not ideal to apply metrics for traditional video to ODV. There are two unique aspects of ODV not present in traditional video that must be taken into account when dealing with ODV. First, ODV has a spherical nature, but it is usually stored in 2D planar formats to be compatible with the existing traditional video storage [78,79] and delivery/streaming [80] solutions. The mapping from spherical to planar representations inevitably introduces spherical projection distortions not present in traditional video. Furthermore, planar representations have discontinuities and borders not present in the spherical representation. Second, there are the interactive viewing characteristics of ODV. The field of view of ODV is much larger than the ones of traditional video, but only a part of the ODV can be freely viewed with an HMD, i.e., the viewport. In [23], it was found that less than 65% of the ODV area is watched by the viewers. Therefore it is important to consider the viewers' behavior while exploring ODVs with an HMD [30,58,81], and to consider visual attention [27,28,82–84], especially when assessing quality since the distortions in salient regions contribute more to the perceived visual quality. Various previous research works emphasize the importance of visual attention in quality assessment [85,86], and existing studies show that visual attention improves the performance of ODV quality assessment [23,29,87–90].

In this chapter, two categories of metrics are presented: full-reference (FR) and no-reference (NR) metrics. FR metrics evaluate the quality of a distorted video with respect to the corresponding undistorted reference video. On the other hand, NR metrics evaluate the quality of a distorted video without accessing the corresponding undistorted reference video. Usually, FR metrics are more accurate than NR metrics, and more widely applied. There is also a third category, called reduced-reference (RR) metrics, which has no access to the undistorted reference video, except for some features extracted from it. To our knowledge, there are not many RR metrics for ODV, and this category is not considered in this chapter.

4.6.2 Metrics overview

This section is divided into three parts. First, we present metrics developed for traditional video that can be applied to ODV stored in spherical projection formats. Then, we introduce metrics for ODV based on traditional visual computing techniques, followed by deep learning-based metrics.

4.6.2.1 Traditional video metrics

A possible approach to assess the quality of ODV consists of applying the metrics for traditional video to ODV stored in spherical projection formats, even if this approach is not ideal since it does not take into account the spherical projection distortions. Common FR metrics for traditional video are peak signal-to-noise ratio (PSNR), structural similarity index measure (SSIM) [91], multiscale SSIM [92] (MS-SSIM), visual information fidelity (VIF) [93], feature similarity index measure (FSIM) [94], detail loss metric (DLM) [95], etc. PSNR is a pixel-based metric based on the mean squared error (MSE). It is commonly used for the performance evaluation of coding and restoration methods due to its simplicity and mathematical convenience [96], even if it is not much correlated with subjective quality perception. SSIM is a perception-based metric that takes into account differences between undistorted and distorted image based on three comparison measurements, namely, luminance, contrast, and structure. The comparison measurements are computed for each pixel location by considering neighboring pixels inside a small window, and they are then combined to obtain the final quality score. A better version of SSIM is MS-SSIM, which considers the SSIM comparison measurements at different scales and not at a single scale, such as SSIM.

Another FR metric for traditional video recently developed by the researchers of Netflix is the video multimethod assessment fusion metric (VMAF) [97]. VMAF is a metric developed to evaluate the distortions introduced by the adaptive streaming systems (i.e., compression and scaling distortions), and characterized by high correlation with subjective scores [98–100]. VMAF first extracts features from each frame based on DLM, VIF, and motion. For each frame, the features are fed to a support vector machine (SVM) regressor [101] that computes a frame quality score. The frame scores are then pooled with arithmetic mean, thereby obtaining the final video quality score. For the training of the SVM regressor, a dataset with 34 reference and 300 distorted videos was created together with subjective quality scores collected during subjective tests. Three recent studies [50,51,87,102] investigated the performance of VMAF applied to ODV. The work in [102] created a dataset of ODVs in ERP format compressed using constant quantization parameters, and showed that VMAF can be used as a metric also for ODVs without modifications. In [50], an alternative version of VMAF, called VMAF-cc, was proposed. VMAF-cc computes the VMAF score from a 360p center crop of the ODV, according to the observation that viewers usually focus on the center of the ODV. It was found that VMAF-cc and VMAF applied to the ERP format have high correlation with subjective scores, and they also have similar performance. On the other hand, [51,87] proposed a framework where VMAF is applied to planar Voronoi patches extracted from the ODV, and they showed that the performance of VMAF can be further improved. This framework is presented in Section 4.7.

So far, only FR metrics were mentioned. But, there are also NR metrics, such as naturalness image quality evaluator (NIQE) [103], distortion identification-based image verity and integrity evaluation (DIIVINE) [104], blind/referenceless image spatial quality evaluator (BRISQUE) [105], blind image integrity notator based in DCT statistics (BLIINDS) [106], six-step blind metric (SISBLIM) [107], etc.

Recent overview papers about metrics for traditional video are [9,108].

4.6.2.2 Omnidirectional video metrics based on traditional techniques

Compared to the metrics for traditional video, the metrics for ODV need to take into account the unique aspects of ODV, namely, the spherical nature and the viewing characteristics. Regarding the spherical nature, the metrics for ODV usually cope with the projection distortions in two ways: with distortion weights [43,109,110] or resampling [111–113]. The distortion weights are related to the level of projection distortion at a particular location, e.g., they can be proportional to the area occupied by a pixel on the spherical representation of the ODV [109]. The metrics based on resampling extract viewports with low projection distortions [114], or convert the ODV into a projection format characterized by low projection distortions [111], or extract uniformly distributed points on the sphere [112]. To consider the ODV viewing characteristics [23,29,88,115], often visual attention weights are computed based on general viewing statistics [115] or on the given content [115]. Different metrics have two components, namely, a feature extraction component followed by a regression component [114,116,117]. The feature extraction component extracts distortion-discriminative features [116,117], while the regression component takes the features and computes the quality score. The regression component is usually implemented by shallow neural networks [116], or random forest regression [114], or support vector regression [117]. In the case of ODV, usually the metrics compute a quality score for each frame. These scores need to be temporally pooled, and for this operation either a simple average or more sophisticated HVS-based pooling techniques [114] are used.

Many quality metrics developed for ODV are the extended versions of the traditional PSNR metric. Sun et al. [109], for instance, developed the weighted spherical PSNR metric (WS-PSNR), a variant of PSNR with weights that consider the projection distortions of the pixels in the planar projection format. These weights are proportional to the area occupied by the pixel on the sphere. Instead of integrating projection distortion weights into PSNR, the Craster parabolic projection PSNR metric (CPP-PSNR) [111] computes PSNR in the Craster parabolic projection format characterized by low projection distortions. Furthermore, the spherical PSNR metric (S-PSNR) [112] estimates the PSNR for uniformly sampled points on the sphere. The number of sampled points in the official implementation is equal to 655362, which is too small compared to the resolution of ODVs, causing massive information loss. This quality metric has two different variants, namely, S-PSNR-NN and S-PSNR-I. When sampling pixels, they use the nearest neighbor or bicubic interpolation, respectively.

Subjective quality studies reported various findings about the PSNR-based quality metrics for ODV. On one hand, Zhang et al. [44] and Sun et al. [85] recently reported that the existing PSNR-based quality metrics for ODV have superior performance than the traditional PSNR. On the other hand, Tran et al. [118] claimed that the traditional PSNR is the most appropriate metric for quality evaluation in ODV communication. Furthermore, Upenik et al. [119] showed that the existing PSNR-based quality metrics for ODV do not have high correlation with subjective scores. A similar conclusion was reached in another study [120].

In addition to the PSNR-based metrics, the structure similarity index measure (SSIM) was also extended to ODV. Zhou et al. [121] proposed the weighted to spherically uniform SSIM (WS-SSIM) based on weights that take into account the projection distortions similar to the ones of WS-PSNR. The researchers at Facebook also developed an alternative version of SSIM similar to WS-SSIM, called SSIM360, and based on projection distortion weights [110]. Another adaptation of SSIM to ODV is the spherical SSIM (S-SSIM) [43]. In this metric, the luminance, contrast, and structure comparison measurements are computed inside small windows in the spherical domain, and weights based on the projection distortions are used.

As already shown in [85,86], visual attention is crucial when evaluating the quality of ODV. Similarly, Li et al. [23] showed that the incorporation of head and eye movement data in objective quality assessment, more specifically in PSNR, increases the prediction performance. Upenik et al. [88] also proposed to incorporate visual attention in PSNR for ODV quality assessment and called their metric VA-PSNR. Furthermore, Ozcinar et al. [29] developed a quality metric based on PSNR that considers visual attention and projection distortions, with the aim of ODV streaming optimization. In [115], two PSNR-based metrics that consider visual attention are proposed, namely the non-content-based perceptual PSNR (NCP-PSNR) and the content-based perceptual PSNR (CP-PSNR). For NCP-PSNR, first a general distribution of the viewport directions along longitude and latitude is computed from the VR-HM48 dataset [115], which contains head movement data. From the viewport direction distribution, a weight map is computed in ERP format considering all the possible viewports that contain each pixel of the weight map in their central region. In the end, the obtained general weight map is integrated into PSNR to obtain the quality score. For CP-PSNR, a viewing direction is first predicted for each frame of the ODV. For the prediction of the frame viewing direction, a random forest model is used that is trained on the head movement data of the VR-HM48 dataset [115]. Next, a viewport binary map is generated for each frame based on the predicted frame viewing direction. The viewport binary map is then multiplied with the weight map computed by NCP-PSNR, and the obtained map is used in PSNR for the computation of the quality score.

In [116], a FR metric for ODV, called back propagation-based quality assessment of panoramic videos in VR system (BP-QAVR), is proposed. The metric is divided into two stages, the extraction of multi-level quality factors and the multi-factor fusion. In the first stage, multi-level quality factors are computed at each frame based on a region of interest (ROI) weighted pixel-wise metric similar to PSNR: $D(d) = 10 \times \log_{10}(255^2/d)$, where d is the distance between reference and distorted frame defined as the sum of pixel-wise Euclidean distances weighted by the ROI map. The factors are extracted at four levels: pixel (low), region (mid), object (high), and projection level. At pixel level, a ROI map corresponding to a saliency map highlighting salient pixels with high color contrast or on edges is used. At region level, maps with the saliency of superpixels are applied for the ROI map. At object level, a ROI map identifying foreground and background based on semantic segmentation is considered. And, at projection level, a ROI map giving more importance to the equator region compared to the pole regions is used. In addition to the mentioned quality factors, also traditional PSNR is considered. After the computation of the quality factors at each frame, they are temporally averaged. In the second stage, the temporally averaged factors are fed to a three-layer back propagation neural network and converted to the final score. The metric was trained and evaluated based on a dataset established in [36] containing encoding distortions, noise, and blurring.

In [122], a spatio-temporal distortion modeling approach is proposed for objectively assessing the quality of ODV by considering the temporal variation of distortions across frames. In particular, a FR metric is proposed, called omnidirectional video PSNR (OV-PSNR). In this metric, the video is subdivided into spatio-temporal segments called tubes, which serve as basic quality assessment units. For the tube extraction, each frame in ERP format is uniformly subdivided into small blocks, and for each block in a frame, this block and the blocks in the closest previous frames along the motion trajectory are assigned to a tube. The duration of each tube corresponds to the eye fixation duration, since HVS integrates visual information at the scale of fixations. Then, the tube distortions are evaluated by taking into account the HVS perception mechanism. Finally, the distortion of a whole ODV is obtained by the spatial and temporal pooling of the tube distortions. Three different versions of OV-PSNR were developed by extending three commonly used spatial distortion metrics—i.e., S-PSNR, CPP-PSNR, and WS-PSNR—to the temporal dimension based on the proposed spatio-temporal distortion model approach. Experimental results demonstrate that OV-PSNR can provide a significant performance improvement compared to other quality metrics for ODV.

In [50], the authors propose two new ODV NR quality metrics, namely, a bitstream meta-data-based metric and a hybrid metric. Whereas the bitstream meta-data-based metric only uses the resolution, bitrate, and framerate to predict the quality score of an ODV, the hybrid metric additionally uses pixel information related to the spatial and temporal complexity, namely, the mean spatial information (SI) and the mean temporal information (TI) [123]. Both NR metrics provide a similar prediction performance as some representative FR metrics evaluated in the paper, whereas the hybrid NR metric shows a slightly better performance. One advantage of the two metrics developed in this paper is that they are computationally less demanding than the commonly used FR quality metrics, hence they could be used, e.g., for video quality monitoring.

In [114], Azevedo et al. propose an improved version of a viewport-based multi-metric fusion (MMF) approach presented in [113]. This FR metric is based on viewports regularly sampled from the ODV that have low projection distortions and that better capture the user experience, in addition to supporting different ODV projection formats. Moreover, since no metric is usually universal for all types of distortions, different spatio-temporal metrics are applied and combined. Another characteristic of this metric, usually absent in other metrics, is the modeling of the HVS temporal quality perception in the form of an HVS-based temporal pooling of the frame scores that takes into account the smooth, asymmetric, and recency effects of the HVS. Specifically, first, N viewports are extracted from each video frame, and different spatio-temporal metrics are applied to the viewports. Then, the scores of corresponding viewports of the different frames are temporally pooled, obtaining for each metric a number of pooled scores equal to the number of viewports N extracted in each frame. In the end, a random forest regression [124] is applied to the pooled scores to compute the final quality score. For the training of the regression model, the ODV dataset VQA-ODV [23] was used.

In [117], a NR metric, called the multifrequency information and local-global naturalness metric (MFILGN), is proposed. MFILGN first extracts two types of features, namely, multifrequency information features and local-global naturalness features. The multifrequency information features are used, because the responses of the neurons in the human visual cortex are frequency-dependent [125], i.e., each neuron responds to specific spatial and temporal frequency signals. For these features, the ODI in ERP format is decomposed into wavelet subbands through the discrete Haar wavelet transform. The entropy intensities of the low-frequency and high-frequency subbands, representing luminance information and textural details, are then computed and used as features. On the other hand, the naturalness features were inspired by other image quality studies [126,127] and are obtained by computing natural scene statistics (NSS) features from both locally viewed field of views and the global ODI in ERP format. After the extraction of the features, the authors use support vector regression [128] to fuse the features and compute the quality score. For the evaluation, the metric MFILGN was trained on the omnidirectional image quality assessment database (OIQA) [86] and the compressed VR image quality database CVIQD2018 [85,129].

4.6.2.3 Omnidirectional video metrics based on deep learning

Recently, in addition to the metrics based on traditional visual computing techniques, also metrics based on deep learning (DL) have been developed demonstrating state-of-the-art performance. The DL-based approaches are usually characterized by two components: a feature extraction component based on convolutional layers, and a score regression component based on fully connected layers [23,90,130–134]. Most of the DL-based metrics are based on the extraction of patches that are processed by networks. These patches are directly extracted from the projection format by image cropping [90,130,131,133], or they are extracted like viewports based on gnomonic projection [132,135]. From the processing of each patch, patch features [90,133,134], or weights [90,133,135], or scores [23,90,130,133,135] are computed, which are then combined and further processed. To cope with the spherical projection distortions, distortion weights [130,131] are used, or patches with low projection distortions are extracted like viewports based on gnomic projection [23,135], or the position coordinates of the patch in the projection format are considered as input [90,133]. Regarding the ODV viewing characteristics, head and eye movement predictions are usually taken into consideration for the computation of patch [23,135] and pixel [135] weights, or for the sampling location of the patches [23,134,135]. The computation of this visual attention data is obtained from pre-trained approaches [23] or integrated and trained in multi-task solutions [135]. The DL-based metrics require training before their deployment, and for that they need large annotated training datasets with subjective scores. Currently, there are not very large datasets. The largest ODV quality dataset with head and eye movement data is VQA-ODV [23], which contains 60 reference and 540 distorted ODVs rated by 221 subjects. To cope with small training datasets, augmentation techniques, such as patch extraction [130] or rotation are used, but it is not clear whether the patches or the rotated content have the same quality of the original content [114]. In addition to traditional training, also adversarial learning has been successfully applied for the problem of quality prediction [90,133].

One of the first DL-based metrics for ODV is the one proposed in [23]. It is a FR metric that takes into account the human viewing behavior, more specifically, it considers head and eye movement weight maps computed in the preprocessing step by DHP [61] and SalGAN [136], respectively. Initially, N patches are randomly sampled from the reference and distorted ODV based on the probability defined by the head movement weight maps. The N patches are then analyzed by a DL-based quality metric for traditional images [137] obtaining N quality scores. Next, the weighted average of the patch scores is computed, where the patch weights are obtained by summing the values of the eye movement weight maps inside each patch. In the end, the weighted average is processed by two fully connected neural layers obtaining the final quality score. For the training and evaluation, the dataset VQA-ODV [23] was created and subjective tests organized to collect quality scores.

The authors of [130] proposed a CNN-based NR metric for ODIs. This metric first divides the ODI in ERP format into non-overlapping patches. Then, each patch is fed to a CNN that computes a quality score. The CNN consists of a feature extraction part with convolutional layers and a regression part with fully connected layers. In the end, a weighted average of the patch scores is computed with patch weights that are maximal for the patches at the equator and that linearly decrease toward the poles. These weights give more importance to the region near the equator since the viewers usually focus on this region [138,139]. In the learning phase, the CNN is trained based on patches whose ground truth quality scores are equal to the ones of the corresponding ODIs.

To consider the viewer bias towards the equator, during training, the patches are non-uniformly randomly sampled so that more patches are extracted from the equator region than from the poles. The metric was trained and evaluated with the dataset provided by [140] with scaling and JPEG compression distortions.

A NR metric for ODV is proposed in [131] based on 3D convolutional layers that preserve the temporal information, instead of 2D convolutional layers. First, spatio-temporal patches are extracted from 10 frames of the input ODV in ERP or equal area projection (EAP) formats. Each patch is then processed by a 3D CNN with three initial blocks consisting of a 3D convolutional layer followed by a 3D maximum pooling layer. After the initial part of the CNN, there are two fully connected layers that compute the patch quality score. Once the patch scores are computed, they are combined based on a weighted average, where the weights take into account the projection distortion of the patches. For the training of the metric, a dataset was created with 147 ODVs. The dataset contains 7 undistorted reference ODVs and 140 compressed ODVs in ERP and EAP formats. Subjective scores for the dataset were collected during a subjective test.

In [132], Sun et al. present a DL-based NR metric for ODIs, called multi-channel convolution neural network for blind 360-degree image quality assessment (MC360IQA). The metric is divided into two parts, a multi-channel CNN and an image quality regressor. In the first part, six equally-sized patches with field of view equal to 90 degrees corresponding to the six faces of the cubemap projection are extracted. The patches are then processed separately by a CNN based on ResNet34 [141] with the last layer replaced by 10 output features obtained with average pooling. In the second part, the features of the six patches are concatenated and a fully connected layer computes the final quality score. A different improved solution, but more computationally demanding, consists of rotating the cubemap projection around the 3D vertical axis and in averaging the scores of MC360IQA applied to the faces of each rotated cubemap projection. For the training of the metric, the compressed VR image quality database (CVIQD2018) [85] with 16 undistorted and 528 compressed ODIs was used.

In [135], a viewport-based CNN (V-CNN) for FR quality assessment of ODV is presented. Besides the computation of the quality score, this solution has two auxiliary tasks, namely, head and eye movement estimation. In the first stage, a spherical CNN [142] and the viewport softer non-maximum suppression (NMS) algorithm are used to extract potential viewports with importance weights taking into account head movement. In the second stage, the saliency map of each viewport is computed by Mini-DenseNet [143], and it is then processed by a CNN together with the viewport to generate the viewport quality score. In the last step, the weighted average of the viewport scores is computed taking into account the viewport importance weights computed in the first stage. The dataset VQA-ODV [23] was used for the training and evaluation since it also includes head an eye movement data.

Another NR metric for ODIs based on DL is presented in [90,133]. This metric is named VR image quality assessment deep learning framework (DeepVR-IQA), and it is a CNN-based metric trained with adversarial learning. DeepVR-IQA has a quality score predictor and a human perception guider. The predictor takes as input 32 equal-sized patches obtained by an uniform subdivision of the ODI in ERP format. From each patch, visual features are extracted based on ResNet50 [141], while from the central coordinate of each patch, positional features are computed that take into account the spherical projection distortions. Next, a patch score is computed from the patch visual features, and a patch weight is computed from the patch visual and positional features. Afterwards, the final quality score is computed by a weighted average of the patch scores. The human perception guider takes as input the distorted and the corresponding undistorted ODI, together with the score of the predictor and the ground truth score. The guider then learns to distinguish between the two types of scores and helps the predictor to improve its performance. For the training of DeepVR-IQA, a dataset was created with 720 compressed ODIs obtained from 60 uncompressed ODIs and with quality scores obtained from 20 subjects.

Another recently developed NR metric for ODI is the viewport oriented graph convolutional network metric (VGCN) [134], which is motivated by the viewing process of ODIs. In this process, the viewers first browse the spherical scenery, and the visual information of different viewports is interacted and aggregated as local quality aggregation. After the image browsing, the viewers reconstruct the spherical scenery in the hallucination based on the viewed viewports and get a general impression of the quality, which is called global quality estimation. Finally, local quality aggregation and global quality estimation are combined into the final perceptual quality. The local quality aggregation is realized in the local branch of VGCN. First, visually salient viewpoints are detected based on the structure information in the ODI, since the HVS is sensitive to it [144]. Specifically, speeded up robust features (SURF) keypoints are computed and filtered by the Gaussian filter obtaining a heatmap, where viewpoints are selected. Then, quality features are extracted from the viewports positioned at the selected viewpoints based on ResNet-18 [141]. Next, a spatial viewport graph is built to model the mutual dependencies of the selected viewports, and the graph is processed by a graph convolutional network obtaining the local quality. The global quality estimation is realized in the global branch of VGCN. In this branch, the entire ODI without viewport sampling is fed to a deep bilinear CNN (DB-CNN) [145], which measures the synthetic and authentic distortions and computes the global quality. In the last part of VGCN, the local and global qualities from the two branches are processed by a regressor consisting of a fully connected layer that computes the final quality. For the evaluation, the OIQA [86] and CVIQD [85] databases were used.

4.7. VIVA-Q: omnidirectional video quality assessment based on planar Voronoi patches and visual attention

This section presents VIVA-Q [51,87], a framework for FR ODV quality assessment that takes into account the unique aspects of ODV, namely, the spherical nature and the interactive viewing characteristics. For the spherical nature and the related spherical projection distortions, VIVA-Q subdivides the ODV into planar Voronoi patches with low projection distortions that are processed by metrics for traditional video, whereas for the interactive viewing characteristics, visual attention is taken into account. Next, the planar Voronoi patches are described, followed by the presentation of the framework VIVA-Q without and with visual attention. Then, the dataset for the evaluation of the framework is introduced, and a comparison study with the most commonly used metrics is presented showing the state-of-the-art performance of VIVA-Q.

4.7.1 Planar Voronoi patches

Planar Voronoi patches can be conceived as a spherical projection format characterized by low projection distortions. For the extraction of M planar Voronoi patches from a given ODV, the spherical Voronoi diagram [146] of M evenly distributed points on the sphere [147] is computed as illustrated in Fig. 4.3(a) and Fig. 4.3(b). The M evenly distributed points $\mathbf{P}_k = (X_k, Y_k, Z_k)$ on the sphere, where $k \in [1, M]$, are obtained according to the following equations: $\alpha_k = (k-1)\pi \left(3 - \sqrt{5}\right)$, $Z_k = \left(1 - \frac{1}{M}\right)\left(1 - \frac{2(k-1)}{M-1}\right)$, $d_k = \sqrt{1 - Z_k^2}$, $X_k = d_k \cos(\alpha_k)$, $Y_k = d_k \sin(\alpha_k)$, where α_k is the azimuthal angle and d_k is the distance of the point from the z-axis.

The spherical Voronoi diagram defines for each input point $\mathbf{P}_k$ the spherical patch Π_k on the surface of the sphere Ω_S that contains all the points that are closer to $\mathbf{P}_k$ than to any of the other input points $\mathbf{P}_l$:

$$\Pi_k = \{\mathbf{P} \in \Omega_S \mid d_S(\mathbf{P}, \mathbf{P}_k) \leq d_S(\mathbf{P}, \mathbf{P}_l) \; \forall l \neq k\}, \tag{4.1}$$

where $d_S(\mathbf{P}, \mathbf{P}_k)$ is the spherical distance between the point $\mathbf{P}$ and the point $\mathbf{P}_k$, i.e., the length of the shortest path on the surface of the sphere connecting these two points. Notice that by using evenly distributed points $\mathbf{P}_k$ on the sphere, we guarantee that the spherical Voronoi patches Π_k have approximately equal size.

After the computation of the spherical Voronoi diagram, for each spherical Voronoi patch Π_k a planar Voronoi patch Π_k' is extracted from the ODV, as illustrated in Fig. 4.3(c). This operation is obtained by first positioning the plane of the planar patch Π_k' on the centroid of the spherical patch Π_k, tangent to the sphere. The points on the sphere and the planar patch Π_k' are related by gnomonic projection [148], and the pixels of Π_k' are computed by sampling the ODV in ERP format using bilinear interpolation. The angular resolution of each planar Voronoi patch Π_k' is defined by the pixels per

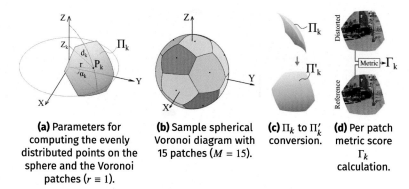

(a) Parameters for computing the evenly distributed points on the sphere and the Voronoi patches ($r \equiv 1$).

(b) Sample spherical Voronoi diagram with 15 patches ($M = 15$).

(c) Π_k to Π'_k conversion.

(d) Per patch metric score Γ_k calculation.

Figure 4.3 Figures of the Voronoi-based quality assessment framework VIVA-Q, showing patch extraction and patch metric score calculation.

visual angle, a parameter that is kept constant for each patch. We use 20 planar Voronoi patches with 10 pixel/degree angular resolution, which is close to the resolution of the HMD used in the VIVA-Q evaluation.

4.7.2 Voronoi-based framework without visual attention

The quality framework presented in this section extends FR metrics for traditional video to ODV. The extended metrics for ODV are called VI-METRIC, where VI stands for Voronoi, and METRIC $\in$ {PSNR, SSIM, MS-SSIM, VMAF, ...} is a FR metric for traditional video. Since we are dealing with FR quality assessment, the inputs of the framework are a distorted (e.g., compressed) ODV and the corresponding undistorted reference ODV. Initially, the quality framework extracts M planar Voronoi patches Π'_k from the distorted ODV and other M from the reference ODV. Then, a FR metric for traditional video is applied to the planar Voronoi patches Π'_k of the distorted and reference ODV, obtaining M patch scores Γ_k as illustrated in Fig. 4.3(d). Here, the following FR metrics are applied: PSNR, SSIM [91], MS-SSIM [92], and VMAF [97]. Since these metrics take rectangular video frames as input, the first three of them are modified, so that they can deal with any patch shape. For VMAF, the bounding box of the patch is taken as input, as it is not straightforward to modify VMAF for different patch shapes. In the end, the final ODV quality score is obtained by computing the arithmetic mean of the patch scores Γ_k as follows:

$$\text{VI-METRIC} = \frac{\sum_{k=1}^{M} \Gamma_k}{M}. \tag{4.2}$$

4.7.3 Voronoi-based framework with visual attention

To take the interactive viewing characteristics into consideration for ODV quality assessment, visual attention is integrated into the quality framework, and its metrics are called VIVA-METRIC, where VA stands for visual attention: VIVA-PSNR, VIVA-SSIM, VIVA-MS-SSIM, VIVA-VMAF, etc.

For the computation of the VIVA-METRICs, first a quality score for each video frame of the distorted ODV is computed based on visual attention, and then the frame scores are temporally pooled into the final quality score. For the computation of the frame scores, initially M planar Voronoi patches Π'_k are extracted from each frame i of the distorted and reference ODVs. Then, a FR metric for traditional video is applied to the planar Voronoi patches Π'_k of each frame i, obtaining M patch scores $\Gamma_{i,k}$ for each frame. At this point, the visual attention map Ψ_i of each frame i of the distorted ODV is estimated. Then, M planar Voronoi patches Π'_k are extracted from each visual attention map Ψ_i, and the sums $v_{i,k}$ of the visual attention pixel values inside each patch Π'_k of each map Ψ_i are computed. The sum $v_{i,k}$ is related to the probability of patch Π'_k of frame i being viewed. Next, the frame scores T_i are obtained through a weighted average of the patch scores $\Gamma_{i,k}$ using the visual attention sums $v_{i,k}$ as weights according to the following equation:

$$T_i = \frac{\sum_{k=1}^{M} v_{i,k} \Gamma_{i,k}}{\sum_{k=1}^{M} v_{i,k}}. \tag{4.3}$$

In the last step, the frame scores T_i are combined using a temporal pooling approach P_{tempo} obtaining the final video score:

$$\text{VIVA-METRIC} = P_{tempo}(T_1, T_2, \ldots, T_N), \tag{4.4}$$

where N is the number of frames. Different pooling approaches P_{tempo} can be applied, like the arithmetic and harmonic mean, the median, the minimum, etc. For VIVA-Q, the arithmetic mean is recommended.

4.7.4 ODV dataset

For the evaluation of VIVA-Q, a dataset of ODVs characterized by scaling and compression distortions was created, and subjective tests were organized to collect subjective scores and visual attention data for the dataset. First, a total of eight uncompressed reference ODVs were selected in YUV420p format of 10 *sec.* length, 8K×4K ERP resolution, and with different characteristics. Then, the reference ODVs were downscaled to three different resolutions in ERP format with the bicubic scaling algorithm: 8128 × 4064, 3600 × 1800, and 2032 × 1016. Next, the ODVs were compressed with the HEVC/H.265 video coding standard [79] using the video buffering verifier method to set the target bitrates. To ensure constant bitrate, each ODV was compressed using two-pass encoding with 150 percent constrained variable bitrate configuration. The buffer size during encoding was defined to limit the output bitrate to twice the maximum bitrate for handling large bitrate spikes. To ensure that the distorted ODVs within the database are uniformly distributed across different quality levels, five different target bitrates were selected independently for each reference ODV in a pilot test with three experts.

To obtain subjective quality scores and visual attention data, subjective tests were conducted with a total of 47 participants, including five outliers identified by the method recommended in ITU-R BT.500-13 [1]. During the experiments, the participants watched each ODV twice with an HMD, according to the chosen modified-absolute category rating with hidden reference (M-ACR-HR) [35] methodology. After the viewing of each ODV, the quality scores were assigned by the participants based on a continuous grading scale in the range [0, 100], with 100 corresponding to the best score, as recommended in ITU-R BT.500-13 [1]. From the participants' quality scores, the difference mean opinion scores (DMOS) [33] were calculated by applying the standard approach described in [149]. During the experiment, the HMD trajectories were also recorded. Afterwards, visual attention maps were computed using the Kent distribution method [83].

4.7.5 Comparison study

For the comparison study, the correlation between metric scores and subjective scores was analyzed. For the correlation analysis, the metric scores were first converted into subjective scores by fitting a logistic function. The logistic function proposed in [150] and defined as follows was used: $S' = \frac{\beta_1 - \beta_2}{1 + e^{-\frac{S - \beta_3}{\|\beta_4\|}}} + \beta_2$, where S' is the predicted subjective score of the metric score S, and $\beta_{1,...,4}$ are the parameters that are estimated during the fitting. Here, the subjective score predicted by the logistic function is the reversed DMOS (i.e., subtracted from 100). To evaluate how well the logistic function predicts the subjective scores, i.e., how well the metric estimates the subjective quality, the following measures were applied to the real and predicted subjective scores: Pearson's linear correlation coefficient (PLCC), Spearman's rank order correlation coefficient (SROCC), root mean squared prediction error (RMSE), and mean absolute prediction error (MAE).

In the comparison study, we evaluated the performance of the Voronoi-based metrics obtained with the VIVA-Q framework and well-known metrics usually considered in ODV quality assessment studies. Four of the chosen well-known metrics were developed for traditional image/video quality assessment: PSNR, SSIM [91], MS-SSIM [92], and VMAF [97]. These metrics were applied to ODVs in two different formats, namely, equirectangular projection (ERP) and cubemap projection (CMP), and to distinguish them we use a subscript, e.g., $PSNR_{ERP}$ and $PSNR_{CMP}$. Moreover, extra four

Table 4.4 Comparison study. The best performance values are in **bold**.

Metrics	PLCC	SROCC	RMSE	MAE
PSNR_{ERP}	0.8408	0.8237	8.2326	6.3169
PSNR_{CMP}	0.8480	0.8323	8.0419	6.2085
S-PSNR-I	0.8580	0.8438	7.8207	5.9715
S-PSNR-NN	0.8584	0.8433	7.8066	5.9648
WS-PSNR	0.8582	0.8430	7.8107	5.9772
CPP-PSNR	0.8579	0.8439	7.8200	5.9779
SSIM_{ERP}	0.7659	0.7551	9.7734	7.7396
SSIM_{CMP}	0.7701	0.7546	9.6583	7.6036
MS-SSIM_{ERP}	0.9224	0.9160	5.8232	4.4205
MS-SSIM_{CMP}	0.9132	0.9081	6.1422	4.7378
VMAF_{ERP}	0.8978	0.8864	6.7433	5.3631
VMAF_{CMP}	0.9063	0.8945	6.5630	5.2229
VI-PSNR	0.8676	0.8551	7.5743	5.8377
VI-SSIM	0.8823	0.8763	7.1172	5.2867
VI-MS-SSIM	0.9486	0.9450	4.8743	3.8475
VI-VMAF	0.9646	0.9581	4.2096	3.1548
VIVA-PSNR	0.8876	0.8712	7.1818	5.5072
VIVA-SSIM	0.9106	0.9007	6.4345	4.8097
VIVA-MS-SSIM	0.9676	0.9635	3.8982	3.1526
VIVA-VMAF	**0.9773**	**0.9717**	**3.3753**	**2.5948**

well-known metrics specifically designed for ODV were analyzed: S-PSNR-I [112], S-PSNR-NN [112], WS-PSNR [109], and CPP-PSNR [111].

Table 4.4 shows the performance of the selected well-known metrics and our Voronoi-based metrics. By looking at the table, it is possible to notice a slightly higher correlation between the subjective and metric scores when the metrics PSNR, SSIM, and VMAF are applied to the CMP format instead of the ERP format. The reason for this could be the lower projection distortions of CMP format compared to ERP format. It can also be observed that the performance of the PSNR-based metrics developed for ODV is better than the performance of traditional PSNR. Furthermore, among all the evaluated metrics in Table 4.4, SSIM is characterized by the worst performance, even worse than PSNR. The reason might be that the inevitable projection distortions negatively affect the performance of SSIM, as some regions on the spherical representation are stretched to much bigger areas on the planar representation (especially the polar regions in ERP format). Therefore SSIM scores could be dominated by these regions, and this could cause SSIM to have lower correlation scores than PSNR, even though, for traditional video, SSIM is much closer to human perception than PSNR. On the other hand, among the selected metrics that are not Voronoi-based, MS-SSIM and VMAF have the best performance. This is not unexpected, since these metrics, which have state-of-the-art performance for traditional video [100], consider scaling and compression distortions that characterize our dataset. Between these two metrics, MS-SSIM is slightly better than VMAF for both projection formats. The reason can be explained by the fact that VMAF was neither modeled for 8K nor ODV.

The results also show that when the metrics are applied to planar Voronoi patches instead of the ERP and CMP formats, they achieve a better performance. This is expected because of the lower projection distortions of the planar Voronoi patches compared to the ERP and CMP formats, and because of the similar angular resolutions of the patches and the HMD used when gathering the subjective scores. Moreover, the Voronoi-based metrics with visual attention (i.e., VIVA-METRICs) achieve better performance than the corresponding ones without visual attention (i.e., VI-METRICs). This improvement shows that visual attention is an important factor to consider in ODV quality assessment in the presence of compression and scaling distortions, i.e., uniform artifacts, and it needs to be taken into account to increase the metric performance. The best performing metric among all compared metrics is VIVA-VMAF followed by VIVA-MS-SSIM.

4.8. Conclusion

This chapter offers an overview on subjective and objective quality assessment for ODV. At the beginning of the chapter, subjective quality assessment is introduced. Specifically, the chapter describes how to conduct subjective tests, such as the test methods, the voting techniques, and the test environments. Furthermore, two classes of subjective quality assessment are presented that depend on the duration of the test videos, i.e., short-term and long-term video quality assessment. The impact of several video-related factors on subjective ODV quality is discussed, as, e.g., video resolution, framerate, bitrate, QP, and motion interpolation algorithms. In addition, it is described how head-rotation data can be captured and why this is needed. Considering its increasing practical relevance, a section is also dedicated to the subjective evaluation of tile-based streaming techniques. With regard to subjective quality assessment for ODV, one of the challenges that remains for future research is the study of the interplay between all the mentioned video-related factors combined with further technological influence factors, such as the display resolution or the FoV of the HMD, especially with regard to high-end and high-resolution HMDs, for instance, the Varjo VR-3.[4] Furthermore, the impact of spatial audio on visual quality and head-rotation behavior is not yet fully considered in the literature. Additionally, state-of-the-art studies don't mention which of the technical factors (e.g., framerate, resolution, or bitrate) is most important to improve the subjective video

---

[4] https://varjo.com/products/vr-3.

quality. Besides this, many subjective tests have been conducted for short-term video quality, but state-of-the-art studies lack in comparing different subjective test methods for long-term video quality.

Regarding objective quality assessment for ODV, the chapter gives an overview of different metrics. The presented metrics are organized into three categories: first, metrics for standard video that are applied to ODV stored in planar formats; second, metrics based on traditional visual computing techniques; third, recent metrics based on deep learning. In particular, the chapter shows how different metrics take into consideration the unique aspects of ODV, i.e., the spherical nature and the related projection distortions of the planar formats, and the interactive viewing characteristics. Different metrics presented in this chapter have a common structure consisting of a component for the extraction of distortion-discriminative features and a regression component that takes the features and computes the quality score. Moreover, a recently developed metric for ODV, called VIVA-Q, is presented, together with its evaluation and a comparison with common metrics for ODV. It is shown how VIVA-Q deals with the spherical nature and interactive viewing characteristics of ODV, namely, with planar Voronoi patches and visual attention, respectively. Recently, different deep learning-based solutions have been developed with state-of-the-art performance. A limitation of these solutions is the relatively small size of the currently available training datasets. In the future, we foresee an effort to create larger annotated datasets that could improve the performance of the deep learning-based metrics.

References

[1] ITU-R Rec. BT.500-14, Methodologies for the subjective assessment of the quality of television images, 2019.

[2] S. Chikkerur, V. Sundaram, M. Reisslein, L.J. Karam, Objective video quality assessment methods: A classification, review, and performance comparison, IEEE Transactions on Broadcasting 57 (2) (2011) 165–182.

[3] U. Engelke, H.-J. Zepernick, Perceptual-based quality metrics for image and video services: A survey, in: 2007 Next Generation Internet Networks, IEEE, 2007, pp. 190–197.

[4] M.-N. Garcia, S. Argyropoulos, N. Staelens, M. Naccari, M. Rios-Quintero, A. Raake, Video streaming, in: Quality of Experience, Springer, 2014, pp. 277–297.

[5] W. Lin, C.-C.J. Kuo, Perceptual visual quality metrics: A survey, Journal of Visual Communication and Image Representation 22 (4) (2011) 297–312.

[6] S. Winkler, P. Mohandas, The evolution of video quality measurement: From PSNR to hybrid metrics, IEEE Transactions on Broadcasting 54 (3) (2008) 660–668.

[7] M. Vranješ, S. Rimac-Drlje, K. Grgić, Review of objective video quality metrics and performance comparison using different databases, Signal Processing. Image Communication 28 (1) (2013) 1–19.

[8] N. Barman, M.G. Martini, QoE modeling for HTTP adaptive video streaming–a survey and open challenges, IEEE Access 7 (2019) 30831–30859.

[9] A. Raake, S. Borer, S.M. Satti, J. Gustafsson, R.R.R. Rao, S. Medagli, P. List, S. Göring, D. Lindero, W. Robitza, G. Heikkilä, S. Broom, C. Schmidmer, B. Feiten, U. Wüstenhagen, T. Wittmann, M. Obermann, R. Bitto, Multi-model standard for bitstream-, pixel-based and hybrid video quality assessment of UHD/4K: ITU-T P.1204, IEEE Access 8 (2020) 193020–193049.

[10] ITU-T Rec. P.1204, Video quality assessment of streaming services over reliable transport for resolutions up to 4K, Recommendation P.1204, Jan. 2020.

[11] ITU-T Rec. P.1204.3, Video quality assessment of streaming services over reliable transport for resolutions up to 4K with access to full bitstream information, Recommendation P.1204.3, Jan. 2020.

[12] ITU-T Rec. P.1204.4, Video quality assessment of streaming services over reliable transport for resolutions up to 4K with access to full and reduced reference pixel information, Recommendation P.1204.4, Jan. 2020.

[13] ITU-T Rec. P.1204.5, Video quality assessment of streaming services over reliable transport for resolutions up to 4K with access to transport and received pixel information, Recommendation P.1204.5, Jan. 2020.

[14] P. Le Callet, S. Möller, A. Perkis (Eds.), Qualinet White Paper on Definitions of Quality of Experience, European Network on Quality of Experience in Multimedia Systems and Services (COST Action IC 1003), Lausanne, CH-Switzerland, 1st Edition (2012).

[15] A. Raake, S. Egger, Quality of Experience. Advanced Concepts, Applications and Methods, Springer, Berlin–Heidelberg–New York, NY, 2014, Ch. Quality and Quality of Experience.

[16] ITU-T Rec. P.10/G.100, Vocabulary for performance, quality of service and quality of experience, 2017.

[17] A. Singla, S. Fremerey, W. Robitza, A. Raake, Measuring and comparing QoE and simulator sickness of omnidirectional videos in different head mounted displays, in: 9th International Conference on QoMEX, 2017, pp. 1–6, https://doi.org/10.1109/QoMEX.2017.7965658.

[18] M. Xu, C. Li, S. Zhang, P. Le Callet, State-of-the-art in 360° video/image processing: Perception, assessment and compression, IEEE Journal of Selected Topics in Signal Processing 14 (2020) 5–26.

[19] I.-T. R. P.919, Subjective test methodologies for 360° video on head-mounted displays, Recommendation P.919, Oct. 2020.

[20] J. Gutierrez, P. Perez, M. Orduna, A. Singla, C. Cortes, P. Mazumdar, I. Viola, K. Brunnstrom, F. Battisti, N. Cieplinska, D. Juszka, L. Janowski, M.I. Leszczuk, A. Adeyemi-Ejeye, Y. Hu, Z. Chen, G. Van Wallendael, P. Lambert, C. Diaz, J. Hedlund, O. Hamsis, S. Fremerey, F. Hofmeyer, A. Raake, P. Cesar, M. Carli, N. Garcia, Subjective evaluation of visual quality and simulator sickness of short 360° videos: ITU-T Rec. P.919, IEEE Transactions on Multimedia 24 (2022) 3087–3100, https://doi.org/10.1109/TMM.2021.3093717.

[21] A. Perkis, C. Timmerer, S. Baraković, J.B. Husić, S. Bech, S. Bosse, J. Botev, K. Brunnström, L. Cruz, K. De Moor, A. de Polo Saibanti, W. Durnez, S. Egger-Lampl, U. Engelke, T.H. Falk, J. Gutiérrez, A. Hameed, A. Hines, T. Kojic, D. Kukolj, E. Liotou, D. Milovanovic, S. Möller, N. Murray, B. Naderi, M. Pereira, S. Perry, A. Pinheiro, A. Pinilla, A. Raake, S. Rajesh Agrawal, U. Reiter, R. Rodrigues, R. Schatz, P. Schelkens, S. Schmidt, S. Shafiee Sabet, A. Singla, L. Skorin-Kapov, M. Suznjevic, S. Uhrig, S. Vlahović, J.-N. Voigt-Antons, S. Zadtootaghaj, QUALINET white paper on definitions of immersive media experience (IMEx), arXiv preprint, arXiv:2007.07032, 2020.

[22] U. Engelke, H. Kaprykowsky, H.-J. Zepernick, P. Ndjiki-Nya, Visual attention in quality assessment, IEEE Signal Processing Magazine 28 (6) (2011) 50–59.

[23] C. Li, M. Xu, X. Du, Z. Wang, Bridge the gap between VQA and human behavior on omnidirectional video: A large-scale dataset and a deep learning model, in: Proceedings of the 26th ACM International Conference on Multimedia, MM '18, Association for Computing Machinery, New York, NY, USA, 2018, pp. 932–940, https://doi.org/10.1145/3240508.3240581.

[24] S. Fremerey, R. Huang, S. Göring, A. Raake, Are people pixel-peeping 360° videos?, Electronic Imaging (2019) pp. 220-1–220-7.

[25] P. Guo, X. Zhao, D. Zeng, H. Liu, A metric for quantifying image quality induced saliency variation, in: 2021 IEEE International Conference on Image Processing (ICIP), IEEE, 2021, pp. 1459–1463.

[26] Y. Meng, Z. Ma, Viewport-based omnidirectional video quality assessment: database, modeling and inference, IEEE Transactions on Circuits and Systems for Video Technology 32 (1) (2022) 120–134.

[27] A. De Abreu, C. Ozcinar, A. Smolic, Look around you: Saliency maps for omnidirectional images in VR applications, in: 2017 Ninth International Conference on Quality of Multimedia Experience (QoMEX), IEEE, 2017, pp. 1–6.

[28] C. Ozcinar, A. Smolic, Visual attention in omnidirectional video for virtual reality applications, in: 2018 Tenth International Conference on Quality of Multimedia Experience (QoMEX), 2018, pp. 1–6, https://doi.org/10.1109/QoMEX.2018.8463418.

[29] C. Ozcinar, J. Cabrera, A. Smolic, Visual attention-aware omnidirectional video streaming using optimal tiles for virtual reality, IEEE Journal on Emerging and Selected Topics in Circuits and Systems 9 (1) (2019) 217–230, https://doi.org/10.1109/JETCAS.2019.2895096.

[30] J. Gutiérrez, E. David, Y. Rai, P. Le Callet, Toolbox and dataset for the development of saliency and scanpath models for omnidirectional/360 still images, Signal Processing. Image Communication 69 (2018) 35–42.

[31] S. Fremerey, A. Singla, K. Meseberg, A. Raake, AVtrack360: An open dataset and software recording people's head rotations watching 360° videos on an HMD, in: Proceedings of the 9th ACM Multimedia Systems Conference, 2018, pp. 403–408.

[32] U. Reiter, K. Brunnström, K. De Moor, M.-C. Larabi, M. Pereira, A. Pinheiro, J. You, A. Zgank, Factors influencing quality of experience, in: Quality of Experience, Springer, 2014, pp. 55–72.

[33] ITU-T Rec. P.910, Subjective video quality assessment methods for multimedia applications, ITU-T Recommendation P.910, Apr 2008.

[34] S. Fremerey, F. Hofmeyer, S. Göring, D. Keller, A. Raake, Between the frames-evaluation of various motion interpolation algorithms to improve 360° video quality, in: 2020 IEEE International Symposium on Multimedia (ISM), IEEE, 2020, pp. 65–73.

[35] A. Singla, S. Fremerey, W. Robitza, P. Lebreton, A. Raake, Comparison of subjective quality evaluation for HEVC encoded omnidirectional videos at different bit-rates for UHD and FHD resolution, in: Proceedings of the on Thematic Workshops of ACM Multimedia 2017, Thematic Workshops '17, ACM, New York, NY, USA, 2017, pp. 511–519, https://doi.org/10.1145/3126686.3126768, http://doi.acm.org/10.1145/3126686.3126768.

[36] B. Zhang, J. Zhao, S. Yang, Y. Zhang, J. Wang, Z. Fei, Subjective and objective quality assessment of panoramic videos in virtual reality environments, in: 2017 IEEE International Conference on Multimedia Expo Workshops (ICMEW), 2017, pp. 163–168, https://doi.org/10.1109/ICMEW.2017.8026226.

[37] A. Singla, W. Robitza, A. Raake, Comparison of subjective quality evaluation methods for omnidirectional videos with DSIS and modified ACR, Electronic Imaging 2018 (2018) 1–6, https://doi.org/10.2352/ISSN.2470-1173.2018.14.HVEI-525.

[38] P. Pérez, J. Escobar, MIRO360: A tool for subjective assessment of 360 degree video for ITU-T P.360-VR, in: 2019 Eleventh International Conference on Quality of Multimedia Experience (QoMEX), 2019, pp. 1–3, https://doi.org/10.1109/QoMEX.2019.8743216.

[39] H.T.T. Tran, N.P. Ngoc, C.T. Pham, Y.J. Jung, T.C. Thang, A subjective study on QoE of 360 video for VR communication, in: IEEE 19th International Workshop on MMSP, 2017, pp. 1–6.

[40] H. Duan, G. Zhai, X. Yang, D. Li, W. Zhu, IVQAD 2017: An immersive video quality assessment database, in: 2017 International Conference on Systems, Signals and Image Processing (IWSSIP), 2017, pp. 1–5, https://doi.org/10.1109/IWSSIP.2017.7965610.

[41] M. Xu, C. Li, Y. Liu, X. Deng, J. Lu, A subjective visual quality assessment method of panoramic videos, in: 2017 IEEE International Conference on Multimedia and Expo (ICME), 2017, pp. 517–522, https://doi.org/10.1109/ICME.2017.8019351.

[42] F. Lopes, J. Ascenso, A. Rodrigues, M.P. Queluz, Subjective and objective quality assessment of omnidirectional video, in: SPIE Conference Series, 2018, https://doi.org/10.1117/12.2321679.

[43] S. Chen, Y. Zhang, Y. Li, Z. Chen, Z. Wang, Spherical structural similarity index for objective omnidirectional video quality assessment, in: 2018 IEEE International Conference on Multimedia and Expo (ICME), 2018, pp. 1–6, https://doi.org/10.1109/ICME.2018.8486584.

[44] Y. Zhang, Y. Wang, F. Liu, Z. Liu, Y. Li, D. Yang, Z. Chen, Subjective panoramic video quality assessment database for coding applications, IEEE Transactions on Broadcasting 64 (2) (2018) 461–473, https://doi.org/10.1109/TBC.2018.2811627.

[45] F. Hofmeyer, S. Fremerey, T. Cohrs, A. Raake, Impacts of internal HMD playback processing on subjective quality perception, Electronic Imaging 2019 (12) (2019) 219, 7pp.

[46] S. Mahmoudpour, P. Schelkens, Visual quality analysis of judder effect on head mounted displays, in: 2019 27th European Signal Processing Conference (EUSIPCO), 2019, pp. 1–5, https://doi.org/10.23919/EUSIPCO.2019.8902665.

[47] S. Katsigiannis, R. Willis, N. Ramzan, A QoE and simulator sickness evaluation of a smart-exercise-bike virtual reality system via user feedback and physiological signals, IEEE Transactions on Consumer Electronics 65 (1) (2019) 119–127, https://doi.org/10.1109/TCE.2018.2879065.

[48] A. Singla, W. Robitza, A. Raake, Comparison of subjective quality test methods for omnidirectional video quality evaluation, in: 2019 IEEE 21st International Workshop on Multimedia Signal Processing (MMSP), 2019, pp. 1–6.

[49] M.S. Anwar, J. Wang, W. Khan, A. Ullah, S. Ahmad, Z. Fei, Subjective QoE of 360-degree virtual reality videos and machine learning predictions, IEEE Access 8 (2020) 148084–148099, https://doi.org/10.1109/ACCESS.2020.3015556.

[50] S. Fremerey, S. Göring, R.R.R. Rao, R. Huang, A. Raake, Subjective test dataset and meta-data-based models for 360° streaming video quality, in: 2020 IEEE 22nd International Workshop on Multimedia Signal Processing (MMSP), 2020, pp. 1–6, https://doi.org/10.1109/MMSP48831.2020.9287065.

[51] S. Croci, C. Ozcinar, E. Zerman, J. Cabrera, A. Smolic, Voronoi-based objective quality metrics for omnidirectional video, in: 11th International Conference on Quality of Multimedia Experience (QoMEX 2019), 2019, pp. 1–6.

[52] S. Fremerey, F. Hofmeyer, S. Göring, A. Raake, Impact of various motion interpolation algorithms on 360° video QoE, in: 2019 Eleventh International Conference on Quality of Multimedia Experience (QoMEX), IEEE, 2019, pp. 1–3.

[53] P. Hanhart, Y. He, Y. Ye, J. Boyce, Z. Deng, L. Xu, 360-degree video quality evaluation, in: 2018 Picture Coding Symposium (PCS), 2018, pp. 328–332, https://doi.org/10.1109/PCS.2018.8456255.

[54] S. Mahmoudpour, P. Schelkens, Omnidirectional video quality index accounting for judder, IEEE Transactions on Circuits and Systems for Video Technology 31 (1) (2020) 61–75.

[55] H. Jiang, D. Sun, V. Jampani, M.-H. Yang, E. Learned-Miller, J. Kautz, Super SloMo: High quality estimation of multiple intermediate frames for video interpolation, in: Proceedings of the IEEE Conference on Computer Vision and Pattern Recognition, 2018, pp. 9000–9008.

[56] T. Tominaga, T. Hayashi, J. Okamoto, A. Takahashi, Performance comparisons of subjective quality assessment methods for mobile video, in: 2010 Second International Workshop on Quality of Multimedia Experience (QoMEX), 2010, pp. 82–87, https://doi.org/10.1109/QOMEX.2010.5517948.

[57] C. Wu, Z. Tan, Z. Wang, S. Yang, A dataset for exploring user behaviors in VR spherical video streaming, in: Proceedings of the 8th ACM on Multimedia Systems Conference, 2017, pp. 193–198.

[58] E.J. David, J. Gutiérrez, A. Coutrot, M.P. Da Silva, P. Le Callet, A dataset of head and eye movements for 360° videos, in: Proceedings of the 9th ACM Multimedia Systems Conference, ACM, 2018, pp. 432–437.

[59] F. Duanmu, Y. Mao, S. Liu, S. Srinivasan, Y. Wang, A subjective study of viewer navigation behaviors when watching 360-degree videos on computers, in: 2018 IEEE International Conference on Multimedia and Expo (ICME), IEEE, 2018, pp. 1–6.

[60] M. Almquist, V. Almquist, V. Krishnamoorthi, N. Carlsson, D. Eager, The prefetch aggressiveness tradeoff in 360 video streaming, in: Proceedings of the 9th ACM Multimedia Systems Conference, 2018, pp. 258–269.

[61] M. Xu, Y. Song, J. Wang, M. Qiao, L. Huo, Z. Wang, Predicting head movement in panoramic video: A deep reinforcement learning approach, IEEE Transactions on Pattern Analysis and Machine Intelligence 41 (11) (2019) 2693–2708, https://doi.org/10.1109/TPAMI.2018.2858783.

[62] A. Covaci, R. Trestian, E.B. Saleme, I.-S. Comsa, G. Assres, C.A.S. Santos, G. Ghinea, 360-degree mulsemedia: A way to improve subjective QoE in 360-degree videos, in: Proceedings of the 27th ACM International Conference on Multimedia, MM '19, Association for Computing Machinery, New York, NY, USA, 2019, pp. 2378–2386, https://doi.org/10.1145/3343031.3350954.

[63] A. Singla, R.R.R. Rao, S. Göring, A. Raake, Assessing media QoE, simulator sickness and presence for omnidirectional videos with different test protocols, in: 2019 IEEE Conference on Virtual Reality and 3D User Interfaces (VR), 2019, pp. 1163–1164, https://doi.org/10.1109/VR.2019.8798291.

[64] A. Singla, S. Fremerey, F. Hofmeyer, W. Robitza, A. Raake, Quality assessment protocols for omnidirectional video quality evaluation, Electronic Imaging 2020 (11) (2020) 69, 7pp., https://doi.

org/10.2352/ISSN.2470-1173.2020.11.HVEI-069, https://www.ingentaconnect.com/content/ist/ei/2020/00002020/00000011/art00003.

[65] I.D. Curcio, H. Toukomaa, D. Naik, Bandwidth reduction of omnidirectional viewport-dependent video streaming via subjective quality assessment, in: Proceedings of the 2nd International Workshop on Multimedia Alternate Realities, AltMM '17, Association for Computing Machinery, New York, NY, USA, 2017, pp. 9–14, https://doi.org/10.1145/3132361.3132364.

[66] R. Schatz, A. Zabrovskiy, C. Timmerer, Tile-based streaming of 8K omnidirectional video: Subjective and objective QoE evaluation, in: 2019 Eleventh International Conference on Quality of Multimedia Experience (QoMEX), 2019, pp. 1–6, https://doi.org/10.1109/QoMEX.2019.8743230.

[67] A. Singla, S. Göring, A. Raake, B. Meixner, R. Koenen, T. Buchholz, Subjective quality evaluation of tile-based streaming for omnidirectional videos, in: Proceedings of the 10th ACM Multimedia Systems Conference, MMSys '19, Association for Computing Machinery, New York, NY, USA, 2019, pp. 232–242, https://doi.org/10.1145/3304109.3306218.

[68] C. Cortés, P. Pérez, J. Gutiérrez, N. García, Influence of video delay on quality, presence, and sickness in viewport adaptive immersive streaming, in: 2020 Twelfth International Conference on Quality of Multimedia Experience (QoMEX), 2020, pp. 1–4, https://doi.org/10.1109/QoMEX48832.2020.9123114.

[69] M.S. Anwar, J. Wang, A. Ullah, W. Khan, S. Ahmad, Z. Li, Impact of stalling on QoE for 360-degree virtual reality videos, in: 2019 IEEE International Conference on Signal, Information and Data Processing (ICSIDP), 2019, pp. 1–6.

[70] C.-L. Fan, W.-C. Lo, Y.-T. Pai, C.-H. Hsu, A survey on 360° video streaming: Acquisition, transmission, and display, ACM Computing Surveys 52 (4) (Aug. 2019), https://doi.org/10.1145/3329119.

[71] V.R. Gaddam, M. Riegler, R. Eg, C. Griwodz, P. Halvorsen, Tiling in interactive panoramic video: Approaches and evaluation, IEEE Transactions on Multimedia 18 (9) (2016) 1819–1831, https://doi.org/10.1109/TMM.2016.2586304.

[72] M. Graf, C. Timmerer, C. Mueller, Towards bandwidth efficient adaptive streaming of omnidirectional video over HTTP: Design, implementation, and evaluation, in: Proceedings of the 8th ACM on Multimedia Systems Conference, 2017, pp. 261–271, https://doi.org/10.1145/3083187.3084016, http://doi.acm.org/10.1145/3083187.3084016.

[73] X. Corbillon, G. Simon, A. Devlic, J. Chakareski, Viewport-adaptive navigable 360-degree video delivery, in: 2017 IEEE International Conference on Communications (ICC), 2017, pp. 1–7, https://doi.org/10.1109/ICC.2017.7996611.

[74] R. van Brandenburg, R. Koenen, D. Sztykman, CDN optimisation for VR streaming, https://www.ibc.org/tech-advances/cdn-optimisation-for-vr-streaming-/2457.article, Oct. 2017. (Accessed 12 June 2018).

[75] R. Monnier, R. van Brandenburg, R. Koenen, Streaming UHD-quality VR at realistic bitrates: Mission impossible?, in: 2017 NAB Broadcast Engineering and Information Technology Conference (BEITC), 2017, pp. 1–8.

[76] S.-C. Yen, C.-L. Fan, C.-H. Hsu, Streaming 360° Videos to Head-Mounted Virtual Reality Using DASH over QUIC Transport Protocol, Association for Computing Machinery, New York, NY, USA, 2019, pp. 7–12, https://doi.org/10.1145/3304114.3325616.

[77] J. van der Hooft, M.T. Vega, S. Petrangeli, T. Wauters, F.D. Turck, Tile-based adaptive streaming for virtual reality video, ACM Transactions on Multimedia Computing, Communications, and Applications (TOMM) 15 (2020) 1–24.

[78] J.-W. Chen, C.-Y. Kao, Y.-L. Lin, Introduction to H.264 advanced video coding, in: Asia and South Pacific Conference on Design Automation, 2006, pp. 736–741, https://doi.org/10.1145/1118299.1118471.

[79] J.-R. Ohm, G. Sullivan, Vision, applications and requirements for high efficiency video coding (HEVC), Tech. Rep. MPEG2011/N11891, ISO/IEC JTC1/SC29/WG11, Geneva, Switzerland, March 2011.

[80] I. 23009-1, Information technology — dynamic adaptive streaming over HTTP (DASH) — part 1: Media presentation description and segment formats, Tech. rep., ISO/IEC JTC1/SC29/WG11, 2014.

[81] A. Singla, S. Fremerey, A. Raake, P. List, B. Feiten, AhG8: Measurement of user exploration behavior for omnidirectional (360°) videos with a head mounted display, Tech. rep., Macau, China, Oct. 2017.

[82] Y. Rai, P. Le Callet, P. Guillotel, Which saliency weighting for omni directional image quality assessment?, in: 2017 Ninth International Conference on Quality of Multimedia Experience (QoMEX), IEEE, 2017, pp. 1–6.

[83] B. John, P. Raiturkar, O. Le Meur, E. Jain, A benchmark of four methods for generating 360° saliency maps from eye tracking data, in: 2018 IEEE International Conference on Artificial Intelligence and Virtual Reality (AIVR), 2018, pp. 136–139, https://doi.org/10.1109/AIVR.2018.00028.

[84] S. Knorr, C. Ozcinar, C.O. Fearghail, A. Smolic, Director's cut: A combined dataset for visual attention analysis in cinematic VR content, in: Proceedings of the 15th ACM SIGGRAPH European Conference on Visual Media Production, CVMP '18, Association for Computing Machinery, New York, NY, USA, 2018, pp. 1–10, https://doi.org/10.1145/3278471.3278472.

[85] W. Sun, K. Gu, S. Ma, W. Zhu, N. Liu, G. Zhai, A large-scale compressed 360-degree spherical image database: From subjective quality evaluation to objective model comparison, in: 2018 IEEE 20th International Workshop on Multimedia Signal Processing (MMSP), 2018, pp. 1–6, https://doi.org/10.1109/MMSP.2018.8547102.

[86] H. Duan, G. Zhai, X. Min, Y. Zhu, Y. Fang, X. Yang, Perceptual quality assessment of omnidirectional images, in: 2018 IEEE International Symposium on Circuits and Systems (ISCAS), 2018, pp. 1–5, https://doi.org/10.1109/ISCAS.2018.8351786.

[87] S. Croci, C. Ozcinar, E. Zerman, J. Cabrera, A. Smolic, Visual attention-aware quality estimation framework for omnidirectional video using spherical Voronoi diagram, Quality and User Experience 5 (2020) 4.

[88] E. Upenik, T. Ebrahimi, Saliency driven perceptual quality metric for omnidirectional visual content, in: 2019 IEEE International Conference on Image Processing (ICIP), 2019, pp. 4335–4339, https://doi.org/10.1109/ICIP.2019.8803637.

[89] G. Luz, J. Ascenso, C. Brites, F. Pereira, Saliency-driven omnidirectional imaging adaptive coding: Modeling and assessment, in: 2017 IEEE 19th International Workshop on Multimedia Signal Processing (MMSP), 2017, pp. 1–6, https://doi.org/10.1109/MMSP.2017.8122228.

[90] H. Lim, H.G. Kim, Y.M. Ro, VR IQA NET: deep virtual reality image quality assessment using adversarial learning, CoRR, arXiv:1804.03943 [abs], 2018.

[91] Z. Wang, A.C. Bovik, H.R. Sheikh, E.P. Simoncelli, Image quality assessment: From error visibility to structural similarity, IEEE Transactions on Image Processing 13 (4) (2004) 600–612, https://doi.org/10.1109/TIP.2003.819861.

[92] Z. Wang, E.P. Simoncelli, A.C. Bovik, Multiscale structural similarity for image quality assessment, in: The Thirty-Seventh Asilomar Conference on Signals, Systems Computers, 2003, vol. 2, 2003, pp. 1398–1402, https://doi.org/10.1109/ACSSC.2003.1292216.

[93] H.R. Sheikh, A.C. Bovik, Image information and visual quality, IEEE Transactions on Image Processing 15 (2) (2006) 430–444, https://doi.org/10.1109/TIP.2005.859378.

[94] L. Zhang, L. Zhang, X. Mou, D. Zhang, FSIM: A feature similarity index for image quality assessment, IEEE Transactions on Image Processing 20 (8) (2011) 2378–2386, https://doi.org/10.1109/TIP.2011.2109730.

[95] S. Li, F. Zhang, L. Ma, K.N. Ngan, Image quality assessment by separately evaluating detail losses and additive impairments, IEEE Transactions on Multimedia 13 (5) (2011) 935–949, https://doi.org/10.1109/TMM.2011.2152382.

[96] H. Sheikh, A. Bovik, G. de Veciana, An information fidelity criterion for image quality assessment using natural scene statistics, IEEE Transactions on Image Processing 14 (12) (2005) 2117–2128, https://doi.org/10.1109/TIP.2005.859389.

[97] Z. Li, A. Aaron, I. Katsavounidis, A. Moorthy, M. Manohara, Toward a practical perceptual video quality metric, https://medium.com/netflix-techblog/toward-a-practical-perceptual-video-quality-metric-653f208b9652, Jan 2019.

[98] N. Barman, S. Schmidt, S. Zadtootaghaj, M.G. Martini, S. Möller, An evaluation of video quality assessment metrics for passive gaming video streaming, in: Proceedings of the 23rd Packet Video Workshop, ACM, 2018, pp. 7–12, https://doi.org/10.1145/3210424.3210434.

[99] R. Rassool, VMAF reproducibility: Validating a perceptual practical video quality metric, in: 2017 IEEE International Symposium on Broadband Multimedia Systems and Broadcasting (BMSB), 2017, pp. 1–2, https://doi.org/10.1109/BMSB.2017.7986143.

[100] C.G. Bampis, Z. Li, A.C. Bovik, Spatiotemporal feature integration and model fusion for full reference video quality assessment, IEEE Transactions on Circuits and Systems for Video Technology 29 (8) (2019) 2256–2270, https://doi.org/10.1109/TCSVT.2018.2868262.

[101] C. Cortes, V. Vapnik, Support-vector networks, Machine Learning 20 (3) (1995) 273–297, https://doi.org/10.1023/A:1022627411411.

[102] M. Orduna, C. Díaz, L. Muñoz, P. Pérez, I. Benito, N. García, Video multimethod assessment fusion (VMAF) on 360VR contents, CoRR, arXiv:1901.06279 [abs], 2019.

[103] A.K. Moorthy, A.C. Bovik, A two-step framework for constructing blind image quality indices, IEEE Signal Processing Letters 17 (5) (2010) 513–516, https://doi.org/10.1109/LSP.2010.2043888.

[104] A. Mittal, A.K. Moorthy, A.C. Bovik, No-reference image quality assessment in the spatial domain, IEEE Transactions on Image Processing 21 (12) (2012) 4695–4708, https://doi.org/10.1109/TIP.2012.2214050.

[105] A. Mittal, R. Soundararajan, A.C. Bovik, Making a "completely blind" image quality analyzer, IEEE Signal Processing Letters 20 (3) (2013) 209–212, https://doi.org/10.1109/LSP.2012.2227726.

[106] M.A. Saad, A.C. Bovik, C. Charrier, Blind image quality assessment: A natural scene statistics approach in the DCT domain, IEEE Transactions on Image Processing 21 (8) (2012) 3339–3352, https://doi.org/10.1109/TIP.2012.2191563.

[107] K. Gu, G. Zhai, X. Yang, W. Zhang, Hybrid no-reference quality metric for singly and multiply distorted images, IEEE Transactions on Broadcasting 60 (3) (2014) 555–567, https://doi.org/10.1109/TBC.2014.2344471.

[108] G. Zhai, X. Min, Perceptual image quality assessment: a survey, Science China Information Sciences 63 (2020) 211301, https://doi.org/10.1007/s11432-019-2757-1.

[109] Y. Sun, A. Lu, L. Yu, Weighted-to-spherically-uniform quality evaluation for omnidirectional video, IEEE Signal Processing Letters 24 (9) (2017) 1408–1412, https://doi.org/10.1109/LSP.2017.2720693.

[110] Facebook, Quality assessment of 360 video view session, https://engineering.fb.com/2018/03/09/video-engineering/quality-assessment-of-360-video-view-sessions/, 2018. (Accessed 11 July 2021).

[111] V. Zakharchenko, K.P. Choi, J.H. Park, Quality metric for spherical panoramic video, Proceedings - SPIE 9970 (2016) 99700C, https://doi.org/10.1117/12.2235885.

[112] M. Yu, H. Lakshman, B. Girod, A framework to evaluate omnidirectional video coding schemes, in: 2015 IEEE International Symposium on Mixed and Augmented Reality, 2015, pp. 31–36, https://doi.org/10.1109/ISMAR.2015.12.

[113] R.G. de, A. Azevedo, N. Birkbeck, I. Janatra, B. Adsumilli, P. Frossard, A viewport-driven multimetric fusion approach for 360-degree video quality assessment, in: 2020 IEEE International Conference on Multimedia and Expo (ICME), 2020, pp. 1–6, https://doi.org/10.1109/ICME46284.2020.9102936.

[114] R.G. Azevedo, N. Birkbeck, I. Janatra, B. Adsumilli, P. Frossard, Multi-feature 360 video quality estimation, IEEE Open Journal of Circuits and Systems 2 (2021) 338–349, https://doi.org/10.1109/OJCAS.2021.3073891.

[115] M. Xu, C. Li, Z. Chen, Z. Wang, Z. Guan, Assessing visual quality of omnidirectional videos, IEEE Transactions on Circuits and Systems for Video Technology 29 (12) (2019) 3516–3530, https://doi.org/10.1109/TCSVT.2018.2886277.

[116] S. Yang, J. Zhao, T. Jiang, J. Wang, T. Rahim, B. Zhang, Z. Xu, Z. Fei, An objective assessment method based on multi-level factors for panoramic videos, in: 2017 IEEE Visual Communications and Image Processing (VCIP), 2017, pp. 1–4, https://doi.org/10.1109/VCIP.2017.8305133.

[117] W. Zhou, J. Xu, Q. Jiang, Z. Chen, No-reference quality assessment for 360-degree images by analysis of multifrequency information and local-global naturalness, IEEE Transactions on Circuits and Systems for Video Technology 32 (4) (2022) 1778–1791, https://doi.org/10.1109/TCSVT.2021.3081182.

[118] H.T.T. Tran, N.P. Ngoc, C.M. Bui, M.H. Pham, T.C. Thang, An evaluation of quality metrics for 360 videos, in: 2017 Ninth International Conference on Ubiquitous and Future Networks (ICUFN), 2017, pp. 7–11, https://doi.org/10.1109/ICUFN.2017.7993736.

[119] E. Upenik, M. Řeřábek, T. Ebrahimi, A testbed for subjective evaluation of omnidirectional visual content, in: Proceedings of the Picture Coding Symposium (PCS), 2016, pp. 1–5.

[120] E. Upenik, M. Rerabek, T. Ebrahimi, On the performance of objective metrics for omnidirectional visual content, in: 2017 Ninth International Conference on Quality of Multimedia Experience (QoMEX), 2017.

[121] Y. Zhou, M. Yu, H. Ma, H. Shao, G. Jiang, Weighted-to-spherically-uniform SSIM objective quality evaluation for panoramic video, in: 2018 14th IEEE International Conference on Signal Processing (ICSP), 2018, pp. 54–57, https://doi.org/10.1109/ICSP.2018.8652269.

[122] P. Gao, P. Zhang, A. Smolic, Quality assessment for omnidirectional video: A spatio-temporal distortion modeling approach, IEEE Transactions on Multimedia (2022) 1–16, https://doi.org/10.1109/TMM.2020.3044458.

[123] I.-T. P.910, Subjective video quality assessment methods for multimedia applications, International Telecommunication Union, 2008.

[124] L. Breiman, Random forests, Machine Learning 45 (1) (2001) 5–32.

[125] F. Heitger, L. Rosenthaler, R. von der Heydt, E. Peterhans, O. Kübler, Simulation of neural contour mechanisms: from simple to end-stopped cells, Vision Research 32 (5) (1992) 963–981.

[126] J. Xiang, G. Jiang, M. Yu, Y. Bai, Z. Zhu, No-reference light field image quality assessment based on depth, structural and angular information, Signal Processing 184 (2021) 108063, https://doi.org/10.1016/j.sigpro.2021.108063, https://www.sciencedirect.com/science/article/pii/S0165168421001018.

[127] W. Zhou, L. Shi, Z. Chen, J. Zhang, Tensor oriented no-reference light field image quality assessment, IEEE Transactions on Image Processing 29 (2020) 4070–4084, https://doi.org/10.1109/TIP.2020.2969777.

[128] B. Schölkopf, A.J. Smola, R.C. Williamson, P.L. Bartlett, New support vector algorithms, Neural Computation 12 (5) (2000) 1207–1245, https://doi.org/10.1162/089976600300015565.

[129] W. Sun, K. Gu, G. Zhai, S. Ma, W. Lin, P. Le Calle, CVIQD: Subjective quality evaluation of compressed virtual reality images, in: 2017 IEEE International Conference on Image Processing (ICIP), 2017, pp. 3450–3454, https://doi.org/10.1109/ICIP.2017.8296923.

[130] T.Q. Truong, H.T.T. Tran, T.C. Thang, Non-reference quality assessment model using deep learning for omnidirectional images, in: 2019 IEEE 10th International Conference on Awareness Science and Technology (iCAST), 2019, pp. 1–5, https://doi.org/10.1109/ICAwST.2019.8923442.

[131] P. Wu, W. Ding, Z. You, P. An, Virtual reality video quality assessment based on 3D convolutional neural networks, in: 2019 IEEE International Conference on Image Processing (ICIP), 2019, pp. 3187–3191, https://doi.org/10.1109/ICIP.2019.8803023.

[132] W. Sun, W. Luo, X. Min, G. Zhai, X. Yang, K. Gu, S. Ma, MC360IQA: The multi-channel CNN for blind 360-degree image quality assessment, in: 2019 IEEE International Symposium on Circuits and Systems (ISCAS), 2019, pp. 1–5, https://doi.org/10.1109/ISCAS.2019.8702664.

[133] H.G. Kim, H.-T. Lim, Y.M. Ro, Deep virtual reality image quality assessment with human perception guider for omnidirectional image, IEEE Transactions on Circuits and Systems for Video Technology 30 (4) (2020) 917–928, https://doi.org/10.1109/TCSVT.2019.2898732.

[134] J. Xu, W. Zhou, Z. Chen, Blind omnidirectional image quality assessment with viewport oriented graph convolutional networks, IEEE Transactions on Circuits and Systems for Video Technology 31 (5) (2021) 1724–1737, https://doi.org/10.1109/TCSVT.2020.3015186.

[135] C. Li, M. Xu, L. Jiang, S. Zhang, X. Tao, Viewport proposal CNN for 360° video quality assessment, in: 2019 IEEE/CVF Conference on Computer Vision and Pattern Recognition (CVPR), 2019, pp. 10169–10178, https://doi.org/10.1109/CVPR.2019.01042.

[136] J. Pan, C. Canton, K. McGuinness, N.E. O'Connor, J. Torres, E. Sayrol, X. Giro-i-Nieto, SalGAN: Visual saliency prediction with generative adversarial networks, arXiv:1701.01081, 2017.

[137] J. Kim, S. Lee, Deep learning of human visual sensitivity in image quality assessment framework, in: 2017 IEEE Conference on Computer Vision and Pattern Recognition (CVPR), 2017, pp. 1969–1977, https://doi.org/10.1109/CVPR.2017.213.

[138] T. Maugey, O. Le Meur, Z. Liu, Saliency-based navigation in omnidirectional image, in: 2017 IEEE 19th International Workshop on Multimedia Signal Processing (MMSP), 2017, pp. 1–6, https://doi.org/10.1109/MMSP.2017.8122229.

[139] Z. Zhang, Y. Xu, J. Yu, S. Gao, Saliency detection in 360° videos, in: ECCV 2018, 2018, pp. 504–520.

[140] M. Huang, Q. Shen, Z. Ma, A.C. Bovik, P. Gupta, R. Zhou, X. Cao, Modeling the perceptual quality of immersive images rendered on head mounted displays: Resolution and compression, IEEE Transactions on Image Processing 27 (12) (2018) 6039–6050, https://doi.org/10.1109/TIP.2018.2865089.

[141] K. He, X. Zhang, S. Ren, J. Sun, Deep residual learning for image recognition, in: 2016 IEEE Conference on Computer Vision and Pattern Recognition (CVPR), 2016, pp. 770–778, https://doi.org/10.1109/CVPR.2016.90.

[142] T.S. Cohen, M. Geiger, J. Köhler, M. Welling, Spherical CNNs, in: International Conference on Learning Representations, 2018, https://openreview.net/forum?id=Hkbd5xZRb.

[143] G. Huang, Z. Liu, L.V.D. Maaten, K.Q. Weinberger, Densely connected convolutional networks, in: 2017 IEEE Conference on Computer Vision and Pattern Recognition (CVPR), IEEE Computer Society, Los Alamitos, CA, USA, 2017, pp. 2261–2269, https://doi.org/10.1109/CVPR.2017.243, https://doi.ieeecomputersociety.org/10.1109/CVPR.2017.243.

[144] Z. Wang, A. Bovik, H. Sheikh, E. Simoncelli, Image quality assessment: from error visibility to structural similarity, IEEE Transactions on Image Processing 13 (4) (2004) 600–612, https://doi.org/10.1109/TIP.2003.819861.

[145] W. Zhang, K. Ma, J. Yan, D. Deng, Z. Wang, Blind image quality assessment using a deep bilinear convolutional neural network, IEEE Transactions on Circuits and Systems for Video Technology 30 (1) (2020) 36–47, https://doi.org/10.1109/TCSVT.2018.2886771.

[146] F. Aurenhammer, Voronoi diagrams - A survey of a fundamental data structure, ACM Computing Surveys 23 (3) (1991) 345–405, https://doi.org/10.1145/116873.116880.

[147] S. Croci, S. Knorr, L. Goldmann, A. Smolic, A framework for quality control in cinematic VR based on Voronoi patches and saliency, in: International Conference on 3D Immersion, Brussels, Belgium, 2017, pp. 1–8.

[148] F. Pearson, Map Projections: Theory and Applications, CRC Press, 1990.

[149] K. Seshadrinathan, R. Soundararajan, A.C. Bovik, L.K. Cormack, Study of subjective and objective quality assessment of video, IEEE Transactions on Image Processing 19 (6) (2010) 1427–1441, https://doi.org/10.1109/TIP.2010.2042111.

[150] VQEG, Final report from the video quality experts group on the validation of objective models of video quality assessment, Tech. rep., ITU, COM 9-80-E, Geneva, Switzerland, 2000.

CHAPTER 5

Omnidirectional video saliency

Fang-Yi Chao[a], Federica Battisti[b], Pierre Lebreton[c], and Alexander Raake[d]
[a]V-SENSE, Trinity College, The University of Dublin, Dublin, Ireland
[b]Department of Information Engineering, University of Padova, Padova, Italy
[c]NTT Network Service Systems Laboratories, Tokyo, Japan
[d]Audiovisual Technology Group, Ilmenau University of Technology, Ilmenau, Germany

5.1. Introduction

How humans (and also other species) perceive and explore the visual world around them has long been of strong scientific interest, first starting from medical and psychological research to quickly become of technological interest, too (see e.g., [1–3]). One key component in visual perception is visual attention. With selective attention, the amount of information provided to the brain can effectively be managed. Obviously, different objects in a scene are differently relevant for a person in a given situation. Selective attention directs the focus of the foveal retinal areas of the eyes to these objects. Along the visual pathway, the information captured by the fovea is magnified in terms of the cortical region associated with foveal vs. peripheral vision [4], enabling a detailed visual inspection of information captured during such *fixation*. Here, two types of visual attention can be distinguished, overt and covert [5]: Overt attention includes focusing, whereas covert does not. Accordingly, overt attention can rather easily be observed using eye and head tracking, whereas covert attention measurement requires more elaborate techniques.

With the advent of more and more sophisticated and accurate, yet also more and more affordable technological solutions for eye and head tracking, systematic research on overt visual attention has emerged over the last decades. When test scenes are presented on a computer display, controlled and repeatable viewing conditions can be achieved. Accordingly, there is a large body of research on overt visual attention for scenes displayed on 2D screens (cf. e.g., [1,6–9]).

Visual attention is steered by two sources of information: On the one hand, *salient* scene information may attract the attention of the viewer in a *bottom-up* manner, leading to the subsequent focusing on a particular region of the scene [1,5,7]. This salient information may be attributed to brightness or motion cues, or auditory or even tactile events that attract the viewer's attention (e.g., hearing a loud sound from behind, or having someone tab one's shoulder). On the other hand, *top-down* attentional processes let the user explore the environment, for example, to find a specific object therein. From an evolutionary vantage point, the relevance of these selective attention mechanisms is

Immersive Video Technologies
https://doi.org/10.1016/B978-0-32-391755-1.00011-0

obvious: While limiting the amount of information to an efficiently restricted stream, and hence saving mental resources and thus energy, important situations—such as having a predator approaching (e.g., sound, visual motion), finding food or engaging into a communication with another person—can effectively be handled [5,10].

In human's daily audiovisual scene analysis, an intertwined mixture of both bottom-up and top-down processes are at play. With head and eye tracking, the associated head and eye movements can be captured. Ultimately, the aim is to identify a representation of what is salient for the observer, trying to identify something close to the *saliency map* of a given scene created at a given time in the person's mind [8].

Besides the scientific investigation of how humans perceive and explore (audio)visual scenes, there are different technical applications where saliency information can be used, such as the following:

- Analysis of viewing image and film content and conclusions on aspects such as the placement of certain scene objects during content production (e.g., [11–13]).
- Layout of a webpage or magazine (e.g., [14,15]).
- Placement of add-on objects in images or videos, such as an added text elements (e.g., [16,17]).
- Marketing, e.g., placement and spatial organization of advertisements or brand information [3].
- User interface design, especially for complex tasks, such as aviation [2].
- Scene-specific evaluation of quality (cf. e.g., [18,19]).
- Content- and perception-aware encoding, assigning higher bitdepth to visually more relevant areas (cf. e.g., [20]).
- Saliency-aware video streaming, with higher-quality processing for more relevant spatio-temporal scene regions. A comprehensive overview about this application that also includes relevant general aspects of saliency and behavior assessment is given in [21]. Associated viewport prediction models are discussed in more detail in Section 5.4.3.

As continuous eye and head tracking on actual users is not practically feasible for many of the aforementioned applications, automatic saliency prediction has garnered substantial scientific attention over the past years (e.g., [6,7,22–26]). Some of the papers belong to the most-cited papers in computer vision (e.g., [6,7]).

Visual attention and saliency assessment comprise different types of information and representations, which are relevant in different contexts (for further details cf. Section 5.3):

- Fixations: During the visual exploration of the scene, the observer focuses on specific points and parts of the scene for a certain amount of time. Typically, this information is represented in terms of saliency maps, that is, heat maps that indicate the relative fixation time (or probability) in certain locations of the visual scene.
- Scanpath information: The observer scans a given scene in a specific manner, with a certain order of objects and areas being focused on in terms of fixations. It is noted

that two different scanpaths for an image may lead to the same fixation pattern in terms of sojourn times in given positions.

• Head position: Especially for omnidirectional images and video (ODI, ODV), the current head position is of relevance. In this case, the surrounding, omnidirectional scene can be explored combining head and eye movements. Head-position information is typically represented regarding the center point of the field of view of a head mounted display (HMD), which also corresponds to the forward viewing direction as the norm of the median plane [27]. The head position is also relevant for 2D screen viewing, for example, for calibration purposes of eye tracking data (see e.g., [28]).

In the recent years, 360° images and video, that is, omnidirectional (OD) visual content has enabled a more holistic assessment of visual attention and saliency (for a related overview see also [29]). Here, with the increasing quality of HMDs and OD content, it is possible to create photo-realistic visual scenes that can be explored in three degrees of freedom (3 DoF). Hence, ODI and ODV saliency measurement is of interest not only for OD imaging technology assessment and optimization, but also to gain a better understanding of how humans explore real-life scenes. The spherical coordinate system underlying head-tracking information is typically represented in the angular coordinates *pitch* (corresponding to elevation), *yaw* (corresponding to head rotations in the horizontal plane), and *roll* (rotations around the norm of the median plane), see Fig. 5.1.

The chapter provides an overview of OD image and video saliency assessment involving empirical studies with users and the development of saliency prediction models based on corresponding ground-truth data. The chapter focuses on the literature on non-stereoscopic OD image and video content, also as very few papers exist that include stereoscopic viewing in HMDs (e.g., [29]).

Besides the tutorial character of the chapter, there are a number of contributions beyond the state of the art. At first, in Section 5.3, the chapter discusses the collection, representation, and analysis of viewing behavior collected from viewers exploring ODI or ODV content. Specific aspects, such as the differences between 2D, on-screen video in comparison to HMD-based viewing, are discussed, for example, regarding the static distribution analysis, and with regard to the change from a central towards an equatorial prior. Another difference is the move from mainly eye tracking, and thus fixation-oriented analysis, as in case of 2D towards the analysis with regard to the viewport center as it is typical for 360° saliency measurement. Moreover, dynamic aspects are discussed, for example, regarding the time it takes a viewer to observe every direction of the 360 images, or the implication of the initial starting point. The relationship between eye and head motion is discussed, in light of the vestibulo-ocular reflex.

As the next step, different types of OD image and video saliency models are reviewed (Section 5.4). The systematic overview first considers ODI models to estimate saliency maps (cf. Section 5.4.1), with a special focus on the characteristics that distinguish

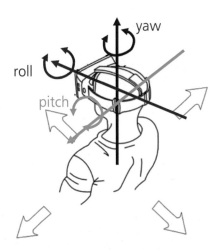

Figure 5.1 Spherical coordinate system typically used to describe OD image and video exploration in 3 DoF by head-rotations. Also indicated are arrows for translatory movement, which is not considered in this chapter.

these saliency models from previous 2D-related ones. Different concepts are addressed, from models that are based on hand-crafted features to machine-learning-based ones. Similarly, Section 5.4.2 reviews a number of ODV saliency models, again ranging from models with hand-crafted features to models employing deep or convolutional neural networks (DNNs, CNNs). The last subsection of the model-related part (Section 5.4.3) provides an extensive overview of viewport prediction models, which are useful for applications such as adaptive streaming [21]. Here, models are distinguished that only include the history of a viewer's behavior, models that also consider saliency or video frame information, and models that are physics-based. Such viewport prediction models can be considered as an application-related counterpart of scanpath prediction models for 2D-screen viewing scenarios.

In the last part of the chapter, Section 5.5, different metrics for the performance evaluation of saliency models are reviewed. Here, it is discussed how metrics should be tuned so as to address omnidirectional content, and how this depends on the underlying projection format. Some of these aspects have been addressed, for example, in [30]. In this chapter, further metrics are added, considering also scanpath and viewport prediction. Furthermore, the chapter is not restricted to the equirectangular projection, and also addressed the cubic projection.

5.2. Collecting user data

A key aspect for the definition of a reliable saliency estimation algorithm is the availability of datasets that include 360° content annotated with eye tracking and/or head motion data. That information is helpful for better understanding the human behavior while exploring the omnidirectional content. Unlike 2D media, omnidirectional images and videos can be viewed in a range that spans 360° horizontally and 180° vertically. For this reason, while looking at an omnidirectional content, the viewer selects only a portion of the scene, the viewport, through his/her head movement (HM) and, within this portion of the space, his/her gaze (collectable through eye movements (EM)) concentrates on salient areas. This is the reason why HM and EM are largely exploited for the definition of saliency models.

The most common technique for collecting HM and EM is to display 360° content through a head mounted display (HMD). Whereas HM can easily be extracted by processing the data provided by the HMD itself, in most cases, EM collection requires being equipped with eye-tracking hardware able to capture EM. The collection of this data requires test protocols and extensive campaigns of subjective testings. Given the peculiarities of the omnidirectional content and of the hardware used to explore it, there are still no well established protocols for collecting such data. A first study towards this research has been carried out by Gutierrez et al. in [31] and later included in the ITU recommendation [32]. Cross-lab tests were carried out in ten laboratories with different types of HMDs and rating methods to validate subjective evaluation methodologies for 360° videos. The main findings of this study suggest the possibility of using 10 s long videos and validating the absolute category rating (ACR) and degradation category rating (DCR) methods. Despite the lack of standardized procedures, the fast spread of the virtual reality (VR) market has pushed the need for 360° algorithms and tools. For this reason, the state-of-the-art presents a number of datasets that can support the development of algorithms dedicated to the 360° pipeline from acquisition and creation to delivery and storage (e.g., optimal omnidirectional coding, saliency estimation, and quality evaluation). As suggested by Xu et al. [33], there are four main aspects that could be considered when preparing a dataset for 360° saliency estimation:

- Consistency among subjects: The exploring behavior of different users should be correlated. The assessment of this agreement can be carried out by analyzing the collected saliency maps among different users and by studying their similarity [29];
- Equator and center bias: Observers replicate the viewing behavior that they have while looking at 2D content and that they usually show in real life; the attention is more focused on the portion of the image/video located in the central part of the scene, the equator. This leads to what is called "equator bias" [34];
- Impact of content: The selection of the content to be displayed highly affects human attention. This aspect has been widely investigated and demonstrated for 2D content, and studies in the literature confirm that the same impact exists for omnidirectional content [29];
- Relationship between HM and EM: Although there is an obvious level of agreement between HMs and EMs, the collected data may differ in a significant way

when adapted for specific applications. One example is given by Rai et al. [35] that evaluated the distributions of HMs and EMs and analyzed the impact of those differences in saliency estimation.

Thanks to the recent spreading of affordable hardware for collecting HM and EM data, an increased number of datasets with varying characteristics have been published. Table 5.1 reports a list of datasets that have been commonly used in the research field for saliency estimation purposes. It is possible to notice that they differ based on the type of displayed content (image or video) in size and number of viewers and also on the collected data (HM, EM or both).

Table 5.1 Available HM and EM datasets for omnidirectional content.

Dataset	Image\Video	Dataset size	Number of viewers	HM\EM
De Abreu et al. [36]	Image	21	32	HM
Bao et al. [37]	Video	16	153	HM
Ozcinar et al. [38]	Video	6	17	HM
Corbillon et al. [39]	Video	7	59	HM
Lo et al. [40]	Video	10	50	HM
Wu et al. [41]	Video	18	48	HM
AVTrack360 [42]	Video	20	48	HM
VR-HM48 [43]	Video	48	40	HM
Wild-360 [44]	Video	85	30	HM
Chao et al. [45]	Video	12	45	HM
Agtzidis et al. [46]	Video	15	13	EM
Garbin et al. [47]	Image	356.649	152	EM
Tabbaa et al. [48]	Video	12	34	EM
Sitzmann et al. [29]	Image	22	169	HM+EM
Salient360 [30]	Image	98	63	HM+EM
Salient360 [34]	Video	19	57	HM+EM
PVS-HM [49]	Video	76	58	HM+EM
Zhang et al. [50]	Video	104	27	HM+EM
VR-EyeTracking [51]	Video	208	45	HM+EM
VQA-ODV [52]	Video	60	221	HM+EM

5.3. User behavior analysis

In this section, the analysis of users' viewing behavior while exploring omnidirectional videos (ODV) is discussed. In the context of images and videos seen on a traditional 2D screen, a lot of work have been performed on the analysis and modeling of visual attention, leading to various models from the original work from Itti [7] up to recent learning-based models, such as DeepGaze II [53] or SalGAN [54]. When dealing with OD contents, new challenges arise as the entire scene cannot be seen at once as it used to be in the case of traditional 2D screens, and it will then result in having both head and eye motion to be involved. In this section different properties of user's viewing behavior when watching OD content will be discussed.

The first consideration that can be addressed is from the point of view of the experimental settings and the differences in viewing behavior, for example, whether users are using the headsets while standing or while seated. In the literature, different works have addressed this problem, and results have shown that in the case of users sitting, how participants are seated has a strong impact on their viewing behavior. Work using a chair that does not allow rotation has shown to result in a strong bias towards a limited exploration from the users [55]. However, using a swivel office chair resulted in a similar exploration to the standing users and showed a high correlation (0.80 Pearson correlation) between the saliency maps obtained from these two different conditions (seated vs. standing) [56]. Further analysis was also performed by comparing VR conditions with a traditional desktop condition, where users could orient the viewport using a mouse, and showed that a relatively high correlation (0.76) could be achieved here, too [29]. A review on system design and user behavior can be found in [57].

When analyzing the distribution of fixations on traditional 2D images, the presence of a center bias has been widely identified [58]. In the context of ODV, this center bias was found to be transformed into an equatorial bias [29,36,59,60]. When studying the distribution of fixation as a function of the latitude, a characterization of this equatorial bias can be made, and previous work has proposed to model it using a Laplace distribution with a mean of 91.30 degrees latitude and a variance of 18.58 degrees [29]. As for the distribution of fixations from the longitude point of view, the results will naturally depend on content. However, one interesting aspect which was studied in the literature is to investigate how quickly users can explore the entire scene shown to them. In the Salient360! dataset [61], the exploration was found to be fast, as it took up to 8 seconds for users to turn their head around the entire longitudinal axis [62]. The speed at which the exploration is performed was found to be dependent of the scene complexity. Results have shown that scenes with low entropy are quickly analyzed and resulted in users quickly focusing on few salient regions. On the other hand, when complexity is increased, it takes a longer time for users to explore the scenes [29]. When analyzing the temporal evolution of the saliency map building process of still images, it was shown that after 30 seconds, a median correlation coefficient score of 0.79 can be achieved while comparing users starting their exploration from different viewport locations [29]. This shows that in the context of medium duration viewing sessions on still images, starting viewport location had a limited impact on the final saliency maps.

Considering that capturing eye motion requires expensive equipment and the majority of head mounted displays (HMD) only provide head-tracking data, the use of head motion as a proxy to head and eye motion was frequently considered when analyzing the viewing behavior of ODV. To investigate the differences between saliency maps produced by head-tracking data only and combined head and eye tracking data, Rai et al. [35] performed a study with an HMD equipped with an eye tracker, and compared the differences of obtained saliency maps. In their work, the authors found a shift between the average location of gaze from the center of the view-port and the average location of fixation with a range from 14 to 20 degrees. The assumption of fixations being in the middle of the viewport was only observed in 2.5% of the scenarios in their dataset [61]. Therefore Rai et al. [35] suggest to take this shift in pitch into account when aiming to approximate eye-motion-based saliency maps from head-motion data.

Going further in the analysis of differences between head and eye motion, the dynamics between these two types of motion have also been analyzed. The head and eye movement are known to interact with each other in a complex manner by involving the vestibulo-ocular reflex. This phenomenon aims to stabilize gaze during head movements [63]. Using this phenomenon, gaze is maintained at the same location by the mean of eye movement, which are performed in the opposite direction of the head movement. This phenomenon is particularly important as head movement occurs frequently, and the vestibulo-ocular reflex will then allow stabilized vision to be achieved. When analyzing viewing behavior of users, previous work was able to model this phenomenon by an inverse linear relationship between head and eye motion data [64]. Therefore this shows that the relationship between eye and head motion is non-trivial, and it may not necessarily be easy to derive one from another.

In this section, key aspects on the distribution of fixation data considering either head-related motion or head- and eye-related motion were summarized. It was shown that these share some similarities, but complex interactions can also be found as well. In the following, the work on modeling these data will be described.

5.4. Modeling

In the literature, a large amount of work can be found on the modeling of how users explore omnidirectional content. This modeling can address a different type of media: images or videos, and be based on different types of modeling, either based on traditional hand-crafted features or newly learned features. Fig. 5.2 shows a 360° image and its fixation map and saliency map from the Salient360! dataset [61]. As mentioned, the fixation points in the fixation map are collected from the subjective tests. A Gaussian filter is used to spread the fixation points to generate a saliency map to account for the gradually decreasing acuity from the foveal vision towards the peripheral vision. The goal of saliency modeling is to predict the saliency map of the given 360° image or video.

In the following, the work done on saliency prediction for omnidirectional images will be introduced. Then, extensions of that work to video will be described. Finally, the specific case of viewport prediction will also be described, considering its significant implication for video streaming.

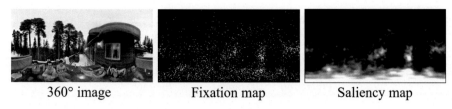

360° image   Fixation map   Saliency map

Figure 5.2 An Example of a 360° image and its fixation map, and saliency map from the Salient360! dataset [61].

5.4.1 Image-based saliency models

Saliency estimation deals with the automatic localization of the areas in a scene having a particular relevance for human observers. This information can be acquired through subjective testing by exploiting the information on fixation points and scan patterns that can be acquired through eye-tracking systems, as described in Section 5.2. As it is well known, subjective tests are time consuming and costly, so many efforts have been devoted to the definition of models able to accurately predict saliency [22,23]. Existing saliency estimation algorithms can be grouped into two classes: top-down approaches rely on the fact that the human visual exploration of a scene is influenced by the specific visual task that is performed; bottom-up methods exploit the evidence that the human attention is unconsciously attracted by local or global features, such as contrast, content, and orientation. However, due to the peculiarities of omnidirectional media and of the different exploration behavior of this type of content, there are still few methods that have been defined for omnidirectional images.

In the following, a non-exhaustive survey of state-of-the-art saliency models for 360° images is reported, and Table 5.2 summarizes all the introduced the models:

- Ling et al. [65] propose an image saliency model, CDSR, that can be applied to 2D and 360° content. It is based on a sparse representation of the image. This is possible by splitting the image in patches and analyzing the inter-patch color differences using a color dictionary trained from natural color images. After the sparse representation is generated, it is used to compute the center–surround differences between image patches. The output of this step is fused with the analysis of the human visual acuity that is used to weight the image patch differences. The obtained saliency map undergoes a latitude-bias enhancement to account for the equator-bias in the human exploration of the content.
- Lebreton et al. [60] propose two new models for 360° image saliency prediction based on the extension of existing and well-established 2D saliency models: BMS [66] and GVBS [67]. The first proposed model, BMS360, implements two main modifications with respect to the 2D algorithm: first it addresses the issue that BMS does not take into account blobs that are in contact with the border of the image. Due to the structure of omnidirectional images in which the content can be con-

Table 5.2 Summary of the presented 360° image saliency prediction methods, where ERP indicates equirectangular projection, RP indicates rectilinear projection, CBP indicates cubic projection, CP indicates cube padding.

Method	Year	Geometric Projection	Derived from 2D model	Tailored for 360°	Techniques
Ling et al. [65]	2018	ERP	✗	✓	Inter-patch color difference
Lebreton et al. [60]	2018	ERP, RP	BMS [66], GVBS [67]	✓	Feature analysis
Startsev et al. [69]	2018	ERP	GBVS [67], eDN [70], SAM-ResNet [71]	✗	Saliency estimation of 'interpretations'
Chao et al. [72]	2018	ERP, CBP	SalGAN [54]	✗	Local and global saliency estimation
Fang et al. [73]	2018	ERP	✗	✓	Gestalt theory
Battisti et al. [74]	2018	ERP	✗	✓	Low and high level feature extraction
Lv et al. [68]	2020	ERP	✗	✓	Spherical graph signal representation

sidered cyclic, saliency can be computed by averaging saliency maps obtained on shifted versions of the 360° image. The second modification takes into account the over-representation of the poles in the ERP in omnidirectional images, which has an impact on the blob normalization procedure performed in BMS. The second proposed model, GVBS360, also includes two modifications with respect to the 2D case: Gabor-based features are computed in the rectilinear domain, and Haversine distance is used instead of the Euclidean distance in the activation and normalization process. Finally, the authors introduce a general framework, ProSal, to adapt 2D saliency estimation algorithms to omnidirectional images.

- Lv et al. [68] propose a saliency estimation method based on the use of convolutional neural networks (CNN). More specifically, the presented approach relies on three steps. The first is the transformation from the equirectangular representation of the image to the spherical graph signal representation. This is the input to a graph saliency prediction network that produces a spherical graph signal representation of the saliency map. Finally, an interpolation module allows to get back to the equirectangular form.

- Startsev et al. [69] base their approach on the concept of "interpretations" of the equirectangular image format. Interpretations are sub-images extracted from the original equirectangular one. For each sub-image the saliency is predicted using state-of-the-art 2D saliency estimation methods. In the presented paper, GBVS [67], eDN [70], and SAM-ResNet [71] are used, but the authors underline the possibility of adopting any other existing 2D saliency estimation model in the proposed framework. The problem that arises when computing the saliency on the sub-images is the fact that pixels on the borders might have a stronger impact since they might be considered more than once in the final saliency estimation. For this reason the authors adopt a pixel-wise maximum operation to select the largest estimated saliency value for these areas.

- Chao et al. [72] propose to extend the SalGAN [54] method developed for 2D images to omnidirectional ones through transfer learning. The first part of the proposed model addresses the problem of reducing the distortions introduced by the equirectangular representation by using multiple cubic representations. The new image representation feeds a generative adversarial networks (GAN) composed of two deep convolutional neural networks (DCNN). Two key aspects of the proposed algorithm are: i) the adoption of a loss function that takes into account three metrics: Kullback–Leibler divergence (KL), Pearson's correlation coefficient (CC) and normalized scanpath saliency (NSS), to optimize the performances on 360° images, ii) the fusion of global and local saliency computed both on the entire image and on the multiple cubic representations.

- Fang et al. [73] exploit the Gestalt theory for 360° images in their proposed approach. They use equirectangular projections that are segmented into superpixels to reduce redundant information and increase spatial structure. After this step, features are extracted to account for saliency. More specifically, the superpixels are converted into the CIELAB color space and luminance and texture are extracted from the L channel, and color features from the a and b channels. Another aspect that is considered is the 360° boundary connectivity that accounts for the difference of saliency between foreground and background. The final saliency map is obtained by combining the extracted features with the boundary connectivity.

- Battisti at al. [74] propose an approach that is based on low-level and high-level features. More specifically, low-level features account for hue, saturation, texture, and saliency within viewports. High-level features concern the presence of human subjects and faces within the scene that are relevant saliency points. Moreover, within the high-level features a more detailed analysis has been carried out to discriminate between the presence of few subjects or of a crowd, to take into account the different impacts that they have on human perception. The final saliency map is obtained by combining the information provided by the features and by performing an equator weighting to include the equator-bias in the human exploration behavior.

Table 5.3 Summary of the 360° video saliency prediction approaches, where ERP indicates equirectangular projection, RP indicates rectilinear projection, CBP indicates cubic projection, CP indicates cube padding.

Method	Year	Geometric Projection	Derived from 2D model	Tailored for 360°	Techniques
Lebreton et al. [62]	2018	ERP	BMS [60]	×	BMS360 with Camera Motion
Nguyen et al. [76]	2018	ERP	Deep ConvNet [77]	×	Transfer Learning
Xu et al. [78]	2018	RP	×	✓	RL
Zhang et al. [50]	2018	3D Sphere	×	✓	Spherical CNN with crown-shape kernels
Cheng et al. [44]	2018	CBP	×	✓	Proposed CP
Zhang et al. [80]	2020	CBP	×	✓	
Dahou et al. [81]	2020	CBP	SalEMA [82]	×	
Chao et al. [84]	2020	CBP	DAVE [85]	✓	CP, Audio-visual Saliency
Qiao et al. [83]	2021	CBP	MT-DNN [83]	×	Multi-Task Learning, CNN, ConvLSTM

5.4.2 Video-based saliency models

Apart from image saliency modeling, which only considers static spatial features, video saliency modeling takes account of static spatial features and dynamic temporal features simultaneously. Dynamic temporal features in 360° video can be extracted by optical flow or 3D CNN, RNN, LSTM, and are then integrated with static spatial features extracted from video frames. In what follow, we survey the state-of-the-art saliency modeling in 360° videos. Table 5.3 summarizes all the introduced the methods.

- Lebreton et al. proposed V–BMS360 [62], which is extended from an image saliency model BMS360 [60] for 360° video. The processing can be divided into the image-based feature maps and the motion-based feature maps, where the image-based feature maps are estimated with BMS360, and the motion-based feature maps are computed from dense optical flow [75]. Both are processed in the equirectangular frames. The key features of camera motion (i.e., motion surroundness and motion source) and user exploration delay are considered in motion-based feature extraction when applying existing image saliency models to head motion prediction for 360° video. Based on a camera-motion analysis, an adaptive motion feature pooling is introduced to merge different motion-based features with different strengths.

- Nguyen et al. proposed a panoramic saliency model PanoSalNet [76] to enhance the head movement prediction for 360° videos. The architecture is derived from Deep ConvNet [77], a saliency prediction model for traditional 2D images. It contains nine convolution and deconvolution layers. Due to the lack of sufficient large 360° video saliency datasets at the time of proposing the method, transfer learning is employed to adapt the 2D saliency model pre-trained with large-scale datasets (i.e., SALICON [24]) for panoramic saliency prediction. The equirectangular frames are fed to the model and after the saliency is predicted by the model, a prior filter [25] is applied to reduce the saliency in areas based on a priori knowledge, such as the four corners of an equirectangular frame.

- Xu et al. [78] proposed to leverage deep reinforcement learning (DRL) to model user's head movement. The approach is based on the observation that users' head movements are highly consistent across different users. The DRL-based head movement prediction (DHP) approach is then proposed to maximize the reward of imitating the user's head movement through the agent's actions. The DRL model contains four convolutional layers, one flatten layer, and LSTM cells. The viewport video frame is extracted based on the head position in the 360° video with rectilinear projection. The DRL network processes the viewport video frame and predicts the head movement in the next frame. The reward measuring the similarity between the predicted and ground-truth head movement is estimated to evaluate the action made by the DRL model. Multiple workflows of models run simultaneously to simulate multiple users watching 360° video and predict users' head movement in the next frame. The predicted head movement of each user at each frame is aggregated as a heat map to generate a saliency map.

- Zhang et al. [50] proposed a spherical CNN to predict saliency for 360° videos. The network is composed of spherical-crown-shape kernels and the convolution is conducted via the stretch and rotation of the kernels along the sphere. Apart from other 2D-derived methods that apply feature extraction on equirectangular video frames, the spherical-crown-shape kernels can be directly applied on the 3D spherical surface without any projection. Hence the spatial features extracted from the spherical CNN are without geometric distortion. The spherical CNN is embedded into U-Net [79], which is referred to as spherical U-Net. The temporal coherence of the viewing process is also taken into account to consider the temporal visual cues in watching a 360° video.

- Cheng et al. [44] proposed a cube padding technique applied on CNN layers to extract visual features on cubic faces without disconnection between every two faces. A spatial-temporal network adopting cube padding as image padding in convolution, pooling, convolutional LSTM layers is designed to predict saliency in 360° video. The method renders the 360° view on six cubic faces with perspective projection and concatenates the faces as the input to the network. By using cube padding connecting features in neighboring cubic faces, the network obtains no image boundary between cubic faces in all convolutional layers. A weakly-supervised training manner is also introduced to refine static features with temporal constraints (i.e., temporal reconstruction loss, smoothness loss, and motion masking loss).

- Zhang et al. [80] proposed a network composed of feature encoding module and saliency prediction module for 360° video saliency prediction. In the feature encoding module, a two-stream structure is used to take video frames and corresponding optical flows in the cubic format as input for spatial and temporal feature extraction. The spatial-temporal features are then processed by a saliency prediction module, which contains a decoding network and a bidirectional convolutional LSTM for saliency map estimation. In light of the finding from existing 360° video visual attention datasets showing that people tend to explore more on the equator area, convolutional Gaussian priors with different horizontal and vertical means and standard deviations are added to the decoding part of the saliency prediction module. The estimated saliency maps in cubic format are back-projected into the equirectangular format for the original video frame.

- Dahou et al. [81] proposed a model ATSal using attention and expert streams to predict 360° video saliency. The attention stream captures static global saliency in equirectangular format, while the expert stream captures temporal local saliency in cubic patches by using an existing 2D saliency model SalEMA [82]. The attention stream utilizes an attention mechanism, where the attention mask is learned in the middle of the stream with an enlarged receptive field to generate the attention map. The feature map extracted in the stream is then combined with the attention map with pixel-wise multiplication followed by pixel-wise summation. The expert's stream operates on local video patches that are projected into cubic faces. Based on the finding that the fixations distribution is highly correlated with the locations of the viewports [83], the expert streams embed two instances of SalEMA on the cube faces for two poles and four equator viewports, respectively. The final saliency map is then obtained by pixel-wise multiplication of the two maps generated by each stream.

- Qiao et al. [83] studied human visual attention over viewport of 360° videos and observed that the distribution of fixations is influenced by the objects and location of the corresponding viewport in 360° videos. Since the user only perceives the content in the viewport when consuming 360° video, a viewport saliency prediction model is proposed to predict the fixation distribution in the viewport over 360° videos. Considering the content and the location of the viewport, a multi-task deep neural network (MT-DNN) is proposed for viewport saliency prediction. The input to MT-DNN includes the spatiotemporally aligned viewport and its corresponding location in longitude and latitude. The viewport frames are fed into shared convolutional layers for extracting the salient features. The features then flow into four branches of a 3-layer CNN and a 3-layer ConvLSTM, each of which corresponds to one task of predicting saliency at a viewport in the 360° region. Then, the output maps of all branches are integrated together, according to their corresponding viewport locations.

- Chao et al. [84] proposed an audio-visual saliency (AVS360) model that incorporates 360° spatial-temporal visual representation and spatial auditory information in 360° videos. Spatial audio displayed in 360° video enables viewers to perceive 360° directions of audio-visual stimuli in the consumption with head-mounted displays (HMDs). The proposed AVS360 model employs two 3D residual networks (ResNets) to encode visual and audio cues separately. The 3D ResNet for visual cues is embedded with a spherical representation technique cube padding [44] to extract 360° visual features, and the 3D ResNet for audio cues extracts the audio features using the log mel-spectrogram. The audio energy map generated from spatial audio description (i.e., ambisonics) is used to indicate sound source locations. Based on the finding [45] that users' visual attention tends to be attracted by sound source locations and the finding [29] that users tend to explore more equator area in 360° video, the audio energy map and equator center bias is integrated with audio and visual features with an attention mechanism.

5.4.3 Viewport predictions

The immersive and interactive technologies in VR have rapidly advanced in recent years. It brings about the surging popularity of 360° video on commercial streaming platforms. Since 360° video captures spherical spatial information in all directions, it requires a massive amount of data to be streamed, e.g., eight times more than traditional videos for the same perceived quality [86]. As users only see a portion of a given video in the viewport of a head-mounted display (HMD), to guarantee high quality of experience (QoE) in the viewport seen by users, the entire 360° video has to be of very high resolution. Recent works have developed viewport-adaptive streaming solutions [38], where the portion of the video in the user's viewport is streamed at the highest possible quality, while the remaining part of the content is streamed at a lower quality for bandwidth saving. Viewport prediction, which predicts the position of the user's viewport in the forthcoming time, has become an essential element to inform the downloading strategy regarding which part of the content should be streamed in high quality at a given point in time. To enable the mechanism in an effective and efficient manner, the tile-based encoding options of modern video codecs, such as HEVC/H.265, can be applied. Accordingly, the approach is often referred to as *tile-based streaming*.

As shown in Fig. 5.3, in viewport prediction, the goal is to predict a viewer's viewport center trajectory (i.e., scanpath) in the forthcoming F seconds, given the viewer's previous viewport center trajectory in the last H seconds. A viewer's viewport scanpath when consuming a 360° video of duration T can be described as $\{P_t\}_{t=0}^{T}$. It can be repre-

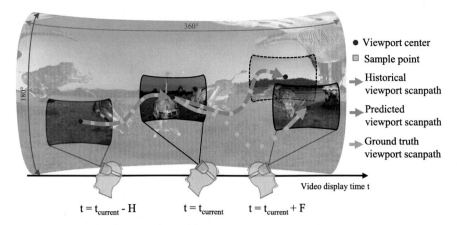

Figure 5.3 Illustration of viewport prediction in 360° video. The goal is to predict the viewport scanpath in the forthcoming *F* seconds, given the past *H*-second viewport scanpath and the video content.

sented in pitch, yaw, and roll, spherical coordinates, or Cartesian coordinates. As shown in Fig. 5.1, a user wearing an HMD can adjust the head orientation by changing the pitch, yaw, and roll, which correspond to rotating along the X, Y, and Z axes in ±180°, respectively. It can be formulated in spherical coordinates longitude θ, and latitude ϕ:

$$\{P_t = [\theta_t, \phi_t]\}_{t=0}^{T}, \quad \text{where } [-\pi < \theta \le \pi, -\pi/2 < \phi \le \pi/2] \tag{5.1}$$

or Cartesian coordinates x, y, and z:

$$\{P_t = [x_t, y_t, z_t]\}_{t=0}^{T}, \quad \text{where } [-1 < x \le 1, -1 < y \le 1, -1 < z \le 1]. \tag{5.2}$$

Let F denote the output prediction window length and H denote the input historical window length. In every timestamp t, the model predicts the forthcoming viewport center position, $\hat{P}_{t+s}$, for all prediction steps $s \in [1, F]$ with the given historical viewport center position P_{t-h} and historical video content V_{t-h} for all past steps $h \in [0, H]$. The historical video content V_{t-h} can be saliency maps or optical flow of video frames, depending on the computation techniques. The problem can be formalized as finding the optimal model f_F^*:

$$f_F^* = \arg\min E_t[\text{Dist}(f_F(\{P_t\}_{t=t-H}^{t}, \{V_t\}_{t=t-H}^{t}), \{P_t\}_{t=t+1}^{t+F})], \tag{5.3}$$

where $\text{Dist}(\cdot)$ measures the geometric distance between the predicted viewport center positions and corresponding ground truth in each time step s, and E_t computes the average distance of every prediction step in interval $t \in [t+1, t+F]$.

Numerous viewport prediction approaches were proposed to benefit 360° streaming systems. They predict a user's viewport center position (i.e., head movement) in the forthcoming seconds during 360° video consumption. Some approaches predict the future viewing position based on the historical viewing information, whereas some approaches also take account of video content to anticipate the future viewports. Since the salient regions attracting visual attention can be estimated by saliency prediction models, some existing viewport prediction methods consider integrating saliency patterns to positional viewing information for achieving better prediction results. In addition to whether a model employs video content or associated saliency maps, existing viewport prediction approaches can also be classified into statistics-based, clustering-based, deep-learning-based, and physics-based, depending on the employed computation techniques. For a comprehensive literature review on viewport-adaptive streaming for 360° video, we refer the reader to [21]. In what follow, we survey the state-of-the-art viewport prediction approaches in 360° videos. Table 5.4 summarizes all the introduced approaches.

- **Statistics-based approaches:** Xie et al. [87] leveraged a linear regression model to estimate the user's future head orientation in yaw, pitch, and roll, which are denoted as α, β, γ, respectively. The least-square method is used to calculate the trends of head movements. The slope over yaw, pitch, and roll are denoted as m_α, m_β, and m_γ. Therefore the estimated value of yaw, pitch, and roll, which are denoted, respectively, as $\hat{\alpha}, \hat{\beta}, \hat{\gamma}$, at time of $t + \delta$, can be predicted using a linear regression model as

$$[\hat{\alpha}(t+\delta), \hat{\beta}(t+\delta), \hat{\gamma}(t+\delta)] = [m_\alpha \delta + \alpha(t), m_\beta \delta + \beta(t), m_\gamma \delta + \gamma(t)]. \qquad (5.4)$$

Qian et al. [88] proposed a weighted linear regression model for viewport prediction. It collects the user's viewport scanpath with a sliding window of 1 second to predict the future head position for each dimension of yaw, pitch, and roll. The weight of each sample is given in a regression model, where the more recent sample obtains a higher weight, to consider if the more recent sample has the biggest impact on the future scanpath. The experimental results obtained by the researchers showed that weighted linear regression outperforms average and simple linear regression methods when predicting viewport for the next 0.5, 1, and 2 seconds.

- **Clustering-based approaches:** As revealed by user behavior analysis [41,78], viewers often share similar viewing behaviors when consuming 360° videos. Clustering-based methods [89–92] group together the trajectories that exhibit similar viewing behaviors into a few clusters for a given 360° video, and a single trend trajectory is calculated for each cluster. When a new user comes to use the system, his/her past scanpath is assigned to one of the clusters and the pre-computed trajectory is subsequently used to predict the future viewport position.

Though users share similar viewing behaviors, the interesting area for users can be multiple in 360° videos [93]. Inspired by such user behavior observations, Ban et al. [89] proposed a k-nearest-neighbors-based (KNN-based) viewport prediction algorithm, namely KVP. It first clusters users by using KNN and incorporates cross-user behavior in the same cluster into the linear regression result to improve viewport prediction accuracy. The linear regression model extrapolates a user's historical viewport scanpath to estimate the possible future viewport position. To amend the estimated result, the KNN-based election picks the nearest K viewport positions of other users in the same cluster. The probability vote mechanism is then applied to calculate each tile's viewing probability.

Rossi et al. [91] argued that minimizing the spherical distance between users' scanpaths does not ensure identifying users who are viewing similar parts of a given 360° video, since viewports with the same center distances may have different overlap rates. The authors then proposed a clique-based clustering using a geometric overlap rate between two viewports on the sphere to quantify the distance. A graph can be built with the nodes representing the centers of the viewports of different users. Two nodes are connected only if the two corresponding viewports have a significant overlap. A clustering method based on the Bron–Kerbosch algorithm [94] is then leveraged to identify clusters that are cliques.

Inspired by the vehicle trajectory prediction [95], Petrangeli et al. [90] employed the spectral clustering algorithm to group similar trajectories by measuring the distance between any two trajectories. A single trend trajectory is then computed to represent each cluster's average trajectory and predict the viewer's following viewport positions.

Taghavi et al. [92] proposed to represent the viewport center with a quaternion. In their method, the distance of a group of viewport centers less than 30° apart in 90% of that interval are clustered together, and a single trend of viewport center in the interval is computed by averaging the quaternion of all viewers in the cluster. After classifying a new user to one of the clusters, a user's future viewport center is predicted based on quaternion rotation extrapolation.

- **Deep-learning-based approaches:** With the rapid development of deep learning technology, numerous viewport prediction methods [51,76,78,96–103] utilized convolutional neural networks (CNN) or/and recurrent neural networks (RNN), including Long Short-Term Memory (LSTM) or Gated Recurrent Unit (GRU) to model a user's head movement in 360° video consumption. Some content-agnostic models [96–98,103] only consider historical viewport scanpaths, while the other content-aware methods [51,76,78,99–102] also incorporate video content information, such as video frames or saliency maps, in addition to the historical trajectory for improving prediction accuracy.

Inspired by the good capability of LSTM for capturing the temporal transition of a sequence, Hou et al. [96] designed a multi-layer LSTM network to model users' head motion patterns and predict the future viewport position based on the past traces. The 2D tile-based format is used to represent the viewpoint feature, where the 360° view in equirectangular format is divided into 72 tiles (6 tiles in vertical and 12 tiles in horizon). The head motion trajectory is represented as a sequence of viewpoints, where each viewpoint is one of the 72 tiles. Note that the viewpoint mentioned here indicates the center of the viewport. Given the previous sequence of viewpoint tiles, the model anticipates the next tile within which the viewpoint will be. The model includes two LSTM layers with 128 LSTM units and a fully connected layer with 72 nodes. To maximize the overlapping rate between the predicted and ground truth viewport, m tiles with the highest probabilities predicted by the model are selected to generate m viewports, and the combination of the m viewports is the final prediction.

The same authors (i.e., Hou et al.) [97] extended the method to 6 DoF for head and body motion prediction in VR content. A multi-task LSTM model is developed for body motion prediction and a multi-layer perceptron model is developed for head motion prediction. The multi-task LSTM model takes account of body motion speed in three axes (x, y, z) simultaneously to predict the body motion for each axis. The multi-layer perceptron model has a similar structure to the multi-task LSTM model but uses fully connected layers to replace LSTM layers.

Heyse et al. [98] proposed to use reinforcement learning of contextual bandits (CB) to predict head orientation in two stages of detection of movement, and prediction of direction. CB is used since its chosen action has no influence on the next state. It is similar to that the predicted position of the agent has no impact on where the user will actually look next. There are four Contextual bandits in a CB bank, one per dimension and decision for motion and direction in longitude and latitude. The predicted actions of the four CB agents are fed to the following algorithmic block to obtain the discrete predicted decisions.

Since LSTM captures temporal dependencies sequentially for each element, it is time-consuming in training and prediction. Sequence-to-sequence Transformer [104] achieves better long-term dependency modeling and larger-batch parallel training by simultaneously taking account of all the elements in a sequence to model the temporal dependencies. Chao et al. [103] proposed a transformer-based viewport prediction model to address viewport prediction as a time series forecasting problem. By leveraging the self-attention mechanism, the model uses only the viewport scanpath without requiring any other content information (e.g., video frames, saliency maps, etc.) to reduce the computational cost and attain superior results compared to other LSTM-based methods.

Instead of considering the historical viewport scanpath only, some methods also take the video content into account for viewport prediction. These content-aware methods process the entire 360° video content, the viewport content, or saliency maps to improve the prediction accuracy.

As mentioned in Section 5.4.2, Xu et al. [78] proposed a DRL model for head motion prediction. The model contains several convolutional layers and LSTM layers to extract video content in the user's viewport and estimate the next head movement in a reinforcement-learning manner. The approach includes multiple workflows of models to simulate multiple users watching 360° video. It is firstly trained offline with a large-scale dataset, and then the trained offline model is used for real-time online prediction. The user's head motion in the current session is collected to fine-tune the model.

Xu et al. [51] explored gaze prediction in 360° videos. By analyzing users' gaze movement in a large-scale dataset that contains at least 31 users watching 208 videos with an HMD, the observation shows that users' gaze movement is related to historical scanpaths and video contents. Based on the observation, a gaze prediction model is proposed to anticipate the user's next gaze position in the forthcoming video frame. To extract salient features in video content, the 2D saliency prediction model SalNet [77] is used to measure saliency maps in the sub-image patch centered at the current gaze point, the sub-image corresponding to the FoV, and the entire 360° image. To extract motion features, FlowNet2.0 [105] is used to compute optical flow in two successive frames. Then, the salient features and motion features are fed to LSTM layers to predict the gaze position in the next frame.

Nguyen et al. [76] designed a saliency model PanoSalNet tailored for 360° video as described in Section 5.4.2. The author then proposed a head movement prediction model which integrates the saliency maps estimated by PanoSalNet and historical head orientation maps with an LSTM network. The historical head orientation maps are generated by first dividing the map into 9×16 tiles and selecting the tile pointed to by the current head-orientation vector. The likelihood of this tile to be viewed is set as 1.0. This tile is used as the center for applying a Gaussian kernel to gradually set other tiles to a lower likelihood to be viewed around the center tile.

Feng et al. [101] developed a live viewport prediction method, namely LiveObj, by detecting and tracking the objects in 360° video. The model is composed of object detection, user view estimation, object tracking, and reinforcement learning-based modeling. The object detection step uses YOLOv3 [106] to detect the objects in videos. The user view estimation step analyzes the user's head orientations and estimates the next viewport position. The object tracking step tracks the objects watched by the user in the recent frames. Finally, the reinforcement-learning-based modeling step is fed with the object tracking results and the estimated user viewport and updates the status of the predicted viewport. The model achieves real-time performance with low processing delays to meet the requirement of live streaming.

- **Physics-based approaches:** In addition to the methods mentioned above that predict future head motion by considering the user's past scanpath and video content,

Table 5.4 Summary of the viewport prediction methods for 360° video. SP denotes scan-path, VF denotes video frame, SM denotes saliency map, VM denotes viewport map.

Method	Year	SP	VF	SM	Prediction Length	Techniques
Statistics-based approaches						
Qian et al. [88]	2016	✓			2 s	Weighted Linear Regression
Xie et al. [87]	2017	✓			3 s	Linear Regression
Clustering-based approaches						
Ban et al. [89]	2018	✓			6 s	KNN-based Clustering
Petrangeli et al. [90]	2018	✓			10 s	Trajectory-based Clustering
Rossi et al. [91]	2019	✓			N/A	viewport Coverage, Clique-based Clustering
Taghavi et al. [92]	2020	✓			10 s	Viewport Coverage, Trajectory-based Clustering
Deep-learning-based approaches						
Hou et al. [96]	2018	✓			2 s	LSTM
Heyse et al. [98]	2019	✓			10 s	RL
Hou et al. [97]	2020	✓			2 s	LSTM, 6 DoF
Chao et al. [103]	2021	✓			5 s	Transformer
Xu et al. [78]	2018	✓	✓		30 ms (1 frame)	RL
Xu et al. [51]	2018	✓	✓	✓	30 ms (1 frame)	CNN, LSTM
Nguyen et al. [76]	2018	✓		✓	2.5 s	LSTM
Feng et al. [101]	2021	✓	✓		1 s	Object Detection, RL
Physics-based approaches						
Romero et al. [108]	2021	✓			5 s	Head Motion Momentum Gravitational Force Field

physics-based [107,108] methods model head movements with angular momentum. These methods assume that head motion follows the inertia of the moving speed and direction. Romero Rondon et al. [108] assumed that the head motion can be described by gravitational physics laws driven by virtual masses created by the video content. They proposed a head motion predictor, namely HeMoG, based on the physics of rotational head motion and gravitation. The rotational head motion is modeled by the user's past head movement with angular velocity and acceleration, while the gravitation is represented by a saliency map. The concept is that all the locations in the current visual scene compete for the user's attention. The capability of a location in the scene to attract user attention can be described as a virtual mass in gravitational models. The head motion is modeled as the torque which indicates the turning effectiveness in a field of gravitational force. The prediction results showed that the head motion momentum is more important than the visual content in the first 2.5 seconds of the prediction window, and the visual content can inform the head motion prediction model only for a time window longer than 3 seconds.

The saliency modeling and viewport prediction approaches introduced in Section 5.4 only focus on monoscopic omnidirectional image/video. Stereoscopic saliency for omnidirectional content is still in its infancy. The dataset [29] proposed by Sitzmann et al. includes gaze and head orientation for users observing 22 stereo omnidirectional images. A larger-scale dataset is required for a more comprehensive study on user behavior, saliency modeling, and viewport prediction. In addition, the datasets and prediction models in this chapter are mainly for 360° video in 3 DoF (i.e., yaw, pitch, and roll). Only Hou et al. [97] considers head and body motion prediction for VR content in 6 DoF (i.e., x, y, z, yaw, pitch, and roll). With the surging popularity in VR multimedia that is built on 3D graphics to allow the users to move their body position freely, extending saliency modeling and viewport prediction from 3 DoF to 6 DoF could significantly benefit the user experience.

5.5. Metrics

In this section, methods to compare predicted saliency and predicted scan paths with ground truth data are addressed, to evaluate model performance. The structure of this section is as follows: at first, methods used for traditional 2D images or videos are introduced. Then, the extensions of these metrics for omnidirectional content using different type of representation formats will be discussed.

5.5.1 2D images/videos saliency

When evaluating the accuracy of a saliency prediction model, different metrics can be used. A classification of these metrics was introduced by Richie [109] dividing them into value-based, location-based and distribution-based metrics. The value-based metrics compare amplitudes between predicted saliency maps and corresponding ground truth eye-fixation maps. The distribution-based metrics consider saliency as distributions, and compare differences between distributions. Finally, the location-based metrics take into account spatial information and are mostly based on *area under the receiver operating characteristic curves* (AU-ROC). In the following, details on the different metrics are provided.

5.5.1.1 *Value-based metrics*

The first metric that can be considered is the normalized scanpath saliency (NSS) [110]. The NSS quantifies the amount of predicted saliency values at the eye-fixation locations (known from ground truth data), and normalizes it with the average and variance of the predicted saliency map. Such process is described in Eq. (5.5), in which p corresponds to the position of each fixation (obtained from ground truth data), and $SM(p)$ is the predicted saliency at the location p. μ_{SM} and σ_{SM} are, respectively, the mean and standard deviation of the predicted saliency map. The NSS score is then obtained by averaging the NSS value of each fixation point. The NSS metric has the benefit of being sensitive to false positives and relative differences in saliency across the entire image. However, due to the normalization by mean and variance, it is invariant to linear transformation.

$$NSS(p) = \frac{SM(p) - \mu_{SM}}{\sigma_{SM}} \tag{5.5}$$

5.5.1.2 Distribution-based metrics

Among distribution-based metrics the Kullback–Leibler divergence (KL-Div) is widely used. The general idea of this metric is to measure the information lost when using the saliency map *(SM)* as an approximation of the ground truth human eye-fixation map probability distribution *(FM)*. Eq. (5.6) describes the computational process of KL-Div, in which the values of x corresponds to every point in the saliency map. One of the challenges with this metric is that it is sensitive to zero values, and miss-detection will be highly penalized [111].

$$KL_{div} = \sum_{x=1}^{X} FM(x) \times \log(\frac{FM(x)}{SM(x) + \epsilon} + \epsilon) \tag{5.6}$$

The earth mover's distance (EMD) [112] is a metric that measures the spatial distance between two probability distributions over a region. It aims at computing the minimal cost to transform the probability distribution described by the predicted saliency maps *(SM)* into the probability distribution obtained from ground truth human eye-fixation data *(FM)*. Eq. (5.7) describes the computational process. In this equation, $f_{i,j}$ is the amount that needs to be transferred from i to j so the predicted saliency map distribution matches with the ground truth fixation distribution. Then, $d_{i,j}$ is the spatial distance between i and j. One of the benefits of the EMD is to penalize false positives proportionally to their spatial distance from the ground truth salient regions. However, it should be noted that this metric is computationally intensive and difficult to use as a criterion for optimizing saliency models [111].

$$EMD = min_{f_{i,j}} \sum_{i,j} f_{i,j} \times d_{i,j} + |\sum_i FM_i - \sum_j SM_j| \times max_{i,j} d_{i,j}$$

under constraints:

$$f_{i,j} > 0, \quad \sum_j f_{i,j} < FM_i, \quad \sum_i f_{i,j} <= SM_j$$

$$\sum_{i,j} f_{i,j} = min(\sum_i FM_i - \sum_j SM_j) \tag{5.7}$$

The linear correlation coefficient (CC) is also a metric that has been used to compare saliency maps. It corresponds to the Pearson correlation coefficient when comparing the predicted and ground truth saliency values, and measures the linear relationship between the considered saliency maps (see Eq. (5.8)). High CC values can be achieved when predicted and ground truth data have similar magnitude. This metric has the benefit of treating false positives and false negatives in a symmetric manner [111].

$$CC = \frac{cov(SM, FM)}{\sigma_{SM} \times \sigma_{FM}} \tag{5.8}$$

The similarity metric (SIM) [112] is a metric that compares the normalized probability distribution of the predicted saliency map (SM) with the probability distribution of the human eye-fixation (FM). This similarity measure sums the minimum values between corresponding points of each distribution (see Eq. (5.9)). The SIM metric is highly sensitive to missing values, and will penalize strongly if areas are not detected as salient. It should also be stated that this metric will not equally penalize false positives as false negatives [111].

$$SIM = \sum_{x}^{X} min(SM(x), FM(x)) \tag{5.9}$$

5.5.1.3 Location-based metrics

Among the location-based metrics, the information gain (IG) [113] can be found. This metric starts from the idea that when different persons see an image, each person will fixate the images at a different location. Therefore fixation can be considered as being derived from a probabilistic process, and it is then possible to address the evaluation of a saliency map using information theory. The general idea of the information gain method is to evaluate the improvement provided by a prediction model by comparing it to the prediction from another baseline that is image independent. Eq. (5.10) describes the computational process. In this equation N is the number of fixations, p are fixation positions, and $B(p)$ is the saliency value for a image-independent baseline saliency prediction model. It should be noted that this metric expects the input saliency maps to be properly regularized (sum of all values equal to one). This metric will then have the property of providing a quantification of the benefit of a given saliency map obtained by a given saliency prediction model compared to another baseline B. Regarding B, in the context of traditional 2D images, a typical approach would be to use the center bias model.

$$IG = \frac{1}{N} \times \sum_{p} [\log_2(\epsilon + SM(p)) - \log_2(\epsilon + B(p))] \tag{5.10}$$

The area under ROC curve (AUC) metric is commonly used for saliency model evaluation. This method is computed by binarizing saliency maps with a given threshold, and computing the trade-off between true and false positives for each threshold.

By varying the threshold value, a ROC curve can be established, and the area under this curve is used to evaluate the accuracy of the saliency prediction. Different variants exist: the AUC-Judd [58] follows the general base principle as previously introduced; the AUC-Borji provides an approximation of this approach by performing the analysis on a random selection of the pixels. Finally, the shuffled AUC (sAUC) [114] is another popular approach. Similarly to the AUC-Borji, sAUC perform the ROC analysis on a subset of the pixels, but instead of being performed on pixels selected randomly, the pixels are chosen based on the fixation map of another image in the dataset. The idea of the sAUC is that in traditional 2D images a central prior can be commonly found, and saliency prediction models that account, for this prior will perform well when the AUC-Judd metric is considered. Results have also shown that the naive center-bias model, although independent of the image under investigation, would already provide compelling results when the AUC-Judd metric is used on a dataset having a strong center-bias [114]. Therefore the idea of using the sAUC metric is to provide a smart sampling so as to mitigate the impact of the center prior bias on the results.

5.5.2 2D images/videos scanpath

When comparing scanpaths, different types of metrics can be used [115–117]. These metrics can be either distance- or vector-based. In the case of distance-based models, only spatial characteristics are used, whereas in the case of vector-based metrics, further considerations, such as frequency and time, can be used as well. In what follow, highlights of two commonly used metrics are presented

At first, the string edit metric can be considered. The general idea of this metric is to represent a sequence of fixations as a sequence of symbols (numbers or letters). This sequence of symbols forms a string, which is then compared to the ground truth data. The comparison process is performed using string edit distances (for example, the Levenshtein distance [118]) and measures the number of deletions, insertions or substitutions that are needed to align the word obtained from ground truth data and the word obtained from the prediction model. A cost is defined for each transformation of each character, and the metric will output the minimum cost that is needed to allow the two words to be matched. This metric has the drawback that it requires to decompose the image into regions of interest, and then fixations need to be considered as belonging to these regions of interest. Such process will then result in a decrease of the spatial resolution of the scanpath analysis. However, it has the benefit of being computationally efficient.

The Jarodzka's metric [119] is a widely used metric to compare scanpaths. This metric is a vector-based approach, which compares scanpaths by considering each of the fixations composing one scan path with the other fixations from the other scan path. The metric can be flexible and can include different features. In [115], three similarity measures are used: the spatial proximity of the starting point of each saccade, the direction and norm of the vector describing the saccades and the proximity in duration of the saccades. Compared to the string edit method, this approach has the advantage that it does not require the area of interest to be defined and that it allows many features about the scanpaths to be considered. However, a limitation is that it assumes the presence of fixations and saccades, and smooth pursuit cannot directly be addressed.

5.5.3 Extensions for omnidirectional content

In the previous section, metrics to evaluate the accuracy of saliency and scanpath prediction models in the case of conventional 2D images was introduced. However, when omnidirectional content is considered, these metrics may not directly be applicable. In this section, two representation formats of omnidirectional images and the corresponding required adjustments for the metrics will be discussed.

5.5.3.1 Equirectangular projection

When using the equirectangular format for representing the omnidirectional images and saliency maps, new challenges are raised as the images and saliency maps suffer from stretching in the poles regions. Therefore if the metrics are computed on such type of images, this will result in erroneous evaluation, as the contribution of the pole regions will be overweighted. Hence, it is not correct to compare the saliency of two equirectangular images directly, and the geometric properties of the equirectangular format need to be considered [30]. To address these issues, a uniform sampling on a sphere should be performed. Fig. 5.4 illustrates such sampling, where points used to evaluate the predicted saliency maps should be selected such that they are uniformly distributed over the surface of the sphere. Performing such sampling results in a nonuniform sampling in the corresponding image in the equirectangular format, as shown in Fig. 5.4.

Below, the consequences of applying such type of sampling on metrics to evaluate saliency maps are discussed. First, let S be the set of points that correspond to a uniform sampling on a sphere. Then, metrics should be adjusted as follows:

- NSS, KL_{div}, CC, SIM: the metrics should be used as defined by their respective equations, but should only be considering the points in S.
- IG: this metric should also be evaluated only using fixation points. It should be noted that it is not affected by the geometric distortions introduced by the use of the equirectangular format. However, instead of using a center bias model as baseline, an equatorial bias model should be used.
- EMD: the earth mover's distance should be applied by considering only points from the uniform sampling on the sphere. Then, regarding the distance measure d, instead of using a Euclidean distance, the orthodromic distance (Eq. (5.11)) should be used.

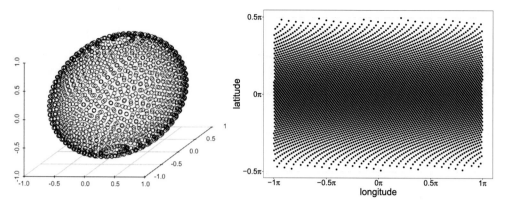

Figure 5.4 Uniform sampling on a sphere. On the left, a uniform distribution of points on a sphere surface is depicted. On the right, the corresponding points on a equirectangular projection are shown.

This allows the geometric properties of the equirectangular format to be addressed. In this equation (ϕ_1, λ_1) and (ϕ_2, λ_2) are the locations of the two considered points.

- AUC-metrics: In the case of AUC-Judd and AUC-Borji, the metrics should be applied using the uniform sampling on a sphere. As for sAUC, no adaptation is required since the sampling is based on another fixation map that is already in the equirectangular coordinate space.

$$\log(d((\phi_1, \lambda_1), (\phi_2, \lambda_2))) = 2 \times a\sin \sqrt{\sin^2 \frac{\Delta\phi}{2} + \cos(\phi_1)\cos(\phi_2)\sin^2 \frac{\Delta\lambda}{2}} \qquad (5.11)$$

$$\Delta\phi = \phi_2 - \phi_1, \ \Delta\lambda = \lambda_2 - \lambda_1$$

Regarding scanpath metrics, extensions to omnidirectional content using equirectangular projection can be performed by changing the distance metrics. The string edit method being based on region of interest can directly be applied to an image in the omnidirectional format. As for the Jarodzka metric [115,119], a direct adaptation to the equirectangular format was proposed by replacing the Euclidean distance by the orthodromic distance [30].

5.5.3.2 Cubic projection

In the previous section, the equirectangular format was discussed. However, in the case of omnidirectional contents, different projections can be used. Among them, the cubic projection can be found. The cubic projection is a mapping, where a portion of the surface of the sphere is projected to flat images. The images are arranged as the faces of a cube, and each face is found using a rectilinear projection. Each projection uses a 90° field of view, which allows the over-representation of the poles regions and corresponding artifacts to be avoided. When applying this type of projection, metrics such as NSS, KL-Div, CC, SIM, AUC-based metrics can be applied directly.

The EMD metric, on the other hand, may be more challenging, as the distance from one point on one projection to another point in a different projection is non-trivial. Performing a conversion of coordinates from Cartesian to polar, and using the orthodromic distance is a way to address this problem.

Regarding the information gain (IG), the baseline model needs to be carefully established. This should be defined as the combination of images with or without equatorial prior depending on the view; the equatorial prior being required for projections where the center of the projection has a null angle of elevation.

As for scanpath measurements, similar to the EMD metric, a key challenge is the handling of distances from one rectilinear projection to another. Using polar coordinates and the orthodromic distance provides a way to address it.

5.6. Conclusion and outlook

The chapter has provided an overview of the state-of-the-art of 360° or omnidirectional image and video saliency research. First, it was discussed how head- and eye-tracking data can be acquired and analyzed. Based on the resulting saliency maps, eye-tracking scan-path data and/or viewport trajectories, three different model types have been reviewed: (i) image-based saliency models, (ii) video saliency models, and (iii) viewport prediction models. For image and video saliency models, (i) and (ii), both more traditional, feature-based and more recent, DNN-based approaches with their implicit feature learning have been presented. For models based on hand-crafted features, these are integrated into the target information domain of the underlying ground-truth data, following the processing path of feature extraction, feature activation, normalization, and aggregation. In the case of DNN-based models, these steps are followed more implicitly. A further criterion that distinguishes modeling approaches is whether they directly operate in the initial projection domain of the available OD images or video sequences, such as the equirectangular projection format, or whether some transformation of the input data into another domain is used, such as a spherical representation or rectilinear format. When the current viewport is to be predicted (iii), as it may, for example, be used for adaptive streaming of ODV, besides future image or saliency information, also a modeling of the human head and eye movements is of interest. This can be done based on the behavioral history and/or the anatomical, and thus physical constraints of the human head and eye movements.

It is interesting to note that for OD image and video saliency, most modeling work has been done for saliency maps rather than scanpaths, or for viewport trajectories. Here, metrics for both saliency and scanpath prediction are still an open topic. Also, most research on OD visual saliency has been conducted for non-stereoscopic content.

This is likely due to the lack of higher-quality stereoscopic OD images and videos. With improving camera technology and resolutions, besides high-quality CGI content, also higher-quality recorded stereoscopic OD video content becomes available. In general, the number of behavior databases for OD visual saliency model development is very limited in comparison to more traditional 2D visual content. Here, approaches such as SALICON [120] have enabled a strong increase in datapoints used as ground truth for 2D saliency modeling. For OD images and video, comparable approaches and larger databases are currently still missing, making it difficult to develop specific, larger-scale DNN-based saliency models.

In terms of OD visual saliency modeling strategy, first attempts have been made using GANs, which are promising for further study. Besides the model algorithms themselves, also the criteria for saliency model performance evaluation are of interest for future research. In particular, the expanded FOV and connectivity of viewports over space and time are novel aspects in comparison to traditional 2D images or video. Appropriate performance evaluation metrics should better reflect such scene- and behavior-related aspects or also perceptual changes coming along with OD visual content.

As was discussed in the chapter, for 2D content and also 360° video, the viewing behavior depends on the actual viewing task; for example, viewing behavior differs between a free exploration and a search or quality evaluation task (e.g., [121]). Though a number of studies exist on this topic for 2D visual content, more research is required for OD images or video. Besides a task as additional trigger of attention, also scene-intrinsic, non-visual information, such as audio may contribute to what a person attends to. Accordingly, first studies have investigated audiovisual saliency for ODV that includes spatial audio (e.g., [84]). More research is needed to get a better understanding of how multisensory perception guides attention in OD scenes. As a first step, the research on saliency of audiovisual spatial scenes should be expanded. Here, saliency and attentional focus will be task-dependent, too, as in the vision-only case. In general, more research is needed to understand the relation between scene content, task, cognitive processes, mediated by saliency and attention. To this aim, OD multisensory scenes can be a key point for creating repeatable and controllable test conditions.

Photorealistic ODV, especially if it includes spatial audio, can be considered as a controlled capture of natural scenes, enabling more ecologically valid research on how humans perceive the world around them than what can be realized with only 2D on-screen video. Current ODV content mainly enables 3 DoF exploration of the scene. In real life, the three additional spatial dimensions for translatory motion principally enable a 6 DoF scene exploration. With CGI-based OD visual content, such as in case of gaming, a 6 DoF interaction is enabled to a certain extent. Accordingly, in future research, acquisition of 6 instead of 3 DoF saliency information will be of interest, to come even closer to a natural exploration of the interaction with a given scene. Based on the resulting trajectory data, 6 DoF saliency prediction models can be developed.

Similarly, the exploration of point cloud or lightfield content by human viewers, or of free-viewpoint visual content could be captured and used for developing even more comprehensive saliency models.

References

[1] M.L. Mele, S. Federici, A psychotechnological review on eye-tracking systems: towards user experience, Disability and Rehabilitation: Assistive Technology 7 (4) (2012) 261–281.

[2] S. Peißl, C.D. Wickens, R. Baruah, Eye-tracking measures in aviation: A selective literature review, The International Journal of Aerospace Psychology 28 (3–4) (2018) 98–112.

[3] M. Wedel, R. Pieters, A review of eye-tracking research in marketing, in: Review of Marketing Research, 2017, pp. 123–147.

[4] D.C. Van Essen, C.H. Anderson, Information processing strategies and pathways in the primate visual system, in: An Introduction to Neural and Electronic Networks, 2nd ed., 1995, pp. 45–76.

[5] M.I. Posner, Orienting of attention, Quarterly Journal of Experimental Psychology 32 (1) (1980) 3–25.

[6] L. Itti, C. Koch, E. Niebur, A model of saliency-based visual attention for rapid scene analysis, IEEE Transactions on Pattern Analysis and Machine Intelligence 20 (11) (1998) 1254–1259.

[7] L. Itti, C. Koch, Computational modelling of visual attention, Nature Reviews. Neuroscience 2 (2001) 194–203.

[8] S. Treue, Visual attention: the where, what, how and why of saliency, Current Opinion in Neurobiology 13 (4) (2003) 428–432.

[9] F. Yan, C. Chen, P. Xiao, S. Qi, Z. Wang, R. Xiao, Review of visual saliency prediction: Development process from neurobiological basis to deep models, Applied Sciences 12 (1) (2022) 309.

[10] W.A. Johnston, V.J. Dark, Selective attention, Annual Review of Psychology 37 (1) (1986) 43–75.

[11] P. Kellnhofer, P. Didyk, K. Myszkowski, M.M. Hefeeda, H.-P. Seidel, W. Matusik, GazeStereo3D: seamless disparity manipulations, ACM Transactions on Graphics (TOG) 35 (4) (2016) 1–13.

[12] P. Marchant, D. Raybould, T. Renshaw, R. Stevens, Are you seeing what I'm seeing? An eye-tracking evaluation of dynamic scenes, Digital Creativity 20 (3) (2009) 153–163.

[13] C. Ramasamy, D.H. House, A.T. Duchowski, B. Daugherty, Using eye tracking to analyze stereoscopic filmmaking, in: SIGGRAPH'09: Posters, 2009, p. 1.

[14] S. Djamasbi, M. Siegel, T. Tullis, Generation Y, web design, and eye tracking, International Journal of Human-Computer Studies 68 (5) (2010) 307–323.

[15] S. Djamasbi, Eye tracking and web experience, AIS Transactions on Human-Computer Interaction 6 (2) (2014) 37–54.

[16] S.C. Boerman, E.A. Van Reijmersdal, P.C. Neijens, Using eye tracking to understand the effects of brand placement disclosure types in television programs, Journal of Advertising 44 (3) (2015) 196–207.

[17] P. Winke, S. Gass, T. Sydorenko, Factors influencing the use of captions by foreign language learners: An eye-tracking study, The Modern Language Journal 97 (1) (2013) 254–275.

[18] U. Engelke, H. Kaprykowsky, H.-J. Zepernick, P. Ndjiki-Nya, Visual attention in quality assessment, IEEE Signal Processing Magazine 28 (6) (2011) 50–59, https://doi.org/10.1109/MSP.2011.942473.

[19] W. Zhang, H. Liu, Study of saliency in objective video quality assessment, IEEE Transactions on Image Processing 26 (3) (2017) 1275–1288.

[20] H. Hadizadeh, I.V. Bajić, Saliency-aware video compression, IEEE Transactions on Image Processing 23 (1) (2013) 19–33.

[21] A. Yaqoob, T. Bi, G.-M. Muntean, A survey on adaptive 360° video streaming: solutions, challenges and opportunities, IEEE Communications Surveys and Tutorials 22 (4) (2020) 2801–2838.

[22] A. Borji, L. Itti, State-of-the-art in visual attention modeling, IEEE Transactions on Pattern Analysis and Machine Intelligence 35 (1) (2013) 185–207, https://www.scopus.com/inward/record.uri?eid=2-s2.0-84870220894&doi=10.1109%2fTPAMI.2012.89&partnerID=40&md5=75e4db707cf19ed79855f26e33653817.

[23] Y. Fang, W. Lin, Z. Chen, C.-M. Tsai, C.-W. Lin, A video saliency detection model in compressed domain, IEEE Transactions on Circuits and Systems for Video Technology 24 (1) (2014) 27–38, https://www.scopus.com/inward/record.uri?eid=2-s2.0-84892587672&doi=10.1109%2fTCSVT.2013.2273613&partnerID=40&md5=ac3c7c7ecc03663d22f050038359e74d.

[24] X. Huang, C. Shen, X. Boix, Q. Zhao, SALICON: Reducing the semantic gap in saliency prediction by adapting deep neural networks, in: 2015 IEEE International Conference on Computer Vision (ICCV), 2015, pp. 262–270, https://doi.org/10.1109/ICCV.2015.38.

[25] M. Cornia, L. Baraldi, G. Serra, R. Cucchiara, A deep multi-level network for saliency prediction, in: 2016 23rd International Conference on Pattern Recognition (ICPR), 2016, pp. 3488–3493, https://doi.org/10.1109/ICPR.2016.7900174.

[26] A. Linardos, M. Kümmerer, O. Press, M. Bethge, DeepGaze IIE: Calibrated prediction in and out-of-domain for state-of-the-art saliency modeling, in: Proceedings of the IEEE/CVF International Conference on Computer Vision, 2021, pp. 12919–12928.

[27] J. Blauert, Spatial Hearing: the Psychophysics of Human Sound Localization, MIT Press, 1997.

[28] P. Lebreton, I. Hupont, M. Hirth, T. Mäki, E. Skodras, A. Schubert, A. Raake, CrowdWatcher: an open-source platform to catch the eye of the crowd, Quality and User Experience 4 (1) (2019) 1–17.

[29] V. Sitzmann, A. Serrano, A. Pavel, M. Agrawala, D. Gutierrez, B. Masia, G. Wetzstein, Saliency in VR: How do people explore virtual environments?, IEEE Transactions on Visualization and Computer Graphics 24 (4) (2018) 1633–1642, https://doi.org/10.1109/TVCG.2018.2793599.

[30] J. Gutiérrez, E. David, Y. Rai, P. Le Callet, Toolbox and dataset for the development of saliency and scanpath models for omnidirectional/360 still images, Signal Processing. Image Communication 69 (2018) 35–42.

[31] J. Gutierrez, P. Perez, M. Orduna, A. Singla, C. Cortes, P. Mazumdar, I. Viola, K. Brunnstrom, F. Battisti, N. Cieplinska, D. Juszka, L. Janowski, M.I. Leszczuk, A. Adeyemi-Ejeye, Y. Hu, Z. Chen, G. Van Wallendael, P. Lambert, C. Diaz, J. Hedlund, O. Hamsis, S. Fremerey, F. Hofmeyer, A. Raake, P. Cesar, M. Carli, N. Garcia, Subjective evaluation of visual quality and simulator sickness of short 360 videos: ITU-T Rec. P.919, IEEE Transactions on Multimedia 24 (2022) 3087–3100, https://doi.org/10.1109/TMM.2021.3093717.

[32] ITU-T, Subjective test methodologies for 360° video on head-mounted displays, ITU-R Recommendation P.919, Oct 2020.

[33] M. Xu, C. Li, S. Zhang, P.L. Callet, State-of-the-art in 360° video/image processing: Perception, assessment and compression, IEEE Journal of Selected Topics in Signal Processing 14 (1) (2020) 5–26, https://doi.org/10.1109/JSTSP.2020.2966864.

[34] E.J. David, J. Gutiérrez, A. Coutrot, M.P. Da Silva, P.L. Callet, A dataset of head and eye movements for 360° videos, in: Proceedings of the 9th ACM Multimedia Systems Conference, MMSys '18, Association for Computing Machinery, New York, NY, USA, 2018, pp. 432–437, https://doi.org/10.1145/3204949.3208139.

[35] Y. Rai, P. Le Callet, P. Guillotel, Which saliency weighting for omni directional image quality assessment?, in: 2017 Ninth International Conference on Quality of Multimedia Experience (QoMEX), 2017, pp. 1–6, https://doi.org/10.1109/QoMEX.2017.7965659.

[36] A.D. Abreu, C. Ozcinar, A. Smolic, Look around you: Saliency maps for omnidirectional images in VR applications, in: Quality of Multimedia Experience (QoMEX), 2017.

[37] Y. Bao, H. Wu, T. Zhang, A.A. Ramli, X. Liu, Shooting a moving target: Motion-prediction-based transmission for 360-degree videos, in: 2016 IEEE International Conference on Big Data (Big Data), 2016, https://doi.org/10.1109/BigData.2016.7840720.

[38] C. Ozcinar, J. Cabrera, A. Smolic, Visual attention-aware omnidirectional video streaming using optimal tiles for virtual reality, IEEE Journal on Emerging and Selected Topics in Circuits and Systems 9 (1) (2019) 217–230, https://doi.org/10.1109/JETCAS.2019.2895096.

[39] X. Corbillon, F. De Simone, G. Simon, 360-degree video head movement dataset, in: Proceedings of the 8th ACM on Multimedia Systems Conference, MMSys'17, Association for Computing Machinery, New York, NY, USA, 2017, pp. 199–204, https://doi.org/10.1145/3083187.3083215.

[40] W.-C. Lo, C.-L. Fan, J. Lee, C.-Y. Huang, K.-T. Chen, C.-H. Hsu, 360° video viewing dataset in head-mounted virtual reality, in: Proceedings of the 8th ACM on Multimedia Systems Confer-

ence, MMSys'17, Association for Computing Machinery, New York, NY, USA, 2017, pp. 211–216, https://doi.org/10.1145/3083187.3083219.

[41] C. Wu, Z. Tan, Z. Wang, S. Yang, A dataset for exploring user behaviors in VR spherical video streaming, in: Proceedings of the 8th ACM on Multimedia Systems Conference, MMSys'17, Association for Computing Machinery, New York, NY, USA, 2017, pp. 193–198, https://doi.org/10.1145/3083187.3083210.

[42] S. Fremerey, A. Singla, K. Meseberg, A. Raake, AVTrack360: An open dataset and software recording people's head rotations watching 360° videos on an HMD, in: Proceedings of the 9th ACM Multimedia Systems Conference, MMSys '18, Association for Computing Machinery, New York, NY, USA, 2018, pp. 403–408, https://doi.org/10.1145/3204949.3208134.

[43] M. Xu, C. Li, Y. Liu, X. Deng, J. Lu, A subjective visual quality assessment method of panoramic videos, in: 2017 IEEE International Conference on Multimedia and Expo (ICME), 2017, pp. 517–522, https://doi.org/10.1109/ICME.2017.8019351.

[44] H.-T. Cheng, C.-H. Chao, J.-D. Dong, H.-K. Wen, T.-L. Liu, M. Sun, Cube padding for weakly-supervised saliency prediction in 360 videos, in: Proceedings of the IEEE Conference on Computer Vision and Pattern Recognition, 2018, pp. 1420–1429.

[45] F.-Y. Chao, C. Ozcinar, C. Wang, E. Zerman, L. Zhang, W. Hamidouche, O. Deforges, A. Smolic, Audio-visual perception of omnidirectional video for virtual reality applications, in: 2020 IEEE International Conference on Multimedia Expo Workshops (ICMEW), 2020, pp. 1–6, https://doi.org/10.1109/ICMEW46912.2020.9105956.

[46] I. Agtzidis, M. Startsev, M. Dorr, 360-degree video gaze behaviour, in: Proceedings of the 27th ACM International Conference on Multimedia, Oct 2019, https://doi.org/10.1145/3343031.3350947.

[47] S.J. Garbin, O. Komogortsev, R. Cavin, G. Hughes, Y. Shen, I. Schuetz, S.S. Talathi, Dataset for eye tracking on a virtual reality platform, in: ACM Symposium on Eye Tracking Research and Applications, ETRA '20 Full Papers, Association for Computing Machinery, New York, NY, USA, 2020, https://doi.org/10.1145/3379155.3391317.

[48] L. Tabbaa, R. Searle, S.M. Bafti, M.M. Hossain, J. Intarasisrisawat, M. Glancy, C.S. Ang, VREED: Virtual reality emotion recognition dataset using eye tracking & physiological measures, Proceedings of the ACM on Interactive, Mobile, Wearable and Ubiquitous Technologies 5 (4) (Dec 2022), https://doi.org/10.1145/3495002.

[49] M. Xu, Y. Song, J. Wang, M. Qiao, L. Huo, Z. Wang, Predicting head movement in panoramic video: A deep reinforcement learning approach, IEEE Transactions on Pattern Analysis and Machine Intelligence 41 (11) (2019) 2693–2708, https://doi.org/10.1109/TPAMI.2018.2858783.

[50] Z. Zhang, Y. Xu, J. Yu, S. Gao, Saliency detection in 360° videos, in: Proceedings of the European Conference on Computer Vision (ECCV), 2018.

[51] Y. Xu, Y. Dong, J. Wu, Z. Sun, Z. Shi, J. Yu, S. Gao, Gaze prediction in dynamic 360° immersive videos, in: 2018 IEEE/CVF Conference on Computer Vision and Pattern Recognition, 2018, pp. 5333–5342.

[52] C. Li, M. Xu, X. Du, Z. Wang, Bridge the gap between VQA and human behavior on omnidirectional video: A large-scale dataset and a deep learning model, in: Proceedings of the 26th ACM International Conference on Multimedia, MM '18, Association for Computing Machinery, New York, NY, USA, 2018, pp. 932–940, https://doi.org/10.1145/3240508.3240581.

[53] M. Kümmerer, T.S.A. Wallis, L.A. Gatys, M. Bethge, Understanding low- and high-level contributions to fixation prediction, in: ICCV, 2017.

[54] J. Pan, C. Canton, K. McGuinness, N.E. O'Connor, J. Torres, E. Sayrol, X. Giro-i-Nieto, SalGAN: Visual saliency prediction with generative adversarial networks, arXiv:1701.01081, 2017.

[55] Y. Hu, M. Elwardy, H. Zepernick, On the effect of standing and seated viewing of 360 degree videos on subjective quality assessment, in: IEEE Conference on Virtual Reality and 3D User Interfaces Abstracts and Workshops (VRW), 2020, pp. 285–286.

[56] N. Coomer, J. Ladd, B. Sanders, Virtual exploration: Seated versus standing, in: VISIGRAPP, 2018.

[57] S. Rossi, C. Ozcinar, A. Smolic, L. Toni, Do users behave similarly in VR? Investigation of the user influence on the system design, ACM Transactions on Multimedia Computing Communications and Applications 16 (2) (2020) 1–26.

[58] T. Judd, K. Ehinger, F. Durand, A. Torralba, Learning to predict where humans look, in: ICCV, 2009.

[59] A. Nuthmann, J.M. Henderson, Object-based attentional selection in scene viewing, Journal of Vision 8 (10) (2010) 1–20.

[60] P. Lebreton, A. Raake, GBVS360, BMS360, ProSal: Extending existing saliency prediction models from 2D to omnidirectional images, in: Salient360: Visual Attention Modeling for 360° Images, Signal Processing. Image Communication 69 (2018) 69–78, https://doi.org/10.1016/j.image.2018.03.006, https://www.sciencedirect.com/science/article/pii/S0923596518302406.

[61] Y. Rai, J. Gutiérrez, P.L. Callet, A dataset of head and eye movements for 360 degree images, in: Proceedings of the ACM Multimedia Systems Conference, MMSys, 2017.

[62] P. Lebreton, S. Fremerey, A. Raake, V-BMS360: A video extention to the BMS360 image saliency model, in: IEEE International Conference on Multimedia & Expo Workshops (ICMEW), 2018.

[63] V.P. Laurutis, D.A. Robinson, The vestibulo-ocular reflex during human saccadic eye movements, The Journal of Physiology 373 (1986) 209–233.

[64] E.G. Freedman, Coordination of the eyes and head during visual orienting, Experimental Brain Research 190 (4) (2008) 369–387.

[65] J. Ling, K. Zhang, Y. Zhang, D. Yang, Z. Chen, A saliency prediction model on 360 degree images using color dictionary based sparse representation, in: Salient360: Visual Attention Modeling for 360° Images, Signal Processing. Image Communication 69 (2018) 60–68, https://doi.org/10.1016/j.image.2018.03.007, https://www.sciencedirect.com/science/article/pii/S0923596518302418.

[66] J. Zhang, S. Sclaroff, Saliency detection: a Boolean map approach, in: 2013 IEEE International Conference on Computer Vision, 2013, pp. 153–160, https://doi.org/10.1109/ICCV.2013.26.

[67] J. Harel, C. Koch, P. Perona, Graph-based visual saliency, in: Proceedings of the 19th International Conference on Neural Information Processing Systems, NIPS'06, MIT Press, 2006, pp. 545–552.

[68] H. Lv, Q. Yang, C. Li, W. Dai, J. Zou, H. Xiong, SalGCN: Saliency Prediction for 360-Degree Images Based on Spherical Graph Convolutional Networks, Association for Computing Machinery, New York, NY, USA, 2020, pp. 682–690.

[69] M. Startsev, M. Dorr, 360-aware saliency estimation with conventional image saliency predictors, in: Salient360: Visual Attention Modeling for 360° Images, Signal Processing. Image Communication 69 (2018) 43–52, https://doi.org/10.1016/j.image.2018.03.013, https://www.sciencedirect.com/science/article/pii/S0923596518302595.

[70] E. Vig, M. Dorr, D. Cox, Large-scale optimization of hierarchical features for saliency prediction in natural images, in: 2014 IEEE Conference on Computer Vision and Pattern Recognition, 2014, pp. 2798–2805, https://doi.org/10.1109/CVPR.2014.358.

[71] X. Corbillon, G. Simon, A. Devlic, J. Chakareski, Viewport-adaptive navigable 360-degree video delivery, in: 2017 IEEE International Conference on Communications (ICC), 2017, pp. 1–7, https://doi.org/10.1109/ICC.2017.7996611.

[72] F.-Y. Chao, L. Zhang, W. Hamidouche, O. Deforges, SalGAN360: Visual saliency prediction on 360 degree images with generative adversarial networks, in: 2018 IEEE International Conference on Multimedia Expo Workshops (ICMEW), 2018, pp. 01–04, https://doi.org/10.1109/ICMEW.2018.8551543.

[73] Y. Fang, X. Zhang, N. Imamoglu, A novel superpixel-based saliency detection model for 360-degree images, in: Salient360: Visual Attention Modeling for 360° Images, Signal Processing. Image Communication 69 (2018) 1–7, https://doi.org/10.1016/j.image.2018.07.009, https://www.sciencedirect.com/science/article/pii/S0923596518307379.

[74] F. Battisti, S. Baldoni, M. Brizzi, M. Carli, A feature-based approach for saliency estimation of omnidirectional images, in: Salient360: Visual Attention Modeling for 360° Images, Signal Processing. Image Communication 69 (2018) 53–59, https://doi.org/10.1016/j.image.2018.03.008, https://www.sciencedirect.com/science/article/pii/S092359651830242X.

[75] C. Zach, T. Pock, H. Bischof, A duality based approach for realtime TV-L1 optical flow, in: F.A. Hamprecht, C. Schnörr, B. Jähne (Eds.), Pattern Recognition, Springer Berlin Heidelberg, Berlin, Heidelberg, 2007, pp. 214–223.

[76] A. Nguyen, Z. Yan, K. Nahrstedt, Your attention is unique: detecting 360-degree video saliency in head-mounted display for head movement prediction, in: ACM Multimedia Conference for 2018 (ACMMM2018), 2018.

[77] J. Pan, E. Sayrol, X. Giro-i-Nieto, K. McGuinness, N.E. O'Connor, Shallow and deep convolutional networks for saliency prediction, in: 2016 IEEE Conference on Computer Vision and Pattern Recognition (CVPR), 2016, pp. 598–606.

[78] M. Xu, Y. Song, J. Wang, M. Qiao, L. Huo, Z. Wang, Predicting head movement in panoramic video: A deep reinforcement learning approach, in: IEEE Transactions on Pattern Analysis and Machine Intelligence, 2018.

[79] O. Ronneberger, P. Fischer, T. Brox, U-Net: Convolutional networks for biomedical image segmentation, in: Medical Image Computing and Computer-Assisted Intervention (MICCAI), in: LNCS, vol. 9351, Springer, 2015, pp. 234–241, arXiv:1505.04597 [cs.CV], http://lmb.informatik.uni-freiburg.de/Publications/2015/RFB15a.

[80] Y. Zhang, F. Dai, Y. Ma, H. Li, Q. Zhao, Y. Zhang, Saliency prediction network for 360° videos, IEEE Journal of Selected Topics in Signal Processing 14 (1) (2020) 27–37, https://doi.org/10.1109/JSTSP.2019.2955824.

[81] Y. Dahou, M. Tliba, K. McGuinness, N.E. O'Connor, ATSal: An attention based architecture for saliency prediction in 360° videos, in: ICPR Workshops, 2020.

[82] P. Linardos, E. Mohedano, J.J. Nieto, K. McGuinness, X. Giro-i-Nieto, N.E. O'Connor, Simple vs complex temporal recurrences for video saliency prediction, in: British Machine Vision Conference (BMVC), 2019.

[83] M. Qiao, M. Xu, Z. Wang, A. Borji, Viewport-dependent saliency prediction in 360° video, IEEE Transactions on Multimedia 23 (2021) 748–760, https://doi.org/10.1109/TMM.2020.2987682.

[84] F.-Y. Chao, C. Ozcinar, L. Zhang, W. Hamidouche, O. Deforges, A. Smolic, Towards audio-visual saliency prediction for omnidirectional video with spatial audio, in: 2020 IEEE International Conference on Visual Communications and Image Processing (VCIP), 2020, pp. 355–358, https://doi.org/10.1109/VCIP49819.2020.9301766.

[85] H.R. Tavakoli, A. Borji, E. Rahtu, J. Kannala, DAVE: A deep audio-visual embedding for dynamic saliency prediction, CoRR, arXiv:1905.10693 [abs], 2019, http://arxiv.org/abs/1905.10693.

[86] S. Afzal, J. Chen, K.K. Ramakrishnan, Characterization of 360-degree videos, in: Proceedings of the Workshop on Virtual Reality and Augmented Reality Network, VR/AR Network '17, Association for Computing Machinery, New York, NY, USA, 2017, pp. 1–6.

[87] L. Xie, Z. Xu, Y. Ban, X. Zhang, Z. Guo, 360ProbDASH: Improving QoE of 360 video streaming using tile-based HTTP adaptive streaming, in: Proceedings of the 25th ACM International Conference on Multimedia, MM '17, Association for Computing Machinery, New York, NY, USA, 2017, pp. 315–323, https://doi.org/10.1145/3123266.3123291.

[88] F. Qian, L. Ji, B. Han, V. Gopalakrishnan, Optimizing 360 video delivery over cellular networks, in: ATC '16, Association for Computing Machinery, New York, NY, USA, 2016, pp. 1–6, https://doi.org/10.1145/2980055.2980056.

[89] Y. Ban, L. Xie, Z. Xu, X. Zhang, Z. Guo, Y. Wang, CUB360: Exploiting cross-users behaviors for viewport prediction in 360 video adaptive streaming, in: 2018 IEEE International Conference on Multimedia and Expo (ICME), 2018, pp. 1–6, https://doi.org/10.1109/ICME.2018.8486606.

[90] S. Petrangeli, G. Simon, V. Swaminathan, Trajectory-based viewport prediction for 360-degree virtual reality videos, in: 2018 IEEE International Conference on Artificial Intelligence and Virtual Reality (AIVR), 2018, pp. 157–160, https://doi.org/10.1109/AIVR.2018.00033.

[91] S. Rossi, F.D. Simone, P. Frossard, L. Toni, Spherical clustering of users navigating 360° content, in: ICASSP 2019 - 2019 IEEE International Conference on Acoustics, Speech and Signal Processing (ICASSP), 2019, pp. 4020–4024.

[92] A.T. Nasrabadi, A. Samiei, R. Prakash, Viewport Prediction for 360° Videos: A Clustering Approach, Association for Computing Machinery, New York, NY, USA, 2020, pp. 34–39, https://doi.org/10.1145/3386290.3396934.

[93] C.-L. Fan, J. Lee, W.-C. Lo, C.-Y. Huang, K.-T. Chen, C.-H. Hsu, Fixation prediction for 360° video streaming in head-mounted virtual reality, in: NOSSDAV'17, Association for Computing Machinery, New York, NY, USA, 2017, pp. 67–72, https://doi.org/10.1145/3083165.3083180.

[94] C. Bron, J. Kerbosch, Algorithm 457: Finding all cliques of an undirected graph, Communications of the ACM 16 (9) (1973) 575–577, https://doi.org/10.1145/362342.362367.

[95] S. Atev, G. Miller, N.P. Papanikolopoulos, Clustering of vehicle trajectories, IEEE Transactions on Intelligent Transportation Systems 11 (3) (2010) 647–657, https://doi.org/10.1109/TITS.2010.2048101.

[96] X. Hou, S. Dey, J. Zhang, M. Budagavi, Predictive view generation to enable mobile 360-degree and VR experiences, in: Proceedings of the 2018 Morning Workshop on Virtual Reality and Augmented Reality Network, VR/AR Network '18, Association for Computing Machinery, New York, NY, USA, 2018, pp. 20–26, https://doi.org/10.1145/3229625.3229629.

[97] X. Hou, S. Dey, Motion prediction and pre-rendering at the edge to enable ultra-low latency mobile 6DoF experiences, IEEE Open Journal of the Communications Society 1 (2020) 1674–1690, https://doi.org/10.1109/OJCOMS.2020.3032608.

[98] J. Heyse, M.T. Vega, F. de Backere, F. de Turck, Contextual bandit learning-based viewport prediction for 360 video, in: 2019 IEEE Conference on Virtual Reality and 3D User Interfaces (VR), 2019, pp. 972–973, https://doi.org/10.1109/VR.2019.8797830.

[99] Q. Yang, J. Zou, K. Tang, C. Li, H. Xiong, Single and sequential viewports prediction for 360-degree video streaming, in: 2019 IEEE International Symposium on Circuits and Systems (ISCAS), 2019, pp. 1–5, https://doi.org/10.1109/ISCAS.2019.8702654.

[100] X. Feng, Y. Liu, S. Wei, LiveDeep: Online viewport prediction for live virtual reality streaming using lifelong deep learning, in: 2020 IEEE Conference on Virtual Reality and 3D User Interfaces (VR), 2020, pp. 800–808, https://doi.org/10.1109/VR46266.2020.00104.

[101] X. Feng, Z. Bao, S. Wei, LiveObj: Object semantics-based viewport prediction for live mobile virtual reality streaming, IEEE Transactions on Visualization and Computer Graphics 27 (5) (2021) 2736–2745, https://doi.org/10.1109/TVCG.2021.3067686.

[102] M.F. Romero Rondon, L. Sassatelli, R. Aparicio-Pardo, F. Precioso, TRACK: A new method from a re-examination of deep architectures for head motion prediction in 360-degree videos, IEEE Transactions on Pattern Analysis and Machine Intelligence (2021) 1–18, https://doi.org/10.1109/TPAMI.2021.3070520.

[103] F.-Y. Chao, C. Ozcinar, A. Smolic, Transformer-based long-term viewport prediction in 360° video: Scanpath is all you need, in: IEEE 23nd International Workshop on Multimedia Signal Processing (MMSP), 2021.

[104] A. Vaswani, N. Shazeer, N. Parmar, J. Uszkoreit, L. Jones, A.N. Gomez, L. Kaiser, I. Polosukhin, Attention is all you need, in: I. Guyon, U.V. Luxburg, S. Bengio, H. Wallach, R. Fergus, S. Vishwanathan, R. Garnett (Eds.), Advances in Neural Information Processing Systems, vol. 30, Curran Associates, Inc., 2017.

[105] E. Ilg, N. Mayer, T. Saikia, M. Keuper, A. Dosovitskiy, T. Brox, FlowNet 2.0: Evolution of optical flow estimation with deep networks, in: IEEE Conference on Computer Vision and Pattern Recognition (CVPR), 2017, http://lmb.informatik.uni-freiburg.de//Publications/2017/IMKDB17.

[106] J. Redmon, A. Farhadi, YOLOv3: An incremental improvement, arXiv:1804.02767 [abs], 2018.

[107] Y.S. de la Fuente, G.S. Bhullar, R. Skupin, C. Hellge, T. Schierl, Delay impact on MPEG OMAF's tile-based viewport-dependent 360° video streaming, IEEE Journal on Emerging and Selected Topics in Circuits and Systems 9 (2019) 18–28.

[108] M.F.R. Rondon, D. Zanca, S. Melacci, M. Gori, L. Sassatelli, HeMoG: A white-box model to unveil the connection between saliency information and human head motion in virtual reality, in: 2021 IEEE International Conference on Artificial Intelligence and Virtual Reality (AIVR), 2021, pp. 10–18, https://doi.org/10.1109/AIVR52153.2021.00012.

[109] N. Riche, M. Duvinage, M. Mancas, B. Gosselin, T. Dutoit, Saliency and human fixations: State-of-the-art and study of comparison metrics, in: ICCV, 2013.

[110] R.J. Peters, A. Iyer, L. Itti, C. Koch, Components of bottom-up gaze allocation in natural images, Vision Research 45 (18) (2005) 2397–2416.

[111] Z. Bylinskii, T. Judd, A. Oliva, A. Torralba, F. Durand, What do different evaluation metrics tell us about saliency models?, IEEE Transactions on Pattern Analysis and Machine Intelligence 41 (3) (2019) 740–757, https://doi.org/10.1109/TPAMI.2018.2815601.

[112] Y. Rubner, C. Tomasi, L.J. Guibas, The Earth mover's distance as a metric for image retrieval, International Journal of Computer Vision 40 (2000) 99–121.

[113] M. Kümmerer, T.S.A. Wallis, M. Bethge, Information-theoretic model comparison unifies saliency metrics, Proceedings of the National Academy of Sciences 112 (52) (2015) 16054–16059, https://doi.org/10.1073/pnas.1510393112.

[114] A. Borji, H.R. Tavakoli, D.N. Sihite, L. Itti, Analysis of scores, datasets, and models in visual saliency prediction, in: ICCV, 2013.

[115] O.L. Meur, T. Baccino, Methods for comparing scanpaths and saliency maps: strengths and weaknesses, Behavior Research Methods 45 (2013) 251–266, https://doi.org/10.3758/s13428-012-0226-9.

[116] C. Xia, J. Han, D. Zhang, Evaluation of saccadic scanpath prediction: Subjective assessment database and recurrent neural network based metric, IEEE Transactions on Pattern Analysis and Machine Intelligence 43 (12) (2021) 4378–4395, https://doi.org/10.1109/TPAMI.2020.3002168.

[117] G. Marmitt, A.T. Duchowski, Modeling visual attention in VR: Measuring the accuracy of predicted scanpaths, in: EUROGRAPHICS, 2002.

[118] V.I. Levenshtein, Binary codes capable of correcting deletions, insertions and reversals, Soviet Physics. Doklady 6 (1966) 707–710.

[119] H. Jarodzka, K. Holmqvist, M. Nyström, A vector-based, multidimensional scanpath similarity measure, in: Proceedings of the Symposium on Eye-Tracking Research & Applications, vol. 1, 2010.

[120] M. Jiang, S. Huang, J. Duan, Q. Zhao, SALICON: Saliency in context, in: Proceedings of the IEEE Conference on Computer Vision and Pattern Recognition, 2015, pp. 1072–1080.

[121] S. Fremerey, S. Göring, R.R.R. Rao, R. Huang, A. Raake, Subjective test dataset and meta-data-based models for 360° streaming video quality, in: 2020 IEEE 22nd International Workshop on Multimedia Signal Processing (MMSP), 2020, pp. 1–6, https://doi.org/10.1109/MMSP48831.2020.9287065.

PART 3

Light fields

Preliminaries on light fields

The position of rays in 3D-space can be described by four parameters in the two-plane parameterization format. An example is given in Fig. 7.1. Even though other approaches are possible, the most intuitive and common parameterization is by means of the intersection of a ray with two planes parallel to the camera plane.

The evolution of light field capturing devices, as introduced in Chapter 6, led to notations that not only differed in the positioning (and hence physical meaning) of the two reference planes, but also in the letters used to express the two 2D intersection points.

To keep the description in the following chapters consistent and to avoid ambiguities in the naming of the parameters, we will use the following nomenclature:

- The coordinates x, y denote the position within each so-called sub-aperture view. When continuous, they are expressed in m in relation to the center of the view, and when discretized, they are expressed in *pixel* relative to the top left corner of the view.

- The coordinates a, b denote the (virtual) camera position. When continuous, they are expressed in m in relation to the center view, and when discretized they are expressed in *view number* relative to the top left camera when viewed through the lens (hence viewing into the direction of the scene).

- The coordinate t denotes the point in time when a ray has been captured. When continuous, it is expressed in s, and if discretized, it is expressed in *sub-frame number*.

The exact conversion between the continuous and discrete values of the coordinates depends on the parameters of the capturing device (pixel size, focal lengths, sub-frame rate, etc.). For better intuition, also the positioning of the two reference planes in 3D scene space can be varied (e.g., the x, y-plane can be on the sensor, on the main lens, or somewhere in the scene, and the a, b-plane can be at the center of the camera plane or at a (virtual) main lens). This positioning, however, does not change the semantic of the two planes, but rather the proportionality factor between the continuous and discrete space. For a concrete example, see Fig. 7.2.

CHAPTER 6

Acquisition of light field images & videos
Capturing light rays

Thorsten Herfet[a], **Kelvin Chelli**[a], **and Mikael Le Pendu**[b]
[a]Saarland Informatics Campus, Saarbruecken, Germany
[b]Inria, Rennes, France

While many of the results achieved through capturing optical parameters of a scene are motivated and defined by the capturing device (e.g. depth maps created by Time of Flight cameras or point clouds created by LIDAR), light fields stem from the physical representation of scenes by assemblies of light rays and hence there is a variety of different methods of capturing light fields.

Already in 1939 with his seminal paper called "*The Light Field*", Andrey Aleksandrovich Gershun [1] introduced the representation of optical scenes by assemblies of photometric rays. It is not surprising that the first papers on light field rendering stem from computer scientists [2] and the first hand-held plenoptic camera has been introduced by the same group roughly 10 years later [3]. Capturing and rendering for the first time in photography included a significant computational element and phrased the term *Computational Photography* [4].

Even though there are many different ways acquiring rays from a light field (e.g., [5]), we will in this chapter restrict ourselves to three major architectural implementations:

- Plenoptic cameras: Due to the long history of photography and the availability of devices, the first implementations of plenoptic imagery have been by adding so-called MLAs (microlens arrays) to standard 2D-cameras. Such hand-held plenoptic photography [3] reused 2D sensors to capture a set of SAIs (sub-aperture images), so that the resolution of the sensor is split between the spatial domain (aka the resolution of each individual SAI) and the angular domain (aka the number of such SAIs).

- Light field gantries: Based on the insight that light fields for sufficient quality do require a large number of rays (actually the spatial resolution should be comparable to 2D-photography so that the overall data-rate is multiplied by the number of SAIs), light field gantries have been proposed. They use high-resolution 2D-cameras and very fine granular positioning systems (down to the 100 μm-domain) to capture a very large number of SAIs with sufficient resolution each.

Immersive Video Technologies
https://doi.org/10.1016/B978-0-32-391755-1.00012-2

- Light field arrays: To overcome the limitation of gantries to still image photography (the scene and illumination need to remain constant during the whole capturing process), most of the recent light field captures have been taken by assemblies of cameras in camera-arrays. Different geometries (from planar to spherical arrays) are used. Since arrays offer the most intuitive capture of light fields (the resolution of each SAI is given by the individual camera, and the angular resolution is given by number and spacing of such individual cameras), in this book, we adapt our nomenclature to light field arrays.

6.1. Plenoptic cameras

6.1.1 Plenoptic 1.0

The initial idea of turning a 2D-single sensor hand-held photographic camera into a light field capturing device stems from Ren Ng (the later founder of the company Lytro), who in his dissertation thesis [3] complemented a consumer SLR (single-lens reflex camera) with a microlens array to create two recording planes:

- The MLA-plane (yielding one microlens per pixel in each SAI and hence defining the *spatial* resolution of the plenoptic camera);
- The sensor plane (yielding several pixels per microlens and hence defining the *angular* resolution of the plenoptic camera);

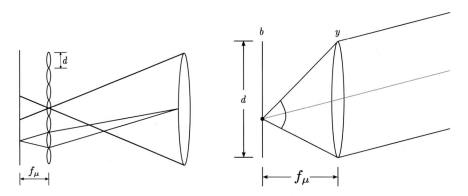

Figure 6.1 Architecture of a single-lens Plenoptic 1.0 camera.

Fig. 6.1 shows the principle architecture of a Plenoptic 1.0 camera: Each microlens acts as a pin-hole camera, spreading rays from different angles over the sensor plane (f_μ and f_M denote the focal lengths of MLA and main lens, d is the diameter of a single microlens and b and y are the vertical component of the SAI-plane (x, y) and the camera plane (a, b)). By careful adjustment of the focal length resp. distance of the MLA with respect to the sensor, Plenoptic 1.0 cameras ensure that the different angular views onto the same scene point are collected in direct neighborhood and behind each microlens. For the angular dimension small angles have been assumed, so that $\tan(\varphi) \approx \sin(\varphi) \approx \varphi$. This is due to the fact that the angular coverage in Plenoptic 1.0 cameras typically is fairly small. With this basic understanding, it is simple to represent the four dimensions in two different 2-dimensional views:

- The SAI-view: This view collects all rays belonging to the same SAI and aligns one SAI besides the other. The sub-aperture view hence is a kind of kaleidoscope, intuitively showing the assembly of images taken from different viewing angles.
- The MLA-view: This view shows the pixels as they appear on the sensor, and, consequently, sometimes is referred to as the RAW–image view (we will stick to MLA-view in this book, since the RAW–image typically requires several post-processing steps from de–Bayering over color-correction to rectification, to be then turned into the MLA-view). It gives an intuitive feeling about the depth of the scene. Scene points at the focal distance of the main lens produce a uniform color, while scene points closer to or further away from the camera produce miniature images in either right-side up (closer) or inverted (further away) version (Fig. 6.3).

Fig. 6.2 shows the difference between MLA- and SAI-view, whereas Fig. 6.3 sheds light on the depth dependent collection behind each of the microlenses.

Figure 6.2 *MLA- vs. SAI-view.* LegoKnights in MLA- (left) and SAI-view (right).

6.1.2 Plenoptic 2.0

Major criticism concerning the design of Plenoptic 1.0 cameras has been the inherent balance between the resolution of each SAI vs. the number of SAIs:

Due to the fact that the resolution of the SAIs is determined by the number of microlenses, changing the balance towards a higher resolution of each of the SAIs would require a significantly larger number of microlenses with two major drawbacks:

Figure 6.3 *MLA-view, closer look.* MLA view at different depths.

- The efficiency suffers: To utilize a large portion of the sensor area, pixels behind each microlens have to approximate a circular shape, which is usually done via a honeycomb (aka hexagonal) structure. Such a structure is hard to approximate with only a few pixels, leaving a significant portion of the sensor unused.
- Due to the geometric relationship between the focal length of the MLA and its distance to the sensor, either the angular coverage per microlens gets smaller or the MLA has to be positioned even closer to the sensor. This distance, however, in existing Plenoptic 1.0 cameras already is fairly small (25 μm in a Lytro Illum camera [6]), so increasing spatial resolution comes at increased complexity in manufacturing.

A solution to this has been proposed with Plenoptic 2.0: [7] overcame the assumption that the microlenses are focused at infinity and act as a pin-hole camera, but rather interpret each microlens as part of an optical system focused at the focal plane of the main lens and acting as a microcamera. The main lens itself is not anymore focused at the microlens array, but rather at an image either in front of or behind it. The ratio of the distances MLA to focal plane (denoted by a in the original paper) and MLA to sensor plane (denoted by b in the original paper) determines the trade-off between spatial and angular resolution. Lumsdaine and Georgiev could show that with this more general Plenoptic 2.0 rendering algorithm, even when applied to images shot with a standard Plenoptic 1.0 camera, the rendering quality is significantly improved (the pinhole microlenses have a very large depth of field so that at the focal plane of the main lens they are still sufficiently focused).

The rendering algorithm is a bit more complex than in Plenoptic 1.0: In Plenoptic 1.0—keep in mind the microlenses are focused at infinity, and hence transform each pixel into a set of parallel rays—each sensor pixel collects rays from a specific direction, but having a spatial span of d. Collecting rays from specific directions hence simply means extracting a fixed coordinate under each microlens. In Plenoptic 2.0, the process of generating SAIs is a bit more complex, since the image under each microlens has a spatial as well as an angular span. Consequently, collecting pixels and averaging over the angular span means averaging across microlenses, rather than just under a single microlens. Given the computational power of most equipment for digital imagery (e.g., mobile phones, whose computational power is driven by high-resolution video encoding), however, this is not a drawback anymore. Plenoptic 2.0 hence overcomes the problem of too low spatial vs. angular resolution. In addition, the balance between spatial and angular resolution is a function of the focal length of the microlenses *and* their distance from the sensor. The production dilemma that for fewer angular views (and consequently larger spatial resolution per view) the number of microlenses needs to increase and the distance of the array from the sensor needs to decrease is solved. Plenoptic 2.0 enables to find a proper balance between the number of lenses in the MLA and its distance from the sensor. (Fig. 6.4.)

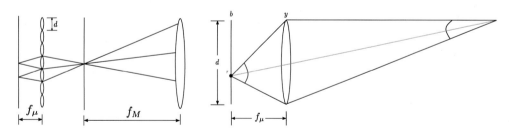

Figure 6.4 Architecture of a single-lens Plenoptic 2.0 camera.

Keep in mind that after post-processing, both Plenoptic 1.0 and 2.0 imagery can be represented in all representation formats introduced in Chapter 7, so this is all about how the spatial and the angular information are mapped to pixels of the image sensor.

6.1.3 Kaleidoscope

A mechanical solution not relying on built in microlens arrays, but rather on external lens accessories is the Kaleidoscopic camera introduced in [8]. It uses kaleidoscopic

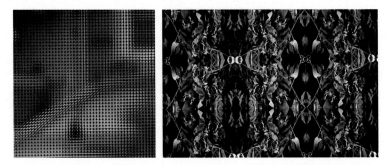

Figure 6.5 *Sensor in Plenoptic Imaging.* Sensor images of Plenoptic 2.0 and kaleidoscopic camera, taken from the original paper [7] and provided by K-Lens.

mirrors to generate a set of microimages at different spatial positions of the sensor. (Fig. 6.5.)

Such kaleidoscopic imaging comes with the advantage of being applicable to standard DSLR cameras, and hence benefit from evolution in sensor technology (a higher resolution of the image sensor directly translates to a higher spatial resolution of the captured light field), but with the disadvantage of expensive manufacturing of the kaleidoscope (pixel positions are determined by the mirror's surfaces, which hence need to be very exact). Therefore kaleidoscopic cameras target the (semi-)professional market[1] and both, kaleidoscopic and Plenoptic 2.0 cameras target the industrial market.[2]

6.2. Light field gantries

Single-lens light field capturing solutions per definition suffer from a limited aperture, and hence a low sensitivity (the light gathered through this aperture has to feed all spatial and angular pixels) as well as a limited parallax (only rays within the aperture can be captured). To overcome these limitations, for a long time light field data-sets have been captured by so-called gantries. The Stanford gantry has been used to acquire dense light fields with nearly 400 views[3] and uses a positioning system based on Lego Mindstorm® with a Canon DSLR, equipped with a wide angle lens (10–22 mm) to stick to pure translational positioning. The sensor resolution has been 3888 · 2592, and the images have been cropped to the part of the scene seen from all positions (ranging from 640–1536 pixel dependent on the overall aperture and the scene itself). Many of the light fields from this archive have become a de-facto standard for the development and evaluation of light field algorithms. Most famous are the following:

---

[1] https://creative.k-lens.de/.
[2] https://industrial.k-lens.de/, https://raytrix.de/.
[3] http://lightfield.stanford.edu/lfs.html.

- LegoKnights
  (http://lightfield.stanford.edu/data/lego_lf/rectified.zip)
- Jelly Beans
  (http://lightfield.stanford.edu/data/jelly_beans_lf/rectified.zip)
- Bracelet
  (http://lightfield.stanford.edu/data/bracelet_lf/rectified.zip)
- Tarot Cards and Crystal Ball
  (http://lightfield.stanford.edu/data/tarot_coarse_lf/rectified.zip)

A gantry with positioning down to the sub-100 μm-domain has been introduced in [9]: The very large gantry covers 4 m horizontally and 0.5 m vertically and can be positioned with an accuracy of 80 μm horizontally and 50 μm vertically.

Light field gantries hence can overcome both shortcomings of single-lens light field capturing devices: due to the sequential capture the sensitivity problem is overcome, since each SAI can exploit the full illumination. Mechanically, large gantries can achieve a very large parallax, and hence capture many 3D-scene points (including those that would be fully occluded with smaller apertures). This all comes with two major drawbacks:

1. The scene must be completely static. Even very small movement leads to occlusion (think of a plant whose leaves just move due to turbulence created by the operator or the moving camera itself).
2. The gantry itself is large and requires a solid installation. Hence this is not suited for capturing in the wild.

6.3. Camera arrays

The most recent and also most widespread technology for light field capture is the so-called camera array. Camera arrays—sometimes also referred to as camera rigs, carrying forward a term used for stereo capturing—are assemblies of several cameras in different geometries:

- Planar arrays are the most common implementation. Fig. 6.6 shows two of those arrays as an example. Planar arrays provide viewing angles in the range of normal viewing, and hence are used to add parallax to scenarios of local head & body motion (looking through a window), as it happens for TV or cinematic viewing.
- Spherical arrays are used for outside-in as well as for inside-out capture. Spherical arrays are used for VR or cave-like viewing (inside-out) or for 3D-capture with the purpose of creating mixed-reality assets (outside-in). (Fig. 6.7.)

So what is the major difference between multiview image resp. video capture and array-based light field capture?

- From the viewpoint of the raw material, array-based light field capture is identical to multiview capture. In analogy to stereo-rigs, the simplest form of multiview capture

Figure 6.6 *Light Field Planar Arrays.* Planar arrays from Fraunhofer IIS (©Fraunhofer IIS) and Saarland University.

Figure 6.7 *Light Field Spherical Arrays.* Spherical arrays from Google [10] and Volucap (www.studiobabelsberg.com).

with known geometry, the major difference is that the pre-processing pipeline of multiview capture to generate light field assets exploits known geometry facts:

- De-Bayering: This is a standard step also in case of single-sensor capture. Multiview capture enables more advanced de-Bayering methods,[4] but de-Bayering can also be done classically and per camera.
- Color-correction: In multiview the different views are captured by different devices. Hence differences in the color mapping have to be corrected to generate reliable color information across the views.
- Rectification: Planar arrays have fixed and carefully adjusted camera positions. Small deviations in the 3D-position, in the camera-rotation, and in the actual focal length, however, create distortions that need to be corrected. Rectification creates virtual camera positions identical to those positions envisaged by the

---

[4] Blatt, Alexander: "Extending Deep Convolutional Demosaicing to Camera Arrays", Master-thesis, Saarland University, 2/2020.

array-designer. Typically lens-distortions are also corrected during the rectification process.

The major difference between general multiview and light field capture therefore is the given geometry. The spatial and temporal relationship between the different views is known, and as a result positions and directions of rays in space and time can be derived.

The next chapter, consequently, will introduce different light field representation formats. Those formats include the spatial and temporal semantics, i.e., ray positions and directions can be extracted, and hence ray-based image processing can take place.

References

[1] A. Gershun, The light field, Journal of Mathematics and Physics 18 (1–4) (1939) 51–151.

[2] M. Levoy, P. Hanrahan, Light field rendering, in: Proceedings of the 23rd Annual Conference on Computer Graphics and Interactive Techniques, 1996, pp. 31–42.

[3] R. Ng, M. Levoy, M. Brédif, G. Duval, M. Horowitz, P. Hanrahan, Light field photography with a hand-held plenoptic camera, Ph.D. thesis, Stanford University, 2005.

[4] R. Raskar, J. Tumblin, Computational photography, in: ACM SIGGRAPH 2005 Courses, ACM, 2005, pp. 1–es.

[5] J. Iseringhausen, B. Goldlücke, N. Pesheva, S. Iliev, A. Wender, M. Fuchs, M.B. Hullin, 4D imaging through spray-on optics, ACM Transactions on Graphics (TOG) 36 (4) (2017) 1–11.

[6] D.G. Dansereau, O. Pizarro, S.B. Williams, Decoding, calibration and rectification for lenselet-based plenoptic cameras, in: Proceedings of the IEEE Conference on Computer Vision and Pattern Recognition, 2013, pp. 1027–1034.

[7] A. Lumsdaine, T. Georgiev, The focused plenoptic camera, in: 2009 IEEE International Conference on Computational Photography (ICCP), IEEE, 2009, pp. 1–8.

[8] A. Manakov, J. Restrepo, O. Klehm, R. Hegedus, E. Eisemann, H.-P. Seidel, I. Ihrke, A reconfigurable camera add-on for high dynamic range, multispectral, polarization, and light-field imaging, ACM Transactions on Graphics 32 (4) (2013) 47–1.

[9] M. Ziegler, R. op het Veld, J. Keinert, F. Zilly, Acquisition system for dense lightfield of large scenes, in: 2017 3DTV Conference: The True Vision-Capture, Transmission and Display of 3D Video (3DTV-CON), IEEE, 2017, pp. 1–4.

[10] M. Broxton, J. Flynn, R. Overbeck, D. Erickson, P. Hedman, M. Duvall, J. Dourgarian, J. Busch, M. Whalen, P. Debevec, Immersive light field video with a layered mesh representation, ACM Transactions on Graphics (TOG) 39 (4) (2020) 86–1.

CHAPTER 7

Light field representation
The dimensions in light fields

Thorsten Herfet[a], **Kelvin Chelli**[a], and **Mikael Le Pendu**[b]

[a]Saarland Informatics Campus, Saarbruecken, Germany
[b]Inria, Rennes, France

Capture is the first step in light field application: Whether in plenoptic cameras or in camera arrays, neither the geometry nor the coloring is perfect. Consequently, light field pre-processing pipelines do include

- De-Bayering: Typical sensors record raw-luminance in Bayer patterns, i.e., single pixels represent one of the three primary colors, and consequently for full color images interpolation techniques need to be applied.
- Color correction: Majorly in arrays, but to a smaller extent also in plenoptic cameras the coloring is not identical for all subaperture views. Color-matching techniques have to be applied to harmonize the colors and to enable the assignment of rays to objects by means of their color.
- De-vignetting: Majorly in plenoptic cameras, but to a smaller extent also in arrays lenses are not adequately effective in avoiding vignetting effects. Consequently, the brightness of rays needs to be harmonized.
- Rectification: To establish the correct relationship between any captured sensor pixel and the respective ray in space, camera positions need to be known perfectly, and lens distortions need to be corrected. The processing step is called rectification, since in many applications (μ-lenses on the MLA in plenoptic cameras, horizontal and vertical alignment in planar camera arrays) the underlying position ideally reflects an equidistantly sampled rectangle. After rectification, all (virtual) extrinsics and intrinsics are known.

After the pre-processing rays can be unambiguously identified by four parameters, plus the known geometry of the capturing device. How these four parameters are defined and what advantages/disadvantages of different representations are will be introduced in this chapter.

7.1. Space domain representation

As elaborated on in Chapter 6 representations of light fields inherently are representations of sets of rays. Since—as in usual photographic cameras—the origin of a ray is not known (it's the point on the convex hull of the scene in the direction of the respective ray, but this hull of the scene is not known apriori), a ray can be unambiguously defined by *four* dimensions.

This can be the intersection with two known 2-dimensional surfaces, a position in space plus two rotation angles or anything else unambiguously defining a ray's position and direction in 3D-space. In the following chapters, we will explain different representation formats; from fairly intuitive ones in the spatial domain to more abstract ones in the frequency- or froxel-domain. Representations typically are optimized for the purpose they intend to serve: light field image and video processing, light field rendering, light field compression, and others.

Bear in mind that in principle and under the assumption of infinitely exact calculations, it is possible to convert one representation into the other. The distribution of actually existing rays over the various dimensions, however, significantly differs. Hence as soon as quantization comes into play, certain representations have advantages over others.

7.1.1 Two-plane model

The most intuitive model for representing position and orientation of a ray is its intersection with two 2D surfaces, whose exact geometry in 3D-space is given:

- For spherical light field capture (e.g., Fig. 6.7 (left)), this can be two spheres of different radius, centered in the origin of the array.
- For a planar array, this most intuitively are two planes parallel to the array. Though actually their position (aka distance from the array) is arbitrary, there is common sense in the literature about how to put semantics to the two planes:
  - For MLA-based Plenoptic 1.0 cameras, one plane is the MLA-plane, whereas the second one is either the main lens plane or a plane within the scene (typically the plane at the focal distance).
  - For camera arrays, one plane is the plane of the camera–centers, and the other is a virtual sensor plane in front of the cameras.

Fig. 7.1 shows, that for this book, and for the sake of consistency, we have decided to name the parameters of pixels in each sub-aperture image x & y, and the parameters describing the camera (aka the viewing position) a & b. For camera arrays, (a, b) hence denotes the camera and (x, y) the pixel on the sensor of that camera. How the discrete parameters relate to real-world coordinates depends on the system parameters as well as on the absolute positioning of the planes.

To give a precise example, Fig. 7.2 sketches the array built by Saarland University. The required system parameters are listed in Table 7.1.

With those parameters and the convention that the (a, b)-plane is in the camera–centers and the (x, y)-plane in front of the (a, b)-plane with a distance of f (here 12.5 mm), we can easily calculate the following:

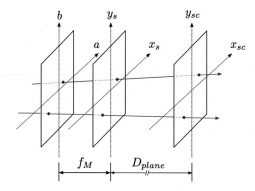

Figure 7.1 Two-plane model geometry and parameters for light field arrays.

Table 7.1 Parameters of the Saarland University array.

Baseline:	$d_x = d_y =$	70 mm
Focal length:	$f =$	12.5 mm
Pixel size:	$sz = p_x = p_y =$	5.86 μm
Resolution:	$S_x \cdot S_y =$	$1920 \cdot 1200$ pixel
Cameras:	$N = 8 \cdot 8 =$	64

- The opening angle of each camera is $2 \cdot atan(\frac{0.960 \cdot 5.86}{12.5}) = 48.46°$.
- The overall baseline of the array is $(\sqrt{N} - 1) \cdot 70 = 490$ mm.
- The frustum hence is given by a virtual single camera with the same opening angle, but $\frac{490}{2} \cdot \frac{12.5}{0.960 \cdot 5.86} = 544.4$ mm behind the camera plane.
- The light field is sparse: Overlapping of adjacent cameras happens at a distance of 77.8 mm and a (single) point is seen by all cameras at a distance of 544.4 mm.
- The disparity in pixel of a point at distance D is given by $d = \frac{70 \cdot 12.5}{0.00586 \cdot D}$ for adjacent cameras. Hence, to have an overlap of, e.g., 1024 pixels between the outermost cameras, we need a depth of at least $\frac{490 \cdot 12.5}{(1920 - 1024) \cdot 0.00586} = 1167$ mm.
- The a, b-plane shows only 64 samples.
- At the focal distance the baseline between the cameras is 490 mm, but only $7 \cdot 1920 \cdot 0.00586 = 78.8$ mm, so only 16%, are covered by the sensors. Starting with the depth of 77.8 mm as calculated above, the whole baseline is covered, and each point of the scene is represented by at least one ray.

7.1.1.1 Ray sets

We can use the two-plane model to shed light on what is actually captured and how this capturing influences the potentially applicable post-processing tools. We have seen that by the intersection with the two planes a, b and x, y, we define a limited set of viewing directions in space. This is why we say light fields are a *set of rays*, rather than

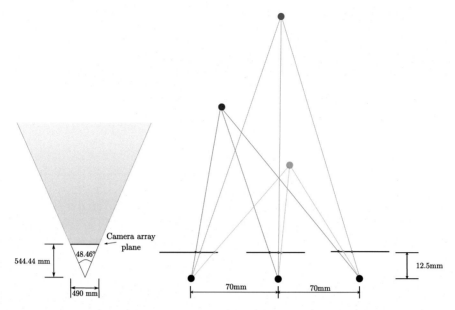

Figure 7.2 *Geometry for Light Field Arrays.* Concrete example of the Saarland University array (as shown in Fig. 6.6).

a set of pixels. Each ray samples the color, as seen from an exact position and in an exact direction in space. Consequently, we have very many different characteristics of rays. The following list shows such different characteristics and how they refer to post-processing tools and to representations, as handled in this book.

- The start of a ray is the opaque point in the scene with the smallest depth. All other points of the scene in the same position and direction are occluded for this specific ray. They might, however, be visible from a different position and direction. This has implications for algorithms such as object removal and view interpolation. The representation with froxels (Section 7.3.3) is an appropriate means to exploit this characteristic.

- The color of a ray is the color of this opaque point in the viewing direction when no transparent objects are in front. Otherwise, the color seen will be a composition of the starting point and the influence of all transparent objects in front. Considering this transparency is one of the biggest merits of the recently introduced neural radiance field (NeRF, Section 7.4).

- Scene points can be hit by 0..N rays. The number of rays hitting a point, however, severely influences the post-processing possible:
  - When a point is not seen at all, in-painting methods are required for view interpolation.

- When a point is seen by only one or very few rays, it presumably is occluded from other positions/directions, and hence can be used for object removal or for view interpolation (looking around the corner).
- When a point is seen by many rays (up to the number of discrete points in the a, b-plane) *and* the color from all those directions is similar, we call the radiation Lambertian and algorithms such as noise-reduction, super-resolution or depth-estimation are possible. When the color is not similar, BRDFs (bidirectional reflectance distribution functions) can be estimated and be exploited for view interpolation. Froxel analysis, as introduced in Section 7.3, enables a classification of ray sets representing the same scene point resp. volume, and hence help avoiding the application of algorithms for which the conditions are hurt.
- Lambertianness is required by many algorithms and also by representations such as the Fourier disparity layers (Section 7.2). Application to non-Lambertian parts of the scene leads to artifacts.

All these observations reveal that the major thread in light field representation and processing is the lack of explicit capture of the starting point of rays, and hence the assignment of a certain scene volume to a ray. This depth information has to be extracted by means of algorithms and/or technical aids, such as time-of-flight cameras. Both, however, are not perfect.

And even when all starting points are known, non-Lambertianness can be due to non-isotropic radiation or due to transparent objects in the scene. With this knowledge we can intuitively understand the merits and shortcomings of different light field representations introduced in this chapter.

7.1.2 Spatio-/angular representation

The example of a light field array (Table 7.1) revealed that the captured set of rays is quite heterogeneous: Even though arrays provide the required resolution of each SAI, the angular sampling is sparse. A significant overlap of all SAIs and, consequently, the availability of a sufficient number of angular rays stemming from the same scene point is only given at large enough distances from the array. Hence for large parts of the scene, rays need to be interpolated, which comes with two major drawbacks:

- Interpolation needs to adhere to Shannon's sampling theorem. This means the coarser the input is sampled, the lower the usable resolution resp. the larger the aliasing (since the capture per definition is not pre-filtered properly). This leads to the well-known aliasing artifacts in (sparse) light field view-interpolation (Fig. 7.3).
- Typical head motion of human observers is small, which leads to the necessity of a very fine angular resolution. Several ten to few hundred views have been shown to provide a smooth parallax perception [1]. This is at least one order of magnitude larger than the number of cameras in one direction of existing light field arrays. Consequently, view interpolation has to be done on the fly.

Figure 7.3 *Aliasing in Light Field Interpolation.* Visible aliasing in parts of the scene near the capturing array: The headlight is more blurry and has more artifacts than the side mirror (top: ground truth, bottom interpolated view).

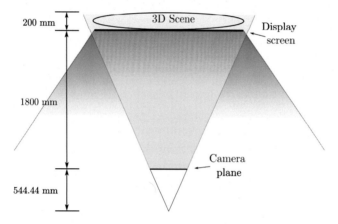

Figure 7.4 *Positioning the LF-Display in the ϕ, θ, x, y-format.* Spatio-/angular LF format.

The authors of [2], looking at light fields from the rendering resp. display-side, introduce an alternative 4D light field representation format: the (ϕ, θ, x, y)-format.[1]

The intuition of this format is analog to the intuition of the a, b, x, y-format stemming from the capture side: Light field rendering is like looking through a window, where rays arrive through different locations of the windowpane (x, y), and the viewer's position defines the angle of the rays perceived by the two eyes (ϕ, θ). In addition, horizontal only parallax displays (where only horizontal head motion leads to natural parallax, whereas vertical head motion leads to the standard experience of looking at a 2D image) can be generated by omitting θ. Fig. 7.4 shows how the display is positioned within the 3D scene to be rendered.

---

[1] Bear in mind that we called the coordinates within each SAI x, y, rather than s, t.

Though for synthetic scenes it is straightforward to produce the rays required for the rendering, natural scenes require a conversion. This is why the authors call this representation a *mezzanine* format: Most applications of light fields will be via light field displays. A format that enables serving different display formats and resolutions and reduces the required computations on the display side hence has advantages. The conversion, however, will inevitably introduce artifacts due to the limited intersection of the ray sets captured and required for rendering.

As in 2D-imagery, to enable sufficient suppression of repeated spectra for excellent perceived quality, the display resolution typically is significantly higher than the captured number of rays. [3] introduce measurements on a projection-based display with a spatial resolution of $1056 \cdot 636$ pixel and an angular resolution of 70. Compared to the light field array used in this chapter, this is a relation of 25 in just one direction (HPO; horizontal parallax only).

$$\frac{N_R}{N_C} = \frac{1056 \cdot 636 \cdot 70}{1920 \cdot 1200 \cdot 8} \approx 25. \tag{7.1}$$

In summary, light fields are represented by four dimensions, which are typically chosen to match the desired purpose best. Capturing—independently of whether by plenoptic cameras or camera arrays—is typically represented by two 2D pixel coordinate systems, which themselves can intuitively be interpreted as two parallel planes, whereas rendering is more intuitively represented by one 2D spatial coordinate system (the display screen) and two angular coordinates for the viewing direction.

It is important to bear in mind that even though for each individual ray the conversion is straightforward and in absence of quantization also lossless, the entire set of rays captured typically very much deviates from the set of rays required for rendering, so that interpolation and conversion losses are inevitable.

7.1.3 Epipolar plane images

With the SAI- and MLA-views (Fig. 6.2), we already introduced two different 2D views of the light field. Obviously other combinations are possible, shedding light onto characteristics of the underlying scene:

- We have seen that for Lambertian parts of the scene, the color of an object is independent of the viewing angle, and hence independent from the SAI, aka the a, b-plane. The position where the scene point is located in the respective SAIs, however, is dependent on its depth, as will be shown in the following chapters (Eq. (7.2)). Stacking different 1D-views of the same part of the scene on top of each other, consequently, creates images where the same object appears at different locations and produces lines with an inclination proportional to the disparity and inverse proportional to the depth. Such images are called *epipolar plane images* or *EPIs* and can be used for the visualization of scenes as well as for depth estimation.

- The resolution of EPIs equals the spatial resolution times the angular resolution. Hence analysis by EPIs is only applicable for light fields with a sufficient number of different views. Using the examples given in Section 7.1.2, the camera array would yield EPIs with a resolution of $1920 \cdot 8$, whereas the display would yield EPIs of size $1056 \cdot 70$ (Fig. 7.5).

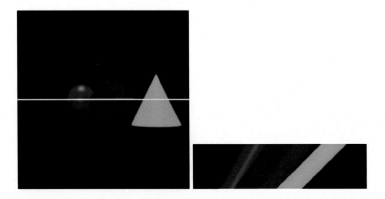

Figure 7.5 *Epipolar Image Example.* EPI for a resolution of $512 \cdot 128$.

7.1.4 Adding time

For now we have introduced sets of rays traversing through the three dimensional volume within the frustum of the capturing device. We did not yet, however, include a notion of time, even though this is very important for the signal processing and the representation of dynamic scenes. To differentiate the set of captured rays also in the temporal domain, we introduce the following notion:

- Light field images are called *4D light fields*. All geometries shown within this chapter of the book refer to instances of 4D light fields (and often are even reduced to one spatial and one angular domain for illustration purposes).
- Light field videos are shot by either plenoptic cameras or camera arrays. In most cases, videos are sequences of 4D light fields, captured at fixed frame times. Hence each light field frame represents a full 4D light field. We call such videos *4.5D light fields*.
- To capture the scene in the best possible way, however, ray sets, as discussed in Section 7.1.1.1, should contain the temporal domain. Especially in areas of fast motion parts of the scene might be occluded at frame instance times, but visible in-between. If those parts are Lambertian—i.e., the color of the scene points is visible from several, potentially adjacent angular positions—sampling them at different points in time can significantly improve the light field. We call those light fields *5D light fields*.

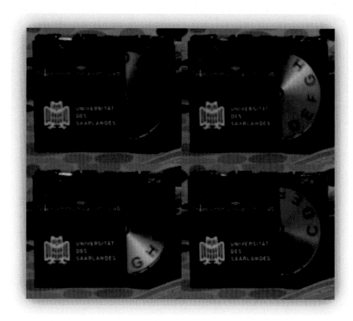

Figure 7.6 *Temporal Sampling of Scenes.* Fast moving object, sampled with 4 sub-frames.

Fig. 7.6 illustrates such a situation: The colored CD is spinning with a velocity of 2400 rpm, leading to a 360°-turn every 25 ms. A 4.5D light field sampled with 40 fps would continuously show the same part of the CD's surface, leaving a large portion of the texture occluded. The figure is an excerpt of a scene captured with the array of Saarland University (Table 7.1) and uses a sub-framing with four sub-frames per frame, creating 160, rather than only 40, different temporal instances for rays. To maximize the probability for Lambertianness, the sub-frames are assigned, as shown in Fig. 7.7. The goal is to maximize the number of motion phases between adjacent cameras, since the probability that all seeing the respective part of the scene is high. For the case of four sub-frames, as used in Fig. 7.6, the top left pattern shows that $2 \cdot 2$ sub-arrays always contain all four phases.

Consequently, light field processing should not prohibit the application of sub-frames, and hence rays should be parameterized by five, rather than four, dimensions: (t, a, b, x, y).

Only few recent light field representations include the notion of time, and even fewer explicitly include the time into their processing pipeline. One such representation is introduced in Section 7.3.3.

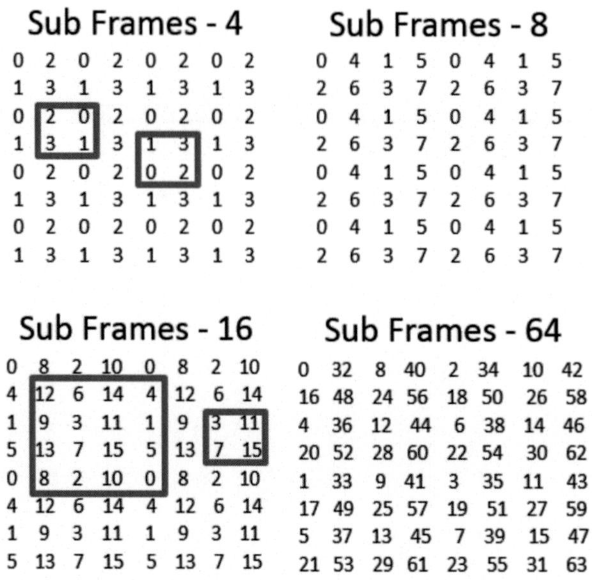

Sub Frames - 4

```
0  2  0  2  0  2  0  2
1  3  1  3  1  3  1  3
0  2  0  2  0  2  0  2
1  3  1  3  1  3  1  3
0  2  0  2  0  2  0  2
1  3  1  3  1  3  1  3
0  2  0  2  0  2  0  2
1  3  1  3  1  3  1  3
```

Sub Frames - 8

```
0  4  1  5  0  4  1  5
2  6  3  7  2  6  3  7
0  4  1  5  0  4  1  5
2  6  3  7  2  6  3  7
0  4  1  5  0  4  1  5
2  6  3  7  2  6  3  7
0  4  1  5  0  4  1  5
2  6  3  7  2  6  3  7
```

Sub Frames - 16

```
0   8  2  10  0   8  2  10
4  12  6  14  4  12  6  14
1   9  3  11  1   9  3  11
5  13  7  15  5  13  7  15
0   8  2  10  0   8  2  10
4  12  6  14  4  12  6  14
1   9  3  11  1   9  3  11
5  13  7  15  5  13  7  15
```

Sub Frames - 64

```
0  32  8  40  2  34  10  42
16 48 24  56 18  50  26  58
4  36 12  44  6  38  14  46
20 52 28  60 22  54  30  62
1  33  9  41  3  35  11  43
17 49 25  57 19  51  27  59
5  37 13  45  7  39  15  47
21 53 29  61 23  55  31  63
```

Figure 7.7 *Subframing for an* 8 · 8 *Camera Array.* Distribution of 4, 8, 16, and 64 sub-frames.

7.2. Frequency domain representation

The full 4D light field representation typically requires complex computations, particularly in the case of dense light fields with high spatial and angular resolutions. Certain properties of the Fourier transform can simplify such computations resulting in more efficient representations in the Fourier domain. Notably, we will see in this section that directly using the 4D Fourier transform of the light field can be advantageous for rendering refocused images. Furthermore, Fourier domain computations make it possible to construct a more compact representation called Fourier disparity layers (FDL) suitable for fast renderings of arbitrary views or refocused images.

In this section, we use the notations $\hat{f}$ for the Fourier transform of a function f, and ω_x and ω_y, the frequency variables in the spatial dimensions x, y, respectively.

7.2.1 4D Fourier transform

Considering the two-plane light field model in Section 7.1.1, rendering a refocused image consists in shearing the 4D space (accounting for the change of focus) and computing an integral over the angular dimensions. The conventional shift-and-sum algorithm explicitly performs these steps in the discrete 4D space by shifting the SAIs, depending on their angular coordinates, and by averaging the shifted SAIs.

However, when representing the light field in the 4D Fourier domain, it becomes possible to accelerate the refocusing process by selecting a 2D slice in the 4D Fourier space, hence removing the need for explicitly computing an integral over all the SAIs. This has been formalized in [4] as a 4D generalization of the Fourier slice theorem, which is commonly used in medical imaging for computed tomography scans. Fig. 7.8 illustrates the principle of the theorem, as originally described for a 1D slice of a 2D space [5]. In this example, the original 2D space is rotated with R_θ before applying the integral projection operator $\mathcal{I}$, which computes the integral over the y-dimension. The theorem states that this sequence of operations is equivalently performed in the Fourier domain by applying R_θ followed by the selection of the 1D slice at coordinate $y = 0$. In other words, it is equivalent to simply selecting a rotated slice.

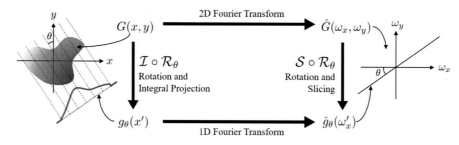

Integral Projection operator: $\mathcal{I}[f](x) = \int_{-\infty}^{+\infty} f(x,y)dy$

Slicing operator: $\mathcal{S}[f](x) = f(x,0)$

Figure 7.8 *Fourier Slice Theorem.* Illustration for a 1D slice of the 2D plane.

The generalized version of the theorem [4] applies to arbitrary numbers of dimensions as well as an arbitrary change of basis in place of the rotation R_θ. This includes the shearing operation involved in refocusing. Therefore given a light field in the 4D Fourier domain, a refocused image is rendered by selecting a sheared 2D slice of the 4D Fourier space, and by applying the inverse 2D Fourier transform. However, this approach has several limitations:

- In discrete space, selecting the sheared slice requires an interpolation in the Fourier domain, which introduces artifacts on top of the angular aliasing that may arise when a too low angular sampling is provided (i.e., not sufficiently dense light field).
- The computation of the 4D Fourier transform is itself a computationally intensive operation. Nevertheless, it can be seen as an offline pre-processing step that only needs to be performed once to render an arbitrary number of refocused images.
- For realistic rendering, it is usually preferable to simulate a realistic camera aperture shape. In the original two-plane light field representation, this is done by integrating over the angular dimensions only within the aperture. However, the 4D Fourier computation does not allow for a control of the aperture shape.

7.2.2 Fourier disparity layers

As we have seen, if a scene point is seen from different views, for planar cameras disparity and depth are related by a simple inverse law:

$$d = \frac{b \cdot f}{sz \cdot D},$$
(7.2)

where b is the baseline between the respective views, f the focal length, sz the pixel size, d the disparity in pixel, and D the depth. Hence for constant depth, there's a fixed and geometry-defined disparity between viewing positions.

The idea of the so-called *Fourier disparity layers* as introduced in [6], hence, is to decompose the scene into a set of discrete layers l_k, each associated with a single disparity value d_k (directly linked to an actual depth with Eq. (7.2)). The layers can be directly used for fast rendering of refocused images with arbitrary aperture shapes and arbitrary change of viewpoint in the camera plane (i.e., change of angular coordinates).

7.2.2.1 Fourier disparity layer rendering

It is first necessary to understand how different images are rendered from the FDL model to derive the layer construction from a 4D light field (presented in Section 7.2.2.2). The simplest form of FDL rendering consists in generating an all-in-focus image (i.e., with infinitely small camera aperture) at given angular coordinates (a, b). This is performed only by shifting each layer l_k by the vector (ad_k, bd_k), and by summing the shifted layers, as illustrated in Fig. 7.9. In the pixel domain, this reads

$$I_{a,b}(x, y) = \sum_k l^k(ad_k x, bd_k y),$$
(7.3)

where $I_{a,b}$ is the rendered image at angular coordinates (a, b). Since images have a discrete pixel sampling, the shift operation requires an interpolation to obtain $l^k(ad_k x, bd_k y)$

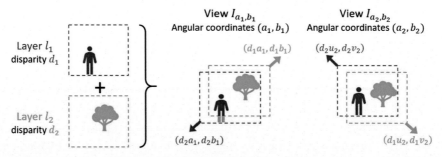

Figure 7.9 *Illustration of Fourier Disparity Layer Rendering.* Shift-and-sum rendering of the layers generates all-in-focus views.

at non-integer coordinates (ad_kx, bd_ky). However, the equivalent operation can be performed in the Fourier domain as frequency-wise operations. Thus given the Fourier representation $\hat{l}^k$ of each layer l_k, no interpolation is required. The Fourier transform $\hat{I}_{a,b}$ of a view $I_{a,b}$ is then computed as

$$\hat{I}_{a,b}(\omega_x, \omega_y) = \sum_k \hat{l}^k(\omega_x, \omega_y) \cdot e^{2i\pi\, d_k\cdot(a\omega_x+b\omega_y)}, \tag{7.4}$$

where the multiplication by the complex exponential accounts for the shift operation.

More generally, for rendering images with arbitrary aperture shapes, each layer can be blurred by a convolution with the aperture shape ψ scaled depending on the disparity of the layer to produce defocus blur (which is depth-dependent). Similarly, to the shift operation, the convolution is more complex to compute in the pixel domain, and the complexity increases with the size of the filter (e.g., size of the aperture here). On the other hand, the equivalent operation is performed in the Fourier domain as a frequency-wise multiplication by the Fourier transform of the filter, hence allowing for fast FDL rendering with a complexity that does not depend on the aperture size. The general rendering equation is then

$$\hat{I}^d_{a,b}(\omega_x, \omega_y) = \sum_k \hat{l}^k(\omega_x, \omega_y) \cdot \hat{\psi}(\omega_x(d - d_k), \omega_y(d - d_k)) \cdot e^{2i\pi\, d_k\cdot(a\omega_x+b\omega_y)}, \tag{7.5}$$

for an image $\hat{I}^d_{a,b}$ focused on the plane of disparity d in the light field, and where $\hat{\psi}$ is the 2D Fourier transform of the camera aperture ψ: if a point (a, b) on the camera plane is within the aperture, $\psi(a, b) = 1$, otherwise $\psi(a, b) = 0$.

Similarly, to the refocusing with the Fourier slice theorem method in Section 7.2.1, the inverse 2D Fourier transform is finally performed to obtain the rendered image.

7.2.2.2 Layer construction in the Fourier domain

The construction of the layers is formulated as the inverse rendering problem: Given a set of light field views with known parameter (angular coordinates, aperture, focus), the layers must be determined so that rendering the views with the same parameters from the FDL optimally reconstructs the input set of views. Since the FDL rendering equation (Eq. (7.5)) is expressed as a linear frequency-wise operation, the inverse problem is also solved independently per frequency component. Let's consider the FDL construction from a set of m light field SAIs $\{I_{a_1,b_1}, ..., I_{a_m,b_m}\}$. The first step consists in computing their 2D Fourier transforms $\{\hat{I}_{a_1,b_1}, ..., \hat{I}_{a_m,b_m}\}$. Knowing the SAI's angular coordinates (a_j, b_j) and given a set of n disparity values $\{d_1, ..., d_n\}$ representative of the disparity range of the scene, the FDL rendering equation for SAIs (Eq. (7.4)) can be written in matrix form $\mathbf{Ax} = \mathbf{b}$ with

$$\mathbf{A}_{j,k} = e^{+2i\pi\, d_k\cdot(a_j\omega_x+b_j\omega_y)}, \quad \mathbf{x}_k = \hat{l}^k(\omega_x, \omega_y), \quad \mathbf{z}_j = \hat{I}_{a_j,b_j}(\omega_x, \omega_y). \tag{7.6}$$

Therefore, at each frequency (ω_x, ω_y), the layers in $\mathbf{x}$ can be determined by solving a linear least squares problem, which has a closed-form solution that can be computed from $\mathbf{A}$ and $\mathbf{z}$. However, this generally results in an ill-posed problem, and a regularization is necessary. In [6], a Tikhonov regularization is used to keep the problem easy to solve with a closed-form solution. In total, the minimization problem is then

$$\mathbf{x} = \arg\min_{\mathbf{x}} \|\mathbf{A}\mathbf{x} - \mathbf{z}\|_2^2 + \lambda \|\mathbf{\Gamma}\mathbf{x}\|_2^2, \tag{7.7}$$

where $\mathbf{\Gamma}$ is the Tikhonov matrix (defined in [6] to prevent strong, non-smooth variations between near viewpoints generated from the layers) and λ is a parameter to control the regularization. The advantage of this Fourier domain formulation is that this problem can be solved in parallel for the different frequency components using conventional matrix arithmetic that can be computed efficiently on modern GPUs.

7.2.2.3 Applications

Though FDLs require significant pre-processing of SAIs (the canonical and mostly original light field format after capturing), view interpolation becomes very simple and fast once the FDL model is computed. The general rendering equation (Eq. (7.5)) also grants the flexibility to fully control defocus blur by adjusting the camera aperture shape and size as well as the disparity of the in-focus plane. Thus FDLs are an excellent light field representation for scenarios that allow off-loading of pre-processing to the edge cloud, but require fast view interpolation on consumer devices (like smart phones).

In addition to the rendering and view interpolation, the FDL model can also serve as the basis for various applications:

- A calibration method described in [6] estimates the angular coordinates of the SAIs and the best set of disparity values for FDL construction. This is performed by determining the parameter values a_j, b_j, and d_k in Eq. (7.6) that yield the best FDL construction according to the minimization function in Eq. (7.7) (averaged over all the frequency components). Stochastic gradient descent is used in practice to solve the minimization efficiently using minibatches of frequency components.
- The FDL construction method was generalized in [7] to generate the layers from SAIs with incomplete spatial sampling, hence enabling light field super-resolution, demosaicing and completion of missing pixels. The approach makes it possible to extract high-resolution images from the RAW data of Plenoptic 1.0 cameras by combining these problems in a single optimization.
- Several FDL-based light field compression schemes have been developed, either by encoding the light field SAIs and using the FDL to predict SAIs from previously encoded ones [8], or by directly encoding the layers [9].
- Once converted back in the pixel domain, the layers can serve to define feature descriptors for light fields, as proposed in [10], to perform robust feature matching between several 4D light fields.

- In [11], a layered saliency model derived from the FDL is used for visual attention prediction of refocused images, given a saliency map of only the central SAI of the light field.

7.2.2.4 Limitations

Despite the various applications and advantages of FDLs, Section 7.1.1.1 also reveals a major disadvantage: FDLs assume a Lambertian scene without occlusion. The model was initially designed for light fields with small baselines, such as those captured with plenoptic cameras. In this case, the optimization-based FDL construction can cope with the small disocclusion areas and non-Lambertian effects without introducing visually disturbing artifacts. However, camera arrays capture light fields with much larger baselines, for which the non-Lambertianness and the large disocclusions become an issue. For instance, since the layers are simply summed together when rendering all-in-focus images, the textures of all the disparity layers are visible, hence the occluder objects appear as transparent as in Fig. 7.10 (left). Nevertheless, this also means that the model can cope with transparent objects in practice, which can be an advantage in some scenarios. It is also worth noting that the issues with large occlusions and non-Lambertian effects are mitigated when rendering refocused images with a sufficiently large aperture (see Fig. 7.10 (right)).

 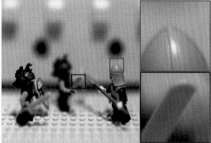

Figure 7.10 *FDL Rendering with large occlusions.* Left: central view rendered with a FDL model constructed from an array of 17x17 views. Right: refocused image rendered with the same FDL (using full aperture covering the angular coordinates of the 17x17 input views).

Another limitation prevents the use of FDLs for light fields with large baselines: The inverse problem of constructing the FDL from a set of views becomes more severely ill-posed when the distance between the input views increases. The construction method presented in Section 7.2.2.2 only considers Tikhonov regularization to keep the problem easy to solve (i.e., with a closed-form solution expressed independently per frequency component). More advanced regularization schemes would be needed to construct FDL models capable of performing higher quality view interpolation from a very sparse set of input views.

7.3. Depth-based representation

Even though the emphasis on *Fourier disparity layers* (Section 7.2) has been on the fact that the anchor images are represented in the frequency rather than spatial domain, they introduced a second, very important component: *Depth*.

As we have seen in Eq. (7.2), knowing the depth of objects tells us where to find them in different views, or vice versa; detecting the disparity of scene point between different views reveals their depth. This depth is an extremely valuable helper for rendering algorithms, since it allows simple (z-buffering) or more complex (volumetric) rendering.

It is hence not surprising that many breakthroughs in light field representation and its major application *view synthesis* make use of depth or disparity in one or the other form. This chapter starts with the introduction of multi-plane and multi-sphere images, presents fristograms (froxel histograms), and concludes with neural radiance fields.

7.3.1 Multi-plane images

[12] & [13] introduced multi-plane images (MPIs). In the same sense as the disparity layers MPIs represent fronto-parallel images at various depths and complemented by an α-value. The semantic behind an MPI is *visibility at a certain depth*. This semantic enables the addition of an α-value, since visibility does not necessarily mean opaque. α adds a notion of transparency to visible parts of the scene. It is this inclusion of transparency that enables a much better treatment of reflections, object boundaries, and scenes with very high depth complexity (when the number of different depths in the scene is much higher than the number of depth planes of the MPI).

As we saw, however, it is already very challenging to estimate disparities and depths; estimating transparency up to now has not been solved with image-based methods. [12] introduce a deep convolutional neural network and a learned gradient descent to solve the problem of mapping a small number of anchor views to the MPI. Fig. 7.11 shows the DeepView architecture, and Fig. 7.12 shows its application to the learning gradient descent.

To apply the same DeepView network to all stages, input images are converted to plane-sweep volumes. A PSV is a stack of warped images: In DeepView, the number of disparity layers is fixed to D, so that $(N - 1) \cdot D$ warped images are created and complemented by the initial D non-warped images, making each PSV an $N \cdot D$ image stack in the same format (but N times "thicker") as the MPIs fed into the second and third stage. As for many other network approaches DeepView requires many GPU–days for training, and also inference is three orders of magnitude beyond real-time. But it has been the first light field representation that includes the notion of visibility, and hence is able to cope with transparent objects and object boundaries.

It is also important to note that the depth layers for DeepView are equally spaced according to inverse depth, i.e., depth layers are denser near to the camera and get sparser

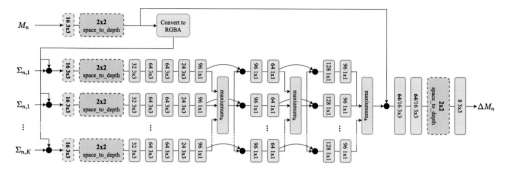

Figure 7.11 *DeepView Update CNN, from [12].* The DeepView convolutional neural network. The overall architecture in figure (redrawn from Fig. 7.12) shows that the CNN is applied three times.

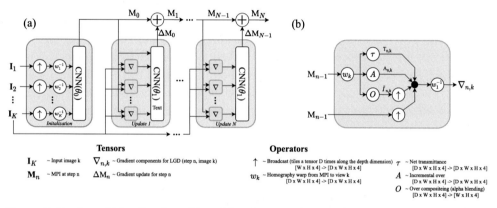

Figure 7.12 *Overall Application of DeepView for Learning Gradient Descent: Redrawn from [12].* Whereas the later stages receive MPIs as inputs, the initial stage is fed by plane-sweep volumes created from the input images.

with growing distance, something in common with the froxel-based representation introduced in Section 7.3.3.

7.3.2 Multi-sphere images

When it comes to non–planar arrays, such as the ones shown in Fig. 6.7, it is more appropriate to align the depth planes to the captured volume. For spherical arrays, consequently, [14] came up with a representation as multi-sphere images (MSIs). Though the fundamental idea remains to be the same (α–compositing of different depth planes), the geometric primitives significantly changed: Whereas for MPIs images could be warped by homographies, for MSIs the different depths have to be warped to spherical shells. This means that in MPIs, the warp fields between the textures of the input views and the MPI planes can be calculated analytically (and straightforward through homographies), for MSIs alternative calculations have to be found. In their implementation Broxton et al. used a ray-tracer to generate warp fields between the textures of the input views and the MSI planes. Since the geometry of the MSIs is fixed, this can be generated once, and then applied, without becoming part of the training and without the requirement of back-propagation. This method hence could be used to modify DeepView to work in an MSI environment. Hence we can summarize that MPIs and MSIs are depth-based light field representations that provide visible textures per plane and add α-values to allow for proper treatment of transparency and object boundaries.

7.3.3 Fristograms

Depth-based representations have advantages in preserving the relationship between the captured rays and the capturing setup. Such a representation emphasizes on the distribution of rays in a scene and the total number of rays originating from a single scene point. The semantic information in the underlying assembly of rays can be a decisive factor for post-processing capabilities. Removal of obstacles is possible if at least one subaperture view (SAI) captures the scene points occluded by the obstacle; looking around corners (optical parallax) is possible when the background can be correctly inpainted; noise reduction can be done by averaging several rays stemming from the same scene point, and refocusing can be done by shift-sum- or hyperfan-filtering [15].

The fristogram-based representation emphasizes the importance of the set of rays captured by a light field the due to the following reasons:

1. Light field capture generates huge amounts of data. A light field camera array consisting of 64 cameras built in the Saarland Informatics Campus, Germany [16] generates 70 Gbps.[2]
2. Most algorithms superimposing (in the simplest cases averaging) different rays assume Lambertian radiation. Consequently, artifacts in refocused or denoised light field images are mostly visible in regions with non-Lambertian radiation.
3. No representation currently available has an explicit notion of time. Especially in regions of very fast motion, it might be advantageous to generate different views over time, rather than over space. A depth-based representation using fristograms contains the spatial and the temporal position of rays.

7.3.3.1 Theory

The major difference between light field and point cloud capture lies in the fact that in light field capture several scene points are captured multiple times. Thus the number of occurrences of the same scene point in the captured set of rays is an important parameter. With the limited resolution of capturing devices—each pixel captures a single ray—and

---

[2] 1920x1200x40x12x64 bps.

assuming knowledge of the camera parameters, we can define a 3-dimensional subspace, whose shape and size follows the frustum. Such a 3-dimensional subspace is called a *froxel*. The term froxel first appeared in [17] and can be defined as a voxel that follows the shape of the frustum [18–20]. As shown in Fig. 7.13, a uniform discretization of the view frustum results in voxels. On the other hand, a depth- and capturing-setup-dependent discretization results in froxels.

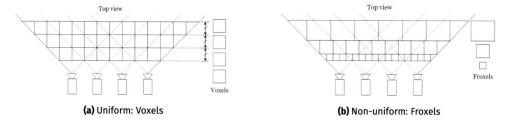

(a) Uniform: Voxels   **(b)** Non-uniform: Froxels

Figure 7.13 Discretization of the View Frustum.

For the sake of simplicity, a froxel is assumed to have an extent of one pixel in each direction. In the camera plane, this describes the frustum of a single pixel, while the extent in the depth is derived by a disparity change of one pixel. Accordingly, the width w_{froxel} and height h_{froxel} are proportional to (i) the pixel size p on the camera sensor (assuming rectangular pixels), and (ii) the distance of the froxel from the camera plane D_{plane}, and inversely proportional to the focal distance of the camera f_M.

Eq. (7.8) is used to compute the width and the height of a froxel. When choosing the scaling factors $n_{hor} = 1$ and $n_{ver} = 1$, the 2D cross section of a froxel is exactly the size of one camera pixel at the distance D_{plane}. Froxels can also be configured to have multiple pixels in the horizontal and vertical dimension by increasing n_{hor} and n_{ver} in (7.8). Consequently, the granularity of the semantic analysis and the computational effort can be optimized for a given application.

$$w_{froxel} = \frac{n_{hor}p}{f_M}D_{plane}, \quad h_{froxel} = \frac{n_{ver}p}{f_M}D_{plane}. \tag{7.8}$$

In the next step, we define the depth of the froxels. When generating a light field, different view points are captured by a camera array. The frustums of the individual cameras overlap and a disparity between the cameras can be calculated. We define the depth of one froxel to be equal to the depth covered by one pixel disparity between the outermost cameras. This way, the frustum is also discretized along the camera rays and gives the froxels a depth. For a given distance D_{plane}, the depth per pixel disparity can be computed using (7.9).

$$d_{froxel} = D^2_{plane} \left/ \left(\frac{f_M \cdot b \cdot (N-1)}{p} - D_{plane} \right) \right. \tag{7.9}$$

Here, b is the camera baseline. We notice that the width and height of a froxel scale linearly with the distance from the camera array, whereas the depth of a froxel scales quadratically. Table 7.2 shows the dimensions of froxels at different depths of a scene point from the camera plane D_{plane}. The set of camera parameters is chosen from the physical camera array described in [16] that has a focal distance $f_M = 12.5$ mm, camera baseline $b = 70$ mm, and the size of a pixel on the sensor to be $p = 5.86$ μm.

Thus assuming the availability of ideal per-view depth maps, the view frustum of the capturing setup can be non-uniformly discretized into froxels. In the next step, the given light field can be parameterized as froxels that preserves the relation between rays and capturing setup to enable semantic aware processing and filtering of light fields.

Table 7.2 Froxel Dimensions (in mm).

D_{plane}	Width (w_{froxel})	Height (h_{froxel})	Depth (d_{froxel})
1000	0.469	0.469	0.9577
1500	0.703	0.703	2.1557
2000	0.938	0.938	3.8343
4000	1.87	1.87	15.3666

7.3.3.2 Semantic analysis methodology

The proposed pipeline to generate fristograms is shown in Fig. 7.14. Initially, the light field along with the parameters of underlying capturing setup are loaded in Matlab®'s workspace. An important prerequisite to semantically analyze light fields using froxels are depth maps. This prerequisite is not unusual, and several well-known standardization activities, such as JPEG PLENO[3] and MPEG[4] extensively leverage disparity resp. depth maps to eliminate redundancy in light fields that stem primarily from Lambertian scene points, while nevertheless maintaining the perceived quality of scene points visible for only few or even one camera. JPEG PLENO in [21] proposes the use of disparity maps to detect occlusions, whereas MPEG uses atlases for texture and depth as explained in [22]. Thus the depth or disparity maps are considered as a common requirement for most of the standard processing of light fields. Thus along with the synthetically rendered light fields used for evaluation, we use synthetically generated depth maps to discretize the view frustum into froxels. Depth maps for the light field scenes are generated using an addon tool in Blender that is implemented based on the works of Honauer et al. [23].

Using the depth maps and the parameters of the capturing setup, the view frustum is non-uniformly discretized into froxels. Once the froxels are defined, all the rays in the

---

[3] https://jpeg.org/jpegpleno/.
[4] https://mpeg.chiariglione.org/sites/default/files/files/standards/parts/docs/w19212.zip.

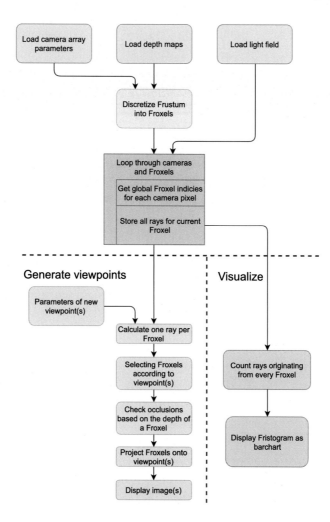

Figure 7.14 Workflow for Fristogram Analysis.

captured light field are assigned to the froxel from which they originate. This provides an alternate representation for the light field, where a direct relation of rays to the capturing setup is achieved. It also provides an insight on the distribution of rays in the scene. Froxels shed light on valuable semantic information that is not available in classical representations, such as

- How densely a froxel of interest is sampled
- How many cameras capture a given scene point
- Origin of rays
- Color distribution of rays in froxels
- Occlusions and dis-occlusions

The data in the froxels can also be used to visualize the ray distribution in the form of fristograms and be leveraged to perform semantically meaningful light field processing. Statistical or learning-based techniques can be applied to deduce material properties, enabling appropriate volumetric filtering and resulting in artifact-free reconstruction. The ray distribution of froxels can also be used to detect and possibly correct inconsistencies in non-perfect depth maps.

Once semantically aware processing is done, the entire light field or new viewpoints can also be generated using the framework. This is done by collecting all the froxels that lie within the frustum of the new view point. In the next step, occlusions are handled by choosing the closest non-empty froxel to the camera. Finally, the froxels are projected onto a camera that lies at the location of the new view point.

7.3.3.3 Applications

Relating the rays in the light field to the cameras in the underlying capturing setup in the form of froxels opens up new avenues to intuitively and semantically analyze light fields in a scalable manner. Some of the application areas are discussed in this section.

- **Denoising** is a common post-processing step in light fields. State-of-the-art denoising techniques, such as in [24] exhibit good results with acceptable complexity. A froxel-based representation of light fields simplifies the task of denoising significantly. For parts of the scene that are sampled with sufficient rays, a simple FIR filter or a median filter can be employed to significantly reduce the effects of noise in the reconstructed light field or viewpoint(s), as described in [25].

- **Volumetric filtering** is usually applied on the entire light field without considering material properties and lighting conditions. Using froxels, the material properties of each part of the scene can be inferred by a simple statistical metric or by a simple neural network architecture, as discussed in [26]. The material properties can be leveraged by volumetric filtering algorithms to appropriately filter the light field and minimize reconstruction artifacts.

- **Compression** light field capture using camera arrays generates a large amount of data. The camera array in [16] that consists of 64 full-HD cameras generate up to 70 GBps of data with a frame rate of 40 fps. This data has to be analyzed, stored, processed, and reconstructed in a computationally viable manner. Thus compression plays a vital role in the success of light fields. A froxel-based representation enables an intuitive approach to reduce the size of the light field by analyzing the ray distribution of every froxels. Froxels with a uniform distribution of rays can be inferred as stemming from a Lambertian radiator and can effectively be represented by a single ray. Thus depending on the scene, the light field can be reduced to a significantly small subset of rays, while maintaining the quality of the reconstructed light field or viewpoint(s).

- **5D light fields,** introduced in Section 7.1.4, are sub-framed light field videos that introduces a controlled adjustment of the temporal behavior of the rig using a sync plane. The goal is to optimize the available rays to maximize the information content in the scene. A froxel-based representation is ideally suited to analyze the scene in a transparent and scalable manner. The outcome of such analysis is a spatio-temporal sampling pattern that maximizes the information content of the underlying scene.

7.4. Alternative representations

7.4.1 Neural radiance fields

A seminal contribution to light field representation formats has been introduced by [27] *neural radiance fields.*

Like froxel-based representations, as introduced in Section 7.3.3, neural radiance fields include the notion of volumes: The space (x, y, z, ϕ, θ) is sampled and a color and volume density ($RGB\sigma$) is assigned to each sample. The main innovation compared to all other representations introduced in this chapter is the encoding of information *along the rays*:

- Neural radiance fields sample the volume (rather than the convex hull of the scene). Each sample contains a color and a density. This allows to deduce the effect of transparent objects in the scene: If several rays cross the same volume, but their respective color as seen during rendering differs, then the influence of as well the starting color—the color of the point on the convex hull of the scene as seen from the spatio-angular position of the respective ray—as the contribution of non-empty volumes along the ray can be deduced.
- Consequently the authors in [27] use volume-rendering, rather than z-buffer-rendering. Though this is more complex (see Eq. (7.10)), since it requires accumulating transmittance along a ray, rather than just overwriting volumes behind others, it is able to deal with non-Lambertian radiance and also transparent materials and objects. This has been a major breakthrough in light field representation formats!

$$C(\mathbf{r}) = \int_{l_{near}}^{l_{far}} T(t)\sigma(\mathbf{r}(t))\mathbf{c}(\mathbf{r}(t), \mathbf{d})dl, \quad T(t) = \exp\left(-\int_{l_{near}}^{l} \sigma(\mathbf{r}(s))ds\right). \quad (7.10)$$

A closer look at Eq. (7.10) reveals the advantages, but also the threads to be addressed for neural radiance fields. It describes the expected color of a camera ray ($C(\mathbf{r})$) by the accumulation of all contributing volume elements, considering their densities (σ) and directional color ($\mathbf{c}(\mathbf{r}(t), \mathbf{d})$):

- It is not known apriori whether a volume element contributes to the radiance field or not. Hence, other than in representations that relate to captured or displayed rays, the set of contributing volume elements is not known. Therefore clever strategies for *importance sampling* are required.

- The number of contributing elements is extremely large: While for *Fourier disparity layers* (Section 7.2) the number is proportional to the number of anchor views and the number of disparity layers, and for *Fristograms* (Section 7.3.3) proportional to the number of camera views and the number of discriminable disparities, neural radiance fields require the representation of as many volume elements as contribute to the final image. This number can by far exceed the number of captured rays. Hence a significant reduction in dimensionality is needed.

To solve the first thread, the authors propose stratified sampling, which is fixing the number of sampled volume elements along a ray, but allowing for positional variance. Stratified sampling quantizes the relevant volume (from l_{near} to l_{far} in Eq. (7.10)) into N evenly-spaced bins, and then draws a single random position from within each bin. This reduces the number of volume elements to N times the number of rays. For rendering, Eq. (7.10) is then available in discrete form and can be simplified, as given in Eq. (7.11).

$$\hat{C}(\mathbf{r}) = \sum_{i=1}^{N} T_i(1 - \exp(-\sigma_i \delta_i))\mathbf{c}_i, \quad T_i = \exp\left(-\sum_{j=1}^{i-1} \sigma_j \delta_j\right). \tag{7.11}$$

The second thread is addressed by the way the authors *create* neural radiance fields and is the name giver. Fig. 7.15 shows that the input to the generator is a set of five dimensional rays: In addition to the four dimensions used in any of the described light field representations, same as for froxel-based representations (Section 7.3), the starting point of the rays is given. For synthetic scenes this is readily available, for real scenes, the authors use a structure-from-motion algorithm (COLMAP, [28]), so that all camera extrinsics and intrinsics as well as the ray sets are given.

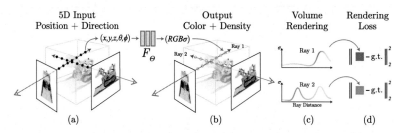

Figure 7.15 *Neural Radiance Fields, from [27].* Pipeline for the Generation and Application of Neural Radiance Fields: Sampling with 5D coordinates (a), Mapping to RGBσ (b), Compositing by accumulating the colors along the rays (c), and Training by comparison to ground truth at known locations (d).

Hence as for all light fields discussed in this chapter, the input is a set of colors (rays) assigned to a position in space and a direction. This is fed into a multilayer perceptron

(MLP), aka a neural network. The network has eight fully connected layers with 256 channels, and hence outputs the volume density σ as a 256-dimensional feature vector. This is then concatenated with the viewing direction (bear in mind that σ is direction-independent) and passed to an output layer with 128 channels to produce the view-dependent RGB color.

The training of the network needs to be done for every scene and in case of light field video for every frame. In the original paper, the authors claim training needs 1–2 GPU-days. Hence neural radiance fields are a very interesting high-quality representation of light fields, and the representation itself is very efficient (input is 100 views with a resolution of $800 \cdot 800$ pixel each, but the network does only have ≈ 615.000 parameters, and hence roughly the number of rays per single view), but transforming a captured light field into NeRF can take very long. Nevertheless, neural radiance fields opened an entire new research field on representations of light fields, and therefore are a very important contribution to light field representation formats.

7.4.1.1 Positional encoding

Besides the sampling strategy and network architecture, neural radiance fields need to be modified to properly represent high-frequency textures. Training of the network without modification due to the large reduction in dimensionality leads to a representation favoring low-resolution textures. Fig. 7.16(d) illustrates that the network tends to lose fine details. Since this is mostly due to the fact that a single position is queried, and the network traces and averages all available volumes along the given position, the network needs to collect information about the effect of positional variations.

$$\gamma(p) = \left(\sin(2^0 \pi p), \cos(2^0 \pi p), \ldots, \sin(2^{L-1} \pi p), \cos(2^{L-1} \pi p) \right). \tag{7.12}$$

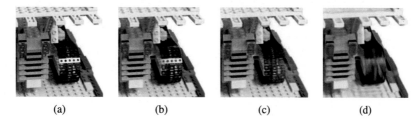

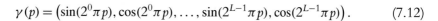

Figure 7.16 *Modifications of NeRF to Optimize Textures, from [27].* A synthesized view of the lego dataset with ground truth (a), the complete NeRF model as introduced in [27] (b), without view dependence of the radiation (c), and without positional encoding (d).

Positional encoding maps the input coordinates $\gamma(\mathbf{x})$ and $\gamma(\mathbf{d})$ to a higher dimensional space, as given in Eq. (7.12). De-facto, this means, for any queried 5D coordinate, the query contains $2L$ coordinate variations, and hence the network learns colors at very many different positions. In [27] the authors propose $L = 10$ for the spatial and $L = 4$ for the angular coordinates. To make the function applicable, space and direction are represented in three dimensions, normalized to $[-1, 1]$, and hence the input of the network has $3 \cdot 20 + 3 \cdot 8 = 84$ elements. Sixty (60) are fed into the input layer, twenty-four (24) are concatenated to the last layer.

References

[1] P. Didyk, T. Ritschel, E. Eisemann, K. Myszkowski, H.-P. Seidel, A perceptual model for disparity, ACM Transactions on Graphics (TOG) 30 (4) (2011) 1–10.

[2] A. Cserkaszky, P.A. Kara, R.R. Tamboli, A. Barsi, M.G. Martini, L. Bokor, T. Balogh, Angularly continuous light-field format: concept, implementation, and evaluation, Journal of the Society for Information Display 27 (7) (2019) 442–461.

[3] P.T. Kovács, R. Bregović, A. Boev, A. Barsi, A. Gotchev, Quantifying spatial and angular resolution of light-field 3-D displays, IEEE Journal of Selected Topics in Signal Processing 11 (7) (2017) 1213–1222.

[4] R. Ng, Fourier slice photography, ACM Transactions on Graphics 24 (3) (2005) 735–744.

[5] R.N. Bracewell, Strip integration in radio astronomy, Australian Journal of Physics 9 (1956) 198–217.

[6] M. Le Pendu, C. Guillemot, A. Smolic, A Fourier disparity layer representation for light fields, IEEE Transactions on Image Processing 28 (11) (2019) 5740–5753.

[7] M. Le Pendu, A. Smolic, High resolution light field recovery with Fourier disparity layer completion, demosaicing, and super-resolution, in: 2020 IEEE International Conference on Computational Photography (ICCP), 2020, pp. 1–12.

[8] E. Dib, M. Le Pendu, C. Guillemot, Light field compression using Fourier disparity layers, in: IEEE International Conference on Image Processing, 2019, pp. 3751–3755.

[9] M. Le Pendu, C. Ozcinar, A. Smolic, Hierarchical Fourier disparity layer transmission for light field streaming, in: IEEE International Conference on Image Processing, 2020, pp. 2606–2610.

[10] Z. Xiao, M. Eng Zhang, H. Jin, C. Guillemot, A light field FDL-HSIFT feature in scale-disparity space, in: IEEE International Conference on Image Processing, Anchorage, United States, 2021, pp. 1–5.

[11] A. Gill, M. Le Pendu, M. Alain, E. Zerman, A. Smolic, Light field visual attention prediction using Fourier disparity layers, in: International Workshop on Multimedia Signal Processing (MMSP), IEEE, 2021, pp. 1–6.

[12] J. Flynn, M. Broxton, P. Debevec, M. DuVall, G. Fyffe, R. Overbeck, N. Snavely, R. Tucker, DeepView: View synthesis with learned gradient descent, in: Proceedings of the IEEE/CVF Conference on Computer Vision and Pattern Recognition, 2019, pp. 2367–2376.

[13] B. Mildenhall, P.P. Srinivasan, R. Ortiz-Cayon, N.K. Kalantari, R. Ramamoorthi, R. Ng, A. Kar, Local light field fusion: Practical view synthesis with prescriptive sampling guidelines, ACM Transactions on Graphics (TOG) 38 (4) (2019) 1–14.

[14] M. Broxton, J. Flynn, R. Overbeck, D. Erickson, P. Hedman, M. Duvall, J. Dourgarian, J. Busch, M. Whalen, P. Debevec, Immersive light field video with a layered mesh representation, ACM Transactions on Graphics (TOG) 39 (4) (2020) 86, 15pp.

[15] D.G. Dansereau, O. Pizarro, S.B. Williams, Linear volumetric focus for light field cameras, ACM Transactions on Graphics 34 (2) (2015) 15.

[16] T. Herfet, T. Lange, K. Chelli, 5D light field video capture, in: Proceedings of the 16th ACM SIGGRAPH European Conference on Visual Media Production, 2019.

[17] A. Evans, Learning from failure: a survey of promising, unconventional and mostly abandoned renderers for 'dreams ps4', a geometrically dense, painterly UCG game, advances in Real-Time Rendering course, in: SIGGRAPH, 2015.

[18] A.-A. Vasilakis, K. Vardis, G. Papaioannou, A survey of multifragment rendering, in: Computer Graphics Forum, vol. 39, Wiley Online Library, 2020, pp. 623–642.

[19] G.G. Slabaugh, T. Malzbender, W.B. Culbertson, Volumetric warping for voxel coloring on an infinite domain, in: European Workshop on 3D Structure from Multiple Images of Large-Scale Environments, Springer, 2000, pp. 109–123.

[20] G. Gkioxari, J. Malik, J. Johnson, Mesh R-CNN, in: Proceedings of the IEEE/CVF International Conference on Computer Vision, 2019, pp. 9785–9795.

[21] P. Astola, L.A. da Silva Cruz, E.A. da Silva, T. Ebrahimi, P.G. Freitas, A. Gilles, K.-J. Oh, C. Pagliari, F. Pereira, C. Perra, et al., JPEG Pleno: Standardizing a coding framework and tools for plenoptic imaging modalities, ITU Journal: ICT Discoveries 3 (1) (2020) 1–15.

[22] J.M. Boyce, R. Doré, A. Dziembowski, J. Fleureau, J. Jung, B. Kroon, B. Salahieh, V.K.M. Vadakital, L. Yu, MPEG immersive video coding standard, Proceedings of the IEEE 109 (9) (2021) 1521–1536.

[23] K. Honauer, O. Johannsen, D. Kondermann, B. Goldluecke, A dataset and evaluation methodology for depth estimation on 4D light fields, in: Asian Conference on Computer Vision, Springer, 2016, pp. 19–34.

[24] M. Alain, A. Smolic, Light field denoising by sparse 5D transform domain collaborative filtering, in: IEEE International Workshop on Multimedia Signal Processing (MMSP 2017), 2017, pp. 1–6, https://v-sense.scss.tcd.ie/wp-content/uploads/2017/08/LFBM5D_MMSP_camera_ready-1.pdf.

[25] T. Herfet, K. Chelli, T. Lange, R. Kremer, Fristograms: Revealing and exploiting light field internals, arXiv:2107.10563, 2021.

[26] K. Chelli, R.R. Tamboli, T. Herfet, Deep learning-based semantic analysis of sparse light field ray sets, in: IEEE 23rd International Workshop on Multimedia Signal Processing (IEEE MMSP), 2021, pp. 1–6.

[27] B. Mildenhall, P.P. Srinivasan, M. Tancik, J.T. Barron, R. Ramamoorthi, R. Ng, NeRF: Representing scenes as neural radiance fields for view synthesis, in: European Conference on Computer Vision, Springer, 2020, pp. 405–421.

[28] J.L. Schonberger, J.-M. Frahm, Structure-from-motion revisited, in: Proceedings of the IEEE Conference on Computer Vision and Pattern Recognition, 2016, pp. 4104–4113.

CHAPTER 8

Compression of light fields

Milan Stepanov, Giuseppe Valenzise, and Frédéric Dufaux
Université Paris-Saclay, CNRS, CentraleSupélec, Laboratoire des signaux et systèmes, Gif-sur-Yvette, France

8.1. Introduction

Light fields (LFs) enable increasing the degree of realism and immersion of visual experience by capturing a scene with a higher number of dimensions than conventional two-dimensional (2D) imaging. Chapter 6 describes various means of capturing LFs, from a plenoptic camera to an array of cameras. The captured information offers novel applications, such as refocusing and a perspective change, at the cost of increased dimensionality and thus storage demand. The necessity of efficient compression methods was acknowledged by the JPEG committee, which started the JPEG Pleno initiative to provide a standard framework for the representation and coding of plenoptic data.

JPEG Pleno organized grand challenges to collect novel LF coding solutions and evaluate them under common conditions following object and subjective quality metrics. These challenges showed that it is possible to exploit correlations in LF images more efficiently using solutions specifically designed to reduce redundancies in LF structure compared to standard image and video codecs.

In the following sections, we will overview different coding solutions for the compression of LF contents. We adopt a classification of LF coding solutions based on a functional part of a codec that is responsible for exploiting LF correlation: transform-based and prediction-based solutions, as presented in Fig. 8.1. Three different transforms are considered in the former group of methods and various prediction-based methodologies based on the type of correlation they are trying to exploit. We mention some promising coding solutions leveraging high modeling capabilities of deep learning methods, and describe the standard coding framework proposed by JPEG Pleno. The chapter is concluded with a discussion on favorable coding methodologies and future prospects.

8.2. Transform-based methods

Transform-based coding tools propose to exploit correlation in LF images using some transformation. In particular, these methods decompose the input vector by representing it as a combination of some basis functions that effectively compact the energy of the input. Some of the transforms proposed in the literature include discrete cosine transform (DCT), discrete wavelet transform (DWT), and Karhunen Loève transform

Immersive Video Technologies
https://doi.org/10.1016/B978-0-32-391755-1.00014-6

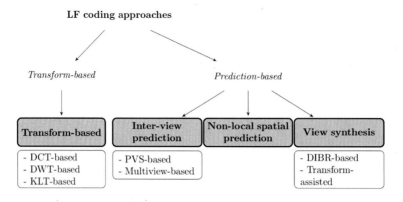

Figure 8.1 Classification of LF coding solutions (inspired by the taxonomy presented in [1]).

(KLT). The initial solution for LF compression proposed to extend transform-oriented image are coding tools, such as JPEG and JPEG2000. These methods are based on DCT and DWT, which rely on fixed basis functions to compute transform coefficients and obtain more compact representations of the input signal. On the other side, KLT computes basis functions for each content, allowing better modeling of input data, but in addition to obtained coefficients, it also needs to transmit basis functions. Unlike image data, LFs present four-dimensional (4D) signals; therefore higher dimensional transformations are typically employed for improved performance, e.g., three–dimensional (3D) or 4D.

8.2.1 Approaches based on DCT

DCT is well known for its application in image coding as it provides a compact representation of the original signal. The frequency representation has most of its energy compacted in a few bands, allowing it to discard high-frequency information efficiently. The deployment of the transform in the standard image codec JPEG demonstrates its utility.

Given the success of JPEG for image coding, some methods propose to extend JPEG functionalities for LF coding. As the micro-lens array (MLA)-view representation (see Chapter 6) facilitates grid-like structure, a natural way of encoding it is to apply DCT on each micro-image (MI), followed by quantization and entropy coding. However, this way, only correlations inside each MI are exploited. Nevertheless, similarities between neighboring MIs can be exploited by creating a volume of MIs and applying 3D-DCT. E.g., [2] studied the impact of 2D scanning patterns that generate the volumes of MIs on coding performance. Following a scanning pattern illustrated in Fig. 8.2, in this study, MIs are organized in a one-dimensional (1D) vector, and a 3D-DCT is applied on blocks of 8 MIs. Among scanning patterns, the 2D Hilbert, shown in Fig. 8.2,

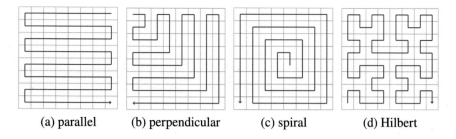

(a) parallel   (b) perpendicular   (c) spiral   (d) Hilbert

Figure 8.2 2D scanning patterns. The individual blocks can be considered as MIs or SAIs.

shows the most promise, suggesting the importance of selecting MIs in such a way that the correlation between MIs inside each 3D block is maximized. At the same time, all schemes show superior performance compared to the JPEG codec confirming higher efficacy in exploiting redundancy in neighboring MIs using the higher-order transform.

The previous coding strategy is sub-optimal when coding 4D LF structure, as it depends on a particular scanning order to exploit the correlation between MIs. Therefore in [3] is proposed to match LF dimensionality by employing 4D-DCT to decorrelate underlying information. After quantization, the coefficients are processed on a bitplane level by grouping zero-valued coefficients using hexadeca-tree clustering. The clustering presents an alternative 4D variant of encoding position of zero coefficients to run-length coding used in the JPEG codec.

8.2.2 Approaches based on KLT

KLT is a data-dependent transformation, which computes transformation coefficients and the basis functions of the transformation for a given input [4]. Thus it is more flexible in adapting to the content than a transformation with fixed basis functions, such as DCT. Typically basis functions are computed by Eigen decomposition or singular value decomposition of the covariance matrix of the underlying data. KLT shows great potential from a compression perspective as it adapts to the input content. On the other hand, the need to transmit both coefficients and basis functions presents a limiting factor, especially in the cases of non-stationary data.

KLT has been proposed for the compression of LF images with the basis functions computed on MIs [5] or sub-aperture images (SAI) [6]. The SAIs are extracted by selecting co-located pixels for every MI. To provide better modeling of MIs, [5] propose clustering MIs using vector quantization and computing and assigning KLT basis vectors to each cluster.

In the KLT coding scheme operating on MIs, [5] experiments show that increasing the number of clusters improves overall performance. Compared to the coding scheme operating on SAIs, the former shows inferior performance as more eigenvectors are needed to obtain similar reconstruction quality. The superior performance of the latter scheme is likely contributed to a higher correlation among SAIs compared to the scheme based on MIs. Each MI captures only a small part of a scene and has different features in different parts of the scene. On the other side, SAIs contain the whole scene and differ slightly due to a change of perspective. Compared to the JPEG codec, both schemes perform better.

8.2.3 Approaches based on DWT

DWT is an alternative to the formerly presented block-based transformations. It iteratively computes low-pass and high-pass representations of an input signal. The final output is a multi-resolution representation of the input signal. As such, it offers resolution scalability as well as quality scalability.

The straightforward application of DWT to LF image compression is via wavelet-based, image-coding tools, e.g., JPEG2000. This strategy is adopted for the coding of LF images captured by a plenoptic camera [7,8]. JPEG2000 shows superior performance when compared to, e.g., legacy JPEG and SPIHT codec [7], or JPEGXR [8]. However, standard image coding tools are not suited to efficiently exploit correlation in the LFs, and a reasonable step would be to use a higher-dimensional transformation, e.g., 4D-DWT. To this end, a separable 1D-DWT is sequentially applied along spatial and angular dimensions resulting in a 4D array of wavelet coefficients and a multi-resolution representation of the LF. The multi-resolution representation allows to reconstruct the LF progressively: low-resolution SAIs can be reconstructed from low-frequency wavelet coefficients. Then, by including high-frequency coefficients, better quality and higher resolution can be achieved. Thanks to this approach, it is possible to trade off rendering speed and quality to meet application demands. Nevertheless, quantitative analysis in terms of peak signal-to-noise ratio (PSNR) shows that this method is inferior to a disparity-compensation based method [9], which suggests that disparity-compensation allows better correction of inter-view differences.

A method called the lifting scheme [10] is proposed as way to facilitate the disparity compensation in wavelet transform across views [11]. The lifting scheme is presented in Fig. 8.3. Given a set of views, two separate sets of even and odd views are created. The high-pass sub-band is obtained in the predict stage by subtracting an odd view from the disparity-compensated even view. The obtained residual is also disparity-compensated to align with the even view and added to it to obtain a low-pass sub-band. This procedure takes advantage of inter-view correlation, and it is followed by an additional step, whereas each sub-band image is processed using a multi-level 2D DWT to take advantage of the remaining intra-view correlations. In the case of full-parallax LFs, i.e., LFs comprised of horizontally and vertically displaced views, the inter-view transformation is carried out by applying the lifting scheme horizontally and vertically across the 2D view grid.

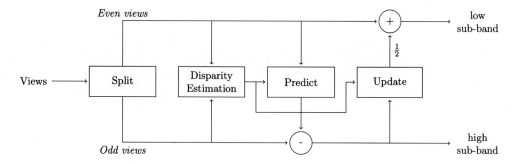

Figure 8.3 Disparity-compensated lifting scheme (redrawn from [12]).

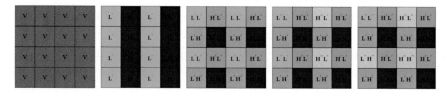

Figure 8.4 Inter-view decomposition carried on horizontal and vertical views alternately. **L** and **H** denote low-pass and high-pass sub-bands, whereas ′ denotes the decomposition level.

In the case of narrow-baseline LFs, e.g., LFs captured by a plenoptic camera, a disparity compensation based on a perspective transformation can be used [12]. In this scenario, it has been shown that among different orders of carrying 1D inter-view transformation, a two-level decomposition applied alternately in horizontal and vertical directions is superior. The 2D inter-view is presented in Fig. 8.4, where a 4×4 LF is shown in the left-most part, whereas each following part shows the decomposition result of the lifting scheme applied alternately to rows and columns of the LF.

As a more sophisticated version of the lifting scheme, [13] propose a hierarchical inter-view transform. It operates in two predict–update steps. First, views are divided in three cosets: corner coset v_c, comprised of views at $(2m, 2n)$ locations; middle coset v_m, comprised of views at $(2m + 1, 2n + 1)$ locations; and perimeter coset v_p, containing views at $(2m, 2n + 1)$ and $(2m + 1, 2n)$ locations. In the first lifting step, views v_p are used to predict views from v_m and the prediction is subtracted from original views v_m, resulting in high-pass sub-band h_m:

$$h_m = \sum_{v_p \in P} \alpha_{p \to m} \cdot W_{p \to m}(v_p), \tag{8.1}$$

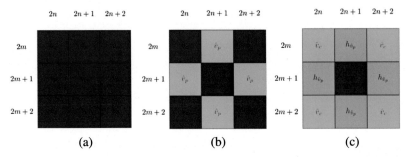

Figure 8.5 Inter-view 2-step lifting scheme: input views (a), coefficients after first predict-update step (b), and the final coefficients after the second step (c). Inspired by [13].

where P is a set of closest perimeter neighbors of a view v_m, as illustrated in Fig. 8.5, and $W_{p \to m}$ is a warping operation that aligns each view at positions p with the views at position m. Low-pass sub-band views $\hat{v}_p$ are computed in similar manner by adding warped high-pass sub-bands to the perimeter views. Then, the residual h_m is added to v_p and low-pass sub-band $\hat{v}_p$ is obtained. The second lifting step is carried out similarly to the previous step among corner views v_c, and low-pass sub-band perimeter views $\hat{v}_p$. High-pass sub-band views $h_{\hat{v}_p}$ are obtained at perimeter view locations by subtracting the low-pass sub-band prediction. Note that there are only two neighboring corner views participating in the prediction of each perimeter view in this case. Finally, the residual signal $h_{\hat{v}_p}$ is added to the corner view to obtain the final low-pass sub-band $\hat{v}_c$. Each sub-band view is afterward encoded using JPEG2000. The procedure is repeated on the final low-pass sub-bands. A hierarchical lifting scheme supported by accurate disparity information proves to be a highly competitive methodology to state-of-the-art methods [13].

8.2.4 Summary

Transform-based methods provide a representation of the input signal, which allows exploiting existing correlation by effectively compacting the energy of the signal in a small range of frequencies. In general, transform-based methods, specifically designed for compression of LF images, outperform image-based codecs, such as JPEG and JPEG2000. Furthermore, 4D transforms proved the most suitable for LF compression as they exploit the intrinsic correlation in a superior manner leading to improved rate-distortion (RD) performance. Namely, LF coding scheme based on 4D-DCT [3] shows superior performance compared to more sophisticated anchors, such as high efficiency video coding (HEVC) applied on an LF arranged in a pseudo–video sequence (PVS). Still, these results stand only for lenslet data, i.e., data captured with a plenoptic camera, with a high correlation between views. On the other hand, 4D-DWT-based methods that leverage disparity compensation to exploit the correlation between views provide improved performance on more challenging data, captured by gantry [13]. In addition, methods based on 4D-DWT offer various scalability levels: quality, viewpoint, and resolution scalability.

8.3. Prediction-based methods

In contrast to transform-based solutions, prediction-based approaches rely on a prediction mechanism that approximates the input signal, which effectively reduces redundancy. Three broad groups of approaches were proposed based on the representation of the input signal and the methodology used to provide an estimate: approaches based on inter-view prediction, non-local spatial prediction, and view synthesis [1].

8.3.1 Inter-view prediction

Inter-view prediction methods refer to approaches that rely on video coding tools to facilitate prediction between views in an LF image. Before coding, an input LF image is converted to a representation acceptable by a video codec. Two representations can be noted, depending on the used video codec. In a PVS representation, an LF image views are picked in a particular scanning order along the 2D view grid and stacked along with the new ("time") dimension. Practically, the views become the frames of the created video sequence and can be processed by, e.g., the HEVC codec. In a multi-view representation, one of the angular dimensions is considered the time dimension. Then, multi-view extensions of standard coding tools, such as advanced video coding (AVC) and HEVC, can be leveraged to exploit correlations along with spatial, inter-view, and pseudo temporal directions.

Over the years, numerous studies have been conducted to evaluate different LF coding pipelines. These studies included contents captured with different systems, testing conditions, and leveraged video coding tools of different generations, which makes getting a universal conclusion on the optimal configuration of the coding system challenging. Nevertheless, partial conclusions and some good practices can be noted.

For lenslet contents, raster and spiral patterns result in a very similar performance, while close behavior is also noticeable when using parallel, raster, or zig-zag patterns [14,15]. Nevertheless, some uncommon coding schemes have shown better performance [15]. These schemes are motivated to reduce the distance between neighboring views to provide similar reference views and improve prediction. Dividing an array of SAIs into different segments before scanning them effectively reduces the distance [16] between scanned views. However, these scanning patterns are fixed and do not consider the content of LF images. The scanning order can be driven by a similarity metric to adaptively decide on the ordering of view into the PVS [17]. A more sophisticated scheme, presented by Imaede et al. [18] searches for an optimal selection order driven by maximization of smoothness between neighboring frames. More precisely, the sum of absolute differences between every pair of views is computed, and the shortest route traversing through all the views is obtained by solving traveling salesman problem. Note, these methods provide a particular scanning order, which needs to be sent to the decoder.

Besides only considering the relations between neighboring frames, the construction of a reference frame list plays a considerable role in the overall performance of PVS-based methods. Namely, the scanning order does not explicitly consider the proximity of views in a reference list; instead, it follows a predefined prediction structure. In [19], it is proposed to set reference frames based on their distance to a current frame. This way, the closer views are used as reference views, and redundancies can be reduced further with experiments reporting on average 36% improvement in terms of bitrate with this addition. Moreover, with the introduction of a distance-driven reference list, the scanning order can be of importance as, e.g., spiral order is evaluated superior to serpentine order [19]. The drawback is extra memory demand to keep all the reference views instead of a small set of reference views. Moreover, it is necessary to provide additional signaling for the type of the scanning order and computational resources to compute optimized reference lists.

Another vital point to consider in PVS-based methods is a coding configuration. E.g., depending on application requirements, a random-access profile or low–delay–P/B profile can be selected. Some results show that random-access and low–delay–B show similar performance on lenslet data in terms of bitrate performance, though the variations might be attributed to content differences. However, in general, low–delay–B tends to offer slightly better performance at very low rates, whereas random-access offers improvements as rates increase [14]. Instead of a fixed scanning order and a fixed coding profile, a hierarchical order can be adopted. E.g., in [20], the central view is selected at the lowest level (coded as I-frame), whereas the rest of the views are organized in hierarchical layers (and coded as P-frames and B-frames).

In addition, a hierarchical scheme can be complemented with a rate allocation methodology, which allows the views used as references to have higher quality than the frames not used as references. E.g., I-frames should have the lowest quantization parameter (QP) as it will serve as a reference for many views, whereas views deeper in the hierarchy can have higher QPs. This dynamic bit allocation reports gains compared to the scenario with constant QP applied across hierarchical levels [20].

Another feature of the hierarchical scheme is possible viewpoint scalability and random-access. The scalability allows support for legacy capturing devices, 2D and 3D/stereo, lenslet, and hight density camera array (HDCA). Also, progressive decoding of each layer would provide higher angular resolution as more layers are decoded. Each hierarchical layer is encoded sequentially, while relying on previously decoded layers and decoded views from the current layer for prediction. Random-access would improve LF navigation efficiency and reduce computational complexity and the decoding time as fewer views need to be processed, but coding efficiency would degrade.

PVS-based schemes present great potential as LF coding tools, and some frameworks have shown impressive performance [19]. However, these methods can exploit correlations in LF images only to some degree as the generation of the PVS disrupts the natural structure, and the codec employs tools originally designed for video signals. Multi-view extensions have been seen as alternatives to standard video codecs, which can exploit inter-view correlation more efficiently. Recently, the multi-view extension of HEVC (MV-HEVC) has been used to compress LF images. In this case, the LF views are classified according to their position in the 2D grid. Views belonging to each row are considered consecutive frames of (pseudo) video captured by cameras located along the first column of views. Similar to PVS-based schemes, prediction orders and rate allocation schemes can be considered to improve performance. Per results by Ahmad et al. [21], MV-HEVC is superior to PVS-based coding on lenslet data, and especially at low rates. A nice feature of these schemes is that they can operate as generic codecs as they do not depend on geometry information and can be applied to both lenslet and HDCA contents.

Video coding-based schemes can be applied to dynamic contents as well. PVSs can be generated at each time instant and merged into the final sequence. Fecker et al. introduce this idea as a transpose picture ordering, though originally for horizontal-direction only LFs [22]. Similarly, all views can be arranged in a 1D array and provided to an MV-HEVC, which can exploit intra-view, inter-view, and temporal correlations.

8.3.2 Non-local spatial prediction

Non-local spatial prediction aims at exploiting similarities in MLA-view. Regardless of the structure of MLA and the design of the optical system, captured MIs exhibit positional correlation as it stores both spatial and angular information on a 2D plane. In the case of the Plenoptic 1.0 camera, each MI samples dense directional light ray information at a single spatial point, whereas in the case of the Plenoptic 2.0 camera, MLA acts as an array of micro-cameras, wherein each micro-camera captures dense spatial information, see Chapter 6. In both cases, besides the highly correlated content inside each MI, neighboring MIs also exhibit a high similarity level due to microlenses' proximity. Non-local spatial prediction drives inspiration from inter-prediction, which exploits the temporal correlation between frames to obtain a motion-compensated prediction for blocks in the current frame. However, as MIs are interleaved on a 2D grid and thus present a 2D image, instead of motion vectors searched across decoded frames, spatial displacement is considered. A similar methodology was proposed in the HEVC extension for screen content coding in the form of a prediction mode, called intra-block copy [23].

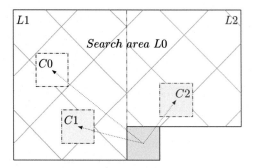

Figure 8.6 Self-similarity prediction. Similarly to motion estimation and compensation in inter-view prediction: block-based matching carries search in a causal, spatial neighborhood. The gray block denotes current block to be coded. *L0* and *C0* denote the search area and a candidate in a native SS method, while the search area *L1* with a candidate *C1* denoted in blue and the search area *L2* with a candidate *C2* denoted in red depict the prediction mode with two independent reference lists. Inspired by [1,24].

For LF compression, standard codecs AVC and HEVC were modified to facilitate MI prediction using the so-called self-similarity (SS) estimation and SS compensation blocks. SS estimation module uses block matching in an area of already processed MIs, i.e., (the whole) causal (picture) area, to find the best match for prediction of the current MI. The idea is illustrated in Fig. 8.6, whereas the SS estimation algorithm searches for the best candidate to match the current coding block (the gray block). Initial experiments show that the addition of SS mode to AVC can improve RD performance and that, for some contents, the new mode gets selected in more than 50% of the time [25]. Instead of a single prediction candidate, multiple prediction candidates can be combined to obtain the final prediction. The idea is illustrated in Fig. 8.6, whereas the search area is divided into two parts, each of which facilitates a list of references, from which the best prediction candidate is obtained. The third prediction candidate is computed as an average between the previous two prediction candidates [24]. Similarly, it has been argued that a bi-directional prediction, where two predictor candidates can be selected from a single search area, can be beneficial when the two best candidates appear close to each other [26]. As an alternative, neighboring blocks can be fixed as prediction candidates instead of searching for a displacement of the best prediction candidates and used in a weighted sum to predict the current block. Jin et al. [27] propose to compute the weights by solving an optimization problem that minimizes the Euclidean distance between the prediction and the current block. A standard displacement-driven template-matching mechanism can also be replaced by high-order prediction models [28]. As MIs capture contents from slightly different perspectives, geometric transforms can be used to model relations between MIs. Compared to two degrees of freedom offered by spatially displaced vectors, the perspective transform can offer up to 8 degrees of freedom.

Most non-local spatial methods propose new prediction methodologies to estimate MI relations. Instead, Jin et al. [29] consider an orthogonal direction, whereas the MI representation itself is transformed into a more coding-friendly version, allowing more efficient employment of already available prediction tools. The processing includes MI alignment, which rearranges MIs such that each MI falls in a separate block on a coding unit grid, interpolation that inpaints missing intensities between aligned MIs, and inverse reshaping that allows to inverse previous operations. Quantitative analysis in terms of Bjøntegaard delta-rate (BD-Rate) shows improved performance of AVC, HEVC, and especially HEVC with SS prediction modes when the reshaping is applied compared to the scenario with the original input.

SS methods offer great potential for compression of contents captured by a plenoptic camera and, in general, show improved performance compared to intra coding. Moreover, as they rely on prediction tools from standard video codecs, they can be extended to plenoptic video sequences by allowing inter coding. However, when compared to other prediction-based coding tools, these methods are generally inferior [19,30].

8.3.3 View synthesis-based prediction

LF schemes based on view synthesis aim at exploiting high inter-view similarity by relying on scene geometry. Typically, a sparse set of reference views and corresponding geometry information is encoded and transmitted, and at the decoder side, the rest of the LF views are reconstructed using transmitted information. In the literature, two distinctive groups of approaches based on view synthesis are presented: depth image based rendering (DIBR) and transform-assisted synthesis.

Disparity compensation proved to be a potent tool in LF coding scheme. Besides radically reducing the number of references and still achieving high-quality prediction, it also offers some scalability in the coding framework. Moreover, it applies to both MI and SAI representation allowing to adapt to a desired scenario.

A scalable coding scheme is of high interest, especially in LFs with many views. Namely, instead of transmitting an entire LF image which would introduce latency, waste of network resources, and increased complexity, a level-wise solution can be adopted to encode/decode the LF progressively. Li et al. [31] subsamples the LF image captured by a focused plenoptic camera by selecting every s-th MI and encodes the subsampled version using a non-local spatial prediction scheme. The rest of the LF image can be predicted at the next layer based on the decoded LF image and estimated disparity maps used to warp the decoded part. As these two layers allow to recover the whole LF image gradually, they provide resolution scalability to the scheme. The decoded and the predicted parts can be added to the reference picture list and allow inter-prediction (and better modeling of the information at the second layer). Therefore the final stage offers quality scalability. Similarly, the hierarchical scheme can be applied to SAIs as well. Moreover, this variant can even provide a more generalized solution with respect to the supported range of disparities; in LFs captured with plenoptic cameras, SAIs have a very small disparity, whereas in the case of HDCA, disparities are larger between views [32]. One implementation could divide views into hierarchical levels with textures and its disparity maps of the lowest hierarchical level being encoded independently, while the rest of the views are processed using warping and merging of warped views. Particular views and their disparity maps from previous hierarchical levels are needed to predict a view at some hierarchical level. The potential of this pipeline has been acknowledged with the adoption in the JPEG Pleno standard.

In addition, a standard coding tool shows great prospects in LF coding solutions. Initially, the 3D extension of HEVC (3D-HEVC) has been proposed to compress the video–plus–depth format more efficiently. For the LF compression, Huang et al. [33] propose a multi–view plus depth architecture based on the 3D-HEVC. Columns of views are organized in video sequences, and computed depth maps are assigned to these sequences. Columns are sampled in a uniform step to select the reference set of views that is encoded using 3D-HEVC. The rest of the columns are synthesized using the DIBR technique. Compared to the PVS-based anchor, the 3D-HEVC-based codec shows superior performance, reporting gains from 55% to almost 70% in terms of BD-rate on contents captured with a plenoptic camera. An important characteristic of schemes relying on depth information is the sensitivity to the quality and the arrangement of depth maps. Namely, 3D-HEVC does not make any assumptions on the arrangement of views, however, it is the most efficient when the views are aligned in 1D or coplanar arrangement.

As an alternative to DIBR-based approaches, transform-assisted approaches exploit sparseness in Fourier domain. In these approaches, the spectrum of the entire LF is recovered from a subset of initial samples. Differently compared to the transform methods presented in Section 8.2, where the entire LF is transformed in a sparser representation and encoded, a sparse representation is recovered from a limited set of samples. It is assumed that LFs have a sparse representation in the angular domain so that the entire LF can be recovered from a limited set of views.

[34] presents an iterative, hierarchical scheme for compression of LF images based on Fourier disparity layers (FDL). An initial set of reference views is encoded using the HEVC codec by arranging views in a PVS. Then, following the decoding, reference views are used to construct the FDL model. The construction of the FDL model starts with the calibration phase, which estimates the angular positions of the input views and the set of disparities for which FDL will be constructed. Then, coefficients of the FDL model can be computed and used to predict the remaining views. In the next step, a scaling factor that provides a global refinement of predicted views is computed, and the final prediction is subtracted from the original views to generate the residual signal.

The obtained residual signal is encoded and transmitted to the decoder side. Depending on the configuration, the remaining views could be the rest of the LF or only a subset. Compared to DIBR- and PVS-based state-of-the-art methods, the proposed scheme shows superior performance in terms of BD-rate and achieves more than 50% bitrate savings.

[35] proposes a coding approach based on Shearlet transform (ST). In ST, each epipolar plane image (EPI) is transformed in the Fourier domain and filtered using a set of passband filters designed to remove aliased components in the frequency domain. The proposed scheme starts by decimating an input $N \times M$ LF image along both angular dimensions and organizing the remaining views in a multi-view PVS, which results in M sequences N frames long. The sequences are encoded using MV-HEVC. Decoded sequences are then used to predict decimated views using a reconstruction algorithm based on ST. The coding approach improves BD metrics performance only at low rates compared to HEVC, where all views are arranged in a PVS and MV-HEVC. At higher rates, the performance of the proposed scheme saturate, and it is proposed that the residual signal of the predicted, decimated views is encoded using MV-HEVC operating in intra-prediction mode.

In [36] a solution based on a graph learning approach is proposed to estimate the disparity between the views in LF. Graph learning is used to model the relation between views based on the observation of strong smoothness between neighboring views in an LF image. Each view is considered a vertex in the graph, and the edges that model the relations between views/vertices are learned from underlying data. The graph is encoded in a lossless manner and transmitted with a set of reference views. The remaining views are reconstructed at the decoder by solving an optimization problem. There are few benefits of this proposed scheme. The graph is learned for each content allowing to adapt to features of different contents. It is computed independently from view selection and compression, which provides high flexibility in selecting the reference views and the applied compression scheme. Furthermore, the independent processing allows for an optimal selection of the reference views, which minimizes the overall quality of the reconstructed LF.

8.3.4 Summary

Predictive coding methods use an approximation of the input signal to reduce correlation in the signal effectively. Among prediction-based methods, schemes leveraging video coding tools' rich and powerful apparatus appeared to be extremely popular. Their versatility and efficiency, coupled with various ways of capturing and representing LF data, offered a massive spectrum of possibilities. Clearly, schemes based on the recent video coding standard, such as HEVC, show high competitiveness. Moreover, multi-view-based coding solutions show state-of-the-art results in recent studies and are highly attractive, as they could be easily extended for a video scenario. Methodologies based on non-local spatial prediction extend standard video coding tools to exploit the intrinsic structure of MI representation. Motion estimation and compensation are leveraged for prediction in the domain of interleaved angular and spatial information and showed improved performance compared to standard image-based coding tools. Finally, view synthesis-based LF compression methodologies have recently received much interest. They rely on the transmission of a sparse set of input views, efficient off-the-shelf coding tools, and the ability to generate a high-quality approximation of the input signal, offering superior RD performance, especially at low bitrates.

Among different prediction methods, it has been reported that the SS-based LF image compression methods cannot achieve comparable performance with the PVS-based methods due to their inflexibility to exploit the correlations among various views, especially in the low bitrate case [19,37]. Comparing PVS-based methods to view synthesis-based approaches in a generalized manner is challenging due to different conditions and limited experiments. Typically, view synthesis methods are compared to native PVS-based methodology and report significant gains, yet, the following works based on PVS show significant improvements. Nevertheless, view synthesis-based approaches show great potential, especially at low rates, as only a few views are transmitted and used to recover the rest of the LF.

PVS-based approaches work well on both lenslet and HDCA contents. Although exploiting HDCA content correlation is more challenging, PVS schemes still perform robustly. This behavior is different compared to, e.g., some transform-based methods (Section 8.2), where performance deteriorates considerably.

8.4. JPEG Pleno

In 2015 the JPEG Committee launched an initiative to explore new immersive imaging modalities [38]. JPEG Pleno is a standardization project within the ISO/IEC JTC 1/ SC 29/WG 1 JPEG Committee. The project is motivated by the committee's vision following the increasing presence of novel immersive technologies. New acquisition technologies capture depth-enhanced, omnidirectional and LF, point cloud, and holographic contents, characterized by richer cues. Moreover, this data introduced novel applications and visualization, which were difficult or impossible to achieve with traditional imagery. As a result, a new processing pipeline emerged, including new variables, such as rendering and interactivity that need to be considered in addition to efficient decoding for the wide adoption of the novel technologies and applications they bring. JPEG Pleno proposes unifying all these technologies by starting from the origin of all these technologies, the light, and the model that describes underlying information, the plenoptic function. Revolving around these ideas, JPEG Pleno aims at deriving a representation framework that provides, in addition to efficient coding tools, support to advanced methodologies for image manipulation, interactivity, random-access, and others supporting emerging applications and services [39].

JPEG Pleno initiative organized two LF coding challenges [40,41] to collect the best available solutions at the time. Proposed solutions are evaluated and compared under the same testing conditions, which are also distributed to encourage further benchmarking of state-of-the-art methods. Perceptual quality was considered the most important criterion when choosing the best solutions.

The first grand challenge was organized at the IEEE International Conference on Image on Multimedia and Expo (ICME) in 2016. It asked for efficient LF compression solutions as alternatives to existing JPEG standards for content captured by the unfocused plenoptic camera. Quantitative performance analysis of the collected solutions showed that it is possible to do much better compared to JPEG anchor by designing schemes that consider LF nature effectively [37].

The second grand challenge was organized at the IEEE International Conference on Image Processing (ICIP) in 2017. In addition to LF solutions for coding the plenoptic content, participants are invited to provide solutions for contents captured by HDCAs. The overall results of the challenge demonstrate that there is much to gain compared to the direct application of video coding tools by designing a methodology that considers LFs structure [30].

It is worth noting that both benchmarks, ICME 2016 Grand Challenge and ICIP 2017 Grand Challenge, considered only perceptual quality and compression efficiency to proclaim a winner, whereas other criteria, such as complexity, latency, and random-access, should be considered depending on the requirements of an application.

The JPEG Pleno project consists of seven parts [42]. Part 1, *Framework*, defines a file format supporting the storage of LFs, point clouds, and holograms. Part 2, *Light field coding*, defines LF coding technology [43]. Part 3, *Conformance testing*, defines a methodology that ensures that an application is compliant with the JPEG standard [42,44]. Part 4, *Reference software*, presents an informative-only implementation designed to help understand methodologies in JPEG Pleno standard [42]. In addition to the mentioned four parts, there are also ongoing activities on point cloud coding, hologram coding, and quality assessment [42]. More about the JPEG Pleno initiative can be found at the web-site.[1]

The following sections provide additional details on LF coding technologies integrated into the standard.

8.4.1 Light field coding

Light field codec can take LF data as input and potentially the corresponding camera parameters and depth maps. JPEG Pleno proposes two modes for encoding LF data: 4D transform mode (4DTM) and 4D prediction mode (4DPM). The former is designed as a transform-based coding tool, inspired by the native JPEG codec and extended to the

[1] https://jpeg.org/jpegpleno/index.html.

Figure 8.7 JPEG Pleno 4D Transform Mode Encoder (inspired by [45]).

4D data structure, while the latter uses the prediction mechanism to exploit similarities in LF data.

4D transform mode

Fig. 8.7 shows the encoder of LF image coding solution based on block partitioning, 4D-DCT, and a hexadeca-tree-oriented bit plane clustering, which allows exploiting redundancy in LF data as a whole.

An LF image is firstly partitioned into fixed-size 4D blocks following a predefined, fixed scanning order. 4D blocks can be partitioned further across spatial dimensions, angular dimensions, or not partitioned, depending on the cost the partitioning generates. 4D-DCT is applied to each block, and the quantized coefficients are encoded using a bitplane-wise hexadeca-tree clustering. The hexadeca-tree clustering groups zero coefficients together at each bitplane by partitioning blocks with more than one non-zero coefficient. This partitioning is implemented across all dimensions and generates 16 4D sub-blocks, hence the name hexadeca-tree. Note that the Lagrangian optimization drives the partitioning, 4D-DCT, and hexadeca-tree clustering. The result is a bitstream that consists of the partition flags, the clustering tree, and kept coefficients and is encoded with binary arithmetic coding.

More information about 4DTM can be found in the overviews of the JPEG Pleno standard framework [43,44]. The initial version of the codec was initially proposed [3], while the improved version, which was adopted as 4DTM, was presented in [45].

4D prediction mode

4DPM exploits the correlation between different views in an LF image using a geometry-driven warping [32]. By relying on geometry information, 4DPM presents a universal LF coding tool as it has a capacity for effective compression of narrow and wide baseline LFs.

The overall block diagram of the prediction mode is illustrated in Fig. 8.8. An LF is divided into disjoint sets of views corresponding to different hierarchical levels. At the lowest hierarchical level, a set of views (the reference views) and a set of corresponding disparity maps are encoded using an external coding tool, such as JPEG2000. At higher hierarchical levels, disparity-based warping and an optimal linear prediction merging of the warped views provide the prediction of current views, denoted as intermediate

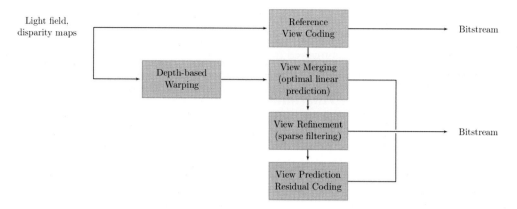

Figure 8.8 JPEG Pleno 4D Prediction Mode Encoder (inspired by [43]).

views. Predicted intermediate views are further refined by applying sparse filtering. Finally, the prediction residual can be encoded using an external codec.

More information about 4DPM can be found in the overviews of the JPEG Pleno standard framework [43,44]. The predecessor of 4DPM is called WaSP, and it is described in the research work of Astola et al. [32]. Merging of the warped views is described in more detail in [46]. A detailed explanation of the design of the sparse predictor and proposed spatial templates are available in [46–48].

4DTM or 4DPM

JPEG Pleno provides two coding modes for LF images. This section briefly summarizes their utility and their strengths and weaknesses.

4DTM offers good performance on the LFs with high inter-view redundancy, LFs captured with a plenoptic camera, while not relying on any additional information about the scene such as its geometry. This scenario offers great simplicity and flexibility in the coding procedure. Furthermore, the scheme is designed to operate independently on fixed-size blocks, which provides random-access capabilities. On the other side, the drawback of the methodology is the lack of expressiveness for sparser LF data.

4DPM uses disparity-based warping and merging, which is different compared to the block-based processing applied in 4DTM. Moreover, the disparity information compresses contents captured by multi-camera arrays or gantries efficiently. Of course, the richer set of functional tools increases the complexity of the approach. 4DPM adopts a hierarchical approach, which provides a high level of flexibility and adaptability to a particular application. For example, if random-access is required, a single view could be assigned to the lowest hierarchical level, and its decoded version can be used to predict the rest of the LF, which are assigned to the second hierarchical level.

The two modes are typically compared only on lenslet contents as 4DTM is not suited for LFs with wider baselines. On widely used test contents, 4DTM achieves from 10% to 30% BD-rate savings compared to 4DPM [44].

8.5. Deep learning-based methods

This section previews LF coding schemes based on deep learning methodologies. Deep learning is highly efficient in learning the finest features in underlying data, as demonstrated across many fields in recent years. From regression to classification tasks, deep learning approaches swiftly outperform conventional methodologies, which were accurately and thoughtfully designed over many years. Nevertheless, there is still a place for improvement, and to explore new fields. This notion especially stands in the case of LF processing, where deep learning brought novelty across various processing applications, including depth estimation, spatial super-resolution, angular super-resolution, and compression. Similar to our initial taxonomy presented in Fig. 8.1, deep learning has been employed to facilitate two functional blocks of the compression pipeline: transform and prediction. This part reviews how deep learning approaches have been employed to enhance some of the LF compression tools described in the previous sections.

Transformation-based

Autoencoders are neural networks trained to reproduce their input at their output. They consist of an encoder that creates an input representation and a decoder that reconstructs the input from the representation. Usually, a constraint is set, which prevents from learning to reproduce the input perfectly and forces to learn essential features in data. This design has been recently proposed for lossy image compression. A new component is added to the autoencoder, which models the probability distribution of the representation. The estimated probability distribution allows computing the bit cost of the representation. Bit cost is minimized together with the reconstruction quality, allowing learning parameters of a lossy codec that operates at a single point on the RD curve. The learning framework is attractive as it offers to learn the parameters of the entire coding system in an end-to-end fashion. In contrast, traditional codecs would require manually designing the framework and independently optimizing different blocks. Recently, autoencoder-based methods for LF compression appeared as well.

For LF compression, a hybrid codec [49] is the first scheme to employ the learned autoencoder-based codec. SAIs are stacked along the channel dimension and fed to the autoencoder. The motivation behind the stacking is two-fold. First, it allows the use of computationally less expensive 2D convolution than 3D or 4D convolutions, which might be more suited for LFs. Second, the channel-wise stacking allows learning filters that jointly consider relations across all views and exploit similarities between views, at least in the case of dense LFs, more efficiently. In addition, an enhancement layer is added for the residual signal coding. The proposed autoencoder yields superior performance compared to state-of-the-art methods and reports more than 37% in terms of BD-Rate compared to HEVC encoding of PVS.

Differently compared to the previous work, Zhong et al. [50] propose 3D convolutional layers as building blocks of the autoencoder architecture. Moreover, MIs are stacked along the third dimension. The scheme performs well at higher rates and consistently outperforms the HEVC anchor. On the contrary, the performance at low rates degrades, suggesting additional considerations are required to achieve superior performance on the entire bitrate range.

Non-local spatial prediction

As mentioned in Section 8.3.2, non-local spatial prediction methods aim to exploit similarities between neighboring MIs. Here we mention schemes designed for the same purpose, but rely on deep learning methods for the prediction mechanism. A MI is considered an elementary coding block that is predicted sequentially from previously decoded MIs, implying the need for explicit modeling of MI structure in deep learning schemes.

With the aim of an improved predictor for lossless LF compression, [51] propose a convolutional neural network that predicts a MI from neighboring MIs. In this scheme, six neighboring MIs are stacked to form a volume of MIs that is processed by a very deep neural network consisting of 2D and 3D convolutional layers. Then, the residual MI is encoded using a modified version of the CALIC codec [52]. Compared to conventional predictors, the proposed predictor allows at least 10% compression gains on LF images captured by a plenoptic camera.

In a more sophisticated variant, Schiopu et al. [53] propose a deep learning method for MI synthesis and prediction. A reference set of views is selected and encoded using an image-based lossless codec. A two-mode neural network is proposed to process the remaining views. The network facilitates two branches, a synthesis branch, and the second for prediction in the coding branch, attached to a shared part of the network. The shared part of the network is inspired by U-net architecture and residual learning. In the first mode, patches are generated by collecting subsampled MIs from reference views and processed by the neural network to estimate a single MI. This mode is used to synthesize the entire LF from the subsampled input sequentially. In the second mode, a neural network processes a 30×60 pixels patch or 2×4 MIs patch generated by collecting six MIs from the causal neighborhood of a current MI and two synthesized MIs in the non-causal neighborhood to obtain the final prediction of the current MI. This prediction is used for predictive coding based on the CALIC architecture. The proposed framework is interesting as it presents an alternative synthesis method that operates on MIs in contrast to typical synthesis methods that synthesize SAIs. Nevertheless, coding performance shows effective improvement of state-of-the-art results.

View synthesis-based prediction

Just as traditional DIBR approaches, deep learning methods were employed to leverage their high modeling capacity in generating novel views using a sparse set of views and geometry information. In addition, some works have shown that geometry can also be estimated at the decoder side, i.e., not transmitted nor estimated from original images, and still provide high-quality reconstruction. These methods typically adopt a similar coding framework, whereas a set of reference views is selected and encoded, whereas at the decoder side, the remaining views are predicted from the decoded reference views.

In [54], a checkerboard pattern is adopted to select the views to be coded and the views to be generated. Authors propose a convolutional neural network, which takes four input views (luminance) arranged along channel dimensions and predicts a view in-between. As the quality of synthesis operation depends on the input quality (affected by coding artifacts), the authors also propose an enhancement network that reduces the artifacts before synthesis. The enhancement network is designed to take as the input coded views and jointly improve the quality of all coded views. Afterward, the enhanced images are provided to the synthesis block that generates new views.

As different methods use different reference view arrangements, and some might perform better than others under different conditions, [55] evaluate the implications of deep learning and optimization-based view synthesis. The experiments show that the combined effort can improve overall performance on some contents compared to scenarios where either approach is independently used. Moreover, the coding performance is improved at lower rates as typically observed in coding methods based on view synthesis.

Similarly, some methods include the residual coding of views predicted by a view synthesis block. [56] propose using the view synthesis method of Kalantari et al. [57] to estimate the non-reference views. The original views subtract the predicted views, and obtained residual frames are encoded by a PVS-based approach. Besides lossy compression, this framework showed great potential for lossless compression. Following a similar strategy, Stepanov et al. [58] propose encoding reference views separately using an image-based coder, while the discarded views are predicted using a views synthesis method. Then, the probability distribution of each pixel is estimated with an autoregressive model and used as the input to the arithmetic coder. Furthermore, by adopting a hierarchical scheme, improved prediction performance is achieved compared to other state-of-the-art lossless methods.

Last but not least, global multi-plane image (MPI) representation, see Chapter 7, has also been successfully employed in LF coding [59]. Similar to previous schemes, reference views are transmitted and used to predict non-reference views. A two-step prediction task is employed at the decoder side to generate non-reference views. First, the MPI representation is constructed from decoded reference views, and in the second step, each non-reference view is predicted based on the obtained MPI representation and its position in LF. A study on the selection of reference views has shown that a particular arrangement of reference views provides superior performance, and, interestingly, adding more reference views beyond some threshold does not improve the quality of reconstructed views. Like other methods in this group, the scheme shows improved performance at low rates. However, it saturates towards higher bitrates.

8.6. Performance analysis

Even though we have witnessed many LF coding solutions in the last three decades, their comparison has been highly challenging. They were compared in different test conditions, using various evaluation metrics and the proposed methodologies were not often publicly available. These diversities make it hard to select a single best approach for LF coding. Moreover, typical comparisons rely on quality evaluation of different methods, while other aspects such as scalability, random-access, complexity, or royalties could add additional weight when determining the quality of an approach.

Recently, there have been some studies that try to compare different methods under common test conditions [37,60]. For the limited set of approaches evaluated in these studies, approaches based on non-local spatial prediction were evaluated less effectively than inter-view prediction and view synthesis-based methods. Methods based on standard video coding tools, especially the MV-HEVC, perform very well and work efficiently on contents captured by plenoptic cameras and multi-camera arrays. Similarly, methods based on view synthesis showed great potential as they significantly reduce the number of views that need to be encoded while exploiting inter-view correlation effectively. Furthermore, a representative of these methods was also adopted in the JPEG Pleno standard. Also, recent deep learning methods proved successful in generating good predictions or geometry information.

JPEG Pleno's coding methodologies did not prove to be superior to other methods unless considered among royalty-free solutions. Among the two modes, the transform-based mode generally performs better on LFs captured by a plenoptic camera than the prediction-based mode. The prediction mode is superior on the contents with wider baselines as the transform-based mode cannot effectively exploit the correlation between views. Moreover, both solutions show highly competitive performance compared to image and video coding standards.

To illustrate the performance of some methods, we consider both modes of the JPEG Pleno codec, 4DTM and 4DPM, PVS coding using the x265 implementation of HEVC, and an autoencoder-based coding method, presented in Section 8.5 [49]. These approaches are compared on one of the contents captured by a plenoptic camera, *Bikes*, and proposed as a test content by JPEG Pleno [61].

As observed in Fig. 8.9, methods specifically designed to explore similarities in the LF structure perform better compared to a scheme based on a standard video coding

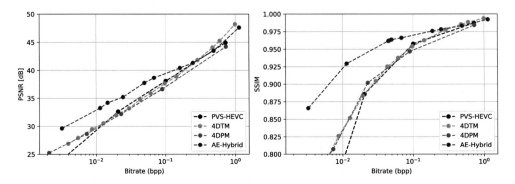

Figure 8.9 RD performance on the LF image *Bikes* in terms of PSNR and SSIM.

tool. Furthermore, 4DTM is slightly superior to its alternative 4DPM, provided by the JPEG Pleno standard. Finally, the autoencoder-based approach outperforms other methods, especially at lower rates in both PSNR and structural similarity index measure (SSIM) objective metrics. More details on the specific coding tools can be found in [49].

8.7. Conclusions and perspectives

This chapter presents an overview of LF coding solutions based on conventional and deep learning methodologies and describes the results of the JPEG Pleno initiative that culminated with two coding solutions. Moreover, a general discussion on the performance of different coding methodologies is covered, and the coding performance of some particular schemes is presented.

Generally speaking, it is not easy to select a single method superior to other methods, considering the broad range of methodologies that appeared. Furthermore, besides typically employing objective or subjective quality metrics in evaluating the potential of a coding scheme, other characteristics, such as scalability, complexity, and random-access capabilities should be considered, depending on an application. As recently suggested by [60], royalty license is another aspect that could play a significant role in determining the potential of a coding solution.

Considering recent advances, LF coding methods based on view synthesis promise excellent compression performance. Its potential comes from the possibility of radically reducing the number of views that needs to be encoded and transmitted. This pipeline has also been adopted in JPEG Pleno coding solutions, where geometry information is used to reconstruct missing views at the decoder side. Moreover, the high modeling power of deep learning methods allows omitting to transmit even geometry information and still recover missing views in high quality. Besides views synthesis, conventional video coding tools were also popular for LF coding, either as the main functional block or as a supporting block, e.g., residual coding. Moreover, the multi-view extension of HEVC is presented as a highly competitive solution for LF compression, with the advantage of being applicable to dynamic contents. Last but not least, transform-based methods show promising results for the compression of contents captured with plenoptic cameras. In particular, the LF coding solution based on 4D-DCT has been adopted in the JPEG Pleno standard.

Although this chapter does not cover in great depth the methodologies for lossless LF coding, it is worth mentioning the recent effort in exploring these approaches. Namely, these methods offer distortion-free reconstruction, which is important in, e.g., medical applications. Among recent methods, coding solutions based on minimum rate predictors offer excellent coding efficiency at the cost of high computational complexity at the encoder side [62], whereas solutions operating on EPIs are computationally efficient and yet provide high coding performance [63].

Another aspect worth mentioning is the coding of dynamic contents. In recent years, significant effort has been put into developing a coding solution for LF images. JPEG Pleno initiative further increased the interest with a call for proposals, grand challenges, and the implementation of the standardized coding solution. LF video coding, on the contrary, stayed somewhat in the shadow of the previous trend. Nevertheless, the recent efforts in MPEG-I on 3 degrees of freedom (3DoF), 3DoF with some limited parallax, 3DoF+, and 6DoF [64] will undoubtedly increase the interest and bring new proposals for coding solutions for LF video technologies.

References

[1] C. Conti, L.D. Soares, P. Nunes, Dense light field coding: A survey, IEEE Access 8 (2020) 49244–49284, https://doi.org/10.1109/ACCESS.2020.2977767.

[2] N.P. Sgouros, D.P. Chaikalis, P.G. Papageorgas, M.S. Sangriotis, Omnidirectional integral photography images compression using the 3D-DCT, in: Digital Holography and Three-Dimensional Imaging, Optical Society of America, 2007.

[3] M.B. de Carvalho, M.P. Pereira, G. Alves, E.A.B. da Silva, C.L. Pagliari, F. Pereira, V. Testoni, A 4D DCT-based lenslet light field codec, in: 2018 25th IEEE International Conference on Image Processing (ICIP), 2018, pp. 435–439, https://doi.org/10.1109/ICIP.2018.8451684.

[4] M.W. Marcellin, D.S. Taubman, JPEG2000: Image Compression Fundamentals, Standards, and Practice, International Series in Engineering and Computer Science, Secs 642, 2002.

[5] J.-S. Jang, S. Yeom, B. Javidi, Compression of ray information in three-dimensional integral imaging, Optical Engineering 44 (12) (2005) 127001.

[6] H.-H. Kang, D.-H. Shin, E.-S. Kim, Compression scheme of sub-images using Karhunen-Loève transform in three-dimensional integral imaging, Optics Communications 281 (14) (2008) 3640–3647.

[7] R.S. Higa, R.F.L. Chavez, R.B. Leite, R. Arthur, Y. Iano, Plenoptic image compression comparison between JPEG, JPEG2000 and SPITH, 2013.

[8] C. Perra, On the coding of plenoptic raw images, in: 2014 22nd Telecommunications Forum Telfor (TELFOR), IEEE, 2014, pp. 850–853.

[9] M.A. Magnor, A. Endmann, B. Girod, Progressive compression and rendering of light fields, in: VMV, Citeseer, 2000, pp. 199–204.

[10] W. Sweldens, The lifting scheme: A construction of second generation wavelets, SIAM Journal on Mathematical Analysis 29 (2) (1998) 511–546.

[11] C.-L. Chang, X. Zhu, P. Ramanathan, B. Girod, Light field compression using disparity-compensated lifting and shape adaptation, IEEE Transactions on Image Processing 15 (4) (2006) 793–806.

[12] J. Garrote, C. Brites, J. Ascenso, F. Pereira, Lenslet light field imaging scalable coding, in: 2018 26th European Signal Processing Conference (EUSIPCO), IEEE, 2018, pp. 2150–2154.

[13] D. Rüefenacht, A.T. Naman, R. Mathew, D. Taubman, Base-anchored model for highly scalable and accessible compression of multiview imagery, IEEE Transactions on Image Processing 28 (7) (2019) 3205–3218.

[14] A. Vieira, H. Duarte, C. Perra, L. Tavora, P. Assuncao, Data formats for high efficiency coding of Lytro-Illum light fields, in: 2015 International Conference on Image Processing Theory, Tools and Applications (IPTA), IEEE, 2015, pp. 494–497.

[15] H.P. Hariharan, T. Lange, T. Herfet, Low complexity light field compression based on pseudo-temporal circular sequencing, in: 2017 IEEE International Symposium on Broadband Multimedia Systems and Broadcasting (BMSB), IEEE, 2017, pp. 1–5.

[16] L. Li, Z. Li, B. Li, D. Liu, H. Li, Pseudo-sequence-based 2-D hierarchical coding structure for light-field image compression, IEEE Journal of Selected Topics in Signal Processing 11 (7) (2017) 1107–1119, https://doi.org/10.1109/JSTSP.2017.2725198.

[17] R. Conceição, M. Porto, B. Zatt, L. Agostini, LF-CAE: Context-adaptive encoding for lenslet light fields using HEVC, in: 2018 25th IEEE International Conference on Image Processing (ICIP), IEEE, 2018, pp. 3174–3178.

[18] K. Imaeda, K. Isechi, K. Takahashi, T. Fujii, Y. Bandoh, T. Miyazawa, S. Takamura, A. Shimizu, LF-TSP: Traveling salesman problem for HEVC-based light-field coding, in: 2019 IEEE Visual Communications and Image Processing (VCIP), IEEE, 2019, pp. 1–4.

[19] J.R. Monteiro, M.N. Rodrigues, M.S. Faria, J.P. Nunes, Optimized reference picture selection for light field image coding, in: 2019 27th European Signal Processing Conference (EUSIPCO), IEEE, 2019, pp. 1–5.

[20] D. Liu, L. Wang, L. Li, Z. Xiong, F. Wu, W. Zeng, Pseudo-sequence-based light field image compression, in: 2016 IEEE International Conference on Multimedia Expo Workshops (ICMEW), 2016, pp. 1–4, https://doi.org/10.1109/ICMEW.2016.7574674.

[21] W. Ahmad, R. Olsson, M. Sjöström, Interpreting plenoptic images as multi-view sequences for improved compression, in: 2017 IEEE International Conference on Image Processing (ICIP), IEEE, 2017, pp. 4557–4561.

[22] U. Fecker, A. Kaup, H.264/AVC-compatible coding of dynamic light fields using transposed picture ordering, in: 2005 13th European Signal Processing Conference, IEEE, 2005, pp. 1–4.

[23] J. Xu, R. Joshi, R.A. Cohen, Overview of the emerging HEVC screen content coding extension, IEEE Transactions on Circuits and Systems for Video Technology 26 (1) (2016) 50–62, https://doi.org/10.1109/TCSVT.2015.2478706.

[24] Y. Li, M. Sjöström, R. Olsson, U. Jennehag, Coding of focused plenoptic contents by displacement intra prediction, IEEE Transactions on Circuits and Systems for Video Technology 26 (7) (2016) 1308–1319, https://doi.org/10.1109/TCSVT.2015.2450333.

[25] C. Conti, J. Lino, P. Nunes, L.D. Soares, P.L. Correia, Spatial prediction based on self-similarity compensation for 3D holoscopic image and video coding, in: 2011 18th IEEE International Conference on Image Processing, IEEE, 2011, pp. 961–964.

[26] C. Conti, P. Nunes, L.D. Soares, Light field image coding with jointly estimated self-similarity bi-prediction, Signal Processing. Image Communication 60 (2018) 144–159.

[27] X. Jin, H. Han, Q. Dai, Plenoptic image coding using macropixel-based intra prediction, IEEE Transactions on Image Processing 27 (8) (2018) 3954–3968.

[28] R.J. Monteiro, P.J. Nunes, N.M. Rodrigues, S.M. Faria, Light field image coding using high-order intrablock prediction, IEEE Journal of Selected Topics in Signal Processing 11 (7) (2017) 1120–1131.

[29] X. Jin, H. Han, Q. Dai, Image reshaping for efficient compression of plenoptic content, IEEE Journal of Selected Topics in Signal Processing 11 (7) (2017) 1173–1186.

[30] I. Viola, T. Ebrahimi, Quality assessment of compression solutions for ICIP 2017 grand challenge on light field image coding, in: 2018 IEEE International Conference on Multimedia & Expo Workshops (ICMEW), IEEE, 2018, pp. 1–6.

[31] Y. Li, M. Sjöström, R. Olsson, U. Jennehag, Scalable coding of plenoptic images by using a sparse set and disparities, IEEE Transactions on Image Processing 25 (1) (2016) 80–91, https://doi.org/10.1109/TIP.2015.2498406.

[32] P. Astola, I. Tabus, WaSP: hierarchical warping, merging, and sparse prediction for light field image compression, in: 2018 7th European Workshop on Visual Information Processing (EUVIP), 2018, pp. 1–6, https://doi.org/10.1109/EUVIP.2018.8611756.

[33] X. Huang, P. An, L. Shen, R. Ma, Efficient light field images compression method based on depth estimation and optimization, IEEE Access 6 (2018) 48984–48993.

[34] E. Dib, M. Le Pendu, C. Guillemot, Light field compression using Fourier disparity layers, in: 2019 IEEE International Conference on Image Processing (ICIP), IEEE, 2019, pp. 3751–3755.

[35] W. Ahmad, S. Vagharshakyan, M. Sjöström, A. Gotchev, R. Bregovic, R. Olsson, Shearlet transform-based light field compression under low bitrates, IEEE Transactions on Image Processing 29 (2020) 4269–4280.

[36] I. Viola, H.P. Maretic, P. Frossard, T. Ebrahimi, A graph learning approach for light field image compression, in: Applications of Digital Image Processing XLI, vol. 10752, International Society for Optics and Photonics, 2018, p. 107520E.

[37] I. Viola, M. Řeřábek, T. Bruylants, P. Schelkens, F. Pereira, T. Ebrahimi, Objective and subjective evaluation of light field image compression algorithms, in: 2016 Picture Coding Symposium (PCS), IEEE, 2016, pp. 1–5.

[38] JPEG PLENO Abstract and Executive Summary, Doc. ISO/IEC JTC 1/SC29/WG1 N6922, Sydney, Australia, February 2015.

[39] T. Ebrahimi, S. Foessel, F. Pereira, P. Schelkens, JPEG Pleno: Toward an efficient representation of visual reality, IEEE MultiMedia 23 (4) (2016) 14–20, https://doi.org/10.1109/MMUL.2016.64.

[40] Grand challenge on light field image compression, Doc. ISO/IEC JTC 1/SC29/WG1 M72022, Geneva, Switzerland, June 2016.

[41] JPEG Pleno Call for Proposals on Light Field Coding, Doc. ISO/IEC JTC 1/SC29/WG1 N74014, Geneva, Switzerland, January 2017.

[42] C. Perra, P.G. Freitas, I. Seidel, P. Schelkens, An overview of the emerging JPEG Pleno standard, conformance testing and reference software, in: P. Schelkens, T. Kozacki (Eds.), Optics, Photonics and Digital Technologies for Imaging Applications VI, in: SPIE, vol. 11353, International Society for Optics and Photonics, 2020, pp. 207–219, https://doi.org/10.1117/12.2555841.

[43] P. Schelkens, P. Astola, E.A. Da Silva, C. Pagliari, C. Perra, I. Tabus, O. Watanabe, JPEG Pleno light field coding technologies, in: Applications of Digital Image Processing XLII, vol. 11137, International Society for Optics and Photonics, 2019, p. 111371G.

[44] P. Astola, L.A. da Silva Cruz, E.A. da Silva, T. Ebrahimi, P.G. Freitas, A. Gilles, K.-J. Oh, C. Pagliari, F. Pereira, C. Perra, et al., JPEG Pleno: Standardizing a coding framework and tools for plenoptic imaging modalities, ITU Journal: ICT Discoveries (2020).

[45] G. De Oliveira Alves, M.B. De Carvalho, C.L. Pagliari, P.G. Freitas, I. Seidel, M.P. Pereira, C.F.S. Vieira, V. Testoni, F. Pereira, E.A.B. Da Silva, The JPEG Pleno light field coding standard 4D-transform mode: how to design an efficient 4D-native codec, IEEE Access 8 (2020) 170807–170829, https://doi.org/10.1109/ACCESS.2020.3024844.

[46] P. Astola, I. Tabus, Light field compression of HDCA images combining linear prediction and JPEG 2000, in: 2018 26th European Signal Processing Conference (EUSIPCO), 2018, pp. 1860–1864, https://doi.org/10.23919/EUSIPCO.20t18.8553482.

[47] I. Tabus, P. Astola, Sparse prediction for compression of stereo color images conditional on constant disparity patches, in: 2014 3DTV-Conference: The True Vision - Capture, Transmission and Display of 3D Video (3DTV-CON), 2014, pp. 1–4, https://doi.org/10.1109/3DTV.2014.6874766.

[48] P. Helin, P. Astola, B. Rao, I. Tabus, Sparse modelling and predictive coding of subaperture images for lossless plenoptic image compression, in: 2016 3DTV-Conference: The True Vision - Capture, Transmission and Display of 3D Video (3DTV-CON), 2016, pp. 1–4, https://doi.org/10.1109/3DTV.2016.7548953.

[49] M. Stepanov, G. Valenzise, F. Dufaux, Hybrid learning-based and HEVC-based coding of light fields, in: 2020 IEEE International Conference on Image Processing (ICIP), IEEE, 2020, pp. 3344–3348.

[50] T. Zhong, X. Jin, K. Tong, 3D-CNN autoencoder for plenoptic image compression, in: 2020 IEEE International Conference on Visual Communications and Image Processing (VCIP), IEEE, 2020, pp. 209–212.

[51] I. Schiopu, A. Munteanu, Macro-pixel prediction based on convolutional neural networks for lossless compression of light field images, in: 2018 25th IEEE International Conference on Image Processing (ICIP), IEEE, 2018, pp. 445–449.

[52] X. Wu, N. Memon, Context-based, adaptive, lossless image coding, IEEE Transactions on Communications 45 (4) (1997) 437–444.

[53] I. Schiopu, A. Munteanu, Deep-learning-based macro-pixel synthesis and lossless coding of light field images, APSIPA Transactions on Signal and Information Processing 8 (2019).

[54] Z. Zhao, S. Wang, C. Jia, X. Zhang, S. Ma, J. Yang, Light field image compression based on deep learning, in: 2018 IEEE International Conference on Multimedia and Expo (ICME), IEEE, 2018, pp. 1–6.

[55] N. Bakir, W. Hamidouche, O. Déforges, K. Samrouth, M. Khalil, Light field image compression based on convolutional neural networks and linear approximation, in: 2018 25th IEEE International Conference on Image Processing (ICIP), IEEE, 2018, pp. 1128–1132.

[56] J. Hou, J. Chen, L.-P. Chau, Light field image compression based on bi-level view compensation with rate-distortion optimization, IEEE Transactions on Circuits and Systems for Video Technology 29 (2) (2019) 517–530, https://doi.org/10.1109/TCSVT.2018.2802943.

[57] N.K. Kalantari, T.-C. Wang, R. Ramamoorthi, Learning-based view synthesis for light field cameras, ACM Transactions on Graphics (TOG) 35 (6) (2016) 1–10.

[58] M. Stepanov, M.U. Mukati, G. Valenzise, S. Forchhammer, F. Dufaux, Learning-based lossless light field compression, in: IEEE International Workshop on Multimedia Signal Processing (MMSP'2021), 2021.

[59] Y. Chen, P. An, X. Huang, C. Yang, D. Liu, Q. Wu, Light field compression using global multiplane representation and two-step prediction, IEEE Signal Processing Letters 27 (2020) 1135–1139.

[60] C. Brites, J. Ascenso, F. Pereira, Lenslet light field image coding: Classifying, reviewing and evaluating, IEEE Transactions on Circuits and Systems for Video Technology 31 (1) (2021) 339–354, https://doi.org/10.1109/TCSVT.2020.2976784.

[61] JPEG PLENO Light field coding common test conditions v3.3, Doc. ISO/IEC JTC 1/SC29/WG1 N84025, Brussels, Belgium, July 2019.

[62] J.M. Santos, L.A. Thomaz, P.A. Assunção, L.A. Cruz, L. Távora, S.M. Faria, Lossless coding of light fields based on 4D minimum rate predictors, arXiv preprint, arXiv:2104.06252, 2021.

[63] M.U. Mukati, S. Forchhammer, Epipolar plane image-based lossless and near-lossless light field compression, IEEE Access 9 (2021) 1124–1136, https://doi.org/10.1109/ACCESS.2020.3047073.

[64] M. Wien, J.M. Boyce, T. Stockhammer, W.-H. Peng, Standardization status of immersive video coding, IEEE Journal on Emerging and Selected Topics in Circuits and Systems 9 (1) (2019) 5–17, https://doi.org/10.1109/JETCAS.2019.2898948.

CHAPTER 9

Light field processing for media applications

Joachim Keinert, Laura Fink, Florian Goldmann, Muhammad Shahzeb Khan Gul, Tobias Jaschke, Nico Prappacher, Matthias Ziegler, Michel Bätz, and Siegfried Fößel
Fraunhofer Institute for Integrated Circuits IIS, Erlangen, Germany

9.1. Light field processing chain overview

Using the light field data captured by camera arrays for a practical application requires an algorithmic processing chain that allows to interpolate between the different views. This chapter focuses on multi-camera setups without active depth measurement. It is assumed that all cameras are synchronized precisely and capture a dynamic scene at interactive rates, i.e., larger than 30 fps.

Fig. 9.1 depicts three possible processing pipelines. Image acquisition and camera calibration is similar for all of them as precise calibration data is mandatory for all subsequent steps of a reconstruction pipeline. Major considerations for the design and implementation of suitable calibration methods will be discussed in Section 9.2.

The leftmost path of Fig. 9.1 depicts the case when a densely sampled light field is available. In this case, re-sampling the plenoptic function results in the desired novel view irrespective of any geometric information. Therefore this type of rendering is also known as "rendering without geometry" or "image-based rendering" [1–3]. As the spatial sampling rate needs to be much higher than the physical spacing between the individual cameras permits, this approach is only suitable for static scenes and not for dynamic scenes. Instead of a regular camera array, a camera mounted on industrial grade robotic arms can be used to capture a static scene with very high density [4,5].

For sparse multi-camera setups, one of the central or rightmost paths of Fig. 9.1 labeled with "image based geometry" or "model based geometry" can be applied. The central path depicts a processing pipeline that renders novel views using image-based geometry represented for instance by depth or disparity maps. Here, depth reconstruction and optional depth refinement form the major processing steps. Typically, the reconstruction step estimates an initial depth map for each input view using a set of adjacent views as input. Pairwise stereo matching [6] yields a set of individual depth maps per view that need to be normalized and finally merged into a single depth map. Subse-

Immersive Video Technologies
https://doi.org/10.1016/B978-0-32-391755-1.00015-8

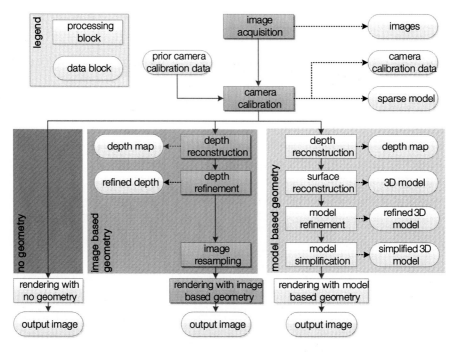

Figure 9.1 Multi-camera image processing pipelines for novel view synthesis from dense (left) and sparse multi-camera setups (center & right). Solid lines indicate consecutive processing steps; dotted lines represent results of a specific processing step.

quently, the resulting depth maps can be refined using a variety of filtering steps. Such filtering may include occlusion checks that test geometric consistency of this image-based 3D model across a set of input views. Inconsistent pixel values can be discarded and need to be concealed using methods such as cross-bilateral or cross-percentile filters [7,8]. The resulting refined depth maps should provide a depth value for every pixel to avoid missing information in rendered images.

The rightmost path of Fig. 9.1 uses 3D models for geometry instead of images. In this branch, a geometric 3D model, e.g., using surface reconstruction techniques [9], is reconstructed. These approaches are able to close possible holes in the initial depth maps allowing those to be sparser than for the previous methods. Surface reconstruction aims to obtain a visual hull of the underlying scene. This is achieved by projecting input disparity maps into a 3D point cloud, a subsequent fusion of nearby points, and finally the creation of surface polygons [10]. Afterwards, this model (e.g., a mesh) forms the basis for subsequent refinement and simplification steps.

The image acquisition and camera calibration shown in Fig. 9.1 is common to all these paths and is explained in the following section.

9.2. Image acquisition and geometric camera calibration

The overall image quality of any output image described above does not only depend on the processing chain itself, but also on the quality of the input images. Besides precise synchronization of all incorporated cameras, including trigger, exposure, gain, and other parameters, colorimetric calibration might be required [11–14].

In addition to those pre-processing steps, efficient depth reconstruction using stereo matching techniques requires precisely aligned images ("rectified images") as it is assumed that corresponding pixels can be found in the same line of a horizontally adjacent image or in the same column of a vertically adjacent image. Even a slight misalignment can significantly degrade the quality of an estimated stereo disparity map. As the required accuracy cannot be achieved solely by mechanical adjustment, extrinsic and intrinsic camera parameters need to be determined [15]. Based on this parameter set, rectifying homographies can be created for a whole set of cameras (in case of a planar camera array) or individually for each pair of cameras. In the resulting rectified images, corresponding points are located in the same row for horizontally neighbored cameras, and in the same column for vertically adjacent cameras.

Determining the camera parameters requires a suitable camera model as well as the basics of projection and re-projection. An overview of the image formation process and camera models has been given by Schoeberl [16]. The concept of multiple view geometry [17] describes the relations between corresponding pixels showing the same object points in different images captured with one or several (pinhole) cameras. Based on these principles, many authors have proposed algorithms that determine position, orientation, focal length, lens distortions, and other parameters of one or several cameras [18–28]. The reconstruction problem is typically formulated as a non-linear optimization that minimizes the re-projection error between an observed point and its re-projected 3D point.

The highest precision as well as a link to absolute metric units can be obtained from active calibration methods that employ calibration objects, such as checkerboards [24,28]. However, even slight modifications to the camera setup can invalidate a parameter set, hindering a later post-processing. Thus active calibration techniques are not optimal for simple use. In contrast to those active methods, Structure-from-Motion (SfM) pipelines [29], for instance, do not require prior knowledge about the objects contained in the scene. Hence they can compute both intrinsic and extrinsic parameters from almost arbitrary images as long as they contain recognizable features [30] and objects in different depths. To this end, SfM pipelines jointly reconstruct camera parameters and a (sparse) 3D model of a scene. This requires capturing a (static) scene from many different perspectives, preferably with a single camera.

For camera arrays, the estimation of the intrinsic and extrinsic parameters can be simplified in case of a precisely manufactured and robust mechanical framework. Thanks to a mechanically stable construction, first estimated values for the camera parameters can be derived from the structural design. They include the focal length of each camera, the ideal orientation as well as the ideal position of each camera. Due to different types of deviations, such as improper focal length or orientation, the real configuration of any camera system will differ from these estimated value. Luckily, for some parameters, such as the position of each camera, deviations to be expected are rather small. This knowledge can be translated into an additional constraint in a non-linear optimization problem reducing the possible degrees of freedom (prior camera calibration data in Fig. 9.1). In contrast to many other calibration techniques, such a method can directly optimize for the remaining vertical error in stereo pairs and neglects the position of a corresponding point in 3D space. Then, only the orientations, relative focal lengths, and principal points need to be determined or approximated [15].

Once the camera parameters have been successfully computed, the geometry of the scene can be reconstructed, as described in the following section.

9.3. Depth reconstruction

Reconstructing a dense representation from a sparsely sampled light field by depth reconstruction techniques forms the central point of a light field processing chain for sparse camera arrays. For each pixel in an image, the goal is to find all corresponding pixels in all other views. The geometric relation between a pair of cameras allows to derive which pixels can be potentially related. Moreover, once the related pixels have been found, the distance between the cameras and the object point depicted by those pixels can be computed. This gain allows to interpolate missing camera views.

Unfortunately, depth reconstruction is an ill-posed problem: stereo matching assumes that a pixel (or a set of pixels surrounding the considered pixel) can be identified unambiguously in a secondary view, e.g., by computing the sum of absolute differences between a block in the primary view and all possible blocks in the secondary view [6]. Such a *cost function* determines the similarity of two pixel sets. In an ideal world, only the corresponding block in the secondary view will have zero difference. However, this assumption is only true if the scene is composed of Lambertian objects only and all surfaces are oriented directly towards the camera array. Otherwise, slight changes either in the viewing angle or due to perspective distortions may create false matches.

In addition to these constraints, occlusions need to be considered as well. A point, being visible in a primary view, might be occluded by some foreground object in a secondary view. Thus it is impossible to find the corresponding pixel. Hence, the cost function will select any other point that suits the optimization criterion (minimum cost function value) best.

Partially, pixels that do not have a valid correspondence in a secondary view due to occlusion can be detected by occlusion testing: considering a pixel in the primary view and its estimated correspondence in a secondary view, the estimated correspondence of the pixel in the secondary view should point back to the considered pixel in the primary view. Otherwise, the estimated correspondence is likely to be wrong.

In regard of these challenges, camera arrays benefit from the fact, that not only one pair of cameras is available for correspondence search. For a single input view, multiple possible secondary views are available to form a stereo pair. For example, a camera in the corner of an array has one horizontal, one vertical, and one diagonal directly adjacent neighbor. A pixel in the primary view might be occluded in one of the secondary views, but might be visible in another secondary view so that a proper matching can still be performed. It is hence not important to interpolate pixels that have been discarded due to consistency problems as other stereo pairs can be selected to provide another set of reliable pixels that fill up unknown pixels. This procedure is also known as disparity merging [31,32].

Stereo matching performs best if the underlying scene is well structured with natural textures that provide high contrast and uniqueness. "Flat" areas, such as homogeneous backgrounds and overexposed areas, need to be avoided when capturing a scene. A detailed introduction into this topic can be found in [6]. Looking at the tables from well-known benchmarks, such as Middlebury [33] or KITTI [34], reveals that the best-performing method often differs from scene to scene. In recent years, state-of-the-art algorithms have increased in complexity [35–37]. Slight parameter changes might improve the result on one scene, but could have a negative effect on another. For instance, such parameters comprise the block size of a block matcher, the threshold of a consistency test, or the kernel size or shape of a filter. In a practical application, it is thus important to quickly find a proper set of parameters that suits the current conditions of the scene and the cameras best (see also Section 9.4).

Once the initial disparity maps have been found, they can be further refined using for instance bilateral filtering [7,8]. Interestingly, experiments have shown that the quality of a refined disparity map does primarily not depend on the complexity of the initial stereo matching method, but more on the following refinement steps [38]. In special cases, stereo matching based on a very simple block matching algorithm can outperform more complex stereo matching methods, such as ADCensus [39] or semi-global matching [40]. This is also beneficial from a computational perspective: instead of executing a complex algorithm N times to obtain N initial results before refinement, a simple yet computationally effective algorithm may save energy and speed up the overall computation.

However, such an approach is only feasible in case a software environment allows to fine-tune the parameters of the algorithm for a specific scene. The following section provides some insights on such an interactive processing.

9.4. Interactive light field processing

As any modern media production requires some sort of post-processing, the employed camera array as well as the implemented software need to be compatible with standard production workflows. For example, this means that operations such as green-screen keying or color grading need to be applied to all input streams. In the best case, one set of parameters is sufficient to optimize the output of the keying operations. In the worst case, however, the parameters need to be adjusted individually for every input stream (e.g., if the raw colors differ from camera to camera).

This means that the underlying software needs to be capable of managing and processing multiple input streams. In a later step, more complex visual effects, such as virtual backgrounds, might be added or the processed material is being integrated into a larger 3D world. All this is only possible if the output of the different algorithms can be understood and controlled by a user such as a post-production artist.

In this regard, traditional signal processing methods excel compared to AI-based methods, explained later on in Section 9.7 as those typically encode the light field in a black box manner that is hardly accessible or adjustable with conventional tools. By allowing for an interactive processing, an experienced user (e.g., a post-production artist) can judge the obtained results based on his know-how. This user may then modify and optimize the processing steps such that the final result meets their requirements. Clearly, this requires a software system that supports changes to the pipeline and parameters. In addition, the software needs to provide intermediate results and interactive modification options to a user.

Node-based software systems, such as Nuke [41,42], Fusion [43,44], or Blender [45, 46], can serve these needs in a favorable manner. By default, such software contains nodes for standard image processing tasks, such as color correction, green-screen keying, image filtering, image transformation, and more. In addition, they support many different input and output formats and can often be extended by custom-designed plug-ins. The basic functionality of this software, in combination with additional plug-ins, forms an excellent basis for a flexible and user-configurable depth reconstruction pipeline.

Realception [15,47], a plug-in suite for Nuke and Unreal Engine [48,49] developed by Fraunhofer IIS, exemplifies such a node-based processing pipeline designed for scene-adapted depth reconstruction from multi-camera arrays. In addition to depth estimation and refinement operations, Realception also provides functionalities for image rectification and novel view synthesis. Nodes for cross-bilateral filtering or cross-percentile filtering [7,50] as well as nodes for geometric and photometric consistency tests allow the improvement of the depth maps. Fig. 9.2 shows an exemplary pipeline in Nuke, where all nodes (gray rectangles) with an RC-prefix denote Realception components. The pipeline first performs some pre-processing steps and reconstructs and refines disparity maps. Finally, it renders a novel view from a light field input dataset. The principles to consider in this last step are discussed in the subsequent section.

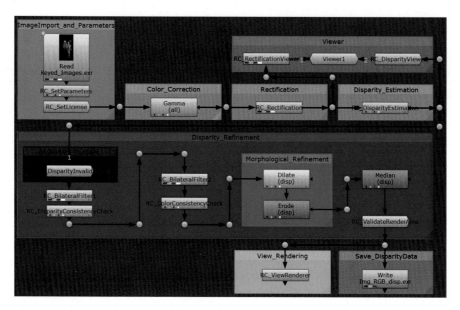

Figure 9.2 Example processing node graph for interactive light field editing within Nuke [41,42] using the plug-in Realception [15,47]. Initially, this graph reads a set of color images. Step by step, the pipeline reconstructs and refines a disparity map for each input image and renders a novel view.

9.5. Light field rendering

Light field rendering or view synthesis is the process of generating a target view from the captured input views. View synthesis can either be done by warping the pixels of the input views to the correct position for the target view, or by first transforming the input views into an intermediate representation (see Fig. 9.1). A 3D mesh as geometry model introduced in Fig. 9.1 combined with a corresponding texture atlas defining the color of each mesh point is an example for the latter. Novel views can then be computed by projecting the textured geometry to the target view, according to the pinhole camera model. Whereas traditional computer graphics use view-independent textures, light fields preserve the view-dependent appearance. In other words, an object point can change its color depending on the viewing direction from which it is observed. Consequently, the texture needs to be view-dependent as well, leading to more complex textures in the form of surface light fields [51,52].

Alternatively, a textureless 3D geometry model can be used to identify for every target pixel, the associated source pixel, showing the same object point, as illustrated in Fig. 9.3. These source pixels can be determined by projecting the intersection point of the target ray with the geometry model back into the source views. The selected source

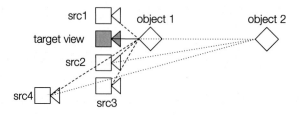

Figure 9.3 Selection of source cameras and pixels. Every ray corresponds to a pixel.

pixels need then to be blended into the target pixel value. Different object locations (object 1 and 2 in Fig. 9.3) lead to different selected source pixels.

In cases where only an image-based geometry is available, source pixels can still be warped to the correct target view pixel based on depth or disparity maps. Together with the intrinsic and extrinsic camera parameters, they define the location of the depicted pixel point in 3D space. Finally, if no geometry information is available, such information needs to be hypothesized. This however will quickly lead to rendering artifacts in cases where the distance between the cameras is too large.

Thus whatever rendering strategy is chosen, a light field view synthesis implementation needs to determine which source cameras should be selected to generate the appearance of a desired target pixel. This is discussed in more detail in the section that follows. Section 9.5.2 will then investigate which target view positions are admissible to avoid missing information in the synthesized image.

9.5.1 Camera selection and blending

As pixel warping requires computation, efficient rendering algorithms try to select relevant source images beforehand and neglect all remaining pixel information. The first criterion to apply for selecting source cameras to be used for view synthesis is frustum visibility. A camera whose field of view frustum does not intersect with the desired target object point can be excluded from the set of possible source views for this object point. Please note that this can only be decided when the location of the target object in 3D space is known.

Secondly, the source view should provide sufficient resolution for the desired target view. Assuming identical intrinsic camera parameters (focal length, pixel size, number of pixels, etc.), camera *src4* in Fig. 9.3 cannot provide enough details for *object 1*, simply because the distance between the object and the source camera is much larger than the distance between the object and the target view.

Thirdly, as the appearance of an object point can change, depending on the target viewing direction, the angle between the source ray and the target ray should be as small as possible. In cases of general source camera placement, this decision depends on the location of the object and the cameras in 3D space. For example, whereas camera *src4* in Fig. 9.3 has a smaller angle with the target ray than camera *src2* for *object 1*, it is the opposite for *object 2*, despite corresponding to the same target ray. Only when the source views are located on a convex or concave surface and a target ray does not intersect this surface more than once, the source camera selection based on the viewing angle is independent of the object location, and only depends on the source and target view positions. This represents a great benefit for regular camera arrays. Please also note that for *src4* and *object 1*, the resolution and the angle criteria come to contradicting conclusions in regard to preference compared to camera *src2*. This makes camera selection a challenge.

Finally, all those cameras in which a desired object point is occluded need also to be excluded from the set of possible source views. Again, this can only be decided when a precise 3D model of the scene is available.

Given that the camera selection depends on the scene geometry, several view synthesis approaches use a proxy mesh during the rendering process. This holds in particular for more irregular camera placements during capture [1,2,53]. For video applications, this would however cause a huge computational burden, as mesh creation is still computationally intensive. Consequently, in such applications more regular camera placements are employed, simplifying both frustum visibility, resolution, and angular camera selection [54–57]. Only the occlusion analysis still requires a 3D model. This can be avoided by rendering from all available source views, and then discarding not needed ones on an individual decision for each target pixel. Obviously, this comes with a significant computation cost when the number of source views is large.

9.5.2 Observation space for planar arrays

Even when following the above principles, the target views cannot be placed arbitrarily in 3D space. Instead, they need to be located in an admissible observation volume, as exemplified for a single object point and a planar light field array in Fig. 9.4. Supposing that the object point intersects the field of view frustum of every camera, the possible target views need to be located in a pyramid, whose cone end is defined by the object point. Target views located outside of this pyramid correspond to an extrapolation, which is prone to disocclusions, and hence rendering artifacts in the case of insufficient inpainting. Please note that according to the previous section, target cameras should not be closer to the object point than the source cameras to avoid a resolution loss. In other words, target cameras should be situated in the pyramid part that is shaded in a darker tone in Fig. 9.4 in the case where target views with insufficient resolution are to be avoided.

Having not only a single object point, but a complete volume containing the objects of the scene, the admissible observation volume for the target views can be computed by intersecting the pyramids whose cone ends are the extreme points of the scene volume.

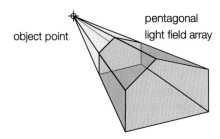

Figure 9.4 Admissible target view volume for a single object point and a pentagonal planar light field array. Each corner corresponds to a camera position.

In practice, this can be done by means of software libraries, such as [58], which are able to compute polytopes based on inequalities.

Fig. 9.5a depicts a corresponding example for a scene located in a volume with a height of 2 m, a depth of 3 m, a front width of 1.4 m, and a back width of 3 m. The minimum distance between the camera array contained in the admissible observation volume and the scene is 2 m. The vertical position of the camera array has to be set in such a way that an observer whose eye height equals 180 cm can move in negative z-direction, as far as possible. In the shown example, this equals to -27 cm, as depicted in Fig. 9.5b. It shows a magnification of the admissible observation volume. In the case where the target view position moves more into negative z-direction, this induces a risk of occlusions.

In summary, light field rendering requires both a careful capture and rendering setup. How this can be achieved in practice in a real-time manner is the subject of the next section.

9.6. Real-time rendering in game engines

With an increasing popularity of computer gaming, the widespread use of state-of-the art game engines, such as Unreal Engine [48,49] or Unity [59,60], comes as no surprise. These engines are not only invaluable tools for the creation of new games, but rather have long surpassed their use as pure 3D game engines and continue to evolve beyond their original purpose. By now, game engines are a tool of choice for a plethora of digital use cases, such as the creation of tech demos, architectural visualization, simulation, education, or as powerful 3D creation platforms for aspiring visual artists [61–66]. In the pursuit of ever-increasing graphical fidelity, methods for integrating photorealistic content into CGI environments are becoming more popular, photogrammetry being one of them [67]. This section will introduce two approaches for the seamless integration of light field footage into virtual environments by rendering new and physically coherent perspectives in real-time.

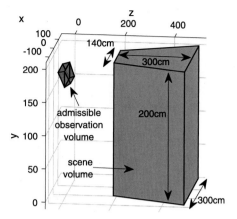

(a) Example scene volume with a depth of 300 cm and a volume height of 200 cm. The front width of the volume is 140 cm, the back width 300 cm.

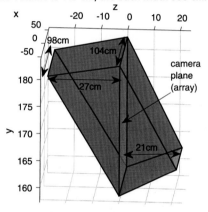

(b) Admissible observation volume for a camera array with 3 rows, each having 10 cameras. The horizontal and vertical distance between the cameras equals 12 cm. The scene volume is located in positive z-direction in a distance of 2 m. The light-gray plane corresponds to the position of the camera array. Its height is 24 cm.

Figure 9.5 Admissible observation volume for a planar light field array.

9.6.1 Pixel-based depth image-based rendering

As already discussed in the previous sections and outlined in Fig. 9.1, there are multiple ways for achieving a novel view synthesis when using multi-camera setups. In the case where a 3D geometry model is not available, pixel-based depth image-based rendering yields promising results [15,38]. The possibility of high parallelization through GPU acceleration of the required pixel-based calculations makes this approach especially feasible for real-time applications, such as virtual reality (VR) experiences. This allows for the integration and composition of real-world light field content into CGI environments,

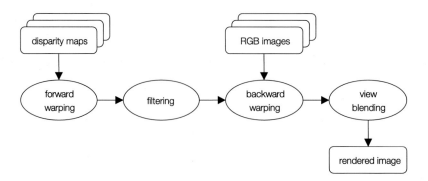

Figure 9.6 Overview of the pixel-based depth image-based rendering pipeline.

where the necessary views are rendered in a perspectively correct fashion. The actual composition is realized by employing an intermediate screen element, which displays a reconstructed view of the light field that is rendered w.r.t. the viewer's current position. The whole processing chain for this rendering approach consists of four components, as outlined in Fig. 9.6.

The input is expected to be N color images and corresponding disparity maps: one for each camera. In the first step, called forward warping, all disparity maps are warped to the camera pose of the target view (see Fig. 9.7, left image). This is done by calculating the pixel position of each source pixel on a new, empty map with the same dimensions as the source map and copying their respective disparity values, resulting in N warped disparity maps. Pixel positions that are outside of the image boundaries are discarded. Special consideration needs to be given to the fact that multiple pixels of a disparity map can be warped to the same target position. In practice, this is often the case when objects occlude each other. Since pixels with higher disparity values in the source disparity map correspond to objects that are closer to the camera, one straightforward approach is to prioritize the source pixel with the highest disparity value, and discarding all others in the case of a warping conflict.

After forward warping, an optional filtering step can be applied to improve the quality of the warped disparity maps by reducing artifacts such as speckles caused by missing or incorrect disparity values in the source maps. Also, since the target pixel positions are discretized, gaps can occur when content is stretched by the warping process.

The following backward warping step can be seen as a texture fetching operation, as it relies on the forward warped disparity maps to get the color information for each target pixel by looking at the corresponding pixel locations in the source images. When attempting to access the color of a source image at a non–integer pixel position, an interpolation using the surrounding pixel values is conducted. The results are exemplified in Fig. 9.7 in the middle image.

Figure 9.7 Left: forward warped and filtered disparity map. Middle: corresponding color image after backward warping using one source camera. Right: final render result after blending multiple backward warped color images together [15]. Both middle and right images are shown before compositing with a potential background, which would smooth the sawtooth-like object borders.

After backward warping, one last blending step combines the backward warped color images to a single target view (Fig. 9.7, right image). Special consideration needs to be taken during the implementation of the blending step to ensure proper handling of occlusions and depth conflicts. Usually, not all N backward warped color images are used, but rather a selection of source views with the least Euclidean distance to the target position, as these views typically show less artifacts, interpolation errors, and occlusions compared to warped images from camera positions that are farther away from the render target. Since a distance-based cut-off criterion for source image selection leads to abrupt changes in the source view selection when the target position is moving through a scene (see Fig. 9.3), the application of a Gaussian distributed weight for each view is a more sensible approach. With this, smooth blending transitions between source view contributions are realized.

9.6.2 Implementation in Unreal Engine

The pixel-based depth image-based rendering approach, as described in Section 9.6.1, can be implemented in Unreal Engine, while using GPU-accelerated compute shaders to facilitate real-time view rendering of video light field content for VR experiences [47,68]. GPU acceleration of the rendering is crucial since the intended use in VR applications requires rendering with at least 90 fps, leaving a maximum time window of 11.1 ms, until the whole light field rendering pipeline has to be completed.

To enable a fast rendering with minimal delay, static memory blocks for both input (RGB images and depth maps) and output are set up in the form of texture buffers that new data can be streamed into or read from in an asynchronous way. One advantage of this texture buffer approach is the capability to also play back videos by constantly streaming new data into the input buffer. The implementation uses a cyclic double buffer, one for RAM and one for VRAM, so as to enable smooth streaming from a comparatively slow (SSD) hard disk drive into the GPU memory. Since the render target is also a texture buffer, this buffer can be assigned as material for any object inside the CG world, enabling this object to serve as display for the most recently rendered view. This object can also be considered as a screen or a light field display inside the virtual environment. With minor adjustments to the computations done in the forward and backward warping, this object can have various shapes, e.g., a sphere or cylinder, and could then also be used to accurately display footage from non-planar arrays, capture domes, or free-hand footage of static scenes. But in the basic use case, when processing data recorded by a planar light field array, the object has the shape of a plane, resulting in a flat light field display with similar properties, like a window.

One remaining challenge of this VR-based approach is that the user and, consequently, the pose of the rendered target view, can be freely chosen. This requires a proper handling of render poses that are not covered by the source footage, because they are outside the admissible observation volume (cf. Section 9.5.2). This can be solved by placing a virtual wall or other opaque objects around the light field display. They naturally block viewing positions and angles from outside the admissible observer space, ensuring valid view renderings from any target pose. The light field display hence represents a window through which the captured content can be watched. This represents an intuitive way of blocking unwanted viewing directions and is easily understood by users, enhancing the feeling of immersion. Fig. 9.8 visualizes this concept with an example. The window analogy holds for all relevant aspects of the rendering, as long as the content displayed by the light field is physically placed behind the display, i.e., the light field display should be located between the viewer and the rendered content.

9.6.3 Mesh-based rendering for view-dependent effects

Render pipelines for meshes are highly optimized on GPUs to deliver remarkable performance for ambitious video game productions. Such pipelines can be extended with image-based rendering techniques for real-time applications to combine the benefits from both worlds for novel view synthesis. The open-source toolkit COLIBRI VR [69] aims to provide a mesh-based implementation for image-based rendering for VR content creators, who use the Unity game engine. Any collection of photographs with either image- or model-based geometry representation (cf. Section 9.1) from COLMAP [29] can be transformed into virtual environments by the custom render pipeline. The main feature of this toolkit is to preserve view-dependent effects, such as specular highlights from the original images and with that, to achieve an accurate rendering of the reconstructed object surface beyond a diffuse texture map, as shown

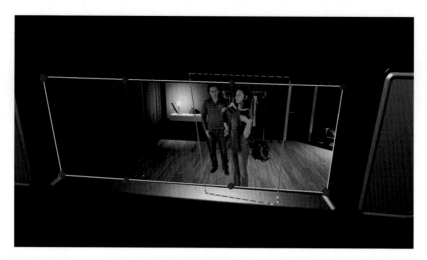

Figure 9.8 Real-time rendering of a light field dataset and integration into a virtual scene using Unreal Engine. The light field video data was captured by a planar 4 × 2 camera array; camera positions are marked with red points. The wall around the window, indicated by a green rectangle in landscape format, blocks viewing angles from outside the admissible observer space. The blue rectangle in portrait format surrounds the rendered content, which is placed "inside" the virtual room [15].

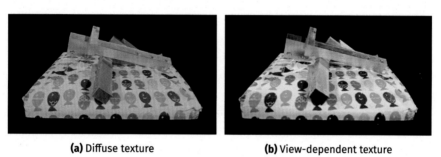

(a) Diffuse texture   **(b)** View-dependent texture

Figure 9.9 Comparison between diffuse texture map and view-dependent texture mapping using the unstructured lumigraph rendering from COLIBRI VR for the same mesh in the Unity game engine. Using the *diffuse texture*, the metal bars look flat and unreal. The *view-dependent texture* can better represent the non-Lambertian surfaces.

in Fig. 9.9. Two different real-time rendering solutions are implemented for still photographs.

The first one is based on the unstructured lumigraph rendering algorithm [1] and requires a global mesh. The key element of this method is an angular and resolution-based blending function to achieve the view-dependent texture mapping. The mesh is being used as a geometry proxy to compute the blending weights. Source cameras

(a) Rendering from original local mesh   **(b)** Rendering from filtered local mesh

Figure 9.10 Local mesh topology can be filtered to compensate stretching artifacts at disocclusion boundaries.

with a location nearby a visible vertex and a viewing angle close to the target view will be assigned a higher weight compared with farther away or even occluded ones. The weights are computed in the vertex stage of the render pipeline (cf. [70] for an overview of a conventional 3D graphics pipeline) for each source camera, where all vertices of the mesh are being processed before the actual primitive assembly. In the fragment stage, the blending of the colors is done after the rasterization of the primitives to compute the final data for the rendered pixel.

To avoid interpolation of the weights between the different pipeline stages, both steps are additionally implemented as a standalone fragment shader, which gives near ray tracing quality based on per-pixel weights. However, due to performance reasons, the actual number of relevant source cameras that contribute to the rendering are just a fraction of the original input and are mostly limited by hardware restrictions. A drawback of this rendering method are the visible ghosting artifacts caused by inaccurate camera calibration or mesh reconstruction.

The second implementation relies on per-view meshes using depth maps similar to [71]. A triangulation produces local meshes with mesh primitives covering several pixels. Those mesh primitives are generated in such a way that loss of accuracy during view rendering can be avoided. As shown in Fig. 9.10, only at disocclusion boundaries, stretching artifacts are likely to appear, which can be eliminated by the user with the toolkit.

For the rendering, the per-view meshes must be processed successively with a custom depth test to blend the projected colors at the target view. Otherwise, artifacts will appear at rendered occlusions if the depth order is not being considered. The blending weights are similar to ones used in the unstructured lumigraph rendering pipeline, and therefore preserve, to some extent, view-dependent effects. The biggest challenge for this method is the geometric inconsistency that cannot be resolved on per-view basis and must be handled during the blending step.

9.7. Neural rendering and 3D reconstruction

After having introduced different light field processing and rendering pipelines using procedural signal processing, this chapter will focus on data-driven methods. Section 9.7.1 starts by introducing learning-based architectures that follow the structure of procedural processing pipelines using an image-based geometry representation. Afterwards, algorithms using implicit geometry representations are introduced in Section 9.7.2. These approaches differ more significantly from the concepts discussed so far, in that information is not stored in a discrete form anymore, but as approximating functions. Finally, Section 9.7.3 shows how neural representations can also be applied to rendering concepts that rely on model-based geometry.

9.7.1 Neural network-based rendering for light field angular super-resolution

This section will explain the image-based rendering (IBR) and depth image-based rendering (DIBR) approaches, as illustrated in Fig. 9.1, which rely on neural networks. These approaches are particularly well suited to increase the limited angular resolution of plenoptic light field cameras [72].

Inspired by the success of deep learning for the task of single-image super-resolution (SR), different IBR methods for light field rendering emerged. Yoon et al. introduced two shallow convolutional neural networks (CNN), each consisting of three convolution layers, to sequentially interpolate both spatial and angular resolution [73]. Similarly, Gul et al. proposed utilizing the raw lenslet image correlation for spatial and angular resolution enhancement [74]. Exploring alternative representations, Wu et al. [75] and Wang et al. [76] reconstruct novel views of the light field by increasing the resolution of the epipolar images using a 2D CNN and a network consisting of both 2D and 3D convolutions.

DIBR methods synthesize novel views based on the recovered underlying geometry, such as depth. Kalantari et al. proposed the first end-to-end neural network-based method to mimic the conventional DIBR pipeline using convolutional neural networks [77]. The whole process is divided into two steps: depth estimation and color reconstruction. They proposed to reconstruct a dense light field using only four corner input images. First, they extracted features by calculating the mean and variance of the warped input images at discrete depth values. Then, a convolutional neural network processed these extracted features to estimate a disparity map at a novel target position. Based on the estimated geometry (i.e., disparity map), all four input views are warped to a target location, which is then fed into another convolutional neural network synthesizing the final target view. As opposed to single view rendering in Kalantari's approach [77], Jin et al. [78] proposed a simultaneous reconstruction of all light field views. Following the two-step process, a CNN-based depth estimation module estimates the 4D light field depth maps to warp the input images to generate warped

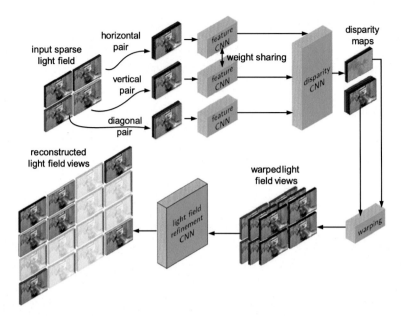

Figure 9.11 Pipeline of the light field view synthesis method *LFVS-AM* [82]. The process is divided into three CNNs: stereo feature extraction, disparity estimation, and light field refinement.

light fields. Then, a novel light field blending module composed of spatio-angular separable (SAS) convolutions [79] generates the final dense light field. A SAS convolution performs a 4D convolution by implementing a sequence of interleaved 2D convolutions (namely 2D spatial and 2D angular convolutions). In contrast to using four corner views, a dense 4D light field rendering from a single image is also possible; however, the quality of the rendered views suffers. Srinivasan et al. [80] estimate the 4D depth map from the center image using a nine-layer CNN consisting of dilated convolutions. Then a 3D convolution-based residual network renders the final light field by processing the warped light field generated using the estimated depth maps. Deviating from a two-step process, Navarro et al. [81] model the view rendering pipeline into three networks, namely feature extraction, depth estimation, and view selection. Rather than using the input views directly for depth estimation, they introduced a neural network to extract features from each image individually. In the end, a view selection network determines the contribution of each warped image to the final result. However, these methods mostly fail to recover fine structures and occluded regions.

This can be improved by an attention mechanism, as presented by *LFVS-AM* [82]. Similar to Navarro et al. [81], the *LFVS-AM* method also models the light field view rendering pipeline using three neural networks, stereo feature extraction, disparity estimation, and light field refinement, as shown in Fig. 9.11. The proposed method consists

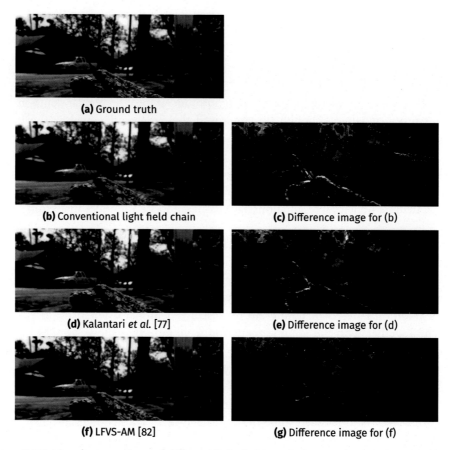

(a) Ground truth

(b) Conventional light field chain   **(c)** Difference image for (b)

(d) Kalantari *et al.* [77]   **(e)** Difference image for (d)

(f) LFVS-AM [82]   **(g)** Difference image for (f)

Figure 9.12 Visual comparison of different light field rendering methods using a test image from [77]. Except for *LFVS-AM* [82], all other methods failed to reconstruct the fine leave structure.

of three main features. First, *LFVS-AM* requires only three out of four corner views relative to the target view position, reducing the computational complexity. Second, *LFVS-AM* extracts features directly from stereo pairs, which helps in estimating accurate disparity maps. Finally, an attention mechanism–based refinement network, incorporating convolutional block attention modules (CBAMs) [83], reconstructs the novel views. CBAMs consist of spatial and channel attention focusing the network on critical regions of the features. Fig. 9.12 shows the visual comparison of different DIBR approaches against the non–learning-based light field chain presented in Section 9.1.

Although these results show that neural networks can deliver good results, all the methods discussed above can only cope with light fields having small base lines. In the case where there are larger base lines, the achievable quality significantly drops. One approach to solve this problem consists of the use of neural implicit representations, as discussed in the following section.

9.7.2 Neural implicit representations

In the previous section, neural networks were introduced into the regular depth image-based rendering pipeline. Though this improved the final render quality, the neural networks are not able to overcome the shortcomings of the depth-based approach itself. Semi-transparencies, for example, are impossible to represent for depth-based approaches, since a single depth value per image pixel is not enough to represent multiple objects that may be visible to that pixel. To address the shortcoming of depth-based approaches, neural implicit representations have garnered more and more interest in recent years.

Specifically, neural radiance fields (NeRF) [84], as introduced in Chapter 7, have shown promising visual fidelity on novel view synthesis tasks. The NeRF-generated depth map, as shown in Fig. 9.13, highlights a NeRF's capability to learn very detailed geometry for a given scene. Even fine details like leaves of plants that usually pose problems for traditional stereo matching are reconstructed properly when using a NeRF approach. Together with the volume rendering technique that allows NeRFs to learn semi-transparent objects and its capability to learn view-dependent effects, NeRF renders can achieve almost photorealistic quality, as can be seen in Fig. 9.13. The original NeRF publication sparked an explosion of follow-up works from the wider field of neural rendering (see Fig. 9.14). These works have further improved upon the original concept of NeRFs and reduced some of their downsides. These downsides include for instance their long training and rendering times, as well being limited to static scenes. While Chapter 7 has made a theoretical introduction to the concept of NeRFs, this section will introduce some of the aforementioned follow-up works, their trade-offs, and highlight some remaining practical challenges in the field of neural implicit scene reconstruction.

Figure 9.13 Results for novel view synthesis using NeRF [84]. Left: rendered image; right: false color depth map.

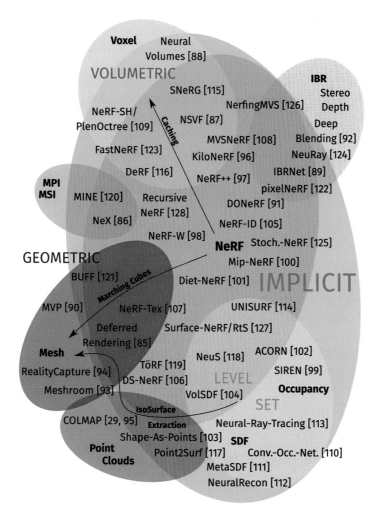

Figure 9.14 Overview map of the neural implicit representation literature [29,85–128] surrounding neural radiance fields [84] as of November 2021. Dynamic, deformable, and relightable representations as well as representations with joint pose estimation have been omitted for clarity.

Practical challenge 1: input data

Like traditional light field rendering techniques, most neural implicit reconstruction approaches assume known camera poses for its input photographs. Since neural implicit approaches optimize a globally consistent geometry and appearance, even a slight misalignment in the poses would introduce conflicting information into the optimization process. While accurate pose estimates are no problem for computer-generated data, the concept of Structure-from-Motion (SfM) that is often used to register cameras for real scenes can fail or give subpar estimates. This would lead to reduced image quality of the final renders.

To avoid this, more recent works such as [129,130] also allow the optimizer to back-propagate the rendering loss to the input camera poses. These are then jointly optimized during training. To allow faster convergence, the poses are usually still initialized with the output of a Structure-from-Motion estimation. The optimizer then only needs to fine-tune the pose estimates. In case no initial estimation is provided, these approaches can compensate for it with a more complex and longer training process. In either case, the final renders are of higher quality than they would be without fine-tuning the poses [129,130].

Similarly, remaining distortion in the input photographs can also give the optimizer conflicting information, leading to degenerated solutions. Either camera distortions need to be modeled in the neural rendering pipeline or the input data for the training process needs to be undistorted beforehand. One neural representation that handles camera distortions in its training process is the Self-Calibrating-NeRF [131].

Since NeRF methods typically expect input photographs from a globally consistent scene, casually photographed scenes with slightly dynamic elements, such as leaves moving in the wind, can cause blurry reconstructions. Deformable neural representations have tackled this problem by introducing a neural deformation field into the rendering pipeline [132,133]. This enables the remapping of points in space into a canonical reference space. The scene in this reference space is assumed to be static. The different input photographs and the slight perturbations in their underlying geometry can then be mapped into this canonical space via a neural network. Consequently, a globally consistent NeRF can be trained in the canonical space. The deformation field is trained jointly with the NeRF network.

Likewise, the deformation field can also be trained to map points from a starting position to a different timestamp in a dynamic sequence, e.g., an animation [134,135]. The deformation field then learns how a scene changes over time. This allows dynamic neural representations to also represent light field video content. Note that the deformation field can readily represent deformation operations, but has trouble to model the sudden appearance or disappearance of objects, such as bursting bubbles. Also note that the literature on dynamic implicit representations is in its early stages, with most dynamic sequences being only few seconds long. The training times for dynamic representations are also significantly longer than for static scenes.

Moreover, the input data for an ordinary NeRF is expected to be consistently lit. Again, different shadows and lighting in the different input photographs would give the NeRF conflicting input information. The NeRF then usually tries to bake the different lighting conditions into the view-dependent appearance of objects, giving them excessive and unrealistic view-dependent effects. To reduce these problems,

NeRF in the Wild (NeRF-W) [98] adds a learned latent embedding vector to all input photographs, that can encode lighting changes and many other inconsistencies. The NeRF-W method can then be trained on input photographs taken under vastly different conditions. Once trained, the embedding vectors can also be interpolated and allow NeRF-W to render a scene under different lighting conditions than those existing during capture. More recent works have also investigated how to model lighting more explicitly [136–138]. While most of them still expect studio-quality input data, once trained, they can dynamically re-light the scene [136,137] and even allow material editing [138].

Another less desirable way for an implicit model to deal with inconsistencies in the input data is through floater artifacts. Since the models are only trained to minimize the rendering error for the training poses, they could theoretically simply learn to place a small 2D photograph of the ground truth training view in front of the corresponding pose. The resulting reconstruction, however, would be degenerated and of little use as the model would be unable to correctly synthesize novel view points. Luckily, the regularization inherent in the neural networks discourages this kind of solution, as explained by [97]. Nevertheless, the above-mentioned floater artifacts can still appear. These are small, but dense artifacts floating in front of the training poses, that minimize the training error. When the NeRF training is presented with slightly conflicting information, e.g., inconsistent shadows, these floater artifacts allow the NeRF to still fit all input data. Recently, Mip-NeRF 360 has tackled this problem by using a specialized distortion loss [139].

Practical challenge 2: training

Another big drawback of most neural representations are their training times for days, even on high-end GPUs. The reason is that the NeRF network needs to be inferred for hundreds of samples per pixel during training. Note that a new model needs to be trained from scratch for every new scene.

As pixels can be rendered independently of each other, and samples along each ray can also be inferred independently of each other, an easy way to speed up rendering and thus training is parallelization. While the original NeRF approach makes limited use of such parallelization, a more recent JAX implementation [140] of NeRF, called JaxNeRF [141], scales the NeRF to multiple GPUs. This allows JaxNeRF to cut training time from days to hours, albeit at additional hardware cost.

Another way to speed up neural implicit training is the use of learned initialization. To this end, a meta-representation is trained on multiple scenes simultaneously, such that it can quickly be fine-tuned to any new scene [142]. This so-called *meta-learning* is broadly used in the field of deep learning. The resulting meta-initialization itself does not represent any scene, but is instead used as a starting point for the training of new scene-specific representations. Since this starting point is optimized to converge towards

Figure 9.15 Results for novel view synthesis using a fine-tuned IBRNet [89]. Left: rendered image; right: false color depth map.

novel scenes quickly, the training is faster than it would be from a random initialization. However, generating a meta-initialization itself is computationally intensive. Additionally, its ability to speed up training convergence depends on how close a novel scene is to the training distribution of the learned initialization.

Using explicit prior information, such as LiDAR point clouds, or point clouds from SfM pipelines have also shown promising results for speeding up training times [106]. Here, the depth values for the points of the point cloud are used as an additional supervisory signal that drives the so-called DS-NeRF more quickly towards convergence. While this can speed up training by a factor of 2-6, DS-NeRF training still takes much longer for a given scene than traditional multi-view stereo approaches [10].

Other approaches, like IBRNet, require no scene-specific training at all. Instead, they learn prior information from a training set, also called *priors* in short. They can then be applied to novel unseen scenes [89,122,124]. Such approaches are hence said to *generalize* to unseen scenes. The learned prior information usually takes the form of trained neural network encoders and their feature extractors. They are trained on large 2D image datasets like ImageNet [143] or from large collections of existing scenes. As such, these approaches suffer from the same problems as a learned initialization: they require a computationally expensive initial training, before they can generalize to new scenes with no additional training. They also provide significantly worse geometric reconstruction, compared to, e.g., NeRF. This can be seen when comparing the depth map of an IBRNet in Fig. 9.15 with a NeRF depth map of the same scene in Fig. 9.13. It is also common to fine-tune these models for a given scene with a short additional training phase to gain a small quality improvement.

The high training cost of NeRFs is also limiting their potential resolution. While the NeRF algorithms make no corresponding assumption and could thus be used to train a NeRF on arbitrarily high input image resolutions, the training time scales at least linearly with the amount of input pixels. If the sample count along the volume rendering ray depth is increased with resolution, as is commonly done with multi-plane image approaches, the training time would scale cubically with the resolution. For high resolution content, NeRFs thus quickly become impractical. Most NeRFs in literature today are limited to less than FullHD resolutions.

Practical challenge 3: rendering

Another problem that limits the application of neural implicit representations is their slow rendering speed. Depending on the resolution, a single frame can take minutes to render.

Early attempts to speed up the rendering divided the 3D scene space into a regular grid of small voxels. Rendering can be sped up by one to three orders of magnitude, when placing learned neural feature embeddings in a sparse subset of these voxels. Such a concept has been proposed by the Neural Sparse Voxel Fields (NSVF) [87]. Alternatively, a separate and smaller NeRF network can be learned for every voxel, as proposed by KiloNeRF [96]. However, both NSVF and KiloNeRF only work for bounded scenes. Unbounded and semi-bounded scenes, including forward-facing scenes, cause problems with the regular grid subdivision of the 3D space. In such cases, a space decomposition using frustum shaped voxels (froxels) [144,145] would serve better (see also Chapter 7).

To facilitate real-time rendering, an implicit representation is usually converted into a format that is easier to render. Usually, this is a more explicit representation. After conversion, the original NeRF network can then be discarded. This new format can for example be a cached NeRF representation, such as a PlenOctree [109]. To cache a NeRF, it is densely sampled. Over-sampling may be applied for anti-aliasing purposes. The obtained outputs are stored in a grid representation such as an octree. Instead of performing a costly inference of the NeRF network multiple times per pixel during rendering, the PlenOctree can simply look up the NeRF output values in the cached octree. Similar to Neural Sparse Voxel Fields (NSVF) which exploit sparsity for a speedup, the PlenOctree also only stores a sparse grid of output values. This avoids the cubic growth of required memory with increasing resolution. Still, most cached representations in literature are limited to less than FullHD resolutions.

Since NeRFs are five-dimensional to allow rendering view-dependent effects (three dimensions for geometry and a base color and two dimensions for view-dependent effects), naively caching the output of a NeRF would require a five-dimensional data structure. The curse of dimensionality would make it practically impossible to cache a NeRF with a very high accuracy. To avoid this problem, the cached values are independent of the actual viewing direction. The view-dependent effects are encoded in these outputs to still allow for instance the rendering of specularities. In the case of PlenOctree, the outputs of a NeRF-SH [109] are cached in the form of spherical harmonics (SH), which gives the methods its name NeRF-SH. Other caching approaches, like Sparse Neural Radiance Grids (SNeRG) [115], predict view-independent neural textures. These allow view-dependent effect reconstruction via deferred rendering.

The faster rendering of PlenOctree compared to the NeRF-SH, which it was extracted from, can also be used to accelerate training. To this end, a NeRF-SH training is stopped early and a PlenOctree is extracted. The PlenOctree is then fine-tuned with a similar rendering error towards convergence. Overall, this can significantly outperform a normal NeRF training [109].

Practical challenge 4: mesh extraction

Alternatively to caching, rendering can be sped up by converting a trained implicit representation into a mesh. Such meshes have been used in computer graphics for decades. Dedicated hardware and optimized rendering pipelines have made meshes a common choice for real-time rendering applications, such as video games. Extracting a lightweight mesh from the detailed density field of a neural representation would allow real-time rendering, even on lower-end consumer devices.

The most simple way to extract a mesh from the density field of an implicit representation is a threshold-based marching cubes approach [146]. However, if the threshold is set too low or high, false-positive or false-negative geometry from artifacts might transfer into the extracted mesh. This is a known problem in literature [114,118]. More sophisticated mesh extraction approaches have been tried in [121]. Still, many fine details from the neural density field are lost during mesh extraction.

To extract detailed meshes from optimized, neural representations, literature has started to incorporate level-sets into the volume rendering pipeline. Level-set modeling implicitly represents surfaces based on a function that maps a point in 3D space to a real value. All points leading to the same and well defined function value are considered to belong to the surface. A signed distance function (SDF), for instance, has a gradient norm of one with its zero level-set defining the surface [147].

Specifically, approaches like [104,114,118] convert a learned level-set function into a density field before volume rendering. This allows them to make use of the superior optimization process of density field approaches and drops the pixel mask requirement common in previous neural implicit level-sets [148]. Once the level-set function has been trained, isosurface extraction can generate a mesh with arbitrarily low quality loss from the level-set geometry. The only downside of level-sets compared to density fields is that they cannot readily support transparencies.

Once extracted, a neural texture for deferred rendering can provide view-dependent color appearance for the mesh geometry [85]. Alternatively, a texture can be extracted from the implicit representation itself. NeuTex [149] instead reformulates the training of the implicit representation such that it jointly learns a texture alongside the geometry. Furthermore, the rendering of the extracted mesh could be sped up by using one of the growing number of differential mesh renderers for mesh simplification, such as [150].

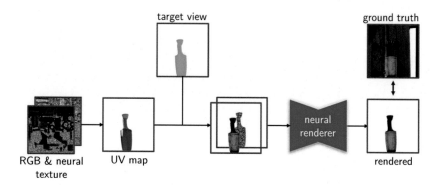

Figure 9.16 Deferred neural rendering pipeline using neural textures.

9.7.3 Neural textures

Using neural textures [85] for novel view synthesis enables high fidelity rendering of objects with complex appearance, including the reproduction of view-dependent effects. Moreover, they can conceal imperfections of the geometry itself without ever touching it, thus being complementary to the methods described in Section 9.7.2.

As the name of the method *deferred neural rendering* suggests, the approach adds a neural component to the traditional computer graphics technique *deferred rendering* [151, 152]. Deferred rendering is commonly used to reduce computations by splitting the rasterization of geometry and the actual shading into two passes. Thus, appearance computations like illumination and material evaluation are only performed for visible fragments.

In the case of deferred neural rendering, shading is performed by a neural network, often referred to as *neural renderer*. This neural renderer interprets neural descriptors that are projected to screen space via the sampling of the neural texture using standard texture coordinates. By doing so, shading is performed from a statistical point of view rather than a physically-based one. An overview of the described pipeline is illustrated in Fig. 9.16. Using traditional computer graphics techniques, the neural and RGB textures are projected into the target view. UV maps establish the relation between the texture images and the geometry primitives. The neural renderer then transforms the projected textures into a rendered image. Both the neural renderer and the neural textures can be trained by comparing the rendered image with the corresponding ground truth.

The neural renderer is often implemented with a U-Net-like [153] architecture [85,154–156], as its skip connections are a favorable design choice for tasks that are framed by a 1-to-1 pixel correlation of in- and output. Thus, the architecture enables fast convergence and the reproduction of high frequency details.

Neural textures are tightly coupled to surface light fields [51,52] and can be seen as a neurally encoded and tightly compressed form of such a light field. Surface light fields are parameterized by the surface position and the view direction – the position it is looked at from. For example, a surface light field may be implemented by storing multiple color samples for each valid texture coordinate, each sample corresponding to a different view direction, respectively. Novel view synthesis can then be performed by rendering the closest sample (with regard to position and angle) that can be found in the texture for a given view ray.

While there is not a neural descriptor stored per view direction, view dependency is achieved by the neural renderer which learns descriptor constellations. The render quality can be further enhanced by "masking out" unnecessary parts of the current view before the textured image is fed into the neural renderer network. To this end, Thies et al. propose the descriptors to be multiplied by the spherical harmonics coefficients of the first three bands of the per-pixel view direction. Thus, neural textures offer a vast compression factor compared to traditional surface light fields that need to store an RGB value for a reasonable amount of directions for any given texture element position.

Note that this view dependency is not limited to view-dependent effects like reflections to mimic complex materials, but also fixes mismatching geometry – solely in screen space – up to some degree. This is an exceptionally interesting feature for novel view synthesis of real scenes as reconstructed meshes from photogrammetry are hardly ever perfect. Also, for highly textured materials like fur or grass which usually have to be modeled by volumes that are expensive to render, this ability is promising.

Using neural feature descriptors to encode information that go beyond standard RGB color is a paradigm seen quite frequently in the state of the art and proves their usability beyond mesh-based geometry representations. Similar to the mesh-based rendering, papers like [155–157] show how such descriptors can be used for point clouds in conjunction with a neural renderer to overcome sparsity and thus, provide great visual fidelity. Others [89] show the feasibility of descriptors for volume-based representations and alike.

Many works [85,155,157] on novel view synthesis propose overfitting to a single or in the best case to only a handful of somewhat similar scenes. Thus, retraining is needed for every new object or in the worst case even for the slightest change in the scene, limiting the use case to learning a single light field by rote. Scene re-composition, especially for objects with specular materials, proves hard as reflections are baked into the descriptors.

However, neural textures can be used beyond their use as compressed light fields. The generalization to unseen scenes, re-lighting, and scene editing is subject of current state-of-the-art methods [89,154,156,158]. Meshry et al. [156] resolve occlusions and achieve re-lighting for touristic scenes by conditioning scene appearance on learned embeddings. Controllable re-lighting for indoor scenes is the subject in the works of Meka et al. [159] and Öchsle et al. [160]. Wang et al. [89] show promising results towards generalization and the applicability for various datasets. Another direction is the incorporation of the plenoptic function's time domain that is usually omitted and thus allowing for controllable animation of faces [161] or replaying video clips from novel view points [135].

In summary, neural textures and related work can be interpreted as highly condensed surface light fields allowing for high fidelity novel view synthesis. However, the direction of ongoing research points to tasks that go beyond the sole reconstruction of known scenes.

9.8. Conclusion and open challenges

Light fields offer a much richer representation of real world scenes in media applications as they enable observation from different perspectives. As a result, the experience is more immersive or realistic compared to a 2D image or video. To make this possible, it is necessary to design and implement a complete processing pipeline, encompassing light field capture, camera calibration, geometry reconstruction, content editing, and real-time rendering approaches. Many solutions have been proposed in this regard, making light field media experiences more and more realistic. Still, a lot of challenges need to be overcome to make light fields applicable in a larger scale. Core aspects include the achievable quality as well as the handling of the large amounts of data and necessary computation. Neural algorithms promise to bring a new way of thinking into these domains. While showing a very high potential to advance light field processing in a significant manner, they currently suffer from huge computation demands and low supported resolutions. Furthermore, a consolidation of the huge variety of possible solutions still needs to be achieved in the future.

Acknowledgments

Parts of this work have been funded by the Free State of Bavaria in the DSAI project and by European Union's Horizon 2020 research and innovation program under the Marie Skłodowska-Curie grant agreement No. 765911 (RealVision).

References

[1] C. Buehler, M. Bosse, L. McMillan, S. Gortler, M. Cohen, Unstructured lumigraph rendering, in: Proceedings of the 28th Annual Conference on Computer Graphics and Interactive Techniques (SIGGRAPH), ACM Press, Los Angeles, CA, USA, 2001, pp. 425–432, https://doi.org/10.1145/383259.383309.

[2] A. Davis, M. Levoy, F. Durand, Unstructured light fields, Computer Graphics Forum 31 (2pt1) (2012) 305–314, https://doi.org/10.1111/j.1467-8659.2012.03009.x.

[3] Image-Based Rendering (IBR), K. Ikeuchi (Ed.), Computer Vision: A Reference Guide, Springer US, Boston, MA, 2014, pp. 399–399, https://doi.org/10.1007/978-0-387-31439-6_100163.

[4] F.S. Zakeri, A. Durmush, M. Ziegler, M. Bätz, J. Keinert, Non-planar inside-out dense light-field dataset and reconstruction pipeline, in: IEEE International Conference on Image Processing (ICIP), Taipei, Taiwan, 2019, pp. 1059–1063, https://doi.org/10.1109/icip.2019.8803402.

[5] M. Ziegler, R. op het Veld, J. Keinert, F. Zilly, Acquisition system for dense lightfield of large scenes, in: 3DTV Conference: The True Vision - Capture, Transmission and Display of 3D Video (3DTV-CON), 2017, IEEE, Copenhagen, Denmark, 2017, pp. 1–4, https://doi.org/10.1109/3DTV.2017. 8280412.

[6] D. Scharstein, R. Szeliski, R. Zabih, A taxonomy and evaluation of dense two-frame stereo correspondence algorithms, in: IEEE Workshop on Stereo and Multi-Baseline Vision (SMBV), Kauai, HI, USA, 2001, pp. 131–140, https://doi.org/10.1109/smbv.2001.988771.

[7] C. Tomasi, R. Manduchi, Bilateral filtering for gray and color images, in: IEEE 6th International Conference on Computer Vision (ICCV), Bombay, India, 1998, pp. 839–846, https://doi.org/10. 1109/iccv.1998.710815.

[8] S. Paris, P. Kornprobst, J. Tumblin, F. Durand, A gentle introduction to bilateral filtering and its applications, in: ACM SIGGRAPH, 2007, p. 130, https://doi.org/10.1145/1281500.1281602.

[9] M. Berger, A. Tagliasacchi, L.M. Seversky, P. Alliez, G. Guennebaud, J.A. Levine, A. Sharf, C.T. Silva, A survey of surface reconstruction from point clouds, Computer Graphics Forum 36 (1) (2017) 301–329, https://doi.org/10.1111/cgf.12802.

[10] Y. Furukawa, C. Hernández, Multi-view stereo: a tutorial, Foundations and Trends in Computer Graphics and Vision 9 (1/2) (2015), Now, Boston Delft.

[11] A. Ernst, A. Papst, T. Ruf, J.-U. Garbas, Check my chart: A robust color chart tracker for colorimetric camera calibration, in: 6th International Conference on Computer Vision / Computer Graphics Collaboration Techniques and Applications, MIRAGE '13, New York, NY, USA, 2013, pp. 1–8, https://doi.org/10.1145/2466715.2466717.

[12] N. Joshi, B. Wilburn, V. Vaish, M. Levoy, M. Horowitz, Automatic Color Calibration for Large Camera Arrays, UC San Diego: Department of Computer Science & Engineering, San Diego, 2005, p. 4.

[13] A. Ilie, G. Welch, Ensuring color consistency across multiple cameras, in: IEEE International Conference on Computer Vision (ICCV), vol. 2, Beijing, China, 2005, pp. 1268–1275, https:// doi.org/10.1109/iccv.2005.88.

[14] K. Li, Q. Dai, W. Xu, High quality color calibration for multi-camera systems with an omnidirectional color checker, in: IEEE International Conference on Acoustics, Speech and Signal Processing (ICASSP), Dallas, TX, USA, 2010, pp. 1026–1029, https://doi.org/10.1109/icassp.2010.5495322.

[15] M. Ziegler, Advanced image processing for immersive media applications using sparse light-fields, Ph.D. thesis, Friedrich-Alexander-Universität Erlangen-Nürnberg (FAU), Erlangen, 2019.

[16] M. Schöberl, Modeling of Image Acquisition for Improving Digital Camera Systems, Ph.D. thesis, Friedrich-Alexander-Universität Erlangen-Nürnberg (FAU), Erlangen, 2013.

[17] R. Hartley, A. Zisserman, Multiple View Geometry in Computer Vision, 2nd edition, Cambridge University Press, Cambridge, 2004, https://doi.org/10.1017/CBO9780511811685.

[18] F. Bajramovic, J. Denzler, Self-calibration with partially known rotations, in: F.A. Hamprecht, C. Schnörr, B. Jähne (Eds.), Pattern Recognition, in: Lecture Notes in Computer Science, vol. 4713, Springer Berlin Heidelberg, Berlin, Heidelberg, 2007, pp. 1–10, https://doi.org/10.1007/978-3-540-74936-3_1.

[19] P. Baker, Y. Aloimonos, Complete calibration of a multi-camera network, in: Proceedings IEEE Workshop on Omnidirectional Vision (Cat. No. PR00704), 2000, pp. 134–141, https://doi.org/10. 1109/omnvis.2000.853820.

[20] M. Brückner, F. Bajramovic, J. Denzler, Intrinsic and extrinsic active self-calibration of multi-camera systems, Machine Vision and Applications 25 (2) (2014) 389–403, https://doi.org/10.1007/s00138-013-0541-x.

[21] A. Bushnevskiy, L. Sorgi, B. Rosenhahn, Multicamera calibration from visible and mirrored epipoles, in: IEEE/CVF Conference on Computer Vision and Pattern Recognition (CVPR), Las Vegas, NV, USA, 2016, pp. 3373–3381, https://doi.org/10.1109/cvpr.2016.367.

[22] X. Chen, J. Davis, P. Slusallek, Wide area camera calibration using virtual calibration objects, in: IEEE Conference on Computer Vision and Pattern Recognition (CVPR), vol. 2, Hilton Head Island, SC, USA, 2000, pp. 520–527, https://doi.org/10.1109/cvpr.2000.854901.

[23] F. Kahlesz, C. Lilge, R. Klein, Easy-to-use calibration of multiple-camera setups, in: International Conference on Computer Vision Systems (ICVS) Camera Calibration Methods for Computer Vision Systems (CCMVS), Dec. 2007, https://doi.org/10.2390/biecoll-icvs2007-177.

[24] G. Kurillo, H. Baker, Z. Li, R. Bajcsy, Geometric and color calibration of multiview panoramic cameras for life-size 3D immersive video, in: International Conference on 3D Vision (3DV), Seattle, WA, USA, 2013, pp. 374–381, https://doi.org/10.1109/3dv.2013.56.

[25] T. Svoboda, D. Martinec, T. Pajdla, A convenient multicamera self-calibration for virtual environments, Presence: Teleoperators & Virtual Environments 14 (4) (2005) 407–422, https://doi.org/10.1162/105474605774785325.

[26] S. Urban, S. Wursthorn, J. Leitloff, S. Hinz, MultiCol bundle adjustment: A generic method for pose estimation, simultaneous self-calibration and reconstruction for arbitrary multi-camera systems, International Journal of Computer Vision 121 (2) (2017) 234–252, https://doi.org/10.1007/s11263-016-0935-0.

[27] V. Vaish, B. Wilburn, N. Joshi, M. Levoy, Using plane + parallax for calibrating dense camera arrays, in: IEEE Conference on Computer Vision and Pattern Recognition (CVPR), vol. 1, Washington, DC, USA, 2004, pp. 2–9, https://doi.org/10.1109/cvpr.2004.1315006.

[28] Z. Zhang, A flexible new technique for camera calibration, IEEE Transactions on Pattern Analysis and Machine Intelligence 22 (11) (2000) 1330–1334, https://doi.org/10.1109/34.888718.

[29] J.L. Schönberger, J.-M. Frahm, Structure-from-motion revisited, in: IEEE Conference on Computer Vision and Pattern Recognition (CVPR), Las Vegas, NV, USA, 2016, pp. 4104–4113, https://doi.org/10.1109/cvpr.2016.445.

[30] J. Ma, X. Jiang, A. Fan, J. Jiang, J. Yan, Image matching from handcrafted to deep features: a survey, International Journal of Computer Vision 129 (1) (2021) 23–79, https://doi.org/10.1007/s11263-020-01359-2.

[31] F. Zilly, Method for the automated analysis, control and correction of stereoscopic distortions and parameters for 3D-TV applications: New image processing algorithms to improve the efficiency of stereo- and multi-camera 3D-TV productions, Ph.D. thesis, Technische Universität Berlin, Berlin, 2015, https://doi.org/10.14279/depositonce-4618.

[32] F. Zilly, C. Riechert, M. Müller, P. Eisert, T. Sikora, P. Kauff, Real-time generation of multi-view video plus depth content using mixed narrow and wide baseline, Journal of Visual Communication and Image Representation 25 (4) (2014) 632–648, https://doi.org/10.1016/j.jvcir.2013.07.002.

[33] Daniel Scharstein, Richard Szeliski, Heiko Hirschmüller, Middlebury stereo vision page, https://vision.middlebury.edu/stereo/. (Accessed 6 December 2021).

[34] A. Geiger, P. Lenz, C. Stiller, R. Urtasun, The KITTI vision benchmark suite, http://www.cvlibs.net/datasets/kitti/eval_scene_flow.php?benchmark=stereo. (Accessed 6 December 2021).

[35] R.A. Hamzah, H. Ibrahim, Literature survey on stereo vision disparity map algorithms, Journal of Sensors (2016) 1–23, https://doi.org/10.1155/2016/8742920.

[36] Z. Tu, W. Xie, D. Zhang, R. Poppe, R.C. Veltkamp, B. Li, J. Yuan, A survey of variational and CNN-based optical flow techniques, Signal Processing. Image Communication 72 (2019) 9–24, https://doi.org/10.1016/j.image.2018.12.002.

[37] M. Zhai, X. Xiang, N. Lv, X. Kong, Optical flow and scene flow estimation: A survey, Pattern Recognition 114 (2021) 107861, https://doi.org/10.1016/j.patcog.2021.107861.

[38] M. Ziegler, A. Engelhardt, S. Müller, J. Keinert, F. Zilly, S. Foessel, K. Schmid, Multi-camera system for depth based visual effects and compositing, in: 12th European Conference on Visual Media Production, CVMP '15, Association for Computing Machinery, New York, NY, USA, 2015, pp. 1–10, https://doi.org/10.1145/2824840.2824845.

[39] X. Mei, X. Sun, M. Zhou, S. Jiao, H. Wang, X. Zhang, On building an accurate stereo matching system on graphics hardware, in: IEEE International Conference on Computer Vision Workshops (ICCV Workshops), Barcelona, Spain, 2011, pp. 467–474, https://doi.org/10.1109/iccvw.2011.6130280.

[40] H. Hirschmuller, Accurate and efficient stereo processing by semi-global matching and mutual information, in: IEEE Computer Society Conference on Computer Vision and Pattern Recognition (CVPR), vol. 2, San Diego, CA, USA, 2005, pp. 807–814, https://doi.org/10.1109/cvpr.2005.56.

[41] Nuke | VFX and Film Editing Software, https://www.foundry.com/products/nuke-family/nuke. (Accessed 6 December 2021).

[42] Nuke (software), Wikipedia. (Accessed 6 December 2021).

[43] Fusion 17 | Blackmagic Design, https://www.blackmagicdesign.com/products/fusion/. (Accessed 6 December 2021).

[44] Blackmagic Fusion, Wikipedia. (Accessed 6 December 2021).

[45] Blender (software), Wikipedia. (Accessed 6 December 2021).

[46] B. Foundation, Blender.org - Home of the Blender project - Free and Open 3D Creation Software, https://www.blender.org/. (Accessed 6 December 2021).

[47] Realception®, https://www.iis.fraunhofer.de/en/ff/amm/content-production/realception.html. (Accessed 6 December 2021).

[48] Unreal Engine | The most powerful real-time 3D creation tool, https://www.unrealengine.com/en-US/. (Accessed 6 December 2021).

[49] Unreal Engine (software), Wikipedia. (Accessed 6 December 2021).

[50] C. Riechert, F.L. Zilly, M. Mã, Real-time disparity estimation using line-wise hybrid recursive matching and cross-bilateral median up-sampling, in: International Conference on Pattern Recognition (ICPR), Tsukuba Science City, Japan, 2012, p. 4.

[51] W.-C. Chen, J.-Y. Bouguet, M.H. Chu, R. Grzeszczuk, Light field mapping: efficient representation and hardware rendering of surface light fields, ACM Transactions on Graphics 21 (3) (2002) 447–456, https://doi.org/10.1145/566654.566601.

[52] D.N. Wood, D.I. Azuma, K. Aldinger, B. Curless, T. Duchamp, D.H. Salesin, W. Stuetzle, Surface light fields for 3D photography, in: 27th Annual Conference on Computer Graphics and Interactive Techniques (SIGGRAPH), New Orleans, LA, USA, 2000, pp. 287–296, https://doi.org/10.1145/344779.344925.

[53] P. Hedman, T. Ritschel, G. Drettakis, G. Brostow, Scalable inside-out image-based rendering, ACM Transactions on Graphics 35 (6) (2016) 1–11, https://doi.org/10.1145/2980179.2982420.

[54] A.P. Pozo, M. Toksvig, T.F. Schrager, J. Hsu, U. Mathur, A. Sorkine-Hornung, R. Szeliski, B. Cabral, An integrated 6DoF video camera and system design, ACM Transactions on Graphics 38 (6) (2019) 1–16, https://doi.org/10.1145/3355089.3356555.

[55] D. Bonatto, S. Fachada, S. Rogge, A. Munteanu, G. Lafruit, Real-time depth video-based rendering for 6-DoF HMD navigation and light field displays, IEEE Access 9 (2021) 146868–146887, https://doi.org/10.1109/access.2021.3123529.

[56] M. Broxton, J. Flynn, R. Overbeck, D. Erickson, P. Hedman, M. DuVall, J. Dourgarian, J. Busch, M. Whalen, P. Debevec, Immersive light field video with a layered mesh representation, ACM Transactions on Graphics 39 (4) (2020) 15, https://doi.org/10.1145/3386569.3392485.

[57] B. Vandame, N. Sabater, G. Boisson, D. Doyen, V. Allié, F. Babon, R. Gendrot, T. Langlois, A. Schubert, Pipeline for real-time video view synthesis, in: IEEE International Conference on Multimedia Expo Workshops (ICMEW), London, UK, 2020, pp. 1–6, https://doi.org/10.1109/ICMEW46912.2020.9105988.

[58] M. Herceg, M. Kvasnica, C.N. Jones, M. Morari, Multi-Parametric Toolbox 3.0, in: European Control Conference (ECC), Zurich, Switzerland, 2013, pp. 502–510, https://doi.org/10.23919/ecc.2013.6669862.

[59] U. Technologies, Unity Real-Time Development Platform | 3D, 2D VR & AR Engine, https://unity.com/. (Accessed 6 December 2021).

[60] Unity (software), Wikipedia. (Accessed 6 December 2021).

[61] F. Lv, C. Hu, Research on simulation of pedestrian flow Unity 3D through multiple exit architecture, in: International Conference on Computer Engineering and Intelligent Control (ICCEIC), Chongqing, China, 2020, pp. 51–54, https://doi.org/10.1109/icceic51584.2020.00018.

[62] F. Valls, E. Redondo, D. Fonseca, P. Garcia-Almirall, J. Subirós, Videogame technology in architecture education, in: M. Kurosu (Ed.), International Conference on Human-Computer Interaction – Human-Computer Interaction. Novel User Experiences, in: Lecture Notes in Computer Science, Springer, Cham, 2016, pp. 436–447, https://doi.org/10.1007/978-3-319-39513-5_41.

[63] D. Chaves, J.R. Ruiz-Sarmiento, N. Petkov, J. Gonzalez-Jimenez, Integration of CNN into a robotic architecture to build semantic maps of indoor environments, in: I. Rojas, G. Joya, A. Catala (Eds.), International Work-Conference on Artificial Neural Networks – Advances in Computational Intelligence, in: Lecture Notes in Computer Science, Springer, Cham, 2019, pp. 313–324, https://doi.org/10.1007/978-3-030-20518-8_27.

[64] W. Qiu, A. Yuille, UnrealCV: connecting computer vision to unreal engine, in: G. Hua, H. Jégou (Eds.), European Conference on Computer Vision – Workshops, vol. 9915, Springer, Cham, 2016, pp. 909–916, https://doi.org/10.1007/978-3-319-49409-8_75.

[65] J. Kang, B.-k. Jeon, S.-h. Kim, S.-y. Park, Exposition of music: VR exhibition, in: ACM SIG-GRAPH Immersive Pavilion, New York, NY, USA, 2021, pp. 1–2, https://doi.org/10.1145/3450615.3464535.

[66] Z. Shen, J. Liu, Y. Zheng, L. Cao, A low-cost mobile VR walkthrough system for displaying multimedia works based on Unity3D, in: 14th International Conference on Computer Science & Education (ICCSE), IEEE, Toronto, ON, Canada, 2019, pp. 415–419, https://doi.org/10.1109/iccse.2019.8845390.

[67] N. Statham, Use of photogrammetry in video games: a historical overview, Games and Culture 15 (3) (2020) 289–307, https://doi.org/10.1177/1555412018786415.

[68] M. Ziegler, M. Bemana, J. Keinert, K. Myszkowski, Near real-time light field reconstruction and rendering for on-line light field evaluation, in: European Light Field Imaging Workshop (ELFI), Borovets, Bulgaria, 2019, p. 4.

[69] G.D. de Dinechin, A. Paljic, From real to virtual: an image-based rendering toolkit to help bring the world around us into virtual reality, in: IEEE Conference on Virtual Reality and 3D User Interfaces Abstracts and Workshops (VRW), Atlanta, GA, USA, 2020, p. 6, https://doi.org/10.1109/vrw50115.2020.00076.

[70] Rendering Pipeline Overview – OpenGL Wiki, https://www.khronos.org/opengl/wiki/Rendering_Pipeline_Overview. (Accessed 6 December 2021).

[71] R.S. Overbeck, D. Erickson, D. Evangelakos, M. Pharr, P. Debevec, A system for acquiring, processing, and rendering panoramic light field stills for virtual reality, ACM Transactions on Graphics 37 (6) (2019) 1–15, https://doi.org/10.1145/3272127.3275031, arXiv:1810.08860.

[72] D. Yue, M.S.K. Gul, M. Bätz, J. Keinert, R. Mantiuk, A benchmark of light field view interpolation methods, in: IEEE International Conference on Multimedia Expo Workshops (ICMEW), London, UK, 2020, pp. 1–6, https://doi.org/10.1109/icmew46912.2020.9106041.

[73] Y. Yoon, H.-G. Jeon, D. Yoo, J.-Y. Lee, I.S. Kweon, Light-field image super-resolution using convolutional neural network, IEEE Signal Processing Letters 24 (6) (2017) 848–852, https://doi.org/10.1109/lsp.2017.2669333.

[74] M.S.K. Gul, B.K. Gunturk, Spatial and angular resolution enhancement of light fields using convolutional neural networks, IEEE Transactions on Image Processing 27 (5) (2018) 2146–2159, https://doi.org/10.1109/tip.2018.2794181.

[75] G. Wu, M. Zhao, L. Wang, Q. Dai, T. Chai, Y. Liu, Light field reconstruction using deep convolutional network on EPI, in: IEEE Conference on Computer Vision and Pattern Recognition (CVPR), Honolulu, HI, USA, 2017, pp. 1638–1646, https://doi.org/10.1109/cvpr.2017.178.

[76] Y. Wang, F. Liu, Z. Wang, G. Hou, Z. Sun, T. Tan, End-to-end view synthesis for light field imaging with pseudo 4DCNN, in: V. Ferrari, M. Hebert, C. Sminchisescu, Y. Weiss (Eds.), European Conference on Computer Vision (ECCV), vol. 11206, Springer, Cham, 2018, pp. 340–355, https://doi.org/10.1007/978-3-030-01216-8_21.

[77] N.K. Kalantari, T.-C. Wang, R. Ramamoorthi, Learning-based view synthesis for light field cameras, ACM Transactions on Graphics 35 (6) (2016) 1–10, https://doi.org/10.1145/2980179.2980251.

[78] J. Jin, J. Hou, H. Yuan, S. Kwong, Learning light field angular super-resolution via a geometry-aware network, Proceedings of the AAAI Conference on Artificial Intelligence 34 (07) (2020) 11141–11148, https://doi.org/10.1609/aaai.v34i07.6771.

[79] S. Niklaus, L. Mai, F. Liu, Video frame interpolation via adaptive separable convolution, in: IEEE International Conference on Computer Vision (ICCV), Venice, Italy, 2017, pp. 261–270, https://doi.org/10.1109/iccv.2017.37.

[80] P.P. Srinivasan, T. Wang, A. Sreelal, R. Ramamoorthi, R. Ng, Learning to synthesize a 4D RGBD light field from a single image, arXiv:1708.03292, Aug. 2017.

[81] J. Navarro, N. Sabater, Learning occlusion-aware view synthesis for light fields, arXiv:1905.11271, May 2019.

[82] M.S.K. Gul, M.U. Mukati, M. Bätz, S. Forchhammer, J. Keinert, Light-field view synthesis using a convolutional block attention module, in: IEEE International Conference on Image Processing (ICIP), Anchorage, AK, USA, 2021, pp. 3398–3402, https://doi.org/10.1109/icip42928.2021.9506586.

[83] S. Woo, J. Park, J.-Y. Lee, I.S. Kweon, CBAM: convolutional block attention module, in: European Conference on Computer Vision (ECCV), Springer, Cham, 2018, p. 17, https://doi.org/10.1007/978-3-030-01234-2_1.

[84] B. Mildenhall, P.P. Srinivasan, M. Tancik, J.T. Barron, R. Ramamoorthi, R. Ng, NeRF: representing scenes as neural radiance fields for view synthesis, in: A. Vedaldi, H. Bischof, T. Brox, J.-M. Frahm (Eds.), European Conference on Computer Vision (ECCV), Springer, Cham, 2020, pp. 405–421.

[85] J. Thies, M. Zollhöfer, M. Nießner, Deferred neural rendering: Image synthesis using neural textures, ACM Transactions on Graphics 38 (4) (2019) 1–12, https://doi.org/10.1145/3306346.3323035, arXiv:1904.12356.

[86] S. Wizadwongsa, P. Phongthawee, J. Yenphraphai, S. Suwajanakorn, NeX: real-time view synthesis with neural basis expansion, in: IEEE/CVF Conference on Computer Vision and Pattern Recognition (CVPR), Virtual, 2021, pp. 8534–8543.

[87] L. Liu, J. Gu, K. Zaw Lin, T.-S. Chua, C. Theobalt, Neural sparse voxel fields, in: H. Larochelle, M. Ranzato, R. Hadsell, M.F. Balcan, H. Lin (Eds.), Conference on Neural Information Processing Systems (NeurIPS), vol. 33, Virtual, 2020, pp. 15651–15663.

[88] S. Lombardi, T. Simon, J. Saragih, G. Schwartz, A. Lehrmann, Y. Sheikh, Neural volumes: learning dynamic renderable volumes from images, ACM Transactions on Graphics 38 (4) (2019) 1–14, https://doi.org/10.1145/3306346.3323020, arXiv:1906.07751.

[89] Q. Wang, Z. Wang, K. Genova, P.P. Srinivasan, H. Zhou, J.T. Barron, R. Martin-Brualla, N. Snavely, T. Funkhouser, IBRNet: learning multi-view image-based rendering, in: IEEE/CVF Conference on Computer Vision and Pattern Recognition (CVPR), Virtual, 2021, pp. 4690–4699.

[90] S. Lombardi, T. Simon, G. Schwartz, M. Zollhoefer, Y. Sheikh, J. Saragih, Mixture of volumetric primitives for efficient neural rendering, ACM Transactions on Graphics 40 (4) (Jul. 2021), https://doi.org/10.1145/3450626.3459863.

[91] T. Neff, P. Stadlbauer, M. Parger, A. Kurz, J.H. Mueller, C.R.A. Chaitanya, A. Kaplanyan, M. Steinberger, DONeRF: towards real-time rendering of compact neural radiance fields using depth oracle networks, Computer Graphics Forum 40 (4) (2021) 45–59, https://doi.org/10.1111/cgf.14340.

[92] P. Hedman, J. Philip, T. Price, J.-M. Frahm, G. Drettakis, G. Brostow, Deep blending for free-viewpoint image-based rendering, ACM Transactions on Graphics 37 (6) (2019) 1–15, https://doi.org/10.1145/3272127.3275084.

[93] C. Griwodz, S. Gasparini, L. Calvet, P. Gurdjos, F. Castan, B. Maujean, G. De Lillo, Y. Lanthony, AliceVision Meshroom: An open-source 3D reconstruction pipeline, in: MMSys: ACM Multimedia Systems Conference, Istanbul, Turkey, 2021, pp. 241–247, https://doi.org/10.1145/3458305.3478443.

[94] RealityCapture: Mapping and 3D Modeling Photogrammetry Software - CapturingReality.com, https://www.capturingreality.com/. (Accessed 6 December 2021).

[95] J.L. Schönberger, E. Zheng, J.-M. Frahm, M. Pollefeys, Pixelwise view selection for unstructured multi-view stereo, in: B. Leibe, J. Matas, N. Sebe, M. Welling (Eds.), European Conference on Computer Vision (ECCV), vol. 9907, Springer, Cham, 2016, pp. 501–518, https://doi.org/10.1007/978-3-319-46487-9_31.

[96] C. Reiser, S. Peng, Y. Liao, A. Geiger, KiloNeRF: speeding up neural radiance fields with thousands of tiny MLPs, in: IEEE/CVF International Conference on Computer Vision (ICCV), Virtual, 2021, pp. 14335–14345.

[97] K. Zhang, G. Riegler, N. Snavely, V. Koltun, NeRF++: analyzing and improving neural radiance fields, arXiv:2010.07492, Oct. 2020.

[98] R. Martin-Brualla, N. Radwan, M.S.M. Sajjadi, J.T. Barron, A. Dosovitskiy, D. Duckworth, NeRF in the wild: neural radiance fields for unconstrained photo collections, in: IEEE/CVF Conference on Computer Vision and Pattern Recognition (CVPR), Virtual, 2021, pp. 7206–7215, https://doi.org/10.1109/cvpr46437.2021.00713.

[99] V. Sitzmann, J. Martel, A. Bergman, D. Lindell, G. Wetzstein, Implicit neural representations with periodic activation functions, in: H. Larochelle, M. Ranzato, R. Hadsell, M.F. Balcan, H. Lin (Eds.), Conference on Neural Information Processing Systems (NeurIPS), vol. 33, Virtual, 2020, pp. 7462–7473.

[100] J.T. Barron, B. Mildenhall, M. Tancik, P. Hedman, R. Martin-Brualla, P.P. Srinivasan, Mip-NeRF: a multiscale representation for anti-aliasing neural radiance fields, in: IEEE/CVF International Conference on Computer Vision (ICCV), Virtual, 2021, pp. 5855–5864.

[101] A. Jain, M. Tancik, P. Abbeel, Putting NeRF on a diet: semantically consistent few-shot view synthesis, in: IEEE/CVF International Conference on Computer Vision (ICCV), Virtual, 2021, pp. 5885–5894.

[102] J.N. Martel, D.B. Lindell, C.Z. Lin, E.R. Chan, M. Monteiro, G. Wetzstein, ACORN: adaptive coordinate networks for neural representation, ACM Transactions on Graphics 40 (4) (2021), https://doi.org/10.1145/3450626.3459785.

[103] S. Peng, C.M. Jiang, Y. Liao, M. Niemeyer, M. Pollefeys, A. Geiger, Shape as points: a differentiable Poisson solver, arXiv:2106.03452, Jun. 2021.

[104] L. Yariv, J. Gu, Y. Kasten, Y. Lipman, Volume rendering of neural implicit surfaces, arXiv:2106.12052, Jun. 2021.

[105] R. Arandjelović, A. Zisserman, NeRF in detail: Learning to sample for view synthesis, arXiv:2106.05264, Jun. 2021.

[106] K. Deng, A. Liu, J.-Y. Zhu, D. Ramanan, Depth-supervised NeRF: fewer views and faster training for free, arXiv:2107.02791, Jul. 2021.

[107] H. Baatz, J. Granskog, M. Papas, F. Rousselle, J. Novák, NeRF-Tex: neural reflectance field textures, in: A. Bousseau, M. McGuire (Eds.), Eurographics Symposium on Rendering - DL-Only Track, The Eurographics Association, 2021, p. 13, https://doi.org/10.2312/sr.20211285.

[108] A. Chen, Z. Xu, F. Zhao, X. Zhang, F. Xiang, J. Yu, H. Su, MVSNeRF: fast generalizable radiance field reconstruction from multi-view stereo, in: IEEE/CVF International Conference on Computer Vision (ICCV), Virtual, 2021, pp. 14124–14133.

[109] A. Yu, R. Li, M. Tancik, H. Li, R. Ng, A. Kanazawa, PlenOctrees for real-time rendering of neural radiance fields, in: IEEE/CVF International Conference on Computer Vision (ICCV), Virtual, 2021, pp. 5752–5761.

[110] S. Peng, M. Niemeyer, L. Mescheder, M. Pollefeys, A. Geiger, Convolutional occupancy networks, in: A. Vedaldi, H. Bischof, T. Brox, J.-M. Frahm (Eds.), European Conference on Computer Vision (ECCV), Springer, Cham, 2020, pp. 523–540, https://doi.org/10.1007/978-3-030-58580-8_31.

[111] V. Sitzmann, E.R. Chan, R. Tucker, N. Snavely, G. Wetzstein, MetaSDF: meta-learning signed distance functions, in: Conference on Neural Information Processing Systems (NeurIPS), Virtual, 2020, pp. 10136–10147.

[112] J. Sun, Y. Xie, L. Chen, X. Zhou, H. Bao, NeuralRecon: real-time coherent 3D reconstruction from monocular video, in: IEEE/CVF Conference on Computer Vision and Pattern Recognition (CVPR), Virtual, 2021, pp. 15598–15607.

[113] J. Knodt, S.-H. Baek, F. Heide, Neural ray-tracing: learning surfaces and reflectance for relighting and view synthesis, arXiv:2104.13562, Apr. 2021.

[114] M. Oechsle, S. Peng, A. Geiger, UNISURF: unifying neural implicit surfaces and radiance fields for multi-view reconstruction, in: IEEE/CVF International Conference on Computer Vision (ICCV), Virtual, 2021, pp. 5589–5599.

[115] P. Hedman, P.P. Srinivasan, B. Mildenhall, J.T. Barron, P. Debevec, Baking neural radiance fields for real-time view synthesis, in: IEEE/CVF International Conference on Computer Vision (ICCV), Virtual, 2021, pp. 5875–5884.

[116] D. Rebain, W. Jiang, S. Yazdani, K. Li, K.M. Yi, A. Tagliasacchi, DeRF: decomposed radiance fields, in: IEEE/CVF Conference on Computer Vision and Pattern Recognition (CVPR), Virtual, 2021, pp. 14153–14161.

[117] P. Erler, P. Guerrero, S. Ohrhallinger, N.J. Mitra, M. Wimmer, Points2Surf learning implicit surfaces from point clouds, in: A. Vedaldi, H. Bischof, T. Brox, J.-M. Frahm (Eds.), European Conference on Computer Vision (ECCV), in: Lecture Notes in Computer Science, Springer, Cham, 2020, pp. 108–124, https://doi.org/10.1007/978-3-030-58558-7_7.

[118] P. Wang, L. Liu, Y. Liu, C. Theobalt, T. Komura, W. Wang, NeuS: learning neural implicit surfaces by volume rendering for multi-view reconstruction, arXiv:2106.10689, Jun. 2021.

[119] B. Attal, E. Laidlaw, A. Gokaslan, C. Kim, C. Richardt, J. Tompkin, M. O'Toole TöRF, Time-of-flight radiance fields for dynamic scene view synthesis, arXiv:2109.15271, Sep. 2021.

[120] J. Li, Z. Feng, Q. She, H. Ding, C. Wang, G.H. Lee, MINE: towards continuous depth MPI with NeRF for novel view synthesis, in: IEEE/CVF International Conference on Computer Vision (ICCV), Virtual, 2021, pp. 12578–12588.

[121] C. Chivriga, B. Wiberg, Y. Shentu, M. Loser, BUFF - Bounding unstructured radiance volumes for free view synthesis, https://github.com/qway/nerfmeshes. (Accessed 6 December 2021).

[122] A. Yu, V. Ye, M. Tancik, A. Kanazawa, pixelNeRF: neural radiance fields from one or few images, in: IEEE/CVF Conference on Computer Vision and Pattern Recognition (CVPR), Virtual, 2021, pp. 4578–4587.

[123] S.J. Garbin, M. Kowalski, M. Johnson, J. Shotton, J. Valentin, FastNeRF: high-fidelity neural rendering at 200FPS, in: IEEE/CVF International Conference on Computer Vision (ICCV), Virtual, 2021, pp. 14346–14355.

[124] Y. Liu, S. Peng, L. Liu, Q. Wang, P. Wang, C. Theobalt, X. Zhou, W. Wang, Neural rays for occlusion-aware image-based rendering, arXiv:2107.13421, Jul. 2021.

[125] J. Shen, A. Ruiz, A. Agudo, F. Moreno, Stochastic neural radiance fields: quantifying uncertainty in implicit 3D representations, arXiv:2109.02123, Sep. 2021.

[126] Y. Wei, S. Liu, Y. Rao, W. Zhao, J. Lu, J. Zhou, NerfingMVS: guided optimization of neural radiance fields for indoor multi-view stereo, in: IEEE/CVF International Conference on Computer Vision (ICCV), Virtual, 2021, pp. 5610–5619.

[127] F. Cole, K. Genova, A. Sud, D. Vlasic, Z. Zhang, Differentiable surface rendering via non-differentiable sampling, in: IEEE/CVF International Conference on Computer Vision (ICCV), Virtual, 2021, pp. 6088–6097.

[128] G.-W. Yang, W.-Y. Zhou, H.-Y. Peng, D. Liang, T.-J. Mu, S.-M. Hu, Recursive-NeRF: an efficient and dynamically growing NeRF, arXiv:2105.09103, May 2021.

[129] C.-H. Lin, W.-C. Ma, A. Torralba, S. Lucey, BARF: bundle-adjusting neural radiance fields, in: IEEE/CVF International Conference on Computer Vision (ICCV), Virtual, 2021, pp. 5741–5751.

[130] Z. Wang, S. Wu, W. Xie, M. Chen, V.A. Prisacariu, NeRF–: neural radiance fields without known camera parameters, arXiv:2102.07064, Feb. 2021.

[131] Y. Jeong, S. Ahn, C. Choy, A. Anandkumar, M. Cho, J. Park, Self-calibrating neural radiance fields, in: IEEE/CVF International Conference on Computer Vision (ICCV), Virtual, 2021, pp. 5846–5854.

[132] K. Park, U. Sinha, J.T. Barron, S. Bouaziz, D.B. Goldman, S.M. Seitz, R. Martin-Brualla, Nerfies: deformable neural radiance fields, in: IEEE/CVF International Conference on Computer Vision (ICCV), Virtual, 2021, pp. 5865–5874.

[133] K. Park, U. Sinha, P. Hedman, J.T. Barron, S. Bouaziz, D.B. Goldman, R. Martin-Brualla, S.M. Seitz, HyperNeRF: a higher-dimensional representation for topologically varying neural radiance fields, arXiv:2106.13228, Jun. 2021.

[134] A. Pumarola, E. Corona, G. Pons-Moll, F. Moreno-Noguer, D-NeRF: neural radiance fields for dynamic scenes, in: IEEE/CVF Conference on Computer Vision and Pattern Recognition (CVPR), Virtual, 2021, pp. 10318–10327.

[135] Z. Li, S. Niklaus, N. Snavely, O. Wang, Neural scene flow fields for space-time view synthesis of dynamic scenes, in: IEEE/CVF Conference on Computer Vision and Pattern Recognition (CVPR), Virtual, 2021, pp. 6498–6508.

[136] P.P. Srinivasan, B. Deng, X. Zhang, M. Tancik, B. Mildenhall, J.T. Barron, NeRV: neural reflectance and visibility fields for relighting and view synthesis, in: IEEE/CVF Conference on Computer Vision and Pattern Recognition (CVPR), Virtual, 2021, pp. 7495–7504.

[137] M. Boss, R. Braun, V. Jampani, J.T. Barron, C. Liu, H.P. Lensch, NeRD: neural reflectance decomposition from image collections, in: IEEE/CVF International Conference on Computer Vision (ICCV), Virtual, 2021, pp. 12684–12694.

[138] X. Zhang, P.P. Srinivasan, B. Deng, P. Debevec, W.T. Freeman, J.T. Barron, NeRFactor: neural factorization of shape and reflectance under an unknown illumination, arXiv:2106.01970, Jun. 2021.

[139] J.T. Barron, B. Mildenhall, D. Verbin, P.P. Srinivasan, P. Hedman, Mip-NeRF 360: unbounded anti-aliased neural radiance fields, arXiv:2111.12077, Nov. 2021.

[140] J. Bradbury, R. Frostig, P. Hawkins, M.J. Johnson, C. Leary, D. Maclaurin, G. Necula, A. Paszke, J. VanderPlas, S. Wanderman-Milne, Q. Zhang, JAX: Composable transformations of Python+NumPy programs, http://github.com/google/jax, 2018.

[141] B. Deng, J.T. Barron, P.P. Srinivasan, JaxNeRF: An efficient JAX implementation of NeRF, https://github.com/google-research/google-research/tree/master/jaxnerf, 2020.

[142] M. Tancik, B. Mildenhall, T. Wang, D. Schmidt, P.P. Srinivasan, J.T. Barron, R. Ng, Learned initializations for optimizing coordinate-based neural representations, in: IEEE/CVF Conference on Computer Vision and Pattern Recognition (CVPR), Virtual, 2021, pp. 2845–2854, https://doi.org/10.1109/cvpr46437.2021.00287.

[143] J. Deng, W. Dong, R. Socher, L.-J. Li, K. Li, L. Fei-Fei, ImageNet: A large-scale hierarchical image database, in: IEEE Conference on Computer Vision and Pattern Recognition (CVPR), 2009 IEEE Conference on Computer Vision and Pattern Recognition, Miami, FL, USA, 2009, pp. 248–255, https://doi.org/10.1109/cvpr.2009.5206848.

[144] Alex Evans, Learning from failure: a survey of promising, unconventional and mostly abandoned renderers for 'Dreams PS4', a geometrically dense, painterly UGC game (presentation), https://www.mediamolecule.com/blog/article/siggraph_2015, 2015.

[145] Sebastien Hillaire, Physically based and unified volumetric rendering in frostbite (presentation), https://www.slideshare.net/DICEStudio/physically-based-and-unified-volumetric-rendering-in-frostbite, 2015.

[146] W.E. Lorensen, H.E. Cline, Marching cubes: A high resolution 3D surface construction algorithm, ACM SIGGRAPH Computer Graphics 21 (4) (1987) 163–169, https://doi.org/10.1145/37402.37422.

[147] Signed distance function, Wikipedia. (Accessed 6 December 2021).

[148] L. Yariv, Y. Kasten, D. Moran, M. Galun, M. Atzmon, B. Ronen, Y. Lipman, Multiview neural surface reconstruction by disentangling geometry and appearance, in: H. Larochelle, M. Ranzato, R. Hadsell, M.F. Balcan, H. Lin (Eds.), Conference on Neural Information Processing Systems (NeurIPS), Virtual, 2020, pp. 2492–2502.

[149] F. Xiang, Z. Xu, M. Hasan, Y. Hold-Geoffroy, K. Sunkavalli, H. Su, NeuTex: neural texture mapping for volumetric neural rendering, in: IEEE/CVF Conference on Computer Vision and Pattern Recognition (CVPR), Virtual, 2021, pp. 7119–7128.

[150] J. Hasselgren, J. Munkberg, J. Lehtinen, M. Aittala, S. Laine, Appearance-driven automatic 3D model simplification, arXiv:2104.03989, Apr. 2021.

[151] M. Deering, S. Winner, B. Schediwy, C. Duffy, N. Hunt, The triangle processor and normal vector shader: A VLSI system for high performance graphics, ACM SIGGRAPH Computer Graphics 22 (4) (1988) 21–30, https://doi.org/10.1145/378456.378468.

[152] Deferred shading, Wikipedia. (Accessed 6 December 2021).

[153] O. Ronneberger, P. Fischer, T. Brox, U-Net: Convolutional networks for biomedical image segmentation, in: N. Navab, J. Hornegger, W. Wells, A. Frangi (Eds.), International Conference on Medical Image Computing and Computer-Assisted Intervention (MICCAI), Springer, Cham, 2015, pp. 234–241, https://doi.org/10.1007/978-3-319-24574-4_28.

[154] G. Riegler, V. Koltun, Stable view synthesis, arXiv:2011.07233, May 2021.

[155] K.-A. Aliev, A. Sevastopolsky, M. Kolos, D. Ulyanov, V. Lempitsky, Neural point-based graphics, in: A. Vedaldi, H. Bischof, T. Brox, J.-M. Frahm (Eds.), European Conference on Computer Vision (ECCV), in: Lecture Notes in Computer Science, Springer, Cham, 2020, pp. 696–712, https://doi.org/10.1007/978-3-030-58542-6_42.

[156] M. Meshry, D.B. Goldman, S. Khamis, H. Hoppe, R. Pandey, N. Snavely, R. Martin-Brualla, Neural rerendering in the wild, in: IEEE/CVF Conference on Computer Vision and Pattern Recognition (CVPR), Long Beach, CA, USA, 2019, pp. 6878–6887, https://doi.org/10.1109/CVPR.2019.00704.

[157] D. Rückert, L. Franke, M. Stamminger, ADOP: approximate differentiable one-pixel point rendering, arXiv:2110.06635, Oct. 2021.

[158] A.W. Bergman, P. Kellnhofer, G. Wetzstein, Fast training of neural lumigraph representations using meta learning, arXiv:2106.14942, Jun. 2021.

[159] A. Meka, R. Pandey, C. Häne, S. Orts-Escolano, P. Barnum, P. David-Son, D. Erickson, Y. Zhang, J. Taylor, S. Bouaziz, C. Legendre, W.-C. Ma, R. Overbeck, T. Beeler, P. Debevec, S. Izadi, C. Theobalt, C. Rhemann, S. Fanello, Deep relightable textures: Volumetric performance capture with neural rendering, ACM Transactions on Graphics 39 (6) (2020) 259, 21pp., https://doi.org/10.1145/3414685.3417814.

[160] M. Oechsle, M. Niemeyer, C. Reiser, L. Mescheder, T. Strauss, A. Geiger, Learning implicit surface light fields, in: International Conference on 3D Vision (3DV), IEEE, Fukuoka, Japan, 2020, pp. 452–462, https://doi.org/10.1109/3dv50981.2020.00055.

[161] J. Thies, M. Elgharib, A. Tewari, C. Theobalt, M. Nießner, Neural voice puppetry: Audio-driven facial reenactment, in: A. Vedaldi, H. Bischof, T. Brox, J.-M. Frahm (Eds.), European Conference on Computer Vision (ECCV), in: Lecture Notes in Computer Science, Springer, Cham, 2020, pp. 716–731, https://doi.org/10.1007/978-3-030-58517-4_42.

CHAPTER 10

Quality evaluation of light fields

Ali Ak and Patrick Le Callet

Nantes Université, École Centrale Nantes, CNRS, LS2N, UMR 6004, Nantes, France

10.1. Introduction

In the last century, a 7D plenoptic function was introduced to define the modern LF, as introduced in Chapter 1. It is described as below:

$$L_{7d} = P(x, y, z, \theta, \phi, t, \lambda), \tag{10.1}$$

which represents the light ray from any given point (x, y, z) in 3D space, to any direction (θ, ϕ) in 3D space for any given time t and wavelength λ. Although the 7D plenoptic function has a comprehensive definition, it is not fully utilized in practical applications due to the high dimensionality of the data. A practically more desirable version, 4D plenoptic function, is introduced as a result. It represents each ray with 4 points defined on two parallel planes. The coordinates are denoted with (x, y) for the image plane and (a, b) for the camera plane.

LF can be represented in a variety of ways, such as sub-aperture views, epipolar plane images (EPI), lenslet image, refocused image stack, pseudo-video sequence (with sub-aperture views or refocused image stack). More details regarding LF representations can be found in Chapter 7. Fig. 10.1 depicts the two most common representations, sub-aperture views and EPIs. On the left, sub-aperture views are displayed on a grid representing the angular domain of the LF with (a, b) coordinates, whereas (x, y) coordinates are used for the spatial dimension of the individual sub-aperture views. EPI slices are drawn on the spatial dimension of each sub-aperture view on horizontal or vertical axis of the angular dimension. In other words, by stacking horizontal or vertical sub-aperture views on top of each other, a rectangular slice can be used to generate a single EPI. By shifting the rectangular slice, we can generate all the EPIs for the corresponding axis. For a LF with resolution $(a, b, x, y, 3)$ (where 3 represents the red, blue, and green color channels), each sub-aperture view has the resolution $(x, y, 3)$, each vertical EPI has the resolution $(a, x, 3)$, and each vertical EPI has the resolution $(b, y, 3)$.

Immersive Video Technologies
https://doi.org/10.1016/B978-0-32-391755-1.00016-X

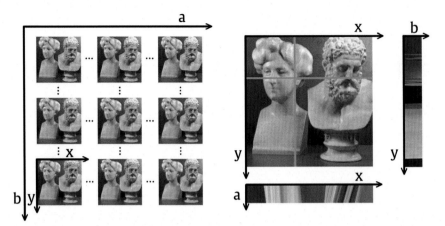

Figure 10.1 Sub-aperture views and EPI representations of a sample LF from the WIN5-LID dataset [1].

10.2. Characteristics of LF-related distortions

Understanding the characteristics of distortions is essential for both objective and subjective quality assessment. In this section, we investigate the impact of various steps in LF imaging pipeline and the impairments occurring at each step.

10.2.1 Acquisition-related distortions

Various methods can be used to capture the LF content, which are introduced in detail in Chapter 6. Depending on the use case, certain capture method may be more advantageous than alternatives. We can categorize them as multiplexed, sequential, and multi-sensor acquisition methods [2]. Multiplexed acquisition relies on cameras known as plenoptic cameras, which utilize a micro-lens array placed between the image sensor and main lens. Sequential acquisition methods rely on a single image sensor placed often on a robotic arm or any other moving system to capture multiple views of the scene with a sequential manner. Time-sequential methodology can only be used to capture static scenes. And finally, multi-sensor acquisition utilizes multiple image sensors and captures the scene from multiple views at the same time. Therefore it is suitable for LF videos and moving scenes.

10.2.1.1 Multiplexed acquisition

Spatially multiplexed cameras are often referred as plenoptic or light-field cameras. Currently, Raytrix [3] is the most commonly known example of such devices. Although plenoptic cameras provide a compact device to capture a light field, they have to have a constant trade-off between the spatial and angular resolution. In other words, increasing the spatial resolution of individual micro-lenses provides a high spatial resolution/low angular resolution LF. Conversely, increasing the number of micro-lenses decreases the spatial resolution and increases the angular resolution of captured LF. Due to the spatial/angular resolution trade-off additional processing steps (e.g., spatial/angular super resolution) might be required that affect the quality of the acquired LF.

LF acquired with plenoptic cameras often suffer from lack of information on the corner sub-aperture views due to micro lens array arrangements. These distortions are visible, and similar to a vignetting. To overcome such distortions, corner views are often omitted from the acquired LF since filling this information is not straightforward.

When it comes to LF video acquisition, current plenoptic camera technology suffers from the lower frame rates (3–4 fps). Although plenoptic cameras can shoot with higher fps than sequential acquisition methods, it has a lower fps than multi-sensor acquisition methods. To overcome this limitation, temporal super resolution methods can be used. These methods often introduce specific distortions on the temporal dimension of the processed video.

10.2.1.2 Time-sequential acquisition

Time-sequential acquisition utilizes a predefined trajectory containing sub-aperture views uniformly distributed on a planar or spherical grid. A robotic arm is often utilized to move the image sensor on this predefined trajectory to capture the LF. The advantage of this method mainly lies within the high spatial angular resolution and the flexibility of the baseline distance. The main disadvantage is the inability to capture LF videos and dynamic LF scenes (i.e., still LF image with moving objects). In the presence of a moving object in the scene, LFs captured with time-sequential method might contain ghosting artifacts due to location difference between consequent captures.

10.2.1.3 Multi-sensor acquisition

The multi-sensor capture requires a set of image sensors ordered on a planar or spherical grid. Ordered image sensors capture an image simultaneously to generate the LF. Each image sensor in this setup corresponds to a sub-aperture view. Main disadvantage of this method is the cost due to high number of image sensors required to capture. On the other hand, based on the number of image sensors, captured LFs do not suffer from low spatial and angular resolutions. Consequently, multi-sensor capture does not lead to any specific impairments. However, baseline of the captured LF is limited by the physical size of the image sensors.

10.2.2 Processing related distortions

Capturing a high spatio-angular resolution light field with high frame rate is limited by at least one of the dimensions in each capturing method. Research often relies on super resolution techniques on various dimensions to mitigate the resolution limitations. For more information, interested readers may refer to Chapter 8.

10.2.2.1 Spatial super resolution

Spatial resolution of a LF content has a similar impact on the QoE as the traditional 2D content. Although it is not a LF specific concern, the content acquired via plenoptic cameras has always a trade-off between the spatial and angular resolution. To this end, spatial super resolution is an alternative solution to cope with this trade-off. Typically, spatially super resolved images contain blur-like distortions and aliasing problems. Learning-based super resolution algorithms may introduce novel distortions, depending on the approach. Moreover, super resolution methods developed for 2D images may introduce additional distortions due to inconsistencies on the angular domain and inconsistency on the temporal domain in cases of LF videos.

10.2.2.2 Angular super resolution

Angular super resolution is commonly called view synthesis in the literature. Similar to spatial super resolution, angular super resolution also helps to cope with the spatial angular resolution trade-off. Moreover, it provides a solution to increase the density of the sub-aperture views of the sparsely captured LF content. View synthesis algorithms shall be categorized into two, based on the presence of the depth map as an input. A recent overview of the view synthesis literature can be found in [2]. Quality of the depth map used for view synthesis may affect the intensity and type of distortions over the synthesized views.

Various factors may affect the performance of view synthesis algorithms. Consequently, the visual quality of the synthesized views may vary. One important factor is the occlusions in the captured scene. Occluded areas in the image need to be filled with information that is unseen previously. Therefore the problem itself (sometimes referred as inpainting) is ill-posed and one of the common inverse imaging problems. Additionally, separating the occluded pixels from the occluding pixels can be another challenge based on the input views. These challenges often lead to structural distortions around the contour of the occluding objects in the scene.

High baseline distances (i.e., the distances between the neighboring sub-aperture views of a LF) further increase the difficulty of the view synthesis task. By increasing the baseline distance, we also increase the disparity between sub-aperture views, resulting in distortions with higher intensity and, consequently, a synthesized view with lower visual quality [4].

Lambertian reflectance model [5] assumes that the light reflects from a surface based on the surface normal and light directions, and the amount of light reflected from the surface is equally bright in every angle. However, complex real-world scenes often do not have this property, which is violated by specular, translucent, and certain reflective surfaces. Pixels that belong to non-Lambertian surfaces cannot be represented with a single depth value. Consequently, view synthesis algorithms encounter yet another challenge on non-Lambertian surfaces. Inconsistencies along the angular dimension of non-Lambertian surfaces can be observed as a result.

10.2.2.3 Temporal super resolution

Temporal super resolution is only a concern for LF video content. Due to slower adoption of LF videos in the literature, the current state of the research regarding to temporal super resolution is somehow limited. However, the characteristics of temporal super resolution distortions are generally common with its 2D counterpart.

Despite similar characteristics, there are two additional complexities for LF video temporal super resolution. First of all, consistency among the 4D LF need to be ensured, as opposed to a 2D image. Furthermore, due to high dimensionality of the LF content, current plenoptic cameras can only shoot up to a limited frame rate. As an example, Lytro Illum 2.0 [6] camera shoots only 3 fps. As an alternative solution, Ting et al. [7] proposed a hybrid system containing a DSLR camera and a plenoptic camera to capture high frame rate LF videos. In cases where such hybrid systems are not applicable, direct use of existing LF cameras can be supported with temporal super resolution algorithms to capture LF videos with an acceptable frame rate.

10.2.2.4 Depth estimation

Depth estimation related distortions are not only visible on acquired depth maps, but also on the LF that is processed with distorted depth maps. Therefore the factors that influence the LF quality due to depth map estimation are harder to isolate and discuss in the imaging pipeline. Depending on the use case, an accurate depth map estimation may become crucial.

Often, depth estimation is done only for the center sub-aperture view [2]. In scenarios where the depth maps for multiple views are estimated, the consistency between the individual depth maps may affect the overall quality. Optimization and evaluation of the acquired depth maps also may influence the quality assessment. Relying on mean squared error as measurement may lower the pixel-based accuracy and promote blurry depth maps. Impact of these errors is also enhanced for LF content with lower baseline. Finally, occluded regions and non-Lambertian surfaces pose a challenge on the depth estimation algorithms, as discussed earlier. An in-depth overview of the literature for depth estimation of the dense LF content can be found in [8].

10.2.3 Compression-related distortions

Compression-related distortions are one of the most common distortion types that are represented in LF image quality datasets [9]. The type of compression scheme dictates the characteristics of the distortions, whereas the compression rate often controls the intensity of distortions. A detailed overview of the LF compression is given in Chapter 7.

One of the common approaches for LF compression is treating the 4D LF as a pseudo video sequence (see Section 10.3.3.2 for more details regarding the pseudo video sequences) and relying on existing hybrid video coding approaches, such as HEVC [10] and VVC [11]. Due to its simplicity and high efficiency, this method is widely adopted in the literature [12]. Distortions that occur with this type of approach share the same characteristics of 2D video compression distortions. They may occur on the spatial dimension with high compression rates. Distortions that occur as irregularities in the temporal domain instead occur in the angular domain for LFs.

Another common approach utilizes the view synthesis algorithms to efficiently compress LF content. A subset of the sub-aperture views (with additional geometry information) is used to reconstruct the full LF. Often, resulting artifacts depend on the utilized view synthesis methodology. Furthermore, occluded regions and non-Lambertian surfaces may alter the geometry information, which may result in structural artifacts on affected regions.

Finally, we have seen an increasing amount of approach utilizing learning-based models in various parts of the coding chain, such as view synthesis, learning-based prediction, and sparse prediction [12]. Their efficiency and the characteristics of the resulting distortions vary greatly from one to another.

10.2.4 Use case specific influencing factors for LF distortions

As it is suggested in [13], based on the state of adoption several use cases emerge in the LF domain, such as industrial, medical, commercial, educational, cultural, and communicational. A detailed analysis of the various key performance indicators [14] and their specific relations to each use case is given in [13]. Since each use case may have different requirements to provide a greater user experience, understanding use case specific parameters for LF quality helps us to allocate resources into more beneficial parts of the imaging pipeline.

For example, in communication scenarios, where the telepresence through mobile devices is concerned, the angular quality and angular resolution of the LF visualization gain importance over other parameters. Medical use cases on the other hand prioritize the accuracy and precision of the displayed content over visual aesthetics. Therefore device characteristics, such as spatial resolution, brightness, contrast are more important for such scenarios.

10.3. Subjective quality assessment

Similar to the other multimedia types, subjective quality assessment is the golden standard for estimating visual quality of LF content. Subjective experiments to collect human preferences on the LF quality are conducted for this purpose. These experiments are often time-consuming and costly. However, they are essential to understand image

Table 10.1 Publicly available LF IQA datasets.

	Method	Distortions	Display	# SRC	# Stim	# Obs	Raw Scores
MPI-LFA [15]	JOD	Compression Super Resolution	2D	14	350	40	✗
VALID [16]	DSIS	Compression Refocusing	2D	5	–	–	✗
SMART [17]	PC/JND	Compression	2D	16	4352 (pairs)	19	✗
WIN5-LID [1]	DSCQS	Compression Super Resolution Refocusing	3D	10	220	23	✗
LFDD [18]	DSIS	Compression Processing Contrast Enhancement	2D	10	–	16	–
Turntable [19]	SSCQE	Compression Additive Noise Gaussian Blur	3D LF	7	168	20	–
FVV [20]	ACR	Compression	2D	6	265	23	✓
VSENSE [21]	Eye Tracking	–	2D	20	–	21	–

quality and develop objective quality metrics that correlates with the human opinion. To this end, researchers collect subjective preferences on the quality of various LF content and made these datasets publicly available to promote research on quality evaluation of LFs. A non-exhaustive list of publicly available datasets is given in Table 10.1.

Unlike other multimedia types, standards and recommendations are not well established for subjective LF quality assessment as of today. Despite the lack of standards, individual efforts are shining light on some of the important research questions. In their study, Darukumalli et al. [22] conducted a series of experiments with different experiment methodologies. The experiments measure the impact of level of zoom on the visual comfort and overall subjective preference. Conducted experiments provide insight regarding the impact of subjective experiment design on QoE experiments conducted on projection based displays, the effect of level of zoom on the subjective preferences, the impact of the presence (or the lack of) background on the perceived quality and the visual discomfort. Two experiment were conducted to measure the acceptance of zoom level. One experiment utilized the absolute category rating (ACR) method, whereas the second experiment is conducted with pair comparison (PC) method. The third experiment measures the visual comfort with a single stimulus (SS) method with varying level of zoom. Results indicate that the pair comparison method reveals the user opinions better than the other two methods. The visual comfort results acquired with the ACR and SS experiments highly correlate, indicating that the design choice between the two has minimal effect on the outcome of the experiment.

A recent work from Kara et al. [23] presents an overview of the viewing conditions of the LF video for subjective experiments. In their work, authors investigate the viewing conditions for static, video, and interactive content separately. The impact of the viewing position of the observers, spatial and angular resolution of the display/content are discussed. The result indicates a higher tolerance of low angular resolution for static LF content compared to LF videos.

10.3.1 Characterization of LF content for subjective assessment

Image quality datasets are expected to be representative in terms of source content (SRC) and the type of distortions. The type of distortions that can occur in LF content were discussed in the previous section, and this section will introduce a set of features that can be used to identify the pristine LF content. A detailed overview of the LF features can be found in [24].

Spatial perceptual information (SI) is a measurement of spatial information in a scene. It is one of the common features that is used for traditional 2D images [25]. Higher SI values indicate a higher spatial complexity for a scene. In SMART LF IQA dataset [17], it is used as the standard deviation over the Sobel [26] filtered luminance image.

Colorfulness (CF) is another feature that is also used for 2D images, which impacts the overall aesthetic of a given content. Many descriptions exist for image colorfulness, and a detailed overview supported by subjective experiments can be found in [27]. For LF content it is described with the mean and standard deviation of the red, green, and blue pixel values [24].

Similar to SI and CF, contrast is also another feature that is commonly used for 2D and LF content. For natural images, an extensive analysis of existing measures and the definition of root mean squared contrast can be found in [28]. For LF images, in [24], gray level co-occurrence matrix (GLCM) is utilized as a contrast descriptor.

Disparity range can be used as a feature to incorporate the 3D information regarding the scene. In [24], the algorithm proposed in [29] is used to estimate the pixel disparity, and the [minimum disparity, maximum disparity] range is used as a feature. Alternatively, 95% range can be used to increase the robustness towards the errors in disparity estimation.

Refocusing range is another feature described in [24], specifically for LF content. Based on the refocusing implementation publicly available in Matlab® light field toolbox [30], a refocusing range is calculated.

The ratio of the occluded regions in the image can be used as another feature related to the 3D structure of the LF scene. In [24], the number of occluded pixels in the LF is calculated with the Matlab light field toolbox [30] and used as a feature. To prevent bias towards the spatial resolution of the LF image, the number of occluded pixels can be normalized with the spatial resolution of a sub-aperture view.

10.3.2 Quality assessment on LF displays

LF displays are still not widely adopted in the commercial market and definitely not available at the consumer level. Consequently, there is a lack of publicly available LF quality datasets that are collected on LF displays.

LF displays can be categorized as back and front projection. Observers and the light source are located on the same side of the screen for front projection displays, whereas the opposite holds for back projection displays. In comparison to back projection displays, front projection displays requires additional attention to experimental conditions in terms of positioning of the observers.

There are various parameters that affect the quality of a LF content when visualized on a LF display. These parameters can be also called key performance indicators in certain literature [14]. Common with the traditional 2D displays, physical size and the spatial resolution, brightness and color space of the LF displays greatly affect the QoE.

On another front, angular resolution is an influencing factor specific to LF displays that affect the visual quality. Angular resolution governs the smoothness of the parallax effect. Currently, commercially available LF displays only take horizontal parallax into consideration, and HoloVizio C80 [31] has the highest angular resolution in the market with 0.5 degrees.

Depth budget defines the perpendicular distance around the LF display, where an object can appear [14]. It is linearly related to the angular resolution and the pixel size of the display. Importance of the depth budget is highly content-dependent and having higher depth may improve the QoE based on the visualized scene.

10.3.2.1 IQA datasets with LF displays

Currently, there are not many publicly available datasets that assess LF quality with LF displays. To the best of our knowledge, turntable dataset [19] by Tamboli et al. is the only publicly available LF IQA dataset that utilizes a LF display. The angular resolution of the LF display was one view per degree. HoloVizio HV721RC display was used for the experiment. This display allows users to experience corresponding viewpoints based on their angle to the display. During the rating task, each observer rated the stimuli on the 5 positions along the viewing arc. Observers rated the stimuli in a quality range from 1 to 5 with the single stimulus continuous quality evaluation (SSCQE) method.

10.3.3 Quality assessment on other displays

Subjective studies can also be conducted on other display types, such as 2D and 3D stereoscopic displays. Majority of the publicly available datasets for LF image quality are collected with 2D displays, thanks to their availability.

LF content can be passively displayed on 2D displays as a pseudo video sequence. Frames of these video sequences are often individual sub-aperture views of the LF content on a pre-defined trajectory. In addition, frames of the pseudo video sequence can be a refocused version of the LF scene. Passive methodology ensures that the same content is being delivered to all observers in the experiment. However, it fails to provide an interactive experience of the LF content.

Interactive experiments on 2D displays require user input to determine the trajectory of the displayed sub-aperture views or refocused image on the focus stack. This allows observers to experience the LF content freely. Due to interactive viewing experience, displayed content varies from one observer to another, resulting in higher variety in subjective preferences.

10.3.3.1 IQA datasets with other displays

Referring back to the Table 10.1, there are many LF IQA datasets in the literature that are collected on 2D displays. In this section, we will introduce these datasets and discuss some of the details. Interested readers are recommended to refer to the recent work from Ellahi et al. [9] for more details.

MPI-LFA dataset [15] consists of 5 real and 9 synthetic dense LF scenes. LF scenes in the datasets contain only horizontal parallax and have the resolution of $960 \times 720 \times 101$. HEVC compression algorithm and various reconstruction-related distortions were used to generate stimuli. The dataset contains 350 LF in total with just objectionable difference (JOD) scores. JOD scores define the amount of objectionable difference between two stimuli. The experiment is conducted with Nvidia glasses to allow stereoscopic display. Acquired results suggest that optical flow-based reconstruction outperforms both the nearest neighborhood and linear interpolation methods. In addition, HEVC compression artifacts were easy to notice by participants in the majority of content.

VALID dataset [16] contains 5 LF scenes with 15×15 angular and 625×434 spatial resolution. Both passive and interactive methodology were utilized with DSIS methodology on a scale of 7 (-3 indicating the poorest quality, +3 indicating best quality). Compression-related distortions and refocusing were evaluated in the dataset. Authors did not share any information regarding the participant demographics.

SMART dataset [17] contains 16 LF scenes that are selected based on content features, such as spatial information, colorfulness, contrast, and brightness. LF scenes were captured with Lytro Illum plenoptic camera. Four (4) compression algorithms were used to generate the stimuli. Pairwise comparison (PC) methodology were used to gather just noticeable difference (JND) steps for each stimulus.

WIN5-LID dataset [1] contains 10 LF scenes (6 real, 4 synthetic scenes) and their quality scores collected with a 3D stereoscopic display. HEVC, JPEG2000 compression algorithms and linear, nearest neighborhood and two learning-based angular super resolution algorithms were used to generate the distorted stimuli. In total, 220 stimuli were rated in the experiment. Picture quality and the overall quality of the LFs were collected with double stimulus continuous quality scale (DSCQS) methodology.

LFDD dataset [18] consists of 8 synthetic LF scenes as the reference stimuli. JPEG, JPEG2000, VP9, AVC, HEVC are some of the compression algorithms that are used to generate the distorted stimuli. Additionally, simple noise and geometrical distortions were tested. Subjective experiment was conducted via crowdsourcing. DSIS was chosen as the subjective testing methodology. A predefined trajectory was used to generate the pseudo video sequences.

FVV dataset [20] contains 6 reference free viewpoint videos with 50 unique views presented as a video sequence from left to right to left in 100 frames. Compression and super-resolution artifacts are used to generate the distorted stimuli. Although it is not named as a LF dataset, the dataset shares the same characteristics with MPI-LFA dataset as it provides a high-resolution horizontal parallax with LF related distortions as the stimuli.

VSENSE dataset [21] investigates the visual attention of refocused LF content. Focus stacks for refocusing were generated via the Fourier disparity level [32] method on 20 different LFs. Although the dataset does not provide any quality evaluation, we have mentioned the dataset due to close relation of visual attention to image quality. The experiment were conducted to investigate the effect of changes in focus on the visual attention of the observers. Visual attention was measured by collecting eye tracking data from the left eye of the observers during the experiment.

10.3.3.2 Impact of visualization trajectory

As stated previously, passive visualization of the LF content can be done by arranging sub-aperture views with a predefined trajectory as pseudo video sequence. In this case, the impact of trajectory can affect the visual quality of the LF. Fig. 10.2 presents 6 different trajectories that are used in a comparative analysis in [33]. The trajectories are visualized with red arrows and explanations are quoted below:

- V1: spiral scan from the external to the internal views in clockwise direction
- V2: diagonal scan in a spiral fashion, starting from the view on the left inferior corner
- V3: horizontal scan from left to right, starting from the view on the left superior corner
- V4: spiral scan in counter-clockwise direction, starting from the center view

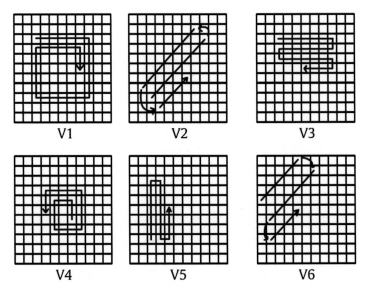

Figure 10.2 A common method to create pseudo video sequences for subjective experiments without user interaction. One of the predefined trajectories above can be used to generate a video sequence from the sub-aperture views.

- V5: vertical scan from bottom to top, starting from the view on the left inferior corner
- V6: diagonal scan from left to right

Twelve (12) LF content from the EPFL LF dataset [34] is used to generate the pseudo video sequences with the 6 trajectories. Twenty-eight (28) participants were recruited to evaluate the quality of the generated video sequences with ACR methodology on a scale from 1 to 5 (1: bad, ..., 5: excellent). A training phase was utilized prior to the experiment to let the observer familiarize with the task. Mean opinion score (MOS) is used to indicate the quality of each video sequence along with the 95 percentile confidence interval (CI).

Fig. 10.3 presents the result of the comparison between the 6 trajectories in terms of MOS and CI values. Overlapping CIs between the 5 trajectories (V1, V3, V4, V5, V6), except V2, indicates a non-significant difference. On the other hand, V2 has significantly lowers the MOS value than the other trajectories. Referring to Fig. 10.2, lower MOS value can be explained; trajectory contains large disparity on both vertical and horizontal dimensions around the corner of the trajectories. This may disturb the observers and consequently lower the MOS value. A more detailed discussion and analysis of the results can be found in [33].

On another front, Fig. 10.4 visualizes a sample rendering trajectory on the LF images with horizontal parallax only. The effect of rendering trajectory on the quality of

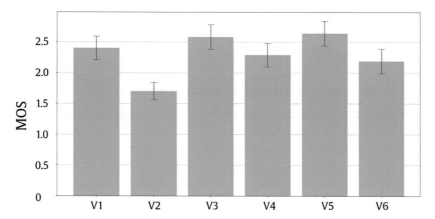

Figure 10.3 Comparison of the MOS scores and their 95% CIs for the 6 predefined trajectories

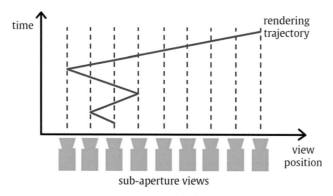

Figure 10.4 Rendering trajectory on LF with only horizontal parallax defined on the temporal dimension.

experience is discussed in detail for free viewpoint videos in [35]. Although they follow a different naming convention, free viewpoint videos are LF with horizontal parallax and the rendering trajectory of this LF is defined over temporal dimension. The results indicate that the observers show significant preference towards certain rendering trajectories. Based on the regions of interest in the content, careful selection of rendering trajectory is required.

10.4. Objective quality assessment

Although subjective experiments are the golden standard for quality assessment, automatically assessing the image quality is still necessary for many applications. It is also not practical to conduct a subjective experiment every time a quality evaluation is required.

Additionally, determining the quality of LF content for real-time applications cannot be done via subjective experiments. To this end, objective quality metrics allow us to estimate the image quality in an automated fashion.

10.4.1 Visibility of LF-related distortions on EPI

We have investigated the LF specific distortions and their sources in LF imaging pipeline in Section 10.2. Many of these distortions were considered when collecting LF image quality datasets in the literature. In this section, we will investigate these distortions on the selected datasets and their visibility on the EPI representations.

A visual inspection of the EPI patches and corresponding edge maps from 5 different LFs in MPI-LFA dataset [15] (see Section 10.3.3.1) is given in Fig. 10.5. Reference EPI patch (i.e., pristine, without distortion) is displayed at the top, meanwhile the 4 EPI patches below contain distortions due to super-resolution algorithms indicated on the left. A brief examination of the EPI patches reveals the characteristics of each super-resolution method. Edge maps acquired with Canny edge detection algorithm [36] provide a binary map emphasizing the visibility of this phenomenon.

Based on this observation, it is natural to investigate the benefit of EPI representations on the image quality metric performances. Therefore next section introduces a set of image quality metrics that leverages structural information within an image to predict the overall quality. Afterwards, we compare the difference between metric performances on EPI and sub-aperture view representations.

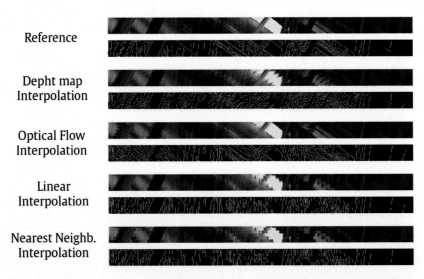

Figure 10.5 Sample EPI patches of 5 different LFs from MPI-LFA dataset [15]. Edge maps of the EPI patches are also presented below to demonstrate the visibility and characteristics of various distortions.

10.4.1.1 Structural image quality metrics

Natural image counter evaluation (NICE) [37] is a full-reference structural image quality metric that relies on the edge maps of reference and distorted image. Extracted edge maps from the reference and distorted images are first dilated with a plus-sign kernel. Later, non-zero elements in the XOR maps between the dilated image pair are calculated to be pooled into a final quality score. Different edge maps might affect the performance of the metric.

Gradient magnitude similarity deviation (GMSD) [38] is another full-reference structural image quality metric that utilizes the directional image gradients. Both reference and distorted images are convoluted with Prewitt [39] filters (horizontal (h_x) and vertical (h_y)):

$$h_x = \begin{bmatrix} 1/3 & 0 & -1/3 \\ 1/3 & 0 & -1/3 \\ 1/3 & 0 & -1/3 \end{bmatrix}, \quad h_y = \begin{bmatrix} 1/3 & 1/3 & 1/3 \\ 0 & 0 & 0 \\ -1/3 & -1/3 & -1/3 \end{bmatrix}.$$

Later, gradient magnitudes at each pixel location for both images are calculated as follows:

$$m_r(i) = \sqrt{(r \circledast h_x)^2(i) + (r \circledast h_y)^2(i)}, \tag{10.2}$$

$$m_d(i) = \sqrt{(d \circledast h_x)^2(i) + (d \circledast h_y)^2(i)} \tag{10.3}$$

to be used to calculate gradient magnitude similarity (GMS) map with the following function:

$$GMS(i) = \frac{2m_r(i)m_d(i)}{(m_r)^2(i) + (m_d)^2(i)}. \tag{10.4}$$

Finally, GMS maps are pooled with standard deviation pooling to estimate the final image quality of the distorted image in comparison to the reference image.

Morphological wavelet peak signal-to-noise ratio (MW-PSNR) [40] calculates the image quality based on morphological wavelet decomposition. PSNR is calculated between each band of decomposed reference and distorted image pairs.

10.4.1.2 Sub-aperture views vs EPI

Structural information present in the EPI regarding the angular dimension of the LF makes it an important representation to understand the presence and the intensity of distortions. With this motivation, we investigate the performance of the three structural image quality metrics that are introduced in the previous section on sub-aperture view

Table 10.2 PCC between metric predictions and MOS scores on FVV dataset [20]. The first column corresponds to PCC values when EPI representations are used, whereas the second column corresponds to PCC values on sub-aperture views.

	EPI	View
MW–PSNR	0.7698	0.7921
GMSD	0.7410	0.6715
NICE	0.5122	0.4310

images and EPIs. Interested readers are recommended to refer to the original work [41] for more information regarding the motivation and the experiment.

Experiment was conducted on FVV dataset [15] (see Section 10.3.3.1). Stimuli in FVV dataset contains content with 50 horizontally arranged sub-aperture views with no vertical parallax. Table 10.2 presents the result of the experiment in terms of Pearson correlation coefficient (PCC) between the metric predictions and MOS values for the three metrics used in the experiments. Higher PCC values indicate a better performance for the metrics. Both sub-aperture views and EPI representations were used to test the metrics. It can be observed that the GMSD and NICE metrics performs better when used over EPI representations instead of sup-aperture views. Structural information, such as directional gradients and edge maps, reveals the distortions that causes inconsistencies in the angular domain. Consequently, GMSD and NICE that rely on filtering the image with Prewitt and Canny kernels perform better on EPI representations. On the other hand, MW-PSNR performance is lower when used over EPI representations. This can be explained by the low spatial resolution of each EPI slice. Multi-scale wavelet decomposition cannot be fully utilized due to the low resolution.

10.4.2 LF image quality metrics

As it stands today, LF is an emerging technology, and quality assessment of LF is an emerging research field. Consequently, there are no well established image quality metrics for LF content. Due to complex imaging pipeline, the ill-defined nature of the LF-related distortions and the higher dimensionality of the LF content, developing objective quality metrics is even more challenging. However, many attempts have been made in the last decade, and more than 30 objective image quality metrics exist in the literature.

Similar to the traditional image quality metrics, we can categorize LF image quality metrics based on the availability of the reference image as an input as full-reference (FR), reduced-reference (RR), or no-reference (NR). When the pristine reference image is present as an input along with the distorted LF, the metric is called a FR metric. Conversely, in the absence of the pristine reference, the metric is called NR. In cases where a set of feature but not the full reference LF is used, the metric is referred to as a RR metric.

On another front, we can categorize the metrics based on the LF representations used as an input. Objective metrics can utilize a variety of LF representations, such as lenslet image, sub-aperture view, EPI, refocused image stack, pseudo video sequence.

The density of the LF (i.e., the baseline distance) can be also used to categorize the objective quality metrics. Currently, due to majority of the publicly available datasets, using dense LFs (i.e., low baseline distance) majority of objective quality metrics are also developed and evaluated on dense LF content. Therefore, at its current state, this categorization might be redundant despite its importance.

The distortions being targeted by the metrics also play an important role, and therefore an informative way to categorize the metrics. Since the datasets used to develop the metrics often dictate the distortions that are targeted by the metric, this categorization can be done via the utilized datasets.

For LF images, metrics often contain two separate streams to evaluate the quality of the spatial and angular dimensions. Two streams are often used to extract features and typically a regression model or a pooling strategy is utilized to merge the two streams into predicting the final quality of the LF content. In addition to the two streams, a third stream can be utilized for LF video content for the temporal dimension. To this date, there are no LF video quality metrics in the literature. Tamboli et al. conducted a study [42] on the use of LF image quality metric [19] to assess LF video frames. Result of the study indicates that the distortions on the temporal space can be separated in the metric space. However, further confirmation with a subjective experiment is required to demonstrate the efficacy of the approach.

A non-exhaustive list of the LF image quality metrics is given in Table 10.3 along with the properties introduced above. At the input column of the table, SAV stands for sub-aperture views, whereas SMV stands for super multi-view. Below we introduce some of these metrics. Note that, the following metrics do not consider any use case. In other words, they evaluate the LF quality independently from the rendering methodology/trajectory. Therefore the results are purely data-driven and various use cases may introduce other complications, which are ignored by the proposed metrics.

The first metric in the table is proposed by Ak et al. [43], and it is a NR metric that takes EPIs from the distorted LF image as an input. It is built on the work illustrated in Section 10.4.1. The metric utilizes the visibility of the LF-related distortions on the EPIs and relies on two set of features as the histogram of oriented gradients (HOG) based bag-of-words codebook and a convolutional sparse coding dictionary. The two sets of features are then used to predict the quality score with a support vector regression model. The model is trained and evaluated on the MPI-LFA dataset, and the results indicate that the metric provides a high correlation to human judgment on LF-content distorted with compression and super resolution distortions with passive display method.

Table 10.3 A non-exhaustive list of LF image quality metrics from the literature.

First Author	Ref	Input	Training Dataset	Evaluation Dataset	LF Density
Ak [43]	NR	EPI	MPI-LFA [15]	MPI-LFA [15]	Dense
Guo [44]	NR	SAV	HCI [45] EPFL [34]	WIN5-LID [1]	Dense
Shi [46]	NR	EPI Cyclopean Img	MPI-LFA [15] SMART [17] WIN5-LID [1]	MPI-LFA [15] SMART [17] WIN5-LID [1]	Dense
Tamboli [19]	FR	SMV	Turntable [19]	Turntable [19]	Sparse
Tian [47]	FR	SAV EPI	MPI-LFA [15]	MPI-LFA [15]	Dense
Zhou [48]	NR	SAV	MPI-LFA [15] SMART [17] VALID [16] WIN5-LID [1]	MPI-LFA [15] SMART [17] VALID [16] WIN5-LID [1]	Dense

Tamboli et al. proposed an objective quality metric [19] that targets the sparse LF content, and, currently, it is the only publicly available objective quality metric that is developed for sparse LF content. Steerable pyramid decomposition over the 3D view of the reference and distorted LF content is used to extract features and quantify the distortions. To assess the quality on the angular dimension, the metric calculates the structural similarity between optical flow arrays obtained from the reference and distorted LFs. The metrics were evaluated on the same dataset [19] proposed in the paper. A cross-validation is used to remove the bias towards the training/test split.

Guo et al. proposed the NR metric [44], which utilizes sub-aperture views with two parallel streams named sub-aperture view fusion and global context perception. The metric is unique in the sense of its training. Pre-training of the metric is done via synthetically generated labels, called ranking-MOS, over a large collection of dense LF content. Finally, the metric is fine-tuned on WIN5-LID dataset [1].

Shi et al. proposed another NR metric [46], which utilizes the cyclopean image array to measure the spatial quality of the LF images and EPIs to measure the angular quality. Similar to [43], the proposed metric relies on the distribution of gradient directions on the EPIs. A support vector regression model is used to combine extracted features to predict final LF image quality.

A FR metric [47] was proposed by Tian et al. relying on two sets of features (symmetry and depth) for quality estimation of LF image content. Symmetry features were calculated over the sub-aperture views of reference and distorted LF in 2 sub-streams as the magnitude-based and orientation-based. Whereas orientation-based symmetry features reveal the distortions on the image details, magnitude-based features emphasize the contour information. For the angular consistency, the proposed metric relies on depth features extracted from the EPIs. Angular quality is quantified by comparing the variance of the lines in a given set of reference and distorted EPI. A weighted average of symmetry and depth scores are then used to predict the final quality.

Zhou et al. proposed a NR quality metric [48], where the LF image is treated as a four-dimensional tensor. The metric operates in CIELAB color space, and Tucker decomposition is used to extract principal components. Principal components spatial characteristics are used to measure the spatial quality, whereas tensor angular variation index is used to quantify the angular consistency. After extracting features from the two streams, a support vector regression model is equipped to predict final quality score.

10.5. Conclusion

Industrial and academical adoption of light field content has widened, thanks to unique opportunities it enables. Last decade brought a great amount of attention to the light field research. Despite the increasing interest, we are still far from light field content reaching out to the consumer market. In the commercial market, we have seen various levels of adoption for different use cases, such as medical, cultural, communicational, industrial [13]. For a given use case, the requirements for a greater user experience may be different than others [14]. This makes the quality assessment of light fields more challenging.

Conducting a subjective study is the ultimate way to assess the quality of experience. There is no exception for the use cases concerning the light field content. To this end, various subjective studies were conducted and shared with the public. Among these, there are studies assessing the quality under varying rendering trajectories, independent of any rendering trajectory, with different focus planes, eye-tracking experiments. A number of testing methodologies have been used in the literature, including DSIS and pairwise comparison. Consequently, subjective preferences are shared as mean opinion scores, pairwise comparison matrices, or just observable differences along the tested stimuli as part of the dataset. Currently, the number of subjective studies with light field displays are low in number in the literature. Majority of the studies uses traditional 2D displays and treat the light field as a pseudo video sequence. Note that though the subjective studies that are not conducted with light field displays may not reflect the effect of all possible influencing factors for all use cases, they still provide a good ground to improve upon.

Objective quality assessment of light field is still developing, and the number of publicly available light field image quality metrics is increasing. To this day, there is no light field video quality metrics as well as an objective quality metric for high dynamic range light field images. The metrics currently do not consider rendering trajectory while assessing the light field quality, and majority of the metrics are targeted for dense light fields. The common scheme for the majority of metrics contains two streams of features assessing the spatial and the angular quality separately. Often a module such as support vector regression model is used to pool the extracted features from the two streams and predict the final light field quality.

With wider adoption of the light field in commercial uses, the key performance indicators will continue to evolve. A wide variety of application will likely to adopt light fields, bringing new use cases and challenges. This creates a need for constant development and improvement of methods and tools to assess light field quality.

References

[1] L. Shi, S. Zhao, W. Zhou, Z. Chen, Perceptual evaluation of light field image, in: 2018 25th IEEE International Conference on Image Processing (ICIP), IEEE, 2018, pp. 41–45.

[2] G. Wu, B. Masia, A. Jarabo, Y. Zhang, L. Wang, Q. Dai, T. Chai, Y. Liu, Light field image processing: An overview, IEEE Journal of Selected Topics in Signal Processing 11 (7) (2017) 926–954, https://doi.org/10.1109/JSTSP.2017.2747126.

[3] Raytrix 3D light-field camera, https://raytrix.de/. (Accessed January 2022).

[4] D. Yue, M.S. Khan Gul, M. Bätz, J. Keinert, R. Mantiuk, A benchmark of light field view interpolation methods, in: 2020 IEEE International Conference on Multimedia Expo Workshops (ICMEW), 2020, pp. 1–6, https://doi.org/10.1109/ICMEW46912.2020.9106041.

[5] S.J. Koppal, Lambertian Reflectance, Springer US, Boston, MA, 2014, pp. 441–443, https://doi.org/10.1007/978-0-387-31439-6_534.

[6] Lytro light-field camera https://www.lytro.com/, currently the website redirects to Raytrix LF camera website.

[7] T. Wang, J. Zhu, N.K. Kalantari, A.A. Efros, R. Ramamoorthi, Light field video capture using a learning-based hybrid imaging system, CoRR, arXiv:1705.02997 [abs], 2017.

[8] O. Johannsen, K. Honauer, B. Goldluecke, A. Alperovich, F. Battisti, Y. Bok, M. Brizzi, M. Carli, G. Choe, M. Diebold, M. Gutsche, H.-G. Jeon, I.S. Kweon, J. Park, J. Park, H. Schilling, H. Sheng, L. Si, M. Strecke, A. Sulc, Y.-W. Tai, Q. Wang, T.-C. Wang, S. Wanner, Z. Xiong, J. Yu, S. Zhang, H. Zhu, A taxonomy and evaluation of dense light field depth estimation algorithms, in: 2017 IEEE Conference on Computer Vision and Pattern Recognition Workshops (CVPRW), 2017, pp. 1795–1812, https://doi.org/10.1109/CVPRW.2017.226.

[9] W. Ellahi, T. Vigier, P.L. Callet, Analysis of public light field datasets for visual quality assessment and new challenges, in: European Light Field Imaging Workshop, Borovets, Bulgaria, Jun 2019, https://hal.archives-ouvertes.fr/hal-02504946.

[10] .-. ISO/IEC, High efficiency video coding, Apr 2013.

[11] .-. ISO/IEC, Versatile video coding, Jul 2020.

[12] C. Conti, L.D. Soares, P. Nunes, Dense light field coding: A survey, IEEE Access 8 (2020) 49244–49284, https://doi.org/10.1109/ACCESS.2020.2977767.

[13] P.A. Kara, R.R. Tamboli, T. Balogh, B. Appina, A. Simon, On the use-case-specific quality degradations of light field visualization, in: C.F. Hahlweg, J.R. Mulley (Eds.), Novel Optical Systems, Methods, and Applications XXIV, vol. 11815, International Society for Optics and Photonics, SPIE, 2021, pp. 81–94, https://doi.org/10.1117/12.2597363.

[14] P.A. Kara, R.R. Tamboli, O. Doronin, A. Cserkaszky, A. Barsi, Z. Nagy, M.G. Martini, A. Simon, The key performance indicators of projection-based light field visualization, Journal of Information Display 20 (2019) 81–93.

[15] V. Kiran Adhikarla, M. Vinkler, D. Sumin, R.K. Mantiuk, K. Myszkowski, H.-P. Seidel, P. Didyk, Towards a quality metric for dense light fields, in: Proceedings of the IEEE Conference on Computer Vision and Pattern Recognition, 2017, pp. 58–67.

[16] I. Viola, T. Ebrahimi, VALID: Visual quality assessment for light field images dataset, in: 2018 Tenth International Conference on Quality of Multimedia Experience (QoMEX), IEEE, 2018, pp. 1–3.

[17] P. Paudyal, R. Olsson, M. Sjöström, F. Battisti, M. Carli, SMART: A light field image quality dataset, in: Proceedings of the 7th International Conference on Multimedia Systems, 2016, pp. 1–6.

[18] A. Zizien, K. Fliegel, LFDD: Light field image dataset for performance evaluation of objective quality metrics, in: Applications of Digital Image Processing XLIII, vol. 11510, International Society for Optics and Photonics, 2020, p. 115102U.

[19] R.R. Tamboli, B. Appina, S. Channappayya, S. Jana, Super-multiview content with high angular resolution: 3D quality assessment on horizontal-parallax lightfield display, Signal Processing. Image Communication 47 (2016) 42–55, https://doi.org/10.1016/j.image.2016.05.010, https://www.sciencedirect.com/science/article/pii/S0923596516300674.

[20] E. Bosc, P. Hanhart, P. Le Callet, T. Ebrahimi, A quality assessment protocol for free-viewpoint video sequences synthesized from decompressed depth data, in: Fifth International Workshop on Quality of Multimedia Experience (QoMEX), Klagenfurt, Germany, 2014, pp. 100–105, https://doi.org/10.1109/QoMEX.2013.6603218.

[21] A. Gill, E. Zerman, C. Ozcinar, A. Smolic, A study on visual perception of light field content, in: The Irish Machine Vision and Image Processing Conference (IMVIP), 2020.

[22] S. Darukumalli, P.A. Kara, A. Barsi, M.G. Martini, T. Balogh, A. Chehaibi, Performance comparison of subjective assessment methodologies for light field displays, in: 2016 IEEE International Symposium on Signal Processing and Information Technology (ISSPIT), 2016, pp. 28–33, https://doi.org/10.1109/ISSPIT.2016.7886004.

[23] P.A. Kara, R.R. Tamboli, A. Cserkaszky, M.G. Martini, A. Barsi, L. Bokor, The viewing conditions of light-field video for subjective quality assessment, in: 2018 International Conference on 3D Immersion (IC3D), 2018, pp. 1–8, https://doi.org/10.1109/IC3D.2018.8657881.

[24] P. Paudyal, J. Gutiérrez, P. Le Callet, M. Carli, F. Battisti, Characterization and selection of light field content for perceptual assessment, in: 2017 Ninth International Conference on Quality of Multimedia Experience (QoMEX), 2017, pp. 1–6, https://doi.org/10.1109/QoMEX.2017.7965635.

[25] ITU-P, Subjective video quality assessment methods for multimedia applications, ITU-P.910, Jan 2022.

[26] N. Kanopoulos, N. Vasanthavada, R.L. Baker, Design of an image edge detection filter using the Sobel operator, IEEE Journal of Solid-State Circuits 23 (2) (1988) 358–367.

[27] C. Amati, N.J. Mitra, T. Weyrich, A study of image colourfulness, in: Proceedings of the Workshop on Computational Aesthetics, CAe '14, Association for Computing Machinery, New York, NY, USA, 2014, pp. 23–31, https://doi.org/10.1145/2630099.2630801.

[28] R.A. Frazor, W.S. Geisler, Local luminance and contrast in natural images, Vision Research 46 (10) (2006) 1585–1598, https://doi.org/10.1016/j.visres.2005.06.038, https://www.sciencedirect.com/science/article/pii/S0042698905005559.

[29] S. Wanner, B. Goldluecke, Variational light field analysis for disparity estimation and super-resolution, IEEE Transactions on Pattern Analysis and Machine Intelligence 36 (3) (2014) 606–619, https://doi.org/10.1109/TPAMI.2013.147.

[30] D.G. Dansereau, O. Pizarro, S.B. Williams, Decoding, calibration and rectification for lenselet-based plenoptic cameras, in: 2013 IEEE Conference on Computer Vision and Pattern Recognition, 2013, pp. 1027–1034, https://doi.org/10.1109/CVPR.2013.137.

[31] HoloVizio C80 glasses-free 3D cinema system, https://holografika.com/c80-glasses-free-3d-cinema/. (Accessed January 2022).

[32] M. Le Pendu, C. Guillemot, A. Smolic, A Fourier disparity layer representation for light fields, IEEE Transactions on Image Processing 28 (11) (2019) 5740–5753.

[33] F. Battisti, M. Carli, P. Le Callet, A study on the impact of visualization techniques on light field perception, in: 2018 26th European Signal Processing Conference (EUSIPCO), 2018, pp. 2155–2159, https://doi.org/10.23919/EUSIPCO.2018.8553558.

[34] M. Rerabek, T. Ebrahimi, New light field image dataset, in: 2016 Eighth International Conference on Quality of Multimedia Experience (QoMEX), Lisbon, Portugal, 2016, https://www.researchgate.net/publication/311924177_New_Light_Field_Image_Dataset.

[35] S. Ling, J. Gutiérrez, K. Gu, P. Le Callet, Prediction of the influence of navigation scan-path on perceived quality of free-viewpoint videos, IEEE Journal on Emerging and Selected Topics in Circuits and Systems 9 (1) (2019) 204–216, https://doi.org/10.1109/JETCAS.2019.2893484.

[36] J. Canny, A computational approach to edge detection, IEEE Transactions on Pattern Analysis and Machine Intelligence PAMI-8 (6) (1986) 679–698, https://doi.org/10.1109/TPAMI.1986.4767851.

[37] D.M. Rouse, S.S. Hemami, Natural image utility assessment using image contours, in: 2009 16th IEEE International Conference on Image Processing (ICIP), 2009, pp. 2217–2220, https://doi.org/10.1109/ICIP.2009.5413882.

[38] W. Xue, L. Zhang, X. Mou, A.C. Bovik, Gradient magnitude similarity deviation: A highly efficient perceptual image quality index, IEEE Transactions on Image Processing 23 (2) (2014) 684–695, https://doi.org/10.1109/TIP.2013.2293423.

[39] J.M.S. Prewitt, Object enhancement and extraction, Picture Processing and Psychopictorics (1970), https://ci.nii.ac.jp/naid/10017095478/en/.

[40] D. Sandić-Stanković, D. Kukolj, P. Le Callet, DIBR-synthesized image quality assessment based on morphological multi-scale approach, EURASIP Journal on Image and Video Processing 2017 (2016), https://doi.org/10.1186/s13640-016-0124-7.

[41] A. Ak, P. Le-Callet, Investigating epipolar plane image representations for objective quality evaluation of light field images, in: 2019 8th European Workshop on Visual Information Processing (EUVIP), 2019, pp. 135–139, https://doi.org/10.1109/EUVIP47703.2019.8946194.

[42] R.R. Tamboli, P.A. Kara, A. Cserkaszky, A. Barsi, M.G. Martini, B. Appina, S.S. Channappayya, S. Jana, 3D objective quality assessment of light field video frames, in: 2018 - 3DTV-Conference: The True Vision - Capture, Transmission and Display of 3D Video (3DTV-CON), 2018, pp. 1–4, https://doi.org/10.1109/3DTV.2018.8478557.

[43] A. Ak, S. Ling, P. Le Callet, No-reference quality evaluation of light field content based on structural representation of the epipolar plane image, in: The 1st ICME Workshop on Hyper-Realistic Multimedia for Enhanced Quality of Experience, London, United Kingdom, 2020.

[44] Z. Guo, W. Gao, H. Wang, J. Wang, S. Fan, No-reference deep quality assessment of compressed light field images, in: 2021 IEEE International Conference on Multimedia and Expo (ICME), 2021, pp. 1–6, https://doi.org/10.1109/ICME51207.2021.9428383.

[45] K. Honauer, O. Johannsen, D. Kondermann, B. Goldlücke, A dataset and evaluation methodology for depth estimation on 4D light fields, in: ACCV, 2016.

[46] L. Shi, W. Zhou, Z. Chen, J. Zhang, No-reference light field image quality assessment based on spatial-angular measurement, IEEE Transactions on Circuits and Systems for Video Technology 30 (11) (2020) 4114–4128, https://doi.org/10.1109/TCSVT.2019.2955011.

[47] Y. Tian, H. Zeng, J. Hou, J. Chen, J. Zhu, K.-K. Ma, A light field image quality assessment model based on symmetry and depth features, IEEE Transactions on Circuits and Systems for Video Technology 31 (5) (2021) 2046–2050, https://doi.org/10.1109/TCSVT.2020.2971256.

[48] W. Zhou, L. Shi, Z. Chen, J. Zhang, Tensor oriented no-reference light field image quality assessment, IEEE Transactions on Image Processing 29 (2020) 4070–4084, https://doi.org/10.1109/TIP.2020.2969777.

PART 4

Volumetric video

CHAPTER 11

Volumetric video – acquisition, interaction, streaming and rendering

Peter Eisert[a,b]**, Oliver Schreer**[a]**, Ingo Feldmann**[a]**, Cornelius Hellge**[a]**, and Anna Hilsmann**[a]

[a]Fraunhofer HHI, Berlin, Germany
[b]Humboldt University Berlin, Berlin, Germany

Due to the rapid development and the advances in extended Reality (XR) technologies and the related devices (e.g., tablets, headsets, etc.), realistic 3D representations of humans have achieved significant attention, especially in use cases, where a convincing visualization of humans is essential. Relevant use cases include interactive teaching and training, new formats for film and cinema, immersive experiences with contemporary witnesses, meet-ups with celebrities, and many more. However, current character animation techniques often do not provide the necessary level of realism. The motion capture process is time-consuming and cannot represent all the detailed motions of a person, especially facial expressions and the motion of clothing and objects. Therefore volumetric video is regarded worldwide as the next important development in media production, especially in the context of rapidly evolving virtual and augmented reality markets, where volumetric video is becoming a key technology.

Though volumetric video offers high visual quality and realism, interaction with the virtual humans is restricted to free viewpoint navigation through a 3D virtual scene. Therefore it would be highly desirable to enable manipulation and animation of the volumetric content similar to classical computer graphics models. We achieve that by automatic rigging of a computer graphics (CG) template mesh that serves as semantic annotation, and can be used as input interface to modify and animate body and face poses. In addition, facial expressions and lip movements can be synthesized from text or speech, allowing the virtual character to react on user behavior. This enables the creation of realistic virtual characters that can interact with potential users in novel application formats and fields, such as e-learning, tele-collaboration, or human machine interaction.

The 3D representation of volumetric video, however, leads to high demands on storage and network capacities. This requires efficient coding and streaming of the 3D mesh and texture sequences. In addition, the content needs to be rendered on virtual (VR) and augmented (AR) reality end user devices with restricted computational capabilities. With our split rendering methods, we decode and render a stereoscopic view on a nearby server and stream these views as 2D videos to the glasses. In this way,

Immersive Video Technologies
https://doi.org/10.1016/B978-0-32-391755-1.00017-1

289

even high-resolution content can be displayed on devices with limited computational resources.

11.1. Creation of volumetric video

For dynamic scenes, virtual characters can be animated by scripts or by motion capture. However, the modeling and animation process of moving characters is time consuming and often it cannot represent all moving details of a real human, especially facial expressions and the motion of clothes. In contrast to these conventional methods, volumetric video is a new technique that scans humans with plenty of cameras from different viewpoints, sometimes in combination with active depth sensors. During a complex volumetric video production process, this large amount of video data is converted to a dynamic 3D mesh sequence, representing a full free-viewpoint video. It has the naturalism of high-quality video, but is represented as a dynamic 3D object, which, for example, can be inserted to a virtual 3D scene, where a user can virtually walk around and arbitrarily change his position and viewing direction.

In recent years, several volumetric studios have been created that are able to produce high-quality volumetric video (e.g., Microsoft's mixed reality capture studios [1], 8i [2], Volucap [3], 4DViews [4], Evercoast [5], HOLOOH [6], Holograms [7], Mantis vision [8] and many more). Most studios focus on a capture volume that is viewed spherically in 360 degrees from the outside. A large number of cameras are placed around the scene, providing input for volumetric video similar to frame-by-frame photogrammetric reconstruction of the actors. The number of cameras varies, ranging from less than 10 cameras to more than 60. The same holds for the resolution. Most of the studios use HD cameras, but some studios focus on high resolution up to 20 MPixel and more. In addition to RGB cameras, active depth sensors are added in some systems to support geometry acquisition. To separate the scene from the background, many studios are equipped with green screens for chroma keying. In contrast, for example, Volucap [3] uses a bright backlit background to avoid green spilling effects in the texture and to provide diffuse illumination. This concept is based on a prototype system developed by Fraunhofer HHI [9] (see Fig. 11.1).

11.1.1 Volumetric video workflow

Our general volumetric video workflow is depicted in Fig. 11.2. The first four blocks refer to modules that perform processing of images from various video streams. The next blocks refer to modules that are dedicated to mesh processing. Finally, the last four blocks assign components, which are related to encoding and streaming of the volumetric assets to the target device, where real-time rendering is required. The amount of raw data after capture is tremendously high, ranging from several GB/min to TB/min, depending on the number of cameras, their resolution and frame rate. Therefore one main purpose and

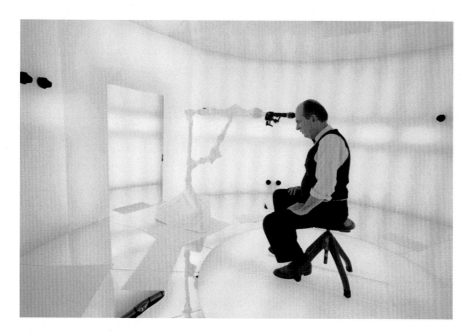

Figure 11.1 Prototype system of Fraunhofer HHI volumetric video capture stage.

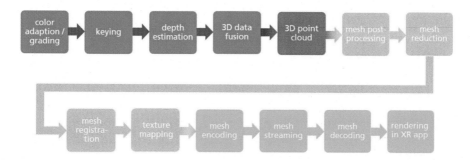

Figure 11.2 Volumetric video workflow diagram.

challenge of this workflow is to reduce the amount of data significantly, while keeping a high level of visual quality and geometrical resolution. The individual processing steps are now described in more detail.

In the first step, usually, **color adaptation** of the different video streams is performed to achieve equal color distribution among all cameras. Further on, a preliminary grading can be performed at this early stage. However, a final artistical color grading is performed at the end of the processing chain, either directly during rendering by using dedicated shaders or by modifying the final texture maps. A next processing step in the workflow is related to the separation of foreground and background to focus the processing resources onto the objects of interest, i.e., persons in the foreground. Usually, this is performed by **chroma keying**. The resulting keying masks optionally can be used to enhance the final mesh quality by applying visual hull constraints.

If video cameras or hybrid RGB-D sensors are used, then depth estimation is performed in parallel on multiple video inputs from different sensors. The output of this step is a related depth map per sensor or stereo camera pair. The resulting **depth information** from different perspectives is transformed to 3D space and combined in a joint 3D point cloud via **3D data fusion**. At this point, depth maps acquired by stereoscopic depth estimation or acquired by RGB-D sensors are treated equally. Afterward, the **3D point cloud** is further processed to perform cleaning and post-processing. In **mesh post-processing**, the 3D point cloud is converted into a consistent mesh. Usually, the resulting mesh is far too complex for real-time rendering on end user devices. Therefore a **mesh reduction** is applied. The target complexity of the mesh can be defined according to the rendering capabilities of the final XR device. So far, for each frame, an individual mesh with different topology is available. To improve the temporal consistency of the geometry and to optimize the data for encoding purposes, a subsequent **mesh registration** is performed. Based on the original input images of the multi-camera capture system, **texture mapping** of the mesh is performed, resulting in a texture atlas and related uv coordinates for each frame. At this stage exists a temporarily aligned mesh sequence, which is still too complex and inappropriate for efficient data streaming. Hence, a **mesh encoding** is applied. The result is a single volumetric video file that allows for efficient **mesh streaming** to the final **XR application**, where the incoming data stream is **decoded** and rendered as dynamic volumetric video assets (see Section 11.3.1).

11.1.2 Calibration

The calibration process measures fixed quantities of the capture setup, which are the following: (1) the intrinsic parameters of the cameras and their positions and orientations in a global coordinate system, (2) the relative color differences between the cameras and the absolute difference to reference colors. The geometric calibration requires a special capture session, in which a calibration target, e.g., a cube with one ChArUco board [10] on each side, is carried around the studio (Fig. 11.3). Many other calibration patterns can be used for this purpose, such as random patterns or chessboards. The cube defines a reference coordinate system, so its detection in all of the cameras allows to solve for their relative position and orientation. Correspondences between world points on the cube and pixels in the images enable the estimation of intrinsic camera parameters, including relative focal length and lens distortion.

Figure 11.3 Calibration cube in the volumetric capture studio (left) and color calibration (right).

11.1.3 Image pre-processing

A high-quality 3D reconstruction can be achieved by a set of pre-processing operations based on the previous calibration step (see Fig. 11.4). After debayering and gamma correction stage, 3D color look-up tables are applied, which match the image colors to a reference camera. Image undistortion reverts any lens distortion caused by wide field-of-view lenses, such that straight lines appear straight in the images again. This correction most notably improves the reconstruction for areas near the image borders. Lastly, the background is removed by obtaining alpha masks from a foreground segmentation algorithm. We use a deep learning approach [11], fine-tuned on hundreds of manually labeled images. The machine learning segmentation outperforms classical approaches, such as [12], most notably at resolving local ambiguities, i.e., when a foreground pixel has a similar color as the clean plate pixel at the same location.

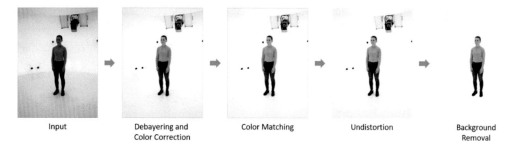

Input   Debayering and   Color Matching   Undistortion   Background
               Color Correction   Removal

Figure 11.4 Pre-processing operations applied on images before 3D reconstruction.

11.1.4 Depth estimation

The depth estimation is the first stage of the 3D reconstruction pipeline. It uses the pre-processed input images and the geometric calibration data to obtain depth information. In the case of multi-view camera setups based on stereo pairs, one depth map is computed per camera pair (see Fig. 11.5). If only information from RGB sensors is available, vision-based stereo approaches are applied. These algorithms can be differentiated by traditional depth estimation algorithms based on correspondence analysis and machine learning-based approaches.

Traditional stereo matching and multi-view stereo (MVS) methods compute pairwise matching costs of raw image patches by a given similarity measure. In recent years, PatchMatch-based stereo matching [13,14] and MVS [15–20] are dominating methods due to inherent parallelism and robust performance. Recently, deep learning shows superior performance in MVS. MVSNet [21] applies a similar idea to stereo matching, by regularizing cost volumes with 3D CNNs. The main difference is that MVS builds cost volumes by warping feature maps from multiple neighboring views. To reduce memory consumption from 3D CNNs, R-MVSNet [22] sequentially regularizes 2D cost maps with a gated recurrent unit (GRU), whereas other works [23–25] integrate multi-stage coarse-to-fine strategies to progressively refine 3D cost volumes. Moreover, Vis-MVSNet [26] explicitly estimates pixel-wise visibility as certainty to guide multi-view cost volume fusion, leading to more robust performance. A current drawback of deep learning-based approaches is the limited availability of training data, memory consumption, and processing time.

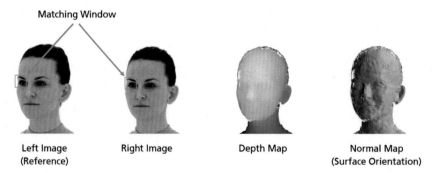

| Left Image (Reference) | Right Image | Depth Map | Normal Map (Surface Orientation) |

Figure 11.5 Stereo depth estimation for a given stereo pair and resulting depth and normal information.

11.1.5 Depth map fusion

After depth estimation, the individual depth maps are fused into a single 3D point cloud. The method described in [27] projects depth maps into 3D space and combines them based on truncated signed distance function (TSDF) representations in a weighted fashion. The TSDF is defined on a discrete 3D grid (Fig. 11.6). An oriented point cloud (i.e., a point cloud with normals) is then extracted from the iso-surface by finding zero-crossings on this grid.

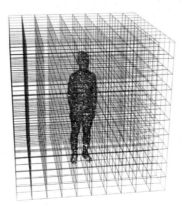

Figure 11.6 The depth map fusion combines all depth maps into a discrete truncated signed distance function and extracts a point cloud from the iso-surface defined on the grid. The grid cells here are enlarged for visualization.

Though the TSDF fusion step approximates the 3D surface reasonably well, the resulting 3D point cloud may still contain outliers originating from depth estimation or segmentation errors. Therefore the point cloud is further processed in multiple cleaning stages [28] (Fig. 11.7): (1) visual hull–like constraints ensure that points falling outside of the foreground masks are discarded consistently for all views, (2) capture volume clipping removes points that are invisible to the majority of cameras, and (3) cylinder cleaning removes points that are outside of a fixed cylinder volume. Although the last two cleaning steps often introduce redundancy, the capture volume clipping can provide more fine-grained control, the cylinder cleaning is usually faster.

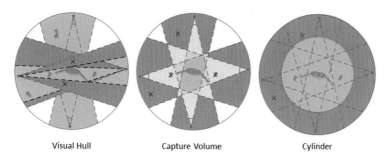

Visual Hull   Capture Volume   Cylinder

Figure 11.7 Different point cloud cleaning stages applied after depth map fusion, here in 2D as seen from above.

11.1.6 Mesh processing

The oriented point cloud extracted in depth map fusion is still an unstructured geometrical representation. It does not contain any information about connectivity and surfaces, respectively. Therefore a dedicated surface reconstruction step follows in the workflow. It first applies the screened Poisson surface reconstruction [29] to the point clouds, resulting in a watertight triangle mesh per frame (see Fig. 11.8).

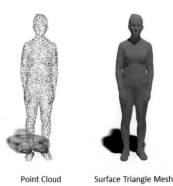

Point Cloud   Surface Triangle Mesh

Figure 11.8 The screen Poisson surface reconstruction extracts a triangle mesh from an oriented point cloud.

Despite the intensive point cloud cleaning, some outliers may remain in the 3D dataset. Thus a last cleaning step removes all connected components, except for the N largest, where N typically equals the number of actors or distinct objects expected in the reconstruction. To further reduce noise on the surface, a Taubin smoothing filter [30] is applied to the mesh. Since the resulting mesh has a large complexity, the number of faces can be reduced with quadric edge collapse (QEC) [31]. The target mesh resolution is configurable and can be adapted according to the capability of the rendering hardware and desired level of geometric detail. See Fig. 11.9 for a visualization of these steps. Optionally, a geometry refinement with a differentiable renderer can be performed at this stage [32].

In the next step, the meshes are prepared for coloring, i.e., transfer of the observed colors in the camera images to the surface geometry. The colors are stored in 2D texture maps that are applied to the geometry during rendering. Therefore a dedicated mapping of the 3D mesh to the 2D domain is computed, leading to a texture atlas with multiple charts for each frame (Fig. 11.10).

For optimization purposes, the charting is performed prior to temporal mesh registration only on key frames, because their parameterization will propagate to the intermediate frames. The applications that perform mesh processing are implemented in C++ and use the libraries OpenMesh [33] and xatlas [34] for mesh data structures, geometry processing, and for charting.

Poisson Surface   Taubin Smoothing   QEC Simplification

Figure 11.9 After Poisson surface reconstruction, the triangle mesh is smoothed and simplified.

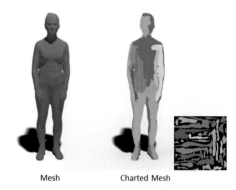

Mesh   Charted Mesh

Figure 11.10 A mesh and its 2D parametrization. It is typically divided into charts that provide an optimal layout in 2D.

11.1.7 Temporal mesh registration

The capture pipeline produces a sequence of 3D surface meshes with all frames being processed individually. Thus while the scene changes gradually over time, the mesh connectivity may be different from frame to frame, which makes editing, processing, and interaction with the volumetric video more difficult and increases data rate for streaming and compression.

Therefore temporal mesh registration is used to create subsequences with consistent mesh topology over time [35]. This can be achieved by tracking and deforming a reference mesh from frame to frame to keep mesh topology constant, while approximating the target surface as close as possible. Additional deformation priors, e.g., via *Laplace diffusion* [36] or *as rigid as possible* [37], constrain relative vertex movements. Larger variations in target topology can be handled by splitting the sequence into subsequences with key frames representing topology for the individual parts [18]. For more compact descriptions, subsequences can also be structured hierarchically in a tree-like manner [38].

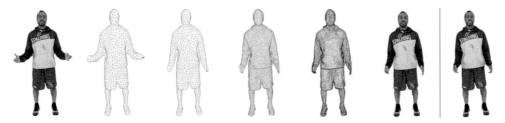

Figure 11.11 The mesh on the left is deformed in a coarse-to-fine approach to closely approximate the surface of the target mesh after the divider on the right.

Our approach for temporal mesh registration [39] is based on a key frame-architecture as in [18], but uses a hierarchical coarse to fine strategy for mesh registration (see Fig. 11.11). First, a number of frames from the sequence are selected based on information on surface area and mesh genus to form a set of key frames, which are not processed further. Then, the chosen key frames are deformed to match the surface of their neighboring meshes progressively forward and backward in the sequence. A subset of frames midway between key frames is registered from both surrounding key frames. By choosing the resulting mesh with the lower registration error, a smooth transition between key frames is ensured.

The pairwise mesh registration is based on the iterative closest point (ICP) algorithm. Working in a hierarchical approach speeds up the convergence towards a global solution, even with large displacements between successive frames, while preserving high-level details. The deformation of a mesh is encoded as transformations on a deformation graph that progressively grows in detail through the hierarchy. The deformation graph is kept as–rigid–as–possible to preserve local stiffness in articulated objects.

The resulting mesh sequence closely resembles the original mesh sequence produced in the previous steps, but has locally consistent topology for simplified further processing and compression.

11.1.8 Use case for volumetric video

Volumetric video offers an authentic and much more realistic digital representation of humans. Besides several other use cases (further discussed in Part V: Applications), this technology is ideal in the context of preserving memories from contemporary witnesses. The stories told by survivors of the Holocaust play a significant role in preservation of our cultural heritage, especially for the young generation. In this context, Fraunhofer Heinrich Hertz Institute and UFA GmbH conceptualized and produced one of the first and longest VR documentaries so far, called "Ernst Grube – The Legacy." Volumetric video is used to retell the stories of Ernst Grube, one of the last German survivors of the Holocaust. It consists of five interviews, each lasting about 10 minutes, in which the Jewish contemporary witness reflects on his life under the Nazi regime, from his youth to his imprisonment in the Theresienstadt concentration camp. In each episode, the protagonists are placed in an authentic virtual recreation of a different historical site (see Fig. 11.12). More details can be found at [28].

Figure 11.12 Screen shot of volumetric video from Ernst Grube in VR. ©The Author(s); Eurographics Proceedings ©2020 The Eurographics Association.

11.2. Animating and interacting with volumetric video

Volumetric video sequences of human performances provide an excellent means for novel applications in VR and AR. The assets can be watched in virtual or real environments from arbitrary viewing directions, providing the user the immersion of being part in the scene. However, visualization is mainly restricted to free viewpoint replay and the virtual characters cannot interact with the users. To allow the virtual humans to react on user behavior (e.g., eye contact, direct verbal address of a real user etc.), more interactive representations have to be developed from this high-quality data that can be manipulated and animated [40].

In this section, we show how volumetric video data can be enriched with semantic information from computer graphics models to establish new possibilities of animation. We treat the body different from the face, as humans are especially sensitive to looking at human faces, and body and face are often handled differently, e.g., body animation via skeleton and face animation though blend shape deformation parameters.

11.2.1 Body animation

The animation of virtual human characters in applications such as computer games, virtual reality or movies is usually done using computer graphics (CG) models, which can be controlled by an underlying skeleton. This enables full control over body motion, but comes at the price of significant modeling effort and sometimes limited realism.

Example-based methods increase realism by relying more on pre-recorded real data. For example, Stoll et al. [41] combine skeleton-based CG models with captured surface data to represent fine details, e.g., wrinkles of apparels on top of the body. Concatenation of captured 3D sequences with view-dependent texturing for real-time interactive animation is addressed by Caras et al. [42]. Similarly, Volino et al. [43] presented a parametric motion graph-based character animation for web applications. An animation synthesis structure for the recomposition of textured 4D video capture, accounting for geometry and appearance, is proposed by Boukhayma et al. [44,45]. This graph structure enables interpolation and traversal between precaptured 4D video sequences.

More recently, the success of deep learning has triggered many approaches to learn body shape and appearance driven by skeleton input data. In [46], Li et al. perform automatic rigging of a template mesh and learn neural blend shapes to reproduce the pose-dependent deformations of the template geometry. Textured models with both pose-dependent geometry and texture are addressed in [47]. Here, appearance and geometric refinements are synthesized from a 2D feature map wrapped around a course template model. This approach is extended in [48] such that also virtual characters with loose clothing can be synthesized dynamically in real-time. For better editing and animation capabilities, Regateiro et al. [49] add a 4D motion graph to a learned character with pose-dependent geometry and appearance to allow navigation through different motion sequences.

Inspired by current approaches for virtual humans, we have developed different methods for body and face synthesis. For body animation, we automatically fit an animatable computer graphics human template model (e.g., the skinned multi-person linear model: SMPL [50]) to the mesh sequence and use the underlying skeleton as input for manipulation of body poses. This enables the animation of the template mesh and transferring surface motion to the volumetric sequence, as described in Section 11.2.1.2. More drastic modification of the content is possible through the concatenation of prerecorded motion sequences (see Section 11.2.1.3) or a learned neural representation, as shown in Section 11.2.1.4.

11.2.1.1 Body model fitting

A volumetric video sequence usually consists of independent meshes for each frame, making it difficult to modify, blend, animate, or learn from the data. Therefore we fit a parametric kinematically animatable human body model (e.g., SMPL [50]) to the volumetric video stream, to closely resemble the shape of the captured subject as well as the pose of each frame. The tracked template mesh, which is aligned to the volumetric video, provides semantic labels and a consistent topology establishing correspondences over time. In addition, it can be animated through an underlying skeleton, and template motion can be transferred to the unstructured mesh sequence.

For the registration of the template to the 3D mesh sequence, we first roughly initialize the body model with an image-based pose estimator followed by a fine-tuning to closely approximate the volumetric video sequence. For initialization, we have extended the SMPL-X framework [50] with temporal consistency constraints to estimate shape and body pose from a monocular image sequence from the capture setup [51]. Instead of a frame by frame estimation, we determine a consistent body shape for the entire sequence with independent body poses for each frame. In addition, a temporal smoothness constraint penalizes deviations of pose parameters from their two temporal neighbors for temporally consistent body shape and motion (see Fig. 11.13).

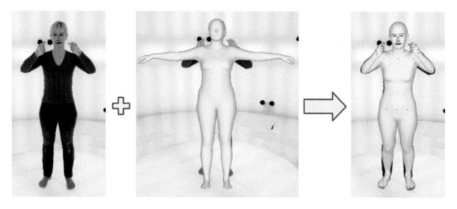

Figure 11.13 Illustration of reprojection loss: Input image with open-pose key points marked in red (left), SMPL-X model in initial rest-pose (middle) and pose and shape adapted SMPL-X model with OpenPose key points (right).

Body model parameters are fitted to the image sequence in three phases. In phase 1, the image sequence is processed consecutively with OpenPose [52] to obtain predicted joint locations as key points at image pixel positions per image. These key points are in turn fed into SMPLify-X [50] to calculate an initialization for the desired temporally consistent body shape and motion. In phase 2, a consistent shape for the image sequence is derived from the initialized body models by parameter optimization of the entire sequence. Finally, in phase 3, the SMPL-X pose parameters are optimized along the sequence with the temporal smoothness constraint for consistent body motion.

The monocular template model initialization is only a rough alignment to the volumetric video in 3D space. Following, the pose parameters are further optimized by minimizing the distances between corresponding vertices of the model and the captured mesh. Both pose and shape are jointly refined in a second step by additionally optimizing the model vertices and skeleton joints to bring the model into better alignment with the captured mesh [53]. To ensure that the natural movement characteristics are not lost, we use a learned pose prior based on Gaussian mixture models. Furthermore, we use a mesh Laplacian constraint to enforce plausible human shapes. With both shape and pose estimation complete, the parameterized human body model closely approximates the original volumetric video sequence (see Fig. 11.14), and the rigged model can be used to animate the volumetric video stream, as described in the next section.

Figure 11.14 Original video from the studio (right) with corresponding fitted template mesh (left).

11.2.1.2 Hybrid animation

Having enriched the volumetric video stream with semantic data by fitting a human body model with an assigned skeleton, it is now possible to kinematically animate the volumetric video. Body poses can be corrected or modified, while keeping the high level of detail in the meshes and textures that were created from real recordings in the capture studio. This is achieved by animating the template model from the skeleton input data and transferring surface motion of the rigged template to the unstructured volumetric sequence.

The kinematic animation of the individual volumetric frames is facilitated through the body model fitted to each frame. For each mesh vertex, the location relative to the closest triangle of the template mesh is calculated, parameterized by the barycentric coordinates of the projection onto the triangle and the orthogonal distance. This relative location is held fixed, virtually gluing the mesh vertex to the template mesh triangle with constant distance and orientation. Thus an animation of the model can directly be transferred to the volumetric video frame [40].

One application for the hybrid animation approach is the interaction with virtual humans in AR or VR, where the virtual human follows the user with his/her head when the user moves in the virtual scene. This substantially enhances the feeling of a true conversation with the virtual character [54]. An example of applying the mesh animation method to head pose correction can be seen in Fig. 11.15. For this correction, the user's position needs to be retrieved in relation to the virtual human's position. This information is usually available from tracking the headset. From that, the joints in the neck of the fitted template model can be modified to orient the actor's face directly towards the user's point-of-view. Artifacts in geometry and the display of unnatural poses can be avoided by restricting the offset of joint rotations to a range around the original pose, or choosing to enforce a human body prior.

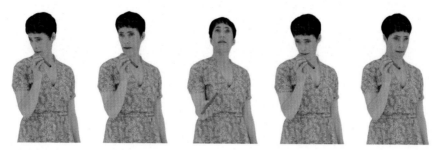

Figure 11.15 Volumetric video sequence with modified head pose.

11.2.1.3 Body pose interpolation

Applying the surface motion of the animated template to the volumetric video sequence is restricted to relatively small corrections, since pose-dependent shape changes taken from the template are smooth. Wrinkles in the clothing do not change and also shading and shadowing effects on the texture remain constant, which becomes apparent if the pose modification is too drastic compared to the original capturing.

Hence, we want to exploit the captured data as much as possible in an example-based approach and only slightly kinematically animate the captured frames. This means, we rely on real measurements that reproduce the fine surface details related to pose modifications as much as possible. Instead of animating a reference mesh to show a target pose, in an example-based approach a similar target motion is searched within a database of prerecorded motion snippets. By temporally concatenating different motion sequences, interactive animations can be produced in a motion graph manner [42,44]. This enables larger variations in animating the virtual human, e.g., directly reacting on user action in AR or VR applications.

Whereas the volumetric video snippets are temporally consistent themselves, the transitions between the concatenated sequences are not, requiring a seamless blending between them. Since the transition point is chosen such that the last frame of the previous sequence is already close to the first pose of the following sequence, only small pose modifications are required, which can be achieved with the animation method described in the previous section, as shown in Fig. 11.16. We establish correspondences between the volumetric video frames through the rigged and tracked template model and defined a transition phase within the pose differences between the sequence, which are smoothly interpolated, transferring template corrections to the mesh vertices. In addition, a blending between surface shape and texture creates a smooth transition between the mismatching sequences [40].

Figure 11.16 Seamless pose interpolation from the last frame (leftmost) of the previous sequence to the first frame (rightmost) of the following concatenated sequence.

The different methods for the generation of new content can be combined; a new sequence that consists of different interpolated subsequences still contains the semantic information of the human body model. It is therefore possible to further animate the newly created sequence, e.g., by additionally applying the gaze correction described in the previous section.

11.2.1.4 Pose-dependent neural synthesis

The fitted body model has a consistent topology and complete texture atlas for any pose. Projecting the texture from the volumetric video to the fitted model and recording a displacement map transfers many of the details of the volumetric video stream onto the model mesh in specific poses. This data can be used to learn person-specific textures and displacements from the volumetric video stream, to be later reproduced for new poses: both interpolated and unseen. We train a convolutional decoder network with a sequence of template meshes with the projected texture from the volumetric video stream to synthesize pose-dependent textures from the input skeleton. This network can then produce textures for previously unseen poses; an example can be seen in Fig. 11.17. Increasing the level of detail and adding learned displacement maps is currently under investigation.

Figure 11.17 Left: original volumetric video frame; middle: animated template with synthesized texture; right: synthesized character with novel pose.

11.2.2 Face animation

Usually, the face is treated differently from the body, as humans are extremely sensitive to looking at human faces. Furthermore, facial expressions are an important part of communication, and for communication it is essential that the synthesized results exhibit the required expressiveness and accuracy. Especially, visual speech synthesis poses several challenges, such as expressiveness and plausibility of the synthesized mouthings as well as inter-dependencies between subsequent visemes, which effect their appearance. Especially, in many applications, e.g., in sign language applications, the synthesized mouthings do not only have to be visually plausible but also accurate in the sense that they carry important information.

For a long time, similar to the full body case, dynamic parametric models have been used for the animation of facial expressions [55–60]. Typically, these models are built by computing a linear basis that reconstructs the 3D face geometry, depending on facial expression and identity parameters. More sophisticated models are even able to capture albedo and diffuse light by incorporating more model parameters [57].

However, though these models are computationally efficient and easy to use, they usually lack expressiveness to capture important details and to represent complex deformations and occlusions/dis-occlusions that occur around eyes, mouth, and in the oral cavity. As a result, purely model-based approaches that use linear face representations employ either hand crafted solutions to visualize these complex areas (e.g., oral cavity) or simply ignore them.

One approach to circumvent these limitations are hybrid models [42,61,62], which incorporate real captured data in the form of high-resolution dynamic textures to capture and reproduce important facial details that cannot be efficiently represented by geometry alone. These dynamic textures are short video textures of facial expressions that can interactively be combined using optimized transitions and seamless temporal blending between them [62]. However, this comes at the cost of high memory requirements during rendering and reduced animation flexibility. With the advent of deep neural networks, more powerful generative models [63–67] have been developed, often based on variational auto-encoders that learn a manifold of facial expression and are capable of jointly reconstructing face geometry or generative adversarial networks (GANs) [68]. These methods usually use large unlabeled datasets of face images and videos to train existing (multi)-linear face models in a self-supervised or unsupervised manner. Often, a differentiable renderer or even a differentiable ray-tracer [69] is employed, while minimizing the color difference between synthesized and target face images. Furthermore, deep generative face models have been developed that provide more detailed and realistic head models of an individual [57,59,60,70], which usually exploit sophisticated capturing setups to produce high-quality training data for their models.

Inspired by these works, we developed a method for generating a personalized and highly realistic 3D head model from captured multi-view footage. Our hybrid model supports animation as well as realistic rendering by combining classical computer graphics with recent methods for deep neural face models and neural rendering, allowing us to synthesize realistic and plausible images of facial expressions in real time. In our hybrid representation (Section 11.2.3), a lightweight statistical head model accounts for approximate geometry, modeling rigid head pose and large-scale deformation of the face. Fine motion and small details are represented with temporally consistent dynamic textures that are computed from multi-view video footage using a graph-cut based approach. By training a joined variational auto-encoder (VAE) for geometry as well as dynamic textures, we obtain a parametric representation of detailed facial expressions. For realistic rendering of the dynamic head model, we train a pixel-to-pixel translation network that refines rasterization-based renderings by computing improved pixel colors as well as an alpha-mask (Section 11.2.5). This introduces more texture details, view-dependent effects, and corrects errors caused by the coarse underlying mesh in complex regions, e.g., oral cavity, ears, hair geometry. Moreover, the alpha-mask simplifies the training process, as pre-computed foreground-segmentation masks are not required. It also facilitates the reconstruction of translucent pixels, which allows for silhouette refinement, the reconstruction of fine structures, such as hair, and the integration of rendered head images into new backgrounds.

11.2.3 Neural hybrid face model

Our hybrid neural face model is learnt from captured multi-view video footage of relevant facial expressions. Our animatable face model is based on linear blend-shapes to represent the approximate face geometry for each captured video frame. As the blend-shapes capture rigid motion and large-scale deformations only, we additionally extract dynamic face textures to represent small motions and details as well as complex areas, such as the oral cavity and the eyes.

Details on the facial performance capture can be found in [71–73]. The result of the facial performance capture is a sequence of textured meshes. Each frame is represented by a rigid motion **T**, blend-shape weights **b**, and an RGB image as texture. To efficiently use the extracted face performance data, we train a neural face model (i.e., a VAE) that is capable of jointly synthesizing geometry as well as texture from a low-dimensional facial expression vector [71]. Fig. 11.18 shows the architecture of the neural face model based on a VAE.

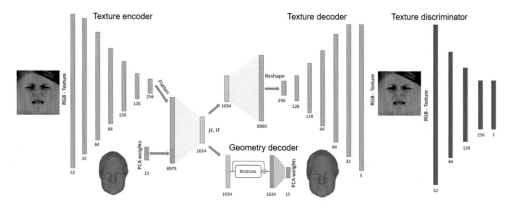

Figure 11.18 Architecture of the deep generative face model.

The auto-encoder receives PCA face shape weights as well as the textures from the performance capture stage as input and transforms them into a 1024-D latent representation of the facial expression. Based on the latent expression vector, we reconstruct face shape weights as well as texture. We use an adversarial training strategy based on a discriminator network, which is trained together with the auto-encoder. The purpose of the discriminator is classifying; it determines whether a texture is synthesized or real. By incorporating the classification error during training, we can improve the visual quality of reconstructed textures. The full training objective function consists of the absolute difference between predicted texture and target texture, the adversarial texture loss, and the mean-squared error between the predicted and the target PCA weights. For a more detailed presentation of our neural facial model, please refer to [71–73].

Using the neural face model, we represent high-dimensional geometry and texture data with a single low-dimensional latent expression vector. Apart from compressing high-dimensional data, the latent representation also allows easy sampling and interpolation of realistic facial expressions without introducing artifacts in texture or geometry.

11.2.4 Text driven facial animation

Though the above described neural face model is capable of reconstructing, sampling, and interpolating captured facial expressions, it does not capture the dynamics. Therefore we train an animation network to learn the dynamics of facial expressions. Such a network can be trained on a sequence of annotated latent expression vectors. In our case, for visual speech synthesis, we annotate the latent vectors with textual labels that describe the displayed viseme or the facial expression [71]. With the annotated data, we train an auto-regressive network (Fig. 11.19) to synthesize sequences of latent expression vectors, given a single label or a sequence of labels. The generated latent expression vectors are then used to reconstruct the geometry and texture using the neural face model. To synthesize animation parameters, the network receives the last animation parameter/timestamp as well as the current sequence label, the next sequence label, and a style vector. Providing subsequent labels helps resolving ambiguities due to coarticulation (a phenomenon in speech when two successive sounds are articulated together) (see Fig. 11.20). Similar effects can occur when animating general facial expressions. To account for that, we condition our network on a style vector that is learned automatically during training. Label and style are zero-based indices that are transformed to a 32-D feature vector by separate embedding layers. We use 19 different feature vectors to represent labels and 514 different style vectors (one style vector for each annotated sequence) [71,73].

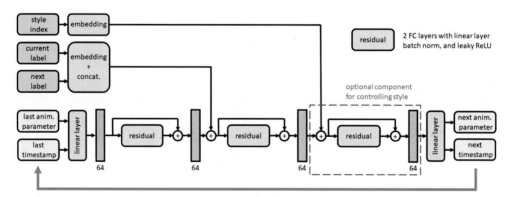

Figure 11.19 Auto-regressive network architecture for the generation of latent animation vectors from text.

During training, the animation network learns an embedding for each label and a rule how to predict the successive facial animation parameters from the previous parameter, a given sequence label, and a style vector. The style vector allows representing different ways of showing the same action. For example, smiling with or without visible teeth.

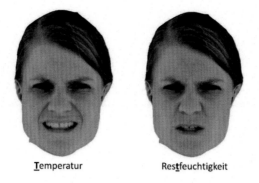

Figure 11.20 Visually different appearances of a "t" in German words.

After training, we are able to synthesize realistic facial animations from a sequence of semantic expression labels. This enables us to (i) animate visual speech directly from text/visemes; (ii) perform simple and fast facial animation based on a high-level description of the content; (iii) capture and adjust the style of facial expressions by modifying the low-dimensional style vector. Fig. 11.21 shows examples of visual speech reconstruction compared to the ground truth.

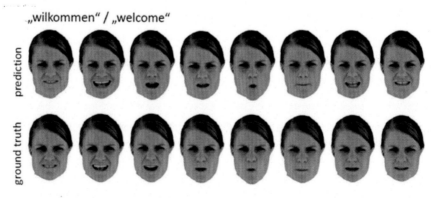

Figure 11.21 Example-based reconstruction of visual speech. Each face corresponds to one viseme of the speech sequence.

11.2.5 Neural face refinement

Though our simple mesh-plus-texture representation is fully capable of capturing and reconstructing facial expressions in 3D, it still lacks realism. Typical problems are a very clean silhouette, missing textural details, lack of geometry details (e.g., bun) at the silhouette, or obviously wrong silhouette geometry (e.g. the open mouth) (Fig. 11.22).

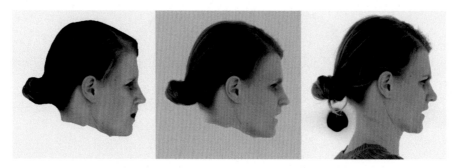

Figure 11.22 Left: approximate head model; (middle): refined rendering with accurate alpha mask and view dependent texture; (right): original camera view.

To improve the rendered face, we train a pixel-to-pixel translation network (UNet [74]). The objective is to reconstruct the captured face image from the rendered version as well as an alpha-mask. The alpha-mask enables the network to modify the face geometry where necessary (i.e., add/remove parts), it allows to use the re-rendered version on new backgrounds and simplifies the training process, since we do not need to pre-compute a foreground/background segmentation for the training data. Moreover, the alpha-mask allows for synthesizing a more realistic silhouette with fine, translucent details, such as hair. Fig. 11.22 shows an example of the improved rendering approach.

11.3. Streaming volumetric video

Raw volumetric video sequences are usually very data intense, requiring efficient encoding and streaming techniques (see also Chapter 16 for further reading on mesh and point cloud streaming). A few recent publications address efficient streaming of volumetric video. Hosseini and Timmerer [75] extended the concepts of HTTP adaptive streaming for point cloud streaming. They proposed different approaches for spatial subsampling of dynamic point clouds to decrease the density of points in the 3D space, and thus reduce the bandwidth requirements. Park et al. [76] proposed using 3D tiles for streaming of voxelized point clouds. Their system selects 3D tiles and adjusts the corresponding load using a rate-utility model that takes into account the user's viewpoint and distance from the object. Van der Hooft et al. [77] proposed an adaptive streaming framework compliant to the recent point cloud compression standard MPEG V-PCC [78]. Their framework PCC-DASH enables adaptive streaming of scenes with multiple dynamic point cloud objects. They also presented rate adaptation techniques that rely on the user's position and focus as well as the available bandwidth and the client's buffer status to select the optimal quality representation for each object. Petrangeli et al. [79] proposed a streaming framework for AR applications that dynamically decides which virtual objects should be fetched from the server as well as their load, depending on the proximity of the user and likelihood of the user to view the object.

Offloading the rendering process to a powerful remote server was first considered in 1990s when PCs did not have sufficient computational power for intensive graphics tasks [80]. A remote rendering system renders complex graphics on a powerful server and delivers the result over a network to a less powerful client device.

With the advent of cloud gaming and mobile edge computing (MEC), *interactive* remote rendering applications have started to emerge, which allow the client device to control the rendering application based on user interaction [81–83]. Mangiante et al. [81] presented a MEC system for field of view (FoV) rendering of 360° videos to optimize the required bandwidth and reduce the processing requirements and battery utilization. Shi et al. [82] developed a MEC system to stream AR scenes containing only the user's FoV, plus a latency-adaptive margin around it. They deployed the prototype on a MEC node connected to a LTE network and evaluated its performance. A detailed survey of remote rendering system is given in [80]. Qian et al. [83] developed a point cloud streaming system that uses an edge proxy to convert point cloud streams into 2D video streams based on the user's viewpoint to enable efficient decoding on mobile devices. They also proposed various optimizations to reduce the motion-to-photon latency between the client and the edge proxy.

11.3.1 Compression and formats

To be able to distribute volumetric video, the textured mesh sequence can be compressed and multiplexed into an MP4 file (see Fig. 11.23). For that purpose, we developed a simple file format, which allows easy download and playback of the volumetric video with standard open-source tools.

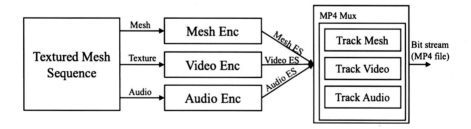

Figure 11.23 MP4 file format for storing mesh, texture, and audio.

For mesh encoding, we use Draco [84], in which the connectivity coding is based on Edgebreaker [85]. Other mesh codecs include Corto [86], open 3D graphics compression of MPEG and Khronos group [87], or MPEG activities on point cloud compression [78] and the recently issued call for proposal from MPEG on dynamic mesh coding [88].

Table 11.1 Exemplary encodings of a volumetric video with mesh and texture format.

Sequence	Basketball player	Boxer
Geometry	20k triangles	65k triangles
Capturing framerate	25 fps	25 fps
Texture resolution	2048x2048	2048x2048
Overall bitrate	**22.6 Mbps**	**47.2 Mbps**
Mesh bitrate (Draco)	12 Mbps	37 Mbps
Video bitrate (H.264)	10 Mbps	10 Mbps
Audio bitrate (AAC)	133 kbps	133 kbps

The texture sequence can be encoded with a regular video encoder, such as H.264/AVC [89], H.265/HEVC [90], or with the most advanced video codec H.266/VVC [91]. Finally, the audio signal is encoded with AAC compression format.

The three different elementary streams (ES) are multiplexed into a common MP4 file, each into a separate track. On the receiver side, plugins for Unity and Unreal allow for easy integration of volumetric video assets into the target AR or VR application. These plugins include the de-multiplexer, as well as related decoders and perform real-time decoding of the mesh sequence. To get an idea of typical data rates with such a format, we encoded two exemplary volumetric video objects. The resulting bitrates can be found in Table 11.1. Of course, the bitrates can be lowered even further by using more advanced codecs. Nevertheless, the figures give a good idea of the order of magnitude of bitrates for streaming volumetric video. Clearly, the transmission of complex scenes with multiple volumetric videos is a challenge for current networks.

11.3.2 Scene description

For the distribution of 3D computer graphics data, scene description formats, such as Khronos glTF [92] or USD [93] can be used. The MPEG glTF 2.0 extension [94] defines a scene description format, which extends glTF 2.0 towards support of timed media, such as volumetric video or audio (see Table 11.2).

To support volumetric video in the glTF file, the MPEG_media, the MPEG_accessor_timed, the MPEG_buffer_circular, and the MPEG_texture_video extensions need to be supported, which enables to access timed video. For instance, the topology of volumetric videos may vary from frame to frame. This dynamicity required accessors to be extended with the MPEG_accessor_timed to indicate the changing properties that define the type and layout of the data in the buffer, e.g., the number of vertices within a mesh of the volumetric video at a particular frame. In addition, the static buffer configuration in glTF is not suitable for dynamic data. Therefore an extension has been included, i.e., MPEG_buffer_circular to indicate that several frames of the content are made available to the presentation engine with an associated presentation time. The same applies to

Table 11.2 List of extensions of the MPEG glTF2.0 extensions.

Extension Name	Description
MPEG_media	Extension for referencing external media sources
MPEG_accessor_timed	Accessor extension to support timed media
MPEG_buffer_circular	Buffer extension to support circular buffers
MPEG_scene_dynamic	Extension to support scene updates
MPEG_texture_video	Extension to support video textures
MPEG_mesh_linking	Extension to link two meshes and provide mapping
MPEG_audio_spatial	Adds support for spatial audio
MPEG_viewport_recommended	Extension to describe a recommended viewport
MPEG_animation_timing	Extension to control animation timelines

texture objects defined in glTF. These texture objects are currently static and require an extension to support video data.

Spatial audio can be enabled by supporting the MPEG_audio_spatial extension, which supports mono and higher-order ambisonics (HOA) and reverb effects.

Animatable volumetric videos using a template mesh, as described in Section 11.2.1.1 and Section 11.2.1.2, are supported by additionally supporting the MPEG_mesh_linking extension. The extension indicates that a particular dynamic mesh, i.e., a dependent mesh, is associated to another static mesh, i.e., a template shadow mesh, and provides access to the correspondences and poses. Furthermore, scene descriptions can be updated by adding the MPEG_scene_dynamic extension, which update the glTF scene document by either providing a new one or applying a JSON patch, whereas MPEG_viewport_recommended allow for signaling a recommended viewport. The extensions further allow synchronizing the glTF animations, which currently are non-timed, with the timed media. This is done by means of the MPEG_animation_timing extension, which specifies the time at which a particular animation needs to be triggered, and further describes how several animations can be applied simultaneously onto an object of the scene.

11.3.3 Remote-rendering for volumetric video

Despite the significant increase in computing power of mobile devices, rendering rich volumetric videos on such devices is still a very demanding task. The processing load is further increased by the presence of multiple volumetric objects in the scene and new challenges are introduced through interactivity. Particularly, interactivity requires changing the volumetric object according to the user input or position, which is especially challenging on mobile devices with low processing power. Another challenge is the lack of efficient hardware implementations for decoding of volumetric data (e.g., point clouds or meshes). Software decoding may drain the battery of mobile devices quickly and fail to meet the real-time rendering requirements.

One way to reduce the processing load on the client is to send a 2D view of the volumetric object rendered according to the viewer's position instead of sending the entire volumetric content. This technique is typically known as remote or interactive rendering [80] or split-rendering. This is achieved by offloading the expensive rendering process to a powerful server and transmitting the rendered views over a network to the client device. Another advantage of this approach is a significant reduction of network bandwidth requirements, because only a single 2D video is transmitted instead of the full 3D volumetric content. The rendering server can be deployed within a cloud computing platform to provide flexible allocation of computational resources and scalability, depending on potential changes in processing load.

Despite these advantages, one major challenge for designing a cloud-based rendering system is the requirement for a low end-to-end latency of the overall system, also known as the motion-to-photon (M2P) latency. In comparison to a client-side only system, the added network latency and additional server-side processing (e.g., video encoding) cause an increase in M2P latency, which may significantly degrade the user experience and cause motion sickness [95]. It is possible to compensate for the increased M2P latency through various optimizations. One promising technique is to move the volumetric content to an edge server geographically closer to the user to reduce the network latency. Edge computing has been gaining importance with the deployment of 5G networks and is considered to be one of the key technologies for interactive use cases that will be enabled by the 5G technology [96]. Secondly, usage of real-time communication protocols, such as WebRTC are also considered to be vital for ultra-low latency video streaming applications [97]. The processing latency at the rendering server is another significant latency component. Therefore using fast hardware-based video encoders is critical for reducing the encoding latency, while providing high video quality. Another way is to predict the future user pose at the remote server and send the corresponding rendered view to the client. Thereby, it is possible to drastically reduce the M2P latency, if the user pose is predicted for a prediction window equal to or larger than the M2P latency of the system. However, accuracy of the prediction algorithms is critical for achieving good results and mispredictions can potentially lead to degradations of user experience.

In this context, we have developed a cloud-based rendering system for interactive streaming of volumetric videos, which includes several of the described optimizations [54][98][99]. Our system reduces the high processing requirements on the client side and significantly decreases the network bandwidth requirements. The next sections describe the key components of our cloud-based volumetric video streaming system as well as the dataflow and interfaces between these components. We implemented a remote-rendering system based on open-source components. The server architecture is discussed in Section 11.3.3.1 and the client architecture in Section 11.3.3.2. The overall system latency is discussed in Section 11.3.3.3.

11.3.3.1 Server architecture

An overview of the server architecture is shown in Fig. 11.24. The server-side implementation is composed of three main parts: a **volumetric player** and a **cloud rendering library**, which are all integrated as a plugin into the **rendering engine**. We describe each block further in detail.

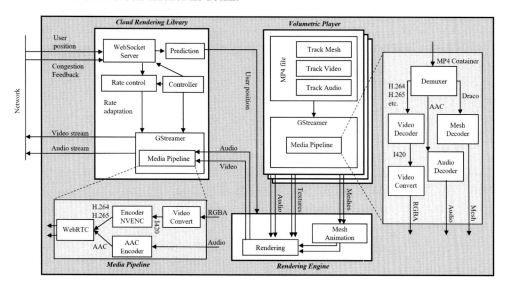

Figure 11.24 Remote rendering: Server architecture.

The **volumetric player** is implemented using Unity with several native plug-ins. The player is able to play multiple volumetric sequences, each stored in a separate MP4 file. We use the MP4 file format, as described in Section 11.3.1, which consists of a video track containing the compressed texture data, a mesh track containing the compressed mesh data and an audio track. After initialization, the player starts playing the available MP4 files by demultiplexing it and feeding the elementary streams to the GStreamer media pipeline with the corresponding video, audio, and mesh decoders. After decoding, the RGBA, audio and mesh data of all available MP4 files are forwarded to the rendering engine.

The **rendering engine** ensures that all objects are rendered in the right place in the scene, based on the position of the user and the objects in the scene. It receives the decoded media streams of all volumetric objects from the volumetric player. From the client, it receives the user position and the position and size of all objects. Then, it renders a separate camera view for each object. In the case of stereo display, as required for VR/AR glasses, two views are rendered, one for the left and one for the right eye. The rendering engine also takes care of rendering the spatial audio from the audio streams of each object. To distribute multiple objects, we use a packed frame format, which packages the rendered textures (left and right view for stereo) of all objects into a single rectangular frame. The rectangular frame is then sent to the encoding media pipeline. To enable animation of objects, we integrate the mesh Animation module that modifies the decoded meshes based on the user position, e.g., to rotate the head towards the user. The volumetric player and the mesh animation module could be replaced by a glTF player that implements the required MPEG extensions for animatable volumetric videos, as described in Section 11.3.2. In our implementation, we use Unity [100] as the rendering engine, but it could also be replaced by any other engine, such as Unreal [101].

The **cloud rendering library** is a cross-platform library written in C++ that can be easily integrated into different applications. In our Unity application, we integrate it as a native plug-in into the player. The library contains various modules for application control, media processing, and the communication interfaces between the server and the client. The main modules of our library are the WebSocket server, GStreamer module, controller, and prediction engine. Each module runs asynchronously in its own thread. The WebSocket server is used for exchanging signaling data between the client and the server. Such signaling data includes the session description protocol (SDP), interactive connectivity establishment (ICE) as well as application-specific metadata for scene description. The WS connection is also used for transmission of control data to modify the position and orientation of any registered object or camera. Our system also allows the usage of WebRTC data channels for control data exchange after a peer-to-peer connection is established. Both plain and secure WebSockets are supported, which is important for real use cases.

The **prediction** module implements a 6DoF user movement prediction algorithm to predict the future head position of the user, based on her past movement patterns. Based on the client interaction and the predictions output by the prediction module, the positions of the registered objects are updated accordingly such that the rendering engine renders a scene matching to the predicted user position that will be attained after a predefined prediction interval. The prediction interval is set to be equal to the estimated M2P latency of the system. Currently, an autoregressive model (as described in [102]) is implemented but the module allows integration of different kind of prediction techniques, e.g., Kalman filtering [103].

The **rate control** receives the congestion feedback from the client and derives from that a target rate for the video encoding in the **Gstreamer** module. We implemented a congestion feedback and related rate control, based on explicit congestion notification (ECN)-based network feedback using L4S flows [104]. Therefore with the direct feedback from the network, our system reacts very fast to changing network conditions, which allows a stable playout for transmission over mobile networks such as 5G.

The **Gstreamer** module contains the media processing pipeline, which takes the rendered textures (at 60 fps) and the rendered audio as input, compresses it as a video and audio stream, and transmits it to the client using WebRTC. Specifically, the unity RenderTexture is inserted into the pipeline using the appsrc element of GStreamer. Since the texture is in RGBA format, it has to be passed through a videoconvert element to bring it to the I420 format accepted by the encoder. We use the Nvidia encoder (NVENC) to compress the texture using H.264/AVC (high profile, level 3.1, IPPP. GOP structure, no B frames), but it is also possible to encode in H.265/HEVC or an advanced encoder using VVC. Finally, the resulting compressed bitstream is packaged into RTP packets, encrypted, and sent to the client using the WebRTC protocol. The resolution of the transmitted video depends on the size of the packed frame and is limited by the capabilities of the hardware decoder on the client side.

The **controller** contains the application logic and controls the other modules, depending on the application state. For example, it closes the media pipeline if a client disconnects and re-initializes the pipeline when a new client is connected. The controller is also responsible for creating response messages for the client. For example, when the client requests the scene description, the WS server notifies the controller that the request has arrived, and the controller creates a response message in JSON format with all available objects from the pool. The response message goes back to the WS server, which deals with the transmission back to client.

11.3.3.2 Client architecture

An overview of the client architecture is shown in Fig. 11.25. Our system targets **mixed-reality** devices, e.g., tablets or glasses. We have implemented both a web player in JavaScript and a native application for android OS, but the system can easily be ported to other operating systems, such as iOS. The easy portability is one of the advantages of our remote-rendering implementation, which relies on widely available open-source protocols, such as WebRTC, and does not require any specific hardware on the client side for processing volumetric media. The only requirement is a hardware video decoder for efficient playback, which is available in most phones or glasses that can play regular 2D video.

The client architecture consists of various connection interfaces, a video decoder, our application logic, and a client application. Before the streaming session starts, the client establishes a WebSocket connection to the server and asks the server to send a description of the rendered scene. The server responds with a list of objects and parameters, which can later be updated by the client. After receiving the scene description, the client replicates the scene and initiates a peer-to-peer (P2P) WebRTC connection to the server. The server and client carry out the WebRTC negotiation process by sending SDP and ICE data over the established WebSocket connection. Finally, the P2P connection is established, and the client starts receiving an audio stream and a video stream corresponding to the current view of the volumetric video. At the same time, the client can use the WebSocket connection (or optionally the RTCPeerConnection)

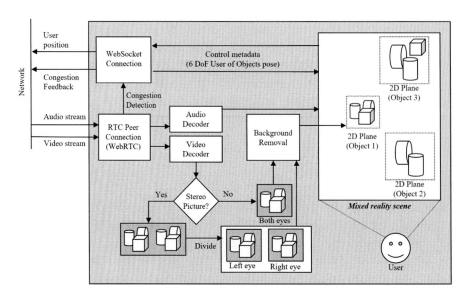

Figure 11.25 Remote-rendering: Client architecture.

for sending the user and objects position to the server and modify the properties of the scene. For example, the client may change its position in the 6DoF space, or it may apply transformations (e.g., rotate, scale) to any volumetric object in the scene. The WebSocket connection is also used to send congestion feedback collected from the received WebRTC streams, either from the packet arrival statistics or through direct feedback from the network via ECN.

The audio and videostreams are forwarded to the specific hardware decoders. After decoding, the packed frame from the video stream is un-packed and each object is treated separately. If the content is stereo, the left and right eye is separated. After the un-packing process, the background needs to be removed from the rendered object. The whole un-packing process and the background removal is happening in the GPU shader, which can be efficiently implemented also on mobile devices.

After removing the background, each object must be placed into the mixed–reality scene, based on the current state of the object position. To enable easy integration into current mixed reality frameworks, we integrate our objects as rendered textures on virtual surfaces in the mixed reality scene (so-called billboards). The app renders the 2D texture of each object on the surfaces held orthogonal to the user's viewpoint. When the user changes position and a new view is rendered on the server, this surface is always rotated towards the user and kept orthogonal. As a result, the user perceives the various 2D views rendered on the orthogonal surface as if a 3D object were present in the scene. For glasses, we integrate two virtual surfaces, one rendered on the left eye and the other on the right eye. The billboard approach also allows for easy drag and drop with all volumetric objects, allowing the user to freely position the objects in the scene. This modification also gets synchronized with the server side to update the camera in the rendering process.

The spatially rendered audio is received as stereo audio on the client side and can be used on regular headsets.

11.3.3.3 Motion-to-photon latency measurement

Characterizing the M2P latency is important for assessing the success of our optimizations towards creating a low-latency streaming framework. The various latency components of the remote-rendering system are shown in Fig. 11.26.

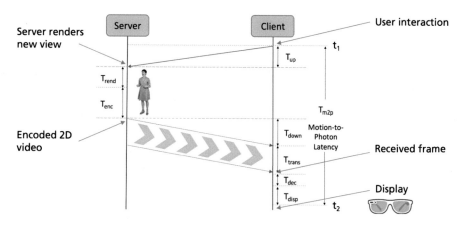

Figure 11.26 Remote rendering: Latency components.

At time instance t_1, the client reports the user position to the server in time T_{up}, where T_{up} depends on the round-trip time (RTT) of the network. On the server side, the rendering engine renders the new view, depending on the user position within time T_{rend} and encodes the rendered view in the media pipeline in time T_{enc}. The encoded 2D video is then transmitted to the client in time T_{down}, which again depends on the RTT of the network, and the transmission delay T_{trans}, which depends on the available channel throughput. Then, the video needs to be decoded in time T_{dec} and displayed in time T_{disp}, where T_{dec} and T_{disp} usually depend on the display refresh rate. The rendered image is then finally shown to the user at time instance t_2, and the overall M2P latency T_{M2P} is then the duration between time instance t_2 and t_1.

To determine T_{M2P} for our system, we developed a framework to measure the latency of our system. Using our cloud rendering library, described in the previous section, we implemented a server-side console application, which sends predefined textures (known by the client), depending on the received control data from the client. Details are outlined in [102]. We deploy this test system on an Amazon EC2 instance.

Once the connection is established, the user can start the session by defining the number of independent measurements. In our setup, we run the server application on an Amazon EC2 instance in Frankfurt, and the client application in a web browser in Berlin. The web browser is connected to the Internet over WiFi. We encode the stream using x264 configured with ultrafast preset and zero latency tuning with an encoding speed of 60 fps. To get statistically accurate results, we set the client to perform 100 latency measurements and calculated the average, minimum, and maximum M2P latency. Fig. 11.27 shows the measured values over 100 cycles. According to our results, the M2P latency T_{M2P} of our system varies between 41 ms and 63 ms. The measured average latency is 58 ms.

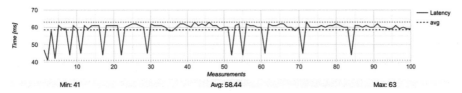

Figure 11.27 Remote rendering: Average latency from an Amazon EC2 instance to a browser implementation.

The total M2P latency is composed of 16.4 ms for the encoding time T_{enc}; the network contributes 15.9 ms to the latency (sum of t_{up}, t_{down} and t_{trans}), and the remaining 27.7 ms comes from the client-side processing T_{dec} and T_{disp}. T_{enc} depends on the encoding frame rate, which depends on what frame rates are supported by the encoder, the hardware video decoder and the display refresh rate of the target device. T_{enc} equal to 16.4 ms means that we have an encoding frame rate of about 60 fps. Increasing the frame rate to 120 fps would reduce T_{enc} to 8.3 ms. The network latency can be further reduced, for example, over a 5G network and using an edge-cloud server. Regarding the client processing delay, we used a non-optimized browser implementation for testing. In a native implementation, this delay is significantly lower and converges towards the delay coming from the display refresh rate T_{disp}. Furthermore, the overall M2P latency can be further reduced by using a user movement prediction, as implemented in our server architecture and discussed in [103] and [102]. As a summary, it can be said that with an optimized end-to-end architecture, the remote rendering approach can be deployed over various kinds of networks, but of course benefit from low latency networks and servers that are deployed very close to the end user.

11.4. Conclusions

Volumetric video has shown to be a major progress for many novel XR technologies. It enables an immersive and highly realistic visualization of virtual humans for applications in teaching and training, film and cinema, as well as human machine interaction. In this chapter, we have presented novel methods for the acquisition, interaction, streaming, and rendering of volumetric video, exemplified along the full processing pipeline developed at Fraunhofer HHI. Recent deep learning technologies increase the quality of the reconstructed assets in terms of geometry and appearance. To go beyond high-quality free viewpoint navigation, the semantic enrichment of volumetric assets by CG models enables the manipulation and animation of the virtual characters, further increasing the immersiveness in XR applications with interactive components. Similarly, progress in neural synthesis allows the control of facial expressions of the virtual human as well as the realistic creation of novel sequences from text and speech input. Finally, efficient encoding and streaming as well as a new split rendering technique enhances usability and operating time on low-power devices, such as VR/AR glasses, paving the way to many practical and novel applications for immersive extended reality.

Acknowledgments

This work has partly been funded by the H2020 European project Invictus under grant agreement no. 952147 as well as by the German Ministry of Education and Research project VoluProf under grant agreement no. 16SV8705.

References

[1] Microsoft, http://www.microsoft.com/en-us/mixed-reality/capture-studios.
[2] 8i, http://8i.com.
[3] Volucap GmbH, http://www.volucap.de.
[4] 4DViews, http://www.4dviews.com.
[5] Evercoast, https://evercoast.com/.
[6] Holooh, https://www.holooh.com.
[7] Volograms, https://volograms.com.
[8] Mantis vision, https://mantis-vision.com.
[9] O. Schreer, I. Feldmann, S. Renault, M. Zepp, P. Eisert, P. Kauff, Capture and 3D video processing of volumetric video, in: Proc. IEEE International Conference on Image Processing (ICIP), Taipei, Taiwan, 2019, pp. 4310–4314, https://doi.org/10.1109/ICIP.2019.8803576.
[10] S. Garrido-Jurado, R. Muñoz-Salinas, F. Madrid-Cuevas, M. Marín-Jiménez, Automatic generation and detection of highly reliable fiducial markers under occlusion, Pattern Recognition 47 (6) (2014) 2280–2292, https://doi.org/10.1016/j.patcog.2014.01.005.
[11] B. Li, L. Heng, K. Koser, M. Pollefeys, A multiple-camera system calibration toolbox using a feature descriptor-based calibration pattern, in: 2013 IEEE/RSJ International Conference on Intelligent Robots and Systems, 2013, pp. 1301–1307, https://doi.org/10.1109/IROS.2013.6696517.
[12] T. Horprasert, D. Harwood, L. Davis, A statistical approach for real-time robust background subtraction and shadow detection, in: Proc. of IEEE Int. Conf. on Computer Vision, Frame-Rate Workshop (ICCV 1999), 1999, pp. 1–19.
[13] M. Bleyer, C. Rhemann, C. Rother, Patchmatch stereo – stereo matching with slanted support windows, in: British Machine Vision Conference (BMVC), 2011, pp. 14.1–14.11.
[14] W. Waizenegger, I. Feldmann, O. Schreer, P. Eisert, Scene flow constrained multi-prior patch-sweeping for real-time upper body 3D reconstruction, in: Proc. IEEE International Conference on Image Processing (ICIP), Melbourne, Australia, 2013, pp. 2086–2090, https://doi.org/10.1109/ICIP.2013.6738430.

[15] S. Galliani, K. Lasinger, K. Schindler, Massively parallel multiview stereopsis by surface normal diffusion, in: 2015 IEEE International Conference on Computer Vision (ICCV), 2015, pp. 873–881, https://doi.org/10.1109/ICCV.2015.106.

[16] J. Schönberger, E. Zheng, J. Frahm, M. Pollefeys, Pixelwise view selection for unstructured multi-view stereo, in: Proc. European Conference on Computer Vision (ECCV), Cham, 2016, pp. 501–518.

[17] Q. Xu, W. Tao, Multi-scale geometric consistency guided multi-view stereo, in: Proc. Computer Vision and Pattern Recognition (CVPR), Long Beach, CA, USA, 2019.

[18] A. Collet, M. Chuang, P. Sweeney, D. Gillett, D. Evseev, D. Calabrese, H. Hoppe, A. Kirk, S. Sullivan, High-quality streamable free-viewpoint video, ACM Transactions on Graphics 34 (4) (2015) 69.

[19] S. Orts, C. Rhemann, S. Fanello, D. Kim, A. Kowdle, W. Chang, Y. Degtyarev, P. Davidson, S. Khamis, M. Dou, V. Tankovich, C. Loop, Q. Cai, P. Chou, S. Mennicken, J. Valentin, P. Kohli, V. Pradeep, S. Wang, S. Izadi, Holoportation: Virtual 3D teleportation in real-time, in: Proc. Annual Symposium on User Interface Software and Technology, 2016, pp. 741–754, https://doi.org/10.1145/2984511.2984517.

[20] K. Guo, P. Lincoln, P. Davidson, J. Busch, X. Yu, M. Whalen, G. Harvey, S. Orts-Escolano, R. Pandey, J. Dourgarian, D. Tang, A. Tkach, A. Kowdle, E. Cooper, M. Dou, S. Fanello, G. Fyffe, C. Rhemann, J. Taylor, P. Debevec, S. Izadi, The relightables: Volumetric performance capture of humans with realistic relighting, ACM Transactions on Graphics 38 (6) (Nov. 2019), https://doi.org/10.1145/3355089.3356571.

[21] Y. Yao, Z. Luo, S. Li, T. Fang, L. Quan, MVSNet: Depth inference for unstructured multi-view stereo, in: Proc. European Conference on Computer Vision (ECCV), Springer International Publishing, Cham, 2018, pp. 785–801.

[22] Y. Yao, Z. Luo, S. Li, T. Shen, T. Fang, L. Quan, Recurrent MVSNet for high-resolution multi-view stereo depth inference, in: 2019 IEEE/CVF Conference on Computer Vision and Pattern Recognition (CVPR), 2019, pp. 5525–5534.

[23] S. Cheng, Z. Xu, S. Zhu, Z. Li, L. Li, R. Ramamoorthi, H. Su, Deep stereo using adaptive thin volume representation with uncertainty awareness, in: Proc. of the IEEE/CVF Conference on Computer Vision and Pattern Recognition, 2020, pp. 2521–2531, https://doi.org/10.1109/CVPR42600.2020.00260.

[24] X. Gu, Z. Fan, S. Zhu, Z. Dai, F. Tan, P. Tan, Cascade cost volume for high-resolution multi-view stereo and stereo matching, in: 2020 IEEE/CVF Conference on Computer Vision and Pattern Recognition (CVPR), 2020, pp. 2492–2501.

[25] J. Yang, W. Mao, J. Alvarez, M. Liu, Cost volume pyramid based depth inference for multi-view stereo, in: Proc. Computer Vision and Pattern Recognition (CVPR), 2020.

[26] R. Chen, S. Han, J. Xu, H. Su, Visibility-aware point-based multi-view stereo network, IEEE Transactions on Pattern Analysis and Machine Intelligence 43 (10) (2021) 3695–3708, https://doi.org/10.1109/TPAMI.2020.2988729.

[27] B. Curless, M. Levoy, A volumetric method for building complex models from range images, in: Proc. of the 23rd Annual Conference on Computer Graphics and Interactive Techniques, 1996, pp. 303–312, https://doi.org/10.1145/237170.237269.

[28] M. Worchel, M. Zepp, W. Hu, O. Schreer, I. Feldmann, P. Eisert, Ernst Grube: A contemporary witness and his memories preserved with volumetric video, in: Eurographics Workshop on Graphics and Cultural Heritage (GCH2020), Granada, Spain, 2020, https://doi.org/10.2312/gch.20201300.

[29] M. Kazhdan, H. Hoppe, Screened Poisson surface reconstruction, ACM Transactions on Graphics 32 (3) (2013) 70–78.

[30] G. Taubin, Curve and surface smoothing without shrinkage, in: Proc. of IEEE International Conference on Computer Vision, 1995, pp. 852–857, https://doi.org/10.1109/ICCV.1995.466848.

[31] M. Garland, P. Heckbert, Surface simplification using quadric error metrics, in: Proc. of SIGGRAPH 97, New York, USA, 1997, pp. 209–216.

[32] M. Worchel, R. Diaz, W. Hu, O. Schreer, I. Feldmann, P. Eisert, Multi-view mesh reconstruction with neural deferred shading, in: Proc. of the IEEE/CVF Conference on Computer Vision and Pattern Recognition, 2022, pp. 6187–6197.

[33] Open mesh, https://www.graphics.rwth-aachen.de/software/openmesh.

[34] X-atlas, https://github.com/jpcy/xatlas/.

[35] G. Tam, Z. Cheng, Y. Lai, F. Langbein, Y. Liu, D. Marshall, R. Martin, X. Sun, P. Ros, Registration of 3D point clouds and meshes: a survey from rigid to nonrigid, IEEE Transactions on Visualization and Computer Graphics 19 (2013) 1199–1217.

[36] K. Varanasi, A. Zaharescu, E. Boyer, R. Horaud, Temporal surface tracking using mesh evolution, in: Proc. European Conference on Computer Vision (ECCV), Marseille, France, 2008, pp. 30–43.

[37] O. Sorkine, M. Alexa, As-rigid-as-possible surface modeling, in: Symposium on Geometry Processing, vol. 4, 2007, pp. 109–116.

[38] C. Budd, P. Huang, M. Klaudiny, A. Hilton, Global non-rigid alignment of surface sequences, International Journal of Computer Vision 102 (1–3) (2013) 256–270.

[39] W. Morgenstern, A. Hilsmann, P. Eisert, Progressive non-rigid registration of temporal mesh sequences, in: Proc. European Conference on Visual Media Production (CVMP), London, UK, 2019, pp. 1–10, https://doi.org/10.1145/3359998.3369411.

[40] A. Hilsmann, P. Fechteler, W. Morgenstern, W. Paier, I. Feldmann, O. Schreer, P. Eisert, Going beyond free viewpoint: Creating animatable volumetric video of human performances, IET Computer Vision, Special Issue on Computer Vision for the Creative Industries 14 (6) (2020) 350–358, https://doi.org/10.1049/iet-cvi.2019.0786.

[41] C. Stoll, J. Gall, E. de Aguiar, S. Thrun, C. Theobalt, Video-based reconstruction of animatable human characters, in: Proc. SIGGRAPH ASIA 2010, ACM Transactions on Graphics 29 (6) (2010) 139–149.

[42] D. Casas, M. Volino, J. Collomosse, A. Hilton, 4D video textures for interactive character appearance, in: Proc. Eurographics, Computer Graphics Forum 33 (2) (Apr. 2014).

[43] M. Volino, P. Huang, A. Hilton, Online interactive 4D character animation, in: Proc. Int. Conf. on 3D Web Technology (Web3D), Heraklion, Greece, 2015.

[44] A. Boukhayma, E. Boyer, Video based animation synthesis with the essential graph, in: Proc. Int. Conf. on 3D Vision (3DV), Lyon, France, 2015, pp. 478–486.

[45] A. Boukhayma, E. Boyer, Surface motion capture animation synthesis, IEEE Transactions on Visualization and Computer Graphics 25 (6) (2019) 2270–2283.

[46] P. Li, K. Aberman, R. Hanocka, L. Liu, O. Sorkine-Hornung, B. Chen, Learning skeletal articulations with neural blend shapes, ACM Transactions on Graphics (TOG) 40 (4) (2021) 1.

[47] L. Liu, M. Habermann, V. Rudnev, K. Sarkar, J. Gu, C. Theobalt, Neural actor: Neural free-view synthesis of human actors with pose control, in: Proc. SIGGRAPH ASIA 2021, ACM Transactions on Graphics 40 (6) (2021), https://doi.org/10.1145/3478513.3480528.

[48] M. Habermann, L. Liu, W. Xu, M. Zollhoefer, G. Pons-Moll, C. Theobalt, Real-time deep dynamic characters, ACM Transactions on Graphics 40 (4) (Aug. 2021).

[49] J. Regateiro, M. Volino, A. Hilton, Deep4D: A compact generative representation for volumetric video, Frontiers in Virtual Reality 2 (132) (2021).

[50] G. Pavlakos, V. Choutas, N. Ghorbani, T. Bolkart, A. Osman, D. Tzionas, M. Black, Expressive body capture: 3D hands, face, and body from a single image, in: Proc. Computer Vision and Pattern Recognition (CVPR), Long Beach, USA, 2019, pp. 10975–10985.

[51] A. Zimmer, A. Hilsmann, W. Morgenstern, P. Eisert, Imposing temporal consistency on deep monocular body shape and pose estimation, Computational Visual Media (2022).

[52] Z. Cao, G. Hidalgo, T. Simon, S. Wei, Y. Sheikh, OpenPose: Realtime multi-person 2D pose estimation using part affinity fields, IEEE Transactions on Pattern Analysis and Machine Intelligence (PAMI) 43 (2021) 172–186.

[53] P. Fechteler, A. Hilsmann, P. Eisert, Markerless multiview motion capture with 3D shape model adaptation, Computer Graphics Forum 38 (6) (2019) 91–109, https://doi.org/10.1111/cgf.13608.

[54] J. Son, S. Gül, G.S. Bhullar, G. Hege, W. Morgenstern, A. Hilsmann, T. Ebner, S. Bliedung, P. Eisert, T. Schierl, T. Buchholz, C. Hellge, Split rendering for mixed reality: Interactive volumetric video in action, in: SIGGRAPH Asia, Demos, 2020, https://doi.org/10.1145/3415256.3421491.

[55] P. Eisert, B. Girod, Analyzing facial expressions for virtual conferencing, IEEE Computer Graphics and Applications 18 (5) (1998) 70–78, https://doi.org/10.1109/38.708562.

[56] P. Eisert, MPEG-4 facial animation in video analysis and synthesis, International Journal of Imaging Systems and Technology 13 (5) (2003) 245–256, https://doi.org/10.1002/ima.10072.

[57] R. Li, K. Bladin, Y. Zhao, C. Chinara, O. Ingraham, P. Xiang, X. Ren, P. Prasad, B. Kishore, J. Xing, H. Li, Learning formation of physically-based face attributes, in: 2020 IEEE/CVF Conference on Computer Vision and Pattern Recognition (CVPR), 2020, pp. 3407–3416.

[58] J. Thies, M. Zollhöfer, M. Nießner, L. Valgaerts, M. Stamminger, C. Theobalt, Real-time expression transfer for facial reenactment, in: SIGGRAPH Asia, ACM Transactions on Graphics 34 (6) (2015), https://doi.org/10.1145/2816795.2818056.

[59] S. Lombardi, J. Saragih, T. Simon, Y. Sheikh, Deep appearance models for face rendering, ACM Transactions on Graphics 37 (4) (July 2018), https://doi.org/10.1145/3197517.3201401.

[60] P. Chandran, D. Bradley, M. Gross, T. Beeler, Semantic deep face models, in: 2020 International Conference on 3D Vision (3DV), 2020, pp. 345–354, https://doi.org/10.1109/3DV50981.2020.00044.

[61] K. Dale, K. Sunkavalli, M. Johnson, D. Vlasic, H. Matusik, H. Pfister, Video face replacement, ACM Transactions on Graphics 30 (6) (Dec. 2011).

[62] W. Paier, M. Kettern, A. Hilsmann, P. Eisert, Hybrid approach for facial performance analysis and editing, IEEE Transactions on Circuits and Systems for Video Technology 27 (4) (2017) 784–797.

[63] A. Tewari, M. Zollhöfer, H. Kim, P. Garrido, F. Bernard, P. Perez, C. Theobalt, MoFA: model-based deep convolutional face autoencoder for unsupervised monocular reconstruction, in: Proc. IEEE International Conference on Computer Vision (ICCV), 2017, pp. 3735–3744.

[64] A. Tewari, M. Zollhöfer, F. Bernard, P. Garrido, H. Kim, P. Perez, C. Theobalt, High-fidelity monocular face reconstruction based on an unsupervised model-based face autoencoder, IEEE Transactions on Pattern Analysis and Machine Intelligence 42 (2018) 357–370, https://doi.org/10.1109/TPAMI.2018.2876842.

[65] A. Tewari, F. Bernard, P. Garrido, G. Bharaj, M. Elgharib, H. Seidel, P. Pérez, M. Zöllhofer, C. Theobalt, FML: face model learning from videos, in: Proc. of the IEEE Conference on Computer Vision and Pattern Recognition, 2019, pp. 10812–10822.

[66] X. Chai, J. Chen, C. Liang, D. Xu, C. Lin, Expression-aware face reconstruction via a dual-stream network, in: 2020 IEEE International Conference on Multimedia and Expo (ICME), 2020, pp. 1–6, https://doi.org/10.1109/ICME46284.2020.9102811.

[67] B. Mallikarjun, A. Tewari, H. Seidel, M. Elgharib, C. Theobalt, Learning complete 3D morphable face models from images and videos, in: Proceedings of the IEEE/CVF Conference on Computer Vision and Pattern Recognition, 2021.

[68] I. Goodfellow, J. Pouget-Abadie, M. Mirza, B. Xu, D. Warde-Farley, S. Ozair, A. Courville, Y. Bengio, Generative adversarial nets, in: Proc. of the 27th International Conference on Neural Information Processing Systems, vol. 2, 2014, pp. 2672–2680.

[69] A. Dib, C. Thébault, J. Ahn, P. Gosselin, C. Theobalt, L. Chevallier, Towards high fidelity monocular face reconstruction with rich reflectance using self-supervised learning and ray tracing, in: Proc. International Conference Computer Vision (ICCV), 2021.

[70] S. Bi, S. Lombardi, S. Saito, T. Simon, S. Wei, K. Mcphail, R. Ramamoorthi, Y. Sheikh, J. Saragih, Deep relightable appearance models for animatable faces, ACM Transactions on Graphics 40 (4) (July 2021), https://doi.org/10.1145/3450626.3459829.

[71] W. Paier, A. Hilsmann, P. Eisert, Neural face models for example-based visual speech synthesis, in: Proc. European Conference on Visual Media Production (CVMP), London, UK, 2020, pp. 1–10, https://doi.org/10.1145/3429341.3429356.

[72] W. Paier, A. Hilsmann, P. Eisert, Interactive facial animation with deep neural networks, IET Computer Vision, Special Issue on Computer Vision for the Creative Industries 14 (6) (2020) 359–369, https://doi.org/10.1049/iet-cvi.2019.0790.

[73] W. Paier, A. Hilsmann, P. Eisert, Example-based facial animation of virtual reality avatars using auto-regressive neural networks, IEEE Computer Graphics and Applications 41 (4) (2021) 52–63, https://doi.org/10.1109/MCG.2021.3068035.

[74] O. Ronneberger, P. Fischer, T. Brox, U-Net: Convolutional networks for biomedical image segmentation, Medical Image Computing and Computer-Assisted Intervention (MICCAI) 9351 (2015) 234–241.

[75] M. Hosseini, C. Timmerer, Dynamic adaptive point cloud streaming, in: Proc. Packet Video Workshop, New York, NY, USA, 2018, pp. 25–30, https://doi.org/10.1145/3210424.3210429.

[76] J. Park, P. Chou, J. Hwang, Rate-utility optimized streaming of volumetric media for augmented reality, IEEE Journal on Emerging and Selected Topics in Circuits and Systems 9 (1) (2019) 149–162, https://doi.org/10.1109/jetcas.2019.2898622.

[77] J. van der Hooft, T. Wauters, F.D. Turck, C. Timmerer, H. Hellwagner, Towards 6DoF HTTP adaptive streaming through point cloud compression, in: Proc. ACM International Conference on Multimedia, 2019, pp. 2405–2413, https://doi.org/10.1145/3343031.3350917.

[78] S. Schwarz, M. Preda, V. Baroncini, M. Budagavi, P. Cesar, P. Chou, R. Cohen, M. Krivokuća, S. Lasserre, Z. Li, J. Llach, K. Mammou, R. Mekuria, O. Nakagami, E. Siahaan, A. Tabatabai, A. Tourapis, V. Zakharchenko, Emerging MPEG standards for point cloud compression, IEEE Journal on Emerging and Selected Topics in Circuits and Systems 9 (1) (2019) 133–148, https://doi.org/10.1109/JETCAS.2018.2885981.

[79] S. Petrangeli, G. Simon, H. Wang, V. Swaminathan, Dynamic adaptive streaming for augmented reality applications, in: Proc. IEEE International Symposium on Multimedia (ISM), 2019, pp. 56–567, https://doi.org/10.1109/ism46123.2019.00017.

[80] S. Shi, C.-H. Hsu, A survey of interactive remote rendering systems, ACM Computing Surveys 47 (4) (2015) 1–29, https://doi.org/10.1145/2719921.

[81] S. Mangiante, G. Klas, A. Navon, Z. GuanHua, J. Ran, M.D. Silva, VR is on the edge: How to deliver 360 videos in mobile networks, in: Proceedings of the Workshop on Virtual Reality and Augmented Reality Network, ACM, 2017, pp. 30–35, https://doi.org/10.1145/3097895.3097901.

[82] S. Shi, V. Gupta, M. Hwang, R. Jana, Mobile VR on edge cloud: a latency-driven design, in: Proceedings of the 10th ACM Multimedia Systems Conference, ACM, 2019, pp. 222–231, https://doi.org/10.1145/3304109.3306217.

[83] F. Qian, B. Han, J. Pair, V. Gopalakrishnan, Toward practical volumetric video streaming on commodity smartphones, in: Proc. International Workshop on Mobile Computing Systems and Applications, 2019, pp. 135–140, https://doi.org/10.1145/3301293.3302358.

[84] Google Draco: a library for compressing and decompressing 3D geometric meshes and point clouds, online, https://github.com/google/draco. (Accessed 27 April 2020).

[85] J. Rossignac, Edgebreaker: Connectivity compression for triangle meshes, IEEE Transactions on Visualization and Computer Graphics 5 (1) (1999) 47–61, https://doi.org/10.1109/2945.764870.

[86] Corto, https://github.com/cnr-isti-vclab/corto. (Accessed 20 June 2019).

[87] Open 3D graphics compression, https://github.com/khronosgroup/gltf/wiki/open-3d-graphics-compression. (Accessed 20 June 2019).

[88] ISO/IEC JTC 1/SC 29/WG 2, N145: CfP for Dynamic Mesh Coding, Oct. 2021.

[89] T. Wiegand, G. Sullivan, G. Bjontegaard, A. Luthra, Overview of the H.264/AVC video coding standard, IEEE Transactions on Circuits and Systems for Video Technology 13 (7) (2003) 560–576, https://doi.org/10.1109/TCSVT.2003.815165.

[90] G.J. Sullivan, J.-R. Ohm, W.-J. Han, T. Wiegand, Overview of the high efficiency video coding (HEVC) standard, IEEE Transactions on Circuits and Systems for Video Technology 22 (12) (2012) 1649–1668, https://doi.org/10.1109/TCSVT.2012.2221191.

[91] B. Bross, Y.-K. Wang, Y. Ye, S. Liu, J. Chen, G.J. Sullivan, J.-R. Ohm, Overview of the versatile video coding (VVC) standard and its applications, IEEE Transactions on Circuits and Systems for Video Technology 31 (10) (2021) 3736–3764, https://doi.org/10.1109/TCSVT.2021.3101953.

[92] glTF 2.0, https://www.khronos.org/gltf.

[93] USD, https://graphics.pixar.com/usd/release/index.html.

[94] MPEG, ISO/IEC DIS 23090-14: Information technology — Coded representation of immersive media — Part 14: Scene Description for MPEG Media, Oct. 2021.

[95] R. Allison, L. Harris, M. Jenkin, U. Jasiobedzka, J. Zacher, Tolerance of temporal delay in virtual environments, in: Proc. IEEE Virtual Reality 2001, 2001, pp. 247–254, https://doi.org/10.1109/VR.2001.913793.

[96] M. Satyanarayanan, The emergence of edge computing, Computer 50 (1) (2017) 30–39, https://doi.org/10.1109/MC.2017.9.

[97] C. Holmberg, S. Hakansson, G. Eriksson, Web real-time communication use cases and requirements, RFC7478, 2015.

[98] S. Gül, D. Podborski, A. Hilsmann, W. Morgenstern, P. Eisert, O. Schreer, T. Buchholz, T. Schierl, C. Hellge, Interactive volumetric video from the cloud, in: Proc. International Broadcasting Convention (IBC), Amsterdam, Netherlands, 2020, https://doi.org/10.1145/3339825.3393583.

[99] S. Gül, D. Podborski, J. Son, G. Bhullar, T. Buchholz, T. Schierl, C. Hellge, Cloud rendering-based volumetric video streaming system for mixed reality services, in: Proc. ACM Multimedia Systems Conference, 2020, pp. 357–360, https://doi.org/10.1145/3339825.3393583.

[100] Unity, https://unity.com.

[101] Unreal, https://www.unrealengine.com.

[102] S. Gül, D. Podborski, T. Buchholz, T. Schierl, C. Hellge, Low-latency cloud-based volumetric video streaming using head motion prediction, in: Proc Workshop on Network and Operating System Support for Digital Audio and Video (NOSSDAV), 2020, pp. 27–33, https://doi.org/10.1145/3386290.3396933.

[103] S. Gül, S. Bosse, D. Podborski, T. Schierl, C. Hellge, Kalman filter-based head motion prediction for cloud-based mixed reality, in: Proc. International Conference on Multimedia, 2020, pp. 3632–3641, https://doi.org/10.1145/3394171.3413699.

[104] Dt. Telekom and Ericsson, Whitepaper: Enabling time-critical applications over 5G with rate adaptation, May 2021.

CHAPTER 12

MPEG immersive video

Patrick Garus[a,e], **Marta Milovanović**[a,b,e], **Joël Jung**[c], **and Marco Cagnazzo**[b,d]

[a]Orange Labs, Guyancourt, France
[b]LTCI, Télécom Paris, Institut polytechnique de Paris, Palaiseau, France
[c]Tencent Media Lab, Palo Alto, CA, United States
[d]Department of Information Engineering, University of Padua, Padua, Italy

The Motion picture experts group (MPEG) has finalized the next iteration of an immersive video coding standard in 2021. Denoted as MPEG immersive video (MIV) [1,2], the new standard is the spiritual successor of the 3D extension of high efficiency video coding (HEVC) [3], targeting the multiview video plus depth (MVD) format. Unfortunately, 3D-HEVC has not been a successful standard, as a widely spread deployment failed to materialize. A paradigm shift was required to satisfy the industrial needs and to lower the hurdle for implementation. The most significant change is the separation of the 2D video codec from the immersive video standard, which means that the utilized 2D codec is out of the scope of the MIV specification. In the case of 3D-HEVC, the 3D extension becomes obsolete if the underlying 2D codec is not deployed. Consequently, MIV has been designed to be compatible with any 2D video codecs that are or will be deployed to consumer devices. Though this choice may increase the chance of industrial success, it sets limitations on the available coding tools. The most characteristic aspects of 3D-HEVC had to be omitted: inter-view and inter-component prediction as well as depth coding tools. Even though prediction-based coding is known to be very efficient in terms of rate-distortion compromise, it requires long prediction structures when coding light fields with many views, which cannot be processed by hardware decoders currently deployed in consumer devices. This matter is quantified by the pixel rate, which is defined as the number of luma pixels that have to be decoded per second to play a video in real-time. Furthermore, memory limitations make it impossible to store all decoded pictures required to predict all views and frames. However, many views are needed to perform high-quality view synthesis and to achieve six degrees of freedom (6DoF), *i.e.,* a free navigation through the scene: the test sequences used in scope of the MIV standardization can entail up to 46 cameras, each providing texture and depth [4]. As a consequence, the reference implementation of the MIV codec, denoted as test model for MPEG immersive video (TMIV) [5], is no longer coding all pixels by prediction, but instead discarding some of them through a pruning process (see Section 12.2.1). The goal of the pruning is to remove redundant information among

---

[e] P.G. and M.M. have contributed equally to this chapter.

Immersive Video Technologies
https://doi.org/10.1016/B978-0-32-391755-1.00018-3

the views, which is not required to render any point of view of the scene. What remains are views containing multiple patches of pixels. The patches are packed together into an entity called the atlas, which is the output format of the TMIV encoder. Therefore an atlas can be seen as a sparse representation of a collection of images. The atlas description and related information is the basis of the MIV bitstream. The pruning process is designed to respect a given pixel rate constraint, enabling the MIV codec implementation to adapt the bitstream to current as well as future capabilities of hardware decoders. The atlas construction is applied to the depth maps as well. An example of texture and depth atlases is shown in Fig. 12.1. The selected full views (*basic views*) are packed into the first atlases and the remaining space is filled with patches (originating from *additional views*). Consequently, one atlas contains mainly full frames, whereas the other atlas contains mainly patches.

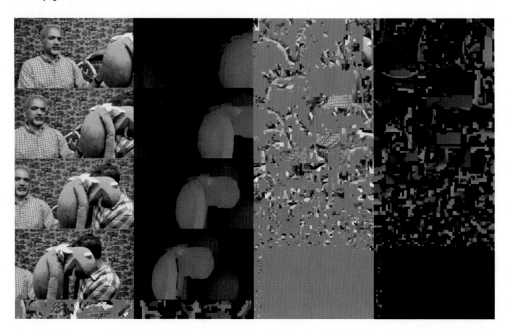

Figure 12.1 An example of texture and depth atlases for Frog sequence. First column: texture atlas with four basic views and patches; second column: depth atlas with four basic views and patches; third column: texture atlas with patches; last column: depth atlas with patches.

The compression of depth maps may harm the synthesis quality, since dedicated depth coding tools are not available in 2D codecs designed for texture coding. As every texture pixel comes with a corresponding depth pixel, the transmission of depth also contributes to the pixel rate limitation. This situation motivated research towards an alternative system, in which depth is recovered at the decoder side instead of being coded, see Section 12.1.2. The MIV bitstream enables the interpretation of the coded patch atlases and provides relevant information (*e.g.,* camera parameters) to perform depth image-based rendering (DIBR). The latter is non-normative, and therefore not part of the MIV standard. This opens the opportunity for the implementers to design their own depth estimation and rendering tools.

MIV has been developed following common test conditions (CTC) [6]. The CTC describes the settings for the TMIV, the configurations for the 2D codec, the test sequences, and the procedure for evaluation. One notable difference to the CTC of 3D-HEVC is the complexity of the test sequences [7]. Whereas 3D-HEVC was limited to rectified images, perspective, and linearly aligned cameras, MIV is challenged by a larger variety of content: natural and computer-generated, perspective and equirectangular, non-rectified images and arbitrarily located cameras. Extended profiles of MIV enable the handling of content with more advanced properties, such as reflections and transparencies.

In summary, the TMIV encoder can be considered as a tool that converts light fields into patch atlases. The TMIV decoder interprets these patch atlases using information parsed from the MIV bitstream to perform light field reconstruction through DIBR.

This chapter presents original results, which highlight that MIV is compatible and competitive with any state-of-the-art 2D codec. Nevertheless, we show that an improvement of the coding performance can be achieved by utilizing screen content coding tools [8], especially for depth atlases. As the tools of the 2D codec cannot be influenced by the MIV standard, our results may encourage the inclusion of dedicated atlas and depth coding tools in future 2D codecs.

The remainder of the chapter is organized as follows: Section 12.1 provides further details of the MIV standard; Section 12.2 describes the TMIV encoder, decoder, and renderer; Section 12.3 presents the CTC and its three anchors; Section 12.4 presents original results related to different codecs and VVC optimization for MIV through screen content coding tools, and Section 12.5 concludes this chapter.

12.1. MIV description and profiles

12.1.1 MIV overview

MIV (ISO/IEC 23090-12) is an extension of the visual volumetric video-based coding (V3C) MPEG standard (ISO/IEC 23090-5 2nd edition), which describes the syntax, semantics, and decoding of any volumetric media. *Volumetric media* refers to formats, which represent a sampled version of the continuous light field or plenoptic function, *e.g.,* MVD, lenslet images or point clouds. The term *video-based* implies that the format is ultimately treated as 2D video. Another example is the video-based point cloud compression (V-PCC) MPEG standard (ISO/IEC 23090-5), which is common with V3C and shares many similarities with MIV. In contrast, the geometry-based point cloud

Table 12.1 The MIV profiles. D: depth, T: texture, A: transparency, O: occupancy sub-bitstreams.

Name	Profiles			
	Main	Extended	Extended - restricted subprofile	Geometry Absent
Video bitstreams	D, T	D, T, A, O	T, A	T
Input format	MVD	MVD+	MPI	MVV MVD

compression (G-PCC) MPEG standard (ISO/IEC DIS 23090-9) processes the point cloud in its own domain, without converting it to a 2D video format.

12.1.2 MIV profiles

Several profiles are defined, allowing adaptation to the input format. The latter is quite flexible since, as shown in Table 12.1; several combinations of texture, geometry, occupancy and transparency are possible.

The first profile is called main profile and is designed for MVD coding: in this case, the only attribute is texture, and the geometry is described by depth information.

The extended profile targets more advanced formats, which, in addition to texture and depth, also include transparency and occupancy. They can be useful to design more sophisticated synthesis algorithms, because DIBR cannot appropriately handle transparent objects, such as windows.

The restricted subprofile of the extended profile has been especially adapted to the multi-plane image (MPI) format [9], which has gained popularity in recent years for providing high-quality view synthesis, despite the very simple synthesis process [10]. Instead of providing a single texture value for an explicitly coded depth value (as in MVD), MPIs provide texture for multiple depth levels, each weighted with a certain alpha/transparency value. To synthesize a view, the MPI is first generated at the target view and each plane is alpha-blended.

Any additional attribute and occupancy in the extended profile are coded as a video bitstream. Though these attributes can improve the view synthesis performance, they increase the general pixel rate and consequently less texture can be coded. Therefore, the overall light field reconstruction can suffer. Especially for MPIs, minimizing the amount of data prior to video-based coding is currently researched [11]. However, removing the redundancy of MPIs for natural content is particularly challenging [12]. As a result, advanced formats have not been able to outperform any MVD-based anchors following the CTC (including MPIs) to this date.

The geometry absent (GA) profile enables the encoding of light fields without geometry. One application concerns densely sampled light fields, for which image-based rendering can lead to sufficient synthesis quality. Another use case is decoder-side depth estimation (DSDE), in which depth maps are estimated at the decoder-side or in the cloud prior to the rendering. This profile provides the most pixel rate for coding of texture as no other attribute is coded. Given that 2D codecs are particularly designed for texture coding, the GA profile allows for coding of the light field with the least harm. The most important requirement for this goal is to have sufficient redundancy in the coded light field to perform depth estimation, which is based on finding matching pixels or blocks among the views. With progress in machine learning-based monocular depth estimation, it can be expected that this requirement will be less stringent in the future.

DSDE is a novel architecture that has been introduced into the MIV standard for the first time. During the standardization activities, significant BD-rate performance gains have been reported [13] compared to an anchor with encoded depth maps. Consequently, the geometry absent profile has been adopted into the MIV. The current implementation of DSDE, with a depth estimator that simultaneously estimates the depth maps of all reference views, does not take into account that the DSDE system, can take advantage of the knowledge of the desired viewport during the depth estimation process, which would result in lower complexity. With complexity being the main concern of DSDE, an extension of DSDE has been proposed in [14], which reduces the runtime of DSDE significantly, while simultaneously improving the view synthesis performance. This approach has been adopted as the geometry assistance SEI message in the MIV standard. However, the concept of MIV seems to contradict the DSDE approach, as MIV avoids sending redundant textures. Nevertheless, it has been shown in [15] that omitting depth additional view atlases improves the BD-rate, especially for low bitrates and natural content. Such a solution requires adaptations of the pruning process and higher compatibility of the depth estimator with additional view texture atlases.

12.2. TMIV description

The TMIV encoder is a non-normative implementation of MIV, which operates on the source material, selects some of the parameters automatically (atlas frame size, number of atlases), preprocesses the textures and depth maps, and packs them into texture and depth atlases. Moreover, it produces the MIV metadata required to decode the atlas video streams. A high-level block scheme of the encoding process is shown in Fig. 12.2.

The TMIV decoder is a reference implementation of a normative process that decodes the MIV metadata, whereas the 2D video decoder decodes the video sub-bitstreams. Afterwards, the decoded atlases and MIV metadata are used to render the desired viewport, with a non-normative rendering technique. A high-level block scheme of the decoding process is shown in Fig. 12.3.

Section 12.2.1 details the TMIV encoder, and Section 12.2.2 describes the TMIV decoder and renderer.

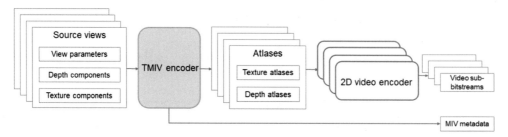

Figure 12.2 High-level block scheme of the immersive video coding paradigm with MIV: encoding.

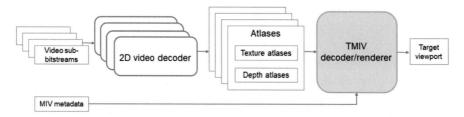

Figure 12.3 High-level block scheme of the immersive video coding paradigm with MIV: decoding.

12.2.1 TMIV encoder

The TMIV encoder can encode the source views in one or multiple subsets (groups), where the number of groups is a user's choice. It consists of a group-based encoder, which is always invoked at the beginning of the encoding process, independently of the number of groups, and a single-group encoder, which encodes each group individually (see Fig. 12.4).

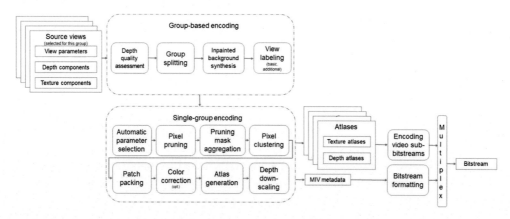

Figure 12.4 Block scheme of the TMIV encoder.

During the first phase (group-based encoding), the quality of depth maps is assessed for each source view. This assessment is done to verify if the level of inter-view consistency among the depth maps is sufficient. The depth map of each source view is reprojected to the others, and the value of a depth pixel of the source view is compared with the depth value of the corresponding pixel neighborhood in the target view. If the difference is higher than a defined threshold, the source pixel is considered inconsistent, and when the total amount of inconsistent pixels is higher than a given threshold, the depth map quality is labeled as low. If the depth map quality is low, the renderer will not use it in the intermediate view synthesis process. Instead, it will warp the texture pixels from the closest source views to fill the holes.

Then, if the user requests more than one group, the source views are organized into multiple separate sub-groups. The grouping process is done by determining the key positions in the scene using the range and distance of cameras, by first finding the dominant axis and the furthest view positions in the pool of views, and then gathering the closest views to the key positions, for each group. The number of key positions is equal to the number of groups. Grouping is beneficial for preserving coherent non-redundant regions of the scene, because it enforces the sampling to be done on the neighboring views.

Afterwards, the synthesized background texture and depth view is prepared, which is to be used instead of the inpainted data at the decoder-side, and it is additionally packed into the atlas. This process is designed to render the background over the foreground. It is utilized to fill the pixels that are lacking after intermediate view synthesis, because at the decoder-side, after view reconstruction, only pruned views are available.

Subsequently, some of the source views are labeled as *basic views*, and the rest of them are labeled as *additional views*. The labeling method is based on the k-medoids algorithm, where the basic views are k medoids among the source views, and the cost function is formed based on the distance between view positions.

The single-group encoding phase is done on each group individually, after all the steps in the group-based encoding phase are done. Therefore it will be done either on all the source views at once or independently for each grouped subset of views.

In the beginning, the automatic calculation of the number of atlases and the atlas frame size is done, which is related to the following constraints: the maximum size of a luma picture, the maximum luma sample rate, and the total number of decoder instantiations.

The next step is atlas construction, which consists of the pruning, mask aggregation and clustering, patch packing, optional color correction of source views, and atlas generation. Basic views are fully packed into atlases, while additional views are being processed further, and their redundancies are pruned before the packing step (see Fig. 12.1). Pruning is essential, because it reduces the interview redundancy in the source multi-view set. It determines which pixels from the additional views are already present in basic or other additional views, and thus, are redundant. A pruning graph is introduced, which describes the hierarchy of the source views where the pruning is done. The basic views are the roots of this graph, whereas the additional views are assigned to the child nodes, in the order of decreasing number of preserved pixels.

Mask aggregation is a process of aggregating masks of active pixels (pixels that were not pruned) frame-by-frame, and this is done for each intra period, whereas clustering is identifying sets of connected active pixels. These clusters are then consecutively packed into the atlases.

The color correction optionally aligns the color characteristics of the source views. Moreover, depth and occupancy atlases can optionally be down-scaled, to allow for a better depth map encoding quality on a fixed bitrate and pixel rate savings.

After atlas construction, the texture atlas and depth atlas video streams are encoded with an arbitrary 2D video encoder. All camera and atlas metadata parameters are formatted as a V3C sample stream [16] with MIV extensions. Finally, these bitstreams are multiplexed into a single MIV bitstream.

12.2.2 TMIV decoder and renderer

The pipeline of a TMIV decoder starts with a client's request for the desired viewport, by giving the viewport position and orientation. Then, the sub-bitstreams are demultiplexed, the MIV bitstream is parsed by the MIV decoder, and the video bitstreams are decoded by a 2D video decoder. Afterwards, the frames are unpacked from the atlases, and the blocks in the frame are organized into a patch map, which guides the recovery of basic and additional views. This process is followed by a non-normative (optional) depth estimation, in the case of decoder-side depth estimation scenario, and, finally, a non-normative rendering of the target viewport.

The process of rendering has multiple steps. First, the culling of the patches takes place to remove the patches that have no overlap with the target view, therefore reducing the complexity of the view synthesis. Furthermore, the occupancy frame is reconstructed, which shows if the pixel is occupied or non-occupied. Subsequently, if the color correction on the source views is done, then the attribute mean value is restored. After these steps, the additional (pruned) views are reconstructed, by mapping the texture and depth patches from the atlases back to the corresponding view.

In the case of the geometry absent profile the depth maps are not transmitted, but just the textures; therefore the estimation of depth maps may be done on the reconstructed textures, using an external depth estimation software, which is not integrated into TMIV. The new reference software used for depth estimation in MPEG-I, according to MIV CTC, is immersive video depth estimation (IVDE) [17]. Previously, depth estimation reference software (DERS) [18,19] was used as the reference software, and it is still a possible alternative for the evaluation purposes.

The view synthesis is implemented in TMIV with two different approaches. The MIV CTC defines the view weighting synthesizer (VWS) as the reference synthesizer. It aims to alleviate the artifacts caused by the inconsistencies in source depth maps and to allow smoother transitions between viewports. To this end, VWS deploys visibility and shading steps. Visibility step generates a target viewport depth map, using splat-based rasterization in the process of pixel reprojection to the target viewport. The selection of the depth pixels is done based on the carefully chosen weighting strategy, where the weights are computed not only using the distance between the source and target view, but also taking into account the weights of the corresponding pruned pixels in other child source views. First, the initial weight is given to the pixel, which is determined based on the mentioned distance. Then, if this pixel is found in one of the pruned pixels of its child views, its weight is added up to the weight of the child view, where the weight of the child view also depends only on its distance from to the target view. Additionally, this process continues to the grandchildren. If the pixel does not reproject into any of the child views, the process moves to the grandchildren. Moreover, if the pixel reprojects into an unpruned pixel of its child view, its weight does not change and the process for this pixel stops.

The second alternative is derived from the reference view synthesizer (RVS) [20]. It projects the source image points onto the target image points, using the triangles method, and blends the pixels independently of the rendering order. The blending is done in such a way to prefer the closer views over views that are further away, to prefer foreground over background objects, and to penalize very elongated triangles, as given in Eq. (12.1):

$$I_{blend} = \sum w\left(\gamma_i, d_i, s_i\right) I_i$$
$$w : (\gamma, d, s) \rightarrow e^{-c_\gamma \gamma + c_d d - c_s s},$$

(12.1)

where I_{blend} is the target pixel, computed from different contributions (pixels I_i); w is an exponential function, which maps the input variables given as a ray angle γ (between the input and target camera); reciprocal geometry d (the reciprocal of the depth value in the target view), and stretching s (the value of unclipped area of the triangle in the target view in respect to the source view).

12.3. Common test conditions

In this section, the CTC for MPEG immersive video is presented, which defines the pipeline and procedure for the fair evaluation of proposals. It describes the MIV anchors, test sequences, and evaluation methodology.

Table 12.2 Test sequences.

Sequence	Type	Format	Resolution	NumViews
Mandatory content				
Painter	NC	LPP	2048 × 1088	16
Frog	NC	LPP	1920 × 1080	13
Carpark	NC	LPP	1920 × 1088	9
ClassroomVideo	CG	ERP	4096 × 2048	15
Museum	CG	ERP	2048 × 2048	24
Fan	CG	LPP	1920 × 1080	15
Kitchen	CG	LPP	1920 × 1080	25
Chess	CG	ERP	2048 × 2048	10
Group	CG	LPP	1920 × 1080	21
Optional content				
Fencing	NC	LPP	1920 × 1080	10
Hall	NC	LPP	1920 × 1088	9
Street	NC	LPP	1920 × 1088	9
Mirror	NC	LPP	1920 × 1080	15
ChessPieces	CG	ERP	2048 × 2048	10
Hijack	CG	ERP	4096 × 2048	10
Cadillac	CG	LPP	1920 × 1080	15

The test material consists of both natural and computer-generated content, created with perspective and omnidirectional cameras. Therefore the views have omnidirectional format (equirectangular projection, ERP) or linear perspective format (linear perspective projection, LPP). In the case of natural content, depth maps are estimated, with some additional post-processing steps, whereas, in the case of computer-generated content, they are produced using mathematical models of the generated 3D scene. In the CTC, the material is separated into mandatory and optional sequences, where optional sequences are more challenging, but not compulsory for the evaluation. A summary of the test sequences' characteristics is presented in Table 12.2.

The test sequences are compressed using TMIV (version 10) and VVenC [21,22], a fast implementation of VVC [23]. The VVenC encoder includes five predefined preset configurations: "slower," "slow," "medium," "fast," and "faster." Each of these configurations offers a different compromise of compression quality with respect to complexity (encoding speed). The "slow" preset has been selected by the MIV group as the best compromise, and the encoder is utilized with the random access configuration [24]. After the video transmission, the MIV metadata and the video bitstreams are decoded using TMIV decoder and VVdeC [25]. The target viewport from a pose trace (predefined navigation positions which imitate the user's motion) is rendered using all available decoded atlases. Finally, the CTC specifies the evaluation of the quality of the synthesized views with both subjective and objective methods.

The CTC defines three different anchors for coding with TMIV. The first one, called the *MIV anchor*, comes in two different configurations depending on the number of frames: A17, which encodes 17 frames, and A97, which encodes 97 frames. This anchor processes the source views, as detailed in the Section 12.2.1, with the goal to obtain the compact representation of the scene packed in the atlases, where some of the views are fully sent, while others are pruned. Secondly, the CTC introduces the *MIV view anchor*, called V17, which, in a view labeling process, automatically decides which subset of views (textures and depth maps) to fully pack and transmit, without further processing of the source views. Finally, the *MIV decoder-side depth-estimation anchor*, called G17, is introduced, which, also in a view labeling process, automatically decides which subset of texture views to fully pack and transmit, whereas the depth maps are estimated using immersive video depth estimation (IVDE) software at the decoder-side before commencing the rendering process. IVDE estimates the depth maps from the arbitrarily positioned views and enables temporal and inter-view consistency of the depth maps. The performance of these three anchors is presented and discussed in Section 12.4.1.

The objective evaluation is done by computing the Bjøntegaard delta (BD) rates [26, 27] in terms of Y-peak signal-to-noise ratio (Y-PSNR) of synthesized views in comparison to the uncoded source views, as well as in terms of immersive video PSNR (IV-PSNR) [28]. Y-PSNR represents the value of the PSNR computed on the luminance channel of the video. IV-PSNR is a PSNR-based metric adapted for immersive video applications, which alleviates the influence of pixel shifts caused by projection errors and the influence of global color differences among the different input views. BD-rate is the metric that shows the average bitrate savings for the same video quality (given with Y-PSNR or IV-PSNR), computed between two rate-distortion curves. The maximum delta PSNR represents the maximum difference between the PSNR of different synthesized views, and it shows the quality variation among the different computed target viewports, which generates visual discomfort.

The quantization parameters $\mathbf{QP_T}$ for the compression of texture videos are chosen to cover the medium and low bitrate range, from 5 Mbps to 50 Mbps, and they are sequence-dependent. Then, the mapping to the quantization parameter $\mathbf{QP_D}$ [29] for the depth is done with Eq. (12.2), applied to five rate points:

$$\forall i \in \{1, 2, 3, 4, 5\}, \quad QP_D(i) = \max\left(1, \lceil -14.2 + 0.8 \cdot QP_T(i) \rceil\right). \qquad (12.2)$$

The pixel rate evaluation is also taken into account, defining low and high constraints that need to be fulfilled according to the HEVC main 10 profile at Level 5.2 and Level 6.2, respectively. The maximum number of decoder instantiations is set to four. All anchors comply with the low pixel rate constraint, which is fixed at 1.070

giga pixels per second. The atlas sizes are automatically computed according to this number. The subjective viewing and evaluation are done on the predefined pose traces, following the recommendations [30] of the MPEG advisory group 5 on visual quality assessment.

12.4. Evaluation of MIV with different configurations and 2D codecs

In this section, we present experimental results related to three cases:

1. The performance of the MIV anchors, as defined by the CTC (see Section 12.4.1).
2. Original results related to the performance of MIV with three state-of-the art 2D video codecs (see Section 12.4.2).
3. Original results related to the performance of screen content coding tools of VVC for MIV atlas coding (see Section 12.4.3).

12.4.1 Performance of MIV anchors

The rate–distortion curves for the A17 anchor (MIV anchor that encodes 17 frames) are shown in Fig. 12.5. We observe a large range of quality as well as bitrate for the mandatory and optional content. For high-rate points, the bitrate ranges from 38 to 68 Mbps, and the synthesis PSNR ranges from 34 to 43 dB. For low-rate points, the bitrate ranges from 2 to 5 Mbps, and the synthesis PSNR ranges from 31 to 43 dB. The IV-PSNR is not always in line with the PSNR, indicating that the perceived quality may be better or worse than expected. The synthesis quality and the amount of needed bitrate typically depend on the complexity of the camera arrangements, the scene, the quality of the textures, and of the depth maps. For some content, such as Frog, Group, and Fan, the view synthesis PSNR may already saturate at low values, independent of further increase of bitrate. This implies that the pixel rate constraint limits the performance of the renderer. Consequently, the synthesis artifacts may outweigh the additional texture and depth quality with an increase in bitrate. In the high bitrate range, maximum delta PSNR peaks to 10.1 dB, whereas in the low bitrate range it is around 2.3 dB. This means that the objective quality across the synthesized views may deviate by up to 10.1 dB and 2.3 dB, respectively.

The V17 and G17 anchors are compared to A17 in terms of BD-rate and video encoding runtime (which is given in percent of the A17 anchor runtime) in Table 12.3. Negative values of BD-rate mean that the tested anchor (G17 or V17) performs better than reference anchor A17, whereas the positive values indicate that the tested anchor performs worse than reference A17. In the case of "---" and "+++," there was not enough overlap to compute BD-rate, where "---" indicates gain, whereas "+++" indicates loss, compared to the anchor A17.

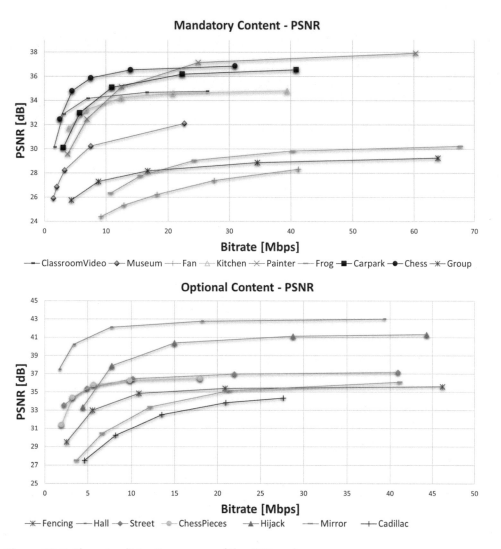

Figure 12.5 The rate-distortion curves of the A17 anchor.

We notice that V17 performs significantly better than the A17 anchor in several cases. The Hall sequence is an interesting exception, as it is the only sequence with significant global camera motion. In such a case, the A17 anchor performs better, as temporal variations may be efficiently included into the atlases. In contrast, the selected views may become sub-optimal over time in V17 and G17. Additionally, when inter-view consistent depth maps are present, as for CGI content, the A17 anchor is able to code the light field more efficiently. However, for CGI content with transparencies in the scene, the depth maps can be misleading, as in the case of Cadillac and Fan.

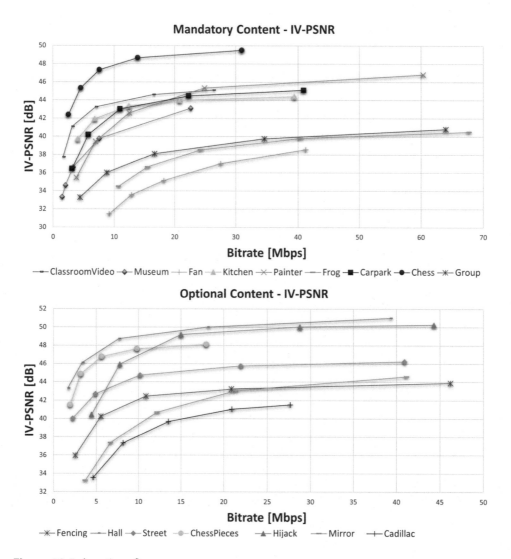

Figure 12.5 (*continued*)

The G17 outperforms the A17 anchor for all natural sequences, except Hall. This is because the depth maps given at the encoder side are not accurate enough, despite best efforts for their estimation and refinements. One can also notice that the G17 anchor can even outperform A17 on CGI content with high-quality depth maps as for the Kitchen sequence. Similar to V17, the performance of G17 is much better for perspective content than for ERP. In the G17 case, however, the limitation is imposed by the used depth estimator (IVDE), which performs much better for perspective content.

Table 12.3 Comparison of the V17 and G17 anchors with respect to the A17 anchor.

Sequence	High BD-Rate PSNR [%]		Low BD-Rate PSNR [%]		High BD-Rate IV-PSNR [%]		Low BD-Rate IV-PSNR [%]		Video encoding [%]	
	V17	G17	V17	G17	V17	G17	V17	G17	V17	G17
Mandatory content										
Painter (NC)	-33.9	-63.2	-31.9	-60.5	-18.6	-33.1	-24.4	-43.0	66.8	80.7
Frog (NC)	-33.5	-67.5	-29.7	-57.5	-9.3	-48.4	-17.0	-48.9	69.2	81.9
Carpark (NC)	31.5	2.1	13.2	-21.1	42.0	18.6	18.1	-10.0	82.6	81.7
Class.Video (CG)	4.0	+++	-20.4	50.3	4.3	158.3	-17.5	4.7	83.1	123.1
Museum (CG)	36.6	320.4	-4.5	73.8	44.4	113.8	0.5	25.1	58.4	88.3
Fan (CG)	-18.9	- - -	-15.6	- - -	-11.0	-69.6	-9.0	-77.5	71.1	131.4
Kitchen (CG)	75.8	-8.8	20.6	-6.5	206.9	105.9	55.0	51.7	63.6	92.2
Chess (CG)	+++	+++	+++	+++	+++	+++	+++	+++	62.5	62.5
Group (CG)	-47.2	+++	-42.4	+++	-11.6	+++	-20.2	+++	54.1	100.2
Optional content										
Fencing (NC)	28.4	67.4	-10.8	-5.4	16.5	25.3	-11.1	-25.7	57.0	82.0
Hall (NC)	1070.3	1060.2	74.6	377.8	119.3	429.3	33.7	177.8	82.9	108.6
Street (NC)	-40.1	-66.0	-17.1	-48.1	7.0	-33.2	11.9	-30.9	74.8	81.0
Mirror (NC)	48.9	-9.5	5.1	-31.2	100.6	16.7	13.2	-16.9	61.2	69.7
ChessPieces (CG)	+++	+++	+++	+++	+++	+++	+++	+++	55.1	66.8
Hijack (CG)	+++	+++	47.1	+++	+++	+++	66.4	+++	56.3	86.4
Cadillac (CG)	-30.6	-58.6	-39.5	-67.8	3.3	-23.9	-30.3	-50.4	55.4	54.8

V17 and G17 outperform A17 in several sequences for low bitrates, *e.g.,* Carpark and Fencing. This reflects that the impact of strong depth compression leads to a higher degradation of synthesis performance, than the estimation of depth maps from compressed textures.

Fig. 12.6 shows the synthesis results on a selected frame of a pose trace, for matching bitrates and for all the anchors. In the first row, we show an example of the synthesis for the Museum sequence, which has a better coding performance for the A17 anchor. The synthesized views clearly confirm that V17 as well as G17 could not recover all the textures. In the case of V17, this is likely due to the pixel rate constraint. As Museum has a resolution of 2048 x 2048, the number of basic views that can be coded in the V17 anchor is far too small to reconstruct all 24 views with sufficient quality. In the case of the G17 anchor, the situation becomes more severe, as the number of transmitted views is too low to do high-performant depth estimation with IVDE. Consequently, a lot of occlusions remain visible in the final views. In the case of A17 anchor, rendered target view has small cracks or patch-level compression block-artifacts. The second row shows the results for Fan sequence. The G17 anchor performs much better than the other anchors, because it preserves well the details of the fan, whereas both A17 and V17 struggle with this task. This is because the impact of depth compression on

Figure 12.6 Comparison of synthesis results obtained by different anchors. First column: A17 anchor; second column: V17 anchor; third column: G17 anchor. First row: Museum; second row: Fan; third row: Carpark.

fine structures as the fan's cage leads to strong synthesis artifacts. In the case of depth estimation at the decoder-side, not all structures could be recovered; however, more details are preserved, and the view is significantly sharper. The third row shows the Carpark sequence as an example of a natural, perspective scene. Even though the A17 anchor provides the best BD-rate performance, many synthesis artifacts are mitigated in the G17 anchor, and the car in the background appears more complete.

In general, the G17 anchor provides sharper rendered views, as the corresponding depth maps do not suffer from compression artifacts. On the other hand, occlusions may harm the perceptual quality if the coded subset of views is too low to perform high-quality depth estimation with IVDE. As the tools used in the A17 anchor have not been designed for non–Lambertian surfaces, the V17 anchor is particularly good for this type of content.

The TMIV encoder is significantly simpler for V17 and G17 than for the A17 anchor, as the complex pipeline of pruning and packing is not required. In addition, the video encoding is faster, as it is easier to encode full-frame atlases than patch atlases.

12.4.2 Codec agnosticism

During the development of MIV, the usage of HEVC or VVC was required according to the CTC. However, the number of available coding standards has never been as large as today, and the market will likely not be dominated by a single codec. Fortunately, MIV is not affected by this competition, as it is designed to be agnostic to any 2D codec on the market. In this section, we aim to confirm the compatibility of MIV with the most recent codecs of the most important video coding standardization organizations in the world: VVC of ISO/IEC MPEG and ITU-T VCEG, AV1 [31] of the Alliance for open media (AOM) [32] and AVS3 [33] of the Audio video coding standard workgroup of China [34]. We verify that the atlases produced by MIV do not contain any specificity that would significantly impact the efficiency of any 2D codec, designed for traditional 2D content.

The reference software alternatives we use in this study are VTM12 for VVC, HPM12 for AVS3, and AV1. For each codec, the random access configuration is utilized as provided by the corresponding standardization body. We did not perform any specific configuration refinements of these codecs, as it is not the goal of this section to provide a competitive comparison between them, but merely highlight the MIV compatibility and overall performance. In all the cases, we compare the alternatives with the main anchor of MIV, which is A17, where VVenC ("slow preset") is utilized.

Fig. 12.7 shows the decoded texture atlas quality, which is ultimately used for view synthesis. The coded texture and depth atlases are shown in Fig. 12.8. The associated encoder runtimes are shown in Table 12.4. For completeness, we provide the results of these experiments in terms of BD-rate in Table 12.5. However, this table should serve as a reference and not as a tool to compare these codecs with each other. Instead, we analyze each codec independently by comparing the performance per sequence with the average.

AV1 shows quite good performance with Painter, Carpark, and Hall sequences. It performs the worst for Group, Kitchen, and ChessPieces. Overall, stronger fluctuations across the sequences are noticeable. HPM12 performs rather stable across all sequences and shows most difficulties with the Fan and Group sequences. Similar to AV1, it performs well for Painter and Hall. VTM12 performs better for Group, ChessPieces, and Frog, instead of Painter and Hall. Similar to HMP12, its performance is rather stable across the sequences. Based on these observations, none of the codecs appears to be incompatible with the specifics of the MIV atlases. Therefore the codec agnosticism, enabled by the MIV standard, is verified in practice.

12.4.3 Atlas coding using SCC tools in VVC

HEVC has been the 2D codec for the evaluation of TMIV throughout most of the development stages of MIV. After being finalized, VVC has replaced HEVC [35]. However, no significant effort to tune the encoder or to take advantage of the *versatility*

Figure 12.7 Details from the compressed texture atlases of the Painter sequence, matching bitrate, all tested encoders. The first row shows the uncompressed source texture. Second row: cropped source; third row: VVenC; fourth row: VTM12; fifth row: AV1; last row: HPM12. The second and fourth columns represent the difference between the encoded atlas and the source.

Table 12.4 Video encoding runtimes for different codecs, compared to the A17 anchor (using VVenC slow preset).

Sequence	Video encoding [%]		
	VTM12	**AV1**	**HPM12**
Mandatory content			
Painter	719.0	131.6	1859.7
Frog	713.4	163.0	2117.2
Carpark	666.7	149.5	1892.0
ClassroomVideo	647.6	171.5	2342.3
Museum	622.6	250.0	1694.3
Fan	659.5	209.2	2241.5
Kitchen	543.9	83.6	1285.3
Chess	666.9	181.6	1479.8
Group	538.7	131.3	1625.7
Average	**642.0**	**163.5**	**1837.5**
Optional content			
Fencing	779.2	143.8	1580.2
Hall	715.9	82.5	1252.5
Street	637.8	130.7	1736.8
Mirror	607.8	142.9	1790.2
ChessPieces	714.0	153.8	1407.3
Hijack	665.8	133.3	1846.7
Cadillac	717.3	152.8	2069.9
Average	**691.1**	**134.3**	**1669.1**

aspect of VVC has been done. Especially for depth coding, VVC comes with interesting edge-preserving tools, such as geometrical partitioning. Screen content coding (SCC) tools have also shown the potential to compress MVD content efficiently with HEVC [36].

In this section, we investigate the performance of intra block copy (IBC), block-based differential pulse-code modulation (BDPCM), and palette mode (PLT) on different types of atlases:

- Basic-view (BV) atlases, containing basic views and a very small amount of patches from additional views,
- Additional-view (AV) patch atlases, containing only small patches from additional views,
- Texture atlases, which consist of only texture component, both for basic view and additional view atlases,
- Depth atlases, which consist of only depth component, both for basic view and additional view atlases.

Table 12.5 MIV objective performance with VTM12, AV1, and HPM12, compared to the A17 anchor (using VVenC slow preset).

Sequence	High BD-Rate PSNR [%]			Low BD-Rate PSNR [%]			High BD-Rate IV-PSNR [%]			Low BD-Rate IV-PSNR [%]		
	VTM12	AV1	HPM12	VTM12	AV1	HPM12	VTM12	AV1	HPM12	VTM12	AV1	HPM12
Mandatory content												
Painter (NC)	-2.0	-35.2	-14.3	-2.3	-45.3	-19.0	5.7	-34.0	-9.8	3.9	-44.0	-14.6
Frog (NC)	-6.9	8.9	6.4	-6.6	-1.8	3.4	7.8	7.8	11.2	5.2	0.1	7.2
Carpark (NC)	-3.6	-11.6	0.5	-3.7	-21.1	-4.9	6.0	-16.7	0.7	4.0	-24.1	-4.9
Class.Vid. (CG)	-1.2	18.4	17.2	1.4	1.8	8.3	7.2	10.0	17.4	7.9	2.6	11.4
Museum (CG)	-2.4	45.1	9.7	-2.8	33.0	5.9	2.5	14.3	5.7	2.5	13.6	5.0
Fan (CG)	-4.3	41.5	60.7	-3.7	19.4	44.4	-1.1	17.7	50.8	0.9	-1.8	37.1
Kitchen (CG)	-4.7	100.1	17.0	-5.5	71.6	16.9	1.7	31.1	10.1	4.1	24.2	6.7
Chess (CG)	-5.6	70.9	21.3	-7.3	28.8	10.5	0.5	10.2	17.1	-0.4	3.6	6.2
Group (CG)	-14.0	155.3	47.6	-11.6	86.4	34.2	-3.0	65.5	28.4	-1.4	42.4	19.5
Average	**-5.0**	**43.7**	**18.4**	**-4.7**	**19.2**	**11.1**	**3.0**	**11.8**	**14.6**	**3.0**	**1.8**	**8.2**
Optional content												
Fencing (NC)	-5.7	-4.3	-3.8	-5.6	-18.6	-9.9	2.1	2.0	-0.5	1.2	-14.2	-8.4
Hall (NC)	-5.6	-67.1	-37.3	-6.4	-68.3	-37.2	4.5	-64.5	-26.1	5.4	-66.2	-28.2
Street (NC)	-1.9	5.4	4.2	-1.8	-11.2	-6.1	6.6	-6.8	2.4	5.9	-14.6	-5.3
Mirror (NC)	-2.7	4.7	9.8	-3.5	-2.6	7.5	3.7	-1.8	11.1	3.1	-5.9	8.9
ChessP. (CG)	-6.6	61.9	14.0	-7.1	26.1	6.1	0.8	9.6	16.5	0.0	5.1	5.8
Hijack (CG)	-4.6	25.0	13.5	-5.5	3.8	7.0	-1.7	-6.0	11.8	-1.5	-11.8	3.0
Cadillac (CG)	-4.5	49.1	20.0	-5.6	32.9	16.9	2.3	11.0	7.8	0.7	3.9	4.8
Average	**-4.5**	**10.7**	**2.9**	**-5.1**	**-5.4**	**-2.2**	**2.6**	**-8.1**	**3.3**	**2.1**	**-14.8**	**-2.8**

IBC searches for the intra-picture similarity on a block basis, where the prediction of the current coding block is done by the reconstructed reference block from the same picture. The search range is restricted to the already coded CTU to the left of the current CTU, which is a strong limitation of atlas coding, as otherwise, IBC may reach similar performance as the multiview extension of HEVC (MV-HEVC). However, we do not perform any normative changes to the codec.

BDPCM is a prediction technique, which is grounded on the residual DPCM [37]. It serves as an alternative intra prediction mode, which is better suitable to avoid errors in predictions of long pixel distances. In intra prediction, the current block is predicted using the filtered reference samples of already decoded block boundaries. This approach can cause high errors, especially in cases where the prediction distance is too long. Typically, this situation is handled by deeper partitioning of the block, reducing the prediction distance and error in the sub-blocks. In BDPCM, however, a given pixel is predicted by the direct neighboring pixels, enabling accurate and efficient predictions with larger blocks, especially for screen content. In VVC, BDPCM is limited to the same block sizes as the transform skip mode.

a)   b)

Figure 12.8 Details from the compressed atlases of the Group sequence, matching bitrate, all tested encoders: a) texture patch atlas; b) depth patch atlas. The first row shows the uncompressed source. Second row: cropped source; third row: VVenC; fourth row: VTM12; fifth row: AV1; last row: HPM12. The second and fourth columns represent cropped images of the difference between the encoded atlas and the source.

Palette mode has proven to be beneficial for CGI content with simple graphics. It is considered as a special coding mode in VVC, together with the intra prediction, inter prediction, and IBC modes. Palette mode encompasses the coding of the palette (different samples) and coding of the spatial position index of its coding unit.

Table 12.6 TMIV+VTM objective performance with IBC, IBC+BDPCM, and IBC+BDPCM+PLT, as compared to the TMIV+VTM anchor.

Sequence	High BD-Rate PSNR [%]			Low BD-Rate PSNR [%]			High BD-Rate IV-PSNR [%]			Low BD-Rate IV-PSNR [%]		
	IBC	IBC BDPCM	IBC BDPCM PLT	IBC	IBC BDPCM	IBC BDPCM PLT	IBC	IBC BDPCM	IBC BDPCM PLT	IBC	IBC BDPCM	IBC BDPCM PLT
Mandatory content												
Painter (NC)	-0.9	-2.1	-3.3	-1.0	-1.9	-3.1	-0.3	-2.1	1.0	-0.4	-1.5	1.3
Frog (NC)	-0.6	-1.1	-2.3	-0.6	-1.1	-2.5	-0.7	-0.8	2.3	-0.9	-0.8	2.2
Carpark (NC)	-1.3	-2.2	-3.2	-1.4	-2.0	-3.1	-1.9	-2.6	0.0	-1.8	-2.2	0.6
Class.Vid. (CG)	-6.3	-8.8	-10.4	-6.8	-9.9	-11.9	-5.9	-7.6	-4.1	-6.8	-9.3	-7.4
Museum (CG)	-1.9	-2.7	-3.5	-2.6	-3.2	-4.0	-1.7	-2.3	2.2	-1.9	-2.7	1.4
Fan (CG)	-7.2	-9.3	-26.3	-7.0	-8.9	-21.7	-6.3	-7.8	-21.3	-6.3	-7.8	-16.6
Kitchen (CG)	-2.1	-3.8	-3.4	-2.8	-3.9	-5.6	-2.3	-3.4	1.2	-2.9	-4.2	0.1
Chess (CG)	-5.0	-5.2	-7.6	-4.6	-5.8	-8.5	-2.7	-4.0	4.0	-3.3	-4.9	1.1
Group (CG)	-2.0	-3.9	-7.3	-2.9	-4.5	-8.3	-1.7	-2.7	1.3	-2.1	-3.4	1.0
Average	**-3.0**	**-4.3**	**-7.5**	**-3.3**	**-4.6**	**-7.6**	**-2.6**	**-3.7**	**-1.5**	**-3.0**	**-4.1**	**-1.8**
Optional content												
Fencing (NC)	-1.2	-0.9	-2.2	-1.1	-1.5	-2.2	-1.2	-1.0	1.8	-1.1	-1.4	2.0
Hall (NC)	0.1	-1.5	-0.7	-0.7	-1.6	-1.4	0.0	-1.3	1.4	-0.4	-1.3	2.4
Street (NC)	-0.2	-0.5	-0.7	-0.6	-0.9	-1.3	-1.7	-1.2	2.4	-1.6	-1.4	3.0
Mirror (NC)	-1.6	-2.2	-3.9	-1.6	-2.3	-4.0	-1.3	-1.7	-1.3	-1.4	-2.0	-1.8
ChessP. (CG)	-6.5	-7.4	-10.0	-5.6	-6.9	-10.5	-4.2	-5.7	1.4	-4.7	-6.4	-2.0
Hijack (CG)	-2.6	-4.2	-6.2	-2.8	-4.5	-6.6	-2.5	-4.0	-3.8	-2.8	-4.4	-4.4
Cadillac (CG)	-2.7	-3.7	-2.7	-2.8	-4.5	-2.8	-2.4	-3.6	-2.4	-2.6	-4.2	-2.6
Average	**-2.1**	**-2.9**	**-3.8**	**-2.2**	**-3.2**	**-4.1**	**-1.9**	**-2.6**	**-0.1**	**-2.1**	**-3.0**	**-0.5**

A summary of the performance of MIV with VTM-SCC tools is shown in Table 12.6. In all the cases, we compare the alternatives with the TMIV+VTM anchor to isolate the impact of the screen content coding tools. Every tool provides additional benefit to the overall coding gain. IBC performs very well on Fan, Classroom video, and ChessPieces. BDPCM provides a small, but consistent gain over all sequences. Taking into account the video encoding runtime, shown in Table 12.7, the benefit of BD-PCM comes with only minor complexity increase over IBC alone. Consequently, we will show these tools jointly in the following sections to reduce the amount of data to present. However, the additional coding gain of PLT for some sequences comes with added complexity. For a few sequences, PLT reduces the performance. Fan is an interesting exception, as the coding gain is significant. To further analyze if these tools are particularly beneficial for certain atlas types, we need to look at each type of content independently.

Table 12.7 Video encoding runtimes for different SCC tools, compared to the TMIV+VTM.

Sequence	Video encoding [%]		
	IBC	IBC BDPCM	IBC BDPCM PLT
Mandatory content			
Painter	115.1	116.6	126.1
Frog	114.5	115.1	125.8
Carpark	115.4	116.4	129.9
ClassroomVideo	112.3	113.5	126.4
Museum	118.3	119.4	141.3
Fan	119.0	123.6	134.9
Kitchen	122.2	122.3	146.1
Chess	116.5	117.6	135.5
Group	123.0	124.1	145.8
Average	**117.4**	**118.8**	**134.6**
Optional content			
Fencing	111.2	112.2	120.4
Hall	112.2	112.8	122.7
Street	115.3	116.0	131.0
Mirror	116.9	118.1	133.7
ChessPieces	112.2	112.8	129.4
Hijack	114.7	114.7	126.6
Cadillac	112.3	112.0	112.3
Average	**113.5**	**114.1**	**125.1**

12.4.3.1 Texture atlas coding

The SCC results for the texture atlases alone are shown in Table 12.8 for IBC and BDPCM as well as in Table 12.9 using additionally PLT. We do not observe significant difference between BV and AV atlases in that case, indicating that there is no particular advantage over different texture atlas types. For BV atlases, IBC is not able to efficiently remove significant amount of redundancies due to limitations of its implementation in the standard. Due to the strong differences between the patches in the AV atlases, the benefit there is also limited. Nevertheless, PLT proves particularly useful for AV atlas coding. The benefit increases with the amount of repetitive textures in the scene as it is the case for Fan, Chess, and ChessPieces. However, following the CTC of MIV, the chroma component is not taken into account in our objective metrics. The Fan sequence shown in Fig. 12.9 indicates that the SCC tools may negatively impact the

Table 12.8 IBC+BDPCM texture atlas results.

Sequence	High BD-Rate PSNR [%]		Low BD-Rate PSNR [%]		High BD-Rate IV-PSNR [%]		Low BD-Rate IV-PSNR [%]	
	BV Atlas	AV Atlas	BV Atlas	AV Atlas	BV Atlas	AV Atlas	BV Atlas	AV Atlas
Mandatory content								
Painter (NC)	0.1	−0.5	0.2	−0.7	0.2	−0.4	0.6	−0.3
Frog (NC)	−0.2	−0.1	−0.2	−0.2	0.1	0.2	0.1	0.2
Carpark (NC)	−2.4	−0.3	−2.3	−0.5	−2.9	−0.9	−2.6	−0.7
Class.Video (CG)	−1.0	−1.2	−0.6	−1.0	−0.4	−0.8	−0.2	−0.8
Museum (CG)	−1.4	−1.0	−1.4	−1.1	−0.9	−0.6	−0.7	−0.5
Fan (CG)	−6.8	−5.8	−5.6	−5.1	−4.0	−3.1	−3.2	−2.9
Kitchen (CG)	−0.8	−1.8	−0.1	−1.1	−0.4	−1.4	−0.5	−1.4
Chess (CG)	−1.9	−2.6	−1.5	−2.5	−0.5	−1.3	−0.5	−1.5
Group (CG)	−2.4	−2.6	−2.5	−2.4	−0.9	−1.3	−1.2	−1.4
Average	**−1.9**	**−1.8**	**−1.6**	**−1.6**	**−1.1**	**−1.1**	**−0.9**	**−1.0**
Optional content								
Fencing (NC)	0.6	0.3	−0.1	−0.4	0.4	0.1	−0.1	−0.3
Hall (NC)	−0.8	−1.3	−1.3	−1.3	−0.4	−1.0	−0.9	−1.1
Street (NC)	−0.5	0.5	−0.9	−0.2	−1.2	−0.1	−1.4	−0.6
Mirror (NC)	−0.8	−0.9	−0.7	−0.9	−0.3	−0.4	−0.3	−0.5
ChessPieces (CG)	−3.1	−3.9	−1.5	−2.7	−0.8	−1.9	−0.9	−2.3
Hijack (CG)	−1.1	−1.7	−0.9	−2.1	−0.7	−1.4	−0.8	−1.9
Cadillac (CG)	−1.1	−0.8	−1.9	−1.7	−1.0	−0.8	−1.4	−1.2
Average	**−1.0**	**−1.1**	**−1.0**	**−1.3**	**−0.6**	**−0.8**	**−0.8**	**−1.1**

color component. Though some structures may be more efficiently recovered using SCC tools, we do not see a general benefit of SCC tools for the usage of texture atlases.

12.4.3.2 Depth atlas coding

The SCC results related to depth atlas coding are shown in Table 12.10 for IBC and BDPCM and in Table 12.11 for PLT additionally. In the case of BV atlases, similar constraints for IBC are given as for texture atlases. However, it is much simpler to find matching structures in the depth domain than in the texture domain. Furthermore, the performance of SCC tools is larger for depth AV atlases. Though variations of colors make the coding of textures more challenging, this is not the case for depth maps. Consequently, AV as well as BV atlases can be efficiently coded using SCC tools. In comparison to the performance for texture atlases, we see a huge benefit of utilizing the

Table 12.9 IBC+BDPCM+PLT texture atlas results.

Sequence	High BD-Rate PSNR [%]		Low BD-Rate PSNR [%]		High BD-Rate IV-PSNR [%]		Low BD-Rate IV-PSNR [%]	
	BV Atlas	AV Atlas	BV Atlas	AV Atlas	BV Atlas	AV Atlas	BV Atlas	AV Atlas
Mandatory content								
Painter (NC)	0.1	−1.2	0.2	−1.3	5.8	4.0	5.5	3.3
Frog (NC)	−0.3	−0.5	−0.3	−0.6	5.7	5.1	6.0	5.3
Carpark (NC)	−2.7	−0.5	−2.9	−0.8	1.8	3.9	2.7	4.2
Class.Video (CG)	−0.3	−1.6	−0.0	−1.1	7.6	3.1	6.3	2.9
Museum (CG)	−1.7	−1.7	−1.7	−1.5	5.3	4.3	5.5	4.3
Fan (CG)	−27.9	−26.2	−20.9	−20.2	−18.2	−16.8	−10.7	−10.1
Kitchen (CG)	0.9	−1.4	−0.6	−2.5	6.5	2.9	6.9	2.7
Chess (CG)	−3.7	−4.7	−3.0	−4.5	11.3	8.9	10.6	7.6
Group (CG)	−6.2	−6.0	−6.9	−6.3	4.9	3.2	6.5	4.1
Average	**−4.6**	**−4.9**	**−4.0**	**−4.3**	**3.4**	**2.1**	**4.4**	**2.7**
Optional content								
Fencing (NC)	−0.5	−0.6	−0.1	−0.7	5.0	4.5	5.8	5.0
Hall (NC)	0.3	−0.2	−0.9	−1.6	2.9	2.5	3.0	1.9
Street (NC)	−0.5	1.9	−1.1	0.1	3.1	4.8	3.9	4.3
Mirror (NC)	−1.3	−1.8	−1.0	−1.4	2.2	1.5	2.3	1.7
ChessPieces (CG)	−4.0	−6.0	−3.4	−6.0	11.8	7.8	8.5	5.1
Hijack (CG)	−1.4	−2.7	−1.1	−3.0	2.5	0.8	2.4	0.7
Cadillac (CG)	−1.4	−0.6	−1.4	−0.4	−1.0	−0.2	−1.0	−0.1
Average	**−1.3**	**−1.4**	**−1.3**	**−1.8**	**3.8**	**3.1**	**3.6**	**2.6**

SCC tools for the coding of depth atlases. The same holds for PLT, as significant coding gain is observed over IBC+BDPCM. An example is shown in Fig. 12.9, which shows that structures of the depth are much better preserved using SCC tools. Consequently, we see a general benefit of SCC tools regarding depth atlas coding. In cases of concerns related to complexity, these tools should be prioritized for the coding of depth atlases instead of texture atlases.

12.5. Conclusion

This chapter presents the MPEG immersive video standard, released in July 2021 by the ISO/IEC MPEG. This new codec enables immersive video services, where natural or computer-generated content captured by real or virtual cameras is processed and transmitted to a client. Its goal is to enable the viewing of a scene with 6 degrees of

Figure 12.9 Details from the compressed atlases of the Fan sequence, matching bitrate: a) texture patch atlas; b) depth patch atlas. First row: source view; second row: cropped source; third row: encoded with VTM; fourth row: encoded with VTM and SCC tools. The blue block highlights an example of color change if SCC tools are used.

freedom, with orientations and view positions varying inside a limited viewing space. After describing the main tools and features of the MIV standard, three different MIV profiles are detailed, and their coding efficiency is assessed under regular common test conditions.

Table 12.10 IBC+BDPCM depth atlas results.

Sequence	High BD-Rate PSNR [%]		Low BD-Rate PSNR [%]		High BD-Rate IV-PSNR [%]		Low BD-Rate IV-PSNR [%]	
	BV Atlas	AV Atlas	BV Atlas	AV Atlas	BV Atlas	AV Atlas	BV Atlas	AV Atlas
Mandatory content								
Painter (NC)	-2.8	-3.1	-2.2	-2.5	-2.8	-3.2	-1.8	-2.2
Frog (NC)	-1.9	-2.5	-1.7	-2.3	-1.7	-2.4	-1.5	-2.2
Carpark (NC)	-2.3	-2.9	-1.8	-2.4	-2.6	-3.2	-1.9	-2.6
Class.Video (CG)	-15.7	-19.0	-12.4	-16.7	-15.8	-19.2	-13.2	-17.2
Museum (CG)	-4.9	-7.6	-4.0	-6.7	-4.9	-7.7	-3.8	-6.6
Fan (CG)	-10.9	-9.6	-10.2	-8.8	-10.1	-8.9	-9.4	-8.0
Kitchen (CG)	-8.7	-12.1	-7.5	-11.4	-8.8	-12.0	-7.6	-11.5
Chess (CG)	-8.9	-11.9	-7.7	-10.9	-8.6	-11.6	-7.6	-10.8
Group (CG)	-7.5	-8.5	-6.2	-7.7	-7.2	-8.2	-6.2	-7.6
Average	**-7.1**	**-8.6**	**-6.0**	**-7.7**	**-6.9**	**-8.5**	**-5.9**	**-7.6**
Optional content								
Fencing (NC)	-1.8	-2.5	-1.9	-2.5	-1.9	-2.6	-1.9	-2.5
Hall (NC)	-1.4	-2.2	-1.4	-2.3	-1.3	-2.0	-1.1	-2.0
Street (NC)	-1.3	-1.3	-1.4	-1.6	-1.8	-1.7	-1.7	-1.8
Mirror (NC)	-3.3	-4.2	-2.9	-3.8	-3.0	-4.1	-2.8	-3.7
ChessPieces (CG)	-8.3	-12.6	-6.2	-10.7	-7.9	-12.2	-6.4	-10.9
Hijack (CG)	-5.6	-7.4	-4.5	-6.3	-5.5	-7.3	-4.5	-6.3
Cadillac (CG)	-5.9	-6.5	-5.9	-6.3	-5.9	-6.5	-5.6	-6.1
Average	**-3.9**	**-5.2**	**-3.5**	**-4.8**	**-3.9**	**-5.2**	**-3.4**	**-4.8**

MIV generates atlases that contain the relevant information for adequate rendering of any viewpoint on the client-side. Advantageously, the standard allows encoding these atlases with any legacy 2D codec. This chapter includes the very first study on this major feature of MIV. The results of encoding MIV atlases with VVC, AV1, and AVS3 are reported, and the MIV agnosticism to the 2D codec is confirmed through experimental results.

It is further investigated whether the coding of atlases with VVC can take advantage of three coding tools designed for screen content coding: intra block copy, BDPCM, and palette mode. Their individual impact is assessed for different components of MIV atlases, texture or depth, and basic or additional views, to provide hints towards encoder optimizations for practical MIV implementations.

Table 12.11 IBC+BDPCM+PLT depth atlas results.

Sequence	High BD-Rate PSNR [%]		Low BD-Rate PSNR [%]		High BD-Rate IV-PSNR [%]		Low BD-Rate IV-PSNR [%]	
	BV Atlas	AV Atlas	BV Atlas	AV Atlas	BV Atlas	AV Atlas	BV Atlas	AV Atlas
Mandatory content								
Painter (NC)	-2.9	-5.3	-2.1	-4.8	0.7	-2.5	2.0	-1.6
Frog (NC)	-3.7	-5.7	-3.3	-5.6	-0.5	-3.4	-0.1	-3.1
Carpark (NC)	-3.9	-5.5	-3.2	-4.7	-2.0	-3.9	-0.8	-2.6
Class.Video (CG)	-17.3	-24.7	-14.1	-21.6	-15.6	-24.3	-13.2	-21.5
Museum (CG)	-5.6	-9.8	-4.4	-8.8	-4.4	-8.9	-3.0	-7.7
Fan (CG)	-23.2	-27.0	-19.6	-22.8	-20.2	-24.7	-16.0	-19.9
Kitchen (CG)	-8.9	-15.7	-8.4	-15.6	-7.5	-14.3	-6.0	-14.0
Chess (CG)	-11.2	-15.4	-10.1	-14.6	-7.7	-12.3	-7.1	-11.8
Group (CG)	-9.1	-11.2	-8.3	-10.6	-6.9	-9.0	-5.9	-8.2
Average	**-9.5**	**-13.4**	**-8.2**	**-12.1**	**-7.1**	**-11.5**	**-5.6**	**-10.0**
Optional content								
Fencing (NC)	-2.7	-4.2	-2.5	-4.0	-0.3	-1.9	0.4	-1.4
Hall (NC)	-0.6	-2.0	-1.0	-2.6	1.3	-0.2	2.7	0.6
Street (NC)	-1.4	-2.4	-1.7	-2.8	0.6	-0.8	1.6	-0.4
Mirror (NC)	-5.5	-7.7	-4.7	-7.0	-4.3	-6.9	-3.7	-6.1
ChessPieces (CG)	-10.8	-16.3	-9.0	-14.9	-6.7	-12.5	-5.8	-11.9
Hijack (CG)	-7.3	-11.1	-5.9	-9.5	-6.6	-10.4	-5.2	-8.9
Cadillac (CG)	-4.4	-4.3	-4.0	-4.1	-4.3	-4.2	-3.8	-4.0
Average	**-4.7**	**-6.9**	**-4.1**	**-6.4**	**-2.9**	**-5.3**	**-2.0**	**-4.6**

References

[1] J.M. Boyce, R. Doré, A. Dziembowski, J. Fleureau, J. Jung, B. Kroon, B. Salahieh, V.K.M. Vadakital, L. Yu, MPEG immersive video coding standard, Proceedings of the IEEE 109 (9) (2021) 1521–1536, https://doi.org/10.1109/JPROC.2021.3062590.

[2] Text of ISO/IEC FDIS 23090-12 MPEG Immersive Video, ISO/IEC JTC1/SC29/WG4 MPEG2021/ N00111, Jul. 2021.

[3] G. Tech, Y. Chen, K. Müller, J.-R. Ohm, A. Vetro, Y.-K. Wang, Overview of the multiview and 3D extensions of high efficiency video coding, IEEE Transactions on Circuits and Systems for Video Technology 26 (1) (2016) 35–49, https://doi.org/10.1109/TCSVT.2015.2477935.

[4] P. Boissonade, J. Jung, [mpeg-i visual] proposition of new sequences for windowed-6dof experiments on compression, synthesis, and depth estimation, ISO/IEC JTC1/SC29/WG11 MPEG2018/m43318, Jul. 2018.

[5] Test Model 10 for MPEG Immersive Video, ISO/IEC JTC1/SC29/WG4 MPEG2021/ N0112, Jul. 2021.

[6] J. Jung, B. Kroon, Common Test Conditions for MPEG Immersive Video, ISO/IEC JTC 1/SC 29/WG 04 N0113, Jul. 2021.

[7] K. Müller, A. Vetro, Common Test Conditions of 3DV Core Experiments, JCTVC ITU-T SG16, Doc. JCT3V-G1100, Feb. 2020.

[8] T. Nguyen, X. Xu, F. Henry, R.-L. Liao, M.G. Sarwer, M. Karczewicz, Y.-H. Chao, J. Xu, S. Liu, D. Marpe, G.J. Sullivan, Overview of the screen content support in VVC: applications, coding tools, and performance, IEEE Transactions on Circuits and Systems for Video Technology 31 (10) (2021) 3801–3817, https://doi.org/10.1109/TCSVT.2021.3074312.

[9] T. Zhou, R. Tucker, J. Flynn, G. Fyffe, N. Snavely, Stereo magnification: learning view synthesis using multiplane images, arXiv:1805.09817, 2018.

[10] B. Mildenhall, P.P. Srinivasan, R. Ortiz-Cayon, N.K. Kalantari, R. Ramamoorthi, R. Ng, A. Kar, Local light field fusion: practical view synthesis with prescriptive sampling guidelines, ACM Transactions on Graphics 38 (4) (Jul. 2019), https://doi.org/10.1145/3306346.3322980.

[11] J. Navarro, N. Sabater, Compact and adaptive multiplane images for view synthesis, in: 2021 IEEE International Conference on Image Processing (ICIP), 2021, pp. 3403–3407, https://doi.org/10.1109/ICIP42928.2021.9506403.

[12] J. Fleureau, R. Doré, B. Chupeau, F. Thudor, G. Briand, T. Tapie, MIV CE1-Related - Activation of a transparency attribute and application to MPI encoding, ISO/IEC JTC 1/SC 29/WG 04 MPEG/m55089, Oct. 2020.

[13] P. Garus, J. Jung, T. Maugey, C. Guillemot, Bypassing depth maps transmission for immersive video coding, in: 2019 Picture Coding Symposium (PCS), 2019, pp. 1–5, https://doi.org/10.1109/PCS48520.2019.8954543.

[14] P. Garus, F. Henry, J. Jung, T. Maugey, C. Guillemot, Immersive video coding: should geometry information be transmitted as depth maps?, IEEE Transactions on Circuits and Systems for Video Technology 32 (5) (2022) 3250–3264, https://doi.org/10.1109/TCSVT.2021.3100006.

[15] M. Milovanović, F. Henry, M. Cagnazzo, J. Jung, Patch decoder-side depth estimation in MPEG immersive video, in: ICASSP 2021 - 2021 IEEE International Conference on Acoustics, Speech and Signal Processing (ICASSP), 2021, pp. 1945–1949, https://doi.org/10.1109/ICASSP39728.2021.9414056.

[16] Text of ISO/IEC DIS 23090-5 Visual Volumetric Video-based Coding and Video-based Point Cloud Compression 2nd Edition, ISO/IEC JTC1/SC29/WG7 MPEG2021/ N00188, Jul. 2021.

[17] D. Mieloch, O. Stankiewicz, M. Domanski, Depth map estimation for free-viewpoint television and virtual navigation, IEEE Access 8 (2020) 5760–5776, https://doi.org/10.1109/ACCESS.2019.2963487.

[18] T. Senoh, N. Tetsutani, H. Yasuda, Depth estimation and view synthesis for immersive media, in: 2018 International Conference on 3D Immersion (IC3D), IEEE, Brussels, Belgium, 2018, pp. 1–8, https://doi.org/10.1109/IC3D.2018.8657842.

[19] S. Rogge, D. Bonatto, J. Sancho, R. Salvador, E. Juarez, A. Munteanu, G. Lafruit, MPEG-I depth estimation reference software, in: 2019 International Conference on 3D Immersion (IC3D), IEEE, Brussels, Belgium, 2019, pp. 1–6, https://doi.org/10.1109/IC3D48390.2019.8975995.

[20] S. Fachada, D. Bonatto, A. Schenkel, G. Lafruit, Depth image based view synthesis with multiple reference views for virtual reality, in: 2018 - 3DTV-Conference: The True Vision - Capture, Transmission and Display of 3D Video (3DTV-CON), 2018, pp. 1–4, https://doi.org/10.1109/3DTV.2018.8478484.

[21] The Fraunhofer Versatile Video Encoder (VVenC), https://github.com/fraunhoferhhi/vvenc/, 2019. (Accessed 30 October 2021).

[22] A. Wieckowski, J. Brandenburg, T. Hinz, C. Bartnik, V. George, G. Hege, C. Helmrich, A. Henkel, C. Lehmann, C. Stoffers, I. Zupancic, B. Bross, D. Marpe, VVenC: an open and optimized VVC encoder implementation, in: 2021 IEEE International Conference on Multimedia Expo Workshops (ICMEW), 2021, pp. 1–2, https://doi.org/10.1109/ICMEW53276.2021.9455944.

[23] Versatile Video Coding (VVC), Doc. ITU-T Rec. H.266, ISO/IEC 23090-3, Feb. 2021.

[24] J. Jung, G. Teniou, X. Li, S. Liu, Moving to VVC for MIV CTC anchor, ISO/IEC JTC 1/SC 29/WG 04 M55823, Jan. 2021.

[25] The Fraunhofer Versatile Video Decoder (VVdeC), https://github.com/fraunhoferhhi/vvdec/, 2018. (Accessed 30 October 2021).

[26] G. Bjontegaard, Calculation of average PSNR differences between RD-curves, ITU-T Q.6/16, Doc. VCEG-M33, Apr. 2001.

[27] S. Pateux, J. Jung, An excel add-in for computing Bjontegaard metric and its evolution, ITU-T SG16 Q 6, Doc. VCEG-AE07, Jan. 2007.

[28] A. Dziembowski, M. Domanski, Objective quality metric for immersive video, ISO/IEC JTC 1/SC 29/WG 11 M48093, Jul. 2019.

[29] B. Kroon, Comments on the common test conditions, ISO/IEC JTC 1/SC 29/WG 11 M54362, Jun. 2020.

[30] J. Jung, M. Wien, V. Baroncini, Draft guidelines for remote experts viewing sessions (v2), JVET of ITU-T VCEG and ISO/IEC MPEG, Doc. JVET-X0204, Oct. 2021.

[31] J. Han, B. Li, D. Mukherjee, C.-H. Chiang, A. Grange, C. Chen, H. Su, S. Parker, S. Deng, U. Joshi, Y. Chen, Y. Wang, P. Wilkins, Y. Xu, J. Bankoski, A technical overview of AV1, Proceedings of the IEEE 109 (9) (2021) 1435–1462, https://doi.org/10.1109/JPROC.2021.3058584.

[32] Alliance for Open Media, https://aomedia.org/. (Accessed 30 December 2021).

[33] J. Zhang, C. Jia, M. Lei, S. Wang, S. Ma, W. Gao, Recent development of AVS video coding standard: AVS3, in: 2019 Picture Coding Symposium (PCS), 2019, pp. 1–5, https://doi.org/10.1109/PCS48520.2019.8954503.

[34] Audio and Video Coding Standard Workgroup of China, http://www.avs.org.cn/english/. (Accessed 30 December 2021).

[35] J. Jung, G. Teniou, X. Li, S. Liu, Moving to VVC for MIV CTC anchor, ISO/IEC JTC 1/SC 29/WG 04 MPEG/m55823, Jan. 2021.

[36] J. Samelak, A. Dziembowski, D. Mieloch, M. Domański, M. Wawrzyniak, Efficient immersive video compression using screen content coding, in: 29. International Conference in Central Europe on Computer Graphics, Visualization and Computer Vision, 2021, pp. 197–206, https://doi.org/10.24132/CSRN.2021.3101.22.

[37] M. Abdoli, F. Henry, P. Brault, P. Duhamel, F. Dufaux, Short-distance intra prediction of screen content in versatile video coding (VVC), IEEE Signal Processing Letters 25 (11) (2018) 1690–1694, https://doi.org/10.1109/LSP.2018.2871872.

CHAPTER 13

Point cloud compression

Giuseppe Valenzise[a], Maurice Quach[a], Dong Tian[b], Jiahao Pang[b], and Frédéric Dufaux[a]
[a]Université Paris-Saclay, CNRS, CentraleSupélec, Laboratoire des signaux et systèmes, Gif-sur-Yvette, France
[b]InterDigital, New York, NY, United States

13.1. Introduction

Point clouds (PCs) are an essential data format for the transmission and storage of immersive visual content and 3D visual data. They are employed in a wide spectrum of applications, including virtual reality [10], mixed reality [19], autonomous driving [78], construction [72], cultural heritage [64], etc. Point clouds represent 3D data as a set of points with (x, y, z) coordinates, also referred to as the point cloud *geometry*, and associated *attributes*, such as colors, normals and reflectance. Furthermore, depending on whether the PC includes a temporal dimension, we can further distinguish between *static* and *dynamic* point clouds.

The number of points in a PC can easily range in the order of millions, and can feature complex attributes. As a result, the bitrate required to transmit raw (uncompressed) point clouds **largely exceeds the available bandwidth** in many communication systems. For example, a dynamic point cloud, such as the one depicted in Fig. 13.1(a), contains around one million points per frame, and is acquired at 30 frames per second. The original PC geometry, obtained, e.g., through photogrammetry (i.e., by estimating the disparity of objects across an array or rig of calibrated cameras), is typically represented with a floating point number (32 bits) per coordinate, to which we need to add the color information (typically 8 bits per channel). This results in a required bandwidth without compression of 3.6 Gbps. Another example comes from LiDAR scans (see Fig. 13.1(c)). A typical LiDAR sensor, such as the Velodyne HDL-64,[1] typically used for autonomous driving applications can acquire over 100k points per sweep, yielding 3 billion points per hour, which is a gargantuan quantity of data to process, store, and transmit. These examples show that lossy and lossless **point cloud compression** (PCC) tools are of paramount importance to enable the practical use of point clouds.

---

[1] https://www.mapix.com/lidar-scanner-sensors/velodyne/velodyne-hdl64/.

Immersive Video Technologies
https://doi.org/10.1016/B978-0-32-391755-1.00019-5
357

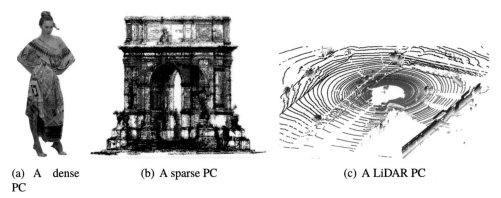

(a) A dense PC   (b) A sparse PC   (c) A LiDAR PC

Figure 13.1 Different kinds of point clouds: (a) is a dense point cloud captured by a camera array, typically used in immersive communication and cinema production [16]; (b) a sparse and noisy point cloud, with spatially varying density [7,23]; (c) a very sparse point cloud dynamically acquired by a LiDAR sensor typically used in autonomous driving [1]. Color indicates elevation from ground; Jiahao Pan.

13.1.1 Challenges in point cloud compression

Coding point clouds poses a number of new challenges compared to traditional image and video coding. The first important difference is the **non-regular sampling** of points in 3D space. In classical signal processing, signals are sampled using a fixed sampling interval (e.g., for the case of audio) or lattice (e.g., the pixel grid). Instead, for point clouds, the sampled locations are part of the signal to be compressed; they define the point cloud geometry. This adds an extra coding cost which, as we will see, can be considerable. Another effect of non-regular sampling is that the point cloud attributes *depend* on the reconstructed geometry. In fact, attributes can be interpreted as a continuous function in 3D space, which is sampled at specific locations during acquisition. After lossy coding of the geometry, the sampling points are moved or suppressed, and the colors need to be re-estimated. We will discuss this phenomenon better in Section 13.3.1.

A second challenge in point cloud compression is represented by the **sparsity** and the **non-uniform density** of points. Sparsity can be due to the acquisition method (e.g., point clouds acquired by camera arrays are typically dense, whereas in LiDAR scans the density of points decreases with the radial distance from the sensor), to occlusions, or other forms of interference and noise. In sparse regions, the correlations between points are weak, which makes it intrinsically difficult to exploit them for prediction or through spatial transforms. Non-uniform density is a consequence of the non-uniform sampling mentioned above. An example of a point cloud with spatially variable density and sparse regions is illustrated in Fig. 13.1(b). We observe that the PC displays "holes" in various regions. Adapting to local PC density is a fundamental requirement of PCC, which is partly solved using tree-based methods.

Finally, a third challenge in point cloud coding is the **lack of structure**. Differently from 2D images and videos, where the concepts of neighborhood and ordering of points are well defined; in the case of point clouds, there is no natural point ordering in general. A notable exception to this general case is LiDAR data, where side information related to the acquisition process is typically available (see Section 13.2.5). The lack of structure requires revisiting classical concepts, such as prediction and transforms. For instance, defining frame-to-frame correspondences between points in dynamic PCs is ill-posed, as the number of points at different time instants might change.

13.2. Basic tools for point cloud compression

Several coding tools have been proposed to solve the challenges mentioned above. In this section, we review some general coding approaches for point clouds, including some of the principles that have been used in standardization (Section 13.3). We leave learning-based methods, which have become popular in the past few years, to a dedicated section (Section 13.4). The interested reader can find more details in numerous literature reviews, which appeared recently, including the taxonomy of PCC methods proposed in [47], the surveys on MPEG PCC standardization in [22] and [58], and the overview on sparse and dense point cloud coding in [11].

13.2.1 2D projections and surface approximations

A simple approach to PCC consists in reducing the dimensionality from 3D to 2D by representing the point cloud using 2D surfaces. There are two ways to implement this principle. One approach, which suits well dense point clouds, assumes that points are sampled from surfaces, i.e., 2D manifolds in 3D space. Therefore the local point distributions can be modeled using surface models, such as planes [18], triangles [17], or Bézier patches [12]. The compression can then be done by fitting the parametric 2D models and transmitting their parameters to the decoder, where points are resampled over these surfaces.

A second strategy based on dimensionality reduction involves projecting the point cloud onto 2D surfaces or planes [29,41,68]. In this way, the compression problem reduces to one of coding 2D images/videos, for which a plethora of methods are available in the literature, including state-of-the-art image/video coding standards. To reconstruct a 3D point cloud, the third dimension needs to be separately coded and transmitted under the form of a *depth map* or *height field* [41]. The projection onto multiple 2D planes is the core idea behind MPEG V-PCC, and we will describe it in more detail in Section 13.3.1.

Finally, notice that the dimensionality could be further reduced to 1D by representing the point cloud as a sequence of points. This approach is specially meaningful when an ordering of the points is known, such as for LiDAR data (see Section 13.2.5). However, in the general case, 1D projections are suboptimal, as correlations between points are exploited only along one dimension. Furthermore, they are difficult to implement, as finding the optimal ordering of points has combinatorial complexity.

13.2.2 Voxelization

Voxelization is a basic tool in point cloud coding. It corresponds to uniformly quantizing the 3D coordinates of points, which are in general real numbers, to a given bit precision. In *voxelized* point clouds, the points lay on a regular 3D lattice, and the geometry is represented through a binary **occupancy** signal over this grid: each voxel is assigned an occupancy bit to indicate whether it contained at least one point. This is in contrast with non-voxelized point clouds, where the 3D coordinates are encoded directly.

Being a form of quantization, voxelization introduces irreversible distortion with respect to the original point cloud. In particular, when the bit depth of voxelization is not sufficiently high to allocate at least a voxel for each original point, geometry information can be lost. PC attributes also need to be resampled over the voxel grid, leading to further distortion. Voxelization can be particularly problematic with *sparse* and variable-density point clouds, since a very high bit depth is necessary to represent them with good fidelity. In addition, since most of the 3D space is empty, voxelization is in general inefficient, as the majority of codewords are unused. We will see in the next section that tree-based space partitioning is an effective way to deal with sparsity.

Finally, notice that voxelization must not necessarily be done in the Cartesian coordinates. For example, it could be applied in spherical or cylindrical coordinates to account for the spatial distribution of the data, e.g., for LiDAR scans [61]. This is essentially equivalent to performing vector quantization in the Cartesian space.

13.2.3 Tree-based partitioning and levels of detail (LoD)

As mentioned before, voxelization alone cannot handle sparse point clouds and empty 3D space efficiently. A more effective solution is using tree-based partitioning, where the 3D space is recursively divided into non-overlapping blocks, which are further partitioned only if they contain at least one point. Commonly used data structures for partitioning include kd-trees [20] or octrees [9,46]. A kd-tree subdivides recursively the space in k-dimensional binary representations. Octrees are a specific kind of kd-trees, where the divisions are dyadic, and are more commonly used for point cloud compression.

An **octree** is the 3D extension of binary trees or quad-trees in 2D. An example of octree partitioning is illustrated in Fig. 13.2. A cubic bounding volume is divided into 8

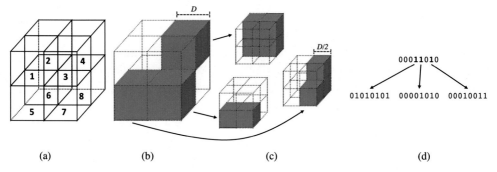

(a)   (b)   (c)   (d)

Figure 13.2 Octree decomposition of a point cloud: (a) a possible scanning order used to index the octants of a bounding volume; (b) the bounding volume is divided into 8 octants. The filled, blue cubes contain at least a point and can be further divided (c), leading to a second level of decomposition. The process is repeated recursively till a desired depth of the tree. The result is an octree (d), where each node is represented with a byte. The octree representation can be also interpreted as a decomposition into different levels of detail (LODs), where the voxel size D is halved at each level to get a finer approximation of the point cloud.

octants, which are ordered according to a certain scanning order (e.g., Fig. 13.2(a)). The occupancy of each octant is signaled with a bit, and the byte representing the sequence of the occupied octants corresponds to a node in the octree (see Fig. 13.2(d)). In other terms, each node in the tree can have 255 possible configurations; the configuration with all zeros is not possible, as this would be an empty node. The position of the bit ones in the node indicates which 3D block is to be further divided. The octree representation is obtained by recursively partitioning the occupied nodes (see Fig. 13.2(b) and (c)) up to a maximum depth given by the voxelization precision. A simple form of lossy compression based on octrees consists in limiting the depth of the tree to be smaller than the maximum possible depth [34]. We will see in Section 13.3.2 that this is also one of the basic mechanism used in G-PCC for lossy coding.

Notice that each level in the octree can be interpreted as a different **level of detail** (LOD) at which the point cloud is represented. In particular, the levels of detail here correspond to a voxel grid with a certain voxel size D, which is halved at each level, increasing the resolution. In addition to octree-based LOD decomposition, other hierarchical structures have been proposed, such as binary trees [73] and quadtrees [28]. These methods also produce a LOD representation of the point cloud, which provides a convenient structure to perform prediction and transforms. These and similar ideas have been employed for modeling entropy contexts and coding attributes in compression schemes, such as G-PCC.

13.2.4 Graph representations

The non-regular nature of point clouds can be well represented by graph structures. The vertexes of the graph correspond to points, and the edges can be inferred in different ways, e.g., based on the Euclidean distance between points, or by approximated distances over the local surfaces. Using a single, fully-connected graph to represent the whole point cloud can be prohibitive for PC sizes typically encountered in practical applications. Therefore points are typically organized as a set of graphs connecting neighboring nodes. Once the graph is built, the attributes can be interpreted as a signal defined over it, and they can be decorrelated using a graph Fourier transform (GFT), which extends the classical Karhunen–Loève transform (KLT) to irregular domains [57]. This approach has been initially proposed in [79], and later extended in several works [13,59,74].

Graphs can be used also for temporal prediction in dynamic point clouds. For instance, Thanou et al. [63] cast motion estimation as a feature-matching problem between consecutive frames, using a spectral graph wavelet descriptor. Alternatively, a spatio-temporal graph can be constructed by using the iterative closest point (ICP) algorithm, and the generalized graph Fourier transform (GGFT) can be employed to perform optimal inter-prediction and transform [75].

Graph transforms are well suited for attribute compression, since the structure of the graph (defined by the geometry) is fixed, and the attributes are variable signals over the graph. Using the same tool for geometry compression is more delicate, as changing the geometry would result in a new graph (not available at the decoder), making this a chicken-and-egg problem. On the other hand, one might consider the occupancy as an additional attribute to code. As this attribute is defined over the whole voxel grid, the dimensionality is too high. This problem can be resolved by encoding a lower resolution point cloud (base layer) and upsampling it via surface reconstruction (upsampled base layer) [14]. This upsampled base layer can then be used as a support, and the original geometry becomes an attribute on this support, similar to residual coding.

13.2.5 Leveraging the acquisition model

In some cases, extra information is available in addition to point cloud geometry and attributes. A relevant example is that of **LiDAR** point clouds, where metadata related to the acquisition, including, e.g., GPS data, timestamps, sensor information, can be accessed at coding time. Fig. 13.3(a) illustrates a typical LiDAR capture system. Points are acquired by a set of laser beams (each with a specific identifier), angularly spaced apart by a certain pitch angle. Each sensor measures the distance of objects in the scene. To capture a complete view of the environment, the sensors rotate across the origin with a certain angular frequency, producing packets of data. The availability of this additional data enables, e.g., to impose an *ordering* over the points, which can be used to code the point cloud using simple delta coding (predictive) schemes [33]. For example, Kohira and Masuda [30] use the GPS timestamps to code point clouds in the context of mobile

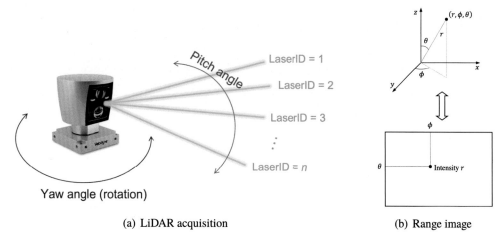

(a) LiDAR acquisition   (b) Range image

Figure 13.3 LiDAR point cloud acquisition employs a set of laser beams (a), which scan the environment circularly to estimate a range (distance) signal. The additional knowledge of the laser beams positions provides valuable side information for coding. In particular, points in spherical coordinates can be mapped to a 2D *range image* (b) reversibly (up to rounding/quantization).

mapping systems. If the sensor makes f rotations per second, a scan line (a full revolution of the sensor) takes $1/f$ seconds. This observation is employed to pack scan lines into a 2D matrix, which is later coded using PNG.

In general, the knowledge of the capturing process allows converting a 3D LiDAR point cloud into a **range image**, as illustrated in Fig. 13.3(b). Specifically, 3D spherical coordinates can be mapped into a 2D image, where the azimuth and elevation angles correspond to rows and columns, and the radial distance is coded as the pixel intensity. In principle, this change of coordinates is reversible (lossless). However, in practice this transformation is often lossy on most LiDAR sensors, albeit some new sensors make it lossless [43] by outputting a range image directly. Range images can be coded using conventional 2D tools, e.g., Ahn et al. [2] compress them with predictive coding in hybrid coordinate systems: spherical, cylindrical, and 3D space. The optimal range prediction mode (direct, via the elevation or using a planar estimation) is chosen with a rate-distortion criterion. Semantic information about the scene can be also used, e.g., by segmenting the range image into ground and objects, prior to predictive and residual coding for compression [62].

LiDAR point cloud packets can be directly compressed in some cases. The point cloud in this format has a natural 2D arrangement with the laser index and rotation (see Fig. 13.3(a)). Since LiDAR packets are typically acquired at high frequency, directly compressing them facilitates low-latency coding. Packets can be compressed using image compression techniques [66]. Hybrid approaches are possible where 2D-based coding is combined with temporal prediction in the 3D space, e.g., using simultaneous localization and mapping (SLAM) to predict intermediate frames between anchor frames for dynamic point clouds [67].

In three dimensions, the structure of the LiDAR sensor can be used as a prior for octree coding. Specifically, sensor information, such as the number of lasers, the position and angle, and angular resolution of each laser per frame can be encoded and exploited to improve compression. Only valid voxels, or plausible voxels, according to the acquisition model, must be encoded when the acquisition process is known. This has been implemented as the angular coding mode in G-PCC (see Section 13.3.2).

13.3. MPEG PCC standardization

Due to the increasing diffusion of 3D point clouds, and in response to the demands for an efficient coding solution for immersive applications, point cloud compression has been the object of standardization by the Moving picture experts group (MPEG). Specifically, in 2013 MPEG first considered point clouds as immersive representation for tele-immersive applications. Fig. 13.4 shows a timeline of the MPEG standardization activities on PCC.

In 2017, MPEG issued a call for proposals (CfP) [38] to solicit new coding solutions for PCC, which would be compared with a simple baseline anchor [34] based on the point cloud library (PCL[2]) to determine the most promising technologies to include in a new standard. These proposals were targeting one or more test model categories (TMC):

- TMC1 addressed the coding of static objects and scenes, e.g., for geographic information systems, cultural heritage;
- TMC2 targeted dynamic point clouds for tele-immersive applications, virtual and augmented reality, etc.;
- TMC3 considered dynamically acquired point clouds, such as LiDAR scans for autonomous vehicles, aerial scans, and large-scale fused point clouds.

After an evaluation of the proposals in 2018, TMC1 and TMC3 were fused into a single TMC13 category, since the proposed coding technologies were mainly based on octree coding and compression in the native 3D domain. TMC13 was later continued as **geometry-based PCC (G-PCC)**. On the other hand, the winning coding approach in TMC2 was based on 2D projection principle to leverage existing efficient video codecs, such as HEVC. TMC2 evolved later into **video-based PCC (V-PCC)**.

The two standards V-PCC and G-PCC were finalized in 2020 and 2021, respectively. At the time of this writing, MPEG is working on a second version of G-PCC, which includes advanced coding tools (e.g., scalability, temporal coding). Also, a new

[2] https://pointclouds.org/.

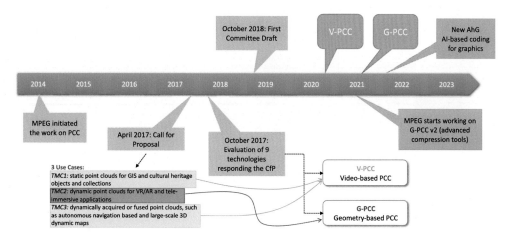

Figure 13.4 The MPEG PCC standardization timeline.

ad hoc group (AhG) on AI-based coding for graphics has been set up to investigate the use of learning-based compression for lossy and lossless point cloud geometry/attributes.

In what follow, we review the two coding standards proposed by MPEG for PCC. It is also worth mentioning that point cloud coding standardization is ongoing as well in the framework of JPEG Pleno [27].

13.3.1 Video-based PCC

V-PCC is based on the 2D projection principle: the 3D geometry and attributes of the point clouds are transformed into a set of 2D patches, which are organized into a sequence of pictures optimized for coding. Fig. 13.5 illustrates a simplified model of the V-PCC codec, which is also referred to as TMC2.

The first step consists in partitioning the 3D point cloud into a set of patches (**patch generation**). The way patches are generated is not normative. As an example, a heuristic approach, adopted in the V-PCC reference implementation [36], first computes the local normals at each point, and associates each point to one of the six faces of a bounding box cube. The association is based on the similarity of the local normals with each of the cube face normals, with the rationale to promote projections that preserve as much as possible the visible surfaces. Points are then clustered based on their normals and plane associations in an iterative process. Three kinds of patches are extracted: the (initial) attribute projections; the geometry projections (which record the distance between the 3D points) and the projection surface in the 3D bounding box; and finally occupancy maps, which indicate which pixels in the 2D projections actually correspond to occupied voxels in the 3D space.

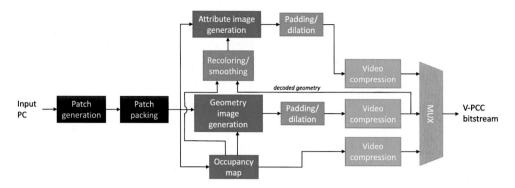

Figure 13.5 A simplified scheme of V-PCC (TMC2).

After the patch generation, **patch packing** aims to place the projected 2D patches into 2D images, and is also outside the scope of the standard, even if many methods have been proposed. The one used in the reference implementation [36] follows an iterative, greedy procedure, in which the patches are first ordered by their size, and they are then assigned to the first available location of the frame in raster-scan order, which guarantees overlap-free insertion. Patches can be rotated or mirrored if necessary. To maintain temporal coherence and improve coding efficiency, patches in different time instants that correspond to the same (or similar) content are placed in similar position across time.

Once the patches have been packed, the attribute, geometry, and occupancy images are **generated**. The conjunction of these images is also referred to as *atlas*. Due to coding, the geometry of the decoded point cloud may differ from the original, i.e., points may have moved or have been suppressed. For this reason, in V-PCC the colors are transferred from the original point cloud to the decoded point cloud in a process called **recoloring**, where the new color of a point is determined based on the nearest point from the original point cloud as well as a neighborhood of points around the reconstructed point. An optional attribute smoothing can be also applied on the attributes to reduce the seams artifacts created by the blocking at patch boundaries. This smoothing is performed as a post-processing in the 3D domain to employ the correct neighborhood information.

The packed images are difficult to code, as they are composed by a collage of disjoint patches and contain a significant amount of hard edges and high frequencies. An example of an attribute frame of the sequence *Longdress* is illustrated in Fig. 13.6(a); a similar phenomenon happens for depth and occupancy images. To render the frame more "coding friendly," the texture and geometry packed images are filtered to fill the discontinuities between patches and smooth the edges, while preserving the contours of objects. Several approaches for **padding** attributes/texture and geometry have been

(a) Packed attribute image   (b) Attribute image after padding

Figure 13.6 Example of attribute image padding in V-PCC. Since the attributes are projected on separated 2D patches, the packed attribute image contains many edges and
empty spaces, which would increase the coding bitrate. Through padding, these artificial
high-frequencies are reduced, while maintaining the original contours and making reconstruction possible.

proposed. For instance, one approach for texture padding available in the reference
G-PCC implementation employs a multi-resolution guided filtering for the texture
image [22]. This results in a smoother image to code, as shown in Fig. 13.6(b). For geometry, the empty space between patches is filled using a padding function to generate
a piece-wise smooth image easier to code, e.g., using directional spatial prediction in
HEVC. This process is also called **geometry dilation**.

Once the atlas images have been constructed and padded, they undergo **video
compression**. In the current V-PCC, the HEVC video compression standard is used;
however, the same architecture would work if more recent standards, such as VVC are
employed. The occupancy maps are coded using the lossless mode of the codec. To
adapt the bitrate, the occupancy images can be packed with a block size bigger than
one pixel, which corresponds to spatial downsampling. The individual bitstreams of the
atlas are then multiplexed, together with metadata information, such as the position and
orientation of the patches, the block size used in packing, etc., to compose the final
V-PCC bitstream.

13.3.2 Geometry-based PCC

Differently from V-PCC, G-PCC encodes point clouds directly in the 3D domain.
A simplified scheme of the G-PCC codec, also referred to as TMC13, is shown in

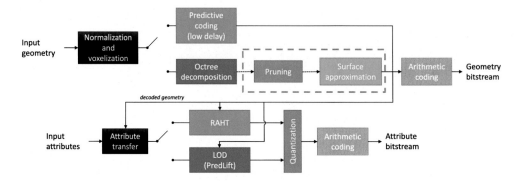

Figure 13.7 A simplified scheme of G-PCC (TMC13).

Fig. 13.7. G-PCC codes separately and with different coding tools the geometry and attributes. However, similarly to V-PCC, attribute coding leverages the *decoded* geometry to avoid drift between original and reconstructed attributes.

13.3.2.1 Geometry coding

G-PCC requires integer coordinates as input. The input point cloud coordinates are first **normalized and voxelized** to a given bit depth. This process consists in first converting the input point cloud coordinates into a frame coordinate system, which essentially defines a 3D bounding box of the point cloud. Next, each of the three dimensions of this bounding box are quantized with a certain number of bits, which corresponds to the voxelization precision of the PC. Notice that voxelization might create duplicate points (due to multiple points quantized to the same coordinates), that are handled by the codec.

G-PCC offers two different encoding modes for geometry: one is based on octrees, with additional modes to optimize the coding performance, whereas the other is a simpler predictive coding mode used for low-latency applications (such as in LiDAR dynamic acquisition), where the points are sequentially traversed, and the value of the current point is predicted based on the previous samples. We present these two modes in more detail in the following.

Octree coding

After voxelization, an **octree decomposition** of the 3D space is carried out, as described in Section 13.2.3. The lossy compression in this scheme is obtained by **pruning** the octree at a certain depth. As a result, in octree coding at low bitrates, the number of reconstructed points is exponentially smaller than in the original point cloud, leading to poor visual quality.

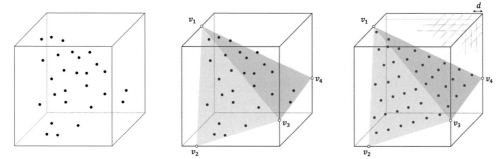

Figure 13.8 Illustration of the trisoup coding principle. Left: At a certain level of decomposition of the octree, a node corresponds to a cube (with size depending on the resolution of the octree) in the 3D space. The points in the cube can be interpreted as samples of a surface in the 3D space. Middle: The surface points are approximated by a set of triangles. The intersections between the triangles and the edges of the cube are coded. Right: The reconstructed surface consists of those voxels (with resolution d) that are intersecting the triangles.

To partially compensate this loss of density, an additional compression tool based on **surface approximation**, known as *triangle soup (Trisoup) coding*, has been proposed.[3] The principle of the trisoup coding is illustrated in Fig. 13.8. At a given level of octree decomposition, a leaf represents a cube in the 3D space, which can be occupied or not. In the trisoup model, the surface corresponding to the points in the cube is represented by its estimated intersections, with the 12 edges of the cube. This results in up to 12 vertices ($v_1, \ldots, v_4$ in the figure) that are entropy coded and transmitted as part of the bitstream. Given the vertices, the surface can be approximated by a non-planar polygon, represented by a set of triangles. The triangulation algorithm is described in [37]. Finally, once the triangles have been determined, they are rasterized to derive a decoded geometry point cloud at a given resolution (voxel size) d by intersecting all possible voxels in the $d \times d \times d$ grid with the triangles (Fig. 13.8, right). This model-based procedure allows the codec to reconstruct piece-wise smooth surfaces with only a limited amount of transmitted information.

G-PCC integrates specific coding tools to optimize the octree coding:

- **Direct coding mode (DCM)**: the octree coding is inefficient when a point cloud presents *isolated points* (which might be due, e.g., to sparse acquisition or noise). In those cases, the 8-bit occupancy code for these points is more expensive than directly coding the coordinates of the point. G-PCC offers mechanisms to infer DCM based on the occupancy of the parent and neighboring nodes of the octree.

---

[3] This tool is not supported in the first G-PCC specification.

- **Planar mode and QT/BT**: when planar surfaces are present in a point cloud (e.g., walls, ground), it is possible to exploit this information and increase the coding efficiency. In particular, by identifying the plane orientation, it is possible to exclude some occupancy configurations and reduce the number of modes. In addition, for some planar configurations, the occupancy division in a node can be expressed through a quadtree (QT) or a binary tree (BT). This enables reducing the number of bits per occupancy symbol from 8 to 4 or 2, respectively, without loss of accuracy.
- **Angular/azimuthal mode**: this mode is used for LiDAR point clouds, for which additional metadata about acquisition, in particular the angular distance between laser beams, are available (see Section 13.2.5). It is applied if the octree node size is sufficiently small to span less than two laser beams. In those cases, it is possible to correct the angular coordinates of a node in such a way that it is coherent with the acquisition constraints, e.g., by projecting it on the closest laser direction. This mode can be used to refine the inferred DCM and the planar mode.

Predictive coding

Predictive coding provides a simpler alternative to octree-based coding, and can be used in low-latency/low-complexity applications, such as the dynamic acquisition scenario targeted in the initial Category 3 content of the MPEG CfP [38]. Specifically, predictive geometry coding assumes that a point ordering in the PC is known, e.g., the LiDAR scanning path. In the low-latency use case, the predictive coding is then applied using a prediction scheme, e.g., delta coding or higher-order filters, on previously decoded data and/or in real time, as data is acquired. In a higher latency scenario, an optimal prediction tree structure can be determined by re-ordering points based on their Morton codes [35], or their polar angles/radius, and by finding the optimal path based on criteria such as the magnitude of the prediction residuals [37].

Arithmetic coding

The final step of geometry coding is context-based arithmetic coding. The contexts depend on the coding tools, e.g., octree, trisoup, or predictive coding. The context-based arithmetic codec is bypassed for DCM, since it is difficult to derive statistical dependencies for isolated points. For octree occupancy, the contexts depend on the *neighbor configuration* (NC), i.e., the occupancy status of the parent node's neighbors. In addition, it is possible to further improve the compression efficiency by exploiting encoded child nodes that are neighbors to the current node. All together, G-PCC offers a large number of contexts, which can be partially reduced by taking into account invariant cases using symmetries and rotations. For a more detailed description of arithmetic coding in G-PCC the reader is referred to the codec description [37].

13.3.2.2 Attribute coding

The current G-PCC supports coding of colors and reflectance attributes. Color attributes are represented using the YCbCr color space, thus a color space conversion is needed if the original color space is different. For reflectance, only one color channel is used. As mentioned above, G-PCC encodes attributes after the decoded geometry is available. When the geometry is coded in a lossy way, the point coordinates after coding might be different from the original input point cloud, and the colors need to be **transferred** to the new geometry. The color transfer follows similar ideas as the recoloring in V-PCC, and since it is performed only at the encoder, it is outside the scope of standardization.

G-PCC offer two kinds of transform/prediction tools for attribute coding: RAHT and LOD.

Region-adaptive hierarchical transform (RAHT)

RAHT is a wavelet-inspired hierarchical spatial transform over the octree, proposed in [15]. The RAHT is applied hierarchically, starting from the leaves of the octree, and producing at each level an approximation and detail coefficient. Similar to wavelet coding, this decomposition compacts the attribute signal energy into a few, low-frequency coefficients, leading to a transform coding gain [26]. For a dense (fully occupied) block of voxels, the RAHT is equivalent to a 3D Haar transform. This Haar transform is modified to take into account empty voxels and the local density of the point cloud. This can be done by modifying the Haar filter coefficients by assigning higher weights to denser nodes, in such a way to adapt to the local density.

Recently, a region-adaptive approach, which builds a hierarchical graph Fourier transform [44], has been considered. An extension of this transform, which adds intra prediction, shows significant gains over the simple RAHT [45].

Level of detail (LOD) generation

A second approach to coding attributes in G-PCC consists in representing the point cloud with multiple levels of detail, adding scalability to the codec. In a first step, the points are separated into several LODs. The LOD can be seen as a progressive approximation of the original point cloud, where each LOD refines the previous one by adding new points. In other terms, the lowest LOD is a subsampling of the PC, whereas the highest LOD contains all the points. The criterion to generate LODs is not specified by the standard, but a typical choice is to use Euclidean distance between points.

Once the LODs are defined, the coding proceeds by applying prediction over neighboring points in the same LOD, or from the previous LOD (the prediction order is

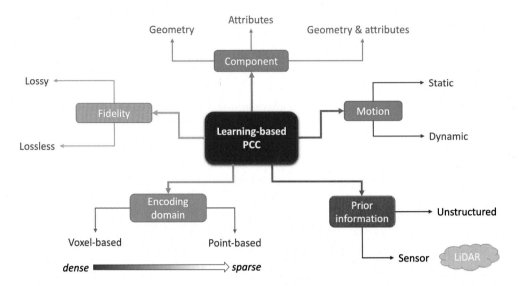

Figure 13.9 A taxonomy of learning-based point cloud compression.

determined by the LOD order). The recursive application of prediction from LOD_j to LOD_{j+1} produces estimations of the residuals between consecutive LODs, which are differentially coded and transmitted to the decoder. This scheme is denoted as **predicting transform** in G-PCC. The predicting transform can be improved by adding a **lifting transform** on top of it. Specifically, the lifting transform introduces an updated operator and an adaptive quantization strategy to take into account the fact that points in lower LODs are used more often, and thus have a higher impact on the coding performance. These predicting and lifting transforms are used jointly in what is called the **PredLift** coding mode in G-PCC. For further details about PredLift, the interested reader can refer to the survey of [22] and the G-PCC codec description [37].

13.4. Learning-based techniques

The recent development of image and video coding methods based on deep neural networks has motivated the study of this kind of techniques for the compression of point clouds. In this section, we propose a taxonomy of learning-based methods for point clouds and review some of the relevant approaches that have been proposed. A more exhaustive survey of recent learning-based PCC methods has been recently proposed in [52].

13.4.1 Taxonomy

Fig. 13.9 proposes a taxonomy of learning-based methods for PCC based on five dimensions.[4] The **fidelity** (lossy/lossless) and **motion** (static/dynamic) dimensions are in common with the 2D image/video coding. On the other hand, the **component** dimension is specific to point clouds. As we have seen for G-PCC and V-PCC, the geometry and attributes are typically coded with separate tools. This is also the case, so far, for the majority of learning-based approaches in PCC, which either target geometry or attribute compression; in the latter case, the geometry is often assumed to be known at the decoder side. Joint geometry and attribute compression has been little studied so far [3].

An important dimension for deep learning-based PCC is the **encoding domain**, which is essentially related to how convolution is carried out in the neural networks to extract significant features to be encoded. Two alternatives have been mainly considered in PCC. One is using *voxel-based* convolution, which basically extends to 3D the conventional 2D convolutions used in convolutional neural networks (CNN). Voxel-based convolution is more suited to dense point clouds, since the receptive field of the convolutional filters almost always includes occupied voxels that can provide useful information. Also, the complexity of voxel-based approaches depends on the dimension of the voxel grid, and might be significantly large when voxelizing sparse or non-uniform-density point clouds (see Section 13.2.2). On the other hand, *point-based* convolutions do not require voxelization and directly operate on point coordinates. A notable example is the PointNet architecture [50], where points are independently processed through an MLP (multilayer perceptron) and the embeddings are pooled by a permutation-invariant function, such as max pooling, to deal with the lack of ordering in the points. A main limitation of PointNet is that it does not consider dependencies between points. Several extensions have been proposed to overcome this problem, e.g., PointNet++ [51] uses a hierarchical approach with set abstraction layers to build a simple graph to extract features from nearest neighbors. Since point-based convolution does not assume any voxelization, it can naturally fit better the coding of sparse point clouds. A third alternative, not reported in Fig. 13.9, consists in using *graph convolutions* [80]. Graph convolution extends conventional 3D convolution to irregular domains, and has been successfully employed in point cloud analysis tasks, e.g., [49]. However, its use in PCC is still to be fully explored.

Finally, a last dimension of the taxonomy involves the availability of **prior information** about the point cloud, in particular related to its acquisition. Most of the PCC literature focuses on *unstructured* point clouds, for which there is no predefined ordering among points. However, as we saw in Section 13.2.5, the case of LiDAR scans is

---

[4] Other taxonomies of PCC algorithms are of course possible, e.g., the one proposed in [47].

different, as additional metadata related to the laser sensors and the scan path are available. This enables developing tailored methods for learning-based LiDAR point cloud coding [65].

In the following, we "sample" this proposed taxonomy and present some methods illustrating relevant work done so far in learning-based PCC.

13.4.2 Deep geometry compression

Inspired by recent advances in learning-based image compression [5,6], deep neural networks have been applied to the compression of point cloud geometry [24,53,55,71].

These schemes mainly rely on **variational auto-encoders**, and in particular the architecture with *hyper-prior* proposed in [6], to learn good data representations for point cloud geometry. To date, the architectures with the most outstanding results are those that assume the point cloud is voxelized to use 3D convolutional neural networks over the voxel grid. A generic scheme of auto-encoder-based geometry coding is shown in Fig. 13.10. The input point cloud geometry is voxelized, as described in Section 13.2.2, and partitioned into nonoverlapping blocks (e.g., with size $64 \times 64 \times 64$ voxels). The partitioning could be done by stopping an octree decomposition at a certain level of detail, which removes the empty space of the point cloud. The voxel values are interpreted as occupancy probabilities (real numbers) and input to an encoder network, which has the goal to produce a latent representation y of the input block. The encoding process is equivalent to computing a (nonlinear) **analysis transform**, using a signal processing terminology.

The latent vector y is quantized, entropy coded, and transmitted to the decoder. To this end, two problems need to be solved. On one hand, the quantizer is a nondifferentiable function, which makes it difficult to use it in end-to-end optimization. To overcome this problem, many approaches have been proposed, with the most commonly used being replacing the quantization noise in the backpropagation with uniform noise [5]. The second problem is how to estimate the symbol probabilities for the arithmetic coder. This can be achieved using a **hyperprior** model to estimate the variance of the quantized latents [6]. The hyperprior model is essentially a variational auto-encoder with a factorized prior, which estimates the variance of a zero-mean multivariate Gaussian latent vector in input. The hyperprior latents are also quantized and entropy coded, and form part of the final bitstream.

At the decoder side, the quantized latent vector $\tilde{y}$ is decoded using the received hyperprior parameters, and input to the decoder network, which implements the **synthesis transform**. The output of the decoder is a set of voxel occupancy probabilities. These continuous quantities are thresholded to obtain a hard occupancy label and reconstruct a voxelized point cloud geometry.

Coding voxelized geometry can be cast as a **classification** problem, i.e., classifying for each voxel, whether it is occupied or not. Thus the auto-encoder can be trained us-

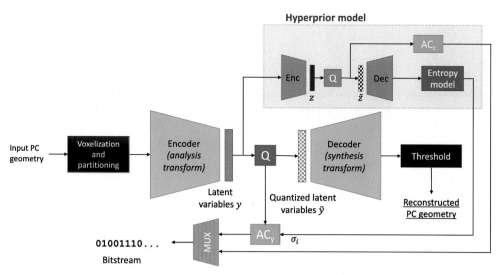

Figure 13.10 General scheme of deep geometry compression based on variational auto-encoders.

ing *binary cross entropy* (BCE) as loss function. In practice, most of the voxels in the point cloud are empty, making the classification problem highly unbalanced. To take into account the class imbalance, Wang et al. [71] propose using weighted binary cross-entropy (WBCE) loss, which balances the classes in BCE using a weight inversely proportional to the class frequency. Most of the empty voxels are easily classified and do not bring much information to learning, which instead would benefit from focusing on hard samples to classify. Quach et al. [53] propose to use a *focal loss* [32] to assign comparatively lower weights to voxels that are already well classified.

The **thresholding** used to reconstruct the point cloud geometry turns out to be critical for coding performance. In fact, a fixed thresholding [53] fails in capturing the variable spatial density of the point cloud. A global threshold may be optimized *per point cloud* [71], or an individual optimal threshold *per block* can be computed at the encoder side and transmitted as side information [55]. An alternative approach consists in training *different models* for different levels of sparsity; the best mode is then selected at the encoder side through rate-distortion optimization and signaled to the decoder [24].

Learning-based point cloud geometry compression has been shown to provide significant coding gains compared to G-PCC, especially for dense point clouds, as shown in Fig. 13.11. In the recent work [69], an improved version of the auto-encoder based codec described above with multi-scale sparse convolutions achieves average rate savings of more than 86% and 77% compared to G-PCC using the D1 and D2 distortion metrics, respectively (see Chapter 18 for a description of these two metrics).

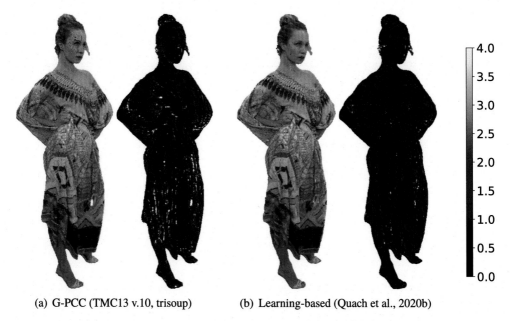

(a) G-PCC (TMC13 v.10, trisoup)   (b) Learning-based (Quach et al., 2020b)

Figure 13.11 Two reconstructed point clouds using a learning-based geometry compression or G-PCC for the *Longdress* point cloud. The reconstructed point clouds are recolored with the original attribute colors for display purposes. The heat maps indicate the D1 errors with respect to the original. The bitrate is about 0.19 bpov for both methods. However, the quality for the learning-based one is significantly higher (D1 PSNR ≈ 70 dB vs. 66 dB). Figure best seen in color.

13.4.3 Generative schemes for lossy compression

Deep neural networks have been used to losslessly code point cloud geometry. If the signal distribution is known, arithmetic coding is typically employed, since it is asymptotically optimal (i.e., it can achieve the entropy rate of the source). Therefore the problem of lossless geometry compression boils down to estimating accurately the geometry probability distribution of the point cloud. Similarly to the lossy geometry compression case discussed above, lossless coding can be carried out after voxelization. Under this assumption, the objective is to estimate accurately the joint probability of voxel binary occupation. Let v_i indicate the occupancy of voxel i. The joint occupancy probability of a block v of $d \times d \times d$ voxels is

$$p(v) = \prod_{i=1}^{d^3} p(v_i | v_{i-1}, v_{i-2}, \ldots, v_1). \tag{13.1}$$

Each term $p(v_i | v_{i-1}, \ldots, v_1)$ above is the probability of the voxel v_i being occupied, given the occupancy of all previous voxels, referred to as a context. The conditional distributions $p(v_i|v_{i-1}, \ldots, v_1)$ can be estimated using a neural network, as proposed in [39]. In practice, since the estimation needs to be causal (only decoded voxels can be used as input to the network), the probability estimation employs masked convolutions [42]. An important difference with respect to lossy geometry compression is that, here, the optimal loss function to use is the binary cross entropy:

$$H(p, \hat{p}) = \mathbb{E}_{v \sim p(v)} \left[\sum_{i=1}^{d^3} - \log \hat{p}(v_i) \right]. \tag{13.2}$$

The cross-entropy represents the bitrate cost to be paid when the approximate distribution $\hat{p}$ is used instead of the true distribution p [21]. More precisely, $H(p, \hat{p}) = H(p) + D_{KL}(p\|\hat{p})$, where D_{KL} denotes the Kullback–Leibler divergence and $H(p)$ is Shannon entropy. Hence, by minimizing (13.2), we indirectly minimize the distance between the estimated conditional distributions and the real data distribution, yielding accurate contexts for arithmetic coding. This approach has been shown to provide rate savings in excess of 35% for dense point clouds compared to G-PCC [39].

The auto-regressive generative model described above can provide accurate context probabilities for arithmetic coding, but entails a high computational cost due to the sequential estimation of the voxel occupancy probabilities. Approximated methods that relax some voxel dependencies to partially parallelize the estimation of voxel occupancies have been proposed, with speedups of about 100x and moderate coding performance losses with respect to the full-complexity model [40].

13.4.4 Point-based methods

In contrast with methods that work on voxels, point-based methods use point coordinates and **multi-layer perceptrons** (MLPs) to extract point features for compression. A notable example of point-based methods is *Octsqueeze* [25]. This method aims at estimating the occupancy probability distributions of nodes in an octree, and is thus specially suited to lossless compression (see previous section). Lossy compression can be obtained by quantizing the geometry prior to lossless compression.

The estimation of node occupancy probabilities follows a similar principle as the voxel-based method presented in Section 13.4.3, with the important difference that the contexts of the entropy model are given by the ancestors of the current node in the octree. More specifically, let x_i denote the 8-bit occupancy symbol of an octree node (see Section 13.2.3), and $\mathbf{x}$ the set of octree nodes. The goal is again to estimate the joint occupancy probability $p(\mathbf{x})$ by minimizing the cross entropy loss:

$$H(p, \hat{p}) = \mathbb{E}_{\mathbf{x} \sim p} \left[- \log_2 \hat{p}(\mathbf{x}) \right], \tag{13.3}$$

where $\hat{p}$ is the estimated distribution. Similarly to the auto-regressive model in Section 13.4.3, the probability $\hat{p}(\mathbf{x})$ is factorized as the product of context conditional probabilities:

$$\hat{p}(\mathbf{x}) = \prod_i \hat{p}_i\left(x_i | \mathbf{x}_{\mathrm{an}}, \mathbf{c}_i\right), \tag{13.4}$$

where $\mathbf{c}_i$ denotes a set of context features of node i, which can include the x, y, z coordinates of the octant, the level in the octree, the parent occupancy, etc.; $\mathbf{x}_{\mathrm{an}}$ is the set of ancestor nodes of the node i. For each octree node x_i, the probability $\hat{p}_i$ is estimated by a cascade of embeddings of a node $\mathbf{h}_i^{(k)}$, with $k = 0, \dots, K - 1$, which are built recursively through a series of MLPs:

$$\mathbf{h}_i^{(0)} = \mathrm{MLP}^{(0)}(\mathbf{c}_i), \tag{13.5}$$

$$\mathbf{h}_i^{(k)} = \mathrm{MLP}^{(k)}\left(\left[\mathbf{h}_i^{(k-1)}, \mathbf{h}_{\mathrm{pa}(i)}^{(k-1)}\right]\right), \tag{13.6}$$

where $\mathbf{h}_{\mathrm{pa}(i)}^{(k-1)}$ is the feature embedding from the parent node of i. The final embedding $\mathbf{h}_i^{(K)}$ is mapped onto an octant occupancy probability $\hat{p}_i$ through a 256-dimensional softmax.

An extension of *Octsqueeze* includes additional contexts to model temporal dependencies [8]. A general limitation of point-based methods for PCC is that they fail to model effectively the local point dependencies, which instead is a key advantage of voxel-based approaches (at least for dense PCs). Hybrid approaches mixing octree and voxel contexts have also been proposed recently [56]. Unfortunately, the comparison of these methods with G-PCC has not been carried out in the standard MPEG common test conditions, which makes it difficult to provide a fair benchmark.

Point processing, under the form of **point convolutions**, has been proposed also for lossy geometry compression in [76], where points are processed using PointNet. The PointNet architecture has proven to be effective for high-level point cloud analysis tasks, such as classification or segmentation. However, its performance for PCC is generally poor, likely because PointNet disregards low-level, local point dependencies, where most of the redundancy is present.

13.4.5 Attribute compression

Recently, deep neural networks have been employed also for the compression of point cloud attributes. Similarly to geometry compression, a simple approach consists in mapping the attributes over a voxel grid and use 3D **voxel convolutions** in an auto-encoder scheme. Alexiou et al. [3] propose joint compression of geometry and attributes defined on a voxel grid. Sparse convolutions are instead used for attribute compression in the recent work [70], where the geometry is assumed to be already available at the decoder side.

Another approach is to use **point-based** neural networks. Sheng et al. [60] propose a point-based auto-encoder architecture for point cloud attribute compression. In par-

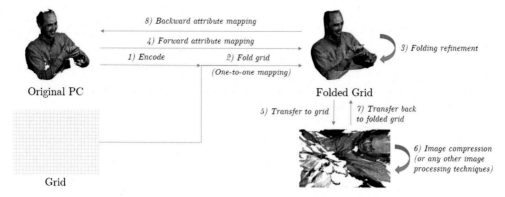

Figure 13.12 Folding-based attribute compression [54]. Attributes are transferred to a 2D grid using a neural network followed by image compression. Figure best seen in colors.

ticular, they propose a second-order point convolution that extends the PointNet++ architecture [51]. As mentioned before, PointNet++ extends PointNet [50] by allowing hierarchical feature aggregation from neighboring points. This scheme is further extended to consider neighbors of neighbors in the aggregation.

A quite different approach has been instead investigated in [54], where the attributes are interpreted as a sampling of a 2D manifold in the 3D space. The method is illustrated in Fig. 13.12. Based on the 2D manifold assumption, a 2D grid can be **folded** on a 3D point cloud (step 2 in the figure), e.g., using the *FoldingNet* model [77]. The mapping between the 2D grid and the 3D points is, in principle, one-to-one; this implies that attributes can be transferred losslessly from the 3D points to the grid (step 5 in the figure), using the inverse folding function. The 2D grid then corresponds to a conventional image, which could be coded using any state-of-the-art image/video codec (step 6 in the figure). In practice, FoldingNet is incapable to provide a perfect geometry folding, and several folding refinements are proposed to overcome this limitation (step 3).

At the time of the writing of this chapter, learning-based attribute compression performance still lags behind the conventional transform/prediction techniques used in G-PCC and described in Section 13.3.2.2.

13.5. Conclusions and perspectives

In this chapter, we have reviewed some basic approaches to code 3D point clouds. In particular, we have presented an overview of the available standard solutions from MPEG, notably geometry-based and video-based PCC. The V-PCC codec has been designed with the specific target of dynamic and dense point cloud compression for applications, such as virtual and augmented reality and telepresence. For this kind of content, V-PCC provides significantly better coding performance than G-PCC in terms of both objective and subjective quality [4,48], thanks to its use of a highly optimized video codec backbone. However, G-PCC is a more flexible and general codec that can be used for other point cloud categories as well, in particular for sparse point clouds, LiDAR scans, and large-scale acquisitions for geographical information systems or cultural heritage. In those cases, G-PCC has been demonstrated to largely improve over previously available 3D coding algorithms, such as the popular Draco codec[5] [11].

Deep point cloud compression is a rapidly evolving domain, and it is likely that several new methods will have been developed at the time this chapter is published. Deep PCC has been strongly inspired by learning-based image compression, in particular by variational auto-encoders and auto-regressive generative models, with some architecture adaptations motivated by handling sparsity, such as the use of sparse convolutions and point-based processing. In recent works, deep learning-based approaches have exhibited outstanding performance on geometry compression and have become comparable to state-of-the-art approaches on attribute compression. However, many challenges remain and **exchange of ideas between traditional and deep learning-based methods** is essential to enable further progress in this field.

A number of research directions are still open in point cloud compression, in particular for learning-based approaches. The **joint coding of attributes and geometry** might bring substantial gains, given the inter-dependence of the two components as well as their interplay in the perception of visual quality. Current deep point cloud compression employs either voxel-based convolutions or point-based processing as learning architectures, which reduces considerably the applicability to sparser point clouds or the ability to capture long-term dependencies among points. To make deep PCC effective on a larger class of real-world uses cases, **graph neural networks** (GNNs) could be a valuable tool as they generalize voxel and sparse convolutions to irregular domains. Nevertheless, compressing the geometry is equivalent to changing the graph topology (and not just the signal defined over it), which does not fit well the current tools used in GNNs. Future work might develop new methodologies to solve these problems and build new coding schemes based on GNNs. The use of more sophisticated **generative models** might also increase significantly the coding performance, at least for specific applications scenarios, as it has been recently shown for 2D video conferencing [31]. Finally, the coding of **dynamic point clouds** has been little studied outside V-PCC, and there is a wide space for improving existing frame-by-frame techniques in G-PCC and deep PCC by considering temporal correlations.

References

[1] S. Agarwal, A. Vora, G. Pandey, W. Williams, H. Kourous, J. McBride, Ford multi-AV seasonal dataset, The International Journal of Robotics Research 39 (2020) 1367–1376.

[5] https://github.com/google/draco.

[2] J. Ahn, K. Lee, J. Sim, C. Kim, Large-scale 3D point cloud compression using adaptive radial distance prediction in hybrid coordinate domains, IEEE Journal of Selected Topics in Signal Processing 9 (2015) 422–434, https://doi.org/10.1109/JSTSP.2014.2370752.

[3] E. Alexiou, K. Tung, T. Ebrahimi, Towards neural network approaches for point cloud compression, in: Applications of Digital Image Processing XLIII, International Society for Optics and Photonics, 2020, p. 1151008, https://doi.org/10.1117/12.2569115.

[4] E. Alexiou, I. Viola, T.M. Borges, T.A. Fonseca, R.L. de Queiroz, T. Ebrahimi, A comprehensive study of the rate-distortion performance in MPEG point cloud compression, APSIPA Transactions on Signal and Information Processing 8 (2019), https://doi.org/10.1017/ATSIP.2019.20, http://www.nowpublishers.com/article/Details/SIP-132.

[5] J. Ballé, V. Laparra, E.P. Simoncelli, End-to-end optimized image compression, in: 2017 5th International Conference on Learning Representations (ICLR), 2017, arXiv:1611.01704.

[6] J. Ballé, D. Minnen, S. Singh, S.J. Hwang, N. Johnston, Variational image compression with a scale hyperprior, arXiv:1802.01436, 2018.

[7] D. Berjón, R. Pagés, F. Morán, Fast feature matching for detailed point cloud generation, in: 2016 Sixth International Conference on Image Processing Theory, Tools and Applications (IPTA), 2016, pp. 1–6, https://doi.org/10.1109/IPTA.2016.7820978.

[8] S. Biswas, J. Liu, K. Wong, S. Wang, R. Urtasun, MuSCLE: multi sweep compression of LiDAR using deep entropy models, Advances in Neural Information Processing Systems 33 (2020).

[9] M. Botsch, A. Wiratanaya, L. Kobbelt, Efficient high quality rendering of point sampled geometry, in: Proceedings of the 13th Eurographics Workshop on Rendering, 2002, pp. 53–64.

[10] G. Bruder, F. Steinicke, A. Nüchter, Poster: Immersive point cloud virtual environments, in: 2014 IEEE Symposium on 3D User Interfaces (3DUI), 2014, pp. 161–162, https://doi.org/10.1109/3DUI.2014.6798870.

[11] C. Cao, M. Preda, V. Zakharchenko, E.S. Jang, T. Zaharia, Compression of sparse and dense dynamic point clouds–methods and standards, Proceedings of the IEEE (2021) 1–22, https://doi.org/10.1109/JPROC.2021.3085957.

[12] R.A. Cohen, M. Krivokuća, C. Feng, Y. Taguchi, H. Ochimizu, D. Tian, A. Vetro, Compression of 3-D point clouds using hierarchical patch fitting, in: 2017 IEEE International Conference on Image Processing (ICIP), 2017, pp. 4033–4037, https://doi.org/10.1109/ICIP.2017.8297040.

[13] R.A. Cohen, D. Tian, A. Vetro, Attribute compression for sparse point clouds using graph transforms, in: 2016 IEEE International Conference on Image Processing (ICIP), 2016, pp. 1374–1378, https://doi.org/10.1109/ICIP.2016.7532583.

[14] P. de Oliveira Rente, C. Brites, J. Ascenso, F. Pereira, Graph-based static 3D point clouds geometry coding, IEEE Transactions on Multimedia 21 (2019) 284–299, https://doi.org/10.1109/TMM.2018.2859591.

[15] R.L. de Queiroz, P.A. Chou, Compression of 3D point clouds using a region-adaptive hierarchical transform, IEEE Transactions on Image Processing 25 (2016) 3947–3956, https://doi.org/10.1109/TIP.2016.2575005.

[16] E. d'Eon, B. Harrison, T. Myers, P.A. Chou, 8i Voxelized Full Bodies - A Voxelized Point Cloud Dataset, in: ISO/IEC JTC1/SC29 Joint WG11/WG1 (MPEG/JPEG) input document WG11M40059/WG1M74006, Geneva, 2017.

[17] A. Dricot, J. Ascenso, Adaptive multi-level triangle soup for geometry-based point cloud coding, in: 2019 IEEE 21st International Workshop on Multimedia Signal Processing (MMSP), 2019, pp. 1–6, https://doi.org/10.1109/MMSP.2019.8901791.

[18] A. Dricot, J. Ascenso, Hybrid octree-plane point cloud geometry coding, in: 2019 27th European Signal Processing Conference (EUSIPCO), 2019, pp. 1–5, https://doi.org/10.23919/EUSIPCO.2019.8902800.

[19] T. Fukuda, Point cloud stream on spatial mixed reality - toward telepresence in architectural field, in: A. Kepczynska-Walczak, S. Bialkowski (Eds.), Computing for a Better Tomorrow - Proceedings of the 36th eCAADe Conference - Volume 2, Lodz University of Technology, Lodz, Poland, 19-21 September 2018, CUMINCAD, 2018, pp. 727–734.

[20] P.M. Gandoin, O. Devillers, Progressive lossless compression of arbitrary simplicial complexes, ACM Transactions on Graphics (TOG) 21 (2002) 372–379.

[21] I. Goodfellow, Y. Bengio, A. Courville, Y. Bengio, Deep Learning, vol. 1, MIT Press, Cambridge, 2016.

[22] D. Graziosi, O. Nakagami, S. Kuma, A. Zaghetto, T. Suzuki, A. Tabatabai, An overview of ongoing point cloud compression standardization activities: Video-based (V-PCC) and geometry-based (G-PCC), APSIPA Transactions on Signal and Information Processing 9 (2020), https://doi.org/10.1017/ATSIP.2020.12.

[23] GTI-UPM, JPEG Pleno Database: GTI-UPM Point-cloud data set, http://plenodb.jpeg.org/pc/upm, 2016.

[24] A. Guarda, N. Rodrigues, F. Pereira, Adaptive deep learning-based point cloud geometry coding, IEEE Journal of Selected Topics in Signal Processing 15 (2) (2021) 415–430, https://doi.org/10.1109/JSTSP.2020.3047520.

[25] L. Huang, S. Wang, K. Wong, J. Liu, R. Urtasun, OctSqueeze: octree-structured entropy model for LiDAR compression, in: 2020 IEEE/CVF Conference on Computer Vision and Pattern Recognition (CVPR), 2020, pp. 1310–1320, https://doi.org/10.1109/CVPR42600.2020.00139.

[26] A.K. Jain, Fundamentals of Digital Image Processing, Prentice-Hall, Inc., 1989.

[27] JPEG, Final Call for Evidence on JPEG Pleno Point Cloud Coding, in: ISO/IEC JTC1/SC29/WG1 JPEG Output Document N88014, 2020.

[28] B. Kathariya, L. Li, Z. Li, J. Alvarez, J. Chen, Scalable point cloud geometry coding with binary tree embedded quadtree, in: IEEE International Conference on Multimedia and Expo (ICME), IEEE, 2018, pp. 1–6.

[29] E.C. Kaya, S. Schwarz, I. Tabus, Refining the bounding volumes for lossless compression of voxelized point clouds geometry, arXiv:2106.00828, 2021.

[30] K. Kohira, H. Masuda, Point-cloud compression for vehicle-based mobile mapping systems using portable network graphics, in: ISPRS Annals of the Photogrammetry, Remote Sensing and Spatial Information Sciences, vol. IV-2/W4, 2017, pp. 99–106, https://doi.org/10.5194/isprs-annals-IV-2-W4-99-2017, https://www.isprs-ann-photogramm-remote-sens-spatial-inf-sci.net/IV-2-W4/99/2017/.

[31] G. Konuko, G. Valenzise, S. Lathuilière, Ultra-low bitrate video conferencing using deep image animation, in: Proc. IEEE Int. Conf. Acoustics, Speech, and Signal Processing, Toronto, Canada, 2021, https://hal.archives-ouvertes.fr/hal-03138045.

[32] T.Y. Lin, P. Goyal, R. Girshick, K. He, P. Dollár, Focal loss for dense object detection, in: 2017 IEEE International Conference on Computer Vision (ICCV), 2017, pp. 2999–3007, https://doi.org/10.1109/ICCV.2017.324.

[33] X. Liu, Y. Wang, Q. Hu, D. Yu, A scan-line-based data compression approach for point clouds: Lossless and effective, in: 2016 4th International Workshop on Earth Observation and Remote Sensing Applications (EORSA), 2016, pp. 270–274, https://doi.org/10.1109/EORSA.2016.7552811.

[34] R. Mekuria, K. Blom, P. Cesar, Design, implementation, and evaluation of a point cloud codec for tele-immersive video, IEEE Transactions on Circuits and Systems for Video Technology 27 (2017) 828–842, https://doi.org/10.1109/TCSVT.2016.2543039.

[35] G.M. Morton, A computer oriented geodetic data base and a new technique in file sequencing, Technical Report, IBM Ltd., Ottawa, Canada, 1966.

[36] MPEG, V-PCC Codec Description, in: ISO/IEC JTC 1/SC 29/WG 7 MPEG Output Document N00100, 2020.

[37] MPEG, G-PCC codec description v12, in: ISO/IEC JTC 1/SC 29/WG 7 MPEG Output Document N00151, 2021.

[38] MPEG 3DG, Call for Proposals for Point Cloud Compression V2. ISO/IEC, JTC 1/SC 29/WG 11 N16763, 2017.

[39] D.T. Nguyen, M. Quach, G. Valenzise, P. Duhamel, Lossless coding of point cloud geometry using a deep generative model, IEEE Transactions on Circuits and Systems for Video Technology 31 (2021) 4617–4629, https://doi.org/10.1109/TCSVT.2021.3100279, https://hal.archives-ouvertes.fr/hal-03321586.

[40] D.T. Nguyen, M. Quach, G. Valenzise, P. Duhamel, Multiscale deep context modeling for lossless point cloud geometry compression, in: IEEE International Conference on Multimedia & Expo Workshops (ICMEW), Shenzhen (virtual), China, 2021, https://hal.archives-ouvertes.fr/hal-03216378.

[41] T. Ochotta, D. Saupe, Compression of Point-Based 3D Models by Shape-Adaptive Wavelet Coding of Multi-Height Fields, The Eurographics Association, 2004, https://doi.org/10.2312/SPBG/SPBG04/103-112.

[42] A. van Oord, N. Kalchbrenner, K. Kavukcuoglu, Pixel recurrent neural networks, in: Proceedings of the 33rd International Conference on Machine Learning, PMLR, 2016, pp. 1747–1756, iSSN: 1938-7228, https://proceedings.mlr.press/v48/oord16.html.

[43] A. Pacala, Lidar as a camera - digital lidar's implications for computer vision, https://ouster.com/blog/the-camera-is-in-the-lidar, 2018.

[44] E. Pavez, B. Girault, A. Ortega, P.A. Chou, Region adaptive graph Fourier transform for 3D point clouds, in: 2020 IEEE International Conference on Image Processing (ICIP), 2020, pp. 2726–2730, https://doi.org/10.1109/ICIP40778.2020.9191183.

[45] E. Pavez, A.L. Souto, R.L.D. Queiroz, A. Ortega, Multi-resolution intra-predictive coding of 3D point cloud attributes, in: 2021 IEEE International Conference on Image Processing (ICIP), 2021, pp. 3393–3397, https://doi.org/10.1109/ICIP42928.2021.9506641.

[46] J. Peng, C.C.J. Kuo, Geometry-guided progressive lossless 3D mesh coding with octree (OT) decomposition, in: ACM SIGGRAPH 2005 Papers, Association for Computing Machinery, New York, NY, USA, 2005, pp. 609–616, https://doi.org/10.1145/1186822.1073237.

[47] F. Pereira, A. Dricot, J. Ascenso, C. Brites, Point cloud coding: A privileged view driven by a classification taxonomy, Signal Processing. Image Communication 85 (2020) 115862, https://doi.org/10.1016/j.image.2020.115862.

[48] S. Perry, H.P. Cong, L.A. da Silva Cruz, J. Prazeres, M. Pereira, A. Pinheiro, E. Dumic, E. Alexiou, T. Ebrahimi, Quality evaluation of static point clouds encoded using MPEG codecs, in: 2020 IEEE International Conference on Image Processing (ICIP), IEEE, Abu Dhabi, United Arab Emirates, 2020, pp. 3428–3432, https://doi.org/10.1109/ICIP40778.2020.9191308, https://ieeexplore.ieee.org/document/9191308/.

[49] F. Pistilli, G. Fracastoro, D. Valsesia, E. Magli, Learning graph-convolutional representations for point cloud denoising, in: European Conference on Computer Vision, Springer, 2020, pp. 103–118.

[50] C. Qi, H. Su, M. Kaichun, L.J. Guibas, PointNet: deep learning on point sets for 3D classification and segmentation, in: 2017 IEEE Conference on Computer Vision and Pattern Recognition (CVPR), 2017, pp. 77–85, https://doi.org/10.1109/CVPR.2017.16.

[51] C.R. Qi, L. Yi, H. Su, L.J. Guibas, PointNet++: deep hierarchical feature learning on point sets in a metric space, arXiv:1706.02413, 2017.

[52] M. Quach, J. Pang, T. Dong, G. Valenzise, F. Dufaux, Survey on deep learning-based point cloud compression, in: Frontiers in Signal Processing, 2022, https://doi.org/10.3389/frsip.2022.846972, https://hal.archives-ouvertes.fr/hal-03579360.

[53] M. Quach, G. Valenzise, F. Dufaux, Learning convolutional transforms for lossy point cloud geometry compression, in: 2019 IEEE International Conference on Image Processing (ICIP), 2019, pp. 4320–4324, https://doi.org/10.1109/ICIP.2019.8803413.

[54] M. Quach, G. Valenzise, F. Dufaux, Folding-based compression of point cloud attributes, in: 2020 IEEE International Conference on Image Processing (ICIP), 2020, pp. 3309–3313, https://doi.org/10.1109/ICIP40778.2020.9191180.

[55] M. Quach, G. Valenzise, F. Dufaux, Improved deep point cloud geometry compression, in: 2020 IEEE 22nd International Workshop on Multimedia Signal Processing (MMSP), 2020, pp. 1–6, https://doi.org/10.1109/MMSP48831.2020.9287077.

[56] Z. Que, G. Lu, D. Xu, VoxelContext-Net: An octree based framework for point cloud compression, arXiv:2105.02158, 2021.

[57] A. Sandryhaila, J.M. Moura, Discrete signal processing on graphs: graph Fourier transform, in: IEEE International Conference on Acoustics, Speech and Signal Processing, IEEE, 2013, pp. 6167–6170.

[58] S. Schwarz, M. Preda, V. Baroncini, M. Budagavi, P. Cesar, P.A. Chou, R.A. Cohen, M. Krivokuca, S. Lasserre, Z. Li, J. Llach, K. Mammou, R. Mekuria, O. Nakagami, E. Siahaan, A. Tabatabai, A.M. Tourapis, V. Zakharchenko, Emerging MPEG standards for point cloud compression, IEEE Journal on Emerging and Selected Topics in Circuits and Systems 9 (1) (2019) 133–148, https://doi.org/10.1109/JETCAS.2018.2885981.

[59] Y. Shao, Z. Zhang, Z. Li, K. Fan, G. Li, Attribute compression of 3D point clouds using Laplacian sparsity optimized graph transform, in: 2017 IEEE Visual Communications and Image Processing (VCIP), IEEE, 2017, pp. 1–4.

[60] X. Sheng, L. Li, D. Liu, Z. Xiong, Z. Li, F. Wu, Deep-PCAC: An end-to-end deep lossy compression framework for point cloud attributes, IEEE Transactions on Multimedia 24 (2022) 2617–2632, https://doi.org/10.1109/TMM.2021.3086711.

[61] S.N. Sridhara, E. Pavez, A. Ortega, Cylindrical coordinates for lidar point cloud compression, in: IEEE International Conference on Image Processing (ICIP), 2021, pp. 3083–3087, iSSN: 2381-8549, https://doi.org/10.1109/ICIP42928.2021.9506448.

[62] X. Sun, H. Ma, Y. Sun, M. Liu, A novel point cloud compression algorithm based on clustering, IEEE Robotics and Automation Letters 4 (2019) 2132–2139, https://doi.org/10.1109/LRA.2019. 2900747.

[63] D. Thanou, P.A. Chou, P. Frossard, Graph-based compression of dynamic 3D point cloud sequences, IEEE Transactions on Image Processing 25 (2016) 1765–1778.

[64] C. Tommasi, C. Achille, F. Fassi, From point cloud to BIM: A modelling challenge in the cultural heritage field, in: ISPRS - International Archives of the Photogrammetry, Remote Sensing and Spatial Information Sciences, vol. XLI-B5, 2016, pp. 429–436, https://doi.org/10.5194/isprsarchives-XLI-B5-429-2016.

[65] C. Tu, E. Takeuchi, A. Carballo, K. Takeda, Point cloud compression for 3D LiDAR sensor using recurrent neural network with residual blocks, in: 2019 International Conference on Robotics and Automation (ICRA), 2019, pp. 3274–3280, https://doi.org/10.1109/ICRA.2019.8794264.

[66] C. Tu, E. Takeuchi, C. Miyajima, K. Takeda, Compressing continuous point cloud data using image compression methods, in: 2016 IEEE 19th International Conference on Intelligent Transportation Systems (ITSC), 2016, pp. 1712–1719, https://doi.org/10.1109/ITSC.2016.7795789.

[67] C. Tu, E. Takeuchi, C. Miyajima, K. Takeda, Continuous point cloud data compression using SLAM based prediction, in: 2017 IEEE Intelligent Vehicles Symposium (IV), 2017, pp. 1744–1751, https://doi.org/10.1109/IVS.2017.7995959.

[68] D.E. Tzamarias, K. Chow, I. Blanes, J. Serra-Sagristà, Compression of point cloud geometry through a single projection, in: 2021 Data Compression Conference (DCC), 2021, pp. 63–72, https://doi.org/10.1109/DCC50243.2021.00014.

[69] J. Wang, D. Ding, Z. Li, X. Feng, C. Cao, Z. Ma, Sparse tensor-based multiscale representation for point cloud geometry compression, arXiv:2111.10633, 2021.

[70] J. Wang, Z. Ma, Sparse tensor-based point cloud attribute compression, arXiv:2204.01023 [eess], 2022.

[71] J. Wang, H. Zhu, H. Liu, Z. Ma, Lossy point cloud geometry compression via end-to-end learning, IEEE Transactions on Circuits and Systems for Video Technology 31 (2021) 4909–4923, https://doi.org/10.1109/TCSVT.2021.3051377.

[72] Q. Wang, M.K. Kim, Applications of 3D point cloud data in the construction industry: A fifteen-year review from 2004 to 2018, Advanced Engineering Informatics 39 (2019) 306–319, https://doi.org/10.1016/j.aei.2019.02.007.

[73] M. Waschbüsch, M.H. Gross, F. Eberhard, E. Lamboray, S. Würmlin, Progressive compression of point-sampled models, in: PBG, 2004, pp. 95–102.

[74] Y. Xu, W. Hu, S. Wang, X. Zhang, S. Wang, S. Ma, W. Gao, Cluster-based point cloud coding with normal weighted graph Fourier transform, in: IEEE International Conference on Acoustics, Speech and Signal Processing (ICASSP), IEEE, 2018, pp. 1753–1757.

[75] Y. Xu, W. Hu, S. Wang, X. Zhang, S. Wang, S. Ma, Z. Guo, W. Gao, Predictive generalized graph Fourier transform for attribute compression of dynamic point clouds, IEEE Transactions on Circuits and Systems for Video Technology 31 (2020) 1968–1982.

[76] W. Yan, Y. shao, S. Liu, T.H. Li, Z. Li, G. Li, Deep AutoEncoder-based lossy geometry compression for point clouds, arXiv:1905.03691, 2019.

[77] Y. Yang, C. Feng, Y. Shen, D. Tian, FoldingNet: point cloud auto-encoder via deep grid deformation, in: 2018 IEEE Conference on Computer Vision and Pattern Recognition (CVPR), 2017, arXiv: 1712.07262.

[78] X. Yue, B. Wu, S.A. Seshia, K. Keutzer, A.L. Sangiovanni-Vincentelli, A LiDAR point cloud generator: from a virtual world to autonomous driving, in: Proceedings of the 2018 ACM on International Conference on Multimedia Retrieval, Association for Computing Machinery, New York, NY, USA, 2018, pp. 458–464, https://doi.org/10.1145/3206025.3206080.

[79] C. Zhang, D. Florêncio, C. Loop, Point cloud attribute compression with graph transform, in: 2014 IEEE International Conference on Image Processing (ICIP), 2014, pp. 2066–2070, https://doi.org/10.1109/ICIP.2014.7025414.

[80] S. Zhang, H. Tong, J. Xu, R. Maciejewski, Graph convolutional networks: a comprehensive review, Computational Social Networks 6 (2019) 1–23.

CHAPTER 14

Coding of dynamic 3D meshes

Jean-Eudes Marvie[a], Maja Krivokuća[a], and Danillo Graziosi[b]

[a]InterDigital INC, Cesson-Sévigné, France
[b]Sony Corporation of America, San Jose, CA, United States

14.1. Introduction

When it comes to *volumetric video coding* (i.e., the compression of three-dimensional (3D) videos obtained from real-life captures of moving subjects), we often see solutions working on *point clouds* or *voxel data*, as discussed in previous chapters. This is due to the fact that the existing devices that are available to capture real-life animated subjects are based on discrete sensors (e.g., cameras, depth sensors, etc.), so a point-based 3D representation is a natural output of such sensors. The signal coming from the acquisition-reconstruction step of these sensors therefore offers a convenient trade-off between the quality of the captured subject (in terms of sufficiently representing its surface details and photometry) and the reconstruction cost, which is relatively low compared to other 3D representations that require additional reconstruction steps. Therefore using the reconstructed signal in this form for its consumption can be an effective approach in the various use cases of *volumetric videos*.

However, 3D *point clouds* are not so convenient to render, especially when targeting real-time playback by leveraging graphics hardware. Indeed, obtaining high-quality renders of point clouds requires accurate *splatting* methods [1] to produce continuous surface projections of the model (which is originally discrete) without holes between the rendered points. Splatting usually requires additional pre-generated information per point, such as the splat radius or stretch vector, normal vector, or other information, which massively increases the cost of storage. Some point cloud rendering approaches also make use of hierarchical representations, such as *octrees* to find point neighborhoods and compute accurate splat stretches at runtime. This reduces the required additional volume of data, but increases the processing complexity for rendering. In the case of *voxel data*, which are equivalent to point clouds aligned within a 3D grid (where each grid element is set to 1 to express the presence of a point or 0 otherwise), rendering can require less additional data than for raw point clouds, thanks to the implicit knowledge of point neighborhoods. However, such grid structures require the storage of points that are regularly organized, and high-resolution grids are needed to accurately represent models that contain many fine (high-frequency) geometric details. Here again, some hierarchical data structures, such as octrees, can be used to lower the data volume, but at the cost of complexity at rendering.

Immersive Video Technologies
https://doi.org/10.1016/B978-0-32-391755-1.00020-1
387

Another approach for 3D object representation is to reconstruct a surface made of triangles, by connecting neighboring points from point clouds (using a *graph* relationship; see Section 14.2), and to encode this additional data, called the *mesh connectivity*, which is used to describe the *topology* of the 3D mesh model.[1] The ensemble of point positions and triangles (described by indices into the array of point positions) is called a *mesh*. The so-connected points are called the *vertices* of the mesh, and any colors associated with the points are called simply the *vertex colors*, or, more generally, the *attributes* of the points. In the context of volumetric video, where real-life captures are used and not computer-generated 3D models, the raw point clouds are usually very dense. Hence, the meshes obtained from such point clouds are also very dense. Throughout this chapter, we will refer to such meshes as *dense meshes with color per vertex*. These meshes can also be generated from *voxel data* by using surface reconstruction algorithms, such as *marching cubes* [2]. In both cases, the mesh is then used at rendering to produce continuous 2D surfaces in the final 2D image that will be displayed on screen for the user, by performing the projection of inter-connected *triangles*, instead of the set of points. Colors per vertex are usually linearly interpolated to produce colors inside the triangle projections. The projection of these triangles can be easily performed by using *ray-tracing* or *rasterization* algorithms. Even though recent 3D graphics hardware is able to execute both of these methods in real-time, the most widely used one is rasterization. By leveraging such modern graphics hardware, which is optimized to work with triangle meshes, it is very easy to render 3D meshes comprising thousands of triangles in real time at 30 frames per second, even on mobile phones. Another strong advantage of using mesh models is the possibility to zoom in at will on the mesh, without introducing holes in the projected (rendered) version of the mesh. There also exist many *multi-resolution representations* of meshes, permitting to adapt the quality on demand at the rendering stage. Meshes are also very convenient to reconstruct normal vectors of the 3D object surface on the fly, whereas point clouds require complex neighborhood searches to do so. In contrast to point clouds, renderers can easily apply lighting to mesh models by using shaders, and generate shadows on and from the meshes, which is important for virtual reality (VR) and augmented reality (AR) applications. More generally, meshes can also be used to model watertight surfaces, which is a useful property for physics simulations. Furthermore, collisions are easy to compute for meshes, which is very convenient for interactions in AR, VR, and game environments (game engines mostly use *textured mesh* representations, explained in the following paragraph).

Even though dense meshes are very good for rendering the original dense signal (captured 3D object) while preserving the captured signal quality, the cost of storage for the vertex positions and connectivity is non-negligible, and such meshes can

---

[1] Note that many different *connectivities* can be used to describe the same surface *topology*, as long as the *genus* of the mesh does not change (see Section 14.2.6).

quickly saturate the renderer with many millions of triangles per second. Preserving such high-resolution models can be of interest in some cases, for instance in the scientific visualization context to render very fine geometric details coming from physics simulations. However, such high geometric precision is usually not needed in most use cases of volumetric videos, such as telepresence or integration within VR or AR environments. In these latter use cases, the geometric precision can be lower, though the photometric precision (the color details, such as the skin pores) must be preserved. Therefore most industrial volumetric video captures today use *textured mesh* representations, instead of *dense meshes with color per vertex* for the 3D content representation. In the case of *textured meshes*, the dense mesh is also usually *simplified*, that is, the original mesh surface is approximated by decimating it to obtain a lower-resolution mesh with fewer triangles, which represents the original surface by *piecewise linear approximation*. The vertex colors of the dense mesh are also projected into a *texture map* made of one or several 2D images. Some mapping coordinates, usually noted *uv*, are assigned to the vertices of the *simplified* mesh to associate the surface of its triangles to different parts of the texture map. At rendering time, the simplified mesh with *uv* coordinates and its associated texture map are used to fill the projected triangles with highly detailed photometry extracted from the texture map. This *textured mesh* representation presents many advantages: for instance, graphics hardware can easily handle meshes with texture maps up to 4 million pixels with good quality filtering using *mipmapping* [3]. The mesh resolution can be set appropriately (at the production or encoding stage) to a desired resolution, without introducing heavy distortions at the photometric level. In terms of compression, the encoding of the image texture can leverage classical 2D image coding schemes, such as PNG (lossless) or JPEG (lossy). Moreover, texture map *sequences* can be encoded using existing 2D video compression schemes, such as HEVC or VVC. For all these reasons, and many others, such as easy editing, the *textured mesh* is the de facto representation for 3D models. All of these advantages can also be leveraged in the context of volumetric video.

Historically, before the recent trend of *sensor*-based acquisition of animated subjects, the only animated meshes that were available were purely synthetic ones, produced using 3D modeling software and eventually human pose scan and motion capture, mostly by gaming, visual effects (VFX), and animated movies industries. Such 3D content, from the computer-generated image (CGI) field, is slightly (but importantly) different from real-life acquisitions. CGI sequences are generally made of a topology, a texture map and *uv* coordinates, which are common to all the frames of the sequence (i.e., static topology, texture map, and *uvs*), with only the vertex positions evolving over time. These *mesh sequences with constant connectivity* are commonly called *animated meshes* (AMs). In contrast, *sensor*-captured 3D sequences are usually made up of positions, topologies, vertex *uvs*, and texture maps, which can all vary for each frame. These *mesh sequences with variable connectivity* are commonly called *time-varying meshes* (TVMs). Note that with TVMs, even the *number of vertices* can vary at each frame, which makes those meshes even more challenging to compress.

The rest of this chapter is organized as follows: After an introduction to some important mesh fundamental concepts in Section 14.2, we present a review of existing techniques for static mesh compression in Section 14.3. We then explain, in Section 14.4, how mesh sequences with *variable connectivity* (i.e., TVMs) can be converted into mesh *sub-sequences* with *constant connectivity* (i.e., sub-sequences of AMs) through *tracking* and *re-meshing*, or directly constructed as sub-sequences of AMs. We review, in this same section, the different AM compression methods currently existing in the literature, and those that have been standardized by international standards organizations. We finally present the existing methods for the coding of TVMs (without any tracking or pre-processing for conversion to AMs) in Section 14.5. Section 14.6 concludes the chapter. In Fig. 14.1, we summarize the different publications related to the compression of AMs and TVMs in the taxonomy that will be used to present these methods in this chapter.

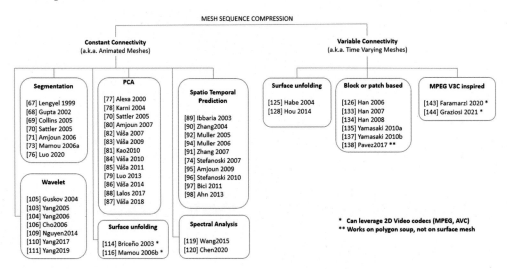

Figure 14.1 A taxonomy of dynamic 3D mesh compression techniques.

14.2. Mesh fundamentals

A 3D *polygonal mesh* model (sometimes also referred to as a *surface mesh*, as it explicitly defines a 3D object's surface, but not its interior volume) consists of a set of planar polygons that are defined by three types of elements: *vertices*, *edges*, and *faces* (or *facets*). The *vertices* constitute a set of points in 3D Euclidean space $\mathbb{R}^3$, which are defined by their (x, y, z) coordinate values, similarly to the *point cloud* representation. These vertices are linked by straight *edges* to form polygonal *faces*. The faces are most commonly triangles, but they can also be other simple convex polygons, e.g., quadrilaterals. Each vertex or face of a mesh may also have additional *attributes* associated with it. These attributes are most commonly (R, G, B) colors (or textures), but there could also be surface normals or other per-vertex or per-face attributes. An example of a triangular surface mesh is shown in Fig. 14.2. Due to the planarity of the mesh faces, a polygonal mesh can only *approximate* a curved (smooth) surface, and a more accurate approximation of this surface can be achieved by increasing the density of vertices and faces in (the corresponding region of) the mesh. Therefore obtaining an increasingly more accurate representation of a smooth surface using a polygonal mesh can easily require a very large amount of data. This is why efficient mesh compression algorithms are crucial to enable the use, storage, and distribution of 3D mesh models. On the other hand, since modern 3D graphics hardware is optimized to deal with triangle mesh representations, such meshes are relatively easy to render and manipulate. Triangle meshes are also easily derived from other surface representations, which makes them a very flexible and portable model type [4]. Another reason for the popularity of triangle meshes (and polygonal meshes in general) is that they are capable of modeling any complex object of arbitrary topology (provided that there is enough computer memory available). For these reasons, the vast majority of 3D models created and used today are triangular surface meshes.

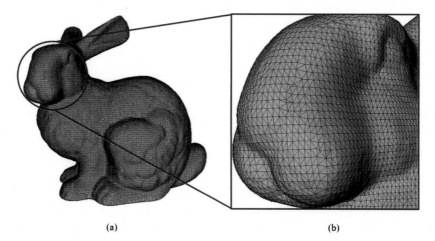

(a)   (b)

Figure 14.2 (a) Triangle mesh representation of the Stanford Bunny; (b) Zoomed-in region of the Bunny's head from (a), to show the triangular faces more clearly.

In the sub-sections below, we introduce some fundamental concepts that are necessary to more fully understand 3D mesh models, and therefore the work on mesh compression that will be presented in later sections in this chapter. Note that the material in the following sub-sections is largely based on the work in [5].

14.2.1 Manifold vs non-manifold meshes

A 3D mesh, being a *boundary* (or *shell*) representation of a solid three–dimensional object, can be viewed as a two–dimensional surface embedded in $\mathbb{R}^3$. The mesh can then be characterized as a *2-manifold* (or simply *manifold*) if every point on its surface has a neighborhood that is *homeomorphic* to an *open disc* of $\mathbb{R}^2$. Two objects are said to be *homeomorphic* if one of the objects can be stretched or bent, without tearing, to form the other object. Intuitively, this means that, at every point on the surface of a 2-manifold, the surface locally looks like the 2D plane. This implies that one edge must be shared by only two faces and not more, and each vertex must have only one ring of connected faces around it. Thus for each vertex, all the faces incident to this vertex must form a *closed fan* (or *disc*). Fig. 14.3 shows a 2D example of such a closed fan (or disc-shaped) neighborhood, along with two examples of non-manifold mesh connectivities.

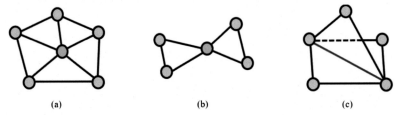

Figure 14.3 Examples of manifold and non-manifold mesh connectivities: (a) manifold (notice the disc-shaped neighborhood around the central, blue vertex); (b) non-manifold, since the neighborhood around the central vertex is not a closed fan; (c) non-manifold, since the edge in red is shared by 3 faces, not 2.

14.2.2 Meshes with and without boundaries

It is possible for a 3D mesh to have one or more *boundaries*, so that it represents an *open* instead of a *closed* mesh. In this case, the mesh can be said to be a *manifold with boundary* if every point on the boundary has a neighborhood that is homeomorphic to a *half-disc* in $\mathbb{R}^2$, while all the points that are not on the boundary have neighborhoods that are homeomorphic to an open disc (as explained in Section 14.2.1, above). A boundary edge is incident to only one face instead of two. For a vertex on the boundary, all the faces incident to this vertex thus form an *open* fan instead of a closed one. Fig. 14.4 illustrates an example of an open fan (or half-disc) neighborhood around a vertex, and it shows an example of a manifold mesh with and without boundaries.

14.2.3 Mesh genus

For a manifold mesh, we can also define its *genus*. The *genus* is the number of "handles" that this mesh has. For example, the Torus mesh in Fig. 14.5(b) has a genus of 1, and

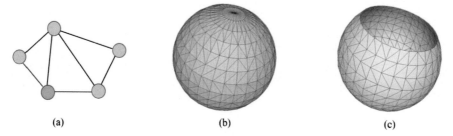

Figure 14.4 (a) Example of a half-disc neighborhood around a vertex (blue) on the boundary of a mesh; the boundary edges are marked in red; (b) Example of a mesh without boundaries (i.e., a closed mesh); (c) Example of a mesh with boundaries (i.e., an open mesh).

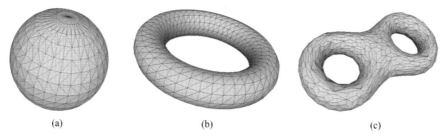

Figure 14.5 Examples of meshes with different topologies: (a) Genus 0; (b) Genus 1; (c) Genus 2.

the Eight mesh in Fig. 14.5(c) has a genus of 2. A mesh that has no handles (i.e., a genus of 0) and no boundary edges is called a *simple mesh*, e.g., see Fig. 14.5(a). A simple mesh is topologically equivalent to a sphere, i.e., it is *homeomorphic* (see Section 14.2.1) to a sphere, as it can be molded into the shape of a sphere, without tearing the mesh's surface.

14.2.4 Types of connectivity in a mesh

We can define the vertex *degree* (or *valence*) for each vertex of a mesh, as the number of edges incident to that vertex. We say that a polygon mesh has a *regular* connectivity if all of its vertices have the same degree (typically 6 for a triangle mesh); an *irregular* connectivity if the vertices have varying degrees; and a *semi-regular* connectivity if all of the vertices have a regular connectivity, except for a few "extraordinary" vertices, which can have an irregular connectivity. Fig. 14.6 shows some examples of regular, irregular, and semi-regular connectivities for a triangular mesh model (note that these examples are shown in 2D for the sake of simplicity, so the vertices on the boundaries appear as if they have fewer edges connected to them than they actually do).

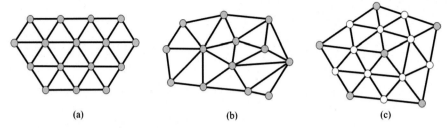

Figure 14.6 Examples of different connectivity types for a triangular mesh: (a) regular connectivity; (b) irregular connectivity; (c) semi-regular connectivity (the "extraordinary" vertices are shown in yellow here, whereas the vertices with regular connectivity are shown in white).

Most 3D mesh models in practice have an *irregular* connectivity, but they are sometimes remeshed to obtain a regular or semi-regular connectivity to facilitate mesh compression.

14.2.5 Representing a mesh as a graph

The *connectivity* of a mesh can be represented as a *planar graph* [6] $G = (V, E)$, where V denotes the set of mesh vertices, and E denotes the set of edges making up the mesh. Each node of the graph represents one vertex, and the links between the different nodes represent the edges that connect these vertices together. In the simplest (and most convenient) case, the connectivity graph is *simple*. This means that (i) the links between the different nodes are *undirected* (i.e., the edges have no orientation), (ii) there are *no loops* around any node (i.e., each edge connects two *different* vertices, not any one vertex to itself), (iii) there are *no multiple links* between any pair of nodes (i.e., there can only be *one edge* connecting any given pair of vertices), and (iv) the graph links are *unweighted* (i.e., the edges have no weights associated with them, as they are all considered equally important). Fig. 14.7 illustrates an example of a simple graph with five nodes, and two examples of non-simple graphs: one with multiple edges, and one with loops. In practice, non-simple graphs could result in degenerate mesh models, e.g., a loop around a vertex (such as in Fig. 14.7(c)) would mean that the edge there is not a straight line (but all edges must be straight lines in a polygonal mesh), and multiple edges between vertices (such as in Fig. 14.7(b)) would create degenerate polygons, as the extra edge would just represent a line segment, rather than a polygon.

Unfortunately, in practice, particularly for meshes generated from scans of real objects (such as in the case of time-varying meshes, covered in Section 14.5), the produced mesh models rarely have *simple* connectivity, and sometimes must be "cleaned up" prior to being processed.

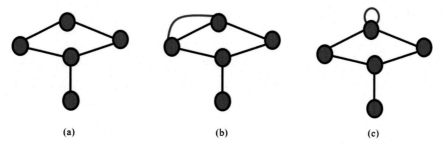

Figure 14.7 (a) Example of a simple graph; (b) example of a non-simple graph with multiple edges between two nodes (the extra edge is shown in red); (c) example of a non-simple graph with a self-loop around one node (shown in red).

A mesh represented as a graph may also have one or more *connected components*. Connected components are essentially sub-meshes, which are disconnected from each other, but are used together to describe a 3D object or scene.

14.2.6 Euler–Poincaré characteristic

Considering a 2-manifold mesh with f faces, v vertices, e edges, genus g, and δ boundary polygons, the Euler–Poincaré characteristic can be used to determine if two 2-manifold meshes are homeomorphic. The Euler–Poincaré characteristic is defined as

$$f + v - e = 2 - 2g - \delta. \tag{14.1}$$

We can say that two 2-manifold meshes *without boundary* ($\delta = 0$) are homeomorphic to each other *if and only if* they have the same Euler–Poincaré characteristic, i.e., if the left-hand side (or right-hand side) of equation (14.1) evaluates to the same value for both meshes. We can see from (14.1) that this is only possible in the case where both meshes have the *same genus g*. Eq. (14.1) also tells us that two 2-manifold meshes *with boundary* ($\delta > 0$) can only be homeomorphic if, in addition to having the same genus g, they also have the *same number of boundary polygons δ*. From these observations, we can conclude that for two 2-manifold meshes to be considered *topologically equivalent*, it does not matter how many vertices, faces, or edges they each have, as long as they have the same number of "handles" (in the case of meshes with genus $g > 0$) and the same number of boundary polygons (for meshes with boundaries). Indeed, this is an intuitive conclusion, because any discrete 3D model of a real-world object, such as a mesh or a point cloud, represents only one possible sampling of the real surface of the 3D object; therefore many such samplings are possible to represent the same surface topology.

In a triangle manifold mesh, we know that each face is constructed from 3 edges. If we then assume that there is a sufficiently large number of edges and triangles and that the ratio of the number of boundary edges (if these exist) to the number of non-boundary edges is negligible [7], we can say that each edge is generally shared by two triangles (as is the case for a manifold mesh without boundary), and thus the number of edges in this mesh is approximately $e \approx 3f/2$. We can then substitute this value for e into the Euler–Poincaré formula in (14.1), to obtain

$$f + v - 3f/2 \approx 2 - 2g - \delta. \tag{14.2}$$

Rearranging (14.2) to solve for v, we get

$$v \approx f/2 + 2 - 2g - \delta. \tag{14.3}$$

Since $f/2$ is much larger than $2 - 2g - \delta$, we can simplify (14.3) to obtain $v \approx f/2$. This tells us that a typical triangle mesh has approximately twice as many faces as vertices. Furthermore, since we have approximated the number of edges as $e \approx 3f/2$, and we also have $v \approx f/2$, this gives us the approximate relationship between the number of edges and the number of vertices as being $e \approx 3v$. From Euler's *degree-sum formula* for graphs [8], we can conclude that the sum of the degrees of all the vertices in a mesh is equal to twice the number of edges in that mesh; thus we have

$$\sum degrees = 2e \approx 6v. \tag{14.4}$$

This tells us that in a typical triangle mesh, the average vertex *valence* (see Section 14.2.4) is 6, which means that, on average, one vertex will be shared by 6 different faces.

14.2.7 Mesh data structures

Several kinds of data structures [9] can be used to represent meshes. Some, such as the *indexed face set*, are more suitable for rendering, whereas some others such as the *half edge*, the *corner table*, or the *adjacency matrix*, are more adapted for geometry processing. A review of these data structures can be found in [9], and Kettner also discusses the different half edge variants in [10]. The half edge and the corner table consume more storage space than the indexed face set, since they store more data to permit efficient traversals of the mesh graph, such as requesting one-ring neighbors of a vertex and other similar operations. Note that both the half edge and corner table cannot represent non-manifold meshes. The adjacency matrix is quite a compact representation, but it does not encode the entire mesh representation and is generally used as an intermediate data structure. Many common file formats for 3D mesh models, such as VRML/X3D [11], OBJ [12], PLY [13], etc., rely on the indexed face set representation.

We know from Section 14.2.6 that in a typical triangle mesh with v vertices and f faces, we can approximate $v \approx f/2$. Thus such a mesh stored as an explicit list of independent triangles, where each triangle is described by the three 32-bit floating-point coordinates for its vertices, requires about $2 \times 3 \times 96v = 576v$ bits. Furthermore, this representation provides no explicit information regarding the adjacency between neighboring triangles or vertices. An indexed face set representation theoretically requires $\log_2(v)$ bits to encode each vertex index, and since we know from Section 14.2.6 that in a typical triangle mesh each vertex will be referenced by 6 different faces on average, this means that around $6v \log_2(v)$ bits will be required for the connectivity data in total. This must be accompanied by a vertex table, which requires a further $96v$ bits, if 32-bit floats are used. As stated in [14], the corner table requires about $12v \log 2(v)$ bits and must be accompanied (as for the indexed face set) by a vertex table, which requires $96v$ bits. However, it was found in [15] that for large, arbitrary surface meshes (e.g., $v > 1000$), the theoretical upper bound for the number of bits required to describe the mesh connectivity is around $3.24v$.

Therefore the indexed face set representation, and the other representations mentioned above, are far from optimal in terms of mesh compression. For this reason, many different mesh compression algorithms have been proposed in the literature to date, which attempt to encode the mesh connectivity and geometry in a more compact manner; some of these compression techniques will be mentioned in the sections that follow.

14.3. Static meshes

The topic of static mesh compression has been extensively studied in the past few decades [7,16,17], and several static mesh compression implementations are freely available [18–21]. Since many of the AM and TVM compression methods (see Sections 14.4 and 14.5) use static mesh compression approaches in parts of their algorithms, in the current section we will briefly review some of the most well known static mesh compression techniques. We will categorize our review into three sub-sections: connectivity compression, vertex (geometry) coding, and standards and software.

14.3.1 Connectivity compression

Connectivity compression methods are usually divided into two categories: *single-rate* and *progressive* compression. *Single rate* methods were traditionally designed to reduce the storage or transmission load between a CPU and a graphics card. These methods encode the entire mesh model (its geometry, connectivity, and attributes) as a whole, so the graphics card cannot render the reconstructed model before the entire bitstream of mesh data has been wholly received. Meanwhile, *progressive* methods are used when a highly detailed mesh is transmitted over bandwidth-restricted channels or consumed by devices with different decoding and rendering capabilities. These methods allow a 3D mesh to be decomposed into a number of different "resolution" or quality levels, so that it can be reconstructed incrementally from coarse to fine levels of detail, or from worse to better quality, by the decoder. In general, *single-rate* compression methods perform a traversal of the mesh elements and identify configurations that can be easily encoded, whereas *progressive* compression methods use mesh simplification tactics to achieve the necessary hierarchical representation.

An efficient way to represent the list of triangles in a mesh is to arrange them into *triangle strips* or *triangle fans*. Instead of three indices per triangle, a triangle strip sends a sequence of triangles connected by one edge and can describe n triangles using $n-2$ indices. In the case of a triangle fan, a series of triangles share a single vertex, and similarly n triangles can be described using $n-2$ indices. Due to their efficiency and simplicity, triangle strips and triangle fans are primitives often used in computer graphics description languages, such as openGL [22] and DirectX [23]. Deering [24], Chow [25], and Bajaj et al. [26] are examples of *single-rate* compression algorithms based on triangle strips and triangle fans.

Meshes can also be represented by graphs such as tree structures. For instance, in a *vertex spanning tree*, the nodes represent the mesh vertices, whereas the branches represent which vertices are connected to each other. In the case of a *face spanning tree*, the nodes correspond to a triangle, and the connected nodes indicate which triangles share an edge. These concepts were used by Taubin and Rossingac [27] in their *topological surgery* algorithm, and by Diaz–Gutierrez et al. [28] in their *hand-and-glove* algorithm.

Some methods use a border line to divide the mesh into two parts: an inner part and an outer part. At first, the face of a single triangle defines the inner part, whereas all the other triangles belong to the outer part. Then triangles are iteratively assimilated by the inner part in a *region-growing* fashion. The growing operations are described by symbols. Once the mesh has been entirely covered by the growing region, processing the symbols in reverse order at the decoding stage reconstructs the connectivity of the mesh. When the region growing operation takes into account the vertices and their respective valences, it is called *valence encoding*, and if the region growing operation takes into account the neighboring triangles, it is known as a *triangle conquest approach*.

The pioneering valence encoding algorithm from Touma and Gotsman [29] is considered to be one of the most efficient *single-rate* mesh compression algorithms, but it is only suitable for oriented manifold 3D meshes. Mamou et al. [30] proposed TFAN, a triangle fan-based compression method that encodes non-manifold and non-oriented triangle meshes by partitioning the mesh into a set of triangle fans. Then, TFAN encodes the configuration of triangle fans using symbols that describe 10 different arrangements and the degree of vertices. In the case of triangle conquest approaches, the *cut-border machine* [31] and *edgebreaker* [32] are examples of coding algorithms that use symbols to indicate the presence of neighboring triangles and also grow the number of traversed triangles. In the *edgebreaker* case, using the valence of the vertices to specify a different entropy context improves the encoding of the symbols [33]. Furthermore, efficient implementations can use data structures, such as the corner table [34].

Usually, *single-rate* compression methods preserve the connectivity of the mesh. But when the lossless criterion is not mandatory, algorithms can use *remeshing* techniques to improve compression performance. The new connectivity is often *regular* and *uniform*, and can therefore achieve higher compression gains, as exemplified in the proposals from Szymczak et al. [35] and Attene et al. [36], among others.

In *progressive* compression methods, a *simplification* operation iteratively modifies the original mesh. The *base mesh*, which results from all the accumulated simplification operations, is then used together with the simplification operations to describe (reconstruct) the original mesh in a progressive manner. By using a reduced set of simplification operations, the resulting coarser mesh can also be used to render a lossy representation of the original mesh. One example of a mesh simplification is the *vertex split* and the *edge collapse* operations used by Hoppe [37] in his *progressive mesh* method. It is also possible to group the vertex split operations together to generate more efficient intermediate representations of the *progressive meshes*, as was done by Taubin et al. [38] in their *progressive forest split* proposal.

Another method for simplifying a triangular mesh and generating a hierarchical representation is to use the *vertex decimation* technique, first introduced by Schroeder et al. [39]. The vertex decimation approach simplifies a mesh by removing a vertex and all its adjacent edges, and then retriangulating the resulting hole with fewer triangles than were originally present in that location. Cohen-Or et al. [40] also used the vertex decimation approach in their patch coloring algorithm for progressive mesh compression.

14.3.2 Vertex (geometry) compression

The mesh vertex coordinates (x, y, z) are usually represented, by default, as IEEE 32-bit floating-point values, but lower resolutions can be used without any visual impairment (for a human observer). A common approach for geometry compression is to first quantize the floating-point values to integers, whereby the quantization resolution is typically 8- to 16-bit. Even though *vector quantization* and *non-uniform quantization* have been used and demonstrated superior performance [5,16], most existing algorithms simply apply *scalar uniform quantization* due to its simplicity and generally adequate performance. Uniform scalar quantization is equivalent to creating a 3D grid inside the bounding box of the mesh, and then snapping the vertices to the nearest grid position to convert the vertex positions to integer values within a chosen integer range.

Following quantization, many methods apply *prediction* strategies to reduce the entropy of the quantized signal, which can then be losslessly encoded with an *entropy encoder*, such as Huffman or an arithmetic encoder [41]. In the case of *single-rate* mesh compression, the mesh traversal produced by coding the connectivity usually influences the prediction, since it imposes a decoding order for the vertices and determines the available reconstructed values. Usually, a combination of previously decoded vertices predicts the current position. *Delta* prediction [24,25] uses the difference between the current and latest decoded vertex in a differential pulse–code modulation (DPCM) fashion. The K previous coefficients of a vertex spanning tree can be used for *linear* prediction [27] of the next vertex position. One of the most popular methods is the *parallelogram* prediction [29]. The latter predicts by using the vertices connected to the predicted position and the vertex opposite to that position, that is, the vertex from the triangle that shares the edge. The prediction is the vertex of a parallelogram formed with the three vertices, which are assumed to be coplanar. To overcome the limitation of coplanar vertices, other methods propose variations of the *parallelogram* prediction by analyzing the angles between triangles [42,43].

Apart from the somewhat standard geometry compression framework of quantization, prediction, and entropy coding, other researchers have proposed alternative methods for geometry compression, which consider more the mesh shape. For example, Karni and Gotsman [44] used the concepts of a graph representation of a mesh, and the Laplacian matrix, for mesh geometry compression. For a mesh with n vertices, the Laplacian matrix (sometimes referred to as the *tutte* Laplacian) is an $n \times n$ matrix with ones on its main diagonal and $-1/deg(v_i)$ in the positions (i, j), where $deg(v_i)$ is the degree of a vertex v_i adjacent to a vertex v_j. The eigenvalues of this matrix can be used as basis functions to obtain a spectral decomposition of the mesh surface, and can thereby be used to compress the mesh geometry. Karni and Gotsman [44] used this principle to propose a *progressive* mesh compression approach for the geometry component. The Laplacian matrix can be generated with the connectivity only, then coefficients resulting from projecting the geometry information onto the eigenvectors of the Laplacian matrix can be sent in a progressive manner (from high to low magnitude) to obtain a progressively better mesh shape reconstruction.

Based on a similar principle of sending coefficients of a transform, Gu et al. [45] proposed *geometry images*, which maps the mesh surface to a regular squared image and uses wavelets to compress and transmit the image. This prioritizes the encoding of the mesh geometry, but the connectivity is converted to a semi-regular mesh. Other algorithms that prioritize geometry over connectivity in a progressive manner use tree structures to create hierarchical representations of the vertices. For instance, Devillers and Gandoin [46] use the *kd-tree* to encode the mesh geometry, whereas Peng and Kuo [47] use an *octree* instead. Both approaches are able to reconstruct the original mesh's connectivity.

Other mesh properties, such as normals and texture coordinates, are usually represented using an array of floating-point values, and similarly to vertex positions, can be encoded by using quantization, prediction, and entropy coding. Since in most cases the connectivity and reconstructed vertex positions are available before compression of other mesh attributes, they can be used when compressing these other mesh properties. For the *parallelogram* prediction of texture coordinates, Isenburg and Snoeyink [48] proposed four different rules considering the presence of texture discontinuities. They can be identified in the mesh connectivity by noticing that one edge for geometry transforms into two edges for the texture connectivity (also known as a *crease* edge). Váša and Brunet [49] also proposed a *parallelogram* prediction modification, but in their case they explicitly use the geometry information to improve the prediction of UV coordinates. Those are two examples of *single-rate* approaches, but *progressive* methods for textured meshes have also been proposed, such as the method from Caillaud et al. [50], which creates the hierarchical representation of the mesh by taking into account the texture seams as well. For per-vertex color compression, Ahn et al. [51] noted that a simple first-order predictor for colors is enough, and they used mapping tables to encode RGB values. In the case of normals, the authors proposed to use a unit sphere representation divided into 6 parts, and to quantize each part into a 4×4 matrix, different from other schemes that usually use the octahedral representation [52] for normal compression. The quantized normals are then predicted by using an average of the normals from vertices in three neighboring triangles.

14.3.3 Standards and software

The Motion picture experts group (MPEG) is well known for producing international ISO standards for video and image compression [53]. In the early 2000s, MPEG published the MPEG-4 standard [54], aimed at compressing multimedia audio-visual scenes, including interactivity with different kinds of multimedia objects, such as synthetic textured meshes. This standard includes static 3D mesh coding tools, such as the *topological surgery* algorithm [27], and several progressive mesh compression tools, for instance the *progressive forest split* [38], the *wavelet subdivision surface* [55], *MeshGrid* [56], and *footprint* [57].

Acknowledging the importance of a trade-off between compression and computational resources, especially with the proliferation of graphics cards in mobile systems, MPEG developed the animation framework extension (AFX), specified in Part 16 of MPEG 4 [58]. The scalable complexity 3D Mesh Compression (SC3DMC) toolset of AFX can choose among three 3D mesh coding techniques: quantization-based compact representation (QBCR), shared vertex analysis (SVA), and triangle FAN (TFAN). Connectivity is not compressed in QBCR, whereas SVA and TFAN apply the proposals from Jang et al. [59] and Mamou et al. [30]. Note that QBCR and SVA maintain the original order of vertices/faces, whereas TFAN reorders them (although one can code the mapping between input and compressed meshes). The geometry is quantized, predicted, and entropy encoded in all three options. Six different predictions are possible (including the *parallelogram* prediction [29]) and five different entropy coding modes may be selected as well. Normals, texture coordinates, color per vertex, and generic attributes can also be encoded, whereby normals are converted to the octahedral representation [50] and texture coordinates are quantized according to the texture map dimension. An open-source and royalty-free implementation of the AFX standard [19] has been included in the glTF, the standard file format for three–dimensional scenes and models from the Khronos group [60].

The glTF standard has also included an extension for mesh compression based on Draco [18], the point cloud and mesh compression tool from Google. Draco has three modes for connectivity compression: a sequential encoder, which encodes the indices directly, the efficient *edgebreaker* algorithm [34], and also an *edgebreaker valence encoding* method [33]. Draco then reorders the vertices and encodes their attributes (geometry, texture coordinates, normals, etc.) following the traditional quantizion, prediction, and entropy encoding steps. For the prediction of vertex positions, Draco can either use the difference from the last decoded position, the *parallelogram* predictor [29], or the *multi-parallelogram* predictor, which uses all the triangular faces opposite to the predictor vertex. For texture coordinates, Draco also includes the *constrained multi-parallelogram* predictor, which explicitly selects which parallelograms to use for prediction by marking the *crease* edges between triangles. For normal coding, Draco uses the octahedral representation [50] and performs prediction by weighting the normals from neighboring triangles by the triangles' areas.

14.4. Constant-connectivity mesh sequences

A so-called *animated mesh* is a sequence of static meshes, where each frame represents the dynamic mesh at a given point in time. The connectivity, topology, and colors of the animated mesh remain constant across all the frames; it is only the geometry (vertex positions) that changes over time. As mentioned in the Introduction of this chapter, such animated meshes are usually computer-generated (not obtained from real-life captures) and are most commonly used in the gaming and film (VFX) industries, but also for medical and scientific visualizations. However, animated meshes are not suited to volumetric video coding, since they do not support varying photometry or topology over time. Nevertheless, we will see in Section 14.4.1 that it is possible to produce or transform some *variable-connectivity mesh sequences* (see Section 14.5) into sub-sequences of meshes with constant connectivity. Once obtained, each sub-sequence (or group of frames) can then be encoded using *animated mesh* compression techniques.

In the current section, we first give a quick overview of possible solutions to obtain *constant-connectivity mesh sequences* from *variable-connectivity mesh sequences*. We then provide a summary of work to date that proposes compression algorithms for constant-connectivity mesh sequences. We will base our presentation of animated mesh compression techniques on the work in [16] from 2015, and extend their taxonomy with more recent publications, using the following categories (see Fig. 14.1): segmentation, principal component analysis (PCA), spatio-temporal prediction, wavelets, surface unfolding, and spectral analysis.

14.4.1 Tracking and re-meshing

At the production stage of real-life volumetric video captures, generating meshes independently for each frame of a mesh sequence produces meshes with variable connectivity. However, to leverage existing AM compression schemes, a consistent connectivity over frames is required. The process of transforming a *variable-connectivity* mesh sequence into a *constant-connectivity* mesh sequence is called mesh *tracking*.

As an example of variable-connectivity mesh sequence conversion into constant-connectivity sequences, Collet et al. [61] present a complete tool chain for acquisition, reconstruction, tracking, and compression. After reconstruction, they obtain a set of frames of variable connectivity. They first subdivide the sequences into sub-sequences of similar topology (recall that different connectivities can define a similar topology). To do so, they compute which frames are the most promising to be used as *keyframes* (i.e., frames whose meshes are well representative of their neighbor frames). They search for frames of higher surface area, of lower *genus* (see Section 14.2.3), and with a higher number of *connected components* (see Section 14.2.5). Once keyframes are found, they use the state-of-the-art non-rigid *iterative closest point* (ICP) algorithm of Li et al. [62] to perform mesh registration, though other approaches [63,64] can be adapted as well. Following this re-meshing, the frames of each sub-sequence have the same connectivity and a stable texture *uv* atlas (i.e., a temporally consistent parameterization). The sub-sequence can then be coded by any AM coding method (in [62] the authors use their own, prediction-based solution). Furthermore, the frame texture atlases are stable over the entire sub-sequence, which leads to higher quality for fixed compression bitrates of the texture stream by using MPEG H.264 or other standard 2D video coding schemes. In [65] Prada et al. extend this tracking method using local re-meshing, to permit tracking over long sequences containing significant deformations or topological changes, which further enhances texture atlas stability. Extracting a spatio-temporally coherent mesh out of a 4D capture is an active area of research, and one can refer to [61–66] for further references.

It should be noted that tracking is a time-consuming process that implies some re-meshing and some texture re-projections, which in turn implies inevitable distortions from the original, non-tracked animated sequence. Thus tracking is better performed at production time during the reconstruction stage, where all the parameters are controlled, rather than at the compression stage. The tracking solution is thus not very practical in the case of a standalone TVM coder. We will see in Section 14.5 other approaches to encode TVMs that do not rely on tracking. But first, let us review the existing AM coding approaches.

14.4.2 Methods based on segmentation

The existing segmentation-based approaches for animated mesh compression consist in partitioning the vertices of the dynamic mesh into groups of vertices, called *clusters*, where each cluster represents a section of the dynamic mesh that has similar movement over time. In 1999, Lengyel proposed the first animated mesh compression algorithm (of all the categories) based on this approach [67]. The clusters in [67] are defined with respect to a reference frame and determined using a heuristic, where a set of seed triangles is chosen at random. The movement of each cluster, estimated by a rigid transformation, is used as a predictor to extrapolate the positions of vertices in the current frame from the reference one. The animation is then encoded using the set of motion parameters for each cluster and the prediction errors associated with each vertex.

Gupta et al. [68] improved the solution in [67] by using the iterative closest point (ICP) algorithm to compute the displacement of the vertices. In their solution, the initial segmentation is based on a topology partitioning algorithm, and is then refined based on some motion coherency criteria. The authors present a compression ratio of 45:1, compared to 27:1 for the Lengyel solution on an animated chicken model.

Later, Collins et al. [69] improved Lengyel's solution by using only rigid transforms without the encoding of residual errors. The authors in [69] introduce a new distortion bound segmentation algorithm based on a weighted least-squares approach that minimizes the number of generated clusters according to the distortion criterion. This solution, however, produces geometric seams between patches, and requires a low-pass filtering of vertex displacements that is performed as a post-processing to attenuate the artifacts.

Sattler et al. [70] also proposed an improved segmentation using clustered vertex trajectories, by integrating a combination of Lloyd's algorithm (also known as Voronoi iteration) and *principal component analysis* (PCA). Each generated cluster is compressed independently using PCA.

Amjoun et al. [71] partitioned mesh vertices into clusters by applying *k-means* clustering [72], where vertex motions can be described by unique 3D affine transforms. The resulting clusters are then encoded using PCA. The algorithm segments the animated mesh into clusters by using a region-growing algorithm, and transforms the original vertex coordinates into the local coordinate frame of their segment. However, the results are seriously dependent on, and affected by, the choice of initial seed vertices.

Mamou et al. [73] also consider a segmentation into almost rigid parts, by performing a hierarchical decimation, which privileges the simplification of neighboring vertices with similar affine motion. The motion of each vertex is then expressed as a weighted linear combination of the cluster motions using a skinning approach adapted from skeletal animation techniques. Motion compensation errors are finally compressed using the *discrete cosine transform* (DCT), which makes the stream spatially scalable if the DCT coefficients are ordered. This approach was later combined with [74] to define the MPEG FAMC [75] standard (see Section 14.4.8).

In [76], Luo et al. make extensive use of a spatio-temporal approach. They first compute an initial temporal cut on the input mesh sequence to obtain a small sub-sequence by detecting the temporal boundary of dynamic behavior. Then, they apply a two-stage vertex clustering on the resulting sub-sequence to classify the vertices into groups with optimal intra-affinities. After that, they perform a temporal segmentation step based on the variations of the principal components within each vertex group. The obtained sub-sequences of clusters are compressed using PCA. They finally perform a lossless compression of the PCA bases and coefficients using ZLib. Their solution generates geometric artifacts at the cluster boundaries, so they generate clusters of a larger size to overlap sibling clusters. They present results ranging from 0.63 to 7 bits per vertex per frame (bpvf) on a range of test models.

14.4.3 Methods based on principal component analysis

Principal component analysis (PCA) methods find a new orthogonal basis to describe the motion of an animated mesh, and achieve compression by using a reduced set of basis eigenvectors. The frames of a mesh sequence are then represented by coefficients obtained from projecting the mesh onto the new (reduced) basis. PCA can be used in two different ways: either by exploiting the temporal correlation of frames and finding the average shape of the sequence (*eigenshapes*), or by exploiting the spatial correlation of the vertices' trajectories and finding the average trajectory (*eigentrajectories*).

Alexa and Muller [77] proposed the first method that applied PCA to obtain the *eigenshapes*. In [77], the vertices of the mesh are arranged in a matrix of size $3v \times f$, where v is the number of vertices, and f is the number of frames. Note that the vertex positions are not the coordinate positions in the corresponding frame, but actually the residual positions after global motion compensation to de-couple the elastic and rigid motion components. By decomposing the matrix using *singular value decomposition* (SVD), the first matrix contains the eigenshapes of the sequence, the second matrix contains the eigenvalues, and the third one contains the coefficients of the frames in the new basis formed by the eigenvectors (i.e., eigenshapes). The animation is compressed by sending the basis vectors for the animation, and the coefficients and global motion estimation per frame. To improve the coding of the coefficients, Karni and Gotsmann [78] proposed a linear predictor based on the *parallelogram* predictor. To better adapt the PCA solution to the motion, Sattler et al. [70] proposed spatial clustering of vertices, whereas Luo et al. [79] proposed temporal clustering of the frames. Amjoun and Straßer [80] also used spatial clustering of vertices, but additionally proposed a rate-distortion allocation by having more eigenvectors at clusters that underwent extreme deformations. A *progressive* animated compression using PCA was also proposed by Kao et al. [81]. With the latter method, the decoder can choose any combination of mesh or motion resolution.

The challenge with PCA methods is that the dimension of the auto-correlation matrix used in the SVD decomposition is dependent on the number of vertices, which can be quite large, usually compared to the sequence of frames that is commonly a couple of seconds long. Furthermore, the PCA eigenvectors need to be precisely encoded, and there is little correlation between them. Therefore Váša and Skala [82] proposed COD-DYAC. This codec uses PCA in the vertex trajectories, instead of their shape, that is, the vertices are arranged in a matrix of size $3f \times v$ instead, which leads to smaller auto-correlation matrices and smaller eigenvectors. The coefficients are then traversed using the *edgebreaker* algorithm, and encoded using the *parallelogram* prediction. Subsequent publications from the same authors [83,84] improved the performance of CODDYAC by compressing the eigentrajectories using motion models and the coefficient predictors by using local neighborhoods. Váša [85] further optimized the mesh traversal, and with that achieved, one of the best performances for CODDYAC. Next, Váša et al. [86,87] used geometric Laplacian and mesh averaging techniques to improve the original COD-DYAC performance, as judged by a perceptual metric.

Even though the compression performance of PCA methods is better than other proposed methods for animated meshes, these are global methods that use *all* the frames to compute the optimal basis. Therefore it is challenging to use PCA in streaming applications. Furthermore, the computation cost of calculating the SVD can be prohibitive as well, for large (dense) mesh models or long sequences. To reduce the computation time of the SVD calculation for both eigentrajectories and eigenshapes, Lalos et al. [88] proposed an efficient method to update the SVD using adaptive orthogonal iterations. They also use intervals of 10 frames, which can be used in low-delay applications, but the compression performance is reduced.

14.4.4 Methods based on spatio-temporal prediction

Due to the fact that the topology of animated mesh sequences is constant over time, the animated vertices generally exhibit strong redundancies and correlations between frames. Differently from global PCA-based methods presented in the previous sub-section, prediction methods for animated mesh compression exploit local coherences, and are thus computationally efficient and more suited for real-time streaming. These methods extend the spatial prediction approaches, such as the parallelogram ones [29,43], to exploit these temporal properties, by either interpolating between spatial or temporal surrounding positions, or by extrapolating from previous frames. Ibarria et al. [89] present two spatio-temporal predictors in their Dynapack framework: extended Lorenzo predictor (ERP) and REPLICA. ERP directly extends the parallelogram method originally introduced by [29] for static mesh compression, whereas REPLICA extends ERP to make it more robust to rotation and scale transformations.

In [90,91], Zhang proposes an alternative approach based on a segmentation method using an octree-based motion representation for each frame. Two consecutive frames are used to generate a small set of motion vectors that represent the motion from the first frame to the other. Quantization and an adaptive arithmetic coder are used to achieve further data reduction. An optimized version of this approach was introduced in [92] by Müller et al. In the solution in [92], called dynamic 3D mesh coder (D3DMC), the authors extract only one representative for a cluster of difference vectors, which provides a significant reduction in the data rate. A *context-adaptive binary arithmetic coder* (CABAC) [93] is finally used to code the representative of the clusters, which have been previously scaled and quantized. Müller et al. [94] later refined their solution with a rate-distortion approach.

Amjoun and Straßer [95] encode delta vectors in local coordinate systems. However, the encoding performance is strongly dependent on the seeds selected for the surface segmentation that they perform.

Stefanoski et al. [74] introduce the decomposition into layers, which are basically mesh levels-of-detail. This approach has become a foundation for several other proposed methods. It was refined by Stefanoski et al. with scalable predictive coding (SPC) in [96], which was the first solution to provide spatio-temporal scalability, and provides an excellent compression ratio as well (between 3.5 and 8 bpvf). The solution in [96] was then further extended by Bici and Akar [97] through novel prediction approaches. Finally, Ahn et al. [98] managed to obtain a 30% gain in performance (compression ratio between 2 and 6 bpvf) compared with SPC, still using the same layered approach.

14.4.5 Methods using wavelets

Wavelet-based mesh compression methods first became popular with the introduction of *subdivision wavelets* by Lounsbery et al. in the mid- to late-1990s [99,100]. In these seminal papers, the authors established a theoretical basis for extending the concept of *multiresolution analysis* (specifically, wavelets) to surfaces of arbitrary topological type, by defining a wavelet-like basis for a mesh surface using the subdivision rules from Loop [101]. The main idea behind subdivision wavelets is to decompose a high-resolution input mesh into a very coarse representation called a *base mesh*, and a set of detail coefficients termed *wavelet coefficients*. At the decoder, the wavelet coefficients can then be used to progressively refine the base mesh at multiple levels of detail (resolution). Because the connectivity of the mesh can be refined in a predictable manner using a set of standard subdivision rules known to both the encoder and decoder, the only connectivity data that needs to be transmitted is the connectivity of the base mesh, which is usually negligible. However, the main restriction with this approach is that the input mesh must have a *semi-regular* connectivity (see Section 14.2.4). This means that the connectivity of the input mesh must be able to be achieved by repeatedly subdividing each face of a coarse base mesh into 4 sub-faces until the resolution of the input mesh is obtained.

Many wavelet-based mesh compression algorithms that exist today are based on a similar principle as the original subdivision wavelets algorithm [99,100]. Since with this technique the mesh connectivity does not need to be encoded separately at each resolution level, the priority of such compression algorithms is on the coding of the mesh *geometry*. Geometry compression is usually achieved by either discarding small, negligible wavelet coefficients at various resolution levels, and/or by quantizing and entropy coding the wavelet coefficients that are chosen for transmission to the decoder. Though subdivision wavelets were originally used for *static* mesh compression [55,99,100,102], they have also been applied to animated mesh compression [103,104]. In both [103] and [104], the hierarchical mesh subdivision is performed on the first frame of the sequence, and then hierarchical motion estimation is used to map the same topology to the other frames. As well as decomposing each frame of the mesh sequence into a base mesh and wavelet coefficients, the wavelet subdivision is applied temporally, along the motion trajectories. The wavelet coefficients are encoded using SPIHT [55].

Although semi-regular remeshing for the subdivision wavelet transform has the obvious advantage that the mesh connectivity data needs no encoding (apart from the base mesh connectivity), in some applications it might be important to preserve the original mesh connectivity. For this reason, several researchers have proposed methods for compressing constant-connectivity animated mesh sequences that have an *irregular* connectivity, without requiring a prior remeshing to a semi-regular connectivity, e.g., [105,106]. In [105], a more compact version of the multiresolution representation presented in [107] (which is based on the *non-uniform* subdivision method of [108]) is introduced. The wavelet coefficients in [105] are computed by using the mesh *geometry*, rather than just the mesh connectivity as in earlier subdivision wavelet schemes. More specifically, the wavelet coefficients are computed based on the geometry of a *parametric* mesh. The first frame of the animated mesh sequence is used as a parametric mesh, and all the other frames are transformed with wavelet coefficients computed from this parametric frame. The parametric frame is encoded separately using a static mesh compression technique. The method in [106] is similar to [105], but it allows lossless compression and lossy.

More recent approaches for animated mesh compression that make use of wavelets consider wavelets defined on *graphs* [109–111]. In [109], *graph wavelet filter banks* (GWFB) [112] are used to compress the geometry and color of animated mesh sequences representing moving human bodies. Both [110] and [111] make use of *spectral graph wavelet transforms* (SGWT) [113].

14.4.6 Methods based on surface unfolding

Inspired by Gu's *geometry images* [45], Briceño extends the principle of unfolding the mesh into an image to animated sequences [114]. The solution is called *geometry videos*. In this solution, the surface is cut and unfolded using stretch minimization [115]. It is first re-sampled and re-organized so that it becomes highly compressible. A strong advantage of the solution is that it can leverage classical 2D video compression techniques (such as MPEG HEVC or VVC) to encode the geometry signal (images). Its drawback resides in the fact that the surface re-sampling and the regular re-meshing introduces some non-negligible distortions in the reconstructed model and the original mesh connectivity is not preserved (unless the mesh happens to have a regular connectivity already, which is rare).

In [116], Mamou proposes the use of multi-chart geometry video, which, similarly to a UV texture atlas, unwraps the surface into several components, instead of only one as in [114]. It then leverages *rigid transforms,* as described in [67], to enhance compression, but using a fixed number of patches. The prediction errors are represented as multi-chart geometry images that can be encoded using standard 2D video encoders. The proposed solution preserves the original topology of the mesh, thus reducing distortions. The use of a piecewise affine predictor leads to better compression than [114]. Finally, the solution in [116] makes use of a low-distortion atlas of parameterization [117], which leads to lower distortion than when using a simple mapping on a 2D square domain.

14.4.7 Methods based on spectral analysis

Karni and Gotsman [44] have shown that spectral methods can be applied to static mesh compression by using the combinatorial graph Laplacian matrix to extract from the mesh's connectivity a basis to encode the geometry. The Laplacian matrix is formed by considering only a one-ring neighborhood of the vertices, which leads to a sparse matrix, whose eigenvectors can be easily extracted. However, this dependence on the mesh's connectivity makes the eingenvectors dependent on the quality of the meshing, which may vary for objects even with the same topology. To circumvent this problem, Vallet and Lévy [118] proposed the *manifold harmonic basis* (MHB), derived as eingenvectors from the Laplace–Beltrami operator. The proposed framework is independent of the meshing and generates an orthogonal basis that can be used in several different applications, from mesh filtering to parameterization, and even compression.

In [119], Wang et al. use spectral analysis to compress animated meshes by projecting on an MHB the field of deformation gradients defined on the surface mesh. The deformation gradient (that is, how the vertices of each triangle rotate and stretch from one frame to another) can be represented by a second-order tensor, or a 3×3 matrix, which can be decomposed into two matrices (rotation and stretching) using polar decomposition. Both matrices are then transformed into coefficients by projecting them onto the MHB. The coefficients are then quantized and arithmetically encoded. Note that the MHB is defined per vertex, whereas the deformation gradient is defined per triangle, so the authors use the average of the functions' values on the vertices.

Another approach that uses spectral analysis for the compression of animated meshes is from Chen et al. [120]. In their proposal, the mesh sequence is divided into clusters of frames with similar pose by using *K-medoids*. Then, for each cluster, the representative frame (i.e., the *keyframe*) is encoded using a static mesh compression technique and transformed into the MHB coefficients. The other frames are projected onto the new basis defined by the keyframe, and the MHB coefficients are encoded with *linear prediction coding* (LPC), which generate values that are then quantized and entropy encoded. At the decoder side, the coefficients are inverse-transformed to generate a low-resolution representation of the non-keyframe. Then the deformation of the low-resolution keyframe to the full-resolution keyframe is determined, and this deformation is transferred from the keyframe to the non-keyframe to recover the high-frequency details.

Both [119] and [120] compare their approaches with PCA-based method COD-DYAC [82]. For higher bitrates, spectral analysis has a better performance, since it does not need to send the eingenvectors (they can be derived from the stored keyframes). Furthermore, it preserves better the shape of the mesh, even if its geometry (vertex positions) is not reconstructed exactly, which is believed to have a higher impact in terms of perceptual quality. However, for lower bitrates, PCA has a better performance, since it is able to achieve a better quality reconstruction than MHB when using the same number of basis vectors. Moreover, frames with sharp protrusions also require a significant number of MHB coefficients for better representation.

14.4.8 The MPEG framework

The first standard to encode animations by the MPEG group, the Face and body animation (FBA) standard [53], targeted human avatars, but was limited to fixed feature points, such as eyes and mouth corners. This standard was later extended to a more generic framework with the bone-based animation (BBA) [58], which includes geometric transform of bones (used in skinning-based animation) and weights (used in morphing animations). For a more generic animation, MPEG first issued the interpolator compression (IC) [121], which is used to compress *key frame animations*, defined by a pair of *keys* indicating the frame index, and *values* indicating, for instance, new positions of vertices. In 2009, MPEG added the frame-based animation mesh compression (FAMC) to the AFX set of animation compression tools. FAMC does not depend on how the animation is obtained (deformation or rigid motion) and compresses an animated mesh by encoding on a time basis the attributes (positions, normal vectors, etc.) of the mesh's vertices. It encodes the first frame with any static mesh compression algorithm, then applies skinning-based motion compensation [73] and layered decomposition [74]. The skinning-based motion compensation is composed of the following steps: global motion encoding (using the barycenter of the meshes to remove the global motion), then vertex partitioning (separating the vertices into clusters using the k-means method), followed by weighted motion compensation (obtaining the prediction by a weighted combination of the K affine transforms for each cluster). The motion-compensated residue is then transformed (using the DCT or lifting transform), and once again the coefficients are predicted by neighboring frames, but using the layered representation [75]. Improvements over the FAMC standard have also been reported in [96,122].

14.5. Variable-connectivity mesh sequences

In contrast to the animated meshes discussed in Section 14.4, *time-varying meshes* (or TVMs) do not have a fixed topology or connectivity across all frames. They are also likely to contain different numbers of vertices in different frames. Though this can make TVMs easier to generate from real-world captures (e.g., from images or 3D scans of real-world objects [123,124], where the mesh for each frame can be generated independently of other frames), it makes the compression problem much more difficult than for animated meshes, as there are usually no explicit correspondences between the vertices or connections across different frames. Furthermore, in a TVM, meshes in successive frames are not necessarily *homeomorphic* (see Section 14.2.1), as the surface reconstruction may be different in different frames. There is also no guarantee that the meshes in a TVM sequence will be manifold, or that the manifold property will continue across different frames.

In this section, we aim to provide an overview of the existing literature on time-varying mesh compression, followed by a discussion on the recent MPEG activities in this area. The problem of compressing time-varying meshes began to be addressed in the literature more than a decade ago (e.g., [125,126]), but it has not progressed much further since then. This is due to both the complexity of the problem, and the fact that the production of TVM content has only begun to gain traction relatively recently as a result of improvements in volumetric capture systems and increasing interest in using real data captures, instead of only computer-generated models (e.g., see [127]).

We categorize the existing literature on TVM compression by the following methods: mesh surface unfolding, subdivision of meshes into blocks, and video-based coding (solutions that leverage standard MPEG V-PCC encoders for compression).

14.5.1 Methods based on mesh surface unfolding

In some of the earliest work on TVM compression [125], the authors propose to cut open the 3D mesh, then flatten the surface by projecting it onto 2D images, similarly to the *geometry images* [45] and *geometry videos* [114], ideas proposed earlier. Conventional 2D video coding methods can then be applied to encode the geometry and associated textures in the 2D images. A notable difference between the method in [125] and geometry images [45] is that the cut path for unfolding the 3D mesh with geometry images is selected so that it passes through high-curvature areas in the mesh, whereas in [125] the cut passes where no significant texture information exists.

Similarly to [125], in [128], the authors also make use of the concept of geometry images [45] and geometry videos [114] to compress TVMs. More specifically, they use the extension of geometry videos proposed in [129], called *conformal geometry videos* (CGVs), which aim to more efficiently represent 3D articulated motion (e.g., human motion) than the traditional geometry videos [114]. As in [129], in [128], salient feature points for the mesh in each frame are first detected (e.g., head, feet, hands, etc.), and corresponding feature points are found in successive frames. Then the marked TVMs are mapped to the *polycube* [130] domain as in [129], the 3D polycubes are cut open, flattened, and reparameterized onto a regular rectangular 2D domain to obtain the CGV representation. Since the CGVs have a regular structure, the original mesh connectivity is not encoded, and therefore cannot be reconstructed losslessly. To compress the CGVs, in [128] the mesh vertices in each frame (2D image) of the CGV are placed as column vectors in a matrix that contains one column vector per frame. Next, *low-rank approximation* (i.e., truncated *singular value decomposition* (SVD)) [131] is applied on this matrix of vertex positions (separately for the X, Y, and Z positions), and the resulting singular values are reshaped back into frames and are named *EigenGVs* by the authors. These EigenGVs are by their nature much more compact than the original CGVs, and they are further compressed in [128] by using a standard 2D video encoder, such as H.264/AVC [132]. The results have been shown to significantly outperform the original geometry videos [114] method in terms of rate-distortion performance and visual quality. Furthermore, the method in [128] naturally offers the possibility of a progressive mesh reconstruction, as the user can choose how many of the EigenGV frames to reconstruct.

14.5.2 Methods based on subdivision of meshes into blocks

In [126,133], the authors propose to extend the idea of 2D block matching from conventional 2D video coding to 3D time-varying mesh coding. Matching blocks across frames are found by comparing the directions of the mean surface normal vectors (SNVs) in those blocks, and the surface normal vectors across the best-matching blocks represent the inter-frame motion vectors. The motion vectors are encoded by using a differential pulse code modulation (DPCM) to obtain predictions of motion vectors between adjacent blocks (which were found to be highly correlated for the mesh data used in [126,133]). Residual values are computed in matching blocks as the minimum sum of the differences of the vertex positions in those blocks. The residual values are decorrelated by using a 1D discrete cosine transform (DCT), and the transform coefficients are uniformly quantized, truncated at the higher frequencies, and entropy coded using Huffman coding.

In [134], the 3D meshes across different frames are first registered (aligned), then the bounding box of the largest mesh in the sequence is subdivided into sub-blocks, which the authors call a *coarse-level quantization* operation. The binary occupancy information for these sub-blocks is encoded using run-length encoding (RLE). The binary occupancy bitstreams are further compared (using an exclusive-OR operation between bitstreams) across different frames to obtain the motion information, and the resulting difference vectors are further encoded using RLE. To compress the vertex positions inside each sub-block, uniform quantization is applied and all the vertices inside a sub-block are quantized to one representative point. The representative points are then also converted to a sequence of occupancy (1 or 0) bits on a regular grid and encoded using RLE. Then the runs that have the same lengths are considered "super-symbols" and further encoded using arithmetic coding. The method in [134] has been shown to outperform the authors' earlier work in [133], in terms of rate-distortion performance.

Contrary to the work in [133,134], where only the geometry data is considered for inter-frame coding, in [135], the authors propose inter- and intra-frame coding approaches that consider the geometry (vertex positions), the connectivity, the color textures, and any other data that is attached to the vertices. In [135], each 3D mesh in the TVM sequence is first subdivided into patches of approximately equal surface area and small enough that they can be considered flat discs. Principal component analysis (PCA) is then applied to place the patches' centers of gravity at the origin of the world coordinate system and to adjust the orientation of the patches so as to align them. These centers of gravity and the rotation parameters for the patches need to be encoded and transmitted to the decoder. For intra-frame coding of the vertex positions, a *spectral compression* [44,136] method is applied since the vertex positions are highly correlated spatially. Only around 10–50% of the lowest-frequency spectral coefficients are kept, with the other values being set to 0, and Huffman coding [41] is used to encode the quantized set of coefficients. To compress the color data per vertex, the authors propose to use either a vector quantization (VQ) on the (R, G, B) color vectors, or a simple scalar quantization, and not spectral compression, since the color values are not usually strongly correlated spatially with other color values. For connectivity compression, the authors employ existing high-performing static 3D mesh connectivity algorithms, such as edgebreaker [32]. For the inter-frame coding, a patch matching approach is proposed to remove the temporal redundancies. Patch matching is achieved by finding the minimum sum of Euclidean distances between a patch in the target frame and all the patches in the reference frame. The residuals between the position and color vectors in the target patch and their corresponding vectors in the matched reference patch are then encoded by a vector or scalar quantization (VQ has generally been found to perform better). Correspondence data between vertices in the target and reference frames must also be encoded, but compared to the bitrate for encoding this data in [133], in [135], the bitrate is very small. Compared to [133,134], for inter-frame geometry coding, the method in [135] has been shown to offer significant rate-distortion improvements.

In [137], the authors present a study on a better bit allocation strategy for their method in [135]. For the mesh models used in [135], the authors demonstrate in [137] that for a good visual quality for the reconstructed 3D meshes, as many bits as possible should be assigned to the vertex positions, whereas for color 8–10 bpvf seems sufficient. This is because the quality of the color reconstruction is highly dependent on the quality of the geometry reconstruction, as the color must be coded on top of lossy geometry. The study in [137] also considers the trade-off in the bit allocations between the target frames and reference frames for the method in [135]. The authors conclude that as many bits as possible should be allocated to the reference frames, whereas the target frames can be allocated a smaller number of bits (e.g., half the bitrate of the reference frames) to achieve the same overall visual quality for inter-frame coding.

More recently, Pavez and Chou [138] propose an alternative representation to surface meshes: a so-called *polygon soup*. They claim that such an unstructured set of triangles, where the triangles are not connected and can overlap, are better at describing surfaces from real-life captures than point clouds or meshes that are on their own. *Polygon soups* can be seen as a trade-off between point-clouds and surface meshes. The authors use an octree encoding to represent the vertices of the reference frames (i.e., the keyframes). They achieve this by quantizing the vertices (i.e., by voxelization) and reordering the quantized vertices by using Morton codes [139]. Using the Morton order, they apply the *region-adaptive hierarchical transform* [140] (RAHT), which is a sequence of orthonormal transforms applied to attribute data living on the leaves of an octree. The output transform coefficients are sorted by decreasing magnitude of weight, quantized by uniform scalar quantization, and entropy coded by using a *run-length-Golomb–Rice* [141] (RLGR) entropy coder. The authors claim that compared to static polygon clouds and a fortiori static point clouds, dynamic polygon clouds can improve color compression by up to 2–3 dB in fidelity, and can improve geometry compression by up to a factor of 2–5 in bitrate. It should be noted that the method in [138] assumes that time-consistent dynamic polygon clouds can be constructed in real time, and therefore that the triangles of the polygon soup are consistent across frames, so that there is a correspondence between colors and vertices within each *group of frames*.

14.5.3 Methods inspired by MPEG V-PCC

In more recent work on TVM compression, solutions that are based on the MPEG video-based point cloud coding (V-PCC) standard from the V3C framework [142] have begun to appear.

Faramarzi et al. [143] propose extending the V-PCC framework to encode dense meshes with per-vertex color data. More specifically, they propose to use V-PCC to encode the mesh geometry and textures, and to encode the connectivity by using edge-breaker [32] and TFAN [30]. Since the order of the reconstructed vertices produced by V-PCC is different to the order of the vertices in the input mesh before compression, but both edgebreaker and TFAN rely on having the same vertex ordering at input and output, so that they can traverse the mesh losslessly, the encoder also needs to encode and transmit the vertex reordering information. Due to this additional coding burden, the proposed solution performs much worse compared to when using Draco to encode the same mesh. The authors thus propose an alternative solution, where vertices and colors are linearly packed into standard video frames, so-called *raw patches* in V-PCC. With this second approach, some V-PCC coding steps, such as patch generation, as well as geometry and attribute smoothing, are skipped; therefore this solution does not leverage the regular patch packing for more efficient coding as proposed in V-PCC. In both the proposed frameworks, V-PCC + edgebreaker is shown to have better compression performance than V-PCC + TFAN; however, Draco usually performs better (on average) than either of the proposed solutions using V-PCC. Moreover, the results in [143] have been demonstrated only for a single frame for each of the meshes in the chosen test set, so it is not yet clear how the proposed solutions might work for time-varying mesh *sequences*.

In [144], the author also proposes an extension of the MPEG V-PCC framework [142] to encode TVMs. Similarly to the case for 3D point clouds, in [144], each vertex position of a 3D mesh is projected onto a pixel position in a 2D patch image, but additionally the *surface* of the 3D mesh is also projected onto the 2D patch projection plane by using rasterization. This produces a dense image representing the mesh connectivity, which is suitable for video coding. Occupancy, geometry, and attributes are encoded as usual by V-PCC. Due to the subdivision into patches and the lossy compression of vertex positions (e.g., quantization), the reconstructed mesh may have gaps between patches. To fix this problem, the author uses an algorithm similar to the mesh zippering approach used in [145], where triangle vertices on the borders of neighboring patches are merged. Note that for both [144] and [143], the input mesh vertex positions must be *voxelized* (converted to integers) before they can be processed by the proposed methods. For geometry compression, the method in [144] has been shown to be outperformed by Draco in terms of rate-distortion performance, whereas for color compression the performance is comparable (or in some cases a little better) to color encoded using HEVC on top of a reconstructed geometry using Draco. The method in [144] has been designed to work both on meshes with per-vertex colors and textured meshes.

14.5.4 The MPEG V-mesh call for proposals

The TVM compression methods inspired by MPEG V-PCC were part of Exploration experiments that were realized during the standardization of the video-based point cloud compression standard, V-PCC [142]. These experiments applied the new point cloud compression standard to the coding of meshes, since both point clouds and meshes are commonly used in the case of VR/AR and volumetric video. It was noted that to encode the connectivity of the meshes, modifications to the new standard would be recommended. Due to the interest of several companies in the mesh data format, the MPEG group decided to issue a call for proposals [146] for TVMs in October 2021. The responses were due in April 2022, and the new standard is expected to be concluded in October 2023.

14.6. Conclusion and future directions

In this chapter, we first motivated the use of 3D triangular *mesh* models to represent animated three-dimensional subjects in the *volumetric videos* that are fast emerging as the newest form of multimedia. Unlike earlier animated mesh sequences, which were generated purely synthetically by computers, the emerging *volumetric videos* are produced from *real-life* captures of moving subjects or objects. With volumetric videos, as for all previous forms of multimedia (1D audio signals, 2D images, and 2D videos), naturally there is a need for efficient compression algorithms to enable such multimedia to be used in a practical manner. In this chapter, we provided an overview of the history of compression techniques that have been proposed over the past few decades for *static* (single-frame) 3D meshes, followed by compression algorithms for synthetically-generated *dynamic* mesh sequences (so-called *animated meshes*), and finally for dynamic mesh sequences produced from real-life captures (so-called *time-varying meshes*, or TVMs). Though we have seen many similarities and patterns in the compression algorithms proposed across these different categories, it is clear that the time-varying meshes are still the most difficult to compress. Indeed, even though research on the compression of such time-varying meshes started more than a decade ago, it is still rather in its infancy. The most difficult problem in compressing such data is the lack of correspondences in the connectivity and geometry of the mesh models across different frames. Tracking algorithms that attempt to find such correspondences are often costly and time-consuming, and therefore not practical to use in the case of a standalone TVM codec. More recently, researchers have begun to propose compression algorithms for TVMs inspired by the recent MPEG V-PCC standard, but the results are still far from the compression rates achievable for animated meshes. Perhaps the recent MPEG call for proposals (CfP) on TVM compression will inspire a flurry of new and creative research in this direction.

Aside from the inherent challenges of designing new compression algorithms, we also have a few other roadblocks that stand in the way of progress, most importantly the following: (i) the lack of a sufficiently large and variable set of TVM datasets to test on (few such datasets currently exist, and they are often proprietary to the companies or institutions that generate them and so can be difficult to acquire); (ii) the fact that different papers in the literature do not all present results on the same datasets, which makes it difficult to compare different compression algorithms; (iii) the frequent lack of sufficient algorithm details in the literature, and/or the lack of available source code for the proposed algorithms, which often makes it difficult or impossible to reproduce the results; and (iv) the lack of agreement on common, reliable error metrics that can be used for the quality assessment of decompressed mesh models and for the fair comparison of different mesh compression algorithms, and which consistently correlate well with human perception of error. To have a more accurate idea of where the research on compression of dynamic 3D meshes truly stands, and therefore to be able to make useful progress, we must also enforce more rigorous presentations of new algorithms that are published in the literature. Indeed, if we cannot accurately reproduce a method, or fairly compare different methods, or even accurately measure the performance of a new method, the usefulness of these methods is limited as we do not have full control over them.

Perhaps the work presented in this chapter will serve as inspiration for new insights and valuable contributions to the field of dynamic mesh compression, and will therefore enable us to reproduce increasingly richer multimedia representations of our world.

References

[1] M. Zwicker, H. Pfister, J. Van Baar, M. Gross, Surface splatting, in: Proceedings of the 28th Annual Conference on Computer Graphics and Interactive Techniques, 2001, pp. 371–378.
[2] W.E. Lorensen, H.E. Cline, Marching cubes: A high resolution 3D surface construction algorithm, ACM SIGGRAPH Computer Graphics 21 (4) (1987) 163–169.
[3] L. Williams, Pyramidal parametrics, in: Proceedings of the 10th Annual Conference on Computer Graphics and Interactive Techniques, 1983, pp. 1–11.
[4] G. Lavoué, 3D Object Processing - Basic Background in 3D Object Processing, John Wiley&Sons, Ltd, 2008, Ch. 1, pp. 5–43, https://doi.org/10.1002/9780470510773.ch1.
[5] M. Krivokuća, Progressive Compression of 3D Mesh Geometry Using Sparse Approximations from Redundant Frame Dictionaries, PhD Thesis, Department of Electrical and Computer Engineering, The University of Auckland, New Zealand, 2015.
[6] M. Fiedler, Algebraic connectivity of graphs, Czechoslovak Mathematical Journal 23 (2) (1973) 298–305.
[7] J. Peng, C.-S. Kim, C.-C.J. Kuo, Technologies for 3D mesh compression: A survey, Journal of Visual Communication and Image Representation 16 (6) (2005) 688–733.
[8] S. Jendrol', H.-J. Voss, Light subgraphs of graphs embedded in the plane—a survey, Discrete Mathematics 313 (4) (2013) 406–421, https://doi.org/10.1016/j.disc.2012.11.007.
[9] M. Ben-Chen, A. Lai Lin, Course on geometry processing algorithms - chapter 2 mesh data structures, https://graphics.stanford.edu/courses/cs468-10-fall/LectureSlides/02_Mesh_Data_Structures.pdf, 2010.
[10] L. Kettner, Using generic programming for designing a data structure for polyhedral surfaces, Computational Geometry 13 (1) (1999) 65–90.
[11] W. Consortium, X3D and VRML, the most widely used 3D formats, https://www.web3d.org/x3d-vrml-most-widely-used-3d-formats, 2000.
[12] P. Bourke, OBJ - polygonal file format, http://paulbourke.net/dataformats/obj/.
[13] P. Bourke, PLY - polygonal file format, http://paulbourke.net/dataformats/ply/.
[14] J. Rossignac, A. Safonova, A. Szymczak, Edgebreaker on a corner table: A simple technique for representing and compressing triangulated surfaces, in: Hierarchical and Geometrical Methods in Scientific Visualization, Springer, 2003, pp. 41–50.
[15] W.T. Tutte, A census of planar triangulations, Canadian Journal of Mathematics 14 (1962) 21–38.
[16] A. Maglo, G. Lavoué, F. Dupont, C. Hudelot, 3D mesh compression: Survey, comparisons, and emerging trends, ACM Computing Surveys (CSUR) 47 (3) (2015) 1–41.
[17] P. Alliez, C. Gotsman, Recent advances in compression of 3D meshes, in: Advances in Multiresolution for Geometric Modelling, 2005, pp. 3–26.
[18] Google, Draco 3D data compression, https://google.github.io/draco/.
[19] K. Mammou, Open 3D graphics compression, https://github.com/KhronosGroup/glTF/wiki/Open-3D-Graphics-Compression, 2013.
[20] M. Geelnard, OpenCTM, http://openctm.sourceforge.net/, 2010.
[21] V. Vidal, E. Lombardi, M. Tola, F. Dupont, G. Lavoué, MEPP2: a generic platform for processing 3D meshes and point clouds, in: EUROGRAPHICS 2020 (Short Paper), 2020.

[22] openGL, openGL primitives, https://www.khronos.org/opengl/wiki/Primitive#Triangle_primitives, 2000.

[23] Microsoft, DirectX primitives, https://docs.microsoft.com/en-us/windows/win32/direct3d9/primitives, 2000.

[24] M. Deering, Geometry compression, in: Proceedings of the 22nd Annual Conference on Computer Graphics and Interactive Techniques, 1995, pp. 13–20.

[25] M.M. Chow, Optimized Geometry Compression for Real-Time Rendering, IEEE, 1997.

[26] C.L. Bajaj, V. Pascucci, G. Zhuang, Single resolution compression of arbitrary triangular meshes with properties, Computational Geometry 14 (1–3) (1999) 167–186.

[27] G. Taubin, J. Rossignac, Geometric compression through topological surgery, ACM Transactions on Graphics (TOG) 17 (2) (1998) 84–115.

[28] P. Diaz-Gutierrez, M. Gopi, R. Pajarola, Hierarchyless simplification, stripification and compression of triangulated two-manifolds, Computer Graphics Forum 24 (2005) 457–467, Blackwell Publishing, Inc., Oxford, UK and Boston, USA.

[29] C. Touma, C. Gotsman, Triangle mesh compression, in: Proceedings-Graphics Interface, Canadian Information Processing Society, 1998, pp. 26–34.

[30] K. Mamou, T. Zaharia, F. Prêteux, TFAN: A low complexity 3D mesh compression algorithm, Computer Animation and Virtual Worlds 20 (2–3) (2009) 343–354.

[31] S. Gumhold, W. Straßer, Real time compression of triangle mesh connectivity, in: Proceedings of the 25th Annual Conference on Computer Graphics and Interactive Techniques, 1998, pp. 133–140.

[32] J. Rossignac, Edgebreaker: Connectivity compression for triangle meshes, IEEE Transactions on Visualization and Computer Graphics 5 (1) (1999) 47–61.

[33] A. Szymczak, Optimized edgebreaker encoding for large and regular triangle meshes, The Visual Computer 19 (4) (2003) 271–278.

[34] J. Rossignac, 3D compression made simple: Edgebreaker with ZipandWrap on a corner-table, in: Proceedings International Conference on Shape Modeling and Applications, IEEE, 2001, pp. 278–283.

[35] A. Szymczak, J. Rossignac, D. King, Piecewise regular meshes: Construction and compression, Graphical Models 64 (3–4) (2002) 183–198.

[36] M. Attene, B. Falcidieno, M. Spagnuolo, J. Rossignac, SwingWrapper: Retiling triangle meshes for better edgebreaker compression, ACM Transactions on Graphics (TOG) 22 (4) (2003) 982–996.

[37] H. Hoppe, Progressive meshes, in: Proceedings of the 23rd Annual Conference on Computer Graphics and Interactive Techniques, 1996, pp. 99–108.

[38] G. Taubin, A. Guéziec, W. Horn, F. Lazarus, Progressive forest split compression, in: Proceedings of the 25th Annual Conference on Computer Graphics and Interactive Techniques, 1998, pp. 123–132.

[39] W.J. Schroeder, J.A. Zarge, W.E. Lorensen, Decimation of triangle meshes, in: Proceedings of the 19th Annual Conference on Computer Graphics and Interactive Techniques, 1992, pp. 65–70.

[40] D. Cohen-Or, D. Levin, O. Remez, Progressive compression of arbitrary triangular meshes, in: IEEE Visualization, vol. 99, 1999, pp. 67–72.

[41] R. Gonzalez, R. Woods, Digital Image Processing, Chapter 8: Image Compression, Pearson Education, Inc., Upper Saddle River, New Jersey, 2008, pp. 525–626.

[42] H. Lee, P. Alliez, M. Desbrun, Angle-analyzer: A triangle-quad mesh codec, Computer Graphics Forum 21 (2002) 383–392, Wiley Online Library.

[43] L. Vasa, G. Brunnett, Exploiting connectivity to improve the tangential part of geometry prediction, IEEE Transactions on Visualization and Computer Graphics 19 (9) (2013) 1467–1475.

[44] Z. Karni, C. Gotsman, Spectral compression of mesh geometry, in: Proceedings of the 27th Annual Conference on Computer Graphics and Interactive Techniques, 2000, pp. 279–286.

[45] X. Gu, S.J. Gortler, H. Hoppe, Geometry images, in: Proceedings of the 29th Annual Conference on Computer Graphics and Interactive Techniques, 2002, pp. 355–361.

[46] O. Devillers, P.-M. Gandoin, Geometric compression for interactive transmission, in: Proceedings Visualization 2000. VIS 2000 (Cat. No. 00CH37145), IEEE, 2000, pp. 319–326.

[47] J. Peng, C.-C.J. Kuo, Geometry-guided progressive lossless 3D mesh coding with octree (OT) decomposition, in: ACM SIGGRAPH 2005 Papers, 2005, pp. 609–616.

[48] M. Isenburg, J. Snoeyink, Compressing texture coordinates with selective linear predictions, in: Proceedings Computer Graphics International 2003, IEEE, 2003, pp. 126–131.

[49] L. Váša, G. Brunnett, Efficient encoding of texture coordinates guided by mesh geometry, Computer Graphics Forum 33 (2014) 25–34, Wiley Online Library.

[50] F. Caillaud, V. Vidal, F. Dupont, G. Lavoué, Progressive compression of arbitrary textured meshes, Computer Graphics Forum 35 (2016) 475–484, Wiley Online Library.

[51] J.-H. Ahn, C.-S. Kim, Y.-S. Ho, Predictive compression of geometry, color and normal data of 3-D mesh models, IEEE Transactions on Circuits and Systems for Video Technology 16 (2) (2006) 291–299.

[52] Z.H. Cigolle, S. Donow, D. Evangelakos, M. Mara, M. McGuire, Q. Meyer, A survey of efficient representations for independent unit vectors, Journal of Computer Graphics Techniques 3 (2) (2014).

[53] L. Chiariglione, The MPEG Representation of Digital Media, Springer Science & Business Media, 2011.

[54] ISO/IEC JTC 1/SC 29/WG 11, ISO/IEC 14496 2:2004, Information technology – Coding of audio-visual objects – Part 2: Visual, https://www.iso.org/standard/73025.html, 2004.

[55] A. Khodakovsky, P. Schröder, W. Sweldens, Progressive geometry compression, in: Proceedings of the 27th Annual Conference on Computer Graphics and Interactive Techniques, 2000, pp. 271–278.

[56] I.A. Salomie, A. Munteanu, A. Gavrilescu, G. Lafruit, P. Schelkens, R. Deklerck, J. Cornelis, MESHGRID – a compact, multiscalable and animation-friendly surface representation, IEEE Transactions on Circuits and Systems for Video Technology 14 (7) (2004) 950–966.

[57] J. Royan, R. Balter, C. Bouville, Hierarchical representation of virtual cities for progressive transmission over networks, in: Third International Symposium on 3D Data Processing, Visualization, and Transmission (3DPVT'06), Citeseer, 2006, pp. 432–439.

[58] ISO/IEC JTC 1/SC 29, Information technology — Coding of audio-visual objects — Part 16: Animation Framework eXtension (AFX), https://www.iso.org/standard/57367.html?browse=tc, 2011.

[59] E.S. Jang, S. Lee, B. Koo, D. Kim, K. Son, Fast 3D mesh compression using shared vertex analysis, ETRI Journal 32 (1) (2010) 163–165.

[60] K. Group, DirectX primitives, https://www.khronos.org/gltf/, 2000.

[61] A. Collet, M. Chuang, P. Sweeney, D. Gillett, D. Evseev, D. Calabrese, H. Hoppe, A. Kirk, S. Sullivan, High-quality streamable free-viewpoint video, ACM Transactions on Graphics (ToG) 34 (4) (2015) 1–13.

[62] H. Li, B. Adams, L.J. Guibas, M. Pauly, Robust single-view geometry and motion reconstruction, ACM Transactions on Graphics (ToG) 28 (5) (2009) 1–10.

[63] E. De Aguiar, C. Stoll, C. Theobalt, N. Ahmed, H.-P. Seidel, S. Thrun, Performance capture from sparse multi-view video, in: ACM SIGGRAPH 2008 Papers, 2008, pp. 1–10.

[64] M. Zollhöfer, M. Nießner, S. Izadi, C. Rehmann, C. Zach, M. Fisher, C. Wu, A. Fitzgibbon, C. Loop, C. Theobalt, et al., Real-time non-rigid reconstruction using an RGB-D camera, ACM Transactions on Graphics (ToG) 33 (4) (2014) 1–12.

[65] F. Prada, M. Kazhdan, M. Chuang, A. Collet, H. Hoppe, Spatiotemporal atlas parameterization for evolving meshes, ACM Transactions on Graphics (TOG) 36 (4) (2017) 1–12.

[66] J. Dvořák, P. Vaněček, L. Váša, Towards understanding time varying triangle meshes, in: International Conference on Computational Science, Springer, 2021, pp. 45–58.

[67] J.E. Lengyel, Compression of time-dependent geometry, in: Proceedings of the 1999 Symposium on Interactive 3D Graphics, 1999, pp. 89–95.

[68] S. Gupta, K. Sengupta, A.A. Kassim, Compression of dynamic 3D geometry data using iterative closest point algorithm, Computer Vision and Image Understanding 87 (1–3) (2002) 116–130.

[69] G. Collins, A. Hilton, A rigid transform basis for animation compression and level of detail, in: Vision, Video, and Graphics, 2005, pp. 21–28.

[70] M. Sattler, R. Sarlette, R. Klein, Simple and efficient compression of animation sequences, in: Proceedings of the 2005 ACM SIGGRAPH/Eurographics Symposium on Computer Animation, 2005, pp. 209–217.

[71] R. Amjoun, R. Sondershaus, W. Straßer, Compression of complex animated meshes, in: Computer Graphics International Conference, Springer, 2006, pp. 606–613.

[72] T. Kanungo, D.M. Mount, N.S. Netanyahu, C.D. Piatko, R. Silverman, A.Y. Wu, An efficient k-means clustering algorithm: Analysis and implementation, IEEE Transactions on Pattern Analysis and Machine Intelligence 24 (7) (2002) 881–892.

[73] K. Mamou, T. Zaharia, F. Prêteux, A skinning approach for dynamic 3D mesh compression, Computer Animation and Virtual Worlds 17 (3–4) (2006) 337–346.

[74] N. Stefanoski, X. Liu, P. Klie, J. Ostermann, Scalable linear predictive coding of time-consistent 3D mesh sequences, in: 2007 3DTV Conference, IEEE, 2007, pp. 1–4.

[75] K. Mamou, T. Zaharia, F. Prêteux, N. Stefanoski, J. Ostermann, Frame-based compression of animated meshes in MPEG-4, in: 2008 IEEE International Conference on Multimedia and Expo, IEEE, 2008, pp. 1121–1124.

[76] G. Luo, Z. Deng, X. Zhao, X. Jin, W. Zeng, W. Xie, H. Seo, Spatio-temporal segmentation based adaptive compression of dynamic mesh sequences, ACM Transactions on Multimedia Computing, Communications, and Applications (TOMM) 16 (1) (2020) 1–24.

[77] M. Alexa, W. Müller, Representing animations by principal components, Computer Graphics Forum 19 (2000) 411–418, Wiley Online Library.

[78] Z. Karni, C. Gotsman, Compression of soft-body animation sequences, Computers & Graphics 28 (1) (2004) 25–34.

[79] G. Luo, F. Cordier, H. Seo, Compression of 3D mesh sequences by temporal segmentation, Computer Animation and Virtual Worlds 24 (3–4) (2013) 365–375.

[80] R. Amjoun, W. Straßer, Efficient compression of 3D dynamic mesh sequences, Journal of WSCG 15 (2007).

[81] C.-K. Kao, B.-S. Jong, T.-W. Lin, Representing progressive dynamic 3D meshes and applications, in: 2010 18th Pacific Conference on Computer Graphics and Applications, IEEE, 2010, pp. 5–13.

[82] L. Váša, V. Skala, CODDYAC: Connectivity driven dynamic mesh compression, in: 2007 3DTV Conference, IEEE, 2007, pp. 1–4.

[83] L. Váša, V. Skala, Cobra: Compression of the basis for PCA represented animations, Computer Graphics Forum 28 (2009) 1529–1540, Wiley Online Library.

[84] L. Váša, V. Skala, Geometry-driven local neighbourhood based predictors for dynamic mesh compression, Computer Graphics Forum 29 (2010) 1921–1933, Wiley Online Library.

[85] L. Váša, Optimised mesh traversal for dynamic mesh compression, Graphical Models 73 (5) (2011) 218–230.

[86] L. Váša, S. Marras, K. Hormann, G. Brunnett, Compressing dynamic meshes with geometric Laplacians, Computer Graphics Forum 33 (2014) 145–154, Wiley Online Library.

[87] L. Váša, J. Dvořák, Error propagation control in Laplacian mesh compression, Computer Graphics Forum 37 (2018) 61–70, Wiley Online Library.

[88] A.S. Lalos, A.A. Vasilakis, A. Dimas, K. Moustakas, Adaptive compression of animated meshes by exploiting orthogonal iterations, The Visual Computer 33 (6) (2017) 811–821.

[89] L.L. Ibarria, J.R. Rossignac, Dynapack: space-time compression of the 3D animations of triangle meshes with fixed connectivity, Tech. rep., Georgia Institute of Technology, 2003.

[90] J. Zhang, C.B. Owen, Octree-based animated geometry compression, in: Proceedings of the IEEE Data Compression Conference, 2004, pp. 508–520.

[91] J. Zhang, C.B. Owen, Octree-based animated geometry compression, Computers & Graphics 31 (3) (2007) 463–479.

[92] K. Muller, A. Smolic, M. Kautzner, P. Eisert, T. Wiegand, Predictive compression of dynamic 3D meshes, in: IEEE International Conference on Image Processing 2005, vol. 1, IEEE, 2005, pp. I–621, https://doi.org/10.1109/ICIP.2005.1529827.

[93] D. Marpe, H. Schwarz, T. Wiegand, Context-based adaptive binary arithmetic coding in the H.264/AVC video compression standard, IEEE Transactions on Circuits and Systems for Video Technology 13 (7) (2003) 620–636.

[94] K. Müller, A. Smolic, M. Kautzner, P. Eisert, T. Wiegand, Rate-distortion-optimized predictive compression of dynamic 3D mesh sequences, Signal Processing. Image Communication 21 (9) (2006) 812–828.

[95] R. Amjoun, W. Straßer, Single-rate near lossless compression of animated geometry, Computer Aided Design 41 (10) (2009) 711–718.

[96] N. Stefanoski, J. Ostermann, SPC: fast and efficient scalable predictive coding of animated meshes, Computer Graphics Forum 29 (2010) 101–116, Wiley Online Library.

[97] M.O. Bici, G.B. Akar, Improved prediction methods for scalable predictive animated mesh compression, Journal of Visual Communication and Image Representation 22 (7) (2011) 577–589.

[98] J.-K. Ahn, Y.J. Koh, C.-S. Kim, Efficient fine-granular scalable coding of 3D mesh sequences, IEEE Transactions on Multimedia 15 (3) (2012) 485–497.

[99] J. Lounsbery, Multiresolution Analysis for Surfaces of Arbitrary Topological Type, PhD Thesis, Department of Computer Science and Engineering, University of Washington, Seattle, Washington, USA, 1994.

[100] M. Lounsbery, T.D. DeRose, J. Warren, Multiresolution analysis for surfaces of arbitrary topological type, ACM Transactions on Graphics (TOG) 16 (1) (1997) 34–73.

[101] C. Loop, Smooth Subdivision Surfaces Based on Triangles, Master of Science Thesis, Department of Mathematics, The University of Utah, Salt Lake City, UT, USA, 1987.

[102] A. Khodakovsky, I. Guskov, Compression of normal meshes, in: Geometric Modeling for Scientific Visualization, Springer, 2004, pp. 189–206.

[103] J.-H. Yang, C.-S. Kim, S.-U. Lee, Progressive coding of 3D dynamic mesh sequences using spatiotemporal decomposition, in: 2005 IEEE International Symposium on Circuits and Systems, IEEE, 2005, pp. 944–947.

[104] J.-H. Yang, C.-S. Kim, S.-U. Lee, Semi-regular representation and progressive compression of 3-D dynamic mesh sequences, IEEE Transactions on Image Processing 15 (9) (2006) 2531–2544.

[105] I. Guskov, A. Khodakovsky, Wavelet compression of parametrically coherent mesh sequences, in: Proceedings of the 2004 ACM SIGGRAPH/Eurographics Symposium on Computer Animation, 2004, pp. 183–192.

[106] J.-W. Cho, M.-S. Kim, S. Valette, H.-Y. Jung, R. Prost, 3-D dynamic mesh compression using wavelet-based multiresolution analysis, in: 2006 International Conference on Image Processing, IEEE, 2006, pp. 529–532.

[107] I. Guskov, W. Sweldens, P. Schröder, Multiresolution signal processing for meshes, in: Proceedings of the 26th Annual Conference on Computer Graphics and Interactive Techniques, 1999, pp. 325–334.

[108] I. Guskov, Multivariate Subdivision Schemes and Divided Differences, Princeton University, 1998.

[109] H.Q. Nguyen, P.A. Chou, Y. Chen, Compression of human body sequences using graph wavelet filter banks, in: 2014 IEEE International Conference on Acoustics, Speech and Signal Processing (ICASSP), IEEE, 2014, pp. 6152–6156.

[110] B. Yang, Z. Jiang, Y. Tian, J. Shangguan, C. Song, Y. Guo, M. Xu, A novel dynamic mesh sequence compression framework for progressive streaming, in: 2017 International Conference on Virtual Reality and Visualization (ICVRV), IEEE, 2017, pp. 49–54.

[111] B. Yang, Z. Jiang, J. Shangguan, F.W. Li, C. Song, Y. Guo, M. Xu, Compressed dynamic mesh sequence for progressive streaming, Computer Animation and Virtual Worlds 30 (6) (2019) e1847.

[112] S.K. Narang, A. Ortega, Compact support biorthogonal wavelet filterbanks for arbitrary undirected graphs, IEEE Transactions on Signal Processing 61 (19) (2013) 4673–4685.

[113] J.D.J.G. Leandro, R.M. Cesar Jr, R.S. Feris, Shape analysis using the spectral graph wavelet transform, in: 2013 IEEE 9th International Conference on e-Science, IEEE, 2013, pp. 307–316.

[114] H.M. Briceno, P.V. Sander, L. McMillan, S. Gortler, H. Hoppe, Geometry videos, in: Eurographics/SIGGRAPH Symposium on Computer Animation (SCA), Eurographics Association, 2003.

[115] P.V. Sander, S. Gortler, J. Snyder, H. Hoppe, Signal-specialized parameterization, in: Proceedings of the Thirteenth Eurographics Workshop on Rendering, Eurographics Association/Association for Computing Machinery, 2002.

[116] K. Mamou, T. Zaharia, F. Prêteux, Multi-chart geometry video: A compact representation for 3D animations, in: Third International Symposium on 3D Data Processing, Visualization, and Transmission (3DPVT'06), IEEE, 2006, pp. 711–718.

[117] K. Zhou, J. Synder, B. Guo, H.-Y. Shum, Iso-charts: stretch-driven mesh parameterization using spectral analysis, in: Proceedings of the 2004 Eurographics/ACM SIGGRAPH Symposium on Geometry Processing, 2004, pp. 45–54.

[118] B. Vallet, B. Lévy, Spectral geometry processing with manifold harmonics, Computer Graphics Forum 27 (2008) 251–260, Wiley Online Library.

[119] C. Wang, Y. Liu, X. Guo, Z. Zhong, B. Le, Z. Deng, Spectral animation compression, Journal of Computer Science and Technology 30 (3) (2015) 540–552.

[120] C. Chen, Q. Xia, S. Li, H. Qin, A. Hao, Compressing animated meshes with fine details using local spectral analysis and deformation transfer, The Visual Computer 36 (5) (2020) 1029–1042.

[121] E.S. Jang, J.D. Kim, S.Y. Jung, M.-J. Han, S.O. Woo, S.-J. Lee, Interpolator data compression for MPEG-4 animation, IEEE Transactions on Circuits and Systems for Video Technology 14 (7) (2004) 989–1008.

[122] O. Petřík, L. Váša, Improvements of MPEG-4 standard FAMC for efficient 3D animation compression, in: 2011 3DTV Conference: The True Vision-Capture, Transmission and Display of 3D Video (3DTV-CON), IEEE, 2011, pp. 1–4.

[123] T. Matsuyama, X. Wu, T. Takai, T. Wada, Real-time dynamic 3-D object shape reconstruction and high-fidelity texture mapping for 3-D video, IEEE Transactions on Circuits and Systems for Video Technology 14 (3) (2004) 357–369, https://doi.org/10.1109/TCSVT.2004.823396.

[124] J. Starck, A. Hilton, Surface capture for performance-based animation, IEEE Computer Graphics and Applications 27 (3) (2007) 21–31, https://doi.org/10.1109/MCG.2007.68.

[125] H. Habe, Y. Katsura, T. Matsuyama, Skin-off: representation and compression scheme for 3D video, in: Picture Coding Symposium, 2004, pp. 301–306.

[126] S.-R. Han, T. Yamasaki, K. Aizawa, 3D video compression based on extended block matching algorithm, in: 2006 International Conference on Image Processing, IEEE, 2006, pp. 525–528.

[127] ISO/IEC JTC 1/SC 29/WG 7, Use cases for Mesh Coding, April 2021.

[128] J. Hou, L.-P. Chau, Y. He, N. Magnenat-Thalmann, A novel compression framework for 3D time-varying meshes, in: 2014 IEEE International Symposium on Circuits and Systems (ISCAS), 2014, pp. 2161–2164, https://doi.org/10.1109/ISCAS.2014.6865596.

[129] D.T. Quynh, Y. He, X. Chen, J. Xia, Q. Sun, S.C. Hoi, Modeling 3D articulated motions with conformal geometry videos (CGVS), in: Proceedings of the 19th ACM International Conference on Multimedia, MM '11, Association for Computing Machinery, New York, NY, USA, 2011, pp. 383–392, https://doi.org/10.1145/2072298.2072349.

[130] J. Xia, I. Garcia, Y. He, S.-Q. Xin, G. Patow, Editable polycube map for GPU-based subdivision surfaces, in: Symposium on Interactive 3D Graphics and Games, Association for Computing Machinery, New York, NY, USA, 2011, pp. 151–158, https://doi.org/10.1145/1944745.1944771.

[131] N. Halko, P.-G. Martinsson, J.A. Tropp, Finding structure with randomness: Probabilistic algorithms for constructing approximate matrix decompositions, SIAM Review 53 (2) (2011) 217–288.

[132] T. Wiegand, G.J. Sullivan, G. Bjontegaard, A. Luthra, Overview of the H.264/AVC video coding standard, IEEE Transactions on Circuits and Systems for Video Technology 13 (7) (2003) 560–576.

[133] S.-R. Han, T. Yamasaki, K. Aizawa, Time-varying mesh compression using an extended block matching algorithm, IEEE Transactions on Circuits and Systems for Video Technology 17 (11) (2007) 1506–1518.

[134] S.-R. Han, T. Yamasaki, K. Aizawa, Geometry compression for time-varying meshes using coarse and fine levels of quantization and run-length encoding, in: 2008 15th IEEE International Conference on Image Processing, 2008, pp. 1045–1048, https://doi.org/10.1109/ICIP.2008.4711937.

[135] T. Yamasaki, K. Aizawa, Patch-based compression for time-varying meshes, in: 2010 IEEE International Conference on Image Processing, IEEE, 2010, pp. 3433–3436.

[136] R. Ohbuchi, A. Mukaiyama, S. Takahashi, A frequency-domain approach to watermarking 3D shapes, Computer Graphics Forum 21 (2002) 373–382, Wiley Online Library.

[137] L. Yamasaki, K. Aizawa, Bit allocation of vertices and colors for patch-based coding in time-varying meshes, in: 28th Picture Coding Symposium, 2010, pp. 162–165, https://doi.org/10.1109/PCS.2010.5702449.

[138] E. Pavez, P.A. Chou, Dynamic polygon cloud compression, in: 2017 IEEE International Conference on Acoustics, Speech and Signal Processing (ICASSP), 2017, pp. 2936–2940, https://doi.org/10.1109/ICASSP.2017.7952694.

[139] G.M. Morton, A computer oriented geodetic data base and a new technique in file sequencing, Tech. rep., 1966.

[140] R.L. De Queiroz, P.A. Chou, Compression of 3D point clouds using a region-adaptive hierarchical transform, IEEE Transactions on Image Processing 25 (8) (2016) 3947–3956.

[141] H.S. Malvar, Adaptive run-length/Golomb–Rice encoding of quantized generalized Gaussian sources with unknown statistics, in: Data Compression Conference (DCC'06), IEEE, 2006, pp. 23–32.

[142] ISO/IEC JTC 1/SC 29, Information technology — Coded representation of immersive media — Part 5: Visual volumetric video-based coding (V3C) and video-based point cloud compression (V-PCC), https://www.iso.org/standard/73025.html, 2021.

[143] E. Faramarzi, R. Joshi, M. Budagavi, Mesh coding extensions to MPEG-I V-PCC, in: 2020 IEEE 22nd International Workshop on Multimedia Signal Processing (MMSP), 2020, pp. 1–5, https://doi.org/10.1109/MMSP48831.2020.9287057.

[144] D.B. Graziosi, Video-based dynamic mesh coding, in: 2021 IEEE International Conference on Image Processing (ICIP), IEEE, 2021, pp. 3133–3137.

[145] G. Turk, M. Levoy, Zippered polygon meshes from range images, in: Proceedings of the 21st Annual Conference on Computer Graphics and Interactive Techniques, SIGGRAPH '94, Association for Computing Machinery, New York, NY, USA, 1994, pp. 311–318, https://doi.org/10.1145/192161.192241.

[146] ISO/IEC JTC 1/SC 29/WG 7, CfP for Dynamic Mesh Coding, 2021.

CHAPTER 15

Volumetric video streaming
Current approaches and implementations

Irene Viola and Pablo Cesar

Centrum Wiskunde en Informatica, Amsterdam, the Netherlands

Since the first ACM multimedia conference in 1993 [1], video streaming over the Internet has been a major research topic for industry and academia. During the last 30 years the focus has shifted [2]: from the early video compression technologies from the late 1980s to media-focused streaming protocols in the 1990s, and from technologies for rate control and shaping based on quality of service (QoS) in the 2000s to dynamic adaptive streaming over HTTP and cloud rendering based on quality of experience (QoE) in the 2010s. The idea of video-on-demand, which was challenged after a number of unsuccessful trials by large media corporations [3], has become an intrinsic part of our daily lives in the 2020s with even a Technology & Engineering Emmy award[1] in 2021 for the standardization of HTTP encapsulated protocols.

The focus of this chapter is on volumetric video streaming, which we anticipate will have a successful journey, even though bumpy and curved, ahead. In retrospect, we can see a number of similarities with video streaming from the 1990s with promising and visionary services [4–7], some remarkable technological solutions [8], and upcoming standards [9,10]. Still, basic research is needed for ensuring the best possible 6 degrees of freedom (6DoF) experience both for immersive consumption of media and for real-time communication. Some existing limitations include real-time compression and delivery techniques that are aware of the context and of the behavior of the users, better modeling techniques of content that allow for dynamic media optimization and tiling, and QoE-based systems that can accommodate different environments and applications.

The chapter does not try to cover all aspects on immersive media technologies, since other chapters already provide an excellent overview on topics. Chapter 3 and Chapter 8 already discuss relevant aspects for 360 videos and light fields, respectively. Other related technological areas, such as RGB-D [11,12] and free-viewpoint video [13] systems, large-scale acquisition and storage systems [14–16], and virtual worlds and environments [17,18], are outside the scope of this chapter.

The benefits of virtual reality and volumetric video are unquestionable, with the potential of radically transforming our lives [19]. Already in the 2000s–2010s, significant effort went into 3D teleimmersion or virtual teleportation with initiatives, such as

---

[1] https://theemmys.tv/tech-73rd-award-recipients/.

Immersive Video Technologies
https://doi.org/10.1016/B978-0-32-391755-1.00021-3

the Office of the Future,[2] TEEVE [20], and viewport [21]. More recently, in 2014, the Moving picture experts group (MPEG), started an ad-hoc group on point cloud compression, MPEG-PCC,[3] where commercial solutions for this type of media mobilized research and industry towards a single direction (Chapter 13). This chapter discusses the most recent different approaches and implementations on volumetric video streaming, in terms of media consumption and communication pipelines. Recent approaches include the reduction of the volume of data by removing redundancies and other non-noticeable aspects of media (e.g., occlusion based on field of view), the optimization based on tiling and progressive streaming approaches, combined with head-motion and movement prediction, and cloud and edge rendering of media for meeting the requirements of low-powered devices [22].

15.1. Theoretical approaches to volumetric video streaming

Volumetric media transmission involves large amounts of data to faithfully represent 3D objects and scenes, several orders of magnitude bigger than traditional images and videos (e.g., a point cloud video with around one million points requires around 5 Gbps). Thus considerable effort has been spent in the literature to design, implement, and evaluate algorithmic solutions that would optimize transmission for the end user, limiting the bandwidth consumption without sacrificing the perceptual quality. In this regard, redundancies in the original data can be exploited to reduce the rate requirements. Moreover, several parts of the data might not be visible at any given time: for example, part of the object might be occluded (think of the back of a cube, which is not visible from the front), hidden by other 3D objects, or outside of the field of view. In this case, being able to predict, and exploit the position and field of view of the user that is visualizing the volumetric content can lead to sensible reductions in network expenditure, with little to no impact on the visual quality. It is no mystery, then, why user-adaptive strategies have become so popular for volumetric video streaming. An example of a generic volumetric video delivery system is depicted in Fig. 15.1. The volumetric content is uploaded into a server, which is in charge of delivering it to the client at a given quality/bitrate level, depending on the network and device constraints. To aid in the delivery, several modules are available: the content might be segmented to exploit occlusions [23–29]; the viewport [22,30] and the bandwidth [31,32] might be predicted to facilitate delivery of upcoming packets; cloud- or edge-based rendering might be used to reduce strain on the client device [33,34]. An overview of challenges and opportunities for volumetric media streaming is presented by van der Hooft et al. [35] and Liu et al. [29].

---

[2] http://www.cs.unc.edu/Research/stc/index.html.
[3] https://mpeg-pcc.org.

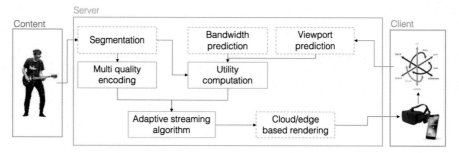

Figure 15.1 Diagram representing a generic server-client architecture for volumetric video streaming. The volumetric content is sent to the server, who is in charge of optionally segmenting it, and then selecting the appropriate encoding for the client, given the network conditions and the user position and rotation. The content can then be streamed in volumetric form to the client, who will perform the rendering, depending on the viewport; alternatively, the rendering can be offloaded to a cloud or edge server, and the viewport can be transmitted to the client as conventional 2D video. The model "Electric guitar player" is taken from [36].

Depending on the type of volumetric content representation that is adopted to transmit and render the data, different streaming strategies can be devised. In the following, we detail streaming strategies for mesh and point cloud contents.

15.1.1 Dynamic mesh streaming strategies

Early attempts at mesh streaming focused on using progressive encoding with several levels of detail to aid in transmission and reception in low-power devices. The seminal work of Hoppe et al. [37] introduces the concept of progressive meshes, which stores any arbitrary mesh M as a coarse baseline M_0 along with n detail layers that can be used to progressively increase the level of detail, up to the original mesh. The key concept at play to obtain the coarse baseline is the so-called *edge collapse*: a transformation that unifies two adjacent vertexes into one. The inverse transformation, *vertex split*, allows to reconstruct the original mesh from the coarser representation through each split record. The result is a lossless compression solution that achieves progressive decoding capabilities, at the expense of additional overhead. Further optimizations have been proposed since then, taking into account the progressive compression of attributes and the decoding time as additional factors. One of such optimizations is used as the basis for a web-based framework to stream meshes [38], which allows for low-latency visualization with limited bandwidth. However, such scenario focuses on lossless delivery of static contents, mainly envisioned for scientific visualization. A strategy for optimizing the delivery of colored meshes in the event of packet loss is proposed by Cheng et al. [39], in which the optimal subsampling factors for geometry and color are derived based on the network conditions; several overlapping subsampled versions of the mesh are created, put into packets, and sent to the receiving side in random order to offer robustness against loss.

In the case of dynamic sequences, it is common to differentiate between *dynamic meshes* and *time-varying meshes* (TMV). The first commonly refers to synthetic animated content, for which vertex and face count, as well as connectivity, remains constant; the varying element is the position of the vertexes. TVMs, inversely, represent meshes with varying geometry, connectivity, vertex, and face counts across frames, which commonly occurs when 3D acquisition of real-life sequences is performed. In this case, the lack of consistent correspondence between vertices across frames leads to complexity in handling the temporal redundancies. To date, several algorithms have been proposed to efficiently encode TVMs [40–44], the most popular in terms of ease of adoption being the open-source library Draco 3D data compression,[4] Corto,[5] O3DGC,[6] and CTM.[7] A benchmarking of open-source mesh codecs for interactive immersive media streaming is presented by Doumanoglou et al. [45]. The codecs are extensively compared based on bitrate, distortion, and processing time, accounting for attribute and normals along with vertexes and connectivity. Results indicate that Draco and O3DGC are the best performing ones in terms of rate-distortion trade-off, whereas Corto offers the fastest decoding time. In addition, theoretical upper- and lower-bounds to the end-to-end latency are computed for each codec, along with an estimate of the achievable frame-rate, for several network conditions, exemplified by the round trip time (RTT) values. Results indicate that, in the case of small RTT, Corto is the best-performing one, both in terms of latency and frame-rate. However, when larger RTT values are considered, Draco outperforms it in terms of latency.

Advanced compression algorithms significantly reduce the bandwidth expenditure needed to transmit meshes. However, to cope with the intense data requirements for low-latency streaming of mesh representations, adaptive solutions are often needed alongside efficient coding solutions. In the case of meshes, network monitoring and optimization have been successfully employed to reduce bandwidth requirements, for example, by designing a network adaptation service to monitor the network performance and consequently adapt the mesh compression parameters [31]. A network optimization system for a centralized immersive gaming setup that targets both the end user's QoE and the production costs for the transcoder are envisioned by Athanasoulis et al. [46]. The authors develop a cognitive network optimizer based on reinforcement learning, which monitors network metrics, such as packet loss, bit- and frame-rate on the receiver side and in the transcoder, as well as the QoE of the transmitted meshes.

---

[4] https://google.github.io/draco/.

[5] http://vcg.isti.cnr.it/corto/.

[6] https://github.com/amd/rest3d/tree/master/server/o3dgc.

[7] http://openctm.sourceforge.net/.

The optimizer analyzes the input and, if needed, instigates changes in the mesh compression level, both in the transcoder and receiver side, and redirects the transcoder processing to either CPU or GPU. The optimizer is demonstrated through two profiles, based on whether it focuses on the QoE or it takes into account production costs, and compared with a baseline greedy approach. The results are evaluated based on the ratio between QoE and production costs, and show that considering both QoE and production cost leads to better performance with respect to the greedy approach in different bandwidth scenarios. Konstantoudakis et al. [32] propose a serverless framework for adaptive transcoding of meshes in a real-time immersive system. As part of the framework, a network optimization strategy to deal with the trade-off between QoE of each spectator and cost to the provider is devised. The model includes parameters such as the probability of a user to join or quit the transmission, the revenue for the provider for each user, the QoE for each user, and the costs of delivering and transcoding. Results demonstrate that the optimization can reduce the transcoding costs by 60% and the delivery by 20%.

In the context of networking optimization, the choice of networking protocol is one key parameter for streaming of volumetric contents. Different protocols might offer more robustness at the expense of larger delays, or more agility when dealing with network changes. The impact of the quality of the mesh reconstruction, as well as the network delay, is studied in the context of a VR game experience with real-time acquisition and reconstruction [47] with respect to the choice of network protocols. In particular, the authors investigate the impact of lag and frame drop on the final QoE, by selecting two different network protocols for the delivery, namely user datagram protocol (UDP) and transmission control protocol (TCP). TCP relies on handshakes to ensure reliability and prevent packet losses. However, this comes at the expense of delays in the transmission chain. On the other hand, UDP is more agile, but does not have a recovery mechanism in place for lost packets; additionally, it does not have congestion control. Results of the experiment show that UDP was preferred to TPC, indicating that packet and frame loss is considered more acceptable with respect to large delays and latency. The use of MPEG-DASH [48] for adaptive streaming of 3D scenes is investigated by Zampoglou et al. [49]. In particular, they propose a framework to arrange X3D scenes in a media presentation description (MPD), which will be used as the base element for the DASH architecture. Similarly, they update the attributes in the adaptation set and representation elements to be used for 3D objects, while being compatible with the DASH architecture. The framework was evaluated in a prototype system against direct HTTP download, demonstrating how the DASH protocol was capable of delivering a first segment of the content, thus initiating the experience for the user, in a fraction of the time required to download the full content. Moreover, the DASH delivery provided the full content in less time with respect to the HTTP counterpart.

Along with network adaptation, the user behavior can be employed to optimize the delivery of meshes. A user adaptation strategy for multiple 3D objects in an AR scenario is proposed in [23]. The authors calculate the priority value of each object in the scene based on the user's field of view, using a method proposed by Chim et al. [50]. Then, assuming that each object is available at several levels of detail, the contribution of each one to the final quality is computed, and a utility value is assigned to each object and level of detail, based on the ratio between quality and size. Finally, the adaptation strategy is formulated as a knapsack problem to maximize the number of objects (and relative levels of detail), based on their priority and utility.

To reduce the amount of data to be sent to the client, cloud-based rendering has also been considered. In this case, the volumetric data is sent to an intermediate server, which renders and transmits the 2D view based on the user's head position and FOV. The approach has the advantage of avoiding the entire mesh to be transmitted to the receiver's side; however, this comes at the cost of increased latency, due to the necessity for the server to receive the user's position before rendering. To alleviate the problem, head motion prediction algorithms have been developed and tested for volumetric streaming. In [30], a framework for head motion prediction, based on Kalman filters, is demonstrated. Khan et al. [33] investigate the use of several neural network architectures to achieve head movement prediction. Zhang et al. [34] extend the problem to multi-user prediction, optimizing the transmission for both the QoE of the users and the network resource utilization. In particular, multicast is used to transmit frames for groups of users with similar viewports.

Immersive streaming applications bring a series of security concerns. In particular, when the 3D objects represent biometrics for identification such as human faces, there is need for secure solutions to maintain the privacy in a streaming scenario. In [51], a volumetric video attack is simulated, and a countermeasure based on adversarial perturbations is devised to dodge the attack without compromising the visual quality.

15.1.2 Dynamic point cloud streaming strategies

Point cloud contents have recently seen a surge in popularity for volumetric video streaming scenarios involving natural acquisition. With respect to meshes, they have the advantage of being easier to process and manipulate, since each point can be treated independently as no connectivity information is required. However, to provide faithful representation of natural scenes, they require large collections of points to be delivered and rendered. Thus first approaches in point cloud streaming focused on improving the compression efficiency for point cloud contents. Similarly to what has been seen for mesh approaches, progressive point cloud encoders have been proposed to allow for refinement as the bandwidth increases, using octree structures that regularly partition the space [52–54]. Meng et al. [55] propose a progressive transmission method, in which the levels of detail of the data are arranged hierarchically, so that the rendering can be performed faster in local areas defined by the users' field of view. Kammerl et al. [56] present one of the first approaches for point cloud compression that is specifically tailored for online streaming. Specifically, they propose to leverage temporal redundancies by creating a double buffer octree structure to find correspondences between consecutive frames. The XOR operation is then applied to encode the differences between the frames. To be able to transmit leaf nodes with resolution greater than the octree resolution, they employ a point detail encoding module, which transmits the difference between the leaf nodes and the voxel center. The same module is used to encode other attributes, such as texture and normals. Mekuria et al. [57] present a compression solution for real-time encoding and decoding of colored point clouds. Their approach is based on an entropy-coded progressive octree structure, which allows to select the appropriate level of detail. Rigid transform estimation is used to perform inter frame prediction, whereas the color attributes are encoded using JPEG. Their solution was adopted as the reference encoder for the MPEG standardization efforts on point cloud compression [9].

Alongside efficient compression solution, adaptive streaming algorithms are needed to optimize delivery of point cloud contents over bandlimited networks. For point cloud contents, user adaptation represents one of the most adopted optimization solutions. As no connectivity information is needed to render them, segmenting the point cloud in non-overlapping regions to be encoded at different qualities is straightforward. An example of user adaptation is shown in Fig. 15.2. Only the regions that fall within the user viewport need to be transmitted and rendered in high quality, allowing for bandwidth savings, while maintaining high visual quality. To allow for such optimization, Hosseini et al. [58] propose an adaptive streaming framework based on MPEG DASH, named DASH-PC. Multiple qualities of the same frame are created to form the *adaptation set*, which is kept on an HTTP server. The client then requests the appropriate *representation*, i.e., a frame at a certain quality level that complies with the bandwidth requirements. Each representation can be split into multiple *segments*, which can help request only the parts of the content that are visible through the user's viewport. To create the representations, three subsampling algorithms are proposed; in addition, a human visual acuity model is employed to incorporate scaling into the adaptive algorithm so as not to waste resources on details that would not be visible. Park et al. [24,25] propose a streaming setup for volumetric contents. They extend the concept of tiling, already used for adaptive streaming of omnidirectional contents, by introducing the concept of *3D tiles*, and they define a utility function to estimate the importance of each tile for a given user. Their utility function takes into account the bandwidth cost of the selected representation, weighted by the number of distinguishable voxels in the tile, and the probability that such tile will be visible. They use a greedy maximization algorithm to select the tiles to be sent. Moreover, a window-based buffer is employed, instead of a simple queue, to offer faster adaptation to user interaction. A low-complexity tiling approach for real-time applications is proposed by Subramanyam et al. [26]. Each point cloud is divided

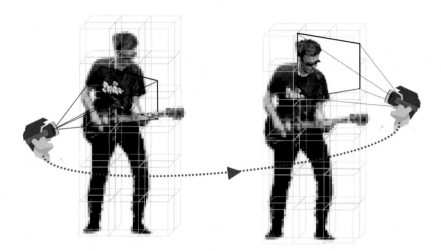

Figure 15.2 Example of user adaptive streaming. Depending on the user viewport, only the portion of the content that falls within the viewing frustum is transmitted in high quality, whereas the remaining segments are transmitted in low quality. As the user changes position and orientation, different segments are selected. The model "Electric guitar player" is taken from [36].

into non-overlapping tiles based on the visibility of each point by the camera that was used to acquire it, and the corresponding orientation of the camera is assigned to each tile. Then, each tile is compressed using a real-time encoder at different quality levels, forming the adaptation set. The utility of each tile is computed as a simple dot product between the orientation of the tile and the user's viewing angle. Three utility heuristics, based on [27], are used to select the proper quality for each tile. The adaptive algorithm is tested under various fixed bitrate constraints, showing that adaptation leads to up to 60% bitrate savings with respect to non-adaptive solutions. Li et al. [59] propose a QoE model to optimize volumetric video streaming. The model is based on the visual quality of the point cloud content, expressed through PSNR on both geometry and color; on the impairments deriving from stalling events, such as downloading and decoding time; and on the quality switch, which happens when a tile of different quality is requested. A viewport prediction framework for mobile streaming of volumetric video is proposed by Han et al. [60]. The authors propose to segment the point cloud contents into cells, which are losslessly compressed using Draco. They employ a lightweight algorithm to perform viewport prediction, and they define three visibility-aware optimization models to select which cell to be transmitted to the user at each time segment: *viewpoint visibility*, which considers an extended viewing frustum with varying level of detail; *occlusion visibility*, which models whether the cell will be visible from the viewpoint; and *distance visibility*, which uses objective quality measurements to understand which level of detail to assign to each cell. They demonstrate their framework on 5G networks and on limited bandwidth scenarios, reporting significant gains on data usage and perceived quality with respect to the baseline.

The previous algorithms tackled adaptation for single point cloud contents. Algorithms for multipoint cloud rate adaptation are proposed by van der Hooft et al. [27]. In particular, the point clouds are ranked based on the distance with respect to the user, the visibility (and potential) of the point cloud, and the ratio between the visible area of the point cloud, and its bandwidth cost. Then, three utility maximization strategies are envisioned: *greedy*, where the highest possible quality is given to the first ranked point cloud before moving down the rank; *uniform*, where the bit budget is spent uniformly on all the point clouds, and the quality is increased one representation at the time; and *hybrid*, where the uniform allocation is used for point clouds within the field of view, and any remaining budget is then used for point clouds outside of it. They test the impact of such heuristic considering different locations for the point clouds and different camera paths to simulate user interactivity. Moreover, a QoE evaluation through subjective studies is performed in a subsequent work [61], which demonstrates the significant impact of the bandwidth allocation strategy on the final perceived quality.

The previous works have focused on providing user adaptation to cope with the bandwidth requirements of the systems. However, network optimization can play a large role in optimizing volumetric video streaming. Ramadan et al. [62] present an adaptive streaming mechanism specifically tailored for 5G networks. In particular, they propose adaptive content bursting in high bandwidth time windows to ensure that the streaming can continue without stalling when low-bandwidth conditions occur. Moreover, they employ dynamic switching between 4G and 5G, depending on the estimated channel conditions, to ensure a more stable streaming experience. Liu et al. [28,29] consider the impact of bandwidth changes, buffer status, and computational resources to design a fuzzy-based delivery system for tiled point clouds. The point cloud tiles are encoded at multiple quality level; however, one main difference with other approaches is that a coarse representation of the full point cloud is stored in the server, along with the *decoded* version of the compressed tiles. The authors consider a quality maximization optimization problem, in which both encoded and decoded versions of the tiles are available to be sent. The decision depends on the predicted bandwidth constraints, on the space availability on the buffer, and on the computational load, which are all modeled using fuzzy logic. They demonstrate gains with respect to the baseline using two point cloud models.

More recently, some machine learning-based models have been employed to further enhance the capabilities of the volumetric video system, especially in adverse conditions, to deliver a better experience to the users. Zhang et al. [63,64] propose a super resolution-aided volumetric video streaming system. The proposed super resolution algorithm is optimized to reduce inference time to cope with real-time streaming constraints, and is specifically designed to promote cross-frame consistency. The integration of the super resolution engine into the volumetric video streaming system is conducted through an adaptation model that takes into account the quality of the point cloud patches, the bandwidth consumption incurring from high-resolution patches, and the computational resources needed to upsample the low-resolution patches, along with the stalling that might derive from them. Huang et al. [65] employ an end-to-end deep neural network, which involves all the steps from acquisition to rendering and playback, thus avoiding traditional encoding, transmission, and decoding solutions. Key features are extracted from the input point cloud content and reconstructed at the receiving side using a lightweight neural network. An online adapter is added to switch between inference models, depending on the bandwidth conditions. Their proposed system is validated through a real-time communication setup, in which contents are acquired by 3D sensors and transmitted through WiFi channels with varying bandwidth.

15.2. Volumetric video streaming systems

In the previous section we have introduced some notable approaches to optimize transmission of volumetric contents for streaming purposes. Orchestrating such a system, however, is far from an easy feat. Technological limitations, network instability, system design constraints, and device consumption costs are all aspects that need to be taken into consideration when constructing a feasible prototype for volumetric video streaming. Incorporating theoretical approaches may lead to the discovery of new vulnerabilities and hard constraints. In the following, we summarize some of the demonstration of volumetric video streaming systems operating on meshes and point clouds.

15.2.1 Mesh-based systems

The majority of the systems proposed in the literature concerns 3D teleimmersion; as such, the focus is on creating a system that can acquire, process, transmit, and render volumetric objects in real-time. A multi-camera system for 3D acquisition and transmission of real-world environments using meshes is described by Vasudevan et al. [66]. The objects are obtained from a cluster of calibrated cameras through disparity estimation; a coarse mesh model is derived through triangularization, and then progressively refined through bisection. The bisection model is used for faster transmission; moreover, fast reconstruction is achieved through parallelization of data and rendering tasks. Mekuria et al. [67] integrate efficient mesh compression and packet loss protection to their system. Their envisioned pipeline consists of a capturing module, an ad-hoc mesh compression module, a rateless coding module for packet loss protection, and a renderer. Beck et al. [68] present a group-to-group teleimmersive system. The participants are captured using multiple calibrated Kinect cameras; then, the data streams are processed using a parallelized and distributed processing pipeline. The rendering is achieved through projection-based multi-user 3D displays, which provides a perspective-corrected 3D scene visualization to each user. The system is evaluated in terms of usability in three scenarios: face-to-face meeting, side-by-side coupled navigation, and independent navigation. Zioulis et al. [69] also employ multiple Kinect cameras to obtain mesh models of their users. Their multi-camera setup captures the RGB-D frames asynchronously and sends them to a centralized server to convert to colored meshes. Additionally, the user's motion is tracked through skeleton data. A server-based networking scheme is employed to transmit the 3D representations, which are compressed using static mesh encoders on a frame-by-frame basis. The system is demonstrated through a 3D gaming scenario. Doumanoglou et al. [70] demonstrate a system architecture for an augmented virtuality scenario, in which users are 3D-captured and can play a game in a teleimmersive system using their body pose as a controller for the game. The system is comprised of a 3D capturing module with integrated pose recognition, player, and spectator clients, and a 3D transcoder component to allow for adaptive streaming for both the players and the spectators. Furthermore, an adaptation for 5G networks is envisioned.

For a broadcasting scenario, a demonstration of a real-time volumetric streaming module for AR synchronized with broadcast video is given by Kawamura et al. [71]. They store the geometry in a binary file comprising of a list of vertexes and normals, to which the texture is attached after JPEG compression; bitrate savings are achieved by mesh simplification. The packets are sent over the Internet using UDP, and synchronization between broadcast video, and AR contents are achieved in their proposed receiver application through sync packets.

Depending on the device that is used to experience the 3D contents, it might not be feasible to deliver the volumetric content directly to the end device. For example, untethered devices might suffer from limited processing power, overheating issues, or battery limitations. Thus it might be necessary to perform the rendering on an edge- or cloud-based server. Orts-Escolano et al. [7] design a volumetric telepresence system called "Holoportation," They use 8 near infrared cameras with active stereo depth estimation to capture the users; the conversion to meshes is done to ensure both spatial and temporal consistency, and to improve the visual quality. Spatial audio is achieved by matching every user source to their relative 3D representation, along with spatialization. Lightweight compression is applied to comply with the real-time requirements. Finally, rendering is performed on the edge servers, employing head motion prediction to reduce latency, and the corresponding views are then transmitted to the rendering device. The system is extensively demonstrated in AR and VR scenarios. Gül et al. [72] propose a volumetric video streaming setup, in which the meshes are sent to a cloud server alongside the user position and rotation. The server performs 6DoF user movement prediction to forecast where the user will be and anticipate which rendered views to send to the user. The effect of the prediction module on the latency is evaluated with respect to the baseline, showing that the rendering error is reduced when employing the prediction mechanism. An additional component that allows animation of volumetric data is designed for the system, which allows the volumetric video character to follow the user as it speaks or moves [73,74].

15.2.2 Point cloud-based systems

A few systems have been proposed in the literature for point cloud video streaming; the main difference laying in whether they involve a real-time telepresence scenario [75,76] or a broadcast volumetric video approach [77,78]. Jansen et al. [75] adopt the DASH framework for real-time transmission of point cloud contents for 3D teleimmersion. Their proposed pipeline uses a multicamera Kinect setup (shown in Fig. 15.3) to acquire RGB-D data, which is converted to tiled point cloud representation at multiple quality levels. The data is sent to the DASH server, which is responsible for sending the selected quality to the receivers, which then decode and render the point cloud contents on the device. Cernigliaro et al. [76] propose a multipoint control unit (MCU) for real-time delivery optimization of multiple point cloud streams, called PC-MCU. The MCU server receives multiple point cloud representations, which are decoded and combined in the virtual scene. To optimize delivery for the receiving devices, the server considers the user's viewport and distance from the point cloud contents to lower the level of detail or remove contents outside of viewing window. The system is evaluated in terms of resource consumption, showing a reduction in both computational resources and necessary bandwidth, at the expense of added latency.

Special attention in the literature has been reserved for systems that are suitable for mobile phone consumption. With respect to tethered devices, there are some considerations that need to be kept in mind: the transmission should be optimized for wireless networks, to allow users to experience the content on the go and move around without constraints; the decoding time needs to be minimized not only for framerate require-

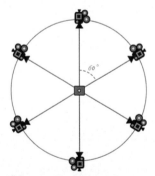

(a) Camera arrangement in the physical space (top view).

(b) Example of user in the capturing setup.

Figure 15.3 Example of acquisition system for real-time transmission of volumetric media, using consumer-grade RGB-D sensors.

ments, but also for memory and power consumption, which are two critical features in mobile devices; the rendering needs to be optimized for fast user adaptation and low motion to photon latency, to maintain a pleasant user experience. Qian et al. [77] present Nebula, a DASH-based system for volumetric streaming on mobile phones. In particular, they encode the point cloud content in layers to achieve progressive streaming through DASH. The decoding and rendering is performed in an edge server to reduce the computational complexity for the mobile device. To reduce the latency, the edge server creates several rendered subframes, based on the current and predicted viewports, which are combined into a packet and sent to the mobile device. Lee et al. [78] present a system architecture for end-to-end streaming of volumetric video to mobile devices, named GROOT, powered by a faster, parallelized encoding and decoding scheme, along with viewport optimization, such as frustum culling and depth-based sampling. Their encoding solution is based on octree geometry. However, instead of encoding the oc-cupancy of the entire tree, they split the octree structure at a predefined maximum breadth depth; then, the leaf nodes are individually encoded, starting from their root at the maximum breadth depth to avoid dependencies with the branches. In practice, this allows to decode the desired leaf nodes without having to traverse the entire point cloud, facilitating faster rendering and removal of unnecessary points for visualization. The color compression efficiency is also improved by reordering the color information from the maximum breadth depth onward to exploit spatial similarities. Frustum culling is applied by checking hierarchically whether the node boundaries fall within the frus-tum; for boundary cases, the children are checked until the entire boundary corners fall within. Finally, the sampling density is adjusted, based on the perceived visual quality.

15.3. Conclusion

This chapter provides an overview of the current approaches of and implementations for volumetric video streaming, considering both media consumption and communication pipelines. Current solutions provide initial working systems that allow a first wave of novel applications from cultural heritage [79] to entertainment experiences [80]. Still, the possibilities are endless, from immersive performances [81] to future exhibitions and conference [82] to medical interventions [83]. Future work is needed for the develop-ment of such novel experiences, as well as the better understanding and modeling of the resulting content for optimization purposes.

A major research area is the optimization of the experience based on progressive streaming and tiling, currently inspired by previous work on 360 videos [84,85]. Volu-metric video, as a 6DoF experience, brings new challenges in terms of predicting and modeling the movement of the user and their relationship with the content. There are some initial investigations about [86], but still more research needs to go in this direc-tion. For example, there is a need for new datasets that focus on navigation patterns

[26,87] for different contexts, which will help the development and validation of more advanced solutions.

Volumetric video will allow for interactive and immersive experiences, palliating existing problems, such as the Zoom fatigue [88]. Future research is needed for the provision of adequate interaction mechanisms and the seamless inclusion of interactive content in the experiences. Though recently works are focusing on trying to better understand the basic constructs on social VR [89,90], further research is needed for considering the volumetric video case. Finally, more datasets centered in interactive activities are missing [36].

Networks, in particular mobile, are evolving, bringing closer to reality futuristic scenarios. Edge rendering, for example, is helping to make volumetric video available in mobile devices. New protocols and infrastructure are coming, increasing the opportunities for everywhere and anytime volumetric video consumption. For example, the European Commission has recently launched an initiative on smart networks and services (SNS)[8] towards 6G, where extended reality will become a core use case.

References

[1] MULTIMEDIA '93: Proceedings of the First ACM International Conference on Multimedia, Association for Computing Machinery, New York, NY, USA, 1993, https://doi.org/10.1145/166266.
[2] ACM Transactions on Multimedia Computing Communications and Applications 9 (1) (2013), https://doi.org/10.1145/2422956.
[3] P. Shenoy, Multimedia systems research: The first twenty years and lessons for the next twenty, ACM Transactions on Multimedia Computing Communications and Applications 9 (1s) (Oct 2013), https://doi.org/10.1145/2490859.
[4] Z. Yang, W. Wu, K. Nahrstedt, G. Kurillo, R. Bajcsy, Enabling multi-party 3D tele-immersive environments with viewcast, ACM Transactions on Multimedia Computing Communications and Applications 6 (2) (mar 2010), https://doi.org/10.1145/1671962.1671963.
[5] C. Kuster, N. Ranieri, Agustina, H. Zimmer, J. Bazin, C. Sun, T. Popa, M. Gross, Towards next generation 3D teleconferencing systems, in: 2012 3DTV-Conference: The True Vision - Capture, Transmission and Display of 3D Video (3DTV-CON), 2012, pp. 1–4, https://doi.org/10.1109/3DTV.2012.6365454.
[6] H. Fuchs, A. State, J. Bazin, Immersive 3D telepresence, IEEE Computer 47 (07) (2014) 46–52, https://doi.org/10.1109/MC.2014.185.
[7] S. Orts-Escolano, C. Rhemann, S. Fanello, W. Chang, A. Kowdle, Y. Degtyarev, D. Kim, P.L. Davidson, S. Khamis, M. Dou, V. Tankovich, C. Loop, Q. Cai, P.A. Chou, S. Mennicken, J. Valentin, V. Pradeep, S. Wang, S.B. Kang, P. Kohli, Y. Lutchyn, C. Keskin, S. Izadi, Holoportation: virtual 3D teleportation in real-time, in: Proceedings of the 29th Annual Symposium on User Interface Software and Technology, UIST '16, Association for Computing Machinery, New York, NY, USA, 2016, pp. 741–754, https://doi.org/10.1145/2984511.2984517.
[8] Y. Alkhalili, T. Meuser, R. Steinmetz, A survey of volumetric content streaming approaches, in: 2020 IEEE Sixth International Conference on Multimedia Big Data (BigMM), 2020, pp. 191–199, https://doi.org/10.1109/BigMM50055.2020.00035.
[9] S. Schwarz, M. Preda, V. Baroncini, M. Budagavi, P. Cesar, P.A. Chou, R.A. Cohen, M. Krivokuća, S. Lasserre, Z. Li, et al., Emerging MPEG standards for point cloud compression, IEEE Journal on Emerging and Selected Topics in Circuits and Systems 9 (1) (2018) 133–148.

---

[8] https://digital-strategy.ec.europa.eu/en/policies/smart-networks-and-services-joint-undertaking.

[10] D. Graziosi, O. Nakagami, S. Kuma, A. Zaghetto, T. Suzuki, A. Tabatabai, An overview of ongoing point cloud compression standardization activities: video-based (V-PCC) and geometry-based (G-PCC), APSIPA Transactions on Signal and Information Processing 9 (2020) e13, https://doi.org/10.1017/ATSIP.2020.12.

[11] S. Dijkstra-Soudarissanane, K.E. Assal, S. Gunkel, F. ter Haar, R. Hindriks, J.W. Kleinrouweler, O. Niamut, Multi-sensor capture and network processing for virtual reality conferencing, in: Proceedings of the 10th ACM Multimedia Systems Conference, MMSys '19, Association for Computing Machinery, New York, NY, USA, 2019, pp. 316–319, https://doi.org/10.1145/3304109.3323838.

[12] S.N.B. Gunkel, R. Hindriks, K.M.E. Assal, H.M. Stokking, S. Dijkstra-Soudarissanane, F. ter Haar, O. Niamut, VRComm: an end-to-end web system for real-time photorealistic social VR communication, in: Proceedings of the 12th ACM Multimedia Systems Conference, ACM, Istanbul, Turkey, 2021, pp. 65–79, https://doi.org/10.1145/3458305.3459595, https://dl.acm.org/doi/10.1145/3458305.3459595.

[13] P. Carballeira, C. Carmona, C. Diaz, D. Berjon, J. Cabrera Quesada, F. Moran, C. Doblado, S. Arnaldo, M. del Mar Martin, N. Garcia, FVV live: A real-time free-viewpoint video system with consumer electronics hardware, IEEE Transactions on Multimedia 24 (2022) 2378–2391, https://doi.org/10.1109/TMM.2021.3079711.

[14] M. Pauly, M. Gross, Spectral processing of point-sampled geometry, in: Proceedings of the 28th Annual Conference on Computer Graphics and Interactive Techniques, SIGGRAPH '01, Association for Computing Machinery, New York, NY, USA, 2001, pp. 379–386, https://doi.org/10.1145/383259.383301.

[15] T. Golla, R. Klein, Real-time point cloud compression, in: 2015 IEEE/RSJ International Conference on Intelligent Robots and Systems (IROS), 2015, pp. 5087–5092, https://doi.org/10.1109/IROS.2015.7354093.

[16] C. Tu, E. Takeuchi, A. Carballo, K. Takeda, Real-time streaming point cloud compression for 3D lidar sensor using u-net, IEEE Access 7 (2019) 113616–113625, https://doi.org/10.1109/ACCESS.2019.2935253.

[17] S. Mondet, W. Cheng, G. Morin, R. Grigoras, F. Boudon, W.T. Ooi, Streaming of plants in distributed virtual environments, in: Proceedings of the 16th ACM International Conference on Multimedia, MM '08, Association for Computing Machinery, New York, NY, USA, 2008, pp. 1–10, https://doi.org/10.1145/1459359.1459361.

[18] P. Lange, R. Weller, G. Zachmann, Scalable concurrency control for massively collaborative virtual environments, in: Proceedings of the 7th ACM International Workshop on Massively Multiuser Virtual Environments, MMVE '15, Association for Computing Machinery, New York, NY, USA, 2015, pp. 7–12, https://doi.org/10.1145/2723695.2723699.

[19] M. Slater, M.V. Sanchez-Vives, Enhancing our lives with immersive virtual reality, Frontiers in Robotics and AI 3 (2016), https://doi.org/10.3389/frobt.2016.00074, https://www.frontiersin.org/article/10.3389/frobt.2016.00074.

[20] Z. Yang, K. Nahrstedt, Y. Cui, B. Yu, J. Liang, S. Hack Jung, R. Bajscy, TEEVE: the next generation architecture for tele-immersive environments, in: Seventh IEEE International Symposium on Multimedia (ISM'05), 2005, 8 pp., https://doi.org/10.1109/ISM.2005.113.

[21] C. Zhang, Q. Cai, P.A. Chou, Z. Zhang, R. Martin-Brualla, Viewport: A distributed, immersive teleconferencing system with infrared dot pattern, IEEE MultiMedia 20 (1) (2013) 17–27, https://doi.org/10.1109/MMUL.2013.12.

[22] B. Han, Mobile immersive computing: research challenges and the road ahead, IEEE Communications Magazine 57 (10) (2019) 112–118, https://doi.org/10.1109/MCOM.001.1800876.

[23] S. Petrangeli, G. Simon, H. Wang, V. Swaminathan, Dynamic adaptive streaming for augmented reality applications, in: 2019 IEEE International Symposium on Multimedia (ISM), 2019, pp. 56–567, https://doi.org/10.1109/ISM46123.2019.00017.

[24] J. Park, P.A. Chou, J.-N. Hwang, Volumetric media streaming for augmented reality, in: 2018 IEEE Global Communications Conference (GLOBECOM), 2018, pp. 1–6, iSSN: 2576-6813, https://doi.org/10.1109/GLOCOM.2018.8647537.

[25] J. Park, P.A. Chou, J.-N. Hwang, Rate-utility optimized streaming of volumetric media for augmented reality, IEEE Journal on Emerging and Selected Topics in Circuits and Systems 9 (1) (2019) 149–162, https://doi.org/10.1109/JETCAS.2019.2898622.

[26] S. Subramanyam, I. Viola, A. Hanjalic, P. Cesar, User centered adaptive streaming of dynamic point clouds with low complexity tiling, in: Proceedings of the 28th ACM International Conference on Multimedia, ACM, Seattle, WA, USA, 2020, pp. 3669–3677, https://doi.org/10.1145/3394171.3413535, https://dl.acm.org/doi/10.1145/3394171.3413535.

[27] J. van der Hooft, T. Wauters, F. De Turck, C. Timmerer, H. Hellwagner, Towards 6DoF HTTP adaptive streaming through point cloud compression, in: Proceedings of the 27th ACM International Conference on Multimedia, ACM, Nice, France, 2019, pp. 2405–2413, https://doi.org/10.1145/3343031.3350917, https://dl.acm.org/doi/10.1145/3343031.3350917.

[28] Z. Liu, J. Li, X. Chen, C. Wu, S. Ishihara, Y. Ji, J. Li, Fuzzy logic-based adaptive point cloud video streaming, IEEE Open Journal of the Computer Society 1 (2020) 121–130, https://doi.org/10.1109/OJCS.2020.3006205.

[29] Z. Liu, Q. Li, X. Chen, C. Wu, S. Ishihara, J. Li, Y. Ji, Point cloud video streaming: challenges and solutions, IEEE Network 35 (5) (2021) 202–209, https://doi.org/10.1109/MNET.101.2000364.

[30] S. Gül, S. Bosse, D. Podborski, T. Schierl, C. Hellge, Kalman filter-based head motion prediction for cloud-based mixed reality, in: Proceedings of the 28th ACM International Conference on Multimedia, ACM, Seattle, WA, USA, 2020, pp. 3632–3641, https://doi.org/10.1145/3394171.3413699, https://dl.acm.org/doi/10.1145/3394171.3413699.

[31] S. Crowle, A. Doumanoglou, B. Poussard, M. Boniface, D. Zarpalas, P. Daras, Dynamic adaptive mesh streaming for real-time 3D teleimmersion, in: Proceedings of the 20th International Conference on 3D Web Technology, ACM, Heraklion, Crete, Greece, 2015, pp. 269–277, https://doi.org/10.1145/2775292.2775296, https://dl.acm.org/doi/10.1145/2775292.2775296.

[32] K. Konstantoudakis, D. Breitgand, A. Doumanoglou, N. Zioulis, A. Weit, K. Christaki, P. Drakoulis, E. Christakis, D. Zarpalas, P. Daras, Serverless streaming for emerging media: towards 5G network-driven cost optimization, Multimedia Tools and Applications (Mar. 2021), https://doi.org/10.1007/s11042-020-10219-7.

[33] M.J. Khan, A. Bentaleb, S. Harous, Can accurate future bandwidth prediction improve volumetric video streaming experience?, in: 2021 International Wireless Communications and Mobile Computing (IWCMC), 2021, pp. 1041–1047, iSSN: 2376-6506, https://doi.org/10.1109/IWCMC51323.2021.9498691.

[34] D. Zhang, B. Han, P. Pathak, H. Wang, Innovating multi-user volumetric video streaming through cross-layer design, in: Proceedings of the Twentieth ACM Workshop on Hot Topics in Networks, ACM, Virtual Event, United Kingdom, 2021, pp. 16–22, https://doi.org/10.1145/3484266.3487396, https://dl.acm.org/doi/10.1145/3484266.3487396.

[35] J. van der Hooft, M.T. Vega, T. Wauters, C. Timmerer, A.C. Begen, F.D. Turck, R. Schatz, From capturing to rendering: volumetric media delivery with six degrees of freedom, IEEE Communications Magazine 58 (10) (2020) 49–55, https://doi.org/10.1109/MCOM.001.2000242.

[36] I. Reimat, E. Alexiou, J. Jansen, I. Viola, S. Subramanyam, P. Cesar, CWIPC-SXR: Point Cloud Dynamic Human Dataset for Social XR, Association for Computing Machinery, New York, NY, USA, 2021, pp. 300–306, https://doi.org/10.1145/3458305.3478452.

[37] H. Hoppe, Progressive meshes, in: Proceedings of the 23rd Annual Conference on Computer Graphics and Interactive Techniques - SIGGRAPH '96, Association for Computing Machinery, 1996, pp. 99–108, https://doi.org/10.1145/237170.237216, http://portal.acm.org/citation.cfm?doid=237170.237216.

[38] G. Lavoué, L. Chevalier, F. Dupont, Streaming compressed 3D data on the web using JavaScript and WebGL, in: Proceedings of the 18th International Conference on 3D Web Technology - Web3D '13, ACM Press, San Sebastian, Spain, 2013, p. 19, https://doi.org/10.1145/2466533.2466539, http://dl.acm.org/citation.cfm?doid=2466533.2466539.

[39] I. Cheng, L. Ying, A. Basu, Packet loss modeling for perceptually optimized 3D transmission, in: 2006 IEEE International Conference on Multimedia and Expo, IEEE, 2006, pp. 1229–1232.

[40] S. Gupta, K. Sengupta, A.A. Kassim, Compression of dynamic 3D geometry data using iterative closest point algorithm, Computer Vision and Image Understanding 87 (1–3) (2002) 116–130.

[41] S. Gupta, K. Sengupta, A. Kassim, Registration and partitioning-based compression of 3-D dynamic data, IEEE Transactions on Circuits and Systems for Video Technology 13 (11) (2003) 1144–1155.

[42] S.-R. Han, T. Yamasaki, K. Aizawa, Geometry compression for time-varying meshes using coarse and fine levels of quantization and run-length encoding, in: 2008 15th IEEE International Conference on Image Processing, IEEE, 2008, pp. 1045–1048.

[43] S.-R. Han, T. Yamasaki, K. Aizawa, Time-varying mesh compression using an extended block matching algorithm, IEEE Transactions on Circuits and Systems for Video Technology 17 (11) (2007) 1506–1518.

[44] A. Doumanoglou, D.S. Alexiadis, D. Zarpalas, P. Daras, Toward real-time and efficient compression of human time-varying meshes, IEEE Transactions on Circuits and Systems for Video Technology 24 (12) (2014) 2099–2116.

[45] A. Doumanoglou, P. Drakoulis, N. Zioulis, D. Zarpalas, P. Daras, Benchmarking open-source static 3D mesh codecs for immersive media interactive live streaming, IEEE Journal on Emerging and Selected Topics in Circuits and Systems 9 (1) (2019) 190–203, https://doi.org/10.1109/JETCAS.2019.2898768.

[46] MMEDIA 2020, The Twelfth International Conference on Advances in Multimedia, Lisbon, Portugal, 23–27 February 2020, ISSN: 2308-4448, ISBN: 978-1-61208-772-6, http://www.thinkmind.org/index.php?view=instance&instance=MMEDIA+2020.

[47] A. Doumanoglou, D. Griffin, J. Serrano, N. Zioulis, T.K. Phan, D. Jiménez, D. Zarpalas, F. Alvarez, M. Rio, P. Daras, Quality of experience for 3-D immersive media streaming, IEEE Transactions on Broadcasting 64 (2) (2018) 379–391, https://doi.org/10.1109/TBC.2018.2823909.

[48] I. Sodagar, The MPEG-DASH standard for multimedia streaming over the internet, IEEE MultiMedia 18 (4) (2011) 62–67.

[49] M. Zampoglou, K. Kapetanakis, A. Stamoulias, A.G. Malamos, S. Panagiotakis, Adaptive streaming of complex Web 3D scenes based on the MPEG-DASH standard, Multimedia Tools and Applications 77 (1) (2018) 125–148, https://doi.org/10.1007/s11042-016-4255-8.

[50] J. Chim, R.W. Lau, H.V. Leong, A. Si, CyberWalk: A web-based distributed virtual walkthrough environment, IEEE Transactions on Multimedia 5 (4) (2003) 503–515.

[51] Z. Tang, X. Feng, Y. Xie, H. Phan, T. Guo, B. Yuan, S. Wei, VVSec: securing volumetric video streaming via benign use of adversarial perturbation, in: Proceedings of the 28th ACM International Conference on Multimedia, ACM, Seattle, WA, USA, 2020, pp. 3614–3623, https://doi.org/10.1145/3394171.3413639, https://dl.acm.org/doi/10.1145/3394171.3413639.

[52] J. Peng, C.J. Kuo, Octree-based progressive geometry encoder, in: Internet Multimedia Management Systems IV, vol. 5242, International Society for Optics and Photonics, 2003, pp. 301–311.

[53] Y. Huang, J. Peng, C.-J. Kuo, M. Gopi, Octree-based progressive geometry coding of point clouds, in: PBG@ SIGGRAPH, 2006, pp. 103–110.

[54] R. Schnabel, R. Klein, Octree-based point-cloud compression, in: PBG@ SIGGRAPH, 2006, pp. 111–120.

[55] F. Meng, H. Zha, Streaming transmission of point-sampled geometry based on view-dependent level-of-detail, in: Fourth International Conference on 3-D Digital Imaging and Modeling, 2003. 3DIM 2003. Proceedings, IEEE, 2003, pp. 466–473.

[56] J. Kammerl, N. Blodow, R.B. Rusu, S. Gedikli, M. Beetz, E. Steinbach, Real-time compression of point cloud streams, in: 2012 IEEE International Conference on Robotics and Automation, 2012, pp. 778–785, iSSN: 1050-4729, https://doi.org/10.1109/ICRA.2012.6224647.

[57] R. Mekuria, K. Blom, P. Cesar, Design, implementation, and evaluation of a point cloud codec for tele-immersive video, IEEE Transactions on Circuits and Systems for Video Technology 27 (4) (2017) 828–842, https://doi.org/10.1109/TCSVT.2016.2543039.

[58] M. Hosseini, C. Timmerer, Dynamic adaptive point cloud streaming, in: Proceedings of the 23rd Packet Video Workshop, PV '18, Association for Computing Machinery, New York, NY, USA, 2018, pp. 25–30, https://doi.org/10.1145/3210424.3210429.

[59] J. Li, X. Wang, Z. Liu, Q. Li, A QoE model in point cloud video streaming, arXiv:2111.02985, Nov. 2021.

[60] B. Han, Y. Liu, F. Qian, ViVo: visibility-aware mobile volumetric video streaming, in: Proceedings of the 26th Annual International Conference on Mobile Computing and Networking, ACM, London, United Kingdom, 2020, pp. 1–13, https://doi.org/10.1145/3372224.3380888, https://dl.acm.org/doi/10.1145/3372224.3380888.

[61] J. van der Hooft, M.T. Vega, C. Timmerer, A.C. Begen, F. De Turck, R. Schatz, Objective and subjective QoE evaluation for adaptive point cloud streaming, in: 2020 Twelfth International Conference on Quality of Multimedia Experience (QoMEX), 2020, pp. 1–6, iSSN: 2472-7814, https://doi.org/10.1109/QoMEX48832.2020.9123081.

[62] E. Ramadan, A. Narayanan, U.K. Dayalan, R.A.K. Fezeu, F. Qian, Z.-L. Zhang, Case for 5G-aware video streaming applications, in: Proceedings of the 1st Workshop on 5G Measurements, Modeling, and Use Cases, ACM, Virtual Event, 2021, pp. 27–34, https://doi.org/10.1145/3472771.3474036, https://dl.acm.org/doi/10.1145/3472771.3474036.

[63] A. Zhang, C. Wang, X. Liu, B. Han, F. Qian, Mobile volumetric video streaming enhanced by super resolution, in: Proceedings of the 18th International Conference on Mobile Systems, Applications, and Services, ACM, Toronto, Ontario, Canada, 2020, pp. 462–463, https://doi.org/10.1145/3386901.3396598, https://dl.acm.org/doi/10.1145/3386901.3396598.

[64] A. Zhang, C. Wang, B. Han, F. Qian, Efficient volumetric video streaming through super resolution, in: Proceedings of the 22nd International Workshop on Mobile Computing Systems and Applications, ACM, Virtual, United Kingdom, 2021, pp. 106–111, https://doi.org/10.1145/3446382.3448663, https://dl.acm.org/doi/10.1145/3446382.3448663.

[65] Y. Huang, Y. Zhu, X. Qiao, Z. Tan, B. Bai, AITransfer: progressive AI-powered transmission for real-time point cloud video streaming, in: Proceedings of the 29th ACM International Conference on Multimedia, ACM, Virtual Event, China, 2021, pp. 3989–3997, https://doi.org/10.1145/3474085.3475624, https://dl.acm.org/doi/10.1145/3474085.3475624.

[66] R. Vasudevan, G. Kurillo, E. Lobaton, T. Bernardin, O. Kreylos, R. Bajcsy, K. Nahrstedt, High-quality visualization for geographically distributed 3-D teleimmersive applications, IEEE Transactions on Multimedia 13 (3) (2011) 573–584, https://doi.org/10.1109/TMM.2011.2123871.

[67] R. Mekuria, M. Sanna, S. Asioli, E. Izquierdo, D.C.A. Bulterman, P. Cesar, A 3D tele-immersion system based on live captured mesh geometry, in: Proceedings of the 4th ACM Multimedia Systems Conference on - MMSys '13, ACM Press, Oslo, Norway, 2013, pp. 24–35, https://doi.org/10.1145/2483977.2483980, http://dl.acm.org/citation.cfm?doid=2483977.2483980.

[68] S. Beck, A. Kunert, A. Kulik, B. Froehlich, Immersive group-to-group telepresence, IEEE Transactions on Visualization and Computer Graphics 19 (4) (2013) 616–625, https://doi.org/10.1109/TVCG.2013.33.

[69] N. Zioulis, D. Alexiadis, A. Doumanoglou, G. Louizis, K. Apostolakis, D. Zarpalas, P. Daras, 3D tele-immersion platform for interactive immersive experiences between remote users, in: 2016 IEEE International Conference on Image Processing (ICIP), IEEE, Phoenix, AZ, USA, 2016, pp. 365–369, https://doi.org/10.1109/ICIP.2016.7532380, http://ieeexplore.ieee.org/document/7532380/.

[70] A. Doumanoglou, N. Zioulis, D. Griffin, J. Serrano, T.K. Phan, D. Jiménez, D. Zarpalas, F. Alvarez, M. Rio, P. Daras, A system architecture for live immersive 3D-media transcoding over 5G networks, in: 2018 IEEE International Symposium on Broadband Multimedia Systems and Broadcasting (BMSB), IEEE, 2018, pp. 11–15.

[71] Y. Kawamura, Y. Yamakami, H. Nagata, K. Imamura, Real-time streaming of sequential volumetric data for augmented reality synchronized with broadcast video, in: 2019 IEEE 9th International Conference on Consumer Electronics (ICCE-Berlin), 2019, pp. 267–268, iSSN: 2166-6822, https://doi.org/10.1109/ICCE-Berlin47944.2019.8966190.

[72] S. Gül, D. Podborski, T. Buchholz, T. Schierl, C. Hellge, Low-latency cloud-based volumetric video streaming using head motion prediction, in: Proceedings of the 30th ACM Workshop on Network and Operating Systems Support for Digital Audio and Video, ACM, Istanbul, Turkey, 2020, pp. 27–33, https://doi.org/10.1145/3386290.3396933, https://dl.acm.org/doi/10.1145/3386290.3396933.

[73] S. Gül, D. Podborski, A. Hilsmann, W. Morgenstern, P. Eisert, O. Schreer, T. Buchholz, T. Schierl, C. Hellge, Interactive volumetric video from the cloud, in: IBC 2020, Amsterdam, The Netherlands, https://www.ibc.org/technical-papers/interactive-volumetric-video-from-the-cloud-/6517.article.

[74] J. Son, S. Gül, G.S. Bhullar, G. Hege, W. Morgenstern, A. Hilsmann, T. Ebner, S. Bliedung, P. Eisert, T. Schierl, T. Buchholz, C. Hellge, Split rendering for mixed reality: interactive volumetric video in action, in: SIGGRAPH Asia 2020 XR, ACM, Virtual Event, Republic of Korea, 2020, pp. 1–3, https://doi.org/10.1145/3415256.3421491, https://dl.acm.org/doi/10.1145/3415256.3421491.

[75] J. Jansen, S. Subramanyam, R. Bouqueau, G. Cernigliaro, M.M. Cabré, F. Pérez, P. Cesar, A pipeline for multiparty volumetric video conferencing: transmission of point clouds over low latency DASH, in: Proceedings of the 11th ACM Multimedia Systems Conference, ACM, Istanbul, Turkey, 2020, pp. 341–344, https://doi.org/10.1145/3339825.3393578, https://dl.acm.org/doi/10.1145/3339825.3393578.

[76] G. Cernigliaro, M. Martos, M. Montagud, A. Ansari, S. Fernandez, PC-MCU: point cloud multipoint control unit for multi-user holoconferencing systems, in: Proceedings of the 30th ACM Workshop on Network and Operating Systems Support for Digital Audio and Video, NOSSDAV '20, Association for Computing Machinery, New York, NY, USA, 2020, pp. 47–53, https://doi.org/10.1145/3386290.3396936.

[77] F. Qian, B. Han, J. Pair, V. Gopalakrishnan, Toward practical volumetric video streaming on commodity smartphones, in: Proceedings of the 20th International Workshop on Mobile Computing Systems and Applications, ACM, Santa Cruz, CA, USA, 2019, pp. 135–140, https://doi.org/10.1145/3301293.3302358, https://dl.acm.org/doi/10.1145/3301293.3302358.

[78] K. Lee, J. Yi, Y. Lee, S. Choi, Y.M. Kim, GROOT: a real-time streaming system of high-fidelity volumetric videos, in: Proceedings of the 26th Annual International Conference on Mobile Computing and Networking, ACM, London, United Kingdom, 2020, pp. 1–14, https://doi.org/10.1145/3372224.3419214, https://dl.acm.org/doi/10.1145/3372224.3419214.

[79] N. O'dwyer, E. Zerman, G.W. Young, A. Smolic, S. Dunne, H. Shenton, Volumetric video in augmented reality applications for museological narratives: A user study for the long room in The Library of Trinity College Dublin, Journal on Computing and Cultural Heritage 14 (2) (may 2021), https://doi.org/10.1145/3425400.

[80] J. Li, S. Subramanyam, J. Jansen, Y. Mei, I. Reimat, K. Ławicka, P. Cesar, Evaluating the user experience of a photorealistic social VR movie, in: 2021 IEEE International Symposium on Mixed and Augmented Reality (ISMAR), 2021, pp. 284–293, https://doi.org/10.1109/ISMAR52148.2021.00044.

[81] A. Beacco, R. Oliva, C. Cabreira, J. Gallego, M. Slater, Disturbance and plausibility in a virtual rock concert: A pilot study, in: 2021 IEEE Virtual Reality and 3D User Interfaces (VR), 2021, pp. 538–545, https://doi.org/10.1109/VR50410.2021.00078.

[82] S.J.G. Ahn, L. Levy, A. Eden, A.S. Won, B. MacIntyre, K. Johnsen, IEEEVR2020: Exploring the first steps toward standalone virtual conferences, Frontiers in Virtual Reality 2 (2021), https://doi.org/10.3389/frvir.2021.648575, https://www.frontiersin.org/article/10.3389/frvir.2021.648575.

[83] G. Riva, Medical clinical uses of virtual worlds, in: The Oxford Handbook of Virtuality, Oxford University Press, 2014, pp. 649–665, https://doi.org/10.1093/oxfordhb/9780199826162.013.014.

[84] M. Zink, R. Sitaraman, K. Nahrstedt, Scalable 360° video stream delivery: Challenges, solutions, and opportunities, Proceedings of the IEEE 107 (4) (2019) 639–650, https://doi.org/10.1109/JPROC.2019.2894817.

[85] C.-L. Fan, W.-C. Lo, Y.-T. Pai, C.-H. Hsu, A survey on 360° video streaming: Acquisition, transmission, and display, ACM Computing Surveys 52 (4) (Aug 2019), https://doi.org/10.1145/3329119.

[86] S. Rossi, I. Viola, L. Toni, P. Cesar, A new challenge: Behavioural analysis of 6-DoF user when consuming immersive media, in: 2021 IEEE International Conference on Image Processing (ICIP), 2021, pp. 3423–3427, https://doi.org/10.1109/ICIP42928.2021.9506525.

[87] E. Zerman, R. Kulnarni, A. Smolic, User behaviour analysis of volumetric video inaugmented reality, in: Thirteenth International Conference on Quality of Multimedia Experience (QoMEX), 2021.

[88] J.N. Bailenson, Nonverbal overload: A theoretical argument for the causes of zoom fatigue, Technology, Mind, and Behavior 2 (1) (2021), https://doi.org/10.1037/tmb0000030, https://tmb.apaopen.org/pub/nonverbal-overload.

[89] A. Yassien, P. ElAgroudy, E. Makled, S. Abdennadher, A Design Space for Social Presence in VR, Association for Computing Machinery, New York, NY, USA, 2020, https://doi.org/10.1145/3419249.3420112.

[90] J. Williamson, J. Li, V. Vinayagamoorthy, D.A. Shamma, P. Cesar, Proxemics and social interactions in an instrumented virtual reality workshop, in: Proceedings of the 2021 CHI Conference on Human Factors in Computing Systems, CHI '21, Association for Computing Machinery, New York, NY, USA, 2021, https://doi.org/10.1145/3411764.3445729.

CHAPTER 16

Processing of volumetric video

Siheng Chen[a] and Jin Zeng[b]
[a]Shanghai Jiao Tong University, Shanghai, China
[b]Tongji University, Shanghai, China

16.1. Introduction

Volumetric video processing is the process of analyzing and modifying a volumetric video to optimize its transmission, storage and quality through various mathematical and computational algorithms. The necessity of processing volumetric videos comes from a wide range of applications, including entertainment, automation, autonomous driving, and metaverse. Appropriate processing techniques would not only significantly improve immersive experience in the 3D world, but also provide better tools to understanding the 3D scene.

This chapter mainly considers two types of volumetric videos: depth images and 3D point clouds. A depth map is an image that contains information relating to the distance of the surfaces of scene objects from a viewpoint. It is usually captured by 3D scanners or reconstructed from multiple images. A 3D point cloud is a set of 3D points, providing discrete representations of continuous external surfaces of scene objects in the 3D space. Since depth images are arranged on a regular grid, whereas 3D points are irregularly scattered in the 3D space, we consider depth images as organized data and 3D point clouds as unorganized data. This difference requires distinct processing approaches. We note that traditional 1D speech data and 2D images are all associated with regular lattices. Therefore we could expand signal processing and image processing methods to handle depth images, but for 3D point clouds, we need new techniques.

Even though the processing algorithms could be significantly different, many processing tasks for volumetric videos are naturally extended from 1D signal processing and 2D image processing. For example, volumetric video denoising is the 3D counterpart of image denoising that aims to remove noise from a volumetric data; volumetric video inpainting is the 3D counterpart of image inpainting that aims to reconstruct missing part in a volumetric data. In this chapter, we start our journey from the fundamental low-level restoration tasks, where we comprehensively compare the difference between processing depth images and 3D point clouds. We further consider high-level processing tasks, including object detection and semantic segmentation, through which we understand the 3D scene better.

Immersive Video Technologies
https://doi.org/10.1016/B978-0-32-391755-1.00022-5

445

16.2. Restoration

Volumetric videos are prone to various degradations during acquisition, editing, compression, transmission, and so on. For instance, when captured by commodity-level RGB-D cameras, such as Microsoft Kinect, Intel RealSense and Google Tango, the resulting depth images will contain noisy or missing pixels in areas where the surfaces have low reflection or are too far from the camera [1]. Moreover, when using structure-from-motion methods to reconstruct 3D model from multi-view images or videos, the resulting 3D point clouds will be incomplete due to the limitations of multiview matching [2,3]. Consequently, numerous studies have been devoted to volumetric video restoration to enhance the accuracy of the geometric information and promote the performance of subsequent 3D applications.

16.2.1 Degradation model

Here we introduce a simple yet general degradation model [4]. Let $\mathbf{p} \in \mathbb{R}^n$ denote the vectorized original (uncorrupted) volumetric data and $\mathbf{q} \in \mathbb{R}^m$ be the corrupted version, and their relation is described as

$$\mathbf{q} = \mathbf{H}\mathbf{p} + \mathbf{n}, \qquad (16.1)$$

where the degradation matrix $\mathbf{H} \in \mathbb{R}^{m \times n}$ ($m \leq n$) is determined by the degradation process and may (or may not) be known, depending on the problem setting, and $\mathbf{n}$ is an additive noise with zero mean following a certain distribution.

The problem of interest is to recover the underlying latent signal $\mathbf{p}$ given the observed signal $\mathbf{q}$ with distortion. In different restoration problems, $\mathbf{H}$ and $\mathbf{n}$ are configured correspondingly. In the following context, we will focus on two fundamental restoration tasks, *i.e.*, *denoising* and *inpainting* (or *completion* in some literature), which can be formulated with the following configuration of $\mathbf{H}$ and $\mathbf{n}$:

1. In the problem of denoising, $\mathbf{H}$ is an identity matrix with $m = n$. In volumetric video denoising, a lot of works assume additive Gaussian model for the noise $\mathbf{n}$ that is signal independent [5–7]. However, in practice, the noise distribution can be signal-dependent and/or device-dependent. For example, the noise contained in the depth image can be caused by occlusion, which appears along the boundary as inaccurate pixels [8] or flying pixels [9]. Moreover, the noise in the three-dimensional model can come from the limitation of multiview image matching algorithms [2,10]. Therefore it remains a challenging task to recover volumetric videos from noise corruption in real practice.

2. In the problem of inpainting, a portion of data points in $\mathbf{p}$ are missing, and we aim at filling in this missing data points via inpainting algorithms. In this case, $\mathbf{H}$ is an square matrix with $m = n$, which zeros out data points in $\mathbf{p}$. The invalid points may be due to the limitation of the depth sensor, where 1) pixel values get over-saturated when surfaces are too glossy, bright, close from the camera, or 2) the sensor fails to

receive the reflected signal when the surfaces are of low reflectance or too far from the camera [1,11]. Furthermore, due the power consumption limitation, the Lidar scans will often have very sparse raw data corresponding to the laser emission pattern [12,13]. In either case, inpainting/completion algorithms are needed to recover the complete and dense depth map or point cloud.

To perform effective restoration of volumetric videos, it requires the methods to either model the signal prior or learn the underlying characteristics of the signal, given data measurements. In the following context, we will briefly introduce these two categories of methods for restoration of depth images and 3D point clouds, then discuss representative methods belonging to each of the two categories.

16.2.2 Model-based methods

The restoration of volumetric video is usually ill-posed, and extra prior knowledge describing the characteristics of the original signal $\mathbf{p}$ is required so as to facilitate the restoration [4,7,14]. The solution considering the signal prior can be formulated as a minimization problem,

$$\mathbf{p}^{\star} = \arg\min_{\mathbf{p}}\ \mathrm{dist}(\mathbf{Hp}, \mathbf{q}) + \lambda \cdot \mathrm{prior}(\mathbf{p}), \tag{16.2}$$

where the first term—$\mathrm{dist}(\mathbf{Hp}, \mathbf{q})$—measures the distance between $\mathbf{Hp}$ and $\mathbf{q}$, often referred to as the data-fidelity term. The second term $\mathrm{prior}(\mathbf{p})$ is the chosen signal prior induced by the model of the signal, which regularizes the restoration problem into a well-posed one.

A large body of research on volumetric video restoration is model-based. **Depth image restoration** recovers clean depth images from degraded observations. Depth image priors reflecting the depth intrinsic properties are usually considered in restoration problems. Similar to natural image denoising, popular priors adopted include low-rank prior [7], sparsity prior [15], and non-local self-similarity prior [6]. To extend priors used in image restoration to **point cloud restoration** is not straightforward due to the irregular structure of point clouds. For example, sparsity prior when used in point cloud restoration will assume local planarity and optimize for sparse representations of certain geometric features [16]. The state-of-the-art methods generalize the notion of non-local self-similarity to point cloud denoising, and are shown to better preserve structural features under high level of noise [17].

In what follows, we will dive into the representative methods, *e.g.*, non-local graph-based transform (NLGBT) for depth image denoising [6], and graph Laplacian regularized point cloud denoising (GLR) [17].

16.2.2.1 Non-local graph-based transform for depth image denoising

As a concrete example, we will discuss a simple yet representative method for depth image denoising, non-local graph-based transform (NLGBT) [6].

Non-local self-similarity prior is widely adopted in image denoising methods, among which the most representative works include non-local means [18] and BM3D [19]. The basic assumption is that similar patches recur throughout an image, thus one patch can be recovered by jointly averaging non-local patches with high similarity.

The assumption can be extended to depth images, where similar edge structures appear throughout the image. Moreover, the piece-wise smooth (PWS) property of depth image perfectly matches the graph Fourier transform [20] (referred to as graph-based transform in [6]) representation, which well preserves PWS signals. In light of this, NLGBT jointly utilizes the above two priors, *i.e.*, the non-local self-similarity and the local piece-wise smoothness of depth images, in the optimization problem.

First of all, to utilize non-local similarity, similar patches are clustered into one group, from which an average patch is computed, as a representation for the average patch statistics in this group. Given the average patch, a graph is constructed by connecting each pixel to its four neighbors, as shown in Fig. 16.1. The edge weight is computed using

$$w_{ij} = \exp\left(-\frac{\text{dist}(i,j)^2}{2\epsilon^2}\right), \tag{16.3}$$

where $\text{dist}(i,j)$ is set to be the intensity difference between pixel i and j, *i.e.*, $|y_i - y_j|$. Given the weighted graph, the adjacency matrix $\mathbf{W}$ is defined with $\mathbf{W}(i,j) = \mathbf{W}(j,i) = w_{ij}$, and the degree matrix $\mathbf{D}$ is a diagonal matrix with the i-th entry $\mathbf{D}(i,i) = \sum_j w_{ij}$. The combinatorial graph Laplacian matrix is then given as $\mathbf{L} = \mathbf{D} - \mathbf{W}$. Then the GFT transform $\mathbf{U}$ is given by the eigenvectors of $\mathbf{L}$ [20]. The averaging process enables the graph to represent non-local statistics, and also performs as a low-pass pre-filtering to the image patches, which contributes to the robustness of the transform matrix $\mathbf{U}$ to noise.

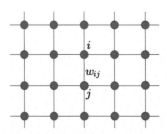

Figure 16.1 A simple grid graph $\mathcal{G}$ connecting each pixel to its four neighbors. This figure has only showed a part of the graph.

Moreover, to preserve local piece-wise smoothness in the recovered image, these patches of high similarity are transformed to the GFT domain, and the denoising is performed by enforcing group sparsity in the GFT domain. Given the noisy patches $\mathbf{y}_p \in \mathbb{R}^n$, where p is the patch index, the formulation becomes

$$\min_{\mathbf{U}, \boldsymbol{\alpha}_p} \Sigma_{p=1}^N \|\mathbf{y}_p - \mathbf{U}\boldsymbol{\alpha}_p\|_2 + \lambda \Sigma_{p=1}^N \|\boldsymbol{\alpha}_p\|_0, \qquad (16.4)$$

where $\boldsymbol{\alpha}_p$ is the GFT coefficients for $\mathbf{y}_p$, and λ is the weighting parameter. The sparsity of $\boldsymbol{\alpha}_p$ is minimized as the smoothness prior to remove noise, because noise often appears as high-frequency components in the GFT domain.

In this way, NLGBT is able to utilize non-local similar geometry by using the same transform $\mathbf{U}$ for all patches and seeking sparse representation for the group, *i.e.*, *group sparsity*. Furthermore, NLGBT preserves textures of individual patches by allowing $\boldsymbol{\alpha}_p$ to be different for each patch. In addition, the transform $\mathbf{U}$ used in NLGBT can be efficiently learned from the average patch, which simplifies the dictionary learning process.

The algorithm based on NLGBT is implemented as follows. First, similar to BM3D, patches with high similarity are clustered into groups. For each group, an average patch is computed and used for graph construction and GFT transform computation. Next, given the GFT, similar patches are transformed to GFT domain and denoised jointly by minimizing the l_0 norm of GFT coefficients, as in Eq. (16.4) by hard-thresholding the coefficients similar to [21]. Iterative approach is adopted in solving the optimization, where graph edge weights and the corresponding GFT transform $\mathbf{U}$ are updated after each iteration. Algorithm 1 summarizes the optimization implementation.

Algorithm 1 Depth Image Denoising With Non-local Graph-based Transform.

Require: Noisy depth image $\mathbf{y}$ and iteration number K
1: Initialize $\mathbf{y}^{(1)} = \mathbf{y}$
2: **for** $k = 1 : K$ **do**
3:     Patch clustering
4:     GFT transform $\mathbf{U}$ computation
5:     Perform denoising by solving Eq. (16.4) via hard-thresholding coefficients
6:     Update $\mathbf{y}^{(k)}$ via inverse GFT
7: **end for**
Ensure: Denoised depth image

Experiment results validate that NLGBT outperforms non-local based schemes, such as non-local means (NLM) and BM3D. In Fig. 16.2, we can see that NLGBT result exhibits clean sharp edges and smooth surface, whereas BM3D result is blurred along the edges to some extent, and the one produced by NLM still looks noisy.

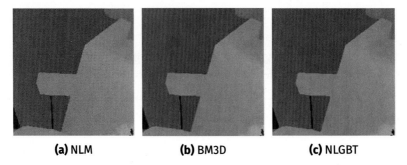

(a) NLM   **(b)** BM3D   **(c)** NLGBT

Figure 16.2 Denoising results of different approaches with depth map Teddy corrupted by AWGN ($\sigma = 10$).

16.2.2.2 Graph Laplacian regularized point cloud denoising

In recent works of 3D point cloud restoration, non-local self-similarity prior is also utilized to achieve state-of-the-art performance [17,22]. In this section, we introduce a recent method, *i.e.*, graph Laplacian regularized point cloud denoising (GLR) [17], which utilizes self-similarity in point cloud patches and enhances robustness to high noise level with better structural detail preservation.

To utilize self-similarity among surface patches, GLR adopts the *low-dimensional manifold (LDMM)* prior [23] and collaboratively denoises the patches by minimizing the manifold dimension. LDMM is first proposed for image processing, assuming that similar image patches are samples of a low-dimensional manifold in high-dimensional space. By using LDMM as the prior, the manifold dimension is used for regularization to recover the image, achieving state-of-the-art results in various image restoration applications, *e.g.*, denoising, inpainting, and super-resolution.

Inspired by LDMM, the proposed GLR assumes surface patches in the point cloud lie on a manifold of low dimension. However, LDMM requires a well-defined coordinate function [23] for manifold dimension computation, which is not straight-forward for surface patches due to the irregular structure of point clouds. Moreover, the point integral method (PIM) in LDMM for solving the dimension optimization is of high complexity, and the linear systems for updating coordinate function are asymmetric, which leads to a large number of iterations to reach convergence [24].

To address the two issues above, GLR approximates the patch-manifold dimension defined in continuous domain with a discrete patch-based graph Laplacian regularizer. In this way, GLR avoids explicitly defining the manifold coordinate functions and enables the LDMM to extend to the point cloud setting. Furthermore, the algorithm implementation is accelerated with a reduced number of iterations, thanks to the symmetric structure of the graph Laplacian matrix.

To be specific, GLR first defines the notion of patch manifold $\mathcal{M}$, given a point cloud $\mathbf{V} = [\mathbf{v}_1, \dots, \mathbf{v}_N]^\top \in \mathbb{R}^{N \times 3}$ with $\mathbf{v}_i \in \mathbb{R}^3$, which is a discrete sampling of a 2D surface of a 3D object. Noise-corrupted $\mathbf{V}$ can be simply modeled as $\mathbf{V} = \mathbf{U} + \mathbf{N}$, where $\mathbf{U}$ contains the true 3D positions, $\mathbf{N}$ is a zero-mean signal-independent noise. Then the graph constructed based on the patches is defined with the symmetric adjacency matrix $\mathbf{W} \in \mathbb{R}^{M \times M}$ with the (m, n)-th entry w_{mn} measuring the similarity between the m-th patch $\mathbf{p}_m$ and n-th patch $\mathbf{p}_n$. $\mathbf{D}$ denotes the diagonal degree matrix, where entry $\mathbf{D}(m, m) = \sum_n w_{mn}$. Then the combinatorial graph Laplacian matrix $\mathbf{L} = \mathbf{D} - \mathbf{W}$ induces the regularizer given as

$$S_{\mathbf{L}}(\boldsymbol{\alpha}_i) = \boldsymbol{\alpha}_i^\top \mathbf{L} \boldsymbol{\alpha}_i = \sum_{m,n} w_{mn}(\alpha_i(\mathbf{p}_m) - \alpha_i(\mathbf{p}_n))^2, \qquad (16.5)$$

where $\boldsymbol{\alpha}_i = [\alpha_i(\mathbf{p}_1) \ldots \alpha_i(\mathbf{p}_M)]^\top$ on the manifold $\mathcal{M}$ is the coordinate function corresponding to the i-th dimension that samples $\mathcal{M}$ at positions of the surface patches. (16.5) is proved to converge to the dimension of $\mathcal{M}$ in [17], thus is used to approximate the patch manifold for optimization regularization.

To accelerate the implementation, the computation of (16.5) is accomplished based on local pairwise correspondence between connected patches, which generates the graph Laplacian $\mathbf{L}_a$, relieving the need for global ordering. The final objective function is given as

$$\min_{\mathbf{U}} \quad \text{tr}(\mathbf{A}^\top \mathbf{L}_a \mathbf{A}) + \mu \|\mathbf{U} - \mathbf{V}\|_F^2, \qquad (16.6)$$

where $\mathbf{A}$ is related to denoised 3D samples $\mathbf{U} \in \mathbb{R}^{N \times 3}$ as follows

$$\mathbf{A} = \mathbf{S}\mathbf{U} - \mathbf{C}, \qquad (16.7)$$

where $\mathbf{S} \in \{0, 1\}^{kM \times N}$ is a sampling matrix to select points from point cloud to form M patches with size k, and $\mathbf{C} \in \mathbb{R}^{kM \times 3}$ is for patch centering, so that the patches are centered at the original point $(0, 0, 0)$. The proposed scheme is shown to have graph spectral low-pass filtering interpretation and numerical stability in solving the linear equation system.

Experimental results suggest that GLR point cloud denoising outperforms competing schemes, including moving least squares (MLS)-based method (APSS [25]), sparsity-based method (moving robust principal components analysis (MRPCA) [26]), and non-local self-similarity based method (LR [22]). Non-local-based LR and GLR in Fig. 16.3(e and f) provide the best results, where the shape of the rifle model is well preserved, validating the effectiveness of patch-similarity based filtering. However, LR tends to over-smoothing, and fine details are lost, such as the ramrod and the muzzle; whereas GLR preserves the salient features without over-smoothing. In sum, experimental results suggest that GLR outperforms existing schemes with better structural detail preservation.

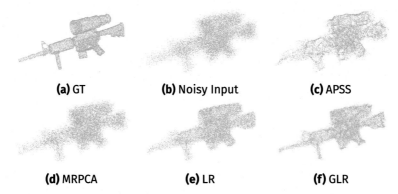

(a) GT   **(b)** Noisy Input   **(c)** APSS

(d) MRPCA   **(e)** LR   **(f)** GLR

Figure 16.3 Denoising results of different approaches with the sample from the ShapeNet dataset [27] corrupted by AWGN ($\sigma = 0.04$).

16.2.3 Learning-based methods

By the virtue of deep learning [28], the capability of volumetric video processing has been escalated to an unprecedented level. In this section, we focus on the recent works addressing depth image and point cloud inpainting/completion with deep neural networks.

16.2.3.1 Non-local spatial propagation network for depth completion

The state-of-the-art algorithm, non-local spatial propagation network (NLSPN) [13], is proposed for depth completion with the RGB image guidance, which predicts non-local neighbors for each pixel and aggregates relevant information using the learnt spatially-varying affinities.

NLSPN is an extension of convolutional spatial propagation network (CSPN) [29], which learns the affinity values via neural network and is applied to depth completion. However, CSPN is inherently limited by the fixed-local neighborhood configuration, ignoring the depth distribution within the local area. Thus it often results in mixed-depth values of foreground and background objects after propagation.

Different from CSPN, NLSPN [13] is trained to predict *non-local* neighbors with corresponding affinities. Furthermore, NLSPN incorporates the confidence of the initial dense depth prediction (which is refined by propagation procedure) into affinity normalization to minimize the propagation of less confident depth values. Fig. 16.4 shows an overview of the NLSPN algorithm. The encoder-decoder network is built upon the residual network. Given RGB and sparse depth images, an initial dense depth and its confidence, non-local neighbors, and corresponding affinities are predicted from the network. Then non-local spatial propagation is conducted iteratively with the affinity normalized by the confidence.

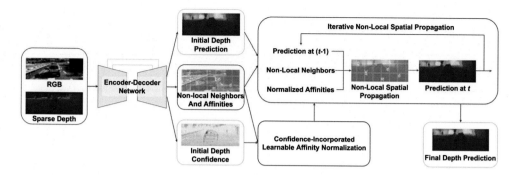

Figure 16.4 Overview of the NLSPN algorithm.

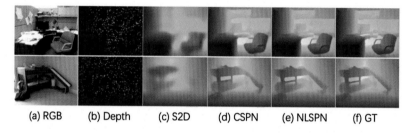

(a) RGB   (b) Depth   (c) S2D   (d) CSPN   (e) NLSPN   (f) GT

Figure 16.5 Depth completion result comparison on the NYUv2 dataset [1].

Fig. 16.5 presents depth completion result comparison among NLSPN, the sparse-to-dense (S2D) [30] and the CSPN [29]. 500 depth pixels were randomly sampled from a dense depth image and used as the input along with the corresponding RGB image. S2D generates blurry depth images, as it is a direct regression algorithm. Compared to S2D, CSPN and NLSPN generate depth maps with substantially improved accuracy, thanks to the iterative spatial propagation procedure. However, CSPN suffers from mixed-depth problems, especially on tiny or thin structures. In contrast, NLSPN well preserves tiny structures and depth boundaries using non-local propagation.

16.2.3.2 Gridding residual network for point cloud completion

Convolutional neural networks (CNN) are widely used in image restoration, *e.g.*, in depth completion in Section 16.2.3.1, but cannot be directly applied to 3D point cloud due to its irregularity. A common approach is to voxelize the point cloud into voxels so that 3D CNN can be applied [31]. However, it is unavoidable to lose geometric information during voxelization. Alternatively, existing works use the multi-layer perceptron (MLP) [32,33] or graph convolutional neural networks (GCN) [34] to aggregate features in point cloud, but the former one neglects the local connectivity, whereas the latter is sensitive to the graph connectivity.

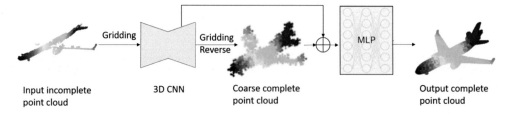

Figure 16.6 Framework of gridding residual network for point cloud completion.

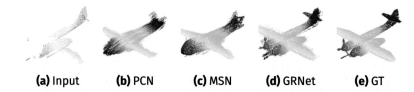

(a) Input   **(b)** PCN   **(c)** MSN   **(d)** GRNet   **(e)** GT

Figure 16.7 Qualitative completion results on the ShapeNet [27] testing example. GT stands for the ground truth of the 3D object.

Motivated by the above-mentioned problems, gridding residual network (GRNet) [35] is proposed for point cloud completion, which adopts 3D grids as intermediate representations to regularize unordered point clouds, and designs gridding and gridding reverse layers to convert between point clouds and 3D grids, without losing structural information. As shown in the framework in Fig. 16.6, the point cloud is first converted to 3D grid structure by *gridding* layer, then fed into the 3D CNN network for completing the missing information in the point cloud. With *gridding reverse* layer, the 3D grid structure data is converted back to the coarse point cloud, which is refined to the final output point cloud by the MLP with additional point cloud features from the 3D CNN decoder.

Fig. 16.7 demonstrates point cloud completion result comparison among GRNet, point completion network (PCN) [32], and morphing and sampling network (MSN) [36]. As can be seen from the comparison, GRNet recovers better details of object than the other methods. PCN and MSN fail to recover the plane head, whereas GRNet preserves the original shape of the plane.

16.3. Semantic segmentation

Semantic segmentation for the 3D point cloud is a fundamental task in 3D scene understanding; it aims to split the point cloud into separate regions, according to the points' semantic meaning, as shown in Fig. 16.8. With the increasing demand for the ability of understanding 3D scene, point cloud semantic segmentation is playing a more im-

Figure 16.8 Semantic segmentation splits the raw 3D point cloud into multiple homogeneous regions. The points in the same region have the same semantic meaning, such as car, road, and building.

portant role in many computer vision and robotics applications, including intelligent vehicles, autonomous mapping, and metaverse.

16.3.1 Point cloud representation

The point cloud semantic segmentation model usually outputs a label indicating the semantic region for each point in a point cloud. Doing such dense prediction task requires a proper data representation. However, unlike 2D images, which are naturally organized as regular grids, point cloud is a collection of irregular arranged points. Although the representation of point cloud has been studied for a long time, there is still no representation that is suitable for all point-cloud-based tasks. Here we will introduce three commonly used point cloud representation for point cloud segmentation: row point, voxel, and projected image. The visualizations of these three representations are shown in Fig. 16.9.

Raw point. The most straightforward representation for 3D point cloud is based on raw 3D points themselves. The matrix representation is

$$\mathbf{P} = [\mathbf{p}_1, \mathbf{p}_2, \dots, \mathbf{p}_n]^T \in \mathbb{R}^{n \times d} \tag{16.8}$$

where $\mathbf{p}_i$ denotes the coordinates and other attributes of the i-th point in the point cloud.

Voxel. The success of CNN in the field of computer vision shows that a discrete representation is both efficient and effective to process. For 3D signal, voxel is a natural discrete representation, which partitions the three-dimensional space into no-overlapping, regularly arranged regions. A straightforward way to represent point cloud

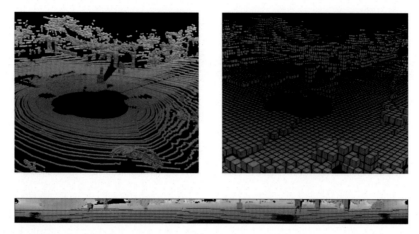

Figure 16.9 Three typical point cloud representations. The representations in top-left, top-right, and bottom are raw point, sparse voxel, and range image separately.

as voxel is to partition the 3D space with the equally-spaced grids, and record the point information into the corresponding voxel. Let the size of voxel be $h \times w \times d$, which separate the 3D space into range H, W, D along the X, Y, Z axes respectively. The (i, j, k)-th voxel represents a 3D voxel space $\mathcal{V}_{i,j,k}^{(\text{voxel})} = \{(x, y, z) | (i - 1)h \leq x \leq ih, (j - 1)w \leq y \leq jw, (k - 1)d \leq z \leq kd\}$. Let $\mathcal{S} = \{(x_i, y_i, z_i), i \in 1, 2, \ldots, n\}$ be the point position set. The element of voxel representation $\mathbf{V} \in \mathbb{R}^{H \times W \times D}$ can be defined as

$$\mathbf{V}_{i,j,k} = \begin{cases} 1, & \text{when } \mathcal{V}_{i,j,k}^{(\text{voxel})} \cap \mathcal{S} \neq \varnothing \\ 0, & \text{otherwise} \end{cases}, \tag{16.9}$$

which indicates whether a voxel space is occupied by the point cloud.

Projected image. Projected image uses 2D regular grids, $\mathbf{I} \in \mathbb{R}^{H \times W}$, to represent point cloud. It maps two axes in 3D space to its horizontal and vertical axes, and embeds the information of the remaining one dimension into a pixel channel. Different projection methods have different embedding functions (definitions of $\mathbf{I}$). For example, the bird's-eye-view (BEV) map is a typical projected image, where the point cloud is projected to the $X - Y$ plane. The (i, j)-th pixel in the BEV map represents a pillar space, $\mathcal{V}_{i,j}^{(\text{BEV})} = \{(x, y, z) | (i - 1)h \leq x \leq ih, (j - 1)w \leq y \leq jw\}$. And the element of BEV map $\mathbf{I}^{(\text{BEV})}$ is defined as

$$\mathbf{I}_{i,j}^{(\text{BEV})} = \begin{cases} \max\limits_{(x,y,z) \in \mathcal{V}_{i,j}^{(\text{BEV})} \cap \mathcal{S}} z, & \mathcal{V}_{i,j}^{(\text{BEV})} \cap \mathcal{S} \neq \varnothing \\ 0, & \text{otherwise} \end{cases}. \tag{16.10}$$

Besides, range image is also a commonly used projected image representation, which projects point cloud into a sphere. The 3D space is partitioned along the azimuth angle $\alpha \in [0, 2\pi)$, and the elevation angle $\theta \in (-\pi/2, \pi/2]$ with the resolution of azimuth angle α_0 and the resolution of elevation angle θ_0. Each pixel in range image corresponds to a frustum space, $\mathcal{V}_{i,j}^{\text{range}} = \left\{ (x, y, z) \mid \alpha_0(i-1) \leq \text{acos}\left(\frac{x}{\sqrt{x^2+y^2}}\right) < \alpha_0 i, \theta_0(j-1) \leq \right.$ $\text{atan}\left(\frac{z}{\sqrt{x^2+y^2}}\right) + \frac{\pi}{2} < \theta_0 j \left.\right\}$. The projection function of range image is

$$\mathbf{I}_{i,j}^{(\text{range})} = \begin{cases} \min_{(x,y,z)\in\mathcal{V}_{i,j}^{(\text{range})}\cap\mathcal{S}} \sqrt{x^2 + y^2 + z^2}, & \mathcal{V}_{i,j}^{(\text{range})} \cap \mathcal{S} \neq \varnothing \\ -1, & \text{otherwise.} \end{cases}$$

(16.11)

Based on the point cloud representation, the current 3D point cloud semantic segmentation model can be roughly divided into four paradigms: projection-based, voxel-based, point-based, and multi-representation-based methods; see an overview in Fig. 16.10.

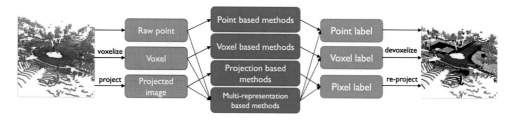

Figure 16.10 Overview of the point semantic segmentation methods.

16.3.2 Projection-based methods

The general paradigm for projection-based methods includes three steps: 1. projecting point cloud to image; 2. doing semantic segmentation at the image level; 3. mapping the semantic label of pixels back to the points.

RangeNet++ [37] is a typical projection-based method, which uses the range map as a intermediate representation of point cloud. The pipeline of RangeNet++ is shown in Fig. 16.11. It first projects the point cloud to a range image as Eq. (16.11), whereas the image coordinates for each point are defined as

$$\begin{pmatrix} u \\ v \end{pmatrix} = \begin{pmatrix} \frac{1}{2}\left[1 - \arctan(y, x)\pi^{-1}\right] w \\ \left[1 - \left(\arcsin\left(zr^{-1}\right) + f_{\text{up}}\right)f^{-1}\right] h \end{pmatrix}.$$

(16.12)

Then RangeNet++ uses a fully convolutional neural network for image-level semantic segmentation. The label of each point is obtained by indexing the range image with

Figure 16.11 The pipeline of RangeNet++ [37]. Each arrow corresponds to a processing step.

all the (u, v) pairs. Finally, RangeNet++ uses an additional kNN-based voting post-processing to solve the shadow problem during the label re-projection procedure.

Besides RangeNet++, [38] use multi-view virtual cameras to project a 3D point cloud onto different 2D planes. PolarNet [39] projects the LiDAR point cloud with BEV, and discretizes the point cloud with a polar coordinate system to align the network attention with the distribution of the original LiDAR point cloud. SqueezeSeg series [40–42] also used range image and designed different network architectures and post-processing methods.

Overall, the projection-based methods can largely utilize the well-studied network design and highly optimized operators for 2D images, but the congenital deficiency of projection inevitably limits their ability to accurately capture stereo geometric information.

16.3.3 Voxel-based methods

Just as the projection-based methods, the voxel-based methods also have three key procedures: 1. voxelizing the point cloud into voxel; 2. doing semantic segmentation at the voxel level; 3. mapping the semantic label of voxels back to the points.

Huang et al. [43] first proposed a 3D-CNN-based framework for voxel-based point cloud semantic segmentation. It first partitions point cloud into dense occupancy voxels as Eq. (16.9). Then a fully convolutional 3D CNN is employed to predict the semantic label of each voxel. In a 3D convolution layer l with kernel size $f \times f \times f$, the m-th channel of output at position (x, y, z) is defined as

$$v_{lm}^{xyz} = b_{lm} + \sum_{i=0}^{f-1}\sum_{j=0}^{f-1}\sum_{k=0}^{f-1} w_{lm}^{ijkT} v_{l-1}^{(x+i)(y+j)(z+k)}, \tag{16.13}$$

where b_{lm} is the bias of channel m, w_{lm}^{ijk} is the weight at position (i, j, k) of channel m. After voxel-level semantic segmentation, each point is directly assigned with the label of the voxel it is in.

There is a lot of room for improvement in the framework of [43]. SEGCloud [44] proposes to use trilinear interpolation to map the voxel feature back to the points, and then uses CRF to refine the point-level predictions. Due to the sparsity of the 3D point cloud, only a small part of voxels is occupied by points, whereas most of the dense grids are empty and invalid for point cloud segmentation. Thus it is inefficient to represent point clouds as dense voxels and apply dense 3D CNNs to them. To address this problem, Graham et al. [45] proposed to restrict the input and output of convolution to the non-empty voxels. To this end, they design a submanifold sparse convolution model, SparseConvNet, based on hash indexing. The sparsity of the model significantly reduces the computation and memory consumption and makes this model suitable for large-scale point cloud segmentation. Choy et al. [46] proposed to extend sparse convolution to high-order sparse data, and proposed a 4D spatio-temporal sparse CNN, named MinkowskiNet [46], for 3D video processing. Besides, Tang et al. [47] implemented the hash indexing operations on the GPU, further accelerating the sparse convolution operation. Cylinder3D [48] proposed to voxelize the LiDAR point cloud with a cylinder coordinate system. It also designs asymmetric sparse convolution to reduce computation.

The voxel-based methods can achieve higher computational efficiency, while maintaining three-dimensional information, and have been widely used in the segmentation of large-scale outdoor point clouds. However, the disadvantage of these methods is that the voxelization of the point cloud will inevitably produce a discrete error, resulting in the loss of the original point cloud information.

16.3.4 Point-based methods

Point-based methods work directly on the unorganized point clouds. The disordered nature of raw point requires the segmentation model to be invariant to point permutation.

The pioneer work PointNet [49] first proposed to use shared multi-layer perception (MLP) to learn point features and symmetric functions to learn permutation invariant global features. The idea behind this design is that a general function defined on a point set can be approximated by applying a symmetric function on transformed elements in the set

$$f(\{x_1, \ldots, x_n\}) \approx g\left(h(x_1), \ldots, h(x_n)\right), \qquad (16.14)$$

where $f : 2^{\mathbb{R}^N} \to \mathbb{R}$, $h : \mathbb{R}^N \to \mathbb{R}^K$ and $g : \underbrace{\mathbb{R}^K \times \cdots \times \mathbb{R}^K}_{n} \to \mathbb{R}$ is a symmetric function. The architecture of PointNet is shown in Fig. 16.12. It uses an MLP as the transformation function to learn point features and a simple global max-pooling layer as the symmetric function to learn global features. Then it concatenates the global and the point features together to predict per-point class score with another MLP.

The success of PointNet inspired a large number of point-based methods. PointNet++ [50], an improved version of PointNet [49], proposed to use symmetric functions to aggregate local spatial information to update the feature of each point. It also

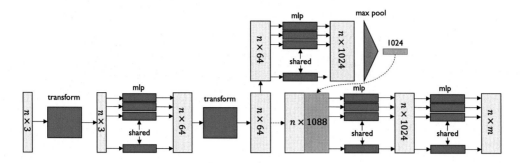

Figure 16.12 The architecture of PointNet [49].

adopts a hierarchical network structure to extract local information at different scales and achieve better adaptability to the density variation of the point cloud. To model the interaction between points, PointWeb [51] established a locally fully connected network in the point cloud, and designed an adaptive feature adjustment (AFA) module based on this network. So that the model can refine the point feature and obtain more discriminative features by interchanging local information. RandLA [52] is a point-based model designed for large-scale point cloud segmentation. It proposed to use random sampling to achieve higher computational efficiency and an effective attention-based local feature aggregation module to learn features from the sampled points. Point transformer [53] brings the self-attention mechanism to the field of 3D point cloud processing. It proposed vector attention to aggregate local feature for point cloud and achieves remarkable improvements on point cloud segmentation.

Besides, there is also some research trying to adapt convolution operation to disordered point clouds. Hua et al. [54] proposed a point-wise convolution operator. The neighbor points are binned to the kernel cell, and the points in the same cell share the same kernel weights during convolution. PCCN [55] proposed to use continuous convolution on point cloud. It parameterizes the continuous kernel function with MLPs, so that the kernel is defined in the entire 3D space. KPConv [56] assigns the kernel weights to a set of kernel points, and the convolution weights of KPConv for neighbor points are determined by their distance to the kernel points. DGCNN [57] regards the point cloud as a dynamic graph and utilizes graph convolution for segmentation. It dynamically builds edges in the point feature space and aggregate graph neighbor feature with EdgeConv to update the point feature.

16.3.5 Multi-representation-based methods

The projection-based, voxel-based, and point-based methods have their own advantages and disadvantages. Some hybrid methods utilize multiple representations to supplement the shortcomings of the single representation methods. PVCNN [58] first uses both point and voxel representation for point cloud segmentation. It uses 3D CNN to learn local features and applies point-wise MLP to complete the discretization loss. Furthermore, RPVNet [59] proposed to simultaneously use point, voxel, and range image in a model. The complementary features from different representations significantly boost the model performance.

16.4. Object detection

The task of 3D object detection is to detect and localize objects in the 3D space with the representation of bounding boxes based on one or multiple sensor measurements, which is an essential task of 3D scene understanding benefiting real-life applications [60], such as autonomous driving and augmented reality. 3D object detection usually outputs 3D bounding boxes of objects, which are the inputs for the component of object association and tracking. Based on the usage of sensor measurements, we can categorize 3D object detection into LiDAR-based detection and fusion-based detection.

Let $\mathcal{S}$ be a real-time LiDAR sweep. A LiDAR-based detector aims to find all the objects in the sweep; that is,

$$\{\mathbf{o}_i\}_{i=1}^{O} = h(\mathcal{S}), \tag{16.15}$$

where $\mathbf{o}_i = [\mathbf{y}_i, \mathbf{b}_i]$ is the i-th object in the 3D scene with $\mathbf{y}_i$ the object's category, such as vehicle, bikes, and pedestrian, and $\mathbf{b}_i$ the corners of bounding box. Now the detection function $h(\cdot)$ is typically implemented with deep-neural-network-based architectures.

The main difference between 2D object detection and 3D object detection is the input representation. Different from a 2D image, a real-time LiDAR sweep could be represented in various ways, leading to corresponding operations in subsequent components. For example, PointRCNN [61] adopts the raw-point-based representation, and then uses PointNet [49] with multi-scale sampling and grouping to learn point-wise features; 3D FCN [62] adopts the 3D-voxelization-based representation and uses 3D convolutions to learn voxel-wise features; PIXOR [63] adopts the BEV-based representation, and then uses 2D convolutions to learn pixel-wise features; and LaserNet [64] adopts the range-view-based representation, and then use 2D convolutions to learn pixel-wise features. Some other methods consider hybrid representations. VoxelNet [65] proposes a voxel-feature-encoding (VFE) layer that combines the advantages of both the raw-point-based representation and the 3D-voxelization-based representation. VFE first groups 3D points, according to the 3D voxel they reside in, then uses PointNet to learn point-wise features in each 3D voxel, and finally aggregates point-wise features to obtain voxel-wise feature for each 3D voxel. The benefit of VFE is to convert raw 3D points to the 3D voxelization-based representation and simultaneously learn 3D geometric features in each 3D voxel.

Similarly to 2D objection detection, there are usually two paradigms of 3D object detection: single-stage detection and two-stage detection. The single-stage detection directly estimates bounding boxes, whereas the two-stage detection first proposes coarse regions that may include objects, and then estimates bounding boxes.

16.4.1 Single-stage detection

The single-stage detection directly follows (16.15). To implement the detection function $h(\cdot)$, a deep–neural–network architecture usually includes two components: a backbone, which extracts deep spatial features, and a header, which outputs the estimations. For a backbone, all these methods use 2D/3D convolutional neural networks with multiscale, pyramidal hierarchical structure. One off-the-shelf backbone structure is feature pyramid networks [66]. A header is usually a multitasking network that handles both category classification and bounding box regression. It is usually small and efficient. Some off-the-shelf header structures are single-shot detector [67] and other small convolutional neural networks.

For example, PointPillars [68], who proposes a new kind of representation of point clouds, utilizes PointNets [49] to extract features in each vertical column (pillar), illustrated in Fig. 16.13. In this way, a point cloud can be encoded into a bird–eye–view pseudo 2D image so that we can conduct detection with any standard 2D convolution detection architecture. To be specific, let l be a point in a point cloud with coordinates x, y, z and reflectance r. We can create a set of pillars $\mathcal{P}$ with $|\mathcal{P}| = B$ by discretizing into an evenly spaced grid in the x-y plane. The points in each pillar are augmented with x_c, y_c, z_c, x_p, y_p, where c subscript denotes distance to the arithmetic mean of all points in the pillar and p subscript denotes the offset from the pillar x, y center. The augmented point l is $D = 9$ dimensional. The number of the non-empty pillars is denoted by P, and the number of points in a pillar is denoted by N. Then PointNet is used to encode point features in each pillar to generate a (C, P, N)-sized tensor from original (D, P, N), followed by a max operation over channels to create an output tensor of size (C, P). Once encoded, these non-empty pillar features are scattered back to the original locations to create a pseudo image. We then use a multi-scale feature extraction backbone illustrated in the backbone part of Fig. 16.13 to get features of the pseudo image. Finally, a SSD detection head finishes the detection pipeline. To summarize, PointPillars proposes a highly efficient end-to-end 3D point clouds detection method by encoding the pillar features.

Recent work [69–71] about 3D object detection also adapts the single-stage detection architecture. 3DSSD [69] presents a point-based 3D single-stage object detector. To address the issue that the localization accuracy and classification confidence may not well align, SASSD [70] presents an auxiliary network in parallel with a sparse convolutional network to regress the box centers and semantic classes for each point with interpolated voxel features, and CIA-SSD [71] proposes confident IOU-aware single-stage detector, which leverage a IoU-aware confidence rectification module to align the two confidence.

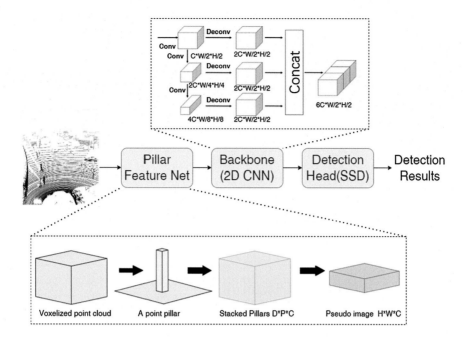

Figure 16.13 The architecture of PointPillars.

16.4.2 Two-stage detection

The two-stage detection implements the detection function $h(\cdot)$ in two stages; that is,

$$\{r_i\}_{i=1}^{R} = h_1(\mathcal{S}), \tag{16.16a}$$
$$\{\mathbf{o}_i\}_{i=1}^{O} = h_2(\mathcal{S}, \{r_i\}_{i=1}^{R}), \tag{16.16b}$$

where r_i is a set of parameters that describes the i-th proposed region in the 3D space.[1] The proposal-generation stage (16.16a) proposes several 3D regions that may include objects inside; and the bounding-box-estimation stage (16.16b) extracts 3D points from those proposed regions and estimates the precise object positions.

For example, PointRCNN [61] is a recent work that follows the two-stage detection, illustrated in Fig. 16.14. In the proposal-generation stage, PointRCNN firstly uses PointNet++ [50] to extract discriminative point-wise features. Based on the point-wise features, foreground point segmentation and bin-based 3D box generation are simultaneously conducted. Through learning to segment the foreground points, the network is forced to capture rich contextual information for better understanding the scene. Eventually, we can get point-wise features, foreground mask and 3D proposals in the first stage. The second stage is the 3D box refinement stage, which targets to

---

[1] There are multiple approaches to parameterizing a 3D region [61].

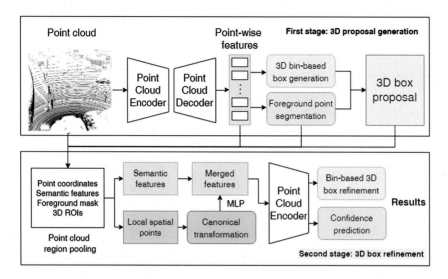

Figure 16.14 The architecture of PointRCNN.

refine the boxes generated in the first stage. In this stage, only features of the points inside the enlarged proposals are kept to be pooled for refinement. An enlarged proposal, $\mathbf{b}_i^e = \left(x_i, y_i, z_i, h_i + \eta, w_i + \eta, l_i + \eta, \theta_i\right)$, generated by slightly enlarge the proposals, $\mathbf{b}_i = \left(x_i, y_i, z_i, h_i, w_i, l_i, \theta_i\right)$, in the first stage, is to encode the additional information, where η is a constant value for enlarging the size of box. Before being fine-tuned, the pooled points belonging to each proposal will be transformed into the canonical coordinate system from original LiDAR coordinate system, which enables better refinement. Finally, the local features and the semantic features from the first stage are concatenated and fed into several fully-connected layers to get the box refinement and confidence prediction.

To summarize, the input representation plays a crucial role in the LiDAR-based detection. The raw-point-based representation provides complete point information, but lacks the spatial prior. PointNet [49] has become a standard method to handle this issue and extract features in the raw-point-based representation. The 3D voxelization-based representation and the BEV-based representation are simple and straightforward, but result in a lot of empty voxels and pixels. Feature pyramid networks with sparse convolutions can help address this issue. The range-view-based representation is more compact, because the data is represented in the native frame of the sensor, leading to efficient processing, and it naturally models the occlusion. But objects at various ranges would have significantly different scales in the range-view-based representation; it usually requires more training data to achieve high performance. VFE introduces hybrid representations that take advantages of both the raw-point-based representations and the 3D voxelization-based representation. PV-RCNN [72] combines 3D voxel CNN with

PointNet-based set abstraction to learn more discriminate point cloud features, which simultaneously utilizes the efficient proposal generation of voxel CNN and flexible receptive fields of PointNet-based methods.

The two-stage detection naturally enjoys a high recall and tends to achieve higher precision [66]. However, the one-stage detection tends to be faster and simpler to meet the demand of real-time processing of some practical applications. In addition to anchor-based methods, anchor-free methods do not need to pre-generate anchors and is a more efficient architecture, recently attracting much attention in the field of object detection. For example, CenterPoint [73], which extends CenterNet [74] from 2D object detection to 3D object detection, achieves high performance of 3D object detection.

16.5. Chapter at a glance

This chapter introduces a series of latest processing techniques for volumetric video. Many of those techniques potentially lay a foundation for prevailing applications, such as autonomous driving and metaverse. Here we specifically focus on three basic tasks, including restoration, object detection, and semantic segmentation. In the low-level task of restoration, we first mathematically formulate a general degradation model, which involves denoising and inpainting (completion) into a formulation. Based on such a model, we consider both non-learning and deep-learning-based processing methods. In the high-level task of semantic segmentation, we first consider various manners of data representation, including voxel-based, projection-based, and point-based representations. Based on each representation, we introduce the latest processing techniques and compare their advantages and disadvantages. In the high-level task of object detection, we consider both single-stage and two-stage detection methods. Hopefully, this chapter provides a broad horizon for readers to get familiar with processing techniques of volumetric videos.

References

[1] N. Silberman, D. Hoiem, P. Kohli, R. Fergus, Indoor segmentation and support inference from RGBD images, in: European Conference on Computer Vision, Springer, 2012, pp. 746–760.

[2] A. Chang, A. Dai, T. Funkhouser, M. Halber, M. Niessner, M. Savva, S. Song, A. Zeng, Y. Zhang, Matterport3D: Learning from RGB-D data in indoor environments, in: International Conference on 3D Vision (3DV), 2017.

[3] R. Ranftl, K. Lasinger, D. Hafner, K. Schindler, V. Koltun, Towards robust monocular depth estimation: Mixing datasets for zero-shot cross-dataset transfer, IEEE Transactions on Pattern Analysis and Machine Intelligence (TPAMI) 44 (2022) 1623–1637.

[4] P. Milanfar, A tour of modern image filtering: New insights and methods, both practical and theoretical, IEEE Signal Processing Magazine 30 (1) (2012) 106–128.

[5] J. Shen, S.-C.S. Cheung, Layer depth denoising and completion for structured-light RGB-D cameras, in: Proceedings of the IEEE Conference on Computer Vision and Pattern Recognition, 2013, pp. 1187–1194.

[6] W. Hu, X. Li, G. Cheung, O. Au, Depth map denoising using graph-based transform and group sparsity, in: 2013 IEEE 15th International Workshop on Multimedia Signal Processing (MMSP), IEEE, 2013, pp. 001–006.

[7] C. Yan, Z. Li, Y. Zhang, Y. Liu, X. Ji, Y. Zhang, Depth image denoising using nuclear norm and learning graph model, ACM Transactions on Multimedia Computing, Communications, and Applications (TOMM) 16 (4) (2020) 1–17.

[8] J. Xie, R.S. Feris, S.-S. Yu, M.-T. Sun, Joint super resolution and denoising from a single depth image, IEEE Transactions on Multimedia 17 (9) (2015) 1525–1537.

[9] I. Chugunov, S.-H. Baek, Q. Fu, W. Heidrich, F. Heide, Mask-ToF: Learning microlens masks for flying pixel correction in time-of-flight imaging, in: Proceedings of the IEEE/CVF Conference on Computer Vision and Pattern Recognition, 2021, pp. 9116–9126.

[10] M. Ji, J. Gall, H. Zheng, Y. Liu, L. Fang, SurfaceNet: An end-to-end 3D neural network for multiview stereopsis, in: Proceedings of the IEEE International Conference on Computer Vision, 2017, pp. 2307–2315.

[11] Y. Zhang, T. Funkhouser, Deep depth completion of a single RGB-D image, in: Proceedings of the IEEE Conference on Computer Vision and Pattern Recognition, 2018, pp. 175–185.

[12] J. Uhrig, N. Schneider, L. Schneider, U. Franke, T. Brox, A. Geiger, Sparsity invariant CNNs, in: International Conference on 3D Vision (3DV), 2017.

[13] J. Park, K. Joo, Z. Hu, C.-K. Liu, I. So Kweon, Non-local spatial propagation network for depth completion, in: Computer Vision–ECCV 2020: 16th European Conference, Proceedings, Part XIII 16, Glasgow, UK, August 23–28, 2020, Springer, 2020, pp. 120–136.

[14] X.-F. Han, J.S. Jin, M.-J. Wang, W. Jiang, L. Gao, L. Xiao, A review of algorithms for filtering the 3D point cloud, Signal Processing. Image Communication 57 (2017) 103–112.

[15] M. Mahmoudi, G. Sapiro, Sparse representations for range data restoration, IEEE Transactions on Image Processing 21 (5) (2012) 2909–2915.

[16] Y. Sun, S. Schaefer, W. Wang, Denoising point sets via L0 minimization, Computer Aided Geometric Design 35 (2015) 2–15.

[17] J. Zeng, G. Cheung, M. Ng, J. Pang, C. Yang, 3D point cloud denoising using graph Laplacian regularization of a low dimensional manifold model, IEEE Transactions on Image Processing 29 (2019) 3474–3489.

[18] A. Buades, B. Coll, J.-M. Morel, A non-local algorithm for image denoising, in: IEEE Conference on Computer Vision and Pattern Recognition, vol. 2, IEEE, 2005, pp. 60–65.

[19] K. Dabov, A. Foi, V. Katkovnik, K. Egiazarian, Image denoising by sparse 3-D transform-domain collaborative filtering, IEEE Transactions on Image Processing 16 (8) (2007) 2080–2095.

[20] A. Ortega, P. Frossard, J. Kovačević, J.M. Moura, P. Vandergheynst, Graph signal processing: Overview, challenges, and applications, Proceedings of the IEEE 106 (5) (2018) 808–828.

[21] D.L. Donoho, J.M. Johnstone, Ideal spatial adaptation by wavelet shrinkage, Biometrika 81 (3) (1994) 425–455.

[22] K. Sarkar, F. Bernard, K. Varanasi, C. Theobalt, D. Stricker, Structured low-rank matrix factorization for point-cloud denoising, in: 2018 International Conference on 3D Vision (3DV), IEEE, 2018, pp. 444–453.

[23] S. Osher, Z. Shi, W. Zhu, Low dimensional manifold model for image processing, SIAM Journal on Imaging Sciences 10 (4) (2017) 1669–1690.

[24] Z. Shi, S. Osher, W. Zhu, Generalization of the weighted nonlocal Laplacian in low dimensional manifold model, Journal of Scientific Computing 75 (2018) 638–656.

[25] G. Guennebaud, M. Gross, Algebraic point set surfaces, ACM Transactions on Graphics (TOG) 26 (3) (2007) 23.

[26] E. Mattei, A. Castrodad, Point cloud denoising via moving RPCA, Computer Graphics Forum 36 (8) (2017) 123–137, https://doi.org/10.1111/cgf.13068.

[27] A.X. Chang, T. Funkhouser, L. Guibas, P. Hanrahan, Q. Huang, Z. Li, S. Savarese, M. Savva, S. Song, H. Su, et al., ShapeNet: An information-rich 3D model repository, arXiv preprint, arXiv:1512.03012, 2015.

[28] Y. LeCun, Y. Bengio, G. Hinton, Deep learning, Nature 521 (7553) (2015) 436–444.

[29] X. Cheng, P. Wang, R. Yang, Depth estimation via affinity learned with convolutional spatial propagation network, in: Proceedings of the European Conference on Computer Vision (ECCV), 2018,
pp. 103–119.

[30] F. Ma, S. Karaman, Sparse-to-dense: Depth prediction from sparse depth samples and a single image, in: 2018 IEEE International Conference on Robotics and Automation (ICRA), IEEE, 2018,
pp. 4796–4803.

[31] A. Dai, C. Ruizhongtai Qi, M. Nießner, Shape completion using 3D-encoder-predictor CNNs and
shape synthesis, in: Proceedings of the IEEE Conference on Computer Vision and Pattern Recognition, 2017, pp. 5868–5877.

[32] W. Yuan, T. Khot, D. Held, C. Mertz, M. Hebert, PCN: point completion network, in: 2018 International Conference on 3D Vision (3DV), IEEE, 2018, pp. 728–737.

[33] J. Pang, D. Li, D. Tian, TearingNet: Point cloud autoencoder to learn topology-friendly representations, in: Proceedings of the IEEE/CVF Conference on Computer Vision and Pattern Recognition,
2021, pp. 7453–7462.

[34] S. Luo, W. Hu, Score-based point cloud denoising, in: Proceedings of the IEEE/CVF International
Conference on Computer Vision, 2021, pp. 4583–4592.

[35] H. Xie, H. Yao, S. Zhou, J. Mao, S. Zhang, W. Sun, GRNet: gridding residual network for dense
point cloud completion, in: European Conference on Computer Vision, Springer, 2020, pp. 365–381.

[36] M. Liu, L. Sheng, S. Yang, J. Shao, S.-M. Hu, Morphing and sampling network for dense point
cloud completion, in: Proceedings of the AAAI Conference on Artificial Intelligence, vol. 34, 2020,
pp. 11596–11603.

[37] A. Milioto, I. Vizzo, J. Behley, C. Stachniss, RangeNet++: Fast and accurate lidar semantic segmentation, in: IROS, 2019.

[38] A. Boulch, B. Le Saux, N. Audebert, Unstructured point cloud semantic labeling using deep segmentation networks, in: 3DOR, 2017.

[39] Y. Zhang, Z. Zhou, P. David, X. Yue, Z. Xi, B. Gong, H. Foroosh, PolarNet: An improved grid
representation for online lidar point clouds semantic segmentation, in: Proceedings of the IEEE/CVF
Conference on Computer Vision and Pattern Recognition (CVPR), 2020.

[40] B. Wu, A. Wan, X. Yue, K. Keutzer, SqueezeSeg: Convolutional neural nets with recurrent CRF for
real-time road-object segmentation from 3D lidar point cloud, in: ICRA, 2018.

[41] B. Wu, X. Zhou, S. Zhao, X. Yue, K. Keutzer, SqueezeSegV2: Improved model structure and unsupervised domain adaptation for road-object segmentation from a lidar point cloud, in: ICRA, 2019.

[42] C. Xu, B. Wu, Z. Wang, W. Zhan, P. Vajda, K. Keutzer, M. Tomizuka, SqueezeSegV3: Spatially-
adaptive convolution for efficient point-cloud segmentation, in: European Conference on Computer
Vision, Springer, 2020, pp. 1–19.

[43] J. Huang, S. You, Point cloud labeling using 3D convolutional neural network, in: ICPR, 2016.

[44] L. Tchapmi, C. Choy, I. Armeni, J. Gwak, S. Savarese, SEGCloud: Semantic segmentation of 3D
point clouds, in: 3DV, 2017.

[45] B. Graham, M. Engelcke, L. van der Maaten, 3D semantic segmentation with submanifold sparse
convolutional networks, in: CVPR, 2018.

[46] C. Choy, J. Gwak, S. Savarese, 4D spatio-temporal convnets: Minkowski convolutional neural networks, in: CVPR, 2019.

[47] H. Tang, Z. Liu, S. Zhao, Y. Lin, J. Lin, H. Wang, S. Han, Searching efficient 3D architectures with
sparse point-voxel convolution, in: European Conference on Computer Vision, 2020.

[48] X. Zhu, H. Zhou, T. Wang, F. Hong, Y. Ma, W. Li, H. Li, D. Lin, Cylindrical and asymmetrical
3D convolution networks for lidar segmentation, in: Proceedings of the IEEE/CVF Conference on
Computer Vision and Pattern Recognition (CVPR), 2021, pp. 9939–9948.

[49] C.R. Qi, H. Su, K. Mo, L.J. Guibas, PointNet: Deep learning on point sets for 3D classification and
segmentation, in: CVPR, 2017.

[50] C.R. Qi, L. Yi, H. Su, L.J. Guibas, PointNet++: Deep hierarchical feature learning on point sets in
a metric space, in: NeurIPS, 2017.

[51] H. Zhao, L. Jiang, C.-W. Fu, J. Jia, PointWeb: Enhancing local neighborhood features for point cloud
processing, in: CVPR, 2019.

[52] Q. Hu, B. Yang, L. Xie, S. Rosa, Y. Guo, Z. Wang, N. Trigoni, A. Markham, RandLA-Net: Efficient semantic segmentation of large-scale point clouds, in: CVPR, 2020.

[53] H. Zhao, L. Jiang, J. Jia, P.H. Torr, V. Koltun, Point transformer, in: Proceedings of the IEEE/CVF International Conference on Computer Vision (ICCV), 2021, pp. 16259–16268.

[54] B.-S. Hua, M.-K. Tran, S.-K. Yeung, Pointwise convolutional neural networks, in: CVPR, 2018.

[55] S. Wang, S. Suo, W.-C. Ma, A. Pokrovsky, R. Urtasun, Deep parametric continuous convolutional neural networks, in: CVPR, 2018.

[56] H. Thomas, C.R. Qi, J.-E. Deschaud, B. Marcotegui, F. Goulette, L.J. Guibas, KPConv: Flexible and deformable convolution for point clouds, in: ICCV, 2019.

[57] Y. Wang, Y. Sun, Z. Liu, S.E. Sarma, M.M. Bronstein, J.M. Solomon, Dynamic graph CNN for learning on point clouds, ACM Transactions on Graphics 38 (5) (2019) 146, https://doi.org/10.1145/3326362.

[58] Z. Liu, H. Tang, Y. Lin, S. Han, Point-Voxel CNN for efficient 3D deep learning, in: NeurIPS, 2019.

[59] J. Xu, R. Zhang, J. Dou, Y. Zhu, J. Sun, S. Pu, RPVNet: A deep and efficient range-point-voxel fusion network for lidar point cloud segmentation, in: Proceedings of the IEEE/CVF International Conference on Computer Vision (ICCV), 2021, pp. 16024–16033.

[60] S. Chen, B. Liu, C. Feng, C. Vallespi-Gonzalez, C. Wellington, 3D point cloud processing and learning for autonomous driving: impacting map creation, localization, and perception, IEEE Signal Processing Magazine 38 (1) (2021) 68–86.

[61] S. Shi, X. Wang, H. Li, PointRCNN: 3D object proposal generation and detection from point cloud, in: 2019 IEEE/CVF Conference on Computer Vision and Pattern Recognition (CVPR), 2019, pp. 770–779.

[62] B. Li, 3D fully convolutional network for vehicle detection in point cloud, in: 2017 IEEE/RSJ International Conference on Intelligent Robots and Systems (IROS), 2017, pp. 1513–1518.

[63] B. Yang, W. Luo, R. Urtasun, PIXOR: real-time 3D object detection from point clouds, in: 2018 IEEE/CVF Conference on Computer Vision and Pattern Recognition, 2018, pp. 7652–7660.

[64] G.P. Meyer, A.G. Laddha, E. Kee, C. Vallespi-Gonzalez, C.K. Wellington, LaserNet: an efficient probabilistic 3D object detector for autonomous driving, in: 2019 IEEE/CVF Conference on Computer Vision and Pattern Recognition (CVPR), 2019, pp. 12669–12678.

[65] Y. Zhou, O. Tuzel, VoxelNet: end-to-end learning for point cloud based 3D object detection, in: 2018 IEEE/CVF Conference on Computer Vision and Pattern Recognition, 2018, pp. 4490–4499.

[66] T.-Y. Lin, P. Dollár, R.B. Girshick, K. He, B. Hariharan, S.J. Belongie, Feature pyramid networks for object detection, in: 2017 IEEE Conference on Computer Vision and Pattern Recognition (CVPR), 2017, pp. 936–944.

[67] W. Liu, D. Anguelov, D. Erhan, C. Szegedy, S.E. Reed, C.-Y. Fu, A.C. Berg, SSD: single shot multibox detector, in: ECCV, 2016.

[68] A.H. Lang, S. Vora, H. Caesar, L. Zhou, J. Yang, O. Beijbom, PointPillars: fast encoders for object detection from point clouds, in: 2019 IEEE/CVF Conference on Computer Vision and Pattern Recognition (CVPR), 2019, pp. 12689–12697.

[69] Z. Yang, Y. Sun, S. Liu, J. Jia, 3DSSD: point-based 3D single stage object detector, in: 2020 IEEE/CVF Conference on Computer Vision and Pattern Recognition (CVPR), 2020, pp. 11037–11045.

[70] C.-H. He, H. Zeng, J. Huang, X. Hua, L. Zhang, Structure aware single-stage 3D object detection from point cloud, in: 2020 IEEE/CVF Conference on Computer Vision and Pattern Recognition (CVPR), 2020, pp. 11870–11879.

[71] W. Zheng, W. Tang, S. Chen, L. Jiang, C.-W. Fu, CIA-SSD: confident IoU-aware single-stage object detector from point cloud, in: AAAI, 2021.

[72] S. Shi, C. Guo, L. Jiang, Z. Wang, J. Shi, X. Wang, H. Li, PV-RCNN: point-voxel feature set abstraction for 3D object detection, in: 2020 IEEE/CVF Conference on Computer Vision and Pattern Recognition (CVPR), 2020, pp. 10526–10535.

[73] T. Yin, X. Zhou, P. Krähenbühl, Center-based 3D object detection and tracking, in: CVPR, 2021.

[74] X. Zhou, D. Wang, P. Krähenbühl, Objects as points, arXiv preprint, arXiv:1904.07850, 2019.

CHAPTER 17

Computational 3D displays

Jingyu Liu[a], Fangcheng Zhong[b], Claire Mantel[a], Søren Forchhammer[a], and Rafał K. Mantiuk[b]
[a]Technical University of Denmark, Kgs. Lyngby, Denmark
[b]University of Cambridge, Cambridge, United Kingdom

17.1. Introduction

This chapter discusses how a volumetric scene can be faithfully rendered with an impression of immersion and realism through emerging three-dimensional (3D) display technologies for virtual reality (VR), which focus on bringing users an isolated experience, and augmented reality (AR), which emphasizes the interaction with the real-world scenes. Typical applications include virtual socialization, entertainment, automotive visualization, and health care.

To describe a volumetric scene, a simple representation can be an omni-directional video, whereas a detailed description can be a *plenoptic function*, which can be expressed as a seven-dimensional (7D) *plenoptic function* that assumes the radiance is constant along the ray:

$$\Phi = P(\theta, \phi, \lambda, t, x, y, z), \tag{17.1}$$

which describes the spectral radiance Φ (Wsr^{-1}m^{-3}) in wavelength λ of a ray traversing the spatial coordinates (x, y, z) along the direction (θ, ϕ) at time t. Unfortunately, the plenoptic function entails unreasonable requirements for storage and processing, as it involves a continuous domain of seven dimensions. A simplification is given by eliminating the z variable giving the *light field* representation. The complexity of the *plenoptic* and the *light field* function, poses a big challenge for 3D display hardware and computation. The challenge is even more significant for AR displays, where interactions between the virtual light field and the physical space must be considered. Nonetheless, human visual system (HVS) is unlikely to perceive minor inaccuracies in the light field. The virtual reproduction of light does not have to be identical to its physical counterpart, provided that it is visually indistinguishable to human eyes.

17.1.1 Outline

This chapter starts with a background on human visual perception, which serves as guidance in designing 3D displays (Section 17.2). Limits of the HVS provide concrete objectives for the targeted display qualities and help better distribute the limited resources, such as hardware, storage, and computation, to where the human vision is most

Immersive Video Technologies
https://doi.org/10.1016/B978-0-32-391755-1.00023-7

sensitive. We also consider the potential artifacts, which may be displayed and perceived, when any of these objectives are not met.

Next, we introduce the mechanisms, architectures, and rendering methods of various designs of 3D displays and evaluate their visual qualities from both the physical and perceptual perspectives (Section 17.3). We categorize such displays into *autostereoscopic* and *stereoscopic* display, according to whether they require any special headgear, glasses, or visual separators in their use. We look into how such displays are designed to reproduce desirable depth information. We discuss a particular type of stereoscopic display for AR applications, optical see-through display (OSTD), which simultaneously presents the virtual and physical light fields by using optical elements that combine light. We explain the unique characteristics, challenges, and solutions of OSTDs. As their objective is not only to reproduce a virtual light field, but also one blended with the physical scene, the perceptual considerations, optical design, and rendering algorithms require different treatments. Besides, we introduce rendering methods designed explicitly for stereoscopic displays, which are distinct from traditional graphics pipelines to use the characteristics of HVS to optimize the computing resource, while maintaining the perceptual quality.

In summary, an illustration of the topics covered in this chapter is depicted in Fig. 17.1.[1]

17.2. Perceptual considerations

This section explains the perceptual considerations relevant to the display systems discussed in Section 17.3. Although the plenoptic function is a 7D continuous function, the HVS does not directly perceive the spectral radiance of individual rays, but the irradiance (projection) of rays coming from all directions on the retina. Moreover, spectral irradiance is integrated over various ranges of wavelengths by the retina's photoreceptors to enable color vision. Finally, the spatial and temporal resolution that the visual system can resolve is limited. In this section, we consider the capabilities of HVS in terms of its perception of the plenoptic function, which guides the designs of 3D display systems. Indeed, by leveraging the limitations of HVS, it is possible to reduce the required precision of the virtual light fields rendered by a 3D display, while recreating identical visual perceptions.

In the discussion that follows, we categorize our considerations into spatial (Section 17.2.1), spectral (Section 17.2.2), temporal (Section 17.2.3), and intensity (Section 17.2.4) aspects of the plenoptic function, each pertaining to the parameters (θ, ϕ, x, y, z), (λ), (t), and the output (P), respectively.

---

[1] Original illustration materials in the Fig. 17.1 (A–C), Fig. 17.3, and Fig. 17.5 were designed by Freepik.

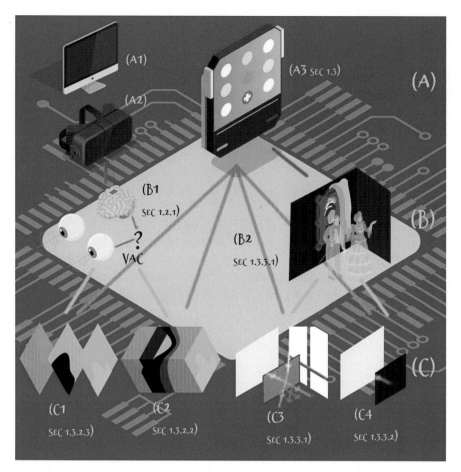

Figure 17.1 A summary of the chapter: (A) lists the display systems that we consider (i.e., (A1) conventional two-dimensional (2D) displays, (A2) 3D displays with stereo cues only, and (A3) computational 3D displays, the primary topic of this chapter which is detailed in Section 17.3); (B) shows two typical problems that display systems suffer from, i.e., (B1) vergence-accommodation conflict (VAC) for 2D displays and 3D displays with stereo cues only (Section 17.2.1), and (B2) ghosting effect (Section 17.3.3.1) from optical see-through displays; (C) shows some typical display technologies to solve the problems listed in (B), such as varifocal displays in (C1) (Section 17.3.2.2), multifocal displays in (C2) (Section 17.3.2.3), and color blending methods in (C3) (Section 17.3.3.1), as well as subtractive methods in (C4) (Section 17.3.3.2) for optical see-through color distortion.

17.2.1 Spatial considerations

Here, we consider the spatial parameters (θ, ϕ, x, y, z) of the plenoptic function Eq. (17.1), which specifies the origin and direction of the rays.

By exploiting the limitations of HVS, we can reduce the number of rays needed to be reproduced for a virtual light field from three aspects. First, due to the limited pupil size and field of view (FOV) of human eyes, only a fraction of light waves from the scene can reach the retina through the pupil, which has a diameter that varies from 2 to 4 mm in daylight to 4 to 8 mm in the dark [119]. The FOV of both eyes combined is approximately 100° vertically and 200° horizontally, with a binocular FOV (i.e., overlapped FOV seen by both eyes) of 120° [18]. An individual eye has a horizontal FOV of about 160°. Second, the visual system does not directly perceive the radiance of individual rays, but the irradiance (projection) of rays from all directions on the retina. Finally, human vision has a limited acuity: the ability to distinguish small details. Visual acuity reaches its highest in the *fovea*, the area on the retina corresponding to the central 2° of the visual field that presents the highest spatial resolution because of a dense distribution of cones. The peak resolving power of the retina is approximately 120 cycles per degree of visual angle [78] corresponding to a display's spatial resolution of 240 pixels per degree. Displays with insufficient spatial resolution result in loss of high-frequency details. When the pixel grid is visible in head-mounted (tracked) displays, we observe a screen-door effect.

Depth perception refers to our ability to perceive a 3D world and infer relative or absolute distances of objects. It arises from a variety of *depth cues* that can be classified into *visual cues*, where retinal images provide the depth information and *oculomotor cues*, where depth judgment is based on eye movements. Depth cues can also be categorized into *binocular cues*, where sensory information is provided by both eyes, and *monocular cues*, where information is observed with a single eye.

Conventional 2D displays can provide a variety of monocular visual cues, such as shading, relative size, occlusion, and perspectives, but there are specific cues unique to 3D displays. For example, *binocular disparity*, or *stereopsis*, is a binocular visual cue, where two retinal images of the same scene are formed from disparate viewpoints of two eyes. When an object is closer, the disparity between its left and right retinal images is larger, and vice versa. Inaccurate disparity causes distortions in perceived depth [31, 132]. *Vergence* is a binocular oculomotor cue, in which the optical axes of the two eyes rotate and converge towards the object's location in focus. Kinaesthetic sensations from extraocular muscles provide information for depth perception as the depth of an object is inversely related to the angle of vergence [93]. Disparity and vergence together are referred to as *stereo cues*. *Defocus blur* is a monocular visual cue, where objects outside the depth of field of the eyes appear blurry on the retina. Evidence has shown that focus cues affect both 3D shape perception and the apparent scale of the scene [6,24,123]. *Accommodation* is the mechanism that modulates the ciliary muscles to stretch or relax the lens and change the curvature of the cornea to focus on objects close or distant. Such muscle movement provides feedback to HVS and a weak depth cue. For young children, accommodation distance can vary from infinity to as near as

6.5 cm [12]. As a depth cue weaker than defocus blur, accommodation is mainly effective within two meters [20]. Accommodation and defocus blur together are referred to as *focus cues*. A regular stereo display where the disparity is provided by presenting two separate planar images to the left and right eyes does not drive the accommodation to the correct depth. Both eyes accommodate to a fixed but incorrect distance since all the rays originate from the screen, rather than the actual depth of the virtual object. Such incorrect accommodation cues lead to vergence-accommodation conflict (VAC) since accommodation and vergence are coupled mechanisms [38]. Their decoupling may cause an unnatural visual experience that results in discomfort [133]. Finally, *motion parallax* is a monocular visual cue, in which the viewers consider closer objects moving faster than further objects. A summary of depth cues can be found in Fig. 17.2. In Section 17.3, we will see how various 3D display systems employ various approaches to support the depth cues mentioned above. It is a great challenge to reproduce all depth cues correctly and collectively without introducing spatial or temporal artifacts.

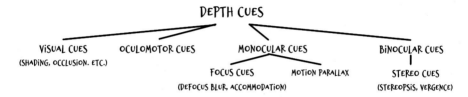

Figure 17.2 A summary of depth cues introduced in Section 17.2.1.

17.2.2 Spectral considerations

Here, we consider the spectral parameter (λ) of the plenoptic function from Eq. (17.1).

The HVS does not directly perceive the spectral radiance of light waves per wavelength λ. Instead, *photoreceptors* on the retina integrate the spectral radiance of light waves over the visible spectrum,[2] and HVS perceives light waves with different spectral distributions as various colors with different brightness. Photoreceptors can be of two types: *cones* and *rods*, with cones predominantly sensitive to daylight and rods active in dark conditions. There are three types of cones: L, M, and S, each peaking at a distinct wavelength in response. In daylight conditions, color vision is driven by LMS cone responses. As mentioned in Section 17.2.1, cones are not uniformly distributed across the retina, but are more densely populated in the fovea. Therefore the fovea is more sensitive to color variations [90], especially those that can be sensed by the L and M cones as they are more concentrated in the fovea.

If two nonidentical light spectra result in the same LMS responses, the HVS would perceive them as the same color despite non-matching spectral power distributions.

---

[2] The visible light spectrum ranges from about 380 to about 750 nanometers in wavelength.

Such colors are referred to as *metamers*. Ignoring changes in luminance, the set of all colors up to a metameric match can be represented by a chromaticity diagram. Thanks to metamerism, displays do not have to generate light waves with physically correct spectra, but only need to achieve a metameric match to reproduce a target color. By generating a unique combination of three primary colors specified in the chromaticity diagram, displays can reproduce the color of arbitrary chromaticity within the convex hull of these primaries.

17.2.3 Temporal considerations

Here, we consider the temporal parameter (t) of the plenoptic function Eq. (17.1).

There is a consensus that a high display refresh rate is essential to maintain a decent visual quality for higher velocities of motion. Motion artifacts, such as judder, ghosting, motion blur, and flicker can be reduced with a higher refresh rate. However, it is difficult to determine a single threshold refresh rate above which any motion artifacts are not perceivable, as it depends on a multitude of factors, such as the persistence and spatial resolution of the display, and the velocity, luminance, and contrast of the stimuli. For example, most AR/VR displays present images with low persistence, where an image is displayed at a higher intensity for a fraction of frame duration, and the display remains blank for the rest of the frame. The stroboscopic effect introduced by such low persistence significantly reduces the motion blur caused by eye gaze moving over a discretely moving image, which is stationary on display throughout a frame for a fixed refresh rate. Though low persistence attenuates the required refresh rate to prevent motion blur, it can introduce visible *flicker* artifacts, the perception of visual fluctuations in intensity, and instability in the presence of a light stimulus if the refresh rate is not high enough [37]. *Critical flicker frequency (CFF)* measures the frequency at which an intermittent light stimulus appears to be utterly steady without flicker artifacts. Low persistence requires a higher CFF for a steady flicker fusion. Therefore it is difficult to determine a threshold refresh rate required for perceptually realistic motion quality for an average scenario, although studies [73] showed that the marginal gain in mean impairment score with a higher refresh rate significantly drops as the refresh rate rises to 300 frames per second and beyond.

17.2.4 Intensity considerations

Here, we consider the light intensity as the output (P) of the Eq. (17.1).

Pupillary light reflex is a mechanism that controls the diameter of the pupil in response to ambient light, resulting in a pupil diameter that varies between 2 mm and 8 mm [119]. The cones and rods are sensitive to different stimulation ranges in terms of luminance: from 0.01 to 10^8 cd/m² for cones and from 10^{-6} to 10 cd/m² for rods [61]. However, the display systems do not target the highest boundary of the luminance stimulation range due to safety concerns. The cones are distributed mainly within the fovea and rods on the peripheral retina. In daylight, the cones' response within fovea maintain high-level activity. In contrast, the peripheral area plays a dominant role under low luminance conditions, as the light is sensed by rods distributed outside the fovea. The *dynamic range* of a scene, natural or displayed, refers to the ratio of its highest and smallest luminance value. In natural scenes, the dynamic range spans approximately 12 to 14 orders of magnitude; the human eye only perceives a portion of this range simultaneously [134]. However, the human eye can adapt dynamically to shift this effective range in response to varying lighting conditions [76]. The most extensive dynamic range a display device can reproduce is also known as the *contrast ratio*. Images with higher contrast are perceived as more realistic and appear to have more depth [117,144].

17.3. Computational 3D displays

Computational displays are an emerging class of displays that integrate computational processing with spatial light modulators (SLMs) so that the system can transcend the limits of purely optical designs. In Section 17.2, we summarized the spatial considerations for a display system, including the FOV, spatial resolution, and depth reproduction. In particular, depth reproduction is unique to 3D displays, as other considerations are the same for conventional 2D displays. In this section, we discuss *computational 3D displays*, a subset of *computational displays* that provide natural reproduction of 3D depth cues.

Whereas 3D display technologies have become increasingly accessible in recent decades, from stereo movies with polarized or active shutter glasses to personal head-mounted VR/AR displays, few fundamental techniques and device architectures have changed. Their designs are mainly based on delivering stereo cues by presenting each eye with a separate planar image. One fundamental issue of this approach is that it results in VAC, as introduced in Section 17.2.1.

Compared to conventional stereo displays, computational 3D displays employ computational resources to deliver essential focus cues in addition to stereo cues. State-of-the-art computational 3D display technologies also introduce novel mechanisms for depth reproduction that exploit the limitations of HVS. We introduce their hardware architectures and rendering algorithms since they are equally crucial for reproducing high-quality volumetric videos. We also review the performance of these display techniques by evaluating the light field they produce and the perceptual requirements they meet from the spatial, spectral, and temporal aspects, as introduced in Section 17.2. In particular, we focus on discussing how focus cues (i.e., accommodation and defocus blur) are reproduced with such displays.

In the discussion that follows, we categorize the computational 3D displays into *autostereoscopic* displays (Section 17.3.1), where stereo cues can be directly provided without a need for any headgear, and *stereoscopic* displays (Section 17.3.2), where the use of special headgear, glasses, or visual separators for eyes is essential to support stereo cues (disparity and vergence). Furthermore, a particular class of stereoscopic displays, optical see-through display (OSTD), is reviewed in Section 17.3.3. OSTDs are mostly applied in AR, where the human eye will fuse the background environment and the virtual scene created by the displays.

Fig. 17.3 is an illustration that shows the structure of Section 17.3.

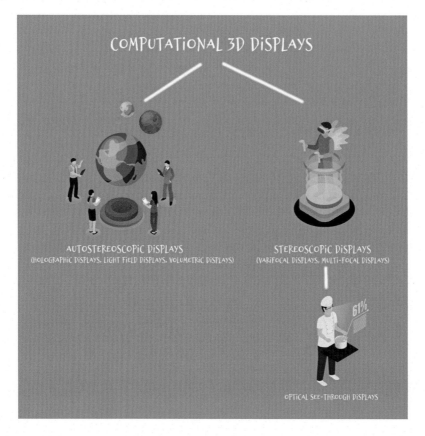

Figure 17.3 A hierarchy of the display systems introduced in Section 17.3.

17.3.1 Autostereoscopic displays

Autostereoscopic displays aim to create accurate stereo cues without special headgear, glasses, or any type of visual separator for the eyes.

In the discussion that follows, we introduce three main types of autostereoscopic displays, distinguished by how they reproduce the light field. Digital *holographic displays* aim to reproduce the entire distribution of light waves, including phase, amplitude, and wavelength, based on the principles of light diffraction and interference (Section 17.3.1.1). *Light field displays* are a close alternative to holographic displays in terms of recreating the original light distribution in a 3D volume (Section 17.3.1.2). The distinction is that light waves created by a holographic display are formed by phase-conjugated rays from each hologram point, while a light field display controls the directional intensity of beams expanding from a 2D panel (usually composed of pixel cells). *Volumetric displays* reduce the light field to a 3D volume composed of voxels (Section 17.3.1.3).

17.3.1.1 Holographic displays

In principle, all depth cues can be automatically and simultaneously achieved by reproducing the light distribution of a 3D scene fully. This is the ultimate objective of a holographic display. Invented by Dennis Gabor [26] in the late 1940s, holograms work on the principles of light diffraction and interference. In acquisition, the object beam of the 3D scene interferes coherently with a reference beam, resulting in interference fringes going through a recording medium that record all the characteristics of lights (phase, amplitude, and wavelength). In rendering, the object beam can be reconstructed in a reverse manner. The reference beam is usually delivered by a single monochromatic laser. Colored holograms can be generated by rendering holograms of three different wavelengths (e.g., red, green, and blue) separately and incoherently superimposing them on one another [5]. Conventional analogue holograms are recorded using non-reconfigurable mediums, such as a photographic emulsion. Modern *computer-generated holography (CGH)* generates holographic interference patterns using SLMs and digital technologies [106]. This enables the rendering of holographic videos [3].

Although ideal holographic display has been regarded as the ultimate form of 3D display, it still faces challenges in both hardware and software. For example, SLMs have limited spatial resolution. Based on a 400 nm blue light, a 127000 pixels per inch (ppi) SLM with a 200 nm pixel size is required to display a fringe width of half the wavelength of light [13]. Current commercial SLMs can only reach 7000 ppi [14]. Even if a dense SLM is physically realizable, displaying a static 3D scene as large as a phone screen would require processing billions of pixels, placing a significant burden on computation and data transmission. For dynamic holograms, the amount of data rises to tens or hundreds of billion pixels per second. Meanwhile, interference of coherent wavefronts results in unavoidable speckle noise that undermines the image quality in contrast and color. Recently, it has been shown that machine learning techniques can be applied to reduce many artifacts of holographic displays, including speckle noise [10,96].

17.3.1.2 Light field displays

In Eq. (17.1), we use five spatial parameters to specify the starting position (x, y, z) and direction (θ, ϕ) of a ray. If we assume a constant radiance along a ray, we only need to know where the ray hits the xy $(z = 0)$ plane and can remove z from the parameterization in Eq. (17.1), reducing it to

$$\Phi = P(\theta, \phi, \lambda, t, x, y). \tag{17.2}$$

A generic light field display generates a four-dimensional distribution of light rays from a planar light source and an optical transmission medium. This way, positional and directional light rays are both recreated and modulated. The simplest method to create directional light rays is to redistribute pixels into N horizontal views. This can be achieved by *parallax barrier* [42,49]—an interlace of transparent and opaque stripes, or *lenticular sheet* [131]—a cylindrical micro-lens array that redirects diffused lights from pixels into specific directions. Of course, both of these approaches prohibit vertical parallax. One advantage of the lenticular sheet over the parallax barrier is that the lenticular sheet does not reduce the display luminance, since the lenticular sheet is comprised of lenses, whereas the parallax barrier blocks light paths. The concept of a lenticular sheet can be generalized to present both horizontal and vertical perspectives and potentially focus cues by replacing it with a 2D micro-lens array. This is the mechanism behind the *integral imaging* [67], where the light field of a 3D object can be recorded by a 2D micro-lens array and reconstructed when viewed at the same distance of the object through the same lens array. As with many other light field display architectures, one fundamental issue of these approaches is the inherent trade-off between spatial and angular resolution (number of distinguishable views). For a display of a finite number of pixels to generate N^2 views, the spatial resolution will be reduced to $1/N^2$ of its full resolution. However, a too low number of views will probably cause discontinuous parallax or break focus cues. Focus cues can only be achieved with a highly dense layout of angular views, as it requires at least two rays to enter the pupil. Another drawback of the lenticular sheet approaches is that they only permit a fixed number of viewing zones, limiting the view box (the range of positions from which the display can be viewed). An incorrect viewing position will probably cause cross-talk and other cues to be wrongly presented. To address these issues, these displays can be integrated with a head tracking system [43], allowing for a dynamic adjustment of the display content to align with the viewing position. This can reduce the essential number of distinguishable views for a fixed head position to maintain a higher spatial resolution and broaden the viewing zone. The drawback is that this is usually limited to a single viewer and requires a highly accurate synchronization between head tracking and rendering to avoid visual artifacts. Directional light rays can also be controlled by *time multiplexing*, designed to overcome the trade-off between spatial and angular resolution by sequentially showing each view [54,63,121]. The downside of time multiplexing is that it requires an overall refresh rate and a scanning rate of the directional device to be the product of the desired perceived refresh rate for each view and the number of views [13].

Due to the large information bandwidth required to express a light field, a fundamental issue of a light field display is that it requires a trade-off of spatial and angular resolution. Although Eq. (17.2) has one parameter less than the full expression, Eq. (17.2) still carries a redundancy of information, since 1) the change of surface color with the viewing direction is highly correlated, and is constant for diffuse surfaces;

2) regions of uniform colors or textures exhibit small variance. *Compressive light field displays* were introduced to leverage computational methods and compressive optics to adaptively maximize the quality of the virtual light field for the displayed content [129]. They are called compressive, because the number of emitted light rays can transcend the number of representing pixels, which are computationally optimized to direct the resulting rays to best approximate the target light field. The compressive optics usually consists of a backlight (uniform or directional) and multiplicative optical layers (e.g., liquid crystal displays (LCDs)). Examples of compressive light field displays include tomographic image synthesis [128], polarization fields [64], and tensor displays [130]. One challenge of these displays is that the multiple layer architecture introduces scattering and inter-reflections, resulting in approximation error, and thus compromising the display contrast and color. Another challenge is compressive light field displays require a scene-based optimization for each frame, causing a high computational cost.

17.3.1.3 Volumetric displays

Volumetric displays produce light originating from voxels in a 3D volume, typically by time multiplexing with image slices emitted or illuminated from switching or mechanically moving surfaces. Examples of volumetric displays include the use of rotating display screens [21], stacks of switchable diffusers [111], the spin of a cylindrical parallax barrier and light-emitting diode (LED) arrays [138], and sweeping diffusers [118]. It is possible to create strong 3D cues with these displays, including stereo, parallax, and focus cues. However, the physical realization of a volumetric display makes it difficult to show occlusions, as voxels appear semi-transparent. Those displays also cannot reproduce view-dependent surface appearance, such as specular reflections, since light is uniformly emitted or reflected from each voxel in all directions. Compared to a holographic or light field display, they also confine the depth of the scene to be within the physical display volume, but they permit a much larger viewing zone.

Discussion

The quality of an autostereoscopic display is highly confined by its limited resolution, dynamic range (contrast), color accuracy, FOV, and computational cost. After all, reproducing a full light field of sufficient size and quality requires control over billions of rays, which is currently infeasible. However, if the number of viewers is limited to a single person and the eye position can be tracked, the subspace of a light field required to be reproduced becomes much smaller. Next, we will discuss stereoscopic displays.

17.3.2 Stereoscopic displays

In contrast to autostereoscopic displays, head-mounted stereoscopic displays (AR/VR headsets) stabilize the eye position relative to the display screens,[3] making them possible to render a 3D scene through a significantly smaller number of required rays. As stereoscopic displays can seamlessly (or with slight variations) integrate existing imaging and rendering techniques, they have been commercially available long before autostereoscopic displays. The most basic design of a stereoscopic display works by showing a separate planar image to each eye to create a stereo vision, while maintaining a decent spatial resolution. This is, for instance, the case of many commercial head-mounted displays (HMDs), such as Oculus Quest 2 [83] and HTC Vive Flow [39], but such a design lacks proper focus cues, as detailed in Section 17.2.1. This section focuses on stereoscopic displays that support focus cues in addition to stereo cues through the help of SLMs and computational methods.

In what follows (Section 17.3.2.1), we first introduce eye-tracking as an essential technology for stereoscopic displays to support focus cues. We then present two variants of stereoscopic displays supporting focus cues: varifocal displays in Section 17.3.2.2 and multifocal displays in Section 17.3.2.3.

17.3.2.1 Eye tracking

Eye-tracking devices can obtain information on the openness of the eyes, the size of the pupils, the position of the eye center, and the gaze direction (or gaze point on a display screen). Current commercial eye trackers can provide eye-tracking information in an embedded manner within VR headset [40]. Eye tracking can be used to allocate computational resources better and improve computing performance when combined with rendering methods, such as foveated rendering [91]. Some displays require information on the position of the eye (or its nodal point) and use eye tracking for that purpose.

Despite these positive perspectives, eye tracking brings many challenges. When looking at the recorded eye movement scan paths, one can notice that the recorded paths appear to be irregular. This is because of *saccades* [9], a rapid eye movement between two fixation points. As saccade is much faster than head or hand movement; tracking reliability is therefore a concern of the eye tracker. Though current commercial eye trackers can reach a high refresh rate as 2000 Hz binocularly [108], other latencies will accumulate when utilizing eye trackers, such as the latency of camera processing (around 8.5 ms), and CPU processing (around 3.5 ms) will add to the system latency [98]. Furthermore, the accuracy of eye tracking can degrade in an environment where lighting conditions vary. The eye needs to adapt to the changing lighting conditions, and the

---

[3] Here, we do not consider regular 3D displays with shutter or polarization glasses, although they can simulate motion parallax with head tracking.

processing method for different luminance levels requires an adaption as well [102]. The awareness of this feature can affect the design of AR applications.

17.3.2.2 Varifocal displays

Varifocal displays can be built upon standard head-mounted stereo displays by actively adjusting the focal distance of the image plane seen by each eye via active optics, such as liquid lenses [1,19,92]. The focal distance adjustment is in accordance with the observer's gaze to show a varying depth of field (DOF) effect. However, these displays introduce undesirable lens distortions caused by the active optics (e.g., deformable membrane mirror [19]). They also require an accurate synchronization of the lens optics and the 2D image source generation (e.g., digital micromirror device (DMD)) with the 3D gaze location. Inaccuracy between the optics and the observers' gaze often leads to errors on the reproduced focal plane. The mechanisms of a varifocal display also require its defocus blur to be synthesized in rendering [135], rather than being optically reproduced, since they only allow for a uniform focal depth throughout the scene for a fixed gaze.

17.3.2.3 Multifocal displays

Multifocal displays can be regarded as a variation of volumetric displays with a fixed viewing position. For each eye, a stack of images is rendered at a fixed number of focal planes at various distances, each plane adding a certain amount of light. Thus a viewer can accommodate appropriately at the desired depth. These focal planes can consist of superimposed image planes with beam-splitters [2] or time-multiplexed image slices that sweep a 3D volume with high-speed switchable lenses [11,69,140]. Compared to a varifocal display, multifocal displays do not require a strict synchronization of the optics and rendering with the gaze location, but still maintain a high resolution and contrast, as they can adopt well-established 2D display techniques [41,143]. Architectures with fixed focal planes also prevent optical aberrations. However, the quality of a multifocal display is susceptible to the accuracy of the eye position, as a misalignment in the focal cues immediately breaks sharp edges and realism. Differences in eye positions of individual observers can be compensated for with a homography correction [82] or a physical calibration [143]. Integration of a multifocal display with high dynamic range (HDR) has been shown to achieve a level of realism that transcends any existing 3D display technique, confusing naive observers between a physical object and its virtual 3D reproduction [143], as shown in Fig. 17.4.

Multifocal decomposition

Despite the previously mentioned improvements, multifocal displays are not free of artifacts. Edges near depth occlusions are particularly difficult to reproduce. Indeed, correctly rendering the images at each focal plane is crucial for multifocal displays to

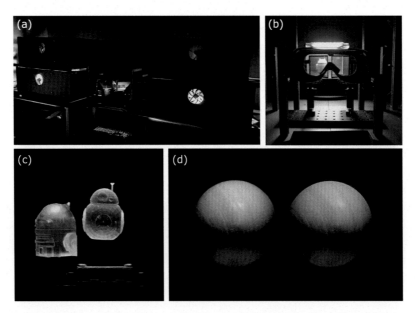

Figure 17.4 (a) A HDR multifocal stereo display [143] (b) which allows for a direct comparison with a physical scene located in front of the observer. (c) (d) The display can reproduce real-world 3D objects with accurate color, contrast, disparity, and a range of focal depth, making it hard to distinguish between real and virtual scenes.

ensure a smooth perception of depth and texture. The algorithm that guides the rendering for multifocal displays is often referred to as *multifocal decomposition*. It approximates a light field of a 3D scene by distributing its content on a discrete number of focal planes. The most straightforward multifocal decomposition approach is to distribute the light across focal planes via a diopter-based linear depth filtering [2,69]. Linear depth filtering can drive accommodation to correct depth with focal plane separations up to one diopter [72], but it produces visible artifacts at occlusion boundaries and for non-Lambertian surfaces. An alternative multifocal decomposition approach is retinal optimization [82,89], which approximates the retinal image of the displayed scene to be as close as possible to its real-world counterpart, especially in terms of defocus blur. It performs better at occlusion boundaries at the expense of a higher computational cost and less accurate accommodation cues [82]. Additionally, a perception-driven hybrid decomposition strategy selects the best existing decomposition method based on the scene content [139]. They show that linear depth filtering typically achieves the best result among all multifocal decomposition algorithms in regions without occlusion boundaries.

17.3.3 Optical see-through displays

Both VR and AR strive to provide an immersive experience in 3D spaces, thus requiring a 3D display in general. VR implies immersing the observer into a virtual environment by fully blocking any environmental light. In contrast, AR involves the interaction of virtual and real scenes and must effectively combine both visual inputs. This can be achieved by using either *video see-through displays*, i.e., displays that compose virtual objects over the reprojection of the physical scene (also referred to as mixed reality), or *optical see-through displays* (OSTD) that overlay virtual objects on light rays coming from the physical scene. In this section, we refer to AR using OSTD as OST-AR.

We can further divide OST-AR into two sub-categories: with or without background subtraction. For additive OST-AR, i.e., without background subtraction, in the design of the display system, all the virtual content is displayed on top of the physical scene in an additive manner. In contrast, OST-AR with background subtraction requires OSTDs with modulation components that block a portion of the incident light from the real environment.

In the discussion that follows, we first introduce additive OST-AR without background subtraction (Section 17.3.3.1), the mechanisms, the perceptual considerations, and a detailed analysis of the color fidelity maintenance. Then we introduce OST-AR with background subtraction (Section 17.3.3.2), with a focus on a topic of how to reproduce occlusion. Then we branch to a discussion on the HDR OSTDs (Section 17.3.3.3). Finally, we discuss the calibration perspective (Section 17.3.3.4).

17.3.3.1 OST-AR without background subtraction

We define additive OSTD as OSTDs, which add the virtual content onto the light path from the environment light to the eyes without modulating the environment light. A typical additive OSTD can project the virtual content to the eyes through retinal projection [65] using Maxwellian view optics (i.e., a combination of optical components to project an image to the pupils [126]), or guide the virtual content to the eyes through waveguides. The waveguide-based solutions have been applied in commercial products already. Lumus Optics is an example [71].

Perceptual consideration for additive OSTD

Besides the general considerations of the perception of the plenoptic function discussed in Section 17.2, OST-AR without background subtraction requires additional perceptual considerations, as the virtual light field is blended and interacts with the physical one. A unique challenge of the additive OSTD is that it is difficult to reproduce dark colors, such as those found in shadows, because of the presence of light from the real environment. An illustration of this challenge is shown in Fig. 17.5. Another challenge is reproducing occlusion, an essential cue for relative positions in 3D space. For exist-

484 Immersive Video Technologies

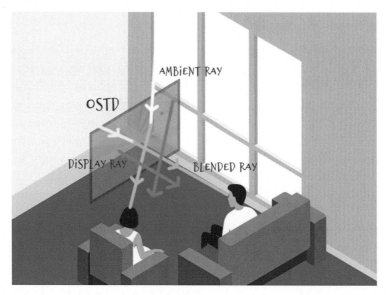

Figure 17.5 Additive feature of the OSTD: Environment light and the displayed light blend together and introduce error in color perception.

ing additive OSTD systems, any perceived transparency for the virtual content, which should be opaque, can break the perception of an occlusion.

Maintaining color fidelity for additive OSTD

Immersive AR experience requires maintaining color fidelity. For additive OSTD, rendering is no longer a video-compositing process as in the video see-through displays. The interference of the environment light and the limitations of optical elements complicate OSTD's imaging model, resulting in various color distortions.

When OSTD uses an optical combiner to blend real and virtual scenes, the perceived color fidelity depends on the accuracy of the additive blending method. A notable side effect of additive blending is the inability to darken the environment. Depending on the properties of the optical combiner, the background always adds a certain amount of intensity to the blended color (for example, the background always contributes 50% to the color when the optical combiner is half reflective and half transparent). [25] described the color blending problem in OSTD. Many research groups have already studied the problem. A straightforward approach is shading the luminance level of the background globally. Some commercial products address this method to reduce background brightness (e.g., Microsoft Hololens 2 [84]). Recent work proposed changing the global opacity of the optical components to suit different environments better [86]. The pixel value for virtual content can be calibrated based on the profile from the lookup table [107]. The work demonstrated that applying a lookup table improves the perceived color fidelity in additive OSTD. [45] proposed a semi-parametric method to improve the coherence of the color appearance of the virtual content with a more consistent color profile. However, the above-mentioned works focused on the color properties of the display, not the color blending with the real background, which assumes the background is black or uniform color. [125] proposed a way to neutralize the real background by capturing the environment with a built-in camera. The captured scene image is used to compensate for the color of the virtual content. This method was limited to only working with the calibrated position and a static scene. An approach to handle complex or dynamic backgrounds was proposed in *smart color system* [35], which extended the previous work in [107] and provided pixel-wise blending simulation with real-time control. A similar method was proposed to neutralize the environment in which the displayed image is calibrated based on the background image [62]. This pixel-wise compensation can be achieved in any environment by pixel-wise mapping from the camera space to the screen space. The compensation method considered the characteristics of the display and camera to reduce artifacts and produce more visually consistent results. [141] proposed a real-time method to enhance the color contrast by utilizing color perception. The work applied a chromatic compensation to the virtual content based on the complementary colors of the background to enhance the color contrast.

17.3.3.2 OST-AR with background subtraction

Hardware-based methods extend the possibilities of OSTD systems. For example, background subtraction is achievable if the optical system is not limited to static semi-transparent components. An optical element, such as SLM, is an option for environment light modulation. For example, LCD can change the transparency of the medium controlling the level of the light passing through. The ELMO series [55,56] inserted an LCD between two coupling lenses so that the environment light first focused on the LCD, and the modulated light then reached the eye through the second lens. Other designs, such as [27], used two-layer curved optical elements with free-form prisms to downsize the form factor, whereas [103] proposed a concept of a binocular OSTD.

A challenge in maintaining color fidelity for OSTDs comes from environment light blending into the light path from virtual content. The problem can be solved if the environment light can be blocked out selectively. A feasible strategy to enhance the color fidelity in subtractive OSTD systems is to modify the transparency of the optical combiner pixel-wise [8,56]. If the pixels are to display virtual objects, the corresponding areas on the optical combiner should be opaque to block out the environment light; whereas for pixels not to display virtual objects, the optical combiner should be transparent. On this basis, one can control the system more finely by adjusting the percentages of the transparency of the pixels [47,51,127].

Occlusion realization from background subtraction

Many factors determine the depth perception among objects in a 3D scene. Depth cues (Fig. 17.2), such as parallax or defocus blur, can be simulated through computer graphics, whereas occlusion and shading simulation is hard to implement in additive OST-AR through software, as explained in the perceptual considerations in Section 17.3.3.1. To make occlusion feasible, modulation of the environment light is necessary. [75] proposed an OST-HMD based on point light projection. The occlusion layer is an LCD that masks the occluded region from the background. An issue with this system is that the edge of occlusion is not sharp since the LCD and the virtual objects are mismatched in depth. To correct the blurry occlusion, [46] proposed a blending algorithm that first calculated how much blurriness the LCD caused due to defocus, and then rendered an image to compensate the blurriness. The compensation image was processed from the background image captured by the camera aligned with the observer's viewpoint. Compared to the methods above, which applied a single modulation layer, [136] proposed a light field display using three layers of the micro-lens array, with two LCDs inserted between the three layers of the micro-lens. The system provided integral imaging with this modulation setup, generating occlusion as a 3D effect. Besides using transmissive LCD, some systems realized occlusion with reflective SLMs. [4] used mirrors in the system to control the light path, which can go either from the viewpoint to the background or from a display. This control allowed pixel-wise state switch, realizing occlusion according to the state of the pixels. [8] used an liquid crystal on silicon (LCOS), which is an LCD with a mirrored backend to modulate the environment light. An additional microdisplay generated the virtual content and an X-cube prism combined the modulated environment light and the virtual content. Another DMD-based OSTD is proposed by [59]. Their approach used DMD for modulation and display simultaneously and LEDs to project virtual content. Then the background and the virtual content were merged through a high-refresh-rate state switch of the DMD, utilizing a binary image factorization. In this approach, the modulation layer was simultaneously used for display, thus decreasing the complexity of the hardware setup.

However, the aforementioned methods suffer from VAC, because the modulation layer is fixed in position and does not adapt to accommodation. A varifocal occlusion approach was proposed in [29]. The system has three relay lenses and an LCD layer sandwiched between two of the lenses. The system can shift the depth of the LCD for adaption. Using focus-tunable lenses, [99] proposed a system in which the LCD placed between the lenses can be focused at different depths.

17.3.3.3 High dynamic range OSTD

Although the extension of the dynamic range of normal displays has been widely discussed in the literature, extending the dynamic range of OST-AR is rarely addressed in research. However, from the visual perception perspective, the dynamic range of the displays is essential for realism. An example among the few studies that specifically addressed the issue of dynamic range using DMDs to display HDR images was presented in [66]. Precise control of each mirror extended the dynamic range to 16-bit. Another prototype targeting for HDR display was proposed in [48]. An HDR projector was used for the retinal projection via a dihedral corner reflector array, and a neutral density filter is used to reduce the amount of light. [143] proposed a high-fidelity AR rendering method, combining the environment capturing with the light field rendering using an HDR OSTD system. However, the above-mentioned benchtop setups have large form factors and require miniaturization for a possible HMD solution.

17.3.3.4 Calibration

Precise calibration for an OSTD system is essential to achieve optimal results. Currently, a reliable method that supports dynamic re-calibration remains a challenge as pixel-level precision is hard to achieve in a dynamic background, even assuming accurate eye tracking and spatial calibration. In contrast, if the background is pre-defined, pixel-level precision can be achieved with an image-based correction. An example is shown in [36] that used a camera that has been calibrated to match the viewpoint of the observer, enabling pixel-level precision in spatial calibration.

17.3.4 Perception-driven rendering techniques

In the part that follows, we introduce two rendering techniques that are beneficial for stereoscopic displays, both based on the perceptual characteristics of the HVS. The first rendering technique presented here, foveated rendering (Section 17.3.4.1), leverages the variation in accuracy across the different zones of the retina to allocate adaptively the limited computing resources. It allows to reduce the computational workload, and thus improve the rendering frame rate, while maintaining or improving the perceived quality. The second rendering technique (Section 17.3.4.2) simulates the defocus for objects outside of the focal plane of the eye. It aims at improving the realism of the rendering through a more accurate stimulation of the HVS.

17.3.4.1 Foveated rendering

As introduced in Section 17.2.1, the retina can be separated into three areas: fovea, parafovea, and periphery with different visual acuity for each. The idea of foveated rendering is to use the gaze location, corresponding to the center of the fovea, to adapt some rendering parameters, such as spatial resolution, shading rate, shading complexity, or level of details. By controlling those parameters of the locally based capacity of the HVS, the computational load can be decreased in the least perceptible manner. For a more detailed review of related publications, the reader is referred to [85]. The approaches presented herein are software-based and consider that gaze tracking/eye tracking is available. Foveated rendering is particularly useful for displays that cover a wide FOV and require high resolution as the fovea covers proportionately a small part of the display ([94] evaluates it to 4% of pixels for consumer grade VR headsets). Therefore VR headsets with a wide FOV are the main application for foveated rendering techniques today. However, as a perception-driven method, foveated rendering has the potential to be applied to other types of 3D display systems as well.

Foveated rendering methods can be organized according to the backend rendering pipeline: rasterization or ray-tracing. Adaptive 3D geometry by usage of different level of details (LOD) has been mainly addressed for raster-based pipelines. The principle of using perceptual models to control the level of details were first set-up with static gaze locations: for polygonal simplification [100] or via a multi-resolution mesh model [70]. More recent approaches integrate it with GPU tessellation, e.g., by adjusting tessellation levels and culling areas [142].

Simplification of the shading step is obtained through adaptation of the shading rate or complexity. The principle of executing shading at different rates was introduced in [116], where the authors apply shading at up to three different rates within a single rendering pass: per groups of pixels (that they name *coarse pixel*), per pixel, and per sample. [30] demonstrate multi-rate shading that controls the coarseness of the shading samples adaptively based on the scene content: lighting, object boundaries, ... [109] couple information from the geometry pass (depth, normal, or texture properties) with a visual perception model (that includes visual acuity and brightness adaptation) to sparsely sample the pixels that will be shaded (while others are interpolated). Modern GPUs allow precise control of the shading rate and *variable rate shading* within a single shading pass, e.g., NVIDIA, allows changing the shading rate from 1×1 to 4×4 across the block size [91]. Another approach to reducing shading complexity is to recycle shading results from previous frames and reproject (or time-warp) the kept pixels. [22] proposed a method that reprojects pixels from the previous frame by adapting a confidence map, where the peripheral area has a higher confidence value. [87] apply shading gradients to determine pixel reuse based on the characteristics of the scene.

Methods for local reduction of the resolution across the FoV have been developed both for rasterization and ray tracing pipelines. The initial raster-based approaches followed a multipass structure, e.g., [28] featured a three-layer foveated rendering with a gradual decrease in peripheral resolution. Lastly, approaches performing the sampling after log-polar mapping to fit the distribution of photoreceptors on the retina have been developed. Building on the log-polar model of the spatial mapping of the retinal image in the striate cortex from [104], Meng et al. apply kernel log-polar conversion to the visual signal of the screen space before performing adaptive sampling, and thus achieve faster computation than by downsampling on the Cartesian coordinates with minimal perceptual distortion [81]. Later, [80] improved this technique by setting different levels of foveation, according to ocular dominance. Ray tracing is straightforward to couple with adaptive sampling because of its flexible sampling strategy. However, decreased ray density introduces artifacts that necessitate post-processing, such as anti-aliasing or denoising. Real-time foveated ray tracing is introduced in [105] using gaze direction to define the sampling distribution of primary rays. Using GPU acceleration for both ray tracing and image reconstruction, they achieve real-time rendering for HTC Vive VR headset. The strong resulting temporal aliasing necessitates filtering. For path tracing, [57] perform the sampling in the log-polar space at an average of 0.4 samples per pixel with a denoising module for real-time rendering. In addition to eccentricity, [114], take into account the characteristics of the content (based on luminance contrast) to define a local spatial resolution. Finally, mixed approaches using both ray tracing for high quality and rasterization or reprojection for increased speed have been developed. In [124], Weier et al. combine ray-tracing in the fovea with reprojection in the peripheral area.

As those approaches are spatial, temporal anti-aliasing filtering is often applied as post-processing to ensure the temporal stability of the content rendered [137]. Modeling spatio-temporal foveation would make that step unnecessary and, additionally, leveraging the temporal characteristics of the HVS would further lead to consequent computational load reduction. In [58], Krajancich et al. model the variation in temporal sensitivity through the critical flicker fusion across the retina. They evaluate the resulting computational load simplification to 7 times that of spatial foveation. Their work is however based on a simplified model of the HVS with fixed fixation point. Another approach using a perceptual model that includes motion perception to simplify the shading complexity was presented in [50]. It does not account for ocular motions, but an extended model coupled with gaze-tracking could be used to guide spatio-temporal foveated rendering.

As detailed in [101], though the performance of the peripheral area of the retina is lower than that of the fovea, it is still key for many visual tasks (e.g., visual search or high-level scene understanding). Therefore, statistics of the content displayed are highly relevant to visual perception. Though most of the previously cited work focus on the loss of acuity in the peripheral area, pattern recognition outside of the fovea is mainly driven by the statistics of larger areas (instead of precise objects) and different objects closer than a certain distance are *pooled* together [95]. That mechanism is named crowding. A direct application to foveated rendering was performed in [120] that transform contents in the peripheral area into ventral metamers, i.e., ensuring they present similar statistics, and are therefore perceived similarly. Crowding also influences cortical maps, and its inclusion in cortical magnification models, as done recently by Strasburger in [110], facilitates making the models more accurate.

Learning-based approaches provide another way to tackle the computational load/perceptual quality trade-off. One example of deep learning based rendering is SideEye from [23] that uses GAN to generate foveated rendered content that includes crowding. In [52], Kaplanyan et al. reconstruct full frames from a sparse subset of pixels with a sampling following the distribution of cones on the retina. They use a U-net

CNN encoder-decoder architecture with added recurrence for temporal stability and the sum of 3 loss function to address spatial quality, temporal stability, and noise. Though the potential of those methods is clear, their lack of explicit control over the rendering pipeline is still a substantial limitation. The fast-paced progresses in application of deep learning to computer graphics, including towards increased control, such as neural rendering [113], are however promising.

17.3.4.2 Synthetic defocus

As presented in Section 17.2.1, the perception of depth relies on visual or oculomotor cues. One such cue, the defocus blur, results from the ability of the human eye to change the shape of its lens and focus light coming from a certain distance. Objects from different focal planes than the one in focus will not be sharply projected onto the retina and will result in a sensation of blur. This cue has been clearly linked to the perception of depth and scale [32,123]. However, defocus blur is an even cue, i.e., it cannot alone inform the observer whether an out-of-focus object is located before or beyond the focal plane. It is therefore most likely used in synergy with other depth cues, such as perspective or chromatic aberrations [7,16]. Vision science studies also suggest that defocus is useful for the control of accommodation [60]. Subjective studies have also showed that synthesizing defocus blur can effectively help visual system to estimate absolute distances to objects [33]. Perceived depth can be enhanced by expanding the range of fixation location as well [53], which is also presented as a more realistic defocus blur simulation. Studies have also shown, specifically for virtual environments, that users prefer when defocus blur is guided by eye-tracking [34,77].

The effectiveness of simulated defocus blur may not assist depth perception [74]. A hardware-based method, which can adjust the focal plane of the display system, instead is a more clear track for solving VAC, such as a method proposed in [82].

The point-spread function of an optical system yields a disc for an out-of-focus point. The diameter of this disc, commonly called circle of confusion (COC),[4] depends on the pupil/aperture of the lens and the distance of the object to the focal plane. This is true for the optical systems of either human eye or for cameras.[5] A main computational cost to model accurately the defocus blur is that the defocus varies according to the depth of the out-of-focus object, thus every point in the scene requires a separate COC calculation. This cost can be high and leads to necessarily choosing a trade-off between accuracy and performance.

The simplest models, used for speed reasons, synthesize blur through either Gaussian kernels [122] or cylinder blur kernel [97]. To model more accurately the optical system,

---

[4] A point in focus will also have a diameter on the retina [44], which is a physical limitation from diffraction, however, the diameter will be smaller than COC.

[5] In photography, the defocus blur resulting from the depth of field of optical lenses is often named Bokeh.

the shape of the aperture can be taken into account, such as was modeled for optical lenses [79] through circular or polygonal Bokeh kernels or by modeling the diffraction from the pupil that spreads a beam of light into the Airy pattern (relevant for pupil diameter under 3 mm). Other imperfections include spherical and chromatic aberrations (due to variation in refractive indices according to wavelength [16]) from the lens (manufactured or in the human eye) and for the human eye, astigmatism. The relative influence of those aspects for depth perception of scenes of constant depth was studied in [15], showing that astigmatism and chromatic aberrations played a significant role, but not spherical aberrations.

In 3D computer graphics, defocus blur simulation is currently built in the standard rendering pipeline in most game engines, such as [115], which realize defocus blur by computing COC from convolution kernel of bokeh filter in the post processing for every frame. A physically correct DOF can be simulated by tracing the ray through a simulated lens (taking cornea and lens as a whole) to simulate DOF in the human eye instead of a single point [17]. However, a ray-tracing based method requires a lot of sample points and is therefore computationally expensive. A deep-learning framework was presented in [88] to model various screen space effects including depth of field using convolutional neural network (CNN). The input features per pixel encompasses various attributes such as pixel geometry, material, lighting but also positions and normals, and higher level attributes such as depth to focal plane or COC radius. More recently, a generic CNN framework to model various depth-related effects such as defocus blur, focal stacks or multilayer decompositions using solely RGB-D as inputs was shown to achieve defocus blur synthesis in 3 to 15 ms for a 512×512 resolution [135]. However, those methods can only achieve results of at most similar perceptual quality of their learning dataset.

A recent psychophysical experiment was conducted in [112]. The work studied the relationship between the fovea and the focus cue to model the eccentricity of visual acuity on top of the low-level visual anatomy model based on the distribution of retinal ganglion cells. The results showed that the discrimination threshold for eccentricity blur is lower than previously reported. Furthermore, the discrimination threshold for depth perception depended on the eccentricity of visual acuity. These conclusions need more supporting experimental data, yet a combination method of foveated rendering and DOF synthesis can support further studies for depth perception with eccentricity in spatial resolution taking into consideration. A proposed hybrid blur solution [68] is a step toward this goal. This work samples the pixels in polar space, in a manner that DOF is presented by a weighted map which determines a Russian Roulette rejection sampling on top of eccentricity sampling for foveation. Later in the post processing it calculates COC to simulate Bokeh blur and longitudinal chromatic aberration. An example of this hybrid method is shown in Fig. 17.6.

Figure 17.6 An example scene rendered with a hybrid synthetic retina blur that combines foveated rendering and defocus blur. In which in fovea & in focus and peripheral / defocus patches are highlighted.

17.4. Summary and discussion

The main purpose of this chapter is to discuss different display systems based on considerations of perception. We first explain the plenoptic function and light field as representations of light emitted from 3D displays. Then we discuss the characteristics of the plenoptic function based on human vision science, including perspectives of spatial resolution, spectral wavelength, temporal resolution and intensity. Next, we focus on the computational 3D displays capable of reproducing 3D scenes and a subset of depth cues. For the discussion of 3D displays, we classify the 3D displays into varifocal and multifocal displays according to whether the depth cues are present in a continuous DOF or separated depth planes. For optical see-through displays, the dominant display systems for AR, we introduce typical examples from the state of the art. Some corresponding rendering methods are discussed, such as foveated rendering and defocus synthesis. In general, for computational 3D display systems, it is essential to reproduce depth cues in coherence with how humans perceive the 3D information to provide an immersive and comfortable visual experience. This is why relieving VAC in conventional 3D display systems has been a widely discussed topic for years, and while solutions in lab settings have been demonstrated, viable commercial solutions are still a challenge.

It is challenging for computational 3D displays to achieve balance in spatial resolution, FOV, temporal resolution, and color fidelity. In addition, a common challenge of the current prototypes is that they need further development to achieve a small form factor if they are to be considered for commercial HMD solutions. While researchers in the literature have been struggling to minimize the trade-off of the above-mentioned factors when designing computational 3D displays, it is promising to combine the latest technologies in the fields of optics and materials science, e.g., utilizing components with smaller form factor, higher precision and less color aberration to improve the performance of the next-generation computational 3D displays.

Acknowledgments

This project has received funding from the European Union's Horizon 2020 research and innovation programme under Marie Skłodowska-Curie Grant Agreement No. 765911 (RealVision).

References

[1] K. Akşit, W. Lopes, J. Kim, P. Shirley, D. Luebke, Near-eye varifocal augmented reality display using see-through screens, ACM Transactions on Graphics 36 (2017), https://doi.org/10.1145/3130800.3130892.

[2] K. Akeley, S.J. Watt, A.R. Girshick, M.S. Banks, A stereo display prototype with multiple focal distances, ACM Transactions on Graphics 23 (2004) 804–813, https://doi.org/10.1145/1015706.1015804.

[3] S.A. Benton, V. Michael Bove Jr., Holographic Imaging, Wiley-Interscience, USA, 2008.

[4] O. Bimber, B. Frohlich, Occlusion shadows: Using projected light to generate realistic occlusion effects for view-dependent optical see-through displays, in: Proceedings. International Symposium on Mixed and Augmented Reality, IEEE, 2002, pp. 186–319.

[5] H.I. Bjelkhagen, E. Mirlis, Color holography to produce highly realistic three-dimensional images, Applied Optics 47 (2008) A123–A133, https://doi.org/10.1364/AO.47.00A123, http://opg.optica.org/ao/abstract.cfm?URI=ao-47-4-A123.

[6] D. Buckley, J.P. Frisby, Interaction of stereo, texture and outline cues in the shape perception of three-dimensional ridges, Vision Research 33 (1993) 919–933.

[7] J. Burge, W.S. Geisler, Optimal defocus estimation in individual natural images, Proceedings of the National Academy of Sciences of the United States of America 108 (2011) 16849–16854.

[8] O. Cakmakci, Y. Ha, J.P. Rolland, A compact optical see-through head-worn display with occlusion support, in: Third IEEE and ACM International Symposium on Mixed and Augmented Reality, IEEE, 2004, pp. 16–25.

[9] B. Cassin, S. Solomon, M.L. Rubin, Dictionary of Eye Terminology, Triad Publishing Company Gainesville, 1990.

[10] P. Chakravarthula, E. Tseng, T. Srivastava, H. Fuchs, F. Heide, Learned hardware-in-the-loop phase retrieval for holographic near-eye displays, ACM Transactions on Graphics (TOG) 39 (2020) 186, https://doi.org/10.1145/3414685.3417846.

[11] J.H.R. Chang, B.V.K.V. Kumar, A.C. Sankaranarayanan, Towards multifocal displays with dense focal stacks, ACM Transactions on Graphics 37 (2018), https://doi.org/10.1145/3272127.3275015.

[12] A.H. Chen, D.J. O'Leary, E.R. Howell, Near visual function in young children. Part I: Near point of convergence. Part II: Amplitude of accommodation. Part III: Near heterophoria, Ophthalmic & Physiological Optics 20 (2000) 185–198.

[13] F. Chen, C. Qiu, Z. Liu, Investigation of autostereoscopic displays based on various display technologies, Nanomaterials 12 (2022), https://doi.org/10.3390/nano12030429, https://www.mdpi.com/2079-4991/12/3/429.

[14] H.M.P. Chen, J.P. Yang, H.T. Yen, Z.N. Hsu, Y. Huang, S.T. Wu, Pursuing high quality phase-only liquid crystal on silicon (LCoS) devices, Applied Sciences 8 (2018), https://doi.org/10.3390/app8112323, https://www.mdpi.com/2076-3417/8/11/2323.

[15] S.A. Cholewiak, G.D. Love, M.S. Banks, Creating correct blur and its effect on accommodation, Journal of Vision 18 (2018), https://doi.org/10.1167/18.9.1.

[16] S.A. Cholewiak, G.D. Love, P.P. Srinivasan, R. Ng, M.S. Banks, ChromaBlur: rendering chromatic eye aberration improves accommodation and realism, ACM Transactions on Graphics 36 (2017).

[17] R.L. Cook, T. Porter, L. Carpenter, Distributed ray tracing, in: Proceedings of the 11th Annual Conference on Computer Graphics and Interactive Techniques, 1984, pp. 137–145.

[18] G. Dagnelie, Visual prosthetics: physiology, bioengineering, rehabilitation, https://doi.org/10.1007/978-1-4419-0754-7, 2011.

[19] D. Dunn, C. Tippets, K. Torell, P. Kellnhofer, K. Akşit, P. Didyk, K. Myszkowski, D. Luebke, H. Fuchs, Wide field of view varifocal near-eye display using see-through deformable membrane mirrors, IEEE Transactions on Visualization and Computer Graphics 23 (2017) 1322–1331, https://doi.org/10.1109/TVCG.2017.2657058.

[20] W. Epstein, S. Rogers, Perception of Space and Motion, Handbook of Perception and Cognition, vol. 5, Academic Press, San Diego, 1995.

[21] G.E. Favalora, J. Napoli, D.M. Hall, R.K. Dorval, M. Giovinco, M.J. Richmond, W.S. Chun, 100-million-voxel volumetric display, in: D.G. Hopper (Ed.), Cockpit Displays IX: Displays for Defense Applications, 2002, pp. 300–312, https://doi.org/10.1117/12.480930.

[22] L. Franke, L. Fink, J. Martschinke, K. Selgrad, M. Stamminger, Time-warped foveated rendering for virtual reality headsets, in: Computer Graphics Forum, Wiley Online Library, 2021, pp. 110–123.

[23] L. Fridman, B. Jenik, S. Keshvari, B. Reimer, C. Zetzsche, R. Rosenholtz, SideEye: a generative neural network based simulator of human peripheral vision, https://arxiv.org/abs/1706.04568, 2017, https://doi.org/10.48550/ARXIV.1706.04568.

[24] J.P. Frisby, D. Buckley, J.M. Horsman, Integration of stereo, texture, and outline cues during pinhole viewing of real ridge-shaped objects and stereograms of ridges, Perception 24 (1995) 181–198.

[25] J.L. Gabbard, J.E. Swan, J. Zedlitz, W.W. Winchester, More than meets the eye: An engineering study to empirically examine the blending of real and virtual color spaces, in: 2010 IEEE Virtual Reality Conference (VR), IEEE, 2010, pp. 79–86.

[26] D. Gabor, A new microscopic principle, Nature 161 (1948) 777–778, https://doi.org/10.1038/161777a0, https://www.nature.com/articles/161777a0.

[27] C. Gao, Y. Lin, H. Hua, Occlusion capable optical see-through head-mounted display using freeform optics, in: 2012 IEEE International Symposium on Mixed and Augmented Reality (ISMAR), IEEE, 2012, pp. 281–282.

[28] B. Guenter, M. Finch, S. Drucker, D. Tan, J. Snyder, Foveated 3D graphics, ACM Transactions on Graphics (TOG) 31 (2012) 1–10.

[29] T. Hamasaki, Y. Itoh, Varifocal occlusion for optical see-through head-mounted displays using a slide occlusion mask, IEEE Transactions on Visualization and Computer Graphics 25 (2019) 1961–1969.

[30] Y. He, Y. Gu, K. Fatahalian, Extending the graphics pipeline with adaptive, multi-rate shading, ACM Transactions on Graphics (TOG) 33 (2014) 1–12.

[31] R.T. Held, M.S. Banks, Misperceptions in stereoscopic displays: A vision science perspective, in: Proceedings of the 5th Symposium on Applied Perception in Graphics and Visualization, Association for Computing Machinery, New York, NY, USA, 2008, pp. 23–32, https://doi.org/10.1145/1394281.1394285.

[32] R.T. Held, E.A. Cooper, M.S. Banks, Blur and disparity are complementary cues to depth, Current Biology 22 (2012) 426–431.

[33] R.T. Held, E.A. Cooper, J.F. O'Brien, M.S. Banks, Using blur to affect perceived distance and size, ACM Transactions on Graphics 29 (2010).

[34] S. Hillaire, A. Lecuyer, R. Cozot, G. Casiez, Using an eye-tracking system to improve camera motions and depth-of-field blur effects in virtual environments, in: 2008 IEEE Virtual Reality Conference, 2008, pp. 47–50, https://doi.org/10.1109/VR.2008.4480749.

[35] J.D. Hincapié-Ramos, L. Ivanchuk, S.K. Sridharan, P. Irani, SmartColor: real-time color correction and contrast for optical see-through head-mounted displays, in: 2014 IEEE International Symposium on Mixed and Augmented Reality (ISMAR), IEEE, 2014, pp. 187–194.

[36] Y. Hiroi, T. Kaminokado, A. Mori, Y. Itoh, DehazeGlasses: optical dehazing with an occlusion capable see-through display, in: Proceedings of the Augmented Humans International Conference, 2020, pp. 1–11.

[37] D.M. Hoffman, G. Lee, Temporal requirements for VR displays to create a more comfortable and immersive visual experience, Information Display 35 (2019) 9–39, https://doi.org/10.1002/msid.1018, https://onlinelibrary.wiley.com/doi/abs/10.1002/msid.1018.

[38] I.P. Howard, B.J. Rogers, Binocular Vision and Stereopsis, Oxford Psychology Series, vol. 29, Oxford University Press, New York, 1995.

[39] HTC, Vive flow, https://www.vive.com/us/product/, 2021.

[40] HTC, Vive pro eye, https://www.vive.com/us/product/vive-pro-eye/overview/, 2021.

[41] X. Hu, H. Hua, High-resolution optical see-through multi-focal-plane head-mounted display using freeform optics, Optics Express 22 (2014) 13896–13903, https://doi.org/10.1364/OE.22.013896, http://opg.optica.org/oe/abstract.cfm?URI=oe-22-11-13896.

[42] K.C. Huang, Y.H. Chou, L.c. Lin, H.Y. Lin, F.H. Chen, C.C. Liao, Y.H. Chen, K. Lee, W.H. Hsu, A study of optimal viewing distance in a parallax barrier 3D display, Journal of the Society for Information Display 21 (2013) 263–270, https://doi.org/10.1002/jsid.172, https://sid.onlinelibrary.wiley.com/doi/abs/10.1002/jsid.172.

[43] T. Huang, B. Han, X. Zhang, H. Liao, High-performance autostereoscopic display based on the lenticular tracking method, Optics Express 27 (2019) 20421–20434, https://doi.org/10.1364/OE.27.020421, http://opg.optica.org/oe/abstract.cfm?URI=oe-27-15-20421.

[44] I. Iglesias, N. López-Gil, P. Artal, Reconstruction of the point-spread function of the human eye from two double-pass retinal images by phase-retrieval algorithms, Journal of the Optical Society of America A 15 (1998) 326–339.

[45] Y. Itoh, M. Dzitsiuk, T. Amano, G. Klinker, Semi-parametric color reproduction method for optical see-through head-mounted displays, IEEE Transactions on Visualization and Computer Graphics 21 (2015) 1269–1278.

[46] Y. Itoh, T. Hamasaki, M. Sugimoto, Occlusion leak compensation for optical see-through displays using a single-layer transmissive spatial light modulator, IEEE Transactions on Visualization and Computer Graphics 23 (2017) 2463–2473.

[47] Y. Itoh, T. Langlotz, D. Iwai, K. Kiyokawa, T. Amano, Light attenuation display: Subtractive see-through near-eye display via spatial color filtering, IEEE Transactions on Visualization and Computer Graphics 25 (2019) 1951–1960.

[48] Y. Itoh, K. Yamamoto, Y. Ochiai, Retinal HDR: HDR image projection method onto retina, in: SIGGRAPH Asia 2018 Posters, 2018, pp. 1–2.

[49] F.E. Ives, A novel stereogram, Journal of the Franklin Institute 153 (1902) 51–52, https://doi.org/10.1016/S0016-0032(02)90195-X, https://www.sciencedirect.com/science/article/pii/S001600320290195X.

[50] A. Jindal, K. Wolski, K. Myszkowski, R.K. Mantiuk, Perceptual model for adaptive local shading and refresh rate, ACM Transactions on Graphics 40 (2021), https://doi.org/10.1145/3478513.3480514.

[51] T. Kaminokado, Y. Hiroi, Y. Itoh, StainedView: variable-intensity light-attenuation display with cascaded spatial color filtering for improved color fidelity, IEEE Transactions on Visualization and Computer Graphics 26 (2020) 3576–3586.

[52] A.S. Kaplanyan, A. Sochenov, T. Leimkühler, M. Okunev, T. Goodall, G. Rufo, DeepFovea: neural reconstruction for foveated rendering and video compression using learned statistics of natural videos, ACM Transactions on Graphics 38 (2019) 212, 13pp., https://doi.org/10.1145/3355089.3356557, http://doi.acm.org/10.1145/3355089.3356557.

[53] P. Kellnhofer, P. Didyk, K. Myszkowski, M.M. Hefeeda, H.P. Seidel, W. Matusik, GazeStereo3D: seamless disparity manipulations, ACM Transactions on Graphics (TOG) 35 (2016) 1–13.

[54] D.S. Kim, S. Shestak, K.H. Cha, S.M. Park, S.D. Hwang, Time-sequential autostereoscopic OLED display with segmented scanning parallax barrier, in: B. Javidi, J.Y. Son, M. Martinez-Corral, F. Okano, W. Osten (Eds.), Three-Dimensional Imaging, Visualization, and Display 2009, International Society for Optics and Photonics, SPIE, 2009, pp. 236–242, https://doi.org/10.1117/12.820313.

[55] K. Kiyokawa, M. Billinghurst, B. Campbell, E. Woods, An occlusion capable optical see-through head mount display for supporting co-located collaboration, in: The Second IEEE and ACM International Symposium on Mixed and Augmented Reality, 2003. Proceedings, IEEE, 2003, pp. 133–141.

[56] K. Kiyokawa, Y. Kurata, H. Ohno, An optical see-through display for mutual occlusion of real and virtual environments, in: Proceedings IEEE and ACM International Symposium on Augmented Reality (ISAR 2000), IEEE, 2000, pp. 60–67.

[57] M. Koskela, A. Lotvonen, M. Mäkitalo, P. Kivi, T. Viitanen, P. Jääskeläinen, Foveated Real-Time Path Tracing in Visual-Polar Space, The Eurographics Association, 2019, https://diglib.eg.org:443/xmlui/handle/10.2312/sr20191219.

[58] B. Krajancich, P. Kellnhofer, G. Wetzstein, A perceptual model for eccentricity-dependent spatio-temporal flicker fusion and its applications to foveated graphics, ACM Transactions on Graphics 40 (2021), https://doi.org/10.1145/3450626.3459784, https://doi-org.proxy.findit.cvt.dk/10.1145/3450626.3459784.

[59] B. Krajancich, N. Padmanaban, G. Wetzstein, Factored occlusion: Single spatial light modulator occlusion-capable optical see-through augmented reality display, IEEE Transactions on Visualization and Computer Graphics 26 (2020) 1871–1879.

[60] P.B. Kruger, S. Mathews, M. Katz, K.R. Aggarwala, S. Nowbotsing, Accommodation without feedback suggests directional signals specify ocular focus, Vision Research 37 (1997) 2511–2526, https://doi.org/10.1016/S0042-6989(97)00056-4.

[61] T. Kunkel, E. Reinhard, A reassessment of the simultaneous dynamic range of the human visual system, in: Proceedings of the 7th Symposium on Applied Perception in Graphics and Visualization, 2010, pp. 17–24.

[62] T. Langlotz, M. Cook, H. Regenbrecht, Real-time radiometric compensation for optical see-through head-mounted displays, IEEE Transactions on Visualization and Computer Graphics 22 (2016) 2385–2394.

[63] D. Lanman, M. Hirsch, Y. Kim, R. Raskar, Content-adaptive parallax barriers: Optimizing dual-layer 3D displays using low-rank light field factorization, ACM Transactions on Graphics 29 (6) (2010) 163, https://doi.org/10.1145/1882261.1866164.

[64] D. Lanman, G. Wetzstein, M. Hirsch, W. Heidrich, R. Raskar, Polarization fields: Dynamic light field display using multi-layer LCDs, in: Proceedings of the 2011 SIGGRAPH Asia Conference, 2011, pp. 1–10, https://doi.org/10.1145/2024156.2024220.

[65] J. Lin, D. Cheng, C. Yao, Y. Wang, Retinal projection head-mounted display, Frontiers of Optoelectronics 10 (2017) 1–8.

[66] P. Lincoln, A. Blate, M. Singh, A. State, M.C. Whitton, T. Whitted, H. Fuchs, Scene-adaptive high dynamic range display for low latency augmented reality, in: Proceedings of the 21st ACM SIGGRAPH Symposium on Interactive 3D Graphics and Games, 2017, pp. 1–7.

[67] G. Lippmann, Épreuves réversibles donnant la sensation du relief, Journal de Physique Théorique Et Appliquée 7 (1908) 821–825, https://doi.org/10.1051/jphystap:019080070082100, http://www.edpsciences.org/10.1051/jphystap:019080070082100.

[68] J. Liu, C. Mantel, S. Forchhammer, Perception-driven hybrid foveated depth of field rendering for head-mounted displays, in: 2021 IEEE International Symposium on Mixed and Augmented Reality (ISMAR), IEEE, 2021, pp. 1–10.

[69] G.D. Love, D.M. Hoffman, P.J. Hands, J. Gao, A.K. Kirby, M.S. Banks, High-speed switchable lens enables the development of a volumetric stereoscopic display, Optics Express 17 (2009) 15716–15725, https://doi.org/10.1364/OE.17.015716, http://www.opticsexpress.org/abstract.cfm?URI=oe-17-18-15716.

[70] D. Luebke, B. Hallen, Perceptually driven simplification for interactive rendering, in: S.J. Gortle, K. Myszkowski (Eds.), Eurographics Workshop on Rendering, The Eurographics Association, 2001, https://doi.org/10.2312/EGWR/EGWR01/223-234.

[71] Lumus, Lumus optics, https://lumusvision.com/products/, 2014.

[72] K.J. MacKenzie, D.M. Hoffman, S.J. Watt, Accommodation to multiple-focal-plane displays: Implications for improving stereoscopic displays and for accommodation control, Journal of Vision 10 (2010) 22, https://doi.org/10.1167/10.8.22, http://www.ncbi.nlm.nih.gov/pubmed/20884597.

[73] A. Mackin, K.C. Noland, D.R. Bull, The visibility of motion artifacts and their effect on motion quality, in: 2016 IEEE International Conference on Image Processing (ICIP), 2016, pp. 2435–2439, https://doi.org/10.1109/ICIP.2016.7532796.

[74] G. Maiello, M. Chessa, F. Solari, P.J. Bex, The (in)effectiveness of simulated blur for depth perception in naturalistic images, PLoS ONE 10 (2015) e0140230.

[75] A. Maimone, D. Lanman, K. Rathinavel, K. Keller, D. Luebke, H. Fuchs, Pinlight displays: wide field of view augmented reality eyeglasses using defocused point light sources, in: ACM SIGGRAPH 2014 Emerging Technologies, 2014, pp. 1–1.

[76] A. Majumder, M.S. Brown, Practical Multi-Projector Display Design, A. K. Peters, Ltd., Natick, MA, USA, 2007.

[77] R. Mantiuk, B. Bazyluk, A. Tomaszewska, Gaze-dependent depth-of-field effect rendering in virtual environments, in: M. Ma, M. Fradinho Oliveira, J. Madeiras Pereira (Eds.), Serious Games Development and Applications, Springer, Berlin, Heidelberg, 2011, pp. 1–12, https://doi.org/10.1007/978-3-642-23834-5_1.

[78] K. Masaoka, Y. Nishida, M. Sugawara, E. Nakasu, Y. Nojiri, Sensation of realness from high-resolution images of real objects, IEEE Transactions on Broadcasting 59 (2013) 72–83.

[79] L. McIntosh, B.E. Riecke, S. DiPaola, Efficiently simulating the bokeh of polygonal apertures in a post-process depth of field shader, in: Computer Graphics Forum, Wiley Online Library, 2012, pp. 1810–1822.

[80] X. Meng, R. Du, A. Varshney, Eye-dominance-guided foveated rendering, IEEE Transactions on Visualization and Computer Graphics 26 (2020) 1972–1980.

[81] X. Meng, R. Du, M. Zwicker, A. Varshney, Kernel foveated rendering, Proceedings of the ACM on Computer Graphics and Interactive Techniques 1 (1) (2018) 5, https://doi.org/10.1145/3203199, http://doi.acm.org/10.1145/3203199.

[82] O. Mercier, Y. Sulai, K. Mackenzie, M. Zannoli, J. Hillis, D. Nowrouzezahrai, D. Lanman, Fast gaze-contingent optimal decompositions for multifocal displays, ACM Transactions on Graphics 36 (2017), https://doi.org/10.1145/3130800.3130846.

[83] Meta, Oculus quest 2, https://store.facebook.com/quest/products/quest-2/, 2020.

[84] Microsoft, Hololens 2, https://www.microsoft.com/en-us/hololens/hardware, 2021.

[85] B. Mohanto, A.T. Islam, E. Gobbetti, O. Staadt, An integrative view of foveated rendering, Computers & Graphics 102 (2022) 474–501.

[86] S. Mori, S. Ikeda, A. Plopski, C. Sandor, BrightView: increasing perceived brightness of optical see-through head-mounted displays through unnoticeable incident light reduction, in: 2018 IEEE Conference on Virtual Reality and 3D User Interfaces (VR), IEEE, 2018, pp. 251–258.

[87] J.H. Mueller, T. Neff, P. Voglreiter, M. Steinberger, D. Schmalstieg, Temporally adaptive shading reuse for real-time rendering and virtual reality, ACM Transactions on Graphics (TOG) 40 (2021) 1–14.

[88] O. Nalbach, E. Arabadzhiyska, D. Mehta, H.P. Seidel, T. Ritschel, Deep shading: Convolutional neural networks for screen space shading, Computer Graphics Forum 36 (2017) 65–78, https://doi-org.proxy.findit.cvt.dk/10.1111/cgf.13225.

[89] R. Narain, R.A. Albert, A. Bulbul, G.J. Ward, M.S. Banks, J.F. O'Brien, Optimal presentation of imagery with focus cues on multi-plane displays, ACM Transactions on Graphics 34 (4) (2015) 59, https://doi.org/10.1145/2766909.

[90] C. Noorlander, J.J. Koenderink, R.J. Den Olden, B.W. Edens, Sensitivity to spatiotemporal colour contrast in the peripheral visual field, Vision Research 23 (1983) 1–11.

[91] NVIDIA, NVIDIA/Variable Rate Shading, https://developer.nvidia.com/vrworks/graphics/variablerateshading, 2018, original-date: 2019-05-30T12:02:24Z.

[92] Oculus, Oculus - Half Dome 3, https://www.oculus.com/blog/half-dome-updates-frl-explores-more-comfortable-compact-vr-prototypes-for-work/.

[93] S.E. Palmer, Vision Science: Photons to Phenomenology, MIT Press, 1999.

[94] A. Patney, M. Salvi, J. Kim, A. Kaplanyan, C. Wyman, N. Benty, D. Luebke, A. Lefohn, Towards foveated rendering for gaze-tracked virtual reality, ACM Transactions on Graphics 35 (2016), https://doi.org/10.1145/2980179.2980246, https://doi-org.proxy.findit.cvt.dk/10.1145/2980179.2980246.

[95] D.G. Pelli, K.A. Tillman, The uncrowded window of object recognition, Nature Neuroscience 11 (2008) 1129–1135, https://doi.org/10.1038/nn.2187.

[96] Y. Peng, S. Choi, N. Padmanaban, G. Wetzstein, Neural holography with camera-in-the-loop training, ACM Transactions on Graphics (SIGGRAPH Asia) 39 (6) (2020) 185, https://doi.org/10.1145/3414685.3417802.

[97] M. Potmesil, I. Chakravarty, A lens and aperture camera model for synthetic image generation, SIGGRAPH Computer Graphics 15 (1981) 297–305.

[98] Pupil Labs, VR/AR eye tracker, https://pupil-labs.com/products/vr-ar/tech-specs/, 2020.

[99] K. Rathinavel, G. Wetzstein, H. Fuchs, Varifocal occlusion-capable optical see-through augmented reality display based on focus-tunable optics, IEEE Transactions on Visualization and Computer Graphics 25 (2019) 3125–3134.

[100] M. Reddy, Perceptually optimized 3D graphics, IEEE Computer Graphics and Applications 21 (2001) 68–75, https://doi.org/10.1109/38.946633.

[101] R. Rosenholtz, Capabilities and limitations of peripheral vision, Annual Review of Vision Science 2 (2016) 437–457, https://doi.org/10.1146/annurev-vision-082114-035733, pMID: 28532349.

[102] W.J. Ryan, A.T. Duchowski, S.T. Birchfield, Limbus/pupil switching for wearable eye tracking under variable lighting conditions, in: Proceedings of the 2008 Symposium on Eye Tracking Research & Applications, 2008, pp. 61–64.

[103] P. Santos, T. Gierlinger, O. Machui, A. Stork, The daylight blocking optical stereo see-through HMD, in: Proceedings of the 2008 Workshop on Immersive Projection Technologies/Emerging Display Technologies, 2008, pp. 1–4.

[104] E.L. Schwartz, Computational anatomy and functional architecture of striate cortex: A spatial mapping approach to perceptual coding, Vision Research 20 (1980) 645–669.

[105] A. Siekawa, M. Chwesiuk, R. Mantiuk, R. Piórkowski, Foveated ray tracing for VR headsets, in: I. Kompatsiaris, B. Huet, V. Mezaris, C. Gurrin, W.H. Cheng, S. Vrochidis (Eds.), MultiMedia Modeling, Springer International Publishing, Cham, 2019, pp. 106–117.

[106] C. Slinger, C. Cameron, M. Stanley, Computer-generated holography as a generic display technology, Computer 38 (2005) 46–53.

[107] S.K. Sridharan, J.D. Hincapié-Ramos, D.R. Flatla, P. Irani, Color correction for optical see-through displays using display color profiles, in: Proceedings of the 19th ACM Symposium on Virtual Reality Software and Technology, 2013, pp. 231–240.

[108] SR_Research, EyeLink 1000 plus, https://www.sr-research.com/eyelink-1000-plus/, 2014.

[109] M. Stengel, S. Grogorick, M. Eisemann, M. Magnor, Adaptive image-space sampling for gaze-contingent real-time rendering, in: Computer Graphics Forum, Wiley Online Library, 2016, pp. 129–139.

[110] H. Strasburger, On the cortical mapping function: Visual space, cortical space, and crowding, Vision Research 194 (2022) 107972, https://doi.org/10.1016/j.visres.2021.107972, https://www.sciencedirect.com/science/article/pii/S0042698921002224.

[111] A. Sullivan, DepthCube solid-state 3D volumetric display, in: A.J. Woods, J.O. Merritt, S.A. Benton, M.T. Bolas (Eds.), Stereoscopic Displays and Virtual Reality Systems XI, 2004, pp. 279–284, https://doi.org/10.1117/12.527543.

[112] Q. Sun, F.C. Huang, L.Y. Wei, D. Luebke, A. Kaufman, J. Kim, Eccentricity effects on blur and depth perception, Optics Express 28 (2020) 6734–6739.

[113] A. Tewari, O. Fried, J. Thies, V. Sitzmann, S. Lombardi, K. Sunkavalli, R. Martin-Brualla, T. Simon, J. Saragih, M. Nießner, R. Pandey, S. Fanello, G. Wetzstein, J.Y. Zhu, C. Theobalt, M. Agrawala, E. Shechtman, D.B. Goldman, M. Zollhöfer, State of the art on neural rendering, Computer Graphics Forum 39 (2020) 701–727, https://doi.org/10.1111/cgf.14022, https://onlinelibrary.wiley.com/doi/abs/10.1111/cgf.14022.

[114] O.T. Tursun, E. Arabadzhiyska-Koleva, M. Wernikowski, R. Mantiuk, H.P. Seidel, K. Myszkowski, P. Didyk, Luminance-contrast-aware foveated rendering, ACM Transactions on Graphics 38 (2019) 98, 14pp., https://doi.org/10.1145/3306346.3322985, http://doi.acm.org/10.1145/3306346.3322985.

[115] Unity, Unity - Manual: Depth of Field, https://docs.unity3d.com/Packages/com.unity.postprocessing@3.2/manual/Depth-of-Field.html, 2022.

[116] K. Vaidyanathan, M. Salvi, R. Toth, T. Foley, T. Akenine-Möller, J. Nilsson, J. Munkberg, J. Hasselgren, M. Sugihara, P. Clarberg, et al., Coarse pixel shading, in: Proceedings of High Performance Graphics, 2014, pp. 9–18.

[117] P. Vangorp, R.K. Mantiuk, B. Bazyluk, K. Myszkowski, R. Mantiuk, S.J. Watt, H.P. Seidel, Depth from HDR: depth induction or increased realism?, in: ACM Symposium on Applied Perception – SAP '14, ACM Press, New York, New York, USA, 2014, pp. 71–78, https://doi.org/10.1145/2628257.2628258, http://dl.acm.org/citation.cfm?doid=2628257.2628258.

[118] Voxon, Voxon VX1, https://voxon.co/technology/, 2020.

[119] H.K. Walker, W.D. Hall, J.W. Hurst (Eds.), Clinical Methods: the History, Physical, and Laboratory Examinations, 3rd ed., Butterworths, Boston, 1990.

[120] D.R. Walton, R.K.D. Anjos, S. Friston, D. Swapp, K. Akşit, A. Steed, T. Ritschel, Beyond blur: real-time ventral metamers for foveated rendering, ACM Transactions on Graphics (TOG) 40 (2021) 1–14.

[121] X. Wang, H. Hua, Time-multiplexed integral imaging based light field displays, in: B.C. Kress, C. Peroz (Eds.), Optical Architectures for Displays and Sensing in Augmented, Virtual, and Mixed Reality (AR, VR, MR) II, International Society for Optics and Photonics, SPIE, 2021, pp. 156–162, https://doi.org/10.1117/12.2576809.

[122] A.B. Watson, A.J. Ahumada, Blur clarified: A review and synthesis of blur discrimination, Journal of Vision 11 (2011) 10, https://doi.org/10.1167/11.5.10.

[123] S.J. Watt, K. Akeley, M.O. Ernst, M.S. Banks, Focus cues affect perceived depth, Journal of Vision 5 (2005) 7, https://doi.org/10.1167/5.10.7.

[124] M. Weier, T. Roth, E. Kruijff, A. Hinkenjann, A. Pérard-Gayot, P. Slusallek, Y. Li, Foveated real-time ray tracing for head-mounted displays, Computer Graphics Forum 35 (2016) 289–298, https://onlinelibrary-wiley-com.proxy.findit.cvt.dk/doi/abs/10.1111/cgf.13026, https://doi-org.proxy.findit.cvt.dk/10.1111/cgf.13026.

[125] C. Weiland, A.K. Braun, W. Heiden, Colorimetric and photometric compensation for optical see-through displays, in: International Conference on Universal Access in Human-Computer Interaction, Springer, 2009, pp. 603–612.

[126] G. Westheimer, The Maxwellian view, Vision Research 6 (1966) 669–682.

[127] G. Wetzstein, W. Heidrich, D. Luebke, Optical image processing using light modulation displays, in: Computer Graphics Forum, Wiley Online Library, 2010, pp. 1934–1944.

[128] G. Wetzstein, D. Lanman, W. Heidrich, R. Raskar, Layered 3D: tomographic image synthesis for attenuation-based light field and high dynamic range displays, ACM Transactions on Graphics (TOG) 30 (2011) 1–12, https://doi.org/10.1145/1964921.1964990.

[129] G. Wetzstein, D. Lanman, M. Hirsch, W. Heidrich, R. Raskar, Compressive light field displays, IEEE Computer Graphics and Applications 32 (2012) 6–11, https://doi.org/10.1109/MCG.2012.99.

[130] G. Wetzstein, D. Lanman, M. Hirsch, R. Raskar, Tensor displays: compressive light field synthesis using multilayer displays with directional backlighting, ACM Transactions on Graphics (Proc. SIGGRAPH) 31 (2012) 1–11.

[131] O.H. Willemsen, S.T. de Zwart, W.L. IJzerman, M.G.H. Hiddink, T. Dekker, 2D/3D switchable displays, in: A. Tervonen, M. Kujawinska, W. IJzerman, H.D. Smet (Eds.), Photonics in Multimedia, International Society for Optics and Photonics, SPIE, 2006, pp. 150–161, https://doi.org/10.1117/12.661911.

[132] A.J. Woods, T. Docherty, R. Koch, Image distortions in stereoscopic video systems, Stereoscopic Displays and Applications IV 1915 (1993) 36–48.

[133] M. Wöpking, Viewing comfort with stereoscopic pictures: an experimental study on the subjective effects of disparity magnitude and depth of focus, Journal of the Society for Information Display 3 (1995) 101–103.

[134] F. Xiao, J. DiCarlo, P. Catrysse, B. Wandell, High dynamic range imaging of natural scenes, Color and Imaging Conference 10 (2002) 337–342.

[135] L. Xiao, A. Kaplanyan, A. Fix, M. Chapman, D. Lanman, DeepFocus: learned image synthesis for computational displays, ACM Transactions on Graphics 37 (2018) 200, 13pp., https://doi.org/10.1145/3272127.3275032, http://doi.acm.org/10.1145/3272127.3275032.

[136] Y. Yamaguchi, Y. Takaki, See-through integral imaging display with background occlusion capability, Applied Optics 55 (2016) A144–A149.

[137] L. Yang, S. Liu, M. Salvi, A survey of temporal antialiasing techniques, Computer Graphics Forum 39 (2020) 607–621, https://doi.org/10.1111/cgf.14018, https://onlinelibrary.wiley.com/doi/abs/10.1111/cgf.14018.

[138] T. Yendo, N. Kawakami, S. Tachi, Seelinder: the cylindrical lightfield display, https://doi.org/10.1145/1187297.1187314, 2005.

[139] H. Yu, M. Bemana, M. Wernikowski, M. Chwesiuk, O. Tursun, G. Singh, K. Myszkowski, R. Mantiuk, H.P. Seidel, P. Didyk, A perception-driven hybrid decomposition for multi-layer accommodative displays, IEEE Transactions on Visualization and Computer Graphics 25 (5) (2019) 1940–1950, https://doi.org/10.1109/TVCG.2019.2898821.

[140] R. Zabels, K. Osmanis, M. Narels, U. Gertners, A. Ozols, K. Rūtenbergs, I. Osmanis, AR displays: next-generation technologies to solve the vergence accommodation conflict, Applied Sciences 9 (2019) 3147, https://doi.org/10.3390/app9153147.

[141] Y. Zhang, R. Wang, E.Y. Peng, W. Hua, H. Bao, Color contrast enhanced rendering for optical see-through head-mounted displays, IEEE Transactions on Visualization and Computer Graphics (2021), https://doi.org/10.1109/TVCG.2021.3091686.

[142] Z. Zheng, Z. Yang, Y. Zhan, Y. Li, W. Yu, Perceptual model optimized efficient foveated rendering, in: Proceedings of the 24th ACM Symposium on Virtual Reality Software and Technology, Association for Computing Machinery, New York, NY, USA, 2018, https://doi.org/10.1145/3281505.3281588, https://doi-org.proxy.findit.cvt.dk/10.1145/3281505.3281588.

[143] F. Zhong, A. Jindal, A.O. Yöntem, P. Hanji, S.J. Watt, R.K. Mantiuk, Reproducing reality with a high-dynamic-range multi-focal stereo display, ACM Transactions on Graphics 40 (2021), https://doi.org/10.1145/3478513.3480513.

[144] F. Zhong, G.A. Koulieris, G. Drettakis, M.S. Banks, M. Chambe, F. Durand, R.K. Mantiuk, DiCE: dichoptic contrast enhancement for VR and stereo displays, ACM Transactions on Graphics 38 (2019), https://doi.org/10.1145/3355089.3356552.

CHAPTER 18

Subjective and objective quality assessment for volumetric video

Evangelos Alexiou[a], Yana Nehmé[b], Emin Zerman[c,g], Irene Viola[a],
Guillaume Lavoué[b], Ali Ak[d], Aljosa Smolic[f], Patrick Le Callet[d], and Pablo Cesar[a,e]

[a]DIS, Centrum Wiskunde en Informatica, Amsterdam, the Netherlands
[b]Origami, LIRIS, Lyon University, Lyon, France
[c]STC Research Center, Mid Sweden University, Sundsvall, Sweden
[d]IPI, LS2N, Nantes University, Nantes, France
[e]Multimedia Computing, TU Delft, Delft, the Netherlands
[f]V-SENSE, School of Computer Science and Statistics, Trinity College Dublin, Dublin, Ireland

As discussed in previous chapters, immersive video technologies create visual content for human consumption, as they "attempt to emulate a real world through a digital or simulated recreation" [1]. The reconstructed volumetric video can be viewed from any angle, providing 6 degrees-of-freedom (DoF) interaction capabilities and is suitable for extended reality (XR) applications, e.g., augmented reality (AR) or virtual reality (VR) applications (see Part 5: Applications). However, the increased level of interactivity offered to the user comes at the cost of a vast amount of data that needs to be processed in a radically different way with respect to traditional video, which in turn prompted further scientific research and active involvement of the MPEG and JPEG standardization bodies [2,3]. Considering that human viewers are the end-users, a thorough understanding of the human visual system (HVS) is necessary to ensure high quality of experience (QoE), as discussed in Chapter 1.

Visual quality assessment is critical to ensure the highest QoE in media technologies. Volumetric video might undergo distortions during processing, compression, transmission, and rendering, which negatively affect the fidelity of the original content. This creates a need for mechanisms that quantify these distortions; that is, new methods to capture subjective quality scores and predict the perceived quality of the content displayed to the viewer. Such mechanisms can be helpful in selection of optimal schemes and tuning of parameters in perceptual terms to improve the QoE. For instance, estimated quality scores are commonly employed to optimize the efficiency of content delivery systems by increasing the effectiveness of compression and transmission methods, considering the trade-off between quality and data size.

---

[g] Emin Zerman was with V-SENSE, School of Computer Science and Statistics, Trinity College Dublin, Dublin, Ireland at the time of writing this chapter.

Immersive Video Technologies
https://doi.org/10.1016/B978-0-32-391755-1.00024-9

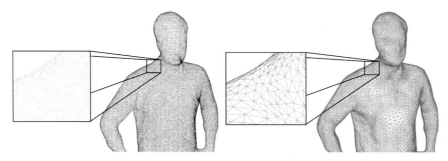

Figure 18.1 Primary elements defining the topology of two commonly used representation methods for volumetric video: point cloud and mesh. Points in 3D space for a point cloud are shown on left, and vertices plus edges for a mesh are shown on right. See Fig. 18.2 for the rendering with color information.

The problem of visual quality assessment has been well-studied for traditional video. Decades of studies on how to assess the quality brought many standards and recommendations, which detail test methodologies, experimental designs, and evaluation procedures for reproducible subjective quality experiments [4–6]. Similarly, many objective quality metrics were developed for the assessment of traditional image and video quality [7]. Despite the breadth of video quality estimation solutions for traditional video, extending the methodologies and algorithms devised for traditional media formats to immersive contents is not trivial. For instance, new subjective quality assessment methods are required to accommodate the higher DoF and to imitate real-life consumption of such richer imaging modalities. Furthermore, since the volumetric video is represented by data types, inherently different than pixels on a regular grid, corresponding objective quality metrics are designed differently.

Volumetric contents are most frequently delivered in the form of 3D polygonal meshes, or 3D point clouds [8]. For a 3D polygonal mesh, the model shape is defined by a set of vertices accompanied by connectivity information to form polygons (typically triangles), whereas the color information for the polygonal (or triangular) faces is determined through texture maps. A 3D point cloud representation is defined by a set of points placed on 3D space, with point coordinates determining the shape, and associated color attributes the color of the model, as shown in Fig. 18.1. Hereafter, we refer to them simply as meshes and point clouds. Both of them have unique characteristics and pose different challenges for visual quality assessment.

Volumetric video is essentially a collection of 3D models, which are played back at a certain frame rate, which gives the viewer the illusion of a continuous movement. This is the same principle still used in traditional video. As the advances and findings in image quality assessment studies were useful for traditional video quality, the findings for static 3D models will bring insight into the quality assessment of dynamic sequences that form volumetric video. Therefore, in this chapter, we cover subjective and objective quality assessment methods for both static and dynamic 3D models, represented as both point clouds and meshes. In particular, we provide the following:

- An overview of subjective quality assessment methodologies with respect to the mode of inspection (i.e., non-interactive and interactive)
- A descriptive list of publicly available subjectively annotated datasets
- A summary of user studies that compare different parameters in the design of subjective quality experiments
- An overview of objective quality metrics grouped per operating principle (i.e., model-based and image-based)
- A unified table with publicly available objective quality metrics
- Advantages and disadvantages of different objective quality assessment approaches

18.1. Subjective quality assessment

As the quality is defined as a subjective trait in the context of multimedia signal processing [9], the golden standard to obtain quality values for the volumetric video is to conduct subjective user studies. Nevertheless, subjective experiments are resource and time expensive to conduct, as they require careful experiment design, expertise on the subject matter, a dedicated space to conduct the user study, and participants' and experimenters' time. Although the objective quality metrics can provide estimated quality scores much faster, subjective evaluations are crucial in quality assessment, as they provide ground truth data for further research and development.

Commonly, subjective experiments are designed according to standards recommended by standardization communities [4,5] or expert groups formed by researchers [6]. The standardization efforts for immersive imaging technologies are still underway. Recently, a new methodology has been standardized for the evaluation of omnidirectional content [10,11]; however, this only takes into account rotational movements in 3DoF, which are not suitable for volumetric videos. Work items currently under study in International Telecommunication Union (ITU) involve subjective methodologies for interactive VR [12] and QoE assessment of XR tele-meetings [13]. Nevertheless, currently, there are no specific standards or recommendations for the new volumetric video.

The existing recommendations and standards for traditional images and video do not take 6DoF interaction into account, as viewers are essentially passive spectators. In other words, in traditional imaging, the viewers can see the entire visual stimulus (i.e., images or video) whenever they are looking at the display. Once they are presented the stimulus, they can inspect it for a fixed duration (e.g., around 10 seconds is a common choice [4]). After this duration, they are asked to either vote on the quality or select the preferred stimulus, depending on the adopted test methodology.

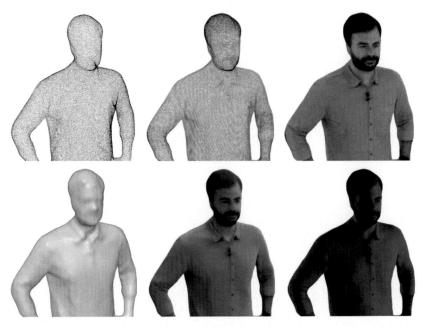

Figure 18.2 Illustration of different aspects affecting the perception of volumetric content: colorless vs colored, point size for point clouds, and lighting for meshes. Top row refers to point cloud representation: (top-left) colorless point cloud, (top-center) colored point cloud with point size 1, (top-right) colored point cloud with point size 3. Bottom row refers to mesh representation: (bottom-left) colorless surface, (bottom-center) textured surface, (bottom-right) textured surface rendered with lighting.

For volumetric video, seeing the whole content at once is not possible, as the content is occluding itself at any given time due to its 3D nature. To ensure that the collected subjective quality scores are representative for the whole volumetric video, the experimenter needs to ensure that the volumetric video is inspected properly by the subjective experiment participants. There are two main ways to facilitate this: let viewers interact with the volumetric video themselves or present a representative stimulus (e.g., a sequence of images from predefined viewpoints) in which the viewer's interaction is non-existent. The former methods better simulate real-life use cases of 3D media consumption, whereas the latter approaches provide the same experience across subjects granting reproducibility, and enable utilization of well-established practices that have been developed for evaluation of traditional video.

There are many aspects that need to be taken into account while designing and conducting subjective user studies, in addition to the user interaction aspect discussed above. The volumetric video can be represented with different 3D formats (e.g., meshes and point clouds), which may contain different attributes; these models can be colorless,

Table 18.1 Various aspects in subjective user studies for volumetric video.

Aspects	Variables
3D Representation	Mesh, Point Cloud
Temporal Variation	Static, Dynamic
Attributes	Colorless, Colored
Mode of Inspection	Passive, Interactive
Methodology	Single stimulus, Double stimulus, Multiple stimulus, Pairwise comparison
Distortion Types	Noise, Compression, Simplification, Smoothing, Sub-sampling, Transmission error
Rendering Parameters	Lighting, Background, Point size (for point clouds)
Display Devices	2D monitors, 3D monitors, Head-mounted displays, Smartphones

colored, or textured. Moreover, there are different rendering parameters that should be configured, which affect the appearance of the models. In Fig. 18.2, examples are presented regarding the effect of the lighting on textures meshes and the point size on point clouds, which, if not carefully chosen, may lead to the appearance of holes (small point size) or patchy areas (large point size). Subjective experiments may also use different display devices or evaluation methodologies to collect quality scores. These experiments make use of either static or dynamic 3D models, and they might feature various types of practical distortions; such as additive or multiplicative noise, mesh simplification or point cloud sub-sampling, compression, transmission, and smoothing. A summary of all these aspects can be seen in Table 18.1.

In this section, we categorize the scientific efforts on subjective quality assessment with respect to the mode of inspection, which dictates if and how the viewer will interact with the visual stimulus. In each subsection, we further divide the studies with respect to the 3D representation.

18.1.1 Non-interactive user studies

One of the ways to collect subjective quality scores for volumetric video is to limit the user interaction completely (i.e., the viewer cannot interact with the stimulus). In this case, a certain visualization technique is used to create visual stimuli, and the volumetric video is represented to the participants of the subjective test in the same manner. There might be various approaches in creating the visual stimuli, which mostly create traditional images or a traditional video that is composed of rendered images of the volumetric video content.

A common way to create these video sequences is to select a certain camera trajectory (e.g., a camera rotating around the object, while staying on the horizontal plane and looking towards the object, as shown in Fig. 18.3). Rendering images from these

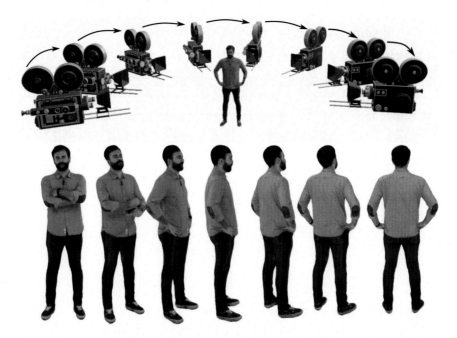

Figure 18.3 One common method to create videos for subjective experiments with no user interaction is to create traditional videos of the volumetric video sequences with a fixed camera trajectory, as shown above. Sample renderings of such a video are shown below. Attribution: The 3D camera model in the figure is created by Jesse Johnson and is licensed under Creative commons attribution (CC BY 4.0).

camera locations and sequencing them as video frames will create a traditional video, which shows the volumetric video from many different viewpoints. Following their creation, these video sequences are shown to the subjective test participants, who in turn determine the quality of the volumetric video sequence. In this setup, the viewer does not and cannot interact with the volumetric video itself, which means that the observer cannot change the viewpoint and can only watch the pre-rendered video. Therefore the user is passive in this scenario.

Although this lack of interaction is a disadvantage for the viewer, it is also an advantage for the experimenter, since this lack of interaction also removes any inter-viewer variation that might occur due to interactivity, i.e., they ensure that the same stimuli will be seen by all participants. Moreover, these approaches do not require complex rendering software or devices, since the resulting still images or videos can be easily visualized on 2D screens using commodity software, and they minimize external biases and conditions that can influence the final results, such as novelty effect or cybersickness.

In the following subsections, we discuss how the subjective user studies are conducted in the literature without user interaction, after grouping them per 3D content representation (e.g., point clouds and meshes).

18.1.1.1 User studies for point clouds

The majority of non-interactive experiments in the literature of point cloud quality assessment, focuses on static contents [14–21]. When evaluating static contents in a non-interactive manner, the experimenter does not have to worry about possible interaction effects between the camera movement and the sequence actions. For example, by simply using circular camera paths, the content will be visualized by all angles without missing information regarding the visual quality of occluded regions. Passive inspection has also been used for dynamic contents [22–24], using predefined camera paths to ensure the same user experience. Moreover, different types of distortions have been studied in the literature: from noise in geometric and textural information of point clouds [15,25–27], to compression artifacts [14–20,22], rendering approaches [19–21,27] and adaptive streaming algorithms [24]. By default, point clouds lead to the perception of holes; hence, the size of points is typically configured so as to enable visualization of watertight objects. In most studies, the experimenters assign the same point size for an entire model, whereas in some experiments different point sizes are assigned based on local densities [14,28,29]. Finally, double stimulus variants denote the most popular evaluation methodologies.

Javaheri et al. [14] evaluate static models representing inanimate objects and human figures at three quality levels, using a spiral camera path moving around a model from a full view to a closer look to capture images from different perspectives. Cubic geometric primitives of adaptive size based on local neighborhoods were employed for rendering purposes. Animated sequences were created and rated by subjects, using the sequential double stimulus impairment scale (DSIS) methodology. The color attributes of the models remained uncompressed to assess the impact of these geometry-only degradations. Su et al. [15] employed a virtual camera orbiting around the point cloud models at a fixed distance to capture the views, which were displayed using the DSIS methodology with simultaneous visualization of the reference and distorted stimuli. A wide set of colored models were distorted using different types of degradations, including Gaussian noise in both topology and texture, octree down-sampling, and compression artifacts from the MPEG test models. More recently, Lazzarotto et al. [16] conducted a crowd-sourced user study to evaluate compression distortions from both conventional and learning-based codecs. The point clouds were rendered using splats of adaptive size, with the camera orbiting at a fixed distance.

Conducting experiments in a single laboratory setting can make questions arise about the generalizability of the results. Even when standardized procedures are adopted to select and screen users, there might be human-related biases that can influence the results. For this reason, cross-laboratory testing helps in checking the validity and in corroborating the outcomes of the test. Cruz et al. [17] report the results of a subjective evaluation campaign that was issued in the framework of the JPEG Pleno [3] activities. Subjective experiments were conducted in three laboratories for quality assessment of colored point clouds under an octree- and a projection-based encoding scheme, using the DSIS methodology. A different camera path was defined per content, and a fixed point size was specified per model and degradation level. This is reported to be the first study making use of contents consumed outer-wise (e.g., objects, human figures) and inner-wise (e.g., scenes). Perry et al. [18] report experiments that were performed in four independent laboratories that participated in the relevant JPEG exploration study activities, evaluating the performance of V-PCC and G-PCC using colored point clouds. The DSIS with side-by-side visualization was employed using fixed-size point primitives to display the models. The experimental setup of each laboratory varied; yet, the collected subjective scores exhibited high inter-laboratory correlation.

In some early studies, conversion to mesh was considered as an alternative for rendering point clouds before being assessed. The degradations under test were applied on the raw point clouds; subsequently, a surface reconstruction algorithm was applied to render the 3D models. Javaheri et al. [27] performed subjective evaluation of de-noising algorithms against impulse noise and Gaussian noise. Video sequences of the reference and the degraded models after reconstruction using the screened Poisson method [30] were sequentially shown to human subjects, before rating the visual quality of the latter. Alexiou et al. [19] present a study where subjective experiments were conducted in five test laboratories to assess the visual quality of colorless point clouds using the same reconstruction algorithm as a rendering methodology. The point clouds were degraded using octree-pruning, and the observers evaluated the mesh models under a simultaneous DSIS methodology. Although different 2D monitors were employed, subjective scores were found to be strongly correlated among the participated laboratories. In [20], the same dataset was evaluated under various 3D display types/technologies (i.e., passive, active, and auto-stereoscopic).

Different point-based and mesh rendering methodologies were employed for subjective quality evaluation by Javaheri et al. [21]. The point clouds were distorted by geometric compression artifacts and rendered using three approaches: colorless point primitives of fixed size with shading; point primitives of fixed size, rendered using the original texture information without shading; and colorless meshes obtained after screened Poisson surface reconstruction, with shading. Each rendering approach was evaluated in separate sessions, using the sequential DSIS methodology.

The aforementioned studies focused on evaluating static contents under various degradations and rendering setups. Few studies have been involved with evaluating dynamic sequences using non-interactive approaches. Schwarz et al. [2] evaluate both static and dynamic colored point cloud models under several encoding categories, settings, and bitrates, from a quality assessment campaign that was conducted in the framework of the call for proposals issued by the MPEG committee [31]. The contents were rendered using cubes as primitive elements of fixed size; animated image sequences of the models captured from predefined viewpoints were generated and assessed using the absolute category rating (ACR) methodology. Subjective evaluations of a volumetric video data set that was acquired and released in the context of the study was performed by Zerman et al. [23], under compression artifacts from the MPEG V-PCC. The point clouds were rendered using primitive ellipsoidal elements of fixed size, and animated sequences were generated from predefined camera paths. The stimuli were subjectively assessed using two methodologies; that is, a side-by-side evaluation with DSIS and a pairwise comparison.

The previous studies focused on evaluating a single point cloud content at the time, which, depending on the context, might not be realistic. For example, several objects can be placed and viewed at the same time in a virtual space, or in a real-time communication scenario, multiple people could be present in the same scene. In [24], subjective quality assessment of dynamic, colored point clouds is conducted in an adaptive streaming scenario hosted by the system described in [32], in which more than one models is placed in the same scene under different arrangements, and were visited with different navigation paths. The streamed cues were subjectively evaluated using an ACR methodology in a desktop setting. For the purposes of the study, volumetric video sequences were selected and encoded at different quality levels using V-PCC. Among the experimental parameters, different bandwidth conditions, bitrate allocation schemes, and prediction strategies were examined.

18.1.1.2 User studies for meshes

Pioneering subjective quality tests involving meshes were conducted on still rendered images [33,34]; those two early studies both assessed the visual impact of simplification artifacts and concerned static and geometry-only meshes; the same applies in [35], which evaluated the impact of geometry compression. Subsequent passive interaction experiments considered meshes with color/texture attributes [36–41] or dynamic meshes [8,42,43]. These studies are detailed below. They considered different types of stimuli (still images or videos) and different protocols (ACR, DSIS, pairwise comparison), adapting existing image/video methodologies for passive inspection of 3D models by observers: 2D still images or generated videos of animated models.

Watson et al. [33] used still rendered images to evaluate the visual impact of mesh simplification using the DSIS methodology. Váša and Rus [35] and Doumanoglou et al. [38] also used still rendered images in their studies to evaluate the impairment of geometry compression and the visual impact of geometry and texture resolution on the quality of textured human body reconstructed meshes, respectively. Both of these studies considered a pairwise comparison methodology. Rogowitz et al. [34] conducted two subjective quality assessment experiments: the first involved 2D static images of simplified 3D objects, whereas the second was performed on rendered videos of these objects in rotation. The results showed that lighting conditions have a strong influence on perceived quality and that observers perceive the quality of still images and animations differently. The authors concluded that the quality of 3D objects cannot be correctly assessed using static 2D projections (still images may mask the effect of light and shading), and thus it is important that the object moves.

Based on these findings, some researchers allowed users to interact freely and in real time with the model by rotating and zooming it, as detailed in Section 18.1.2.2. However, others decided to control the viewpoints visualized by the user showing an animation of the 3D object to avoid cognitive overload that can alter human judgments.

Guo et al. [37] opted for this approach to assess the influence of lighting, shape, and texture on the perception of artifacts for textured meshes. They animated each object in the dataset with a low-speed rotation and generated videos that were displayed to observers during the test. The subjective study was conducted using the pairwise comparison method. The same experimental procedure was adopted by Vanhoey et al. [44] to investigate the impact of light-material interactions on the perception of geometric distortion of 3D models.

Pan et al. [36] conducted a subjective experiment on textured meshes to assess the perceptual interactions between the geometry and color information. They considered only geometry and texture sub-sampling distortions. They animated their meshes with a slow rotation and the experiment was based on the DSIS methodology. Nehmé et al. [39] provide the first public dataset for meshes with vertex colors produced in VR. The dataset was obtained through a subjective study based on the DSIS methodology. The stimuli were rendered at a fixed viewing distance from the observer in a virtual scene, under different viewpoints and animated in real-time with either slow rotation or slow zoom-in. The study allowed to analyze the impact of several factors, such as viewpoints and animations on both quality scores and their confidence intervals.

The above works considered quality assessment of static meshes. Váša and Skala [42] and Torkhani et al. [43] were the first authors to propose quality assessment experiments involving dynamic meshes (without color/texture). Distortions included diverse types of noise and compression. The rated stimuli were videos of mesh sequences, rendered from fixed viewpoints. Used methodologies were respectively single stimulus rating [43] and multiple stimulus rating [42].

More recently, Zerman et al. [8] considered the ACR with Hidden Reference (ACR-HR) methodology to compare dynamic textured meshes and colored point clouds in the context of a VV compression scenario utilizing the appropriate state-of-the-art compression techniques for each 3D representation. They built a database and collected user quality opinion scores using rendered version of VVs, shown to the participants on an LCD display.

The previous experiments were conducted in laboratories, under controlled environments and with high-end equipment. Along with laboratory subjective experiments, crowd-sourcing experiments have become very popular in recent years, especially during COVID-19 pandemic, where participants could not be physically present in the lab. However, conducting subjective quality assessment tests in a crowd-sourcing setting imposes several challenges, notably those related to the lack of control over the participants' environment and the reliability of the participants, since the latter are not supervised. A recent study was conducted to investigate whether a crowd-sourcing test can achieve the accuracy of a laboratory test for 3D graphics [45]. For this purpose, the authors designed a crowd-sourcing experiment that replicates as much as possible the lab experiment presented in [40], which was conducted in VR. Specifically, they used the same dataset of 3D models and the same experimental methodology (i.e., DSIS). Since in crowd-sourcing the test environment cannot be fully controlled, videos of rotating stimuli were displayed to the participants to limit their interactions with the 3D objects. The results of this study showed that under controlled conditions and with a proper participant screening approach, a crowd-sourcing experiment based on the DSIS method can be as accurate as a laboratory experiment. It is worth mentioning that crowd-sourcing is quite faster to evaluate large datasets, yet the most time intensive task is building and designing the experimental framework (or setup) (user-friendly tool, control viewer environment, add screening test, etc.). Based on these findings, a large-scale crowd-sourcing experiment was conducted to rate the perceived quality of the largest dataset of textured meshes to this date [41]. This dataset allowed to analyze the impact of the distortions and model characteristics (geometric and color complexity) on the perceived quality of textured meshes.

18.1.2 Interactive user studies

An alternative way to collect subjective user quality scores is to conduct user studies in more interactive experimental settings, which account for more realistic scenarios of consumption for 3D content. Considering that there are no recommendations for interactive protocols, most of the efforts make use of well-established methodologies (e.g., ACR or DSIS) in experimental setups ranging from desktop arrangements to XR applications, which accommodate interactivity with varying DoF.

In all cases, the contents are placed in a virtual scene, designed by the experimenter depending on the task at hand (i.e., background, lighting, etc.). Moreover, the users are given the means to handle the camera position and orientation at any given moment to inspect the contents under evaluation at their will. For instance, in desktop setups the contents are displayed on flat-screen monitors with user interactions typically being registered through the mouse cursor or computer keyboards. In XR settings, the contents are visualized through a head-mounted display (HMD), with the users controlling their viewpoint either by physical movements in the real world, or by controllers.

By design, interactive evaluation protocols lead to individual visual experiences across users, which ultimately affect their opinion regarding the visual quality of the content under inspection. However, it is advocated that such methodologies are better adjusted to the interactive nature of richer imaging modalities, with user quality scores inherently containing the preferred type of interaction. To compensate this uncertainty in user ratings, it is common for the experimenters to either recruit more participants or to allow interactions without imposing time limitations. Finally, enabling interactive protocols allows the experimenter to analyze the behavior of users with 3D visual data, and explore inter-dependencies between interactivity patterns and perception of quality.

In the following subsections, we discuss subjective user studies using interactive evaluation protocols reported in the literature, clustered per 3D content representation.

18.1.2.1 User studies for point clouds

The interactive user studies for point clouds generally use three different platforms: desktop devices [25,28,29,46–49], AR [26], and VR [50–52] headsets. Many studies focus on static point clouds [25,26,28,29,46–48,50], whereas only a couple of the studies focus on dynamic point clouds [49,51]. Similarly to passive inspection experiments, studies on both colorless [25,26,46] and colored [28,29,47–52] models have been conducted, while different types of distortions and point size selection strategies have been employed. Lastly, double stimulus methodologies are more frequently used.

Interactive variants of the DSIS and ACR methodologies were first proposed by Alexiou et al. [25,46] to assess the quality of geometry-only point clouds in a desktop setting, using the mouse cursor to change the viewpoint. In both studies, Gaussian noise and octree-pruning were employed to simulate position errors from sensor inaccuracies and compression artifacts, respectively. In these user studies, the models were displayed side-by-side using points of minimum size.

The visual quality of colored point clouds was evaluated by Torlig et al. [47] in subjective experiments that were performed in two separate laboratories. Orthographic projections after real-time voxelization of both the reference and the distorted models were shown to the subjects, using the simultaneous DSIS methodology. Point clouds representing both inanimate objects and human figures were selected and compressed using the CWI-PCL codec [49]. The results showed that subjects rate more severely distortions on human models. Moreover, using this codec, marginal gains are brought by color improvements at low geometric resolutions, indicating that the visual quality is rather limited at high sparsity. In a study that followed [28], the same dataset was assessed under the same methodology using a different rendering scheme. The point clouds were rendered using cubes of locally adaptive sizes, with the rating trends being found very similar to those of Torlig et al. [47].

A comprehensive quality assessment study of the MPEG point cloud compression test models is presented with subjective evaluation experiments conducted in two independent laboratories [29]. Static, colored point clouds with diverse characteristics were employed and compressed following the MPEG common test conditions. The encoded models were displayed using splats of adaptive size based on local sparsity, and evaluated in an interactive platform using the simultaneous DSIS methodology. As part of the study, subjective experiments under a pairwise comparison protocol were performed to conclude on preferable rate-allocation strategies for geometry, and geometry-plus-color encoding. Based on the findings, human subjects prefer the distortions from regular down-sampling (Octree) over triangulated surface approximations (TriSoup), at both low and high bitrates.

In previous studies, the users were able to rotate, zoom and translate the models, and interact without timing constraints. Yang et al. [48] conducted subjective quality assessment on a large set of widely-employed colored models, allowing only rotation under a fixed distance. Several degradation types affecting both the geometry and the color information were introduced, consisting of octree-pruning, noise injection in the coordinates and the RGB values, random down-sampling, and combinations of the above to further augment the visual impairments. The experiments were conducted using a single stimulus protocol.

Despite the convenience of desktop environments to perform interactive testing, their setup is often less realistic when compared to immersive, XR environments. The first attempt was made by Alexiou et al. [26], making use of an AR setting to evaluate the visual quality of colorless point clouds, subject to octree-pruning and Gaussian noise. A simultaneous DSIS methodology was employed, and a separate session was issued per distortion type. The models were displayed using point primitives of minimum size and were placed as virtual assets in the real world, with users perceiving them via an HMD, and interacting with 6DoF via physical movements.

Perceptual quality of static point clouds in VR was evaluated in a recent study [50]. The users were able to interact with the stimuli with 6DoF via both physical movements and using the controllers, in a virtual scene that was designed to avoid distractions. The color encoding modules of the MPEG G-PCC test model were evaluated using octree-based geometry compression under two double stimulus protocols. The models were displayed using quads of adaptive size that were interpolated before rendering to smooth the surfaces. The user behavior during evaluation was also analyzed to provide further insights. Wu et al. [52] present a study evaluating a large set of colored, static point cloud contents in a 6DoF VR viewing condition. Separate sessions were issued for point clouds depicting human figures and objects. The DSIS methodology with side-by-side inspection was used in all cases, including hidden references to compute DMOS. The point clouds were rendered using minimum point size, while the subjects were able to navigate in the virtual space only by physical movements.

Desktop-based setups were also used for quality assessment of dynamic point clouds. In the work of Mekuria et al. [49], subjective experiments were conducted in the proposed 3D tele-immersive system, where the users were able to interact with naturalistic (dynamic point cloud) and synthetic (computer generated) models in a virtual scene. The participants were able to navigate in the virtual environment through the use of the mouse cursor in thw desktop setting. The proposed encoding solution (CWI-PCL) that was employed to compress the naturalistic content of the scene was evaluated, among several other aspects of quality (e.g., level of immersiveness and realism).

Visual quality assessment using dynamic point cloud contents in VR under both 3DoF and 6DoF interaction scenarios is presented in the work of Subramanyam et al. [51]. Human figures from real-life acquisition and artificially generated were encoded using the V-PCC and the CWI-PCL, which denotes the anchor codec of the MPEG studies [49]. The models were displayed in the virtual scene using quads of fixed size and evaluated under an ACR-HR protocol. The users were able to navigate by physical movements in the 6DoF scenario, while remaining sited in the 3DoF counterpart. Results showed the superiority of V-PCC at low bitrates, whereas statistical equivalence was found with the MPEG anchor at higher bitrates, depending on the content. Finally, the inability of the codecs to achieve transparent visual quality was remarked. In a subsequent study [53], the subjective quality scores between these 3DoF and 6DoF VR settings were compared to pre-recorded videos visualized on common 2D screens to conclude on the effects of different viewing conditions.

18.1.2.2 User studies for meshes

Many authors have adopted for free interaction in their subjective tests for evaluating the quality of meshes. The majority of these works were performed on 2D screen: Lavoué et al. [54], Corsini et al. [55], and Torkhani et al. [43] conducted subjective experiments based on single stimulus methods (derived from ACR), whereas Lavoué et al. [56] and Silva et al. [57] implemented double stimulus methods (derived from DSIS). In these experiments, the observers were able to freely interact (i.e., free-viewpoint interaction) with the 3D models to evaluate and rate their quality. All those studies considered meshes without color or texture, and they evaluated the impairments introduced by various geometry distortions (e.g., noise, compression, smoothing, watermarking).

An early attempt of a 3D tele-immersive system allowing real-time communication between natural representations of humans and synthetic avatars, was presented by Mekuria et al. in [58]. The natural representations in this setting were rendered as meshes. For purposes of subjective quality evaluation, a pre-recorded natural human moving was employed as the test stimulus. The original representation and three degraded versions after encoding with three real-time mesh coding solutions were subjectively evaluated from near and far distance.

Few experiments involving meshes have been conducted in immersive environments. Christaki et al. [59] subjectively assessed the perceived quality of meshes (without color/texture) subject to different compression codecs in a VR setting using the pairwise comparison method. The content was viewed freely as a combination of natural navigation (i.e., physical movement in the real-world) and user interaction. Gutiérrez et al. [60] used the dataset of textured meshes provided in [37] to evaluate the perception of geometry and texture distortions in mixed reality (MR) scenarios. They also analyzed the impact of environment lighting conditions on the perceived quality of 3D objects in MR. The experiment was based on the ACR-HR method and the observers were asked to freely explore the displayed 3D models.

18.1.3 Publicly available datasets

Some of the works presented above have publicly released their datasets. Table 18.2 outlines the publicly available subjective quality datasets for 3D content. For meshes, the available datasets concern mostly geometry-only content [19,35,42,43,54,56,57] and are all rather small (see the first 7 rows in Table 18.2). The only public dataset involving meshes with vertex colors is provided by Nehmé et al. [39] and contains 480 distorted stimuli. For textured meshes, three datasets exist: [37], [8] and [41]. The first two datasets contain, respectively, 136 and 28 stimuli, whereas the latter contains more than 343k stimuli, of which 3000 (a generalized and challenging subset) are associated with mean opinion scores (MOS) derived from subjective experiments, and the rest with predicted quality scores (pseudo-MOS), making it the largest quality assessment dataset of textured meshes to date.

Regarding point clouds, only two datasets concern colorless models: [25,26] and [21], with the rest considering colored models. Among the latter, the largest available datasets are the WPC by Su et al. [15], the SJTU-PCQA by Yang et al. [48] and the SIAT-PCQD by Wu et al. [52]. The WPC is composed of point clouds captured in a laboratory setting by the authors, which are degraded by different types of distortions; the SJTU-PCQA makes use of contents that have been extensively utilized in standardization activities under various compression distortions; the SIAT-PCQD involves point clouds from the MPEG and JPEG repositories and a publicly accessible 3D content sharing platform, which are encoded using only V-PCC.

The majority of the reported datasets for both meshes and point clouds were generated through experiments that were conducted on desktop settings. In particular, only the studies presented in [26] and [39,50,52,53] were conducted in immersive environments, with the former performed in AR, and the latter in VR platforms, respectively.

As discussed in Section 18.1, there are various aspects that differ for subjective experiments during the data collection step. All these aspects and different parameters are listed in the columns of Table 18.2. Most of these aspects are either self-describing or introduced at the beginning of this chapter.

Regarding the "Methodology" column, although subjective evaluation methodologies have specific instructions and distinctions among themselves, for the sake of simplicity, we only consider the number of stimuli test participants see to provide a vote. For single stimulus methodologies, the participants decide on the subjective quality by

Table 18.2 Publicly available subjectively annotated datasets for meshes & point clouds.

Dataset	3D Representation	Temporal Variation	Attributes	Mode of Inspection	Methodology	Distortion Types	# Stimuli rated	# Ratings per Stimulus	Raw Scores
LIRIS / EPFL [54]	Mesh	Static	Colorless	Interactive	Single stimulus	Noise addition Smoothing	84	12	✓
LIRIS Masking [56]	Mesh	Static	Colorless	Interactive	Double stimulus	Noise addition	24	11	✓
IEETA Simplification [57]	Mesh	Static	Colorless	Interactive	Double stimulus	Simplification	30	65	X
UWB #1 [35]	Mesh	Static	Colorless	Passive	Pairwise comparison	Compression	63	69	✓
RG-PCD [19]	Mesh	Static	Colorless	Passive	Double stimulus	Octree-pruning	30	126	✓
UWB #2 [42]	Mesh	Dynamic	Colorless	Passive	Multiple stimulus	Compression Noise addition	36	37~49	X MOS&CI
3D Mesh Animation Quality [43]	Mesh	Dynamic	Colorless	• Passive • Interactive	Single stimulus	Noise addition Compression Transmission error	286	• 16 • 25	✓
LIRIS Textured Mesh [37]	Mesh	Static	Texture maps	Passive (Generated videos)	Pairwise comparison	- On geometry: Compression Simplification Smoothing - On texture: Compression Sub-sampling	• 100×2 renderings • 36×2 renderings	• 11~15 (Exp.1) • 10~11 (Exp.2)	X preference matrices
Nehmé et al. [41]	Mesh	Static	Texture maps	Passive (Generated videos)	Double stimulus	Compression Simplification	• 3000 (MOS) • 340750 (Pseudo-MOS)	45	✓

continued on next page

Table 18.2 (continued)

Dataset	3D Repre-sentation	Temporal Variation	Attributes	Mode of Inspection	Methodology	Distortion Types	# Stimuli rated	# Ratings per Stimulus	Raw Scores
3D Meshes with Vertex Colors [39]	Mesh	Static	Vertex colors	Passive in VR (Slow animations)	Double stimulus	Compression Simplification	480	24	X MOS&CI
G-PCD [25,26]	Point cloud	Static	Colorless	• Interactive • Interactive in 6DoF AR	• Single & Double stimulus • Double stimulus	Noise addition Octree-pruning	50	• 2×20 • 21	✓
M-PCCD [29]	Point cloud	Static	Colored	Interactive	• Double stimulus • 2×Pairwise comparison	Compression	• 240 • 40 & 30	• 40 • 2×25	✓
IRPC [21]	Point cloud	Static	• 2×Colorless • Colored	Passive (Generated videos)	Double stimulus	Compression	• 54 • 54	• 2×20 • 20	X MOS
WPC [15]	Point cloud	Static	Colored	Passive (Generated videos)	Double stimulus	Compression Noise addition Octree-pruning	740	30	X MOS
VsenseVVDB [23]	Point cloud	Dynamic	Colored	Passive (Generated videos)	Double stimulus & Pairwise comparison	Compression	32	19	✓

continued on next page

Table 18.2 (*continued*)

Dataset	3D Representation	Temporal Variation	Attributes	Mode of Inspection	Methodology	Distortion Types	# Stimuli rated	# Ratings per Stimulus	Raw Scores
VsenseVVDB2 [8]	• Point cloud • Mesh	Dynamic	• Colored • Texture maps	Passive (Generated videos)	Single stimulus	Compression	• 136 • 28	23	✓
ICIP2020 [18]	Point cloud	Static	Colored	Passive (Generated videos)	Double stimulus	Compression	96	15~27	X MOS&CI
PointXR [50]	Point cloud	Static	Colored	Interactive in 6DoF VR	2×Double stimulus	Compression	40	2×20	✓
SJTU-PCQA [48]	Point cloud	Static	Colored	Interactive	Single stimulus	Compression Noise addition Scaling	378	16	X MOS
SIAT-PCQD [52]	Point cloud	Static	Colored	Interactive in 6DoF VR	Double stimulus	Compression	340	38	X DMOS
LB-PCCD [16]	Point cloud	Static	Colored	Passive	Double stimulus	Compression	105	48	✓
2DTV-VR-QoE [53]	Point cloud	Dynamic	Colored	• Interactive in 6DoF VR • Interactive in 3DoF VR • Passive (Generated videos)	Single stimulus	Compression	72	• 26 • 26 • 25	✓

seeing only one stimulus. Similarly, for double stimulus methodologies, participants provide a rating after seeing two stimuli, one of which is generally the reference stimulus (or source model). In multiple stimulus, this number is more than two, and in pairwise comparison, participants choose the better quality stimulus from two stimuli presented to them.

The "# Stimuli Rated" column includes the reference stimuli if they were rated during the test (e.g., as hidden reference). Some datasets might have quality labels in addition to the MOS values that are collected from participants. These quality labels are generally estimated using a quality metric that shows very high correlation to the MOS values. These labels are called pseudo-MOS, and their purpose is to increase the number of labels for metrics training and evaluation.

The "# Ratings per Stimulus" column indicates the number of unique observations made during the experiment, or the number of unique votes that was collected for every stimulus.

Another important parameter for multimedia content quality datasets (images, videos, audios, 3D graphics, etc.) is whether the individual quality scores of each participant were shared and made publicly available. Although all the quality datasets share MOS or preference scores, these values might not be enough to characterize the statistical attributes and distributions of the individual votes [61]. Providing individual votes can allow for further statistical analysis and research into the weaknesses of certain stimuli, use cases, or objective quality metrics [62,63]. Therefore, in Table 18.2, we identify whether the indicated datasets share individual votes from participants in the "Raw Scores" column.

18.1.4 Comparative studies

There are several studies focused on addressing the impact of different aspects (Table 18.1), in subjective quality evaluation of volumetric content. The usage of different types of *3D representation*, the *mode of inspection*, the *display devices*, the *rendering parameters*, and the evaluation *methodologies*, are among the most relevant and popular in the literature. Although some knowledge may be transferred from 2D imaging, which has been well-studied, the effect of different variables for quality assessment of volumetric video can only be quantified through scientific research and experimentation using such contents. Hence, these studies are particularly important, as they can help us better understand and identify interactions between influencing factors.

The first user study aiming at comparing point cloud against mesh *representations* for compression of volumetric video is presented by Zerman et al. in [8]. The Google Draco and JPEG encoding engines were employed for geometry and texture of mesh, respectively, whereas V-PCC and G-PCC were recruited to encode geometry and color of point cloud versions of the contents. As part of the study, the efficiency of the latter MPEG point cloud codecs was also analyzed. All models were evaluated in a passive protocol using the ACR–HR for both content representations, while point clouds were displayed using fixed-size point primitives. Results show that the point cloud encoding-plus-rendering pipeline leads to better performance at low bitrates, whereas higher quality levels are achieved by the mesh-based counterpart. However, the latter is attained for bitrates that well-exceed the point cloud ones. Finally, among the MPEG alternatives, the superiority of the V-PCC was confirmed.

Similarly, a subjective evaluation of volumetric videos using both point cloud and mesh technologies is detailed in the work of Cao et al. [64]. Several additional factors were considered in the experimental design, among which were the target bitrate, the content resolution, and the viewing distance. To decrease the parameter space, for every target bitrate, a manual identification of the optimal combination for model resolution and compression parameters per viewing distance was performed in a perceptual sense. The selected stimuli were evaluated following passive inspection in two experiments that were carried out. In the first, the subjects rated the visual quality of models that were displayed using both types of content representations under an ACR methodology. In the second, a pairwise comparison between the same models represented as point clouds and meshes was issued. Based on the results, subjects favored the point cloud alternative at lower bitrates. Moreover, the viewing distance was found to be an important factor, and mesh modeling was preferred at closer distances. At higher bitrates and distant inspection, human opinions expressed equal preference.

In the study of Javaheri et al. [21], particular combinations of *representations*, *attributes*, and *rendering* methodologies were examined for quality evaluation of static point clouds, subject to compression distortions. In particular, the experiments were conducted using (a) colorless point clouds, (b) colored point clouds, and (c) colorless meshes, to evaluate the same point cloud distortions. Results show that different scoring behaviors might be observed for the same compression impairments under a different selection. Moreover, the scoring deviations might vary per codec. Finally, it was suggested that texture information might mask underlying geometric distortions.

Regarding the effect of adopting different *modes of inspection* for subjective quality assessment, very few comparisons have been performed. Torkhani et al. [43] performed both passive and interactive experiments for the same dataset of dynamic meshes, using a single stimulus protocol. They concluded that under most kinds of distortions user interaction can affect the perceived quality; however, this impact depends on the nature of the distortion (e.g., global vs local) and is hard to predict. Viola et al. [53] conducted subjective experiments in 3DoF and 6DoF VR as well as with pre-recorded videos in conventional monitors. Two sets of point clouds were employed, subject to compression distortions. For one of the two sets, the viewing condition was deemed to have a significant effect on the distribution of the scores, indicating differences between interactive and non-interactive inspection. For the other set, however, the inspection method had no effect on the scores. The study suggests that conclusions derived from either a non-interactive or interactive experiment can be roughly generalized, since the effect of the inspection method on the collected scores was, if existent, marginal. In particular, the interaction between codec and inspection method was not significant, meaning that you would draw the same conclusions about the relative performance of one codec with respect to the other in either interactive or non-interactive scenarios. However, this study highlights that other factors, besides visual quality, might be important for the selection of inspection method; for example, the level of presence or immersion, or the discomfort caused by cyber sickness.

Regarding the influence of different *display devices*, the collected user ratings from an AR setting and an interactive desktop setup were compared in [65]. In both experiments, colorless point clouds of minimum size were employed. The results revealed similar rating trends in the presence of Gaussian noise, and differences under octree-pruning. In particular, the authors claim that the former type of degradation leads to clearly perceived artifacts independently of the type of devices, hence leading to high correlation. Differences were also observed with respect to the shape of the models. Finally, higher confidence intervals, associated with subjective scores from the AR setting, suggest a larger number of users to be involved in such experimental setups. Results from a collaborative effort in the framework of the JPEG Pleno on point clouds were reported in [20], where reconstructed mesh models from compressed, colorless point clouds were assessed using various 3D display types/technologies (i.e., passive, active, and auto-stereoscopic) in different laboratories. Inter-laboratory correlations and comparisons with quality scores for the same dataset evaluated in 2D monitors, show very high correlation, suggesting that human judgments are not significantly affected by the display equipment.

The majority of current comparative studies is focused on understanding the impact of employing a different evaluation *methodology* on the obtained quality scores and their accuracy. Specifically, Alexiou et al. [25] compared the results of an ACR and a DSIS test, in which subjects were able to interact with the point clouds viewed on screen. They found that, the DSIS method is more consistent in identifying the level of impairments. The sequential DSIS and a newly proposed variant, namely alternating DSIS, were employed to evaluate point cloud contents subject to color compression distortions in [50]. In the former protocol, the reference model is presented to the user followed by the distorted, whereas in the latter, the user is allowed to toggle between the reference and the distorted at will. The experiments were conducted in VR with users interacting with 6DoF. The results indicated that the alternating DSIS protocol leads to lower uncertainty for the perceived distortions; it is faster, and generally preferred by the participants. Recently, a comprehensive study [40] compared the performance of three of the most prominent subjective methodologies, with and without explicit references, namely ACR-HR, DSIS and SAMVIQ, to determine the best one for evaluating the perceived quality of 3D graphics, especially in VR. The study was conducted in a VR environment using a dataset of meshes with vertex colors animated with slow rotation. Results assert that the presence of an explicit reference is necessary to improve the accuracy and the stability of the method. DSIS tends to be the most suitable method, in terms of accuracy and time-efficiency, to assess the quality of 3D graphics. Authors recommended the use of at least 24 observers for DSIS tests.

18.2. Objective quality assessment

Although subjective quality assessment provides ground truth quality scores for visual stimuli, it is not feasible to carry out user studies for each scenario, especially when there is a need to determine the quality for a large number of contents or for real-time applications. In these cases, objective quality assessment methods (or objective quality metrics) are particularly useful, enabling algorithmic quality estimation using mathematical calculations and signal processing approaches.

Simple geometric or color distances/errors between 3D models are weakly correlated with human perception, since they ignore perceptual characteristics of the HVS [23,54,66], analogously to the mean square error (MSE) and peak signal-to-noise ratio (PSNR) measurements in 2D imaging. Therefore current efforts are concentrated on perceptually driven visual quality metrics, which can be primarily distinguished in top-down and bottom-up approaches. The former treat the HVS as a black box and capture modifications in content features that are induced by distortions to estimate perceived quality. The latter rely on computational models that describe properties of the HVS, mainly to determine the visibility of errors caused by distortions. With the rise of machine learning, a third category has recently emerged, consisting of metrics that rely on purely data-driven approaches, which do not demand any explicit model.

Independently of the design, objective quality metrics can be categorized based on their requirement for the original content (i.e., reference) at execution time as full-reference (FR), reduced-reference (RR), and no-reference (NR). For FR metrics, the distorted model is compared to its reference. For RR metrics, some reference data are required as inputs, whereas for NR, no reference information is necessary. FR metrics are generally employed to drive lossy processing operations, such as compression, transmission, simplification, and watermarking. However, they have higher computational overhead and are not always applicable, as the original content is not always available. RR metrics make use of lightweight, descriptive features that are extracted from both the reference and the distorted contents for comparison purposes. They are typically employed when it is inefficient, or impractical to provide the entire original content, such as in a video streaming scenario. NR metrics are the most practical in terms of usage, yet they are often rather limited in terms of scope, i.e., tuned for a particular type of distortion with limited generalization capabilities.

Finally, considering their operating principle, 3D quality metrics can be classified as model-based and image-based (also known as rendering-based or projection-based) metrics. The model-based metrics operate on the 3D model itself (either mesh or point cloud) and its attributes, such as texture maps or color values. The image-based metrics function on the image domain and usually on projected views of 3D models on 2D planar arrangements; i.e., they often apply image quality metrics (IQMs) on 2D snapshots of the rendered 3D model. The rest of this section is structured according to this classification: In Section 18.2.1, model-based methods for point clouds and meshes are described, whereas in Section 18.2.2, image-based metrics are reported for both types of content representations.

18.2.1 Model-based quality metrics

The majority of model-based quality metrics are based on top-down FR approaches. In FR quality metrics, a correspondence function is essential to enable comparisons between the original (or reference) and the distorted contents. In conventional 2D imaging, this is easily achieved by matching the pixel grids of the reference and the distorted contents. However, this is not the case for 3D data, whose topology is altered by geometric distortions that typically introduce dislocation and/or removal of 3D points. Given the different 3D point (or vertex) populations and coordinates, the point matching (i.e., correspondence) step between the reference and the distorted models becomes an ill-posed problem. After establishing a correspondence, errors between attributes or features associated to the matched points are computed.

Often, 3D data quality metrics identify point matches using the nearest neighbor algorithm for simplicity reasons. In particular, following the most common conventions, the original model is selected as the reference $\mathcal{R}$ and the distorted model is set under evaluation $\mathcal{T}$. Considering point clouds (or meshes), for every point (or vertex) $\mathbf{t} \in \mathcal{T}$, the nearest reference point (or vertex) $\mathbf{r_t} \in \mathcal{R}$ is identified, and a local error $e(\phi_t, \phi_{r_t})$ is computed between corresponding features ϕ_t and ϕ_{r_t}. A global quality score $q_{\mathcal{T} \to \mathcal{R}}$ is obtained by pooling the local errors, as given in Eq. (18.1):

$$q_{\mathcal{T} \to \mathcal{R}} = \frac{1}{|\mathcal{T}|} \left(\sum_{t \in \mathcal{T}} e(\phi_t, \phi_{r_t})^m \right)^{1/n}, \tag{18.1}$$

where $|\mathcal{T}|$ is the number of points (or vertices) of $\mathcal{T}$ and $m, n \geq 1$. Using $n = 1$, and $m = 1$ or $m = 2$, the average or the MSE are obtained, respectively.

Note that $q_{\mathcal{T} \to \mathcal{R}}$ is an asymmetric measurement, as $q_{\mathcal{T} \to \mathcal{R}} \neq q_{\mathcal{R} \to \mathcal{T}}$. That is, by selecting the distorted model as the reference, different sets of matched points (or vertices) are obtained, resulting in different global quality scores. To obtain quality predictions that are independent of the reference selection, it is common to use both models as reference and apply a symmetric operation $f(\cdot)$ on the exported global quality scores, such as the average or the maximum, as shown in Eq. (18.2).

$$q = f\left(q_{\mathcal{T} \to \mathcal{R}}, q_{\mathcal{R} \to \mathcal{T}}\right). \tag{18.2}$$

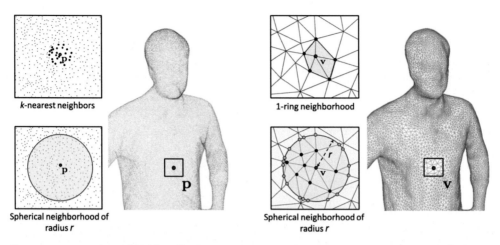

Figure 18.4 Local neighborhood computation around a point **p** in a point cloud (left) and a vertex **v** in a mesh (right). For the point cloud, the *k*-nearest neighbors with $k = 24$ and the range search with radius *r* (*r*-search) approaches are depicted. The 1-ring neighborhood as well as the *r*-search are illustrated for the mesh.

Another approach that has been widely used to provide a global quality score, is the Hausdorff distance. It is defined as the greatest out of all the distances between the points (or vertices) of $\mathcal{T}$ and the nearest/corresponding points (or vertices) of $\mathcal{R}$. It can be derived by using max pooling (instead of the aggregation in Eq. (18.1)) of local errors that measure the Euclidean distance between a point (or vertex) **t** and its nearest $\mathbf{r_t}$. The Hausdorff distance of the point cloud (or mesh) under evaluation $\mathcal{T}$ from the reference $\mathcal{R}$ is computed as follows:

$$q_{\mathcal{T} \to \mathcal{R}} = \max_{\mathbf{t} \in \mathcal{T}} \{ \min_{\mathbf{r} \in \mathcal{R}} \{ d(\mathbf{t}, \mathbf{r}) \} \} = \max_{\mathbf{t} \in \mathcal{T}} \{ d(\mathbf{t}, \mathbf{r_t}) \}, \qquad (18.3)$$

where $d(\cdot)$ is the Euclidean distance.

Finally, it is rather frequent for both point cloud and mesh model-based metrics to take into consideration local neighborhoods around a queried point (or vertex) to compute an attribute or a feature ϕ. For point clouds, the most common algorithms are the *k*-nearest neighbor and the range search with radius *r*, denoted as *k*-nn and *r*-search, respectively, and shown on the left side of Fig. 18.4. The former identifies the nearest *k* points to a queried point **p**, whereas the latter returns all points enclosed in a sphere with center **p** and radius *r*. For meshes, the 1-ring neighborhood and the *r*-search, illustrated on the right side of Fig. 18.4, are employed. The first refers to the set of all vertices connected with the queried vertex **v** by an edge. The second, is defined as the connected set of vertices belonging to the sphere with center **v** and radius *r*. In this case, the intersections between this sphere and the edges of the mesh are also added to the neighborhood. Note that the k-nn (for point clouds) and 1-ring (for meshes) approaches lead to neighborhoods of arbitrary extent, depending on the point density or vertex sampling of the model. The k-nn approach has a fixed population (equal to k), and the 1-ring is straightforward to compute. Concurrently, the r-search approach identifies same volumes that may enclose varying number of samples.

In what follows, we first discuss the model-based metrics for point clouds, and then those for meshes.

18.2.1.1 For point clouds

The development of point cloud objective quality metrics has been an active research field the last five years. This interest was fueled by the MPEG and JPEG standardization activities on point cloud compression [2,3], which required reliable solutions for quality assessment of point cloud compression distortions.

Early developments of model-based predictors employed simple distances between attributes of matched points to measure local errors, as shown in Fig. 18.5. The point-to-point metric denotes the earliest attempt, with the geometric variant computing the Euclidean distance between point coordinates to measure the geometric displacement of distorted samples from their reference positions [67]. Setting $n = 1$ and $m = 2$ in Eq. (18.1), the point-to-point metric with MSE is computed, also known as D1 [68]:

$$D1 = \frac{1}{|\mathcal{T}|} \sum_{t \in \mathcal{T}} d(\mathbf{t}, \mathbf{r_t})^2,$$

(18.4)

where $d(\cdot)$ is the Euclidean distance. Analogously, the point-to-point variant for color distortions measures the error between RGB color values or YUV intensities of matched points, effectively simulating the MSE that has been widely used for 2D images [69], while the PSNR version of this measurement is obtained straightforwardly..

The point-to-point metrics have low complexity; however, they do not account for perceptual characteristics of the HVS. An early alternative to capture geometric distortions based on distances that are more perceptually relevant, is the point-to-plane metric [67]. This method relies on the projected error of distorted points across reference normal vectors. Thus local errors measure the deviation of distorted points from linearly approximated reference surfaces. A global degradation score is typically obtained using the MSE, as given below following the conventions of Fig. 18.5, which is also referred to as D2 [68]:

$$D2 = \frac{1}{|\mathcal{T}|} \sum_{t \in \mathcal{T}} |\vec{u} \cdot \vec{n}_{\mathbf{r_t}}|^2.$$

(18.5)

Beyond MSE, the Hausdorff distance (Eq. (18.3)) has been additionally used with both point-to-point and point-to-plane metrics. Finally, the geometric PSNR has been proposed for both metrics to account for differently scaled contents [70], using either

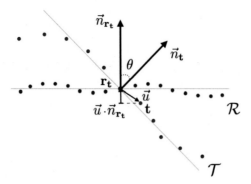

Figure 18.5 Error quantification between a distorted point **t** and a reference point $\mathbf{r_t}$ from simple point-wise distances. Setting $\vec{u} = \mathbf{t} - \mathbf{r_t}$ and θ the angle between corresponding normal vectors, the local error for point-to-point is $d(\mathbf{t}, \mathbf{r_t}) = \|\vec{u}\|^2$, for point-to-plane is $|\vec{u} \cdot \vec{n}_{r_t}|$, and for plane-to-plane is $1 - 2\min\{\theta, \pi - \theta\}/\pi$.

the voxel grid's diagonal or the maximum nearest-neighbor distance of the original content as the peak value.

The above metrics were employed in the MPEG standardization activities since the beginning. As a consequence, they were widely used and tested by the research community, attracting interest and inspiring submissions to improve their performance. For instance, the generalized Hausdorff distance was proposed to mitigate the sensitivity of the Hausdorff distance in outlying points by excluding a percentage of the largest individual errors [71]. A revised geometric PSNR calculation was proposed in [72], setting as peak value the average over distances between neighbors in 3D space, or after projection onto local planes, to represent the intrinsic resolution or rendering resolution of the content, respectively.

Another early-developed method evaluating geometry-only distortions is the plane-to-plane metric, proposed by Alexiou et al. [73]. This metric estimates the difference in orientation between local surface approximations of the original and the distorted point clouds. This is achieved by computing the angular similarity between unoriented normal vectors from locally fitted surfaces. In particular, the angle between the two normal vectors is computed as follows:

$$\theta = \arccos\left(\frac{\vec{n}_{r_t} \cdot \vec{n}_t}{\|\vec{n}_{r_t}\| \|\vec{n}_t\|}\right), \tag{18.6}$$

where the angular similarity is given as

$$\text{Angular similarity} = 1 - \frac{2\min\{\theta, \pi - \theta\}}{\pi}. \tag{18.7}$$

The plane-to-plane metric relies on the computation of normal vectors and its performance is affected by how they approximate the underlying surfaces. An insightful analysis for the calibration of this metric is provided in [74].

In the same list of geometry-only model-based quality metrics lies the point-to-distribution, introduced by Javaheri et al. [75], which computes the Mahalanobis distance between a point and a reference neighborhood. In this case, the geometric deviation is measured with respect to the distribution of reference samples, thus accounting for the local reference topology. This metric was lately extended to capture color degradations by applying the same formula to luminance attributes [76]. The two quality scores obtained for geometry and texture were simply averaged to provide a final predicted quality score.

More recent proposals rely not only on surface properties extracted from point samples, but also on the utilization of statistics to capture relations between points that lay in the same local neighborhood. For that purpose, a correspondence is established between points in the point cloud under evaluation $\mathcal{T}$, and the relative reference point cloud $\mathcal{R}$. Then, statistics are computed based on the neighborhood surrounding the points, as seen in Fig. 18.6. An initial metric towards this direction is PC-MSDM by Meynet et al. [77], which is based on the relative difference between local curvature statistics (mean, standard deviation and covariance of curvature). The PC-MSDM was later extended to colored point clouds by incorporating local statistical measurements of luminance, chrominance, and hue components to evaluate textural impairments. A proposed weighting function regularizes the contributions of each feature in the final quality prediction. The new metric is called PCQM [78]. Both PC-MSDM and PCQM, instead of using nearest neighbors, employ the reference points and their projections onto the quadric surfaces fitted to the distorted model as correspondences.

Alexiou et al. proposed PointSSIM [79], which relies on a similar logic, capturing perceptual degradations based on the relative difference of statistical dispersion estimators applied on local populations of location, normal, curvature, and luminance data. An optional pre-processing step of voxelization is proposed to enable different scaling effects and reduce intrinsic geometric resolution differences across contents. The VQA-CPC metric, by Hua et al. [80] depends on statistics of geometric and color quantities. These quantities are obtained by computing the Euclidean distance between every sample from the arithmetic mean of the point cloud, considering geometric coordinates and color values, respectively. The color point cloud metric based on geometric segmentation and color transformation (CPC-GSCT) denotes an extension, involving a partition stage of the point cloud, before the extraction of features per region [81]. The geometric features consist of statistical moments applied on Euclidean distances, angular distortions, and local densities, which are weighted according to the roughness of a region. The textural features rely on the same statistics after conversion to the HSV color model.

More recently, the PointPCA metric was presented by Alexiou et al. [82], making use of statistics applied on a series of geometric and textural descriptors. The former are

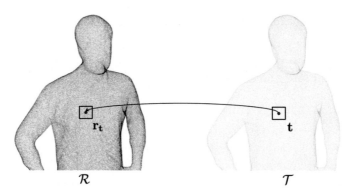

Figure 18.6 Computation of statistics considering a neighborhood around every point. Points that belong to the point cloud under evaluation $\mathcal{T}$ are matched with points from the reference $\mathcal{R}$, and corresponding statistics are compared to obtain local errors. Normally, a global quality score is computed by pooling, per Eq. (18.1).

extracted from measurements obtained after performing principal component analysis (PCA) in support regions defined around point samples, while the latter consist of luminance intensities. The proposed geometric descriptors capture the dispersion of points distribution, the dimensionality, variation, and roughness of the underlying surface, as well as the parallelity with respect to the coordinate system axes. An individual prediction is obtained from every geometric and textural descriptor, with a final quality score obtained via a weighted average.

The GraphSIM by Yang et al. [83] denotes a graph signal processing-based approach, which evaluates statistical moments of color gradients computed over graphs. The graphs are constructed around keypoints of the reference content, and are identified after high-pass filtering on its topology. A more recent, multi-scale version of this metric, namely MS-GraphSIM, is presented by Zhang Y. et al. [84] The proposed multi-scale point cloud representation is achieved by low-pass filtering on color, point down-sampling, and region shrinking. The FQM-GC by Zhang K. et al. [85] is another solution that extracts geometry features from graphs constructed per partition after geometry segmentation, with the graph signal considering normal vectors. Moreover, a color segmentation step is employed and a colorfulness index is computed to weight the obtained segments accordingly. Color histograms and the relative difference of several moments of chrominance components are employed to estimate color distortions per segment.

Xu et al. [86] present the EPES, a point cloud quality metric based on potential energy. In this method, a number of points are selected, called origins, after applying a high-pass filtering operation in the topology of a point cloud. Local neighborhoods are formed around these origins, and the potential elastic energy needed to move the enclosed points from the origin to their current state (considering both geometry and color) is computed. A global score is obtained by aggregating the individual elastic potential energies across origins. Additionally, a local score is obtained as the cosine similarity between the direction of forces needed to transfer a reference and a corresponding distorted point from their origin to their current positions. Global and local features are pooled together to provide a final quality score.

In the work of Diniz et al. [87], local binary patterns on the luminance channel are applied in local neighborhoods. This work is later extended [88] to additionally take into consideration the point-to-plane distance between point clouds, and the point-to-point distance between corresponding feature maps in the quality prediction. A variant descriptor, namely, local luminance patterns, is proposed in [89]. This work also introduces a voxelization stage in the metric's pipeline to alleviate its sensitivity to different voxelization parameters. In [90], a texture descriptor to compare neighboring color values using the CIEDE2000 distance is proposed. The color differences are coded as bit-based labels, which denote frequency values of predefined difference intervals. An extension is presented in [91], namely, BitDance, which incorporates a geometric descriptor that relies on the comparison of neighboring normal vectors, resulting in bit-based labels similarly to the texture counterpart.

A set of texture-only metrics has been proposed by Viola et al. [92], which relies on histograms or correlograms of luminance and chrominance components to characterize the color distributions of distorted and reference point cloud data. A global quality score is obtained by weighted combination of the proposed color-based predictor and the point-to-plane metric.

The previous works refer to FR quality metrics. Regarding RR approaches, the first attempt was reported by Viola et al. in [93]. The algorithm is based on global features extracted from the location, luminance, and normal data, with a weighted average used to combine the distortions into a single quality score. More recently, an RR metric for point clouds encoded with V-PCC was presented by Liu et al. [94]. The prediction is a linear model of geometry and color quantization parameters, with parameters determined by a local and a global color fluctuation feature that accounts for the different impact of compression artifacts on contents.

An NR method was recently proposed by Hua et al. in [95], namely, BQE-CVP. This method relies on geometric features based on point distances, normals, curvatures and point density, which are estimated after segmentation and weighted according to local roughness, similarly to the same authors' previous work in [81]. Texture degradations are computed as statistical moments of distortion maps obtained after applying the just noticeable distortion [96] on point cloud projections. Moreover, features based on gray-texture variations, color entropy, and color contrast, are extracted. Finally, a joint feature based on a geometric-color co-occurrence matrix is proposed.

The performance of well-established, pre-trained convolutional neural network (CNN) architectures for classification, was investigated to assess the quality of the point clouds, after necessary adjustments by Chetouani et al. in [97]. Geometric distance, mean curvature, and luminance values are employed and form patches. A patch quality index is computed using a CNN model, and a global quality index is obtained after pooling. Quach et al. [98] extend the use of perceptual loss from 2D images to point clouds, which are represented as voxel grids with binary occupancy or truncated distance fields. The perceptual loss is applied on the latent space, after passing through a simple auto-encoding architecture that is composed of convolution layers.

18.2.1.2 For meshes

Many mesh visual quality metrics have been proposed in the literature in the past 15 years [99,100]. Existing metrics are mostly FR. Most of them also follow the classical top-down approach used in image quality assessment: local feature differences between the reference and distorted meshes are computed at vertex level, and then pooled over the entire 3D model to obtain a global quality score. Whereas pioneering techniques were limited to evaluating geometry distortions only, most recent ones incorporate color/texture information. Moreover, machine learning and, more recently, deep learning approaches are gaining in popularity. This allows, among other benefits, the emergence of NR methods. The paragraphs that follow detail existing mesh quality metrics.

As mentioned earlier, pioneering metrics evaluated only geometric distortions, i.e., they rely on geometric characteristics of the mesh without considering its appearance attributes. Primary works used simple geometric measures, such as Hausdorff distance [101], MSE, root mean squared (RMS) error [102] and PSNR. These measures quickly demonstrated a poor correlation with the human vision, since they ignore perceptual information [103]. Hence, encouraging the development of more perceptually driven visual quality metrics. One of the first proposed metrics combined the RMS geometric distance between corresponding vertices with the RMS distance of their Laplacian coordinates, which reflect the degree of surface smoothness [104]. A strain energy field-based measure (SEF) was also developed by Bian et al. in [105]. This metric is based on the energy introduced by a specific mesh distortion; that is, the more the mesh is deformed, the greater the probability of perceiving the difference between the reference and distorted meshes. Some authors were inspired by IQMs. For instance, Lavoué et al. [54,66] proposed two metrics, called mesh structural distortion measure (MSDM) and MSDM2, inspired by the well-known SSIM [106]. In particular, the authors extended the SSIM to meshes by using the mesh curvature as an alternative for the pixel intensities. MSDM2 is adapted for meshes with different connectivities. Torkhani et al. [107] also proposed a metric based on local differences in curvature statistics. They included a visual masking model to their metric. Other works considered the dihedral angle differences between the compared meshes to devise their metric, such as the dihedral angle mesh error (DAME) metric [35]. The above metrics consider local variations at the vertices or edges. Corsini et al. [55] proceeded differently. They computed one global roughness value per 3D model considering dihedral angles and variance of the geometric Laplacian, and then derived a simple global roughness difference. In a similar approach, Wang et al. [108] proposed a metric called fast mesh perceptual distance (FMPD) based on global roughness computed using the Gaussian curvature. A survey [99] detailed these works and showed that MSDM2 [66], DAME [35], and FMPD [108] are excellent predictors of visual quality.

Besides these works on global visual quality assessment (top-down approaches adapted for supra-threshold distortions), few works based on bottom-up approaches were proposed. Nader et al. [109] introduced a bottom-up visibility threshold predictor for 3D meshes. Guo et al. [110] also studied the local visibility of geometric artifacts and showed that curvature could be a good predictor of distortion visibility.

Several works used machine learning techniques in assessing the quality of meshes, with multi-linear regression adopted to optimize the weights of several mesh descriptors [111], or support vector regression (SVR) used to fuse selected features to obtain a quality metric [112]. Recently, a machine learning-based approach for evaluating the quality of 3D meshes was proposed, in which crowd-sourced data is used, while learning the parameters of a distance metric [113].

Moving to dynamic meshes, Váša et al. [42] proposed a metric, called STED, based on the comparison of mesh edge lengths and vertex displacements between two animations. Torkhani et al. [43] devised a quality metric for dynamic meshes, which is a combination of spatial and temporal features. In more recent work, Yildiz et al. [114] developed a bottom-up approach incorporating both the spatial and temporal sensitivity of the HVS to predict the visibility of local distortions on the mesh surface.

For some use cases, the reference might not be available. Therefore NR quality assessment metrics are needed. Unlike FR metrics, few NR quality metrics for meshes have been proposed in the literature. These metrics are based on data-driven approaches (machine learning). Abouelaziz et al. [115] proposed an NR metric that relies on the mean curvature features and the general regression neural network (GRNN) for quality prediction. The blind mesh quality assessment index (BMQI), proposed in [116], is based on the visual saliency and SVR, whereas that proposed in [117] is based on dihedral angles and SVR. Abouelaziz et al. [118] also used CNNs to assess the quality of meshes. The CNN was fed with perceptual hand-crafted features (dihedral angles) extracted from the mesh and presented as 2D patches.

All the works presented above consider only the geometry of the mesh, and therefore only evaluate geometric distortions. Regarding 3D content with color or material information, little work has been published. For meshes with diffuse texture, Pan et al. [36] derived from the results of a subjective experiment a quantitative metric that approximates perceptual quality based on texture and geometry (wireframe) resolution. Tian et al. [119] and Guo et al. [37] proposed metrics based on a weighted combination of a global distance on the geometry and a global distance on the texture image. Tian et al. [119] combined the MSE computed on the mesh vertices with that computed on the texture pixels, whereas Guo et al. [37] linearly combined MSDM2 [66] (for mesh quality) and SSIM [106] (for texture quality) metrics. These metrics combine errors computed on different domains (mesh and texture image). Very recently, Nehmé et al. [39] introduced the color mesh distortion measure (CMDM), which, to this date, is the only model-based quality metric for meshes with colors attributes that works entirely on the mesh domain. This metric incorporates perceptually relevant geometry and color features and is based on a data-driven approach. It can be viewed as the mesh version of the point cloud metric PCQM [78].

As can be seen, most existing model-based quality metrics ignore the visual saliency information, yet finding salient regions (regions that attract the attention of observers) has become a useful tool for many applications, such as mesh simplification [120] and segmentation [121], and quality control of VR videos (360 videos) [122,123]. A recent work has investigated how incorporating saliency information into a model-based metric can improve the predicted quality [124]. Authors devised an extension of the CMDM metric [39] by combining its geometry and color features with the visual attention complexity (VAC) feature based on visual saliency dispersion proposed in [125]. Integrating the VAC was found to improve the overall performance of CMDM, especially when assessing the quality of geometrically quantized stimuli.

18.2.2 Image-based approaches

To evaluate the quality of 3D content, several authors considered IQMs computed on rendered snapshots, as depicted in Fig. 18.7. These approaches can be efficient since the field of image quality assessment is highly developed, and many successful IQMs have been introduced, such as the Sarnoff VDM [126], SSIM [106] (and its derivatives), VIF [127], FSIM [128], HDR-VDP2 [129], iCID [130], BLIINDS [131], GMSD [132], DeepSIM [133], LPIPS [134], WaDIQaM [135], NIMA [136], and PieAPP [137].

The image-based approach was first used to drive perceptually based tasks, such as mesh simplification [138,139]. So far, mainly FR approaches have been proposed for quality evaluation of 3D data of both meshes and point clouds. That is, views of the original and the distorted contents are captured under identical camera parameters, and a quality prediction is obtained as an average, or a weighted average of individual objective scores.

Image-based metrics allow holistic capture of both topology and color distortions as reflected by the corresponding rendering application. However, several factors affect the image-based metrics' computations. In particular, the rendering scheme that is employed to display the 3D data together with the environmental and lighting conditions, the number of cameras (or viewpoints), the configuration of each camera's parameters for the acquisition of model views, and the pooling of quality scores obtained for differ-

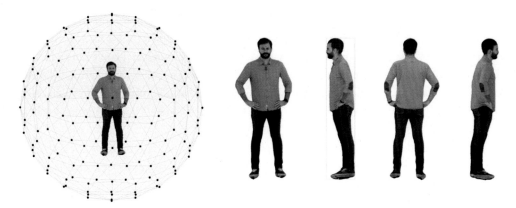

Figure 18.7 A common camera arrangement to capture views of a 3D model is illustrated on the left. The camera positions (i.e., black points) are typically selected to be uniformly distributed across a surrounding sphere. Snapshots of the 3D model are presented on the right, as captured from the front, right, back, and left cameras.

ent views into a single global quality score. Hence, image-based metrics are considered to be rendering-dependent and view-dependent solutions [29,54], which are opposed to the rendering-agnostic, model-based methods. The impact of such factors is further discussed in subsection 18.2.3.

In what follow, we first present the image-based metrics for point clouds, then those for meshes.

18.2.2.1 For point clouds

Image-based approaches were first used for point cloud imaging in the work of de Queiroz et al. [140]. Their prediction accuracy on point cloud contents was initially examined by Torlig et al. [47]. Concretely, the PSNR, SSIM [106], MS-SSIM [141], and VIF [127] (applied on the pixel domain) were executed on images after orthographic projection of the reference and distorted point clouds on the faces of a surrounding cube. The results showed that the MS-SSIM was the best candidate, achieving better performance than the model-based alternatives available at the time. The same conclusions regarding the effectiveness of MS-SSIM were drawn in another study using the same point cloud contents, but under a different rendering technique; that is, the point clouds were rendered using cubic primitives of locally adaptive size both for subjective evaluation and for the computation of image-based metrics; [28].

The first image-based metric tailored for point cloud contents was proposed by Yang et al. [48], relying on a weighted combination of global and local features extracted from texture and depth images. Specifically, the Jensen-Shannon divergence on the luminance channel serves as the global feature, whereas a depth edge map that reflects discontinuities, a texture similarity applied on color components, and an estimated content complexity factor account for the local features. Another approach, proposed by He et al. [142] was to project color and curvature values on planar surfaces. In this case, color impairments are evaluated using probabilities of local intensity differences, together with statistics of their residual intensities, and similarity values between chromatic components. The geometric distortions are evaluated based on statistics of curvature residuals.

A hybrid method that uses both image- and model-based algorithms is presented by Chen et al. [143]. In particular, the point clouds are divided into non-overlapping partitions, called layers. A planarization process takes place at each layer, before applying the IW-SSIM [144] to assess geometric distortions. Color impairments are evaluated using RGB-based variants of similarity measurements defined in [78]. A linear model is employed to assign optimal weights on the defined features.

A deep neural network architecture, namely PQA-Net, was proposed by Liu et al. [145] for NR quality assessment of point clouds. In this method, features are extracted from multiple views after a series of CNN blocks and, after fusion, they are shared between a distortion identifier and a quality predictor to obtain a final quality score.

Wu et al. [52] apply popular IQMs on patches from geometry and texture images. The patches are obtained after segmenting the reference point cloud into point clusters based on normal vectors. To ensure pixel matching between the reference and the distorted patch, for every reference point, its nearest distorted point is identified, and both are projected on the same pixel locations. Results show substantial improvements with respect to the application of the same IQMs on the six sides of models' bounding boxes. The IW-SSIM was found to achieve best performance.

A learning-based approach based on patches from projected maps of geometry and texture, as implemented in V-PCC, is presented by Tao et al. [146]. The proposed network makes use of a joint color-geometric feature extractor, two-stage multi-scale feature fusion, and spatial pooling. The extractor is composed of sequential CNNs to extract multi-scale features from geometry and color patches separately, with corresponding features maps subsequently fused. The spatial pooling module consists of two fully-connected layer branches that perform (a) quality prediction and (b) weight allocation, per patch. The final score is obtained as a weighted average across all patches.

18.2.2.2 For meshes

IQMs, notably VDP [147] and SSIM [106], were used to study the relationship between the viewing distance and the perceptibility of model details to optimize the level-of-detail (LoD) design of complex 3D building facades [148]. SSIM [106] was also used to optimize textured mesh transmission [149]. Considering a view-independent approach, the RMS error was computed on snapshots taken from different viewpoints (different camera positions regularly sampled on a bounding sphere) to evaluate the impact of simplification on 3D models [150].

Recently, several authors have started to exploit CNNs to assess the quality of meshes using an image-based approach. Most of the existing works considered geometry-only meshes (without color attributes). In [151], the CNN was fed with 2D rendered images of the mesh generated by rotating the object. Another quality metric for meshes was devised by extracting feature vectors from 3 different CNN models and combining them using an extension of the compact bi-linear pooling (CMP) [152]. The authors used a patch-selection strategy based on mesh saliency to give more importance to perceptually relevant (attractive) regions. In fact, not all regions of the 3D model image receive the same level of attention from observers.

A more recent metric called graphics-LPIPS was proposed for assessing the quality of rendered 3D graphics [41]. The metric is an extension of the LPIPS metric (originally designed for images and perceptual similarity tasks) [134], which has been adapted to 3D graphics and quality assessment tasks based on DSIS. Graphics-LPIPS is computed on patches of snapshots of the rendered 3D models and employs a CNN (the AlexNet architecture more precisely) with learning linear weights on top. The overall quality of the 3D model is derived by averaging local patch qualities.

18.2.3 Comparison between model-based and image-based approaches

Several works compared the performance of image-based metrics and model-based approaches for quality assessment of 3D models [16–18,28,29,39,47,52,103]. Results indicate that both approaches are having their merits, with model-based generally showing higher generalization capabilities across contents and distortions. Table 18.3 summarizes advantages and disadvantages, as well as use cases of each approach.

The main advantage of using image-based metrics to evaluate the visual quality of 3D objects is their natural handling of complex interactions between different data properties involved in the appearance (geometry, color or texture information, and normals), which avoids the problem of how to combine and weight them [150]. For instance, using IQMs on projected views of 3D models simultaneously captures geometric and chromatic degradation as reflected in the renderer, in addition to the natural incorporation of the complex rendering pipeline (computation of light material interactions and rasterization), thus capturing 3D content as experienced/perceived by users.

On the other hand, these methods require prior knowledge of the final rendering of the stimuli, i.e., the lighting conditions and the viewpoint, since they operate on 2D rendered snapshots. Additionally, they depend on the choice of 2D views employed to estimate a quality score. In particular, the selection of camera positions, camera parameters, number of viewpoints, and pooling applied across different views, will lead to different quality characterizations for the same 3D model.

Table 18.3 Overview of the advantages, disadvantages, and use cases of the image-based and model-based approaches.

	Model-based approaches	Image-based approaches
Advantages	• Independent of the final rendering & the displayed viewpoint • Practical for driving processing operations	Natural ability to handle: • multimodal nature of data • complex rendering pipeline
Disadvantages	Sophisticated algorithms to handle: • multimodal nature of data • complex rendering pipeline	• Prior knowledge of the final rendering & the displayed viewpoint • The choice of 2D views, their number, and the pooling method
Use cases	• Evaluating different distortions applied to different 3D models • Driving perceptually based tasks	• Evaluating the quality of different versions of the same object under a single type of distortion

In these frameworks, the number of views and the camera parameters are set to cover the maximum surface of a model under evaluation. However, using a large number of views/cameras leads to redundancies and extra computational costs, without guaranteeing performance improvements, as indicated in [28]. When applying IQMs on projected views of a 3D model, excluding pixels that don't belong to the effective part of the displayed model (i.e., background filtering), was found to improve the accuracy of the predicted quality [28]. Moreover, non-uniform weightings that increase the impact of quality scores from views that are more relevant may improve the prediction performance. Alexiou et al. [28] showed that estimating the global quality score by incorporating importance weights based on user inspection time is beneficial in terms of prediction accuracy (i.e., better performance than uniform weighting) and computational costs (i.e., less views are required to be captured, especially in dense camera arrangements). Wu et al. [52] incorporated a weighting function based on the ratio of projected area of that model view with respect to the total amount, observing performance improvements. Weighted views have been also considered in [103] for objective quality evaluation of meshes, with importance weights obtained based on a surface visibility algorithm [153], typically used for viewpoint preference selection [154].

Overall, image-based metrics are not practical for driving processing operations (e.g., mesh simplification). Model-based metrics are better suited instead, since they operate on the same representation space with the corresponding processing algorithms; thus it is possible to control processing operations both globally (on the entire model) and locally (on the vertex/point level). At the same time, they typically require complex processes to effectively capture perceptually relevant features. Moreover, it is not straightforward how to fuse information extracted from different attributes (e.g., geometry, texture) to obtain a total quality score.

Last but not least, the performance of image-based metrics greatly depends on distortions and contents. They are less accurate in differentiating and ranking different distortions, or distortions applied to different 3D models, which is not the case for model-based metrics [39,103].

18.2.4 Objective quality assessment in volumetric video

As video is a collection of still frames, volumetric video is also a collection of 3D models aggregated together, which are played back at a certain frame rate to create the motion perception. Temporal sub-sampling rate (i.e., frame rate) can be defined as the frequency of the consecutive models in the temporal axis of the volumetric video sequence. Utilizing all available frames in the volumetric video sequence is the common approach for objective quality evaluation. After predicting quality of each frame in the sequence, a temporal pooling method (e.g., arithmetic mean) is necessary to merge individual frame scores into a final quality score [23,24]. This is also commonly done in traditional video quality assessment, while extending the quality metrics that are developed for images to video [155]. However, one of the challenges for objective quality assessment of volumetric video is that the sizes of volumetric video sequences are big, and estimating objective quality can be time-consuming and computationally heavy. Reducing temporal sub-sampling rate and choosing appropriate pooling strategy may reduce the computational complexity without sacrificing from the prediction accuracy.

In a recent study, Ak et al. [156] investigated the performance of 30 quality metrics for 7 different temporal sampling methodologies over 8 different temporal sub-sampling rates. The study was conducted on the VsenseVVDB2 dataset [8], only on the point cloud sequences. The VsenseVVDB2 dataset contains 8 point cloud volumetric video sequences of 10 seconds length with 30 frames per second (fps). The utilized pooling methods are summarized in Table 18.4. Each pooling method was used with the following 8 different frame rates: {1, 2, 3, 5, 6, 10, 15, 30}. The frame rates were selected to ensure a uniform sampling.

Results are presented in Fig. 18.8, where SROCC is used to measure the performance of objective quality metrics. 11 image-based, 19 model-based metrics were evaluated on 56 combinations of 7 sub-sampling methods and 8 sub-sampling frequencies. Lighter colors indicate higher correlation with subjective opinions. Each row corresponds to a different quality metric indicated by the row number. Each column shows a different combination of temporal sub-sampling frequency and temporal sub-sampling method. Columns are divided into 7 groups by the sub-sampling method indicated at the bottom of the figure. For each sub-sampling method, frame rate increases from left to right.

Table 18.4 Definitions and selected parameters for pooling methods.

Sampling method	Formula	Parameter
Arithmetic mean	$Q = \dfrac{1}{N} \sum_{i=1}^{N} q_i$	–
Harmonic mean	$Q = \left(\dfrac{1}{N} \sum_{i=1}^{N} q_i^{-1} \right)^{-1}$	–
Minkowski mean	$Q = \left(\dfrac{1}{N} \sum_{i=1}^{N} q_i^{p} \right)^{1/p}$	$p = 2$
VQ pooling	$Q = \dfrac{\sum_{i \in G_L} q_i + w \cdot \sum_{i \in G_H} q_i}{|G_L| + w \cdot |G_H|},\ w = \left(1 - \dfrac{M_L}{M_H} \right)^2$	–
Percentile pooling	$Q = \dfrac{1}{|P_{low}|} \sum_{i \in P_{low}} q_i$	Percentile = 10%
Primacy pooling	$Q = \sum_{i=1}^{N} w_i q_i,\ w_i = \dfrac{\exp(-\alpha i)}{\sum_{j=1}^{L} \exp(-\alpha j)},\ 0 \le i \le L$	$L = 360,\ \alpha = 0.01$
Recency pooling	$Q = \sum_{i=1}^{N} w_i q_i,\ w_i = \dfrac{\exp(-\alpha (L-i))}{\sum_{j=1}^{L} \exp(-\alpha (L-j))},\ 0 \le i \le L$	$L = 360,\ \alpha = 0.01$

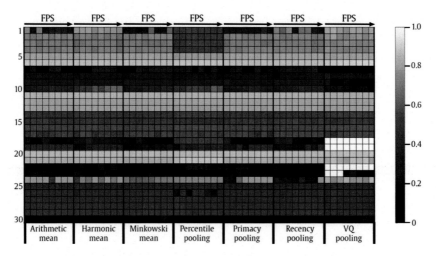

Figure 18.8 Metric performances in terms of SROCC for a number of sampling methodologies and sub-sampling rates. 1) MP-PSNR-FR, 2) MP-PSNR-RR, 3) MW-PSNR-FR, 4) MW-PSNR-RR, 5) PSNR, 6) SSIM, 7) NIQSV, 8) NIQSV+, 9) APT, 10) EM-IQM, 11) SI-IQM, 12) Color-Y, 13) Color-Y-PSNR, 14) Color-U, 15) Color-U-PSNR, 16) Color-V, 17) Color-V-PSNR, 18) point-to-point-Haus, 19) point-to-point-Haus-PSNR, 20) point-to-point-RMS, 21) point-to-point-RMS-PSNR, 22) point-to-plane-Haus, 23) point-to-plane-Haus-PSNR, 24) point-to-plane-RMS, 25) point-to-plane-RMS-PSNR, 26) plane-to-plane-MSE, 27) plane-to-plane-RMS, 28) plane-to-plane-Mean, 29) plane-to-plane-Median, 30) plane-to-plane-Min.

Results indicate, for any given temporal sampling method, using a lower frame-rate does not result in a lower performance. Even by sub-sampling by 1 fps, metrics performances do not show a significant difference compared to the full frame rate available (i.e., 30 fps). This observation indicates that compression artifacts affect the perceived quality of the volumetric video uniformly in time. For similar distortions, with no significant loss in the accuracy of objective quality metrics, calculations can be sped up to 30 times for stimuli.

Each considered pooling method has a different priority for the temporal dimension. Results in Fig. 18.8 show non-significant changes in metric performances with various pooling methods. Similar to the sub-sampling rate analysis, this occurs due to uniform presence of the compression distortions on the point clouds in the volumetric video sequences. Considering the non-significant performance difference of the quality metrics for various temporal sampling methods, arithmetic mean is the most efficient alternative due to computational simplicity.

It is worth noting that only point clouds of human bodies are used in this study, and early trials show that these findings might be valid for meshes and other types of 3D graphics as well. Although this needs further experimentation and validation by peer-review processes, using a reduced number of 3D models without sacrificing the metric accuracy can be very beneficial for wide deployment of volumetric video streaming.

18.2.5 Publicly available software implementations

As described in previous subsections, there are many different approaches in estimating the visual quality of volumetric video. In most cases, during the development of new objective quality metrics, a comparison is needed to validate the newly developed metrics's performance. To help future scientists and developers in their goals to propose more accurate quality metrics, publicly available implementations of existing methods are listed in Table 18.5. As can be seen, objective quality metrics for volumetric video can be grouped in different categories, with respect to 3D representation (i.e., mesh or point cloud); whether they demand color attributes or not; metric class in terms of reference data requirement; and domain of operation (i.e., model or image). Furthermore, a brief description of the features that each metric relies upon are indicated, along with a link to the open-source code.

18.3. Conclusion

Volumetric video is a novel form of visual representation that enables us to view at reconstructed 3D models from any viewpoint, which brings different challenges and limitations for visual quality assessment. The most important challenges are in understanding and estimating user interaction, selecting the correct 3D representation, and setting various conditions in applications such as rendering parameters and display

Table 18.5 Publicly available objective quality metric implementations for meshes & point clouds.

Metric	3D Representation	Attributes	Class	Domain	Features	Open-source code
Metro (1998) [102]	Mesh	Colorless	FR	Model-based	Mean error	https://sourceforge.net/projects/vcg/
Mesh (2002) [101]	Mesh	Colorless	FR	Model-based	Hausdorff distance	https://github.com/arnaudgelas/mesh
MSDM2 (2011) [54,66]	Mesh	Colorless	FR	Model-based	Local differences in curvature statistics	https://github.com/MEPP-team/MEPP2
TPDM (2014) [107]	Mesh	Colorless	FR	Model-based	Local differences in curvature tensor	http://www.gipsa-lab.fr/~fakhri.torkhani/software/TPDM.rar
DAME (2012) [35]	Mesh	Colorless	FR	Model-based	local differences in dihedral angles	http://meshcompression.org/software-tools
FMPD (2012) [108]	Mesh	Colorless	FR	Model-based	Global roughness using Gaussian curvature	http://www.gipsa-lab.grenoble-inp.fr/~kai.wang/publications_en.html
JND (2016) [109]	Mesh	Colorless	FR	Model-based	(bottom-up) visibility threshold predictor based on local contrast and spatial frequency	https://github.com/MEPP-team/MEPP2
Yildiz et al. (2020) [113]	Mesh	Colorless	FR	Model-based	Learning geometric parameters of a distance metric using crowd-sourced data	https://www.dropbox.com/s/m3bnb93vun91763/Learning.VQA.zip?dl=0

continued on next page

Table 18.5 (*continued*)

Metric	3D Representation	Attributes	Class	Domain	Features	Open-source code
STED (2011) [42]	Dynamic mesh	Colorless	FR	Model-based	Local differences in edge length (spatial and temporal parts)	http://meshcompression.org/software-tools
CMDM (2021) [39]	Mesh	Colored	FR	Model-based	Local differences in curvature and color statistics	https://github.com/MEPP-team/MEPP2
Graphics-LPIPS (2022) [41]	Mesh	Colored	FR	Image-based	CNN with linear weights on top	https://github.com/YanaNEHME/Graphics-LPIPS
Plane-to-plane (2018) [73]	Point cloud	Colorless	FR	Model-based	Angular similarity between normal vectors	https://github.com/mmspg/point-cloud-angular-similarity-metric
PC-MSDM (2019) [77]	Point cloud	Colorless	FR	Model-based	Curvature statistics	https://github.com/MEPP-team/PC-MSDM
PCQM (2020) [78]	Point cloud	Colored	FR	Model-based	Curvature and color statistics	https://github.com/MEPP-team/PCQM
Hist_Y (2020) [92]	Point cloud	Colored	FR	Model-based	Luminance histogram	https://github.com/cwi-dis/point-cloud-color-metric
PointSSIM (2020) [79]	Point cloud	Colored	FR	Model-based	Location, angular similarity, curvature, or luminance statistics	https://github.com/mmspg/pointssim
Point-to-distribution (2020) [75]	Point cloud	Colored	FR	Model-based	Mahalanobis distance of point coordinates and luminance	https://github.com/AlirezaJav/Point_to_distribution_metric

continued on next page

Table 18.5 (*continued*)

Metric	3D Representation	Attributes	Class	Domain	Features	Open-source code
PCM_RR (2020) [93]	Point cloud	Colored	RR	Model-based	Location, angular similarity and luminance histograms	https://github.com/cwi-dis/PCM_RR
GraphSIM (2020) [83]	Point cloud	Colored	FR	Model-based	Color gradient statistics around keypoints using graphs	https://github.com/NJUVISION/GraphSIM
Perceptual loss (2021) [98]	Point cloud	Colorless	FR	Model-based	Differences in latent space after auto-encoding voxel grids with binary or truncated distance fields	https://github.com/mauriceqch/2021_pc_perceptual_loss
BitDance (2021) [91]	Point cloud	Colored	FR	Model-based	Bit-based differences of colors using CIEDE2000 and normal vectors	https://github.com/rafael2k/bitdance-pc_metric
MS-GraphSIM (2021) [84]	Point cloud	Colored	FR	Model-based	Color gradient statistics on multi-scale representations around keypoints using graphs	https://github.com/zyj1318053/MS_GraphSIM
PointPCA (2021) [82]	Point cloud	Colored	FR	Model-based	Statistics on PCA-based geometric descriptors and luminance	https://github.com/cwi-dis/pointpca
PQA-Net (2021) [145]	Point cloud	Colored	NR	Image-based	Multi-view CNN-based features fed to a distortion identifier and a quality predictor	https://github.com/qdushl/PQA-Net

devices. This chapter provides a wide overview of quality assessment and estimation methodologies through subjective user studies and objective quality estimators for volumetric content.

With the increased degrees of freedom, users need to interact with the media itself. This makes user interaction a crucial part of subjective quality assessment. Nevertheless, there are no recommendations or standards for conducting user studies for volumetric video in 6DoF. Therefore experimenters adapted various methodologies for subjective user studies that were developed for traditional image and video quality assessment with different parameters for various aspects. These involve the 3D representation, temporal variation, attributes, mode of inspection, subjective test methodology, distortion types, rendering parameters, and display devices, among others. Ground truth subjective quality scores were collected as part of these studies, with publicly released datasets reported in this chapter. Comparative studies show that there are certain cases that selecting one approach is more efficient than others. When compressed with state-of-the-art codecs, point clouds seem to be better at low-bandwidth conditions, whereas meshes are better at high-bandwidth conditions or storage cases. Interactive and non-interactive experiments generally do not have statistically significant differences. Nevertheless, interactive visualization approaches might be more suitable, as they better simulate targeted use cases, with human judgments implicitly incorporating effects of display devices, rendering parameters, higher DoF, and immersion, to name a few. Among the commonly used subjective methodologies, the DSIS seems to be more accurate by yielding lower uncertainty regarding the level of impairment perceived in a stimulus. However, such a methodology may lead to comparative scores.

Automatic estimation of volumetric video quality via objective quality metrics is still under development. Model-based approaches rely on the primary 3D data structure. The unique nature of volumetric video enables its representation with meshes and point clouds. Since point clouds do not have connectivity information, the majority of corresponding metrics focus on capturing underlying 3D surfaces. Early attempts for both point clouds and meshes are based on simple error measurements, whereas more recent efforts combine various features from geometry and/or texture domain. Image-based approaches, on the other hand, focus on projecting the 3D model onto planar arrangements and often making use of 2D quality metrics. Comparative studies show both approaches have different advantages and disadvantages. Although image-based approaches require rendering and camera parameters to be set beforehand, they take all the rendering effects into account, while estimating the quality. Model-based approaches generate scores that are independent of the viewpoint; however, they need to be rather complex to take human visual perception into account, which usually results in high computational demands. The selection of either approach depends on the application, as they both have strengths and weaknesses. Recent studies also show that to estimate volumetric video quality for compression scenarios, we do not need to compute the metric results for all of the frames (i.e., consecutive 3D models in a volumetric video). Since most compression methods generate distortions that do not change by time, selecting fewer frames yields as accurate quality estimations as computing it over all frames, although further experimentation is required at this front.

With the popularization of XR technologies and applications on the Internet, social media, and metaverse(s), the volumetric video will become more popular. Volumetric video will be used in different mixed XR applications alongside other types of 3D graphics, and there will be a need for new methodologies to capture the human perception and predict human opinions about visual quality within these mixed-media environments. This makes the field of visual quality assessment very relevant, and open to the new challenges the upcoming advances will bring.

References

[1] A. Perkis, C. Timmerer, S. Baraković, J. Baraković Husić, S. Bech, S. Bosse, J. Botev, K. Brunnström, L. Cruz, K. De Moor, A. de Polo Saibanti, W. Durnez, S. Egger-Lampl, U. Engelke, T.H. Falk, J. Gutiérrez, A. Hameed, A. Hines, T. Kojic, D. Kukolj, E. Liotou, D. Milovanovic, S. Möller, N. Murray, B. Naderi, M. Pereira, S. Perry, A. Pinheiro, A. Pinilla, A. Raake, S.R. Agrawal, U. Reiter, R. Rodrigues, R. Schatz, P. Schelkens, S. Schmidt, S.S. Sabet, A. Singla, L. Skorin-Kapov, M. Suznjevic, S. Uhrig, S. Vlahović, J.-N. Voigt-Antons, S. Zadtootaghaj, QUALINET white paper, on definitions of immersive media experience (IMEx), European Network on Quality of Experience in Multimedia, Systems and Services, 14th QUALINET meeting (online), https://arxiv.org/abs/2007.07032, May 2020.
[2] S. Schwarz, M. Preda, V. Baroncini, M. Budagavi, P. Cesar, P.A. Chou, R.A. Cohen, M. Krivokuća, S. Lasserre, Z. Li, J. Llach, K. Mammou, R. Mekuria, O. Nakagami, E. Siahaan, A. Tabatabai, A.M. Tourapis, V. Zakharchenko, Emerging MPEG standards for point cloud compression, IEEE Journal on Emerging and Selected Topics in Circuits and Systems 9 (1) (2019) 133–148, https://doi.org/10.1109/JETCAS.2018.2885981.
[3] T. Ebrahimi, S. Foessel, F. Pereira, P. Schelkens, JPEG Pleno: Toward an efficient representation of visual reality, IEEE MultiMedia 23 (4) (2016) 14–20, https://doi.org/10.1109/MMUL.2016.64.
[4] ITU-T, Subjective video quality assessment methods for multimedia applications, ITU-T Recommendation P.910, Apr 2008.
[5] ITU-R, Methodology for the subjective assessment of the quality of television pictures, ITU-R Recommendation BT.500, Jan 2012.
[6] F. Kozamernik, V. Steinmann, P. Sunna, E. Wyckens, SAMVIQ—A new EBU methodology for video quality evaluations in multimedia, SMPTE Motion Imaging Journal 114 (4) (2005) 152–160.
[7] N. Ponomarenko, L. Jin, O. Ieremeiev, V. Lukin, K. Egiazarian, J. Astola, B. Vozel, K. Chehdi, M. Carli, F. Battisti, et al., Image database TID2013: Peculiarities, results and perspectives, Signal Processing. Image Communication 30 (2015) 57–77.
[8] E. Zerman, C. Ozcinar, P. Gao, A. Smolic, Textured mesh vs coloured point cloud: A subjective study for volumetric video compression, in: 2020 Twelfth International Conference on Quality of Multimedia Experience (QoMEX), IEEE, 2020, pp. 1–6.
[9] P. Le Callet, S. Möller, A. Perkis, Qualinet white paper on definitions of quality of experience, European Network on Quality of Experience in Multimedia Systems and Services (COST Action IC 1003), Lausanne, Switzerland, Version 1.2, Mar 2013.
[10] ITU-T, Subjective test methodologies for 360° video on head-mounted displays, ITU-T Recommendation P.919, Oct 2020.
[11] J. Gutierrez, P. Perez, M. Orduna, A. Singla, C. Cortes, P. Mazumdar, I. Viola, K. Brunnstrom, F. Battisti, N. Cieplinska, et al., Subjective evaluation of visual quality and simulator sickness of short 360 videos: ITU-T Rec, IEEE Transactions on Multimedia (2021) 919.

[12] ITU-T, Subjective test method for interactive virtual reality applications, ITU-T Work Programme P.IntVr, https://www.itu.int/itu-t/workprog/wp_item.aspx?isn=17045. (Accessed 19 January 2022).

[13] ITU-T, QoE assessment of extended reality (XR) meetings, ITU-T Work Programme P.QXM, https://www.itu.int/itu-t/workprog/wp_item.aspx?isn=15113. (Accessed 19 January 2022).

[14] A. Javaheri, C. Brites, F. Pereira, J. Ascenso, Subjective and objective quality evaluation of compressed point clouds, in: 2017 IEEE 19th International Workshop on Multimedia Signal Processing (MMSP), 2017, pp. 1–6, https://doi.org/10.1109/MMSP.2017.8122239.

[15] H. Su, Z. Duanmu, W. Liu, Q. Liu, Z. Wang, Perceptual quality assessment of 3D point clouds, in: 2019 IEEE International Conference on Image Processing (ICIP), 2019, pp. 3182–3186.

[16] D. Lazzarotto, E. Alexiou, T. Ebrahimi, Benchmarking of objective quality metrics for point cloud compression, in: 2021 IEEE 23rd International Workshop on Multimedia Signal Processing (MMSP), 2021, pp. 1–6.

[17] L.A. da Silva Cruz, E. Dumić, E. Alexiou, J. Prazeres, R. Duarte, M. Pereira, A. Pinheiro, T. Ebrahimi, Point cloud quality evaluation: Towards a definition for test conditions, in: 2019 Eleventh International Conference on Quality of Multimedia Experience (QoMEX), 2019, pp. 1–6, https://doi.org/10.1109/QoMEX.2019.8743258.

[18] S. Perry, H.P. Cong, L.A. da Silva Cruz, J. Prazeres, M. Pereira, A. Pinheiro, E. Dumic, E. Alexiou, T. Ebrahimi, Quality evaluation of static point clouds encoded using MPEG codecs, in: 2020 IEEE International Conference on Image Processing (ICIP), 2020, pp. 3428–3432, https://doi.org/10.1109/ICIP40778.2020.9191308.

[19] E. Alexiou, T. Ebrahimi, M.V. Bernardo, M. Pereira, A. Pinheiro, L.A. Da Silva Cruz, C. Duarte, L.G. Dmitrovic, E. Dumic, D. Matkovics, A. Skodras, Point cloud subjective evaluation methodology based on 2D rendering, in: 2018 Tenth International Conference on Quality of Multimedia Experience (QoMEX), 2018, pp. 1–6, https://doi.org/10.1109/QoMEX.2018.8463406.

[20] E. Alexiou, A.M.G. Pinheiro, C. Duarte, D. Matković, E. Dumić, L.A. da Silva Cruz, L.G. Dmitrović, M.V. Bernardo, M. Pereira, T. Ebrahimi, Point cloud subjective evaluation methodology based on reconstructed surfaces, in: A.G. Tescher (Ed.), Applications of Digital Image Processing XLI, vol. 10752, International Society for Optics and Photonics, SPIE, 2018, pp. 160–173.

[21] A. Javaheri, C. Brites, F. Pereira, J. Ascenso, Point cloud rendering after coding: impacts on subjective and objective quality, arXiv preprint, arXiv:1912.09137, 2019.

[22] R. Mekuria, S. Laserre, C. Tulvan, Performance assessment of point cloud compression, in: 2017 IEEE Visual Communications and Image Processing (VCIP), 2017, pp. 1–4, https://doi.org/10.1109/VCIP.2017.8305132.

[23] Emin Zerman, Pan Gao, Cagri Ozcinar, Aljosa Smolic, Subjective and objective quality assessment for volumetric video compression, in: Proc. IS&T Int'l. Symp. on Electronic Imaging: Image Quality and System Performance XVI, 2019, pp. 323-1–323-7, https://doi.org/10.2352/ISSN.2470-1173.2019.10.IQSP-323.

[24] J. van der Hooft, M.T. Vega, C. Timmerer, A.C. Begen, F. De Turck, R. Schatz, Objective and subjective QoE evaluation for adaptive point cloud streaming, in: 2020 Twelfth International Conference on Quality of Multimedia Experience (QoMEX), 2020, pp. 1–6.

[25] E. Alexiou, T. Ebrahimi, On the performance of metrics to predict quality in point cloud representations, in: A.G. Tescher (Ed.), Applications of Digital Image Processing XL, vol. 10396, International Society for Optics and Photonics, SPIE, 2017, pp. 282–297.

[26] E. Alexiou, E. Upenik, T. Ebrahimi, Towards subjective quality assessment of point cloud imaging in augmented reality, in: 2017 IEEE 19th International Workshop on Multimedia Signal Processing (MMSP), 2017, pp. 1–6, https://doi.org/10.1109/MMSP.2017.8122237.

[27] A. Javaheri, C. Brites, F. Pereira, J. Ascenso, Subjective and objective quality evaluation of 3D point cloud denoising algorithms, in: 2017 IEEE International Conference on Multimedia Expo Workshops (ICMEW), 2017, pp. 1–6.

[28] E. Alexiou, T. Ebrahimi, Exploiting user interactivity in quality assessment of point cloud imaging, in: 2019 Eleventh International Conference on Quality of Multimedia Experience (QoMEX), 2019, pp. 1–6, https://doi.org/10.1109/QoMEX.2019.8743277.

[29] E. Alexiou, I. Viola, T.M. Borges, T.A. Fonseca, R.L. de Queiroz, T. Ebrahimi, A comprehensive study of the rate-distortion performance in MPEG point cloud compression, APSIPA Transactions on Signal and Information Processing 8 (2019) e27.

[30] M. Kazhdan, H. Hoppe, Screened Poisson surface reconstruction, ACM Transactions on Graphics 32 (3) (2013) 29, 13pp.

[31] MPEG 3DG and Requirements, Call for proposals for point cloud compression v2, ISO/IEC JTC1/SC29/WG11 Doc. N16763, Apr. 2017.

[32] J. van der Hooft, T. Wauters, F. De Turck, C. Timmerer, H. Hellwagner, Towards 6DoF HTTP adaptive streaming through point cloud compression, in: Proceedings of the 27th ACM International Conference on Multimedia, MM '19, Association for Computing Machinery, New York, NY, USA, 2019, pp. 2405–2413.

[33] Benjamin Watson, Alinda Friedman, Aaron McGaffey, Measuring and predicting visual fidelity, in: Proceedings of the 28th Annual Conference on Computer Graphics and Interactive Techniques, SIGGRAPH '01, Association for Computing Machinery, New York, NY, USA, 2001, pp. 213–220, https://doi.org/10.1145/383259.383283.

[34] B.E. Rogowitz, H.E. Rushmeier, Are image quality metrics adequate to evaluate the quality of geometric objects?, in: Human Vision and Electronic Imaging VI, in: Proc. SPIE, vol. 4299, 2001, https://doi.org/10.1117/12.429504.

[35] L. Váša, J. Rus, Dihedral Angle Mesh Error: a fast perception correlated distortion measure for fixed connectivity triangle meshes, Computer Graphics Forum 31 (5) (2012).

[36] Y. Pan, I. Cheng, A. Basu, Quality metric for approximating subjective evaluation of 3-D objects, IEEE Transactions on Multimedia 7 (2) (2005) 269–279, https://doi.org/10.1109/TMM.2005.843364.

[37] J. Guo, V. Vidal, I. Cheng, A. Basu, A. Baskurt, G. Lavoué, Subjective and objective visual quality assessment of textured 3D meshes, ACM Transactions on Applied Perception 14 (2016) 1–20, https://doi.org/10.1145/2996296.

[38] A. Doumanoglou, N. Zioulis, E. Christakis, D. Zarpalas, P. Daras, Subjective quality assessment of textured human full-body 3D-reconstructions, in: 2018 10th International Conference on Quality of Multimedia Experience, QoMEX 2018, 2018.

[39] Y. Nehmé, F. Dupont, J.-P. Farrugia, P. Le Callet, G. Lavoué, Visual quality of 3D meshes with diffuse colors in virtual reality: Subjective and objective evaluation, IEEE Transactions on Visualization and Computer Graphics 27 (3) (2021) 2202–2219, https://doi.org/10.1109/TVCG.2020.3036153.

[40] Y. Nehmé, J.-P. Farrugia, F. Dupont, P.L. Callet, G. Lavoué, Comparison of subjective methods for quality assessment of 3D graphics in virtual reality, ACM Transactions on Applied Perception 18 (1) (2020) 1–23, https://doi.org/10.1145/3427931.

[41] Y. Nehmé, F. Dupont, J.-P. Farrugia, P. Le Callet, G. Lavoué, Textured mesh quality assessment: Large-scale dataset and deep learning-based quality metric, arXiv preprint, arXiv:2202.02397, 2022.

[42] L. Váša, V. Skala, A perception correlated comparison method for dynamic meshes, IEEE Transactions on Visualization and Computer Graphics 17 (2011) 220–230, https://doi.org/10.1109/TVCG.2010.38.

[43] F. Torkhani, K. Wang, J.-M. Chassery, Perceptual quality assessment of 3D dynamic meshes: Subjective and objective studies, Signal Processing. Image Communication 31 (2) (2015) 185–204, https://doi.org/10.1016/j.image.2014.12.008.

[44] K. Vanhoey, B. Sauvage, P. Kraemer, G. Lavoué, Visual quality assessment of 3D models: On the influence of light-material interaction, ACM Transactions on Applied Perception 15 (1) (2017), https://doi.org/10.1145/3129505.

[45] Y. Nehmé, P.L. Callet, F. Dupont, J.-P. Farrugia, G. Lavoué, Exploring crowdsourcing for subjective quality assessment of 3D graphics, in: IEEE International Workshop on Multimedia Signal Processing (MMSP), 2021.

[46] E. Alexiou, T. Ebrahimi, On subjective and objective quality evaluation of point cloud geometry, in: 2017 Ninth International Conference on Quality of Multimedia Experience (QoMEX), 2017, pp. 1–3, https://doi.org/10.1109/QoMEX.2017.7965681.

[47] E.M. Torlig, E. Alexiou, T.A. Fonseca, R.L. de Queiroz, T. Ebrahimi, A novel methodology for quality assessment of voxelized point clouds, in: A.G. Tescher (Ed.), Applications of Digital

Image Processing XLI, vol. 10752, International Society for Optics and Photonics, SPIE, 2018, pp. 174–190.

[48] Qi Yang, Hao Chen, Zhan Ma, Yiling Xu, Rongjun Tang, Jun Sun, Predicting the perceptual quality of point cloud: A 3D-to-2D projection-based exploration, IEEE Transactions on Multimedia 23 (2020) 3877–3891, https://doi.org/10.1109/TMM.2020.3033117.

[49] R. Mekuria, K. Blom, P. Cesar, Design, Implementation, and Evaluation of a Point Cloud Codec for Tele-Immersive Video, IEEE Transactions on Circuits and Systems for Video Technology 27 (4) (2017) 828–842.

[50] E. Alexiou, N. Yang, T. Ebrahimi, PointXR: A toolbox for visualization and subjective evaluation of point clouds in virtual reality, in: 2020 Twelfth International Conference on Quality of Multimedia Experience (QoMEX), 2020, pp. 1–6, https://doi.org/10.1109/QoMEX48832.2020.9123121.

[51] S. Subramanyam, J. Li, I. Viola, P. Cesar, Comparing the quality of highly realistic digital humans in 3DoF and 6DoF: A volumetric video case study, in: 2020 IEEE Conference on Virtual Reality and 3D User Interfaces (VR), IEEE, 2020, pp. 127–136.

[52] X. Wu, Y. Zhang, C. Fan, J. Hou, S. Kwong, Subjective quality database and objective study of compressed point clouds with 6DoF head-mounted display, IEEE Transactions on Circuits and Systems for Video Technology 31 (12) (2021) 4630–4644.

[53] I. Viola, S. Subramanyam, J. Li, P. Cesar, On the impact of VR assessment on the quality of experience of highly realistic digital humans, Quality and User Experience 7 (1) (2022) 3, https://link.springer.com/article/10.1007/s41233-022-00050-3.

[54] G. Lavoué, E. Drelie Gelasca, F. Dupont, A. Baskurt, T. Ebrahimi, Perceptually driven 3D distance metrics with application to watermarking, in: Applications of Digital Image Processing XXIX, vol. 6312, 2006, pp. 150–161, https://doi.org/10.1117/12.686964.

[55] M. Corsini, E.D. Gelasca, T. Ebrahimi, M. Barni, Watermarked 3-D mesh quality assessment, IEEE Transactions on Multimedia 9 (2007) 247–256.

[56] G. Lavoué, A local roughness measure for 3D meshes and its application to visual masking, ACM Transactions on Applied Perception 5 (4) (2009), https://doi.org/10.1145/1462048.1462052.

[57] S. Silva, B.S. Santos, C. Ferreira, J. Madeira, A Perceptual Data Repository for Polygonal Meshes, in: 2009 Second International Conference in Visualisation, 2009, pp. 207–212.

[58] R. Mekuria, P. Cesar, I. Doumanis, A. Frisiello, Objective and subjective quality assessment of geometry compression of reconstructed 3D humans in a 3D virtual room, in: A.G. Tescher (Ed.), Applications of Digital Image Processing XXXVIII, vol. 9599, International Society for Optics and Photonics, SPIE, 2015, pp. 537–549, https://doi.org/10.1117/12.2203312.

[59] K. Christaki, E. Christakis, P. Drakoulis, Subjective visual quality assessment of immersive 3D media compressed by open-source static 3D mesh codecs, in: 25th International Conference on MultiMedia Modeling (MMM), 2018, pp. 1–12.

[60] J. Gutiérrez, T. Vigier, P. Le Callet, Quality evaluation of 3D objects in mixed reality for different lighting conditions, Electronic Imaging 2020 (2020), https://doi.org/10.2352/ISSN.2470-1173.2020.11.HVEI-128.

[61] T. Hoßfeld, P.E. Heegaard, M. Varela, S. Möller, QoE beyond the MOS: an in-depth look at QoE via better metrics and their relation to MOS, Quality and User Experience 1 (1) (2016) 1–23.

[62] E. Zerman, G. Valenzise, F. Dufaux, An extensive performance evaluation of full-reference HDR image quality metrics, Quality and User Experience 2 (1) (2017) 5.

[63] L. Krasula, K. Fliegel, P. Le Callet, M. Klíma, On the accuracy of objective image and video quality models: New methodology for performance evaluation, in: 2016 Eighth International Conference on Quality of Multimedia Experience (QoMEX), IEEE, 2016, pp. 1–6.

[64] K. Cao, Y. Xu, P. Cosman, Visual Quality of Compressed Mesh and Point Cloud Sequences, IEEE Access 8 (2020) 171203–171217.

[65] E. Alexiou, T. Ebrahimi, Impact of visualisation strategy for subjective quality assessment of point clouds, in: 2018 IEEE International Conference on Multimedia Expo Workshops (ICMEW), 2018, pp. 1–6, https://doi.org/10.1109/ICMEW.2018.8551498.

[66] G. Lavoué, A multiscale metric for 3D mesh visual quality assessment, Computer Graphics Forum 30 (5) (2011) 1427–1437.

[67] D. Tian, H. Ochimizu, C. Feng, R. Cohen, A. Vetro, Geometric distortion metrics for point cloud compression, in: 2017 IEEE International Conference on Image Processing (ICIP), 2017, pp. 3460–3464, https://doi.org/10.1109/ICIP.2017.8296925.

[68] MPEG 3DG Group, Common test conditions for point cloud compression, ISO/IEC JTC1/SC29/WG11 Doc. N18474, Mar. 2019.

[69] D. Tian, H. Ochimizu, C. Feng, R. Cohen, A. Vetro, Updates and integration of evaluation metric software for PCC, ISO/IEC JTC1/SC29/WG11 Doc. MPEG2017/M40522, Apr. 2017.

[70] D. Tian, H. Ochimizu, C. Feng, R. Cohen, A. Vetro, Evaluation metrics for point cloud compression, ISO/IEC JTC1/SC29/WG11 Doc. M39966, Jan. 2017.

[71] A. Javaheri, C. Brites, F. Pereira, J. Ascenso, A generalized Hausdorff distance based quality metric for point cloud geometry, in: 2020 Twelfth International Conference on Quality of Multimedia Experience (QoMEX), 2020, pp. 1–6, https://doi.org/10.1109/QoMEX48832.2020.9123087.

[72] A. Javaheri, C. Brites, F. Pereira, J. Ascenso, Improving PSNR-based quality metrics performance for point cloud geometry, in: 2020 IEEE International Conference on Image Processing (ICIP), 2020, pp. 3438–3442, https://doi.org/10.1109/ICIP40778.2020.9191233.

[73] E. Alexiou, T. Ebrahimi, Point cloud quality assessment metric based on angular similarity, in: 2018 IEEE International Conference on Multimedia and Expo (ICME), 2018, pp. 1–6, https://doi.org/10.1109/ICME.2018.8486512.

[74] E. Alexiou, T. Ebrahimi, Benchmarking of the plane-to-plane metric, ISO/IEC JTC1/SC29/WG1 Doc. M88038, Jul. 2020.

[75] A. Javaheri, C. Brites, F. Pereira, J. Ascenso, Mahalanobis based point to distribution metric for point cloud geometry quality evaluation, IEEE Signal Processing Letters 27 (2020) 1350–1354, https://doi.org/10.1109/LSP.2020.3010128.

[76] A. Javaheri, C. Brites, F. Pereira, J. Ascenso, A point-to-distribution joint geometry and color metric for point cloud quality assessment, arXiv preprint, arXiv:2108.00054, 2021.

[77] G. Meynet, J. Digne, G. Lavoué, PC-MSDM: A quality metric for 3D point clouds, in: 2019 Eleventh International Conference on Quality of Multimedia Experience (QoMEX), 2019, pp. 1–3, https://doi.org/10.1109/QoMEX.2019.8743313.

[78] G. Meynet, Y. Nehmé, J. Digne, G. Lavoué, PCQM: A full-reference quality metric for colored 3D point clouds, in: 2020 Twelfth International Conference on Quality of Multimedia Experience (QoMEX), 2020, pp. 1–6, https://doi.org/10.1109/QoMEX48832.2020.9123147.

[79] E. Alexiou, T. Ebrahimi, Towards a point cloud structural similarity metric, in: 2020 IEEE International Conference on Multimedia Expo Workshops (ICMEW), 2020, pp. 1–6, https://doi.org/10.1109/ICMEW46912.2020.9106005.

[80] L. Hua, M. Yu, G. Jiang, Z. He, Y. Lin, VQA-CPC: a novel visual quality assessment metric of color point clouds, in: Q. Dai, T. Shimura, Z. Zheng (Eds.), Optoelectronic Imaging and Multimedia Technology VII, vol. 11550, International Society for Optics and Photonics, SPIE, 2020, pp. 244–252.

[81] Lei Hua, Mei Yu, Zhouyan He, Renwei Tu, Gangyi Jiang, CPC-GSCT: Visual quality assessment for coloured point cloud based on geometric segmentation and colour transformation, IET Image Processing 16 (4) (2022) 1083–1095, https://doi.org/10.1049/ipr2.12211.

[82] E. Alexiou, I. Viola, P. Cesar, PointPCA: Point cloud objective quality assessment using PCA-based descriptors, arXiv preprint, arXiv:2111.12663, 2021.

[83] Qi Yang, Zhan Ma, Yiling Xu, Zhu Li, Jun Sun, Inferring point cloud quality via graph similarity, IEEE Transactions on Pattern Analysis and Machine Intelligence 44 (6) (2022) 3015–3029, https://doi.org/10.1109/TPAMI.2020.3047083.

[84] Y. Zhang, Q. Yang, Y. Xu, MS-GraphSIM: Inferring Point Cloud Quality via Multiscale Graph Similarity, Association for Computing Machinery, New York, NY, USA, 2021, pp. 1230–1238, https://doi.org/10.1145/3474085.3475294.

[85] K.-x. Zhang, G.-y. Jiang, M. Yu, FQM-GC: Full-reference quality metric for colored point cloud based on graph signal features and color features, in: ACM Multimedia Asia, MMAsia '21, Association for Computing Machinery, New York, NY, USA, 2021, https://doi.org/10.1145/3469877.3490578.

[86] Y. Xu, Q. Yang, L. Yang, J.-N. Hwang, EPES: Point cloud quality modeling using elastic potential energy similarity, IEEE Transactions on Broadcasting (2021) 1–10, https://doi.org/10.1109/TBC.2021.3114510.

[87] R. Diniz, P.G. Freitas, M.C.Q. Farias, Towards a point cloud quality assessment model using local binary patterns, in: 2020 Twelfth International Conference on Quality of Multimedia Experience (QoMEX), 2020, pp. 1–6, https://doi.org/10.1109/QoMEX48832.2020.9123076.

[88] R. Diniz, P.G. Freitas, M.C. Farias, Multi-distance point cloud quality assessment, in: 2020 IEEE International Conference on Image Processing (ICIP), 2020, pp. 3443–3447, https://doi.org/10.1109/ICIP40778.2020.9190956.

[89] R. Diniz, P.G. Freitas, M.C. Farias, Local luminance patterns for point cloud quality assessment, in: 2020 IEEE 22nd International Workshop on Multimedia Signal Processing (MMSP), 2020, pp. 1–6, https://doi.org/10.1109/MMSP48831.2020.9287154.

[90] R. Diniz, P.G. Freitas, M. Farias, A novel point cloud quality assessment metric based on perceptual color distance patterns, Electronic Imaging 2021 (9) (2021) 256, 11pp., https://doi.org/10.2352/ISSN.2470-1173.2021.9.IQSP-256.

[91] R. Diniz, P.G. Freitas, M.C.Q. Farias, Color and geometry texture descriptors for point-cloud quality assessment, IEEE Signal Processing Letters 28 (2021) 1150–1154, https://doi.org/10.1109/LSP.2021.3088059.

[92] I. Viola, S. Subramanyam, P. Cesar, A color-based objective quality metric for point cloud contents, in: 2020 Twelfth International Conference on Quality of Multimedia Experience (QoMEX), 2020, pp. 1–6, https://doi.org/10.1109/QoMEX48832.2020.9123089.

[93] I. Viola, P. Cesar, A reduced reference metric for visual quality evaluation of point cloud contents, IEEE Signal Processing Letters 27 (2020) 1660–1664, https://doi.org/10.1109/LSP.2020.3024065.

[94] Q. Liu, H. Yuan, R. Hamzaoui, H. Su, J. Hou, H. Yang, Reduced reference perceptual quality model with application to rate control for video-based point cloud compression, IEEE Transactions on Image Processing 30 (2021) 6623–6636, https://doi.org/10.1109/TIP.2021.3096060.

[95] L. Hua, G. Jiang, M. Yu, Z. He, BQE-CVP: Blind quality evaluator for colored point cloud based on visual perception, in: 2021 IEEE International Symposium on Broadband Multimedia Systems and Broadcasting (BMSB), 2021, pp. 1–6, https://doi.org/10.1109/BMSB53066.2021.9547070.

[96] X. Yang, W. Ling, Z. Lu, E. Ong, S. Yao, Just noticeable distortion model and its applications in video coding, Signal Processing. Image Communication 20 (7) (2005) 662–680, https://doi.org/10.1016/j.image.2005.04.001.

[97] A. Chetouani, M. Quach, G. Valenzise, F. Dufaux, Deep learning-based quality assessment of 3D point clouds without reference, in: 2021 IEEE International Conference on Multimedia & Expo Workshops (ICMEW), 2021, pp. 1–6, https://doi.org/10.1109/ICMEW53276.2021.9455967.

[98] M. Quach, A. Chetouani, G. Valenzise, F. Dufaux, A deep perceptual metric for 3D point clouds, Electronic Imaging 2021 (9) (2021) 257, 7pp., https://doi.org/10.2352/ISSN.2470-1173.2021.9.IQSP-257.

[99] M. Corsini, M.C. Larabi, G. Lavoué, O. Petrik, L. Váša, K. Wang, Perceptual Metrics for Static and Dynamic Triangle Meshes, Computer Graphics Forum 32 (1) (2013) 101–125.

[100] G. Lavoué, R. Mantiuk, Quality assessment in computer graphics, in: Visual Signal Quality Assessment: Quality of Experience (QoE), 2015, pp. 243–286.

[101] N. Aspert, D. Santa-Cruz, T. Ebrahimi, MESH: measuring errors between surfaces using the Hausdorff distance, in: Proceedings. IEEE International Conference on Multimedia and Expo, 2002, https://doi.org/10.1109/ICME.2002.1035879.

[102] P. Cignoni, C. Rocchini, R. Scopigno, Metro: Measuring error on simplified surfaces, Computer Graphics Forum 17 (1998).

[103] G. Lavoué, M.C. Larabi, L. Vasa, On the Efficiency of Image Metrics for Evaluating the Visual Quality of 3D Models, IEEE Transactions on Visualization and Computer Graphics 22 (8) (2016) 1987–1999.

[104] Z. Karni, C. Gotsman, Spectral compression of mesh geometry, in: Proceedings of the 27th Annual Conference on Computer Graphics and Interactive Techniques, 2000, pp. 279–286, https://doi.org/10.1145/344779.344924.

[105] Z. Bian, S.-M. Hu, R. Martin, Evaluation for small visual difference between conforming meshes on strain field, Journal of Computer Science and Technology 24 (2009), https://doi.org/10.1007/s11390-009-9198-3.

[106] Z. Wang, A.C. Bovik, H.R. Sheikh, E.P. Simoncelli, Image quality assessment: from error visibility to structural similarity, IEEE Transactions on Image Processing 13 (4) (2004) 600–612.

[107] F. Torkhani, K. Wang, J.-M. Chassery, A curvature-tensor-based perceptual quality metric for 3D triangular meshes, Machine Graphics & Vision 23 (1) (2014) 59–82.

[108] Kai Wang, Fakhri Torkhani, Annick Montanvert, A fast roughness-based approach to the assessment of 3D mesh visual quality, Computers & Graphics 36 (7) (2012) 808–818, https://doi.org/10.1016/j.cag.2012.06.004.

[109] G. Nader, K. Wang, F. Hétroy-Wheeler, F. Dupont, Just noticeable distortion profile for flat-shaded 3D mesh surfaces, IEEE Transactions on Visualization and Computer Graphics 22 (11) (2016) 2423–2436, https://doi.org/10.1109/TVCG.2015.2507578.

[110] J. Guo, V. Vidal, A. Baskurt, G. Lavou, Evaluating the local visibility of geometric artifacts, in: ACM Symposium in Applied Perception, 2015.

[111] G. Lavoué, I. Cheng, A. Basu, Perceptual quality metrics for 3D meshes: Towards an optimal multi-attribute computational model, in: 2013 IEEE International Conference on Systems, Man, and Cybernetics, 2013, pp. 3271–3276, https://doi.org/10.1109/SMC.2013.557.

[112] A. Chetouani, Three-dimensional mesh quality metric with reference based on a support vector regression model, Journal of Electronic Imaging 27 (4) (2018) 1–9, https://doi.org/10.1117/1.JEI.27.4.043048.

[113] Z.C. Yildiz, A.C. Oztireli, T. Capin, A machine learning framework for full-reference 3D shape quality assessment, Visual Computer 36 (1) (2020) 127–139.

[114] Z.C. Yildiz, T. Capin, A perceptual quality metric for dynamic triangle meshes, EURASIP Journal on Image and Video Processing 2017 (12) (2017).

[115] I. Abouelaziz, M. El Hassouni, H. Cherifi, A curvature based method for blind mesh visual quality assessment using a general regression neural network, in: 2016 12th International Conference on Signal-Image Technology Internet-Based Systems (SITIS), 2016, pp. 793–797, https://doi.org/10.1109/SITIS.2016.130.

[116] A. Nouri, C. Charrier, O. Lézoray, 3D Blind Mesh Quality Assessment Index, IS&T International Symposium on Electronic Imaging, Jan. 2017.

[117] I. Abouelaziz, M. El Hassouni, H. Cherifi, No-reference 3D mesh quality assessment based on dihedral angles model and support vector regression, Image and Signal Processing (2016) 369–377.

[118] I. Abouelaziz, M.E. Hassouni, H. Cherifi, A convolutional neural network framework for blind mesh visual quality assessment, in: 2017 IEEE International Conference on Image Processing (ICIP), 2017, pp. 755–759, https://doi.org/10.1109/ICIP.2017.8296382.

[119] D. Tian, G. AlRegib, Batex3: Bit allocation for progressive transmission of textured 3-D models, IEEE Transactions on Circuits and Systems for Video Technology 18 (1) (2008) 23–35.

[120] Y. Zhao, Y. Liu, R. Song, M. Zhang, A saliency detection based method for 3D surface simplification, in: 2012 IEEE International Conference on Acoustics, Speech and Signal Processing (ICASSP), 2012, pp. 889–892, https://doi.org/10.1109/ICASSP.2012.6288027.

[121] X. Jiao, T. Wu, X. Qin, Mesh segmentation by combining mesh saliency with spectral clustering, Journal of Computational and Applied Mathematics 329 (2018) 134–146.

[122] S. Croci, S.B. Knorr, L. Goldmann, A. Smolic, A framework for quality control in cinematic VR based on Voronoi patches and saliency, in: 2017 International Conference on 3D Immersion (IC3D), 2017, pp. 1–8.

[123] S. Croci, C. Ozcinar, E. Zerman, S. Knorr, J. Cabrera, A. Smolic, Visual attention-aware quality estimation framework for omnidirectional video using spherical Voronoi diagram, Quality and User Experience 5 (2020), https://doi.org/10.1007/s41233-020-00032-3.

[124] Y. Nehmé, M. Abid, G. Lavoué, M.P.D. Silva, P.L. Callet, CMDM-VAC: Improving a perceptual quality metric for 3D graphics by integrating a visual attention complexity measure, in: 2021 IEEE International Conference on Image Processing (ICIP), 2021, pp. 3368–3372, https://doi.org/10.1109/ICIP42928.2021.9506662.

[125] M. Abid, M. Perreira Da Silva, P. Le Callet, Perceptual characterization of 3D graphical contents based on attention complexity measures, in: QoEVMA'20: Proceedings of the 1st Workshop on Quality of Experience (QoE) in Visual Multimedia Applications, 2020, pp. 31–36, https://doi.org/10.1145/3423328.3423498.

[126] J. Lubin, A visual discrimination model for imaging system design and evaluation, in: Vision Models for Target Detection and Recognition, 1995, pp. 245–283, https://doi.org/10.1142/9789812831200_0010.

[127] H.R. Sheikh, A.C. Bovik, Image information and visual quality, IEEE Transactions on Image Processing 15 (2) (2006) 430–444.

[128] L. Zhang, L. Zhang, X. Mou, D. Zhang, FSIM: A feature similarity index for image quality assessment, IEEE Transactions on Image Processing 20 (8) (2011) 2378–2386, https://doi.org/10.1109/TIP.2011.2109730.

[129] R. Mantiuk, K.J. Kim, A.G. Rempel, W. Heidrich, HDR-VDP-2: A calibrated visual metric for visibility and quality predictions in all luminance conditions, ACM Transactions on Graphics 30 (4) (Jul. 2011), https://doi.org/10.1145/2010324.1964935.

[130] J. Preiss, F. Fernandes, P. Urban, Color-image quality assessment: From prediction to optimization, IEEE Transactions on Image Processing 23 (3) (2014) 1366–1378, https://doi.org/10.1109/TIP.2014.2302684.

[131] M.A. Saad, A.C. Bovik, C. Charrier, A DCT statistics-based blind image quality index, IEEE Signal Processing Letters 17 (6) (2010) 583–586, https://doi.org/10.1109/LSP.2010.2045550.

[132] W. Xue, L. Zhang, X. Mou, A.C. Bovik, Gradient magnitude similarity deviation: A highly efficient perceptual image quality index, IEEE Transactions on Image Processing 23 (2) (2014) 684–695, https://doi.org/10.1109/TIP.2013.2293423.

[133] F. Gao, Y. Wang, P. Li, M. Tan, J. Yu, Y. Zhu, DeepSim: Deep similarity for image quality assessment, Neurocomputing 257 (2017) 104–114, https://doi.org/10.1016/j.neucom.2017.01.054, Machine Learning and Signal Processing for Big Multimedia Analysis.

[134] R. Zhang, P. Isola, A.A. Efros, E. Shechtman, O. Wang, The unreasonable effectiveness of deep features as a perceptual metric, in: 2018 IEEE/CVF Conference on Computer Vision and Pattern Recognition (CVPR), 2018, pp. 586–595, https://doi.org/10.1109/CVPR.2018.00068.

[135] S. Bosse, D. Maniry, K.-R. Müller, T. Wiegand, W. Samek, Deep neural networks for no-reference and full-reference image quality assessment, IEEE Transactions on Image Processing 27 (1) (2018) 206–219, https://doi.org/10.1109/TIP.2017.2760518.

[136] H. Talebi, P. Milanfar, NIMA: Neural image assessment, IEEE Transactions on Image Processing 27 (8) (2018) 3998–4011, https://doi.org/10.1109/TIP.2018.2831899.

[137] E. Prashnani, H. Cai, Y. Mostofi, P. Sen, PieAPP: Perceptual image-error assessment through pairwise preference, in: Proceedings of the IEEE Conference on Computer Vision and Pattern Recognition (CVPR), June 2018.

[138] L. Qu, G.W. Meyer, Perceptually guided polygon reduction, IEEE Transactions on Visualization and Computer Graphics 14 (5) (2008) 1015–1029, https://doi.org/10.1109/TVCG.2008.51.

[139] N. Menzel, M. Guthe, Towards perceptual simplification of models with arbitrary materials, Computer Graphics Forum 29 (2010).

[140] R.L. de Queiroz, P.A. Chou, Motion-compensated compression of dynamic voxelized point clouds, IEEE Transactions on Image Processing 26 (8) (2017) 3886–3895, https://doi.org/10.1109/TIP.2017.2707807.

[141] Z. Wang, E. Simoncelli, A. Bovik, Multiscale structural similarity for image quality assessment, in: The Thirty-Seventh Asilomar Conference on Signals, Systems Computers, 2003, vol. 2, 2003, pp. 1398–1402, https://doi.org/10.1109/ACSSC.2003.1292216.

[142] Z. He, G. Jiang, Z. Jiang, M. Yu, Towards a colored point cloud quality assessment method using colored texture and curvature projection, in: 2021 IEEE International Conference on Image Processing (ICIP), 2021, pp. 1444–1448, https://doi.org/10.1109/ICIP42928.2021.9506762.

[143] T. Chen, C. Long, H. Su, L. Chen, J. Chi, Z. Pan, H. Yang, Y. Liu, Layered projection-based quality assessment of 3D point clouds, IEEE Access 9 (2021) 88108–88120, https://doi.org/10.1109/ACCESS.2021.3087183.

[144] Z. Wang, Q. Li, Information content weighting for perceptual image quality assessment, IEEE Transactions on Image Processing 20 (5) (2011) 1185–1198, https://doi.org/10.1109/TIP.2010.2092435.

[145] Qi Liu, Hui Yuan, Honglei Su, Hao Liu, Yu Wang, Huan Yang, Junhui Hou, PQA-Net: Deep no reference point cloud quality assessment via multi-view projection, IEEE Transactions on Circuits and Systems for Video Technology 31 () (2021) 4645–4660, https://doi.org/10.1109/TCSVT.2021.3100282.

[146] W.-x. Tao, G.-y. Jiang, Z.-d. Jiang, M. Yu, Point Cloud Projection and Multi-Scale Feature Fusion Network Based Blind Quality Assessment for Colored Point Clouds, Association for Computing Machinery, New York, NY, USA, 2021, pp. 5266–5272.

[147] S.J. Daly, Visible differences predictor: an algorithm for the assessment of image fidelity, in: Human Vision, Visual Processing, and Digital Display III, vol. 1666, 1992, pp. 2–15.

[148] Q. Zhu, J. Zhao, Z. Du, Y. Zhang, Quantitative analysis of discrete 3D geometrical detail levels based on perceptual metric, Computers & Graphics 34 (1) (2010) 55–65, https://doi.org/10.1016/j.cag.2009.10.004.

[149] F. Caillaud, V. Vidal, F. Dupont, G. Lavoué, Progressive compression of arbitrary textured meshes, Computer Graphics Forum 35 (7) (2016) 475–484.

[150] P. Lindstrom, G. Turk, Image-driven simplification, ACM Transactions on Graphics 19 (3) (2000) 204–241, https://doi.org/10.1145/353981.353995.

[151] Ilyass Abouelaziz, Aladine Chetouani, Mohammed El Hassouni, Hocine Cherifi, A blind mesh visual quality assessment method based on convolutional neural network, in: Proc. IS&T Int'l. Symp. on Electronic Imaging: 3D Image Processing, Measurement (3DIPM), and Applications, 2018, pp. 423-1–423-5, https://doi.org/10.2352/ISSN.2470-1173.2018.18.3DIPM-423.

[152] I. Abouelaziz, A. Chetouani, M. El Hassouni, L.J. Latecki, H. Cherifi, No-reference mesh visual quality assessment via ensemble of convolutional neural networks and compact multi-linear pooling, Pattern Recognition 100 (2020) 107174.

[153] D. Plemenos, M. Benayada, Intelligent display in scene modelling. New techniques to automatically compute good views, in: Proceedings of the International Conference GraphiCon'96, 1996.

[154] X. Bonaventura, M. Feixas, M. Sbert, L. Chuang, C. Wallraven, A survey of viewpoint selection methods for polygonal models, Entropy 20 (5) (2018), https://doi.org/10.3390/e20050370, https://www.mdpi.com/1099-4300/20/5/370.

[155] K. Seshadrinathan, R. Soundararajan, A.C. Bovik, L.K. Cormack, A subjective study to evaluate video quality assessment algorithms, in: Human Vision and Electronic Imaging XV, vol. 7527, International Society for Optics and Photonics, 2010, p. 75270H.

[156] A. Ak, E. Zerman, S. Ling, P.L. Callet, A. Smolic, The effect of temporal sub-sampling on the accuracy of volumetric video quality assessment, in: 2021 Picture Coding Symposium (PCS), 2021, pp. 1–5, https://doi.org/10.1109/PCS50896.2021.9477449.

PART 5

Applications

CHAPTER 19

MR in video guided liver surgery

Rafael Palomar[a,b], Rahul Prasanna Kumar[b], Congcong Wang[c], Egidijus Pelanis[b,d], and Faouzi Alaya Cheikh[a]

[a]The Department of Computer Science, The Norwegian University of Science and Technology, Gjøvik, Norway
[b]The Intervention Centre, Oslo University Hospital, Oslo, Norway
[c]The Engineering Research Center of Learning-Based Intelligent System, Ministry of Education, and the School of Computer Science and Engineering, Tianjin University of Technology, Tianjin, China
[d]Institute of Clinical Medicine, University of Oslo, Oslo, Norway

19.1. Introduction

Liver cancer is one of the most common types of cancer, and its frequency is increasing in geographical areas where, traditionally, the incidence has been low [1]. Surgical resection, which consists of the surgical removal of tumor tissue (and surroundings) in the liver, is the only curative treatment for large tumors—such as hepatocellular carcinoma (HCC) [2]—and it is a potential curative therapy for cancer spread to the liver from other organs, notably colorectal metastases [3].

To support the decision-making process in liver resections, computer-aided systems providing surgeons with tools for planning and navigation [4–7] have been developed. These systems for planning and navigation rely on processing medical images to generate 3D models that can be used in both virtual reality and augmented reality environments. These techniques are not only used for computing 3D virtual models representing the patient's anatomy, but also provide the necessary means for the specification of resections, this is, the surgical path separating the tumor and its surroundings from the healthy tissue

Recent advances in medical imaging and image processing allow not only a more accurate representation of the patient's anatomy, but also the inclusion of non-anatomical (functional) information. In addition, recent trends in computing, such as general-purpose GPU computing, leverage a remarkable amount of computational power, which allows the performing of very complex computational operations in parallel (e.g., organ deformations in real-time). All these improvements are portraying a new clinical reality, where 3D models computed pre-operatively (before the operation starts), are adapted intra-operatively (during the operation) to the patient's anatomy to provide a more accurate representation of the target organ [8]. Optimization of the 3D models in terms of simplification and reduction of elements, keeping the accuracy, is important for the real-time use of the models in the applications. Furthermore, the adaptation of the underlying processing algorithms to new computing trends can maximize the number of operations performed on these models.

Together with these technological developments, surgeons have continued improving and developing new surgical techniques, which do not only employ the new technologies used by their predecessors, but also demand further technological innovations. In the context of virtual reality and augmented reality systems, this demand translates into the development of new systems able to cope with organ deformations during surgery, and introduce more complex models, which can include functional information. To be sure, the adoption of new computing paradigms combined with new geometric modeling tools is a necessary step to advance computer-assisted surgical systems towards a new reality, in which models will not only increase their complexity, but also become deformable. Careful consideration of deformations is important for navigation applications, where the soft tissue organs are continuously deforming due to motion, patient positioning (e.g., gravity), and physical interactions during surgery are involved.

19.1.1 Liver surgery

Liver surgical resection is considered to be the treatment of choice for patients with HCC (primary liver cancer), which account for 70% to 80% of the liver cancer cases worldwide [9]. For these cases, surgical resection is considered to be a safe and effective therapy [10]. In addition, selected patients with metastatic liver tumors (secondary cancer), which develops in 50% of the cases of colorectal cancer, present up to 58% increased 5-year survival rate after surgical resection [11].

Broadly speaking, there exists two approaches to perform liver surgical resection: open surgery and laparoscopic surgery [12]. In open surgery, a large incision is performed on the patient's abdomen to give the surgeon access to the organ. In such operations, the surgeon can visually inspect the organ and can directly interact with it to perform the surgical actions. In laparoscopic surgery, however, the operation takes place through small incisions and with the use of elongated instruments and camera that are inserted through the incisions into the patient's abdomen. This makes the surgery a great challenge for the operator due to the lack of direct sight and direct physical contact with the organ. The visualization of the surgical site is carried out with the use of a laparoscopic camera inserted into the patient's abdomen at the tip of an instrument.

Laparoscopic liver surgery has been applied successfully to a wide variety of cases, such as HCC [13] and colorectal metastases [14], and it is associated with a reduction of post-operative pain, shorter hospitalization, and faster patient recovery. During surgery, laparoscopic liver resection is associated with technical challenges related to the exploration and mobilization of the liver, the vascular control, and parenchymal transection [15]. Laparoscopic liver surgery and its comparison to the open surgery has been a subject of significant research efforts [14,16,17].

Regardless of the open/laparoscopic nature of the surgery, there exist different types of resections. The classification and typology of resections are still based on

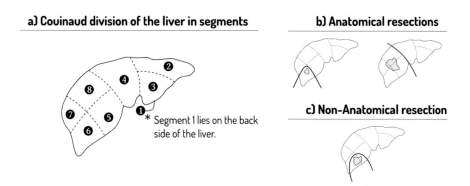

a) Couinaud division of the liver in segments

⑧ ④ ② ③ ① ⑦ ⑤ ⑥

* Segment 1 lies on the back side of the liver.

b) Anatomical resections

c) Non-Anatomical resection

Figure 19.1 Liver resections: a) Couinaud division of the liver in segments; b) anatomical resections, following the Couinaud division; and c) non-anatomical resection, not following the Couinaud division.

the Couinaud eight-segments model [18], which divides the liver in segments or volumes, according to the organization of the blood supply by the portal vein (Fig. 19.1a). Broadly speaking, there exist two groups of resections: anatomic resections, where one or more complete segments are removed, in respect to the boundaries established by the Couinaud division (Fig. 19.1b); on the contrary, non-anatomic resections do not respect boundaries established by the Couinaud model (Fig. 19.1c). According to Strasberg and Phillips [19], anatomic resections can be further classified according to three orders: hemilivers (order 1), sections (order 2), and segments (order 3); the authors also consider extended resections, which can be composed by a combination of a hemiliver and a section.

19.1.2 Overview of planning and navigation in liver resection procedures

Computer-assisted surgical planning and navigation systems have been supporting surgical interventions for more than two decades [20,21]. Surgery planning refers to the definition of a plan prior to the operation. This plan, which is often specified as a trajectory to be followed during surgery, may include indicators of risk and surgical outcome; in the case of liver resection, measures related to the distance to anatomical structures, as well as volumetry of the resected/remnant tissue are employed. Surgery navigation, on the other hand, is concerned with the correct execution of the plan during surgery, this is, the control of correct movement and position of the surgical instruments. Planning and navigation of liver resection procedures have proven to be beneficial for the localization of tumors, the precision of surgery planning [22–24], and for the improvement of orientation and confidence of surgeons during the operation [25].

Surgery planning and navigation can be combined, and both rely on the generation of three-dimensional (3D) models derived from pre-operative imaging. As shown in Fig. 19.2, a typical work-flow involving planing and navigation starts from the acquisition of pre-operative images from either computed tomography (CT) or magnetic resonance imaging (MRI). A volumetric medical image, regardless of its modality, is a 3D scalar field, where its elements represent intensity values. The process of labeling (separating) the different anatomical structures in the image is known as segmentation and produces a new scalar field, known as a *label map*, where its elements take a set of discrete values associated to different types of anatomical/functional structures. In liver surgery, the label map is usually constrained to the set $L = \{l_b, l_p, l_h, l_o, l_t\}$, where l_b represents a value indicating tissue not relevant for the procedure (image background), and the rest represents values for *parenchyma, hepatic venous system, portal venous system,* and *tumor* tissue, respectively. In some cases, this set of labels can be further extended to consider multiple separate tumors[1] and other anatomical structures, such as the bile ducts. Segmentation has traditionally been considered a major bottleneck for the processing workflow [26]; however, recent developments on machine learning, and particularly deep learning, are opening for the possibility of automatic segmentation. To date, many segmentation tasks still require some degree of human correction.

While segmentation (label map) inherently describes the geometry of the anatomical structures, its visualization is performed by 3D surface models comprised of triangular meshes. 3D surface models are not only used for visualization, but also for the definition of *virtual resections* [27]. Virtual resections define the cutting path separating tumor and healthy tissue, as well as other anatomical structures affected by the resection, such as vessels. The geometric information contained in the 3D models and the virtual resection can be used in computer-assisted systems to calculate volumetric information of the resection, which can be used as an indicator of adequacy of the surgical plan.

3D models and virtual resections can be used during surgery (intra-operatively) through computer-assisted navigation systems. As described in Terry and Peters [17], these systems utilize a localizer to track the surgical instruments; optical and electromagnetic tracking systems are the two main technologies employed in the clinical routine and the former is still the more widely used of the two. To mitigate the geometric discrepancies between the pre-operative reality (medical images, segmentations and 3D models) and the intra-operative reality (the patient on the operating table) produced by differences in coordinate systems and deformations, registration (the process of aligning two coordinate systems) is performed. Registration can be broadly classified into two categories, rigid and non-rigid; for a detailed review of registration methods, we refer to the extensive work by Markelj et al. [28].

19.2. Medical images pre-processing

During image acquisition, noise and artifacts are introduced, making image analysis difficult both for doctors as well as for the computer vision algorithms. Therefore it is

---

[1] Different tumors can be indicated by further extending the set L to add more values.

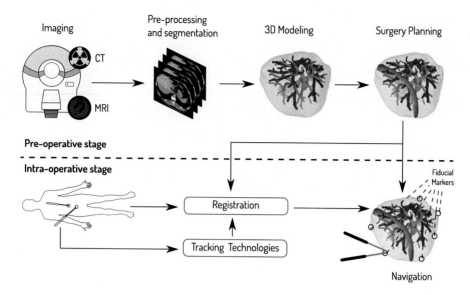

Figure 19.2 Processing workflow, including surgical planning and navigation.

essential to enhance image quality of pre- and intra-operative images to provide high quality multimodal data for feature extraction, personalization of computational biomechanical models, optimal image registration, and improved image-guided interventions. In a surgery navigation system, pre-processing is required at two stages: 1) pre-operative stage, where CT and MRI images are processed; 2) intra-operative stage, where laparoscopic video are processed.

19.2.1 Medical image enhancement

In pre-operative stage, in the context of cancer treatment, CT imaging remains widely accepted as a primary preoperative evaluation tool. MRI is influential in characterizing nondeterministic lesions due to its higher sensitivity in comparison with CT [29]. It is a usual practice to acquire both CT and MRI during therapeutic procedures. Though a CT image acquisition system is inexpensive and has faster acquisition, it is not safe for specific patients. MRI is prone to contain motion artifacts and has acquisition time as long as 1.5 hours. Nevertheless, the concordance of MRI and CT findings also becomes essential in case of suspicion. Computational methods are thus investigated and developed to improve the quality of medical images, such as CT and MRI. The enhancement improves the visibility of the internal anatomical structures of the organs; furthermore, it makes the medical images more suitable for subsequent image processing tasks and analysis, such as segmentation, registration, feature extraction, and classification.

For intra-operative stage, high quality laparoscopic video is essential for surgery. However, the captured video quality is very often affected by different artifacts. Typical

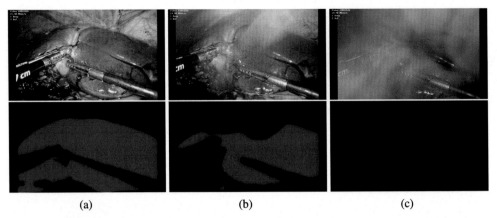

(a)   (b)   (c)

Figure 19.3 Laparoscopic images and the corresponding segmentation results, red indicates liver and black stands for the background. (a) Smoke free images. (b) Images with low density smoke. (c) Images with high density smoke. Original images are provided by Oslo University Hospital and processed by the segmentation algorithm proposed in [32,33].

artifacts include specular reflections, blood, surgical smoke, dynamic illumination conditions, etc. [30]. In particular, surgical smoke is one major artifact, which is caused by energy-generating devices during for example electrocautery or laser ablation. It significantly deteriorates the image quality by reducing the contrast and radiance information for large areas of the surgical field, as shown in the first row of Fig. 19.3. This creates uncomfortable view for the surgeons, which may not only increase surgical risk [31], but also degrades the performance of computer-assisted surgery algorithms, such as segmentation, reconstruction, tracking, etc. Fig. 19.3 illustrates an example where segmentation fails due to surgical smoke.

Many numerical methods are proposed for medical image enhancement [33–35]. Whereas image enhancement approaches are critical, image quality assessment is also important for the automation of the processing. As throughout the image processing phases, it is of great importance to have control of the quality of the medical images used in each step, starting from acquisition, to ensure that the useful information is not lost. Image quality is commonly defined in terms of visible distortions in an image, such as color shifts, blurriness, noise, and blockiness [36]. Image quality can be assessed either subjectively using human feedback or objectively. However, the use of human feedback is time-consuming and prone to inconsistency, and may not always be feasible in real-world applications, such as video-guided surgery. Hence, some efficient algorithms are required for objective image quality assessment. Moreover, it is also useful to have evaluation metrics for assessing the results and performance of other steps in the processing pipeline, such as image registration, enhancement, and segmentation [36].

19.2.2 Segmentation

Image segmentation is one of the most widely studied topics in computer vision, which can be classified into binary segmentation, semantic segmentation, and instant segmentation. The result of conventional image segmentation is a set of meaningful segments (regions, edges or groups of pixels, tokens) sharing the same low-level spatial properties/characteristics defined for a predefined objective or representation of the observed scene. The segments are obtained based on the feature attributes of their pixels, such as intensity, texture, color, edge, etc. Semantic segmentation is to classify each pixel into a specific category by trying to understand the image at a pixel level. Compared to simple image segmentation, which only splits the image into different segments, semantic segmentation tells, for example, that segment one is a bottle, segment two is a cube, etc. Moreover, instance segmentation algorithm gives more precise category information, which can differentiate instances by giving a different label to each instance. Thus if we have several similar objects in the scene, instance segmentation will give each of them a different label, whereas semantic segmentation would give them the same label.

Segmentation is an essential step to understand the contents of a scene. Abdomen organs segmentation is an essential step for computer-assisted diagnosis, surgery navigation, visual augmentation, radiation therapy, and bio-marker measurement systems to site a few. Similar to enhancement, two segmentation steps are required: 1) segmentation of pre-operative stage, where CT and MRI images are processed; 2) segmentation of intra-operative stage, where laparoscopic videos is processed. The former includes segmentation of liver, liver vessels, and lesions, whereas the latter can only provide information about the liver surface.

In preoperative plannings, good segmentation can lead to a smaller resection margin, and hence, sparing more tissue. Due to varying acquisition protocols, different contrast agents, varying scanner resolution, and different enhancement techniques, robust and automatic segmentation of liver parenchyma, vessels, and lesions still remains an open challenge and has recently attracted considerable research attention.

In intra-operative video analysis, extracting regions of interest for registration is essential. For surface-based registration, one is only interested in the organ part, thus segmenting the background and the target organ before registration is necessary [37,38]. Moreover, for instrument tracking, the target instrument needs to be recognized [39,40]. Therefore segmenting and semantically understanding the laparoscopic images is an essential step of a surgery navigation system.

Semantic segmentation is a challenging problem, and most of the earlier segmentation methods are unable to predict the semantic information of their output segments. The majority of the successful methods for semantic segmentation in the past decade rely on hand-crafted features with classic machine learning methods as classifiers [41,42]. Hand-crafted features include local binary pattern [43], scale-invariant feature transform [44], histogram of oriented gradients [45], bag-of-visual-words [46], etc. After feature

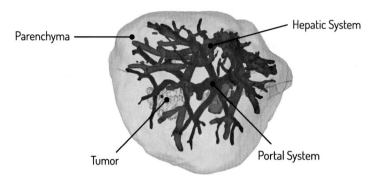

Figure 19.4 Complete 3D patient-specific model obtained from segmented CT featuring parenchyma, portal, and hepatic systems, and a single tumor.

extraction, classifiers such as support vector machine (SVM) [47], conditional random field [48,49], random forests [50], or boosting [51] are employed to predict the semantic information.

However, the performance of classic methods is limited by the quality of the hand-crafted features used. The rapid advances we are witnessing in deep learning are leading to breakthroughs in semantic segmentation. A milestone work is the U–Net and FCN proposed in [52]. This method employs fully convolutional layers to replace the fully connected layers of classification models, which can output per-pixel dense segmentation map, rather than classification scores.

19.3. 3D liver modeling

The aim of 3D modeling is to construct surface models (∂M_i with $i = 1, ..., k$) from label maps containing k different tissues encoded as labels. The most common representation form of surface models is triangular meshes, which can be denoted as sets $\mathcal{M} = \{V, T\}$ with the set of vertices $V = \{0, 1, 2, ...\}$, having associated position coordinates in space $\mathbf{p}_i \in \mathbb{R}^3$, edges $E = \{(i, j)|i, j \in V\}$, indicating connectivity, as well as triangles $T = \{(i, j, k)|(i, j), (j, k), (k, i) \in E\}$. Due to the nature of the underlying data (medical images), the models resemble the anatomical structures of the patient; the models are patient-specific.

A complete 3D patient-specific model (Fig. 19.4) used for planning and navigation of liver resection procedures consist of the following anatomical structure:
- the parenchyma, or the functional tissue of the liver;
- the vessels, which typically are separated into portal system, and hepatic vessel system according to an in-flow/out-flow of blood;
- and the tumor(s).

Due to their geometric structure (tubular structures with high curvature and convex features), vessels are the most complex geometric anatomical structures involved in the reconstruction of 3D patient-specific models, and hence, the topic has been the subject of extensive research. Preim et al. [27], which provides a comprehensive overview of available reconstruction methods, separates the reconstruction strategies into two categories:

- *model-based* methods, which work on the basis of assumptions (e.g., vessels present circular cross-sections) and either generate parametric or implicit surfaces or fit primitives such as cylinders or truncated cones;
- *model-free* methods, which are not based in any assumption. Marching cubes [53], multi-level partition of unity (MPU) implicit [54] and subdivision surfaces [55] are evaluated and compared in [56].

Model-based methods provide smooth models, which are easy to interpret; however, these might lead to inadequate results for the analysis and representation of certain pathologies (e.g., aneurysms). On the other hand, model-based methods adhere to the underlying data, and therefore, in some cases they might lead to lower mesh quality resulting in poor visualization (e.g., original image with low resolution or noise).

Though reconstruction of vascular structures has been subject to extensive research, reconstruction of parenchyma and tumors have been given very little attention in the literature. For the reconstruction of these anatomical structures, marching cubes is the *de-facto* standard and is often followed by decimation [57] (reduction of triangles) and smoothing [58]. However, some authors, such as Palomar et al. [59] propose the use of geometric modeling methods that can better adhere to the geometric characteristics of the specific anatomical structures and particularly the use of Poisson surface reconstruction (**PSR**) as a method for modeling the liver parenchyma. PSR was first proposed by Kazhdan et al. [60] as a method for reconstruction of watertight surfaces models ∂M from oriented clouds of points. The method combines the advantages of global and local approximation schemes, and it is known for its noise resiliency.

PSR is based on the reconstruction of an indicator function $\mathcal{X} : \mathbb{R}^3 \rightarrow \mathbb{R} \in [0, 1]$, whose gradient $\nabla \mathcal{X}$ resembles the structure of the oriented cloud of points $\vec{V}$ to be reconstructed. Hence, the problem pivots around finding the scalar function $\mathcal{X}$, whose gradient best matches that cloud of points $\vec{V}$:

$$\tilde{\mathcal{X}} = \arg \lim_{\mathcal{X}} \|\nabla \mathcal{X} - \vec{V}\|, \tag{19.1}$$

where $\|.\|$ is the Euclidean norm. By making use of the divergence operator, Kazhdan et al. [60] transforms this problem into a variational problem optimized by the Poisson equation:

$$\Delta \mathcal{X} \equiv \nabla \cdot \nabla \mathcal{X} = \nabla \cdot \vec{V}. \tag{19.2}$$

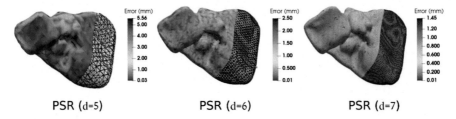

Figure 19.5 Liver surface models computed by Poisson surface reconstruction with different depth (d) values.

The implementation of this can be based on an adaptive and multi-resolution structure, such as an octree $\mathcal{O}$, in which every point sample of the cloud of points falls into a leaf node at a depth d. An intuitive way of thinking about the parameter d is a mechanism to control the granularity of the mesh, where high depth values lead to complex models able to represent smaller features, and *vice versa*. Finally, to obtain the model ∂M, isosurface extraction is applied to the average value of the approximated indicator function $\tilde{\mathcal{X}}$. Fig. 19.5 shows the parenchyma 3D models obtained using PSR, indicating the complexity and the reconstruction error for different depths.

19.4. Model-organ registration

In surgical navigation, the purpose of registration is to align the pre- and intra-operative data, meanwhile updating the pre-operative model to reduce the task of mentally matching different information sources of the surgical scene. In particular, typical intra-operatively available data includes US, iMRI, iCT, and laparoscopic videos, which can be used for registration purpose [61]. An example of pre-operative CT model and intra-operatively reconstructed point cloud registration process is shown in Fig. 19.6.

It is observed that intra-operative navigation relies on overlay between pre-operative information and intra-operative information, which relies on precise pre-operative and intra-operative registration. Registration thus becomes one of the critical components for the navigation system. So far, optical and electromagnetic tracking systems are most widely used, where real-time localization of the surgical instrument is provided during surgery, for which optical tracking system (OTS) is regarded as the most reliable and accurate tracking technique [62]. These navigation techniques have been commercially used and became standard procedures in surgeries such as neurosurgery, where the structure is supposed to be rigid. These techniques have successfully revolutionized surgery navigation [62,63].

There also exist commercial systems for navigation for liver surgery. Such as, IQQA-Liver (EDDA Technology, Inc., New Jersey, USA), which provides quantitative analysis

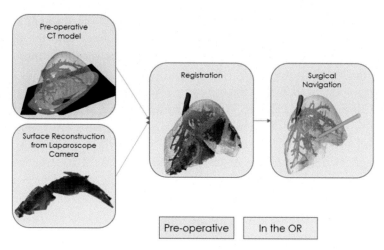

Figure 19.6 Example of the use of stereo point cloud reconstruction to perform model-to-patient registration for surgical navigation [66].

for pre- and post-operative assessment of liver. CAS-ONE Surgery and CAS-ONE IR (CAScination, Bern, Switzerland) are navigation systems designed for ablation of tumors for liver, kidney, lung, etc. Moreover, several open-source platforms are developed: CustusX can localize intra-operative location of the tumor through navigated US by electromagnetic position sensor [64], and NorMIT Navigation is a platform for image guided interventions based on 3D slicer [65].

19.5. Mixed reality guided surgery

Mixed reality (MR) is considered a subset of extended reality using head mounted displays. In MR, the real world and virtual worlds are merged, with physical and digital objects co-existing and interacting with each other. This allows users to visualize and interact with 3D models alongside real objects, and walk around a virtual model similar to a real object. Although there are many MR head mounted displays (HMD) that are currently in development or production, only two such devices stand out in terms of their wide-spread use:

- Microsoft Hololens [67]. It was the first commercially available HMD (2016) that brought the usage of MR into the market. Later (in 2019), the 2nd generation of the device was released, which was lighter, with better center of gravity, faster processor, longer battery life, and wider field of view.
- MagicLeap 1 [68]. It was released in 2018 with similar battery life to HoloLens 2 and higher field of view than the Hololens 1.

Both HMDs use an optical projection of 3D models on its see-through lenses. Also, both HMDs can create a spatial map of the user's surroundings with the use of multiple cameras and sensors. Nevertheless, Microsoft Hololens is still the most used MR platform for medical purposes [69].

Depending on the need for specific use cases, different applications have to be created with the MR devices. Unity engine [70] is the common core development platform for such devices, where custom interaction and visualization options can be programmed. For the use in liver surgery, the main needs are in the surgery planning and navigation. Though many methods as described in Section 19.1.2 have been developed for liver surgery planning and navigation, very few methods are available with the use of MR.

19.5.1 Surgery planning

Visualizing 3D patient specific models as holograms in MR could provide the surgeons with a better anatomical overview. Also, with the added depth information in MR, visualizing and surgery planning in MR could greatly influence the decision-making process leading to better decisions in surgical planning. Nevertheless, there are very few works in the literature on the use of MR-based liver surgery planning [71–73]. In them, many consider just MR for just viewing the 3D models, in contrast to using it for direct surgery planning, as by Kumar et al. [73].

Kumar et al. show how a surgery planning MR application can be built and subsequently tested under a clinical setting. In this work, custom interactions and visualizations, such as scale, rotation and movement of 3D models, marker placements, CT/MR viewer, and specific surgery planning interactions for heart and liver were implemented. Here, the liver surgery planning is reimplemented based on the work on liver resection planning using deformable Bezier surfaces [74]. The process starts with a Bezier plane being initialized in the liver model, which is then deformed accordingly to the required resection. The deformation can be performed using interactive manipulation of coordinates of the control points that are distributed on a grid, as shown in Fig. 19.7. Apart from the deformable plane, a safety indicator is also provided, which is visualized in red for the area that violates the resection margin. In addition to liver surgery planning, the paper also describes a heart surgery planner.

19.5.2 Navigation

With the use of MR-based navigation, surgeons have the possibility to directly observe 3D virtual patient specific models registered and overlaid on the real patients. Thus enabling the surgeons to concentrate and engage in the true surgical environment, and thereby greatly benefiting the surgeons' operation efficiency and precision. Fig. 19.8 shows how a 3D model can be registered and overlaid on to a real body, making an "X-ray vision" for the user. Though navigation with MR is starting to be heavily

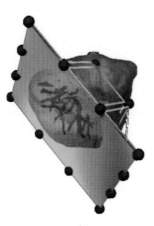

Figure 19.7 Liver resection planning in MR [73].

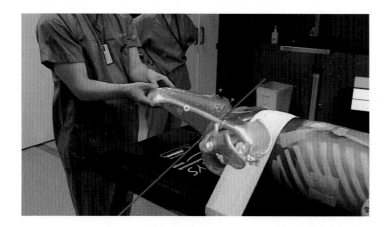

Figure 19.8 3D model registered and overlaid on the model in MR [79].

researched for many clinical applications [75–80], it is yet to be extended to liver surgery. This might be due to be fact that liver is a soft-tissue, and its movement registrations are a big challenge to solve.

Li et al. proposed a manual registration method using mixed reality with an optical tracker to superimpose 3D liver models on patients for liver tumor puncture naviga-tion to address the problem of incorrect needle placement [81]. Here, optical markers rigidly attached to the HoloLens, anatomical marks on the patient and a k-wire with attached reflective spheres serve as an optical marker for the initial manual registration step. Then, for an automatic temporal registration during the procedure, the tracked k-wire was used. Finally, a 3D-printed skull with 10 landmarks was used for a registration accuracy validation experiment, which reported an average target registration error of 2.24 mm.

19.6. Medical validation

As previously mentioned in the introduction of this chapter, liver surgery has been transiting towards more laparoscopic interventions, which involves the use of new technological solutions. This includes continued improvements and development of laparoscopes and related hardware and software systems, such as improvements in resolution in 4k compatible scopes, depth presentation by using of stereoscopy, and enhanced imaging with indocyanine green (ICG) compatible probes. The use of ICG in liver surgery can assist in several ways, such as in visualizing vascular territories, and assisting in detection and definition of liver lesions, to mention a few. Fluorescent glow from the ICG is shown as a colorful augmentation to the laparoscopic view [82].

By bringing patient-specific models to the operating room, patient anatomy and pathology could be shown and used as a map to possibly improve some aspects of the communication and enhance spatial understanding. This can be on a separate screen with and without interaction [59], or using a head-mounted device, such as Hololens providing a holographic view of the patient anatomy to interact with, by the surgeon using his own hands [73]. It has also been shown that the use of HoloLens to localize lesions in the liver reduced time needed compared to conventional medical images [83].

With tracked instruments (e.g., using OTS) and model-organ registration procedure, these 3D models can be shown on a separate screen in a 3D scene, shown in Fig. 19.9, or overlaid as AR. The use of AR during interventions has been demonstrated during liver surgery [84–86]. Though demonstrated in clinical use, these lack quantitative evaluation of accuracy in terms of the target, which, in this case, could be guidance accuracy to a lesion or a specific location of a vascular structure.

Above-mentioned approaches for navigated laparoscopic liver resection bring errors already from the patient-specific model, which are normally based on pre-operative image due to the time required to create a 3D model. During laparoscopic liver surgery, surgeons introduce gas into the abdomen (pneumoperitoneum), which deforms and changes patient anatomy compared to the pre-operative images. Such changes have a significant effect on navigation accuracy [87]. Based on these findings in previous study, to achieve a navigation approach with improved accuracy should limit dependency on the user to drive the registration and utilize intra-operative imaging modalities, such as intra-operative CT.

Another important aspect of the navigation system is the ability to update model-organ registration once insufficient accuracy has been suspected due to organ manipulation and deformation. One option is to perform the whole registration process with

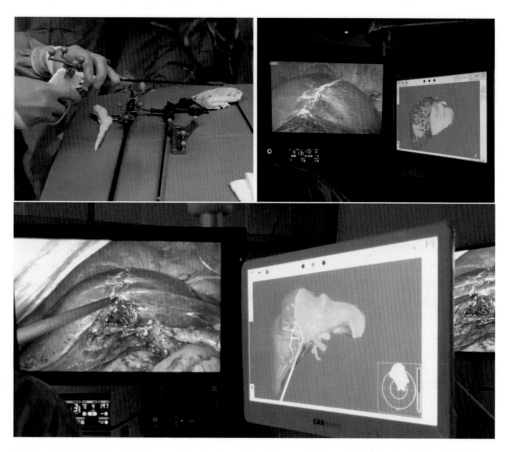

Figure 19.9 Navigated laparoscopic liver resection utilizing optical tracking and point-based registration method to perform model-organ registration. The image on the top left shows sterile trackers attached on-top of the laparoscopic instruments. The image on the top right shows a laparoscopic view of the liver with a marked resection line and a second screen showing a patient specific 3D model with a resection plan. The image on the bottom shows the tracked laparoscopic instrument, shown as a white line on the screen, with the 3D model to provide the surgeon with the location of the instrument tip and the surrounding anatomy underneath the liver surface.

extensive manual labor, alternatively it has been shown to be possible to drive a registration, mostly a user independent registration, by fluoroscopic imaging [88] and surface reconstruction combined with biomechanical model [89]. At the current state of development, introduction of such new methods and techniques to the clinical routines might prolong and complicate the surgical procedure without a documented quantitative improvement to the patient care.

19.7. Conclusion

AR has shown a huge potential that is set to revolutionize video-guided surgery planning and navigation. The example of laparoscopic liver resection presented in this chapter, has proven its validity, even for such a complicated intervention on a soft organ. Obviously, it is easier to apply such technology in more rigid organs' surgery, such as bones or the brain. The extended use of these HMDs is associated with side effects, such as headache, motion sickness, and claustrophobia. Furthermore, the limited field of view and the image quality of the HoloLens AR headset produces head discomfort and ocular fatigue. Therefore there are several hurdles to be removed before the use of MR in surgery becomes a widespread practice in the operation rooms. From the hardware side, there is a need for lightweight HMD with better field of view, battery life, and a robust interface for intuitive and precise interaction with the models during surgery planning and navigation. A solution that provides haptic feedback to the surgeon would greatly improve the realism of organ manipulation. In addition to such hardware, it is critical to have automatic software tools for the rapid creation of detail rich 3D models of patient organs from multi-modal medical images, and for easily registering them to the patient's organs, with the ability to accommodate to any changes of organs' shapes during the operation.

References

[1] L.A. Torre, F. Bray, R.L. Siegel, J. Ferlay, J. Lortet-Tieulent, A. Jemal, Global cancer statistics, 2012, CA: A Cancer Journal for Clinicians 65 (2) (2015) 87–108, https://doi.org/10.3322/caac.21262.

[2] J. Belghiti, R. Kianmanesh, Surgical treatment of hepatocellular carcinoma, HPB Official Journal of the International Hepato Pancreato Biliary Association 7 (1) (2005) 42–49, https://doi.org/10.1080/13651820410024067.

[3] P.C. Simmonds, J.N. Primrose, J.L. Colquitt, O.J. Garden, G.J. Poston, M. Rees, Surgical resection of hepatic metastases from colorectal cancer: A systematic review of published studies, British Journal of Cancer 94 (7) (2006) 982–999, https://doi.org/10.1038/sj.bjc.6603033.

[4] O. Konrad-Verse, A. Littmann, B. Preim, Virtual resection with a deformable cutting plane, SimVis 1 (2004).

[5] L. Ruskó, I. Mátéka, A. Kriston, Virtual volume resection using multi-resolution triangular representation of B-spline surfaces, Computer Methods and Programs in Biomedicine 111 (2) (2013) 315–329, https://doi.org/10.1016/j.cmpb.2013.04.017.

[6] M. Peterhans, A. vom Berg, B. Dagin, D. Interbitzin, C. Baur, D. Candinas, S. Weber, A navigation system for open liver surgery: design, workflow and first clinical applications, The International Journal of Medical Robotics and Computer Assisted Surgery 7 (1) (2011) 7–16, https://doi.org/10.1002/rcs.

[7] R. Palomar, F.A. Cheikh, B. Edwin, Å. Fretland, A. Beghdadi, O.J. Elle, A novel method for planning liver resections using deformable Bézier surfaces and distance maps, Computer Methods and Programs in Biomedicine 144 (2017) 135–145.

[8] S. Rohl, S. Bodenstedt, S. Suwelack, R. Dillmann, S. Speidel, H. Kenngott, B.P. Muller-Stich, Dense GPU-enhanced surface reconstruction from stereo endoscopic images for intraoperative registration, Medical Physics 39 (3) (2012) 1632–1645, https://doi.org/10.1118/1.3681017.

[9] E. Vanni, E. Bugianesi, Obesity and liver cancer, Clinics in Liver Disease 18 (1) (2014) 191–203, https://doi.org/10.1016/j.cld.2013.09.001.

[10] J.H. Zhong, A.C. Rodriguez, Y. Ke, Y.Y. Wang, L. Wang, L.Q. Li, Hepatic resection as a safe and effective treatment for hepatocellular carcinoma involving a single large tumor, multiple tumors, or macrovascular invasion, Medicine (Baltimore) 94 (3) (2015) e396, https://doi.org/10.1097/md.0000000000000396.

[11] E.P. Misiakos, N.P. Karidis, G. Kouraklis, Current treatment for colorectal liver metastases, World Journal of Gastroenterology: WJG 17 (36) (2011) 4067–4075, https://doi.org/10.3748/wjg.v17.i36.4067.

[12] E. Vibert, T. Perniceni, H. Levard, C. Denet, N.K. Shahri, B. Gayet, Laparoscopic liver resection, British Journal of Surgery 93 (1) (2006) 67–72, https://doi.org/10.1002/bjs.5150.

[13] H. Kaneko, S. Takagi, Y. Otsuka, M. Tsuchiya, A. Tamura, T. Katagiri, T. Maeda, T. Shiba, Laparoscopic liver resection of hepatocellular carcinoma, American Journal of Surgery 189 (2) (2005) 190–194, https://doi.org/10.1016/j.amjsurg.2004.09.010.

[14] A.D. Guerron, S. Aliyev, O. Agcaoglu, E. Aksoy, H.E. Taskin, F. Aucejo, C. Miller, J. Fung, E. Berber, Laparoscopic versus open resection of colorectal liver metastasis, Surgical Endoscopy 27 (4) (2013) 1138–1143, https://doi.org/10.1007/s00464-012-2563-2.

[15] I. Ahmed, P. Paraskeva, A clinical review of single-incision laparoscopic surgery, Surgeon 9 (6) (2011) 341–351, https://doi.org/10.1016/j.surge.2011.06.003.

[16] A.A. Fretland, A.M. Kazaryan, B.A. Bjornbeth, K. Flatmark, M.H. Andersen, T.I. Tonnessen, G.M.W. Bjornelv, M.W. Fagerland, R. Kristiansen, K. Oyri, B. Edwin, Open versus laparoscopic liver resection for colorectal liver metastases (the Oslo-CoMet study): study protocol for a randomized controlled trial, Trials 16 (1) (2015) 1–10, https://doi.org/10.1186/s13063-015-0577-5.

[17] K. Cleary, T.M. Peters, Image-guided interventions: technology review and clinical applications, Annual Review of Biomedical Engineering 12 (1) (2010) 119–142, https://doi.org/10.1146/annurev-bioeng-070909-105249.

[18] C. Couinaud, Le foie: études anatomiques et chirurgicales, Masson & Cie, 1957.

[19] S.M. Strasberg, C. Phillips, Use and dissemination of the brisbane 2000 nomenclature of liver anatomy and resections, Annals of Surgery 257 (3) (2013) 377–382, https://doi.org/10.1097/SLA.0b013e31825a01f6.

[20] H.K. Gumprecht, D.C. Widenka, C.B. Lumenta, BrainLab VectorVision Neuronavigation System: technology and clinical experiences in 131 cases, Neurosurgery 44 (1) (1999) 97–104.

[21] H. Staecker, B.W. O'malley, H. Eisenberg, B.E. Yoder, Use of the LandmarX™ surgical navigation system in lateral skull base and temporal bone surgery, Skull Base 11 (04) (2001) 245–256.

[22] W. Lamadé, G. Glombitza, L. Fischer, P. Chiu, C.E. Cárdenas, M. Thorn, H.P. Meinzer, L. Grenacher, H. Bauer, T. Lehnert, C. Herfarth, The impact of 3-dimensional reconstructions on operation planning in liver surgery, Archives of Surgery (Chicago, Ill.: 1960) 135 (11) (2000) 1256–1261.

[23] H. Lang, A. Radtke, M. Hindennach, T. Schroeder, N.R. Frühauf, M. Malagó, H. Bourquain, H.-O. Peitgen, K.J. Oldhafer, C.E. Broelsch, Impact of virtual tumor resection and computer-assisted risk analysis on operation planning and intraoperative strategy in major hepatic resection, Archives of Surgery (Chicago, Ill.: 1960) 140 (7) (2005) 629–638, https://doi.org/10.1001/archsurg.140.7.629.

[24] C. Hansen, S. Zidowitz, B. Preim, Impact of model-based risk analysis for liver surgery planning, International Journal of Computer Assisted Radiology and Surgery 9 (3) (2014) 473–480, https://doi.org/10.1007/s11548-013-0937-0.

[25] P. Lamata, F. Lamata, V. Sojar, P. Makowski, L. Massoptier, S. Casciaro, W. Ali, T. Stüdeli, J. Declerck, O.J. Elle, B. Edwin, Use of the resection map system as guidance during hepatectomy, Surgical Endoscopy 24 (9) (2010) 2327–2337, https://doi.org/10.1007/s00464-010-0915-3.

[26] A. Zygomalas, D. Karavias, D. Koutsouris, I. Maroulis, D.D. Karavias, K. Giokas, V. Megalooikonomou, Computer-assisted liver tumor surgery using a novel semiautomatic and a hybrid semiautomatic segmentation algorithm, Medical & Biological Engineering & Computing (2015), https://doi.org/10.1007/s11517-015-1369-5.

[27] B. Preim, C.P. Botha, Visual Computing for Medicine: Theory, Algorithms, and Applications, 2nd edition, Newnes, 2013.

[28] P. Markelj, D. Tomaževič, B. Likar, F. Pernuš, A review of 3D/2D registration methods for image-guided interventions, Medical Image Analysis 16 (3) (2012) 642–661, https://doi.org/10.1016/j.media.2010.03.005.

[29] J. Chalela, C. Kidwell, L. Nentwich, M. Luby, J. Butman, A. Demchuk, M. Hill, N. Patronas, L. Latour, S. Warach, Magnetic resonance imaging and computed tomography in emergency assessment of patients with suspected acute stroke: a prospective comparison, Lancet 369 (2007) 293–298, https://doi.org/10.1016/S0140-6736(07)60151-2.

[30] B. Sdiri, A. Beghdadi, F.A. Cheikh, M. Pedersen, O.J. Elle, An adaptive contrast enhancement method for stereo endoscopic images combining binocular just noticeable difference model and depth information, Electronic Imaging 2016 (13) (2016) 1–7.

[31] H. Carbajo-Rodríguez, J.L. Aguayo-Albasini, V. Soria-Aledo, C. García-López, Surgical smoke: risks and preventive measures, Cirugía Española (English Edition) 85 (5) (2009) 274–279.

[32] C. Wang, F.A. Cheikh, A. Beghdadi, O.J. Elle, Adaptive context encoding module for semantic segmentation, Electronic Imaging 2020 (10) (2020) 27, 7pp.

[33] C. Wang, Intra-operative image enhancement and registration for image guided laparoscopic liver resection, PhD Thesis at The Norwegian University of Science and Technology, Gjøvik, Norway, 2021.

[34] R. Naseem, Cross-modality guided image enhancement, PhD Thesis at The Norwegian University of Science and Technology, Gjøvik, Norway, 2021.

[35] B. Sdiri, 2D/3D endoscopic image enhancement and analysis for video guided surgery, PhD Thesis at Université Sorbonne Paris Nord, Paris, France, 2018.

[36] Z.A. Khan, Learning based quality assessment for medical imaging in the context of liver cancer treatment, PhD Thesis at Université Sorbonne Paris Nord, Paris, France, 2021.

[37] N. Haouchine, S. Cotin, Segmentation and labelling of intra-operative laparoscopic images using structure from point cloud, in: IEEE International Symposium on Biomedical Imaging, IEEE, 2016, pp. 115–118.

[38] E. Gibson, M.R. Robu, S. Thompson, P.E. Edwards, C. Schneider, K. Gurusamy, B. Davidson, D.J. Hawkes, D.C. Barratt, M.J. Clarkson, Deep residual networks for automatic segmentation of laparoscopic videos of the liver, in: Medical Imaging 2017: Image-Guided Procedures, Robotic Interventions, and Modeling, vol. 10135, International Society for Optics and Photonics, 2017, p. 101351M.

[39] M. Allan, A. Shvets, T. Kurmann, Z. Zhang, R. Duggal, Y.-H. Su, N. Rieke, I. Laina, N. Kalavakonda, S. Bodenstedt, et al., 2017 robotic instrument segmentation challenge, arXiv preprint, arXiv:1902.06426, 2019.

[40] A. Mohammed, S. Yildirim, I. Farup, M. Pedersen, Ø. Hovde, StreoScenNet: surgical stereo robotic scene segmentation, in: Medical Imaging 2019: Image-Guided Procedures, Robotic Interventions, and Modeling, vol. 10951, International Society for Optics and Photonics, 2019, p. 109510P.

[41] X. Liu, Z. Deng, Y. Yang, Recent progress in semantic image segmentation, Artificial Intelligence Review (2018) 1–18.

[42] F. Garcia-Lamont, J. Cervantes, A. López, L. Rodriguez, Segmentation of images by color features: A survey, Neurocomputing 292 (2018) 1–27.

[43] D.-C. He, L. Wang, Texture unit, texture spectrum, and texture analysis, IEEE Transactions on Geoscience and Remote Sensing 28 (4) (1990) 509–512.

[44] D.G. Lowe, Distinctive image features from scale-invariant keypoints, International Journal of Computer Vision 60 (2) (2004) 91–110.

[45] L. Bourdev, S. Maji, T. Brox, J. Malik, Detecting people using mutually consistent poselet activations, in: European Conference on Computer Vision, Springer, 2010, pp. 168–181.

[46] G. Csurka, C. Dance, L. Fan, J. Willamowski, C. Bray, Visual categorization with bags of keypoints, in: ECCV Workshop on Statistical Learning in Computer Vision, vol. 1, Prague, 2004, pp. 1–2.

[47] B. Fulkerson, A. Vedaldi, S. Soatto, Class segmentation and object localization with superpixel neighborhoods, in: IEEE International Conference on Computer Vision, IEEE, 2009, pp. 670–677.

[48] X. He, R.S. Zemel, M.Á. Carreira-Perpiñán, Multiscale conditional random fields for image labeling, in: IEEE Computer Society Conference on Computer Vision and Pattern Recognition, vol. 2, IEEE, 2004, pp. II–II.

[49] C. Russell, P. Kohli, P.H. Torr, et al., Associative hierarchical CRFs for object class image segmentation, in: IEEE International Conference on Computer Vision, IEEE, 2009, pp. 739–746.

[50] J. Shotton, M. Johnson, R. Cipolla, Semantic texton forests for image categorization and segmentation, in: IEEE Conference on Computer Vision and Pattern Recognition, IEEE, 2008, pp. 1–8.

[51] J. Shotton, J. Winn, C. Rother, A. Criminisi, TextonBoost for image understanding: Multi-class object recognition and segmentation by jointly modeling texture, layout, and context, International Journal of Computer Vision 81 (1) (2009) 2–23.

[52] J. Long, E. Shelhamer, T. Darrell, Fully convolutional networks for semantic segmentation, in: IEEE Conference on Computer Vision and Pattern Recognition, IEEE, 2015, pp. 3431–3440.

[53] T.S. Newman, H. Yi, A survey of the marching cubes algorithm, Computers & Graphics 30 (5) (2006) 854–879, https://doi.org/10.1016/j.cag.2006.07.021.

[54] Y. Ohtake, A. Belyaev, M. Alexa, G. Turk, H.-P. Seidel, Multi-level partition of unity implicits, ACM Transactions on Graphics 22 (3) (2003) 463, https://doi.org/10.1145/882262.882293.

[55] J. Wu, R. Ma, X. Ma, F. Jia, Q. Hu, Curvature-dependent surface visualization of vascular structures, Computerized Medical Imaging and Graphics: Official Journal of the Computerized Medical Imaging Society 34 (8) (2010) 651–658, https://doi.org/10.1016/j.compmedimag.2010.07.006.

[56] J. Wu, Q. Hu, X. Ma, Comparative study of surface modeling methods for vascular structures, Computerized Medical Imaging and Graphics: Official Journal of the Computerized Medical Imaging Society 37 (1) (2013) 4–14, https://doi.org/10.1016/j.compmedimag.2013.01.002.

[57] W.J. Schroeder, J.A. Zarge, W.E. Lorensen, Decimation of triangle meshes, in: Proceedings of the 19th Annual Conference on Computer Graphics and Interactive Techniques, 1992, pp. 65–70.

[58] R. Bade, J. Haase, B. Preim, Comparison of fundamental mesh smoothing algorithms for medical surface models, SimVis 1 (c) (2006) 1–16.

[59] R. Palomar, F.A. Cheikh, B. Edwin, A. Beghdadhi, O.J. Elle, Surface reconstruction for planning and navigation of liver resections, Computerized Medical Imaging and Graphics 53 (2016) 30–42, https://doi.org/10.1016/j.compmedimag.2016.07.003, https://www.sciencedirect.com/science/article/pii/S0895611116300684.

[60] M. Kazhdan, M. Bolitho, Poisson surface reconstruction, in: Proceedings - Eurographics Symposium on Geometry Processing, 2006.

[61] L. Maier-Hein, P. Mountney, A. Bartoli, H. Elhawary, D. Elson, A. Groch, A. Kolb, M. Rodrigues, J. Sorger, S. Speidel, et al., Optical techniques for 3D surface reconstruction in computer-assisted laparoscopic surgery, Medical Image Analysis 17 (8) (2013) 974–996.

[62] T. Peters, K. Cleary, Image-Guided Interventions: Technology and Applications, Springer Science & Business Media, 2008.

[63] T. Ungi, A. Lasso, G. Fichtinger, Open-source platforms for navigated image-guided interventions, Medical Image Analysis 33 (2016) 181–186.

[64] C. Askeland, O.V. Solberg, J.B.L. Bakeng, I. Reinertsen, G.A. Tangen, E.F. Hofstad, D.H. Iversen, C. Våpenstad, T. Selbekk, T. Langø, et al., CustusX: an open-source research platform for image-guided therapy, International Journal of Computer Assisted Radiology and Surgery 11 (4) (2016) 505–519.

[65] S. Pieper, M. Halle, R. Kikinis, 3D slicer, in: IEEE International Symposium on Biomedical Imaging: Nano to Macro, IEEE, 2004, pp. 632–635.

[66] T. Andrea, Accurate and effective model-to-patient registration for navigation in image guided laparoscopic liver resection, PhD Thesis at Oslo University Hospital, Oslo, Norway, 2020.

[67] Microsoft HoloLens | Mixed Reality Technology for Business, https://www.microsoft.com/en-us/hololens.

[68] Magic Leap 1, https://www.magicleap.com/magic-leap-1.

[69] S. Barteit, L. Lanfermann, T. Bärnighausen, F. Neuhann, C. Beiersmann, Augmented, mixed, and virtual reality-based head-mounted devices for medical education: systematic review, JMIR Serious Games 9 (3) (2021) e29080, https://doi.org/10.2196/29080, https://games.jmir.org/2021/3/e29080.

[70] J.K. Haas, A History of the Unity Game Engine, Worcester Polytechnic Institute, 2014.

[71] Y. Saito, M. Sugimoto, S. Imura, Y. Morine, T. Ikemoto, S. Iwahashi, S. Yamada, M. Shimada, Intraoperative 3D hologram support with mixed reality techniques in liver surgery, Annals of Surgery 271 (1) (2020) e4–e7.

[72] I.M. Sauer, M. Queisner, P. Tang, S. Moosburner, O. Hoepfner, R. Horner, R. Lohmann, J. Pratschke, Mixed reality in visceral surgery: development of a suitable workflow and evaluation of intraoperative use-cases, Annals of Surgery 266 (5) (2017) 706–712.

[73] R.P. Kumar, E. Pelanis, R. Bugge, H. Brun, R. Palomar, D.L. Aghayan, A.A. Fretland, B. Edwin, O.J. Elle, Use of mixed reality for surgery planning: Assessment and development workflow, Journal of Biomedical Informatics 112 (2020) 100077.

[74] R. Palomar, Geometric modeling for planning of liver resection procedures, PhD thesis, 2018.

[75] X. Wu, R. Liu, J. Yu, S. Xu, C. Yang, Z. Shao, S. Yang, Z. Ye, Mixed reality technology–assisted orthopedics surgery navigation, Surgical Innovation 25 (3) (2018) 304–305.

[76] Z. Zhou, Z. Yang, S. Jiang, X. Ma, F. Zhang, H. Yan, Surgical navigation system for low-dose-rate brachytherapy based on mixed reality, IEEE Computer Graphics and Applications 41 (3) (2020) 113–123.

[77] C.F. Davrieux, M.E. Giménez, C.A. González, A. Ancel, M. Guinin, B. Fahrer, E. Serra, J.-M. Kwak, J. Marescaux, A. Hostettler, Mixed reality navigation system for ultrasound-guided percutaneous punctures: a pre-clinical evaluation, Surgical Endoscopy 34 (1) (2020) 226–230.

[78] E.Z. Cai, Y. Gao, K.Y. Ngiam, T.C. Lim, Mixed reality intraoperative navigation in craniomaxillofacial surgery, Plastic and Reconstructive Surgery 148 (4) (2021) 686e–688e.

[79] A. Teatini, R.P. Kumar, O.J. Elle, O. Wiig, Mixed reality as a novel tool for diagnostic and surgical navigation in orthopaedics, International Journal of Computer Assisted Radiology and Surgery 16 (3) (2021) 407–414.

[80] M. Birlo, P.E. Edwards, M. Clarkson, D. Stoyanov, Utility of optical see-through head mounted displays in augmented reality-assisted surgery: A systematic review, Medical Image Analysis (2022) 102361.

[81] R. Li, W. Si, X. Liao, Q. Wang, R. Klein, P.-A. Heng, Mixed reality based respiratory liver tumor puncture navigation, Computational Visual Media 5 (4) (2019) 363–374.

[82] P. Gavriilidis, B. Edwin, E. Pelanis, E. Hidalgo, N. De'Angelis, R. Memeo, L. Aldrighetti, R.P. Sutcliffe, Navigated liver surgery: State of the art and future perspectives, Hepatobiliary and Pancreatic Diseases International 21 (2) (2022) 226–233, https://doi.org/10.1016/j.hbpd.2021.09.002.

[83] E. Pelanis, R.P. Kumar, D.L. Aghayan, R. Palomar, Å.A. Fretland, H. Brun, O.J. Elle, B. Edwin, Use of mixed reality for improved spatial understanding of liver anatomy, Minimally Invasive Therapy & Allied Technologies 29 (3) (2020) 154–160, https://doi.org/10.1080/13645706.2019.1616558.

[84] C. Conrad, M. Fusaglia, M. Peterhans, H. Lu, S. Weber, B. Gayet, Augmented reality navigation surgery facilitates laparoscopic rescue of failed portal vein embolization, Journal of the American College of Surgeons 223 (4) (2016) e31–e34, https://doi.org/10.1016/j.jamcollsurg.2016.06.392.

[85] J. Hallet, L. Soler, M. Diana, D. Mutter, T.F. Baumert, F. Habersetzer, J. Marescaux, P. Pessaux, Transthoracic minimally invasive liver resection guided by augmented reality, Journal of the American College of Surgeons 220 (5) (2015) e55–e60, https://doi.org/10.1016/j.jamcollsurg.2014.12.053.

[86] G.A. Prevost, B. Eigl, I. Paolucci, T. Rudolph, M. Peterhans, S. Weber, G. Beldi, D. Candinas, A. Lachenmayer, Efficiency, accuracy and clinical applicability of a new image-guided surgery system in 3D laparoscopic liver surgery, Journal of Gastrointestinal Surgery (2019), https://doi.org/10.1007/s11605-019-04395-7.

[87] A. Teatini, E. Pelanis, D.L. Aghayan, R.P. Kumar, R. Palomar, Å.A. Fretland, B. Edwin, O.J. Elle, The effect of intraoperative imaging on surgical navigation for laparoscopic liver resection surgery, Scientific Reports 9 (1) (2019) 1–11, https://doi.org/10.1038/s41598-019-54915-3.

[88] E. Pelanis, A. Teatini, B. Eigl, A. Regensburger, A. Alzaga, R.P. Kumar, T. Rudolph, D.L. Aghayan, C. Riediger, N. Kvarnström, O.J. Elle, B. Edwin, Evaluation of a novel navigation platform for laparoscopic liver surgery with organ deformation compensation using injected fiducials, Medical Image Analysis 69 (2021) 101946, https://doi.org/10.1016/j.media.2020.101946.

[89] A. Teatini, J.-N. Brunet, S. Nikolaev, B. Edwin, S. Cotin, O.J. Elle, Use of stereo-laparoscopic liver surface reconstruction to compensate for pneumoperitoneum deformation through biomechanical modeling. To cite this version: HAL Id: hal-03130613. Use of stereo-laparoscopic liver surface reconstruction to compensate for (2021).

CHAPTER 20

Immersive media productions involving light fields and virtual production LED walls

Volker Helzle
Filmakademie Baden-Württemberg, Ludwigsburg, Germany

20.1. Light fields in media production

Light fields deal with many stereo-related aspects and creative opportunities for visual storytelling. XR headsets and holographic displays are particularly suitable for light field data. In addition, light fields have the potential to provide more flexibility and possibilities in professional visual effects (VFX) post-productions as well as providing a base asset that can be reused beyond the initially targeted use case. Acquisition of light fields, however, appears, for now, even more challenging as for stereo productions.

We will take a close look at implications of the "Unfolding" production and working with a light field camera rig in a professional TV studio. Data acquisition and use in a creative pipeline with standardized tools will be addressed. We will, furthermore, discuss results on different output displays, such as auto-stereoscopic displays.

20.1.1 The creation of "Unfolding"

The Unfolding production investigated the creative potential of light fields from capture over processing to finally display. It features the international cellist Isabel Gehweiler[1] performing one of her own musical creations. The scenario reflects a typical VFX setup "subject in front of a green screen." Foreground and background elements can be separated and allow modification in a post-production process. The produced footage was used to demonstrate how light field data can simplify and enrich this creative process. The data also served as a foundation for further research and tool development. The light field rig created by Saarland University was tested in terms of usability in media productions, both on-set and in post-production. The fundamental preprocessing (de-bayering, color calibration, rectification) was developed and provided by Trinity College Dublin (TCD), specifically for the requirements of light fields.

The concept was developed in close collaboration with a professional director of photography (DoP) who also led the studio production. This was essential since the

---

[1] https://www.isabelgehweiler.com.

Immersive Video Technologies
https://doi.org/10.1016/B978-0-32-391755-1.00026-2
575

intention was to define the needs of creatives and identify "real world" problems as well as the potential in handling the light field camera and data.

The entire production was planned by creating a virtual version of the scenery in the DCC application *Blender*. It enabled the team to plan the physical recording, including cameras and timing. The process also allowed for the creation of a virtual light field camera according to the specifications of the Saarland University rig. It allowed us to produce synthetic data of the 64 virtual cameras without involving challenges of a real recording test, including physical setup and data management. This process was carried out in close collaboration with the DoP, allowing multiple iterations to define and achieve the creative vision. In addition, the gathered data gave other project partners a head start for tuning their post processing algorithms towards the specific data the physical light field camera would produce.

With a *Blender* plugin to generate light field cameras based on physical parameters, such as disparity between cameras, field of view, amount of cameras, shape of camera grid, and position in the scene, a complete previsualization video has been developed (Fig. 20.1). This workflow allowed multiple fast iterations between DoP and a technical department.

Figure 20.1 Light field previsualization using *Blender*.

The actual recording was done at a TV studio of Saarländischer Rundfunk, featuring the light field camera rig engineered by Saarland University. The rig consists of 64 individual cameras with global shutter, 1/1.2" sensors at 1920 x 1200 resolution. The cameras were placed with an even distance of 90 mm in an 8 x 8 matrix. (See Fig. 20.2.)

Each camera captures at up to 41 frames per second at max resolution. Custom electronics allow triggering at 10 µs precision. Each camera is connected to a NUC6i5SYK (Core i5, 8GB RAM and 256GB SSD). The custom hardware rig allows for various

Figure 20.2 64 camera light field rig by Saarland University.

configurations (shape and size), such as 60×60 cm, 2×2 m or 1×4 m. Recording required up to 72.5 Gb/s, which equals 2 min per TB and a maximum recording time of 12 minutes at maximum frame rate until the SSD caches filled up. Unfolding was recorded with 25 fps, resulting in a data rate of 44.2 Gbps. Four (4) takes were recorded with a total data of 3.86 TB.

In cooperation with the DoP and the staff from the studio, a 5×5 meter greenstage, adequate lighting, and multi channel audio recording was realized. To illuminate the green screen as evenly as possible and at the same time light the actress visually pleasant, a huge butterfly light rig from the top and some indirect light reflectors from the sides were set up. To synchronize the images with the sound, a visible timecode clap on stage and a metronome tick provided via headphones were used. To avoid any maladjustment of the camera, the setup and calibration was done on stage shortly before the recording started. Instead of using a checkerboard for calibration, a plane with a textured motive (Fig. 20.4) was used. The additional texture plane added necessary natural features to the green screen dominated scene. These features were used to rectify the cameras in post-production.

The Unfolding filming was realized within a realistic production environment of a TV studio. Based on the preproduction, we recorded four runs, one for each cellist voice in the play. The data was then used in varying post-production processes to craft two versions. Version 1.0 was intended to evaluate the usefulness and added benefits of light fields in a 2D production pipeline using professional post-production software, such as *Foundry's Nuke*. Additionally we investigated which requirements had to be met by the preprocessing of the RAW light field capturings to use them efficiently. This production was used as reference and provided ground truth data. It served several SAUCE partner developments, such as the preprocessing and calibration developed by Trinity College Dublin. Version 2.0 makes extended use of the light field data in an offline and real-time application for auto-stereoscopic display output. Combining light field data with 3D renderings and displaying the results way beyond 2D were the key aspects. (See Fig. 20.3.)

Figure 20.3 Final image from Unfolding 1.0. Full video: https://youtu.be/UnsmKQjO4ro.

The vision of the first production was centered around using focus as a creative tool guiding the viewers attention throughout the musical performance. The scenery starts in a white room, where the cellist sits at her instrument, all out of focus. With the first notes, the focus slowly expands. During the cellists performance, the focus adjusts to the scenery through tilt-shift simulations, focus shifts, and t-stop variations. All those effects were created and animated in post-production by exploiting the possibilities of the captured light field. Based on the light field, the camera perspective could be chosen in post-production and depth information was generated to steer the focus. Initially only the strings of the chello are visible. The focus moves perfectly with the musician's hand movements. Then the entire bow is in focus, and the face of the cellist becomes visible. Finally, the area of focus expands completely over the musician. Clones of her join in the canon. Four identical musicians play at the same time and fill the room with sound.

20.1.2 Post-production of Unfolding 1.0

To be able to make use of the captured light field material, the RAW data had to be processed. This preprocessing started with debayering all frames of all cameras. By debayering, color information for each pixel is interpolated based on the intensity values of neighboring pixels. This is a standard process normally executed by any camera internally. For the light field camera, the processing overhead, while capturing, was designed to be as small as possible, while no compromises were made regarding recording quality. After debayering, the calibration of all cameras towards each other had to be addressed. The geometric calibration (also known as rectification) has been performed with a SLAM++ implementation developed by Brno University.

Two methods for color calibration, developed by SAUCE partners, have been evaluated with the captured light field material. For light field camera arrays, a color equalization step is important to account for differences in color between the different cameras. Two color equalization schemes were proposed. They use correspondences between reference and test image pairs to estimate color correction functions, which ensure that color consistency is maintained across all views.

The first method is an extension of the color stabilization method of Vazquez-Corral and Bertalmío (2014) [1], originally intended to conform footage of common scene elements from multiple cameras/color encoding schemes. It equalizes the colors between a test and reference image pair by determining an optimal 3 x 3 matrix and non-linear correction term (inspired by the camera encoding pipeline), which minimizes the difference in colors between them. A second method has also been investigated when a color chart is present in the scene. TCD extended the method in Grogan and Dahyot (2019) [2], which uses color correspondences between images to compute a thin plate spline transformation, which maps the color distribution of one image to match the others. TCD extended this approach to account for both correspondences between test and reference image pairs, as well as correspondences between the captured and ground truth color charts. This ensures that colors across the light field remain consistent, while also matching the ground truth colors. With both methods, the center view is taken as the reference view, and all other view's colors are aligned to it. A color propagation scheme has also been considered to account for high disparities, in which each concentric circle of views around the center is corrected and later used as references for the following circle. Colors captured by each camera are found to be temporally consistent, so the color correction function that is estimated for a single light field video frame can be applied to the whole video sequence without introducing temporal inconsistencies.

The method by Grogan and Dahyot (2019) [2] has been chosen for the Unfolding production, since a color checker has been captured in all shots, and a calibration to a known color space of adjusting all cameras to the center camera is superior for the intended post-production. All preprocessing steps (debayering, rectification, and color equalization) were calculated on the computing cluster belonging to the light field camera itself. The 64 computers work jointly to process all frames. This was not done while capturing, but as an additional step later on. The actual post-production was carried out at Filmakademie. By using a combination of tools developed by SAUCE partners and established post-production software (*Nuke*), the Unfolding 1.0 video[2] was generated, showcasing the potential and possibilities of light field video material. For this purpose it was first tested whether light field data offer advantages in existing

[2] https://youtu.be/UnsmKQjO4ro.

Figure 20.4 Recording setup at studio. Notice the textured background for automatic calibration.

workflows. The test results also served as a basis to compare more traditional, stereo 3D post-production workflows with light field ones. The *Nuke*-based production was completed within three months. The background extraction and compositing utilized chroma keying, and the tilt-shift lens effect were realized based on a depth controlled blur. Light fields also provide the possibility to generate physically correct depth of field effects without calculating an intermediate depth map. This is achieved by blending the different views captured in a light field. However, this approach required a dense enough captured light field with minimal disparity between neighboring cameras. Otherwise block artifacts can appear. Interpolation and other optimizations to generate artifact-free results have been advanced within the SAUCE project by TCD. Further details of the Unfolding production can be found in Trottnow et al. [3].

To establish light field data in workflows of creative productions, several aspects should be addressed in the future. Primarily, efficient compression methods to reduce the amount of captured data appear desirable to apply them in traditional post-production pipelines. The light field system in use produced 64 individual raw video streams. This data required a well prepared pipeline to be processed for the final result. The initial step of working with the data was to eliminate inconsistencies. This involved color correction and geometric calibration of all cameras involved.

Future use of light field data should allow for high quality dynamic and temporal consistent depth maps as well as 3d reconstructions of objects captured. This would remove constraints using green screen workflows, allowing for creative procedures directly manipulating the geometric data and associated parameters, such as lighting and surface characteristics in a post process. In addition to separating foreground from background objects, it appears desirable to simulate lens characteristics and their associated effects. Ideally, an operator would gain full access over focus, the associated focus plane (tilt shift), and blur appearance (f-stops) embedded in a post-production workflow. Additionally functionality to alter the camera perspective would be beneficial, as they cope with the physical limitations of the light field rig. Other useful tools can be the representation of light field data through auto-stereoscopic displays. First prosumer solutions are available on the market. An example is the *looking glass*, which provides an auto-stereoscopic display capable of 45 horizontal views.

20.1.3 Post-production of Unfolding 2.0

The output of the original Unfolding 1.0 production was a compositing of parts of the light field footage in front of a white background, which demonstrated some advantages of refocus and tilt-shift effects. For Unfolding 2.0, we decided to go for more elaborate results by displaying the footage on the *Looking Glass* auto-stereoscopic display and replacing the background with an immersive 3D environment. The goal was to further showcase the versatile nature of light field footage.

To achieve this, several *Nuke* scripts were developed to help with the automatic processing of the light field footage. This included preprocessing, such as chroma key, retiming and rectification as well as calculating depth maps for the post-production. Additionally we needed new or adapted plug-ins for *Unity* to display footage on the auto-stereoscopic display.

The device has its own format for displaying light field footage. It's called "Quilt" and consists of 45 images arranged in a specific order on a contact sheet. Since we only had one row consisting of 8 cameras, the best way to get to 45 images seemed to be to interpolate some frames in between. We achieved this with the *Nuke Kronos* plugin. (See Fig. 20.5.)

After we got our first Quilt-footage on the auto-stereoscopic display, we realized that the disparity between the original light field camera array was way too high to be looked at comfortably. It caused some eyestrain, and most of the scene seemed to be out of focus. Therefore we decided to go for a real-time 3D scene in *Unity* instead. This gave us way more flexibility in setting up the camera to achieve the best visual experience on the device.

A Quilt is a 4k image, containing 5×9 smaller sub images. One for each of the required 45 views of the holo display. The quilts are defined as static images, so we had to modify the existing plugin to support video. We also had to add support for transparencies, as this was needed for the integration of the individual cellists into the 3d scenery. To make this possible, the high performance video (HPV) player was used.

Figure 20.5 Unfolding version 2.0 on auto-stereoscopic display.

The HPV eco-system was originally created within the former Dreamspace project[3] funded by the European Union. The HPV is a cross-platform C++ toolset for playing back high-resolution and high frame rate video content. HPV also supports alpha masks. Unfolding version 2.0 for the *Looking Glass* can be obtained from the SAUCE project website.[4]

20.2. Immersive LED wall productions

During the SAUCE project, Filmakademie explored possibilities of immersive virtual production setups featuring large scale LED walls. The technology of LED walls has the potential to provide multiple advantages for modern movie productions, including VFX. These range from time savings, environmental aspects over visual feedback on set, and minimized post-production efforts. In this chapter, we will share an overview of the productions carried out at cave and flat wall studio setup, as well as insights into challenges and solutions.

20.2.1 LED cave production

Filmakademie ran experimental productions on immersive movie productions at the LED cave built by RentEventTec in Mannheim Germany and a reduced setup in one of the Filmakademie studios.

---

[3] https://www.dreamspaceproject.eu/.
[4] https://www.sauceproject.eu/Downloads.

The LED cave[5] is a D shaped construction of 3 large screens (front, back, top) with an overall size of 18 m by 9.5 m and a height of 4 m. The curved front screen consisted of 464 LED modules with 1.9 mm pixel pitch (pp) and had a resolution of 14.848 x 2.048 pixels. The top screen used 594 modules, also with 1.9 mm pp, but a reduced resolution of 9.216 x 4.864 pixels. For the back screen 288 brighter, but also less dense modules with 3.9 mm pp and an overall resolution of 9.216 x 4.864 pixel were used. Seven synchronized workstations were needed to fill this amount of pixels in a sufficient manner. The render nodes ran either *Unreal* or *Unity* to generate the displayed scenes. For the recorded image to look correct in the camera, it had to be distorted due to the camera position and rotation. For this purpose, it was necessary to be able to determine this data from the camera at any time. A 12 camera *Optitrack Prime41* motion capturing system with passive markers was used. (See Fig. 20.6.)

Figure 20.6 Left: LED cave is a D shaped construction of 3 large screens (front, back, top); Right: car illuminated by autumn environment.

As an initial scenario, we tested using the LED wall by utilizing static pre-captured real footage, instead of real-time rendered artificial environments. We were able to test the pipeline of quickly changing background and lighting in a car shoot scenario. In a second stage, we ran tests on how to interact with virtual, rendered content on the LED wall in real-time on tablet clients using a software environment developed by Filmakademie.

To preserve the light characteristics created by the cave and at the same time reduce image artifacts, such as moiré, a professional cinema camera and fast lenses (Sony Venice, Zeiss ultra prime lenses) were used during the production.

One big advantage of using a LED wall in a movie production was that it provided not just imagery for the background, but also the lighting. The LED wall thereby mostly replaced the need for other light sources on set. Complex reflections on objects (e.g.,

---

[5] https://www.ledcave.de/.

car paint, windows) in the studio were generated effortlessly, while having full control over the scenery being displayed on the wall. Imagery displayed on the LED screen could be exchanged quickly. This quick exchange though required tools to easily search and find appropriate content.

Imagine for example a DoP, set dresser, creative director, etc., requesting a change of the background and lighting. While technically quickly possible, the content also needed to be generated or reused from a database. A search framework attached to a diverse and holistic database, probably even capable of performing transformations, such as file format conversions, is needed. For our use case a database of 360 HDR images enriched with descriptive labels was searchable through a search and transformation framework developed by DNEG within the SAUCE project. Within moments, it was possible to search, e.g., for an autumn forest in the search frontend, extract the image from it and display it on the LED cave, changing the entire scenery and lighting.

Virtual productions become increasingly common in modern movie productions. The possibilities to visualize, edit, and explore virtual 3D content directly on a movie set make it increasingly attractive for VFX productions. Some of the virtual production scenarios also involve animated characters and motion capturing. But the complexity of animation systems prohibits it's usage on a film set. Though most of the virtual production tools and frameworks are not publicly available or open source, none of them has the possibility to interactively and intuitively animate characters on set.

The research and development team of Filmakademie Baden-Württemberg engineered the open source "Virtual Production Editing Tools"[6] (VPET) [4] [5] over the last years. With as little hardware overhead as possible, VPET offers the possibility to stream an arbitrary 3D scene to tablet clients. On the tablets, the 3D scene can be aligned with the real world in augmented reality (AR), making the tablet a window to the provided set extension. Users can explore and edit 3D elements, lighting as well as rigid body animations. The scene host and all clients communicate changes among themselves through a synchronization server, keeping the scene consistent. In addition, approaches were developed and tested to make procedural character animation on set possible by using machine learning and providing high level control over a character. It does not make sense to author a complete animation from scratch with an on-set virtual production tool set, as it requires too much time and expertise to produce a convincing result. Nevertheless, the possibility to easily direct virtual characters on a film set appears desirable. Tablets offer an intuitive way to interact with elements during a virtual production, e.g., in augmented reality being useful for directing characters. Flexibility and ease of use are the main targets for this work.

Towards this goal, Filmakademie and Pompeu Fabra University have been working on a joint effort within the SAUCE project. On set, only high level commands should

---

[6] http://vpet.research.animationsinstitut.de/.

be used to drive a character. Commands such as "Go there" and "Run" should be used on the VPET tablet tools. (See Fig. 20.7.) This requires that procedural animations are generated on an arbitrary host application and that the character is animated in a scene-aware manner. Obstacles should be avoided, and uneven grounds need to be compensated. This technology is also known from game creation, but only slowly introduced into the film industry. Such complex, highly adaptable animation solving, required for virtual productions, cannot be executed on a tablet conveniently. Therefore an API was introduced to plug arbitrary animation-solving engines into the VPET ecosystem; different solutions are continuously explored. This API is part of the open-source release and can be obtained from the project public repository.[7]

Figure 20.7 VPET offers real-time on-set light, asset and animation editing via an intuitive interface.

To be able to make the best use of an LED wall setup, there is a high demand for fast and intuitive tools that allow adding, directing, and editing assets on set. VPET was developed to edit and explore 3D sceneries on set, and therefore already proved to be an essential tool in such a LED wall-based virtual production scenario. With the added character animation interface, VPET becomes even more valuable and makes it possible to also direct virtual characters intuitively and on a high level in real-time on set, especially for the previsualization phase, but also in the final production. The developed search and transformation framework provides an essential architecture to stay agile and fast in a demanding virtual production process. Reusable assets can be found and added to the scenery quickly.

[7] https://github.com/FilmakademieRnd/VPET.

20.2.2 Flat LED wall production

Another LED wall production was carried out at studio facilities on the Filmakademie campus realizing the short movie "Snowflower."[8] This time the focus was on 3D real-time rendered content and character animation being used, in addition to a real set. Rendering was realized in *Unity 3D*.

The room itself as well as all interior objects were built in *Cinema 4D*, further refined in *Maya*, and then textured in *Substance Painter*. *Unity* was the backbone of the production, since the machine learning framework had been set up here. *Unity* would also handle the communication with the tablet clients to allow for animation control and set editing. Consequently shading, lighting, and further scene preparation were done in the game engine. For every object in the scene, a duplicate had to be created with lower resolution iOS-ready textures to be streamed to the tablet clients.

The ape creature was originally built for a student production at Animationsinstitut. To be able to use the character in the context of a game engine, it had to be simplified, re-textured, and re-rigged. As a backup, the character was also exported with baked mocap animation out of *Motionbuilder*.

The studio setup encompassed a flat LED wall with 7 meters width and 4 meters height, consisting of 14 by 8 individual panels with a pixel pitch of 1.9 mm, resulting in a total resolution of 3584 by 2048 pixels. As maximal brightness, 1200 nit are stated.[9] Three additional panels with a size of 0.8 by 1.8 meters, a pixel pitch of 8.33 mm, and a maximal brightness of 7000 nit[10] got mounted on wheels and were mainly used as additional movable light sources and for casting reflections. The camera and the three light panels were tracked live in the studio. For this purpose an *Optitrack* motion capturing system with passive markers was used. The markers were placed on top of the camera and on the three movable panels. To cover the entire area, 24 motion capturing cameras were installed on all four walls of the studio. This allowed us to determine the exact position and orientation of the camera and the light panels at all times. The acquired data was transmitted via network to a workstation running *Unity* and the VPET server and infrastructure.

To avoid artifacts in the animations and the captured image, the rendering, animation, camera, and LED wall had to be synchronized. The systems used were connected to an external genlock, which provided a world clock of 50 frames per second. Despite the comparatively bright LED technology, it turned out to be advantageous to use particularly light sensitive cameras and bright lenses. This helped to make creative use of the lighting provided by LEDs. Due to the low depth of field, such a setup also helped to maintain a cinematographic look and prevented image artifacts such as moire.

---

[8] https://youtu.be/FuGF8AexFY0.
[9] https://www.leditgo.de/files/pdf/LEDitgo_rXone_Datenblatt.pdf.
[10] https://www.leditgo.de/files/pdf/LEDitgo_sB8_Datenblatt.pdf.

Therefore a Sony Venice camera[11] in combination with Leica Summicron C[12] lenses were chosen as the main camera. To underline the soft and warm scenery and to further reduce resolution-related artifacts an additional softening filter was installed in front of the camera. For the interaction with the digital set elements iPads with VPET clients were used. Such were connected to the VPET server workstation via a WiFi network.

For the production, a professional DoP-supported camera setup and cinematography, also giving essential feedback on the virtual production environment in general, as well as on the quality of the content, were displayed on the LED wall. The first setting established a vase on a table with a slow forward track, gradually revealing the ape creature approaching in the distance. Since the scene would serve as reference for following scenes of the short film, it was thoroughly arranged. The team tested different lenses and LED levels and paid attention to every reflection. In multiple takes, the ape got animated using both pre-recorded motion capturing and machine learning data. The latter required the input of the tablet-based editing tools developed by Animationsinstitut (Fig. 20.8 right).

The second shot showed the ape only as reflection on the water surface, while the camera moved gently to induce parallax. The grabbing of the flower was held out of frame; the audience would only see the stem being pulled out of the vase. Here a precise positioning of both the ape and the environment was needed to achieve the desired look. The third scene picked up the framing of the first one and, by slowly moving the camera backwards, followed the creature as it strode away into the forest. For all shots a video of a flickering fireplace was screened on two of the three mobile LED panels, providing natural refractions and reflections, especially on the vase, which was furthermore held in focus to avoid moiré. Apart from one extra back light, the LED wall and the movable panels were the only light source and sufficient for illuminating the foreground. A black pro-mist filter was used to soften lights and contrasts. This halation helped to further harmonize foreground and virtual background. By adding some depth blur to the images rendered by the game engine, the overall depth of field looked slightly more convincing, although simply adding virtual defocus and real bokehs usually does not end up in realistic results.

In general, the idea of screening characters on a LED wall and combining them with live action foregrounds proved to be feasible with some limitations. As soon as the character got too prominent in the image, one would expect it to be in focus, which is not possible, since the LED panels should stay de-focused to avoid moiré. Implicitly, a real interaction between virtual characters and live action foreground was not advisable. Also, the fact that the LED wall was in a fixed distance to the camera, and thus all screened content holds a constant level of bokeh, which further detracted from the

---

[11] https://pro.sony/de_DE/products/digital-cinema-cameras/venice.
[12] https://www.leitz-cine.com/product/summicron-c.

Figure 20.8 The "Snowflower" production was a test drive for virtual production with interactive AI powered character animation tools.

credibility of the captured images. Our use case was constructed around these limitations, and therefore produced acceptable results. For real productions, such screened virtual characters will only be suitable sporadically, for example, for background crowds. Future VFX productions could make use of characters via LED screens to engage all actors in the scenery with virtual protagonists. Not being able to focus on the screen and character could be solved by an additional compositing step. As virtual production processes can be applied not just to VFX productions but also to fully animated CG productions, the proposed workflow could lead to completely new production processes. Sceneries could be prepared accordingly and animations be blocked instantly in line with the directors expectations. Animators could refine this data in a post process. This proposed workflow would combine motion capture, machine learning-powered tools and traditional (hand) animation.

The "Snowflower" production showed machine learning, smart assets, and interactive interfaces are key to be able to run virtual productions, especially when the goal is to capture "everything in camera" by, e.g., using an LED wall. This reduces or eliminates the need for extensive post-production, but adds high demands on pre-production. All virtual assets need to be available in the final quality, before the actual production on set. Any adjustments to the scene need to be done on set in parallel to the actual production. A search and transformation framework can become a very helpful tool in this process, as it allows artists to quickly add new, reusable assets matching the requirements of the production. More and more virtual characters are used in modern productions. In a virtual production scenario they should be directable on set just as an actor. This can only be achieved by providing tools to direct the virtual characters with high-level commands.

20.2.3 Summary

The SAUCE experimental productions carried out by Filmakademie Baden-Württemberg have indicated current and future potential of light field data and the use of large scale LED wall setups. However, the application of these new technologies demands for a fundamental reconfiguration of production processes, tools, and skill set among creative talent. In particular, the challenges of photo realistic real-time content creation appear rather difficult for traditional VFX artists. This further applies to on-set movie creation methodology, where (final) image composition, including VFX, can now be an interactive team effort. This however demands for new procedures and a global understanding of technological challenges in all departments.

References

[1] J. Vazquez-Corral, M. Bertalmío, Color stabilization along time and across shots of the same scene, for one or several cameras of unknown specifications, IEEE Transactions on Image Processing 23 (10) (2014) 4564–4575, https://doi.org/10.1109/TIP.2014.2344312.

[2] M. Grogan, R. Dahyot, L2 divergence for robust colour transfer, Comput. Vis. Image Underst. 181 (2019) 39–49, https://doi.org/10.1016/j.cviu.2019.02.002.

[3] J. Trottnow, S. Spielmann, T. Lange, K. Chelli, M. Solony, P. Smrz, P. Zemcik, W. Aenchbacher, M. Grogan, M. Alain, A. Smolic, T. Canham, O. Vu-Thanh, J. Vázquez-Corral, M. Bertalmío, The potential of light fields in media productions, in: SIGGRAPH Asia 2019 Technical Briefs, SA '19, Association for Computing Machinery, New York, NY, USA, 2019, pp. 71–74, https://doi.org/10.1145/3355088.3365158.

[4] S. Spielmann, V. Helzle, A. Schuster, J. Trottnow, K. Götz, P. Rohr, VPET: Virtual production editing tools, in: ACM SIGGRAPH 2018 Emerging Technologies, SIGGRAPH '18, Association for Computing Machinery, New York, NY, USA, 2018, https://doi.org/10.1145/3214907.3233760.

[5] S. Spielmann, A. Schuster, K. Götz, V. Helzle, VPET: A toolset for collaborative virtual filmmaking, in: SIGGRAPH ASIA 2016 Technical Briefs, SA '16, Association for Computing Machinery, New York, NY, USA, 2016, https://doi.org/10.1145/3005358.3005370.

CHAPTER 21

Volumetric video as a novel medium for creative storytelling

Gareth W. Young, Néill O'Dwyer, and Aljosa Smolic
V-SENSE, School of Computer Science and Statistics, Trinity College Dublin, Dublin, Ireland

This chapter discusses the V-SENSE[1] project's contribution to volumetric video (VV) production as a novel medium for creative storytelling. As discussed in previous chapters, VV facilitates the 3D representation and visualization of dynamic, kinetic content (people, animals, objects, etc.) using live-action video, instead of computer graphics and animation. VV can be recorded via several vision capture technologies, including infrared, RGB video, and LIDAR. For high-definition footage, dedicated studios have been created that surround the performance space with multiple cameras, capturing millions of data points for 3D digital reconstruction. Combined with 3D modeling techniques, VV contributes to imaginative story worlds for playback, broadcast, and display as dynamic 3D visual media that can be viewed across various platforms.

21.1. Volumetric video and creative practice

VVs are different from traditional video media in two distinctive ways. Firstly, VVs are 3D and typically represented as 3D point clouds or 3D meshes (polygons). Secondly, VV offers 3D rendering capabilities with six-degree-of-freedom (6DoF), making them interactive, immersive, and expressive from a viewer-controlled first-person perspective. VV facilitates 6DoF by allowing audiences to freely change their viewing position (X, Y, Z) and orientation (pitch, yaw, roll). By contrast, conventional and modern 360° videos are presented on a two-dimensional (2D) plane, or a three-degree-of-freedom (3DoF) sphere. Thus classic 2D videos provide no viewport freedom, and 360° videos only allow 3DoF (pitch, yaw, roll), with the viewer's normal, transverse, and longitudinal positions are permanently fixed or "baked in."

The VV pipeline is discussed in detail in other chapters of this book from capture to display. Despite significant progress, the technology still has limitations that may affect the visual quality and experience. These factors are related to the production costs of hardware (number of cameras, other sensors, studio equipment, etc.) and labor in post-production (interactive processing and refinement by experts using dedicated software

---

[1] https://v-sense.scss.tcd.ie/.

Immersive Video Technologies
https://doi.org/10.1016/B978-0-32-391755-1.00027-4
591

Figure 21.1 Patrick Prendergast, the 44th Provost of Trinity College Dublin (2011–2021): (left) in the capture studio and (right) his keynote presentation via Microsoft's Hololens v1.

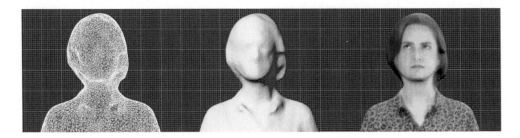

Figure 21.2 Wireframe, solid, and textured 3D model (left-to-right).

tools). Whereas high-end professional productions are expensive and well-equipped studios lead to professional quality results, lower-budget productions may compromise. Fig. 21.1 illustrates an example of a person in V-SENSE's affordable VV capture studio (left) and the resulting VV viewed through AR glasses (right). Fig. 21.2 illustrates the reconstruction process in post-production.

Maximizing quality and minimizing efforts in post-production, VV pre-production design typically considers some of the current limitations of the technology. This process includes the creation and use of costumes, accessories, hair, makeup, materials, etc. Certain colors and reflective or transparent materials may cause problems. Textured surfaces are well suited, whereas loose clothes may be problematic. Furthermore, the specific movements of the performers may lead to inaccuracies, so choreography is also necessary concerning the speed and the nature of motion. Also, most studios are restricted by the number of individuals captured simultaneously (usually only 1 or 2 people concurrently). Despite these limitations, VV is increasingly used in multiple domains, with professional applications being developed for education, fashion, advertising, entertainment, and video games, indicating the stakeholders' interest in investing in the short-term with a view to the long-term gain.

VV can be regarded as a significant development in media production. Content for XR is becoming more pervasive in modern society for entertainment, healthcare, government, military, education, and industry training. With the rapid development and adoption of VR and AR technology in these areas, VV is also becoming a key technology for communicating meaning and artistic expression. Financial forecasts envision a positive future for the global VV market, estimating that it will grow from $1.4 billion in 2020 to $5.8 billion by 2025 [1]. This growth leads one to conclude that the future of VV for artists and producers is a bright one.

21.2. Case studies

The V-SENSE project—extending visual sensation through image-based visual computing (2016–2022)—was funded by the Science Foundation of Ireland (SFI) for research in creative technologies. The core technology enabling the creative productions presented in this chapter, i.e., VR/AR content creation based on 3D VV techniques, was developed by V-SENSE researchers [2] who spun out an innovative VV production company called Volograms.[2]

During the life of the V-SENSE project, there have been numerous tests and creative experiments, eight of which could be classified as significant standalone works of art: *MR play* (2017–19), *The Trinity library long room mixed reality project, featuring Jonathan Swift* (2018), *Faoladh* (2018), *Bridging the Blue* (2019), *The virtual field trip* (2021), and *Image technology echoes* (2020), as well as the forthcoming *Mixed-reality Ulysses: Pilot episode I* (2020) and *Episode II* (2022) and *XR music videos: featuring New Pagans* (2022). Six of these significant productions were made applying VV. What follows is a brief synopsis of these projects.

21.2.1 MR play trilogy (2017)

MR play consists of a three-year trilogy of research experiments linking the performing arts and computer science disciplines [3]. Each part of the trilogy reimagines Samuel Beckett's groundbreaking theatrical text, *Play* (1963), for various formats of digital culture, including 1) a webcast (*Intermedial play*), 2) virtual reality (*Virtual play*) and, 3) augmented reality (*Augmented play*). Play was chosen, because it specifically engages the questions of dialogue and interactivity. In the original *play*, the dramaturgy operates on the basis that the sequence of the actors speaking is determined by a moving spotlight, which Beckett likens to an "inquisitor" [4, p. 318]; they speak when the light is

---

[2] https://www.volograms.com/.

Figure 21.3 MR play VV assets.

on them, and fall silent when the light is off. So, *play* is a game of interaction between the light operator and the actor, mediated by light technology.

In the theater, the audience passively observes the interaction between the light operator and the actors. The objective of the series of research experiments was to incrementally increase the audience's sense of immersion in the drama by exploring qualities such as agency and interactivity. In *Intermedial play*, the audience is drawn closer to the action through the employment of a pan-tilt-zoom (PTZ) robotic camera, where film grammar, such as super-close-up and sound effects, are used to create the illusion that the audience is complicit in the Pavlovian trail. *Intermedial play* was the precursor, inspiration, and catalyst of *Virtual play* and *Augmented play*. *Intermedial play* was a collaboration between Néill O'Dwyer (V-SENSE artist in residence) and Nicholas Johnson, Associate Professor in Trinity College's Department of Drama and secretary and co-director of the newly established Trinity Centre for Beckett Studies. An online video recording is available.[3]

Virtual play was a reinterpretation of *play*, intending to engage a contemporary viewership via VR technologies (see Fig. 21.3). In this version, we acknowledge the interactive specificities of digital VR technologies and the role of the user as active; we recognize new opportunities for narrative and give the power of activation over to the end user, whose gaze becomes the spotlight. The user thus embodies the "inquisitor" and is empowered to independently discover the story by looking at the characters and provoking them to speak.

This work was V-SENSE's inaugural arts and culture project under the creative technologies remit. The project was conceived to demonstrate how VR content could be produced cheaply and expertly, thereby challenging the notion that sophisticated

---

[3] https://youtu.be/R11lT65HCZg.

Figure 21.4 *Virtual play* (left) and *Intermedial play* (right).

VR content is exclusively the domain of wealthy institutes and production houses. This virtual reality response to *play* pushed the limits of possibility in consumable video and film by eliciting the new power of digital interactive technologies to respond to Samuel Beckett's deep engagement with the stage technologies of his day.

A central goal was to address ongoing concerns in the creative cultural sector regarding managing narrative progression in an immersive environment. The solution implemented here operated on the basis that users activated the virtual actors into speaking through their gaze, so the artwork acknowledged the new condition of active audiences and recognized new opportunities for narrative by affording audiences a central role in its unfurling. It was believed that by placing the audience at the center of the storytelling process, they were more appropriately assimilated to the virtual world and subsequently empowered to explore, discover, and decode the story, instead of passively watching and listening. The gaming sector has effectively harnessed this narrative approach using procedural graphics and animation, but film and video (fundamentally based on live-action capture technologies) have struggled to engage this problem effectively. As such, this project investigated new narrative possibilities for interactive, immersive environments using live-action VV. (See Fig. 21.4.)

This VR version was, to our knowledge, the first full-length production of a VR drama using VV techniques. It is highly commended by both the computer science and digital arts communities, having been competitively selected for exhibition at some of the top art–science conferences and festivals in the world, including Beckett and Intermediality 2017 (where it premiered), New European Media 2017 (where it won first prize for the "Art and Design Award"), SIGGRAPH 2018, Beyond Festival 2018 (at ZKM), the Prague Quadrennial 2019, and DRHA 2021 (where Professors Smolic and Johnson were invited to co-present a keynote on the subject). The work also produced a raft of publications on varying topics that intersect both the arts and computer sciences, including a description of the process [3]; two aesthetic reflections on practice that articulate the perspectives of the theater practitioners and cogitate on the significance of the technological development [5]; a poster paper at a top computer science conference [6], which catalyzed a commission to expand the essay into an entire article for the world's leading art–science journal [7]; and, finally, a deep-dive human-computer interaction (HCI) study [8] that draws on the subjective opinions of industry and academic subject-matter experts, and which teases out the potentialities, pitfalls, and areas for further research in this exciting, emerging genre of digital arts.

Augmented play was the third and final part of the trilogy. The user and narrative paradigms were the same as the VR version; that is, users were invited to don the AR head-mounted display (HMD), embody the interrogator, and explore the narrative by confronting Beckett's characters virtually. This version had much in common with the earlier VR edition, because it used the same VV assets, user interaction, and narrative development mode. However, the viewing paradigm was different, because the content was displayed using cross-platform AR technology. Using AR allowed audiences to visually merge virtual, graphical, computer-rendered objects with real-world objects and scenes using a mobile phone, a tablet, or an HMD. Unlike VR, this approach allows users to see the world around them, as it does not close off the outside world or fully immerse the audience in an "other" computerized world. Therefore the AR version elicited the exploratory specificities of the story by allowing people to interact with Beckett's characters in context-relevant, site-specific locations, meaning that it was ideal for location-based role-play and site-specific drama. As such, as a result of the afterlife and sepulchral nuances of the story, *Augmented play* was premiered in the vaulted, cavernous basement of the CHQ center in the historic Dublin Docklands quarter to thematically engage the audience through contextualized, tangible architectural qualities to embellish notions of mystery, discovery, and reward.

21.2.2 Jonathan Swift at the Trinity library long room

As well as holding a special place in the hearts of students, staff, alumni, and the wider Dublin community, the Trinity library long room is a major destination for cultural heritage tourists. The objective of the Jonathan Swift project was to create an anecdotal XR narrative that would embellish and humanize the visitor experience by creating a welcoming and friendly digital character who is contextually relevant to the CH site and who adopts a "humorous and playful mode of communication" via AR technology [9, p. 22]. Because there is no substitute for the genuine experience of being physically present in the long room's breath-taking space, replacing the experience of visiting the library was not the initial goal of this project. Therefore AR was deemed the most appropriate solution.

Specifically, visitors were to augment their real-world visit using an AR application that ran on a mobile phone, tablet, or an HMD device. These users were to be wel-

Figure 21.5 A visitor wearing the Hololens (left) and a screenshot of a user's point of view when wearing the Hololens (right).

comed to the long room by a friendly VV representation of the famous Dean Jonathan Swift, who proceeds to divulge an embarrassing, whimsical, and humorous memory of his youthful escapades, while studying at the university. The application consists of a monologue about 1 minute in length. As in the previous *MR play* project, both AR and VR prototypes were created using the same VV assets. Therefore the XR technologies enabled an interactive narrative, whereby a visitor could also remotely encounter the Swift character in a VR simulation of the long room.

The interactive VR prototype visualized the long room building and its contents, allowing the user to be immersed in the world of cultural heritage through simulation. The virtual architectural environment was built using a combination of manual 3D modeling and the computer vision process of photogrammetry, comprising a static 3D model that could be imported into a game engine, and then combined with the dynamic VV content. This approach meant that the visitors could be located anywhere on the planet and, by putting on an HMD, they could remotely enter the virtual long room and explore it via the various VR platforms available today.

The Trinity long room's Jonathan Swift XR project exemplifies V-SENSE's innovative approach to content creation, showcasing original technologies in real-world productions. The AR version occurs within the long room library's physical space using an AR HMD or a handheld mobile device (such as a smartphone or tablet). Using the spatial tracking features of AR devices, the digital volumetric video character appears standing beside a marble bust of Dean Swift (a permanent exhibit of the museum), as seen in Fig. 21.5. The goal was to provide the various exhibitions with greater context and meaning, enhancing the overall visitor experience. This AR version was developed in the second phase of the project and only used the dynamic VV content. There was no need to virtually reconstruct the long room's internal, architectural spaces (the static content), because the user was already physically present in the geometric area. This production demonstrates VV content's versatility and illustrates novel tools and pipelines for creative digital content design.

The project's conceptual basis was founded on the idea that visualization technologies could create an engaging, interactive digital tour guide of the long room, featuring representations of famous historical personalities, such as Swift. The vision for the project was that the interactive tour would provide visitors with "peripheral stories that help draw their attention to the multitude of historical, architectural and archival details, procuring a deeper, more enriching experience of the world heritage site" [10]. The project was developed as a scalable pilot study, focusing on a single example, with the view that it may one day be expanded to take in the entire museum by including multiple characters and personalities apt to the various exhibits [11]. Developing a commercial industry-ready AR tour guide application was beyond the means and remit of V-SENSE, but a quality of experience and grounded theory study was conducted, which presented, measured, and discussed "the appeal, interest, and ease of use of this ludic AR storytelling strategy mediated via AR technology in a cultural heritage context" [9]. The study's findings indicated "that humorous, playful storytelling is both appropriate and effective in this context because it enriched the visitors' experiences, and more of this type of work was encouraged" by such projects, either in this museum or in others.

21.2.3 Bridging the Blue

In this work, V-SENSE explored the role of immersive content creation in technologically mediated perspective-taking experiences of VR. *Bridging the Blue* was a creative experiment that explored VR as "the ultimate empathy machine" [12], where users could explore an imaginary world and experience personal depictions of clinical depression, experienced first hand by the artist. The experience harnesses VR as a new type of human-orientated technology that can be used for perspective-taking by applying a volumetric capture of real-world human performance to assess the effects of empathy-building experiences achieved via new media [13]. Audience attitudes towards the protagonist were augmented to re-evaluate their experiences of perceived oneness and increase the amount of effort spent on helping oneself, others, and meaningfully engaging with society. From an industry perspective, this technological intervention was used to discuss production methodologies and interaction techniques when applied in XR content creation and to inform future creative technology projects.

The philosophies of augmented virtuality [14] were explored through the live-action capture and representation of the performer, who was projected into and interacted with the virtual world; that is, objects from the physical world could co-exist with digital objects within the immersive virtual environment (IVE) (Fig. 21.6). By merging the real—the volumetric capture of the narrator—and the virtual, the born-digital world designed and built using game engines and 3D modeling software, *Bridging the Blue* produced a VR platform to explore experiences of clinical depression.

Figure 21.6 Bridging the Blue scene selection (Left) and narrative experiences (Right).

Bridging the Blue was presented as an interactive VR experience that transported the viewer to a familiar yet imaginary world. The user begins on a small, rocky island out at sea (Fig. 21.6), and they are surrounded by symbols that have significance to the artist and their experience of clinical depression. These artifacts act as interactive keys that allow the user to teleport to linked narratives (7 in total) that employ two main narrative methods: 1) the fly-on-the-wall method, where the (unseen) user observes a VV representation of the artist/subject in the middle of an episode without being able to interact with the scene, and 2) the first-person narrative method, where the artist/subject directly addresses the user in a sort of lecture format, describing the experiences and divulging information comprised of her ordeal and clinical facts. "Here, the technology has been harnessed as a device to catalyze shifts, prompting the viewer to evaluate and recalibrate modes of listening in the context of mental health" [15, p. 17]. This goal is pursued through the organization of three main principles: 1) by assigning agency to the user, whereby they can navigate between narratives without the promise of rewards or an overall linear goal; 2) through heightened awareness and flow catalyzed by the novelty-factor of the technology; and 3) by simulating an embodied, experiential encounter with the artist that is pivotal to the transformative intentions of the work. Interaction with the artist/subject is limited to listening. The intention is to model "responses more consistent with empathy, support, and validation in the context of non-professional conversations about mental health where the natural tendency is often to attempt to offer solutions or advice without having the requisite professional expertise" [15, p. 18]. The project is an exercise in employing immersive technologies as a tool for subconsciously training best practice techniques, such as listening skills for people with no knowledge of mental health support protocols or skills in navigating such conversations.

Within each scene, the work challenges common misconceptions of and responses to depression and offers subjective playback and validation to those who have also been affected by this condition. In this context, the work demonstrates VR's new, innate capabilities and its capacity to inform the viewer. The artist [15] argues this in the context of the literary technique of defamiliarization, an aesthetic philosophy championed by the Russian formalists, perhaps most notably by Viktor Shklovsky in his 1917 essay "Art as Technique" [16]. Given that Bridging the Blue is an immersive experience permitting an embodied, first-person encounter Arielle argues that under Held and Hein's technology–perception experiments [17], the venture enables a neurobiological basis for changes in perception. Human perception is a faculty of awareness that is malleable and subjective, and ordinarily, it is "habitual, economical, automatic—too familiar, in fact" [18, p. 28]. Defamiliarization describes the literary technique of taking the audience out of their comfort zone by making ordinary and familiar objects appear different, causing them to question their preconceptions about the thing under regard, ultimately transforming perception. Arielle's strategy in Bridging the Blue is to challenge the audience's expectations of what they believe clinical depression to be by challenging them to witness symptoms and listen to its effects from a different perspective.

21.2.4 Image Technology Echoes

In the immersive experimental fiction *Image Technology Echoes*, the user enters a quiet gallery inside a cavernous museum space (Fig. 21.7). *Image Technology Echoes* asks how we experience perception and embodiment and how much could be happening below the surface of those we meet. Real actors are captured using VV techniques and perform all of the characterizations and representations of the three scenes. The script for each set is written in collaboration with deep learning frameworks that use natural language processing (NLP) algorithms. The text generated by the algorithms was supervised and edited by the director/playwright Lauren Moffat and periodically reprocessed until the machine-human-machine partnership developed a suitably nuanced text that evoked the spirit of the artist's vision. In this regard, in terms of visual computing and the playwriting process, *Image Technology Echoes* shows provocative new ways of creating work in collaboration with machines.

The narrative comprises three scenes: the gallery, which is constituted by a dialogue between the two main protagonists, and the two subconscious scenes formed by monologues. The gallery is empty, except for an older man and a younger woman, who have a conversation about the painting they are looking at: a large expressionist canvas depicting a stormy ocean. The starched conversation circulates indefinitely unless the visitor enters the body of one of the two figures, at which time they are transported into the respective subconscious mental space of that character. These mental spaces manifest as messy rooms with a large window that overlooks a humongous version of the painting, which appears very different from each character's point of view. Each room contains a character that echoes the personality of its owner. The user has a fly-on-the-wall perspective in these rooms, watching the character's doppelgänger or homunculus reciting a stream of consciousness. In a voyeuristic dynamic, the audience witnesses a personal, introspective, and slightly obsessive rant.

Figure 21.7 Image Technology Echoes.

In September 2020, *Image Technology Echoes* was included in the competitive Vancouver International Film Festival as one of its featured projects, Volumetric Market. It was also displayed as a prototype demonstration at the Espronceda Institute for Arts and Culture in Barcelona in October 2020. *Image Technology Echoes* celebrated its world festival premiere at the International Film Festival Rotterdam in June 2021 and has been very well received across many of the top global VR communities since. In May 2021, *Image Technology Echoes* won first place at the prestigious VR ART PRIZE, awarded by Deutsche Kreditbank (DKB) in cooperation with the Contemporary Arts Alliance (CAA) Berlin featured in an exhibition at Haus am Lützowplatz April–June 2021. It also received acclaim during this time in the American Business Magazine, Forbes [19].

21.2.5 Mixed reality Ulysses

In the *mixed reality Ulysses* XR application, users were invited to enter James Joyce's literary world Ulysses through AR and VR technology (Fig. 21.8). The VR application allowed audiences from any part of the globe to experience the sites and associated scenes from the story via a VR headset. On the other hand, the AR application encouraged audiences to physically go to those locations and witness the VV as dramatic recreations of the scenes using mobile phones, tablets, or AR HMDs. At SIGGRAPH Asia 2021 [20], these experiences were fully prototyped as XR storytelling applications for a broader project that aims to depict multiple scenes of the book using VV capture techniques for the dynamic content and photogrammetric practices for the 3D scenic construction.

Figure 21.8 MR Ulysses.

The pilot episode depicts a recreation of the book's opening scene, featuring a dialogue between Buck Mulligan and Stephen Dedalus (Joyce's pseudonymous doppelgänger) on the roof of the Martello Tower at Sandycove. The mode of audience interaction (in the pilot episode) consists of the user embodying Dedalus's character with Mulligan positioned opposite as the interlocutor. Therefore Mulligan is the only visible character in the scene. The user is not required to articulate the words of Dedalus; these sections were delivered by the application and were heard (in full stereo), as if spoken in the first person. Mulligan's voice is perceived as coming from the other dialoguing character; his voice is subjected to 3D spatial audio—simulating distance and direction—to enhance immersion and embellish the sense of presence. The excerpt is a reinterpretation of the section, where Stephen accuses Mulligan of speaking insultingly about his mother's death. Mulligan, a doctor by profession, scrambles to defend his position, but his attempt to justify himself, in a speech about the normality of death, only causes further offense to his sensitive listener. Though only three minutes long, the address and dialogue are profoundly expressive and provide an insight into Joyce's dexterous handling of language.

Although hindered by the onset of the COVID-19 pandemic, the project was auspiciously timely, because it provided insights into many of the vocational problems creative artists and performers encountered during the 2020/21 global lockdown. For example, in the AR instance, *MR Ulysses* demonstrates a site-specific theatrical paradigm, where audiences could experience theater and performance en plein air using mobile and wearable technologies. Furthermore, Bloomsday's annual literary festival, which since 1963 celebrates the book through site-specific reenactments of text passages, was canceled for the first time in 2020. In the VR instance, MR Ulysses provided a means for audiences to immerse themselves in a simulated spatial experience of Bloomsday without having to travel to Dublin physically by applying open-source photogrammetry processes [21,22]. *MR Ulysses* does not claim to be a replacement for the joy of site-specific physical gatherings that celebrate literature, but it does help provide an insight into how the vocational disenfranchisement (suffered by theater/performing arts practitioners as a result of the global lockdown) can be eased by harnessing the global interconnectivity of electronic networks [23]. As such, *MR Ulysses* demonstrates how the paradigm of spatialized storytelling that is unique to MR can be effectively integrated with VV techniques in a way that challenges our current understanding of physical experiences of live theater [23].

21.2.6 XR music videos

Finding new ways to visualize and express musical performance in VR is driven by artistic creativity, a desire to innovate technologically, and a need to capture new and existing audience attention. If "Artificial reality is the authentic postmodern condition, and virtual reality its definitive technological expression" [24, p. 169], then postmodernist representations of art can be expressed from within VR. Immersive XR music videos were studied at V-SENSE as an emergent art form in and of themselves, as many emergent XR technologies are being applied in this endeavor, such as stereoscopic and 360° audiovisual spatial recording technology. These capture technologies expanded the traditional viewing medium to include further dimensions of immersion, interaction, and imagination for the audience, and were closely tied to advancements being made in home PC GPU/CPU speeds, HMD optics, software data processing capabilities, and AI.

Music videos are short films that integrate songs and imagery produced for artistic and promotional purposes. Modern music videos apply various media capture techniques and creative post-production technologies to provide a myriad of stimulating and artistic approaches to audience entertainment and engagement for viewing across multiple devices. Within this domain, VV capture technologies have become a popular means of recording and reproducing musical performances for new audiences to access via traditional 2D screens and emergent XR platforms, such as AR/VR. These 3D digital reproductions of live musical performances are captured and enhanced to deliver cutting-edge audiovisual entertainment. However, the precise impact of VV in music video entertainment was still in need of exploration from a user perspective. The XR music video project demonstrated how users responded to VV representations of music performance via XR technology. This approach explored how audiences were likely to react to music videos in an XR context and offered insights into how future music videos may be developed. The findings were a formative starting point for more sophisticated, interactive music videos that could be accessed and presented via emergent platforms, for example, how VV XR music videos may be captured, edited, and accessed for live performance. (See Fig. 21.9.)

Figure 21.9 Imaginative XR music video experiences can take you anywhere.

The study of XR music videos was used to inform V-SENSE's user-centered design of a custom-made VV VR music video experience [25], featuring the New Pagans' track *Lily Yeats*. The project's pilot study initially highlighted the specific qualities that audiences seek during the consumption of such materials. Iterations of this novel application area are expected to focus on differences between traditional media and new XR experiences and expose and build upon existing HCI studies that focus on music and technology in use, specifically those concerning how users experience music videos presented via 6DoF XR technologies.

21.3. Reflection on V-SENSE practices

The aforementioned collection of V-SENSE's creative experiments has highlighted the potential of XR technology to shift artist and audience engagement paradigms. This context-specific focus spotlights how new uses for creative technology can bring further understanding and meaning to XR within the film, theater, and performance domain. From exploring the innovative works of the V-SENSE project, we have observed a potential disruption to the creative cultural sector caused by the increasing adoption of XR technologies in emerging modes of creative practice and evolving audience consumption behaviors. Following a series of user studies that use these experiments as stimuli, we can also understand and identify the explicit need to establish a new storytelling grammar [8].

A new storytelling grammar for XR must first balance the artist and audience perspectives and prioritize specialization and mise-en-scene over traditional temporal paradigms. XR must also facilitate entertainment by employing those specificities that come into their own in digital media: interaction, dialogue, exploration, discovery, networking, etc. Therefore further research is required to explore and define these qualities and reveal how these disruptive technologies will affect the creation and consumption of future performing arts practices.

This chapter highlights numerous considerations for the deployment of VV techniques in creative performance practice and the establishment of a storytelling grammar, surfacing in the cross-section of presented works and the qualitative and quantitative findings they produced. For example, careful consideration should be given to the role of temporality, spatiality, and the mixing of physical and digital realities when creating IVE experiences for VR and to site-specificity when using AR. However, these specificities of the XR platform also need to be meaningfully contextualized to the content to avoid the presented works being overwhelmed by novelty and technical exhibitionism. Existing performances will need to be re-established to engage audiences effectively. This factor mainly concerns timing and pace, interactive narrative models, and reconciling the shared audience experience.

In summary, it can be asserted that each VV-XR production engages the emerging genre uniquely and experimentally by tackling different aspects of the content-versus-technique relation, contributing to the definition of a nascent storyworlding grammar. The MR play series engages audience interaction by placing the user at the center of the story's unfolding. The Jonathan Swift app for the Trinity library explores the embellishment of the museological experience. Bridging the Blue investigates employing the technology to educate through a combination of listening and exploration. Images Technology Echoes explores the use of NLP for script development and also uses exploratory devices but, in this context, to challenge the subjectivities of the unconscious and human relations. In the context of intangible cultural heritage, XR Ulysses explores, on the one hand, geospatial AR technologies for site-specific performance and, on the other, VR technologies as a means of simulating site-specific performance. Finally, the XR music video investigates the potential of audiences as a creative agent by giving them control over some aspects of the musical tracks and the spatial relationship to the characters (aka the musician's avatars).

Though our collection of experiments contributes to defining a new taxonomy and can help us begin to map the grammar of VV-XR, they by no means come close to covering the totality of the emerging genre. Just as filmmaking took half a century to solidify a widely accepted grammar and vocabulary, so will XR take a similarly long time for its language to be defined. In terms of history and the artistic avant-garde, what is certain is that with the emergence of new technologies, there follow a plethora of creative productions that attempt to harness them towards creative expression. Just as technology is a continually evolving phenomenon, so too does art continually evolve; the grammar that emerges is determined by the gradual interplay of successes and failures that often swap position, depending on the audience's subjectivity.

21.4. Conclusion

XR as a media entertainment platform can be much more than immersive gaming, just as film entertainment is more than blockbuster cinema. Contemporary XR productions offer an expansive entertainment value to existing and emergent 3D media practices and beyond. By approaching the use of technology creatively, objects of attention within an IVE can be presented so that audiences can move around, interact, and engage with creative materials, making the XR experience fundamentally unique and rewarding to the audience. However, this technological intervention can arguably only add further value over more traditional multimedia practices as a supplement to the main creative focus, such as music, cinema, gaming, and so forth, by making full use of the 6DoF experience as well as implementing engaging interactions and introducing player/audience agency. Although highly immersive and engaging, VV also brings light to issues concerning conventional performance practice in and for IVEs and how artists can entertain audiences with artistic content remaining as intended.

References

[1] Market and Markets Research, Volumetric video market with COVID-19 impact by volumetric capture (hardware, software, services), application (sports, events, and entertainment, medical, advertisement, and education), content delivery & region - global forecast to 2026, https://www.marketsandmarkets.com/Market-Reports/volumetric-video-market-259585041.html.

[2] R. Pagés, K. Amplianitis, D. Monaghan, J. Ondřej, A. Smolić, Affordable content creation for free-viewpoint video and VR/AR applications, Journal of Visual Communication and Image Representation 53 (2018) 192–201.

[3] N. O'Dwyer, N. Johnson, E. Bates, R. Pagés, J. Ondřej, K. Amplianitis, D. Monaghan, A. Smolić, Virtual play in free-viewpoint video: reinterpreting Samuel Beckett for virtual reality, in: 2017 IEEE International Symposium on Mixed and Augmented Reality (ISMAR-Adjunct), IEEE, 2017, pp. 262–267.

[4] S. Beckett, Play, in: The Complete Dramatic Works of Samuel Beckett, Faber & Faber, London, 2006, pp. 305–320.

[5] N. O'Dwyer, N. Johnson, Exploring volumetric video and narrative through Samuel Beckett's play, International Journal of Performance Arts and Digital Media 15 (1) (2019) 53–69.

[6] N. O'Dwyer, N. Johnson, R. Pagés, J. Ondřej, K. Amplianitis, E. Bates, D. Monaghan, A. Smolić, Beckett in VR: Exploring narrative using free viewpoint video, in: SIGGRAPH 2018 Posters, ACM, 2018, pp. 1–2.

[7] N. O'Dwyer, N. Johnson, E. Bates, R. Pagés, J. Ondřej, K. Amplianitis, D. Monaghan, A. Smolic, Samuel Beckett in virtual reality: Exploring narrative using free viewpoint video, Leonardo 54 (2) (2021) 166–171.

[8] G.W. Young, N. O'Dwyer, N. Johnson, E. Zerman, A. Smolic, Mixed reality and volumetric video in cultural heritage: Expert opinions on augmented and virtual reality, in: International Conference on Human-Computer Interaction, Springer, 2020, pp. 195–214.

[9] N. O'dwyer, E. Zerman, G.W. Young, A. Smolic, S. Dunne, H. Shenton, Volumetric video in augmented reality applications for museological narratives: A user study for the long room in The Library of Trinity College Dublin, Journal on Computing and Cultural Heritage (JOCCH) 14 (2) (2021) 1–20.

[10] N. O'Dwyer, J. Ondřej, R. Pagés, K. Amplianitis, A. Smolić, Jonathan Swift: augmented reality application for Trinity library's long room, in: International Conference on Interactive Digital Storytelling, Springer, 2018, pp. 348–351.

[11] E. Zerman, N. O'Dwyer, G.W. Young, A. Smolic, A case study on the use of volumetric video in augmented reality for cultural heritage, in: Proceedings of the 11th Nordic Conference on Human-Computer Interaction: Shaping Experiences, Shaping Society, 2020, pp. 1–5.

[12] C. Milk, Ted2015: How virtual reality can create the ultimate empathy machine, https://www.ted.com/talks/chris_milk_how_virtual_reality_can_create_the_ultimate_empathy_machine?language=en, 2015.

[13] G.W. Young, N. O'Dwyer, A. Smolic, Exploring virtual reality for quality immersive empathy building experiences, Behaviour & Information Technology (2021) 1–17.

[14] P. Milgram, F. Kishino, A taxonomy of mixed reality visual displays, IEICE Transactions on Information and Systems 77 (12) (1994) 1321–1329.

[15] L.G. Arielle, Bridging the Blue, in: R. Brown, B. Salisbury (Eds.), The Art Exhibit at ICIDS 2019 Art Book: The Expression of Emotion in Humans and Technology, Carnegie Mellon University, Pittsburgh, 2020, Ch. 1, pp. 15–28.

[16] L. Crawford, Viktor Shklovskij: Différance in defamiliarization, Comparative Literature (1984) 209–219.

[17] R. Held, A. Hein, Movement-produced stimulation in the development of visually guided behavior, Journal of Comparative & Physiological Psychology 56 (5) (1963) 872.

[18] D.P. Gunn, Making art strange: A commentary on defamiliarization, The Georgia Review 38 (1) (1984) 25–33.

[19] S. Rabimov, Why first virtual reality art prize is perfect for 2020 e, https://www.forbes.com/sites/stephanrabimov/2020/11/27/why-first-virtual-reality-art-prize-is-perfect-for-2020/, 2020.

[20] N. O'Dwyer, G.W. Young, A. Smolic, M. Moynihan, P. O'Hanrahan, Mixed reality Ulysses, in: SIGGRAPH Asia 2021 Art Gallery, SA '21, Association for Computing Machinery, New York, NY, USA, 2021, p. 1, https://doi.org/10.1145/3476123.3487880.

[21] O. Dawkins, G.W. Young, Engaging place with mixed realities: Sharing multisensory experiences of place through community-generated digital content and multimodal interaction, in: International Conference on Human-Computer Interaction, Springer, 2020, pp. 199–218.

[22] O. Dawkins, G.W. Young, Workshop—ground truthing and virtual field trips, in: 2020 6th International Conference of the Immersive Learning Research Network (iLRN), IEEE, 2020, pp. 418–420.

[23] N. O'Dwyer, G.W. Young, A. Smolic, XR Ulysses: Addressing the disappointment of canceled site-specific re-enactments of Joycean literary, cultural heritage on Bloomsday, International Journal of Performance Arts and Digital Media (2022) 1–19, https://doi.org/10.1080/14794713.2022.2031801.

[24] B. Woolley, Virtual Worlds: A Journey in Hype and Hyperreality, Benjamin Woolley, 1993.

[25] G.W. Young, N. O'Dwyer, M. Moynihan, A. Smolic, Audience experiences of a volumetric virtual reality music video, in: Proceedings of the IEEE Conference on Virtual Reality and 3D User Interfaces, 2022, pp. 1–7.

CHAPTER 22

Social virtual reality (VR) applications and user experiences

Jie Li[a,b] **and Pablo Cesar**[b,c]

[a]EPAM Systems, Hoofddrop, the Netherlands
[b]Centrum Wiskunde en Informatica, Amsterdam, the Netherlands
[c]Delft University of Technology, Delft, the Netherlands

22.1. Introduction

There is a growing need for effective remote communication, which has many positive societal impacts, such as reducing environmental pollution and travel costs, supporting rich collaboration by remotely connecting talented people. Video conferencing tools, such as *Zoom*[1] and *Google Hangouts*,[2] are low-cost, allow multiple users to have conversations at the same time, and provide face-to-face-like experiences compared to audio-only phone calls [1,2]. Some high-end video conferencing systems, such as *HP Halo* and *Cisco Telepresence* are designed to link two physically separated rooms through wall-size screens, high-fidelity audio, and video, which enable users to feel co-present in a single conference room [3,4]. However, all the video conferencing tools still restrict users in front of screens with "talking heads experiences," and limit physical activities that naturally arise from social interactions and spontaneous collaborations [2,5].

Social VR has the potential to afford more social interaction than video conferencing, such as the ability to organically break off into small groups, or interact with virtual objects in the scene [6]. Many commercial social VR platforms have implemented novel social mechanics to stimulate social activities, such as designing a virtual environment (VE) to simulate a group discussion atmosphere, implementing built-in tools to enable users to stay in VEs and focus on the social tasks. Existing social VR platforms vary widely in affordances, fidelity, scale, and accessibility. On commercial platforms, such as *Facebook Horizon*,[3] *AltSpaceVR*,[4] and *VRChat*,[5] the facial expressions, voice, eye direction, and body gestures of a user are captured and mapped to the virtual avatar of

---

[1] Zoom (https://zoom.us) is a video conferencing tool, enabling a large group of people meeting online at the same time.

[2] Google Hangout (https://hangouts.google.com) is a multiple-user video conferencing tool.

[3] *Facebook Horizon* (https://www.oculus.com/facebook-horizon) is an invite-only virtual community where users can explore the virtual worlds and do creative activities together.

[4] *AltSpaceVR* (https://altvr.com) is a commercial virtual reality community for virtual live shows, meetups, and classes.

[5] *VRChat* (https://www.vrchat.com) is an online massively multiplayer social environment.

Immersive Video Technologies
https://doi.org/10.1016/B978-0-32-391755-1.00028-6
609

that user in real-time. Platforms such as *Mozilla Hubs*,[6] *Gather Town*[7] also enable social experiences, but result in dramatically different experiences. *Facebook Horizon* requires users to have a head-mounted display (HMD). *AlterSpaceVR*, *VRChat*, and *Mozilla Hubs* provide fully 3D environments that can be experienced on a desktop or using an HMD. *Gather Town* uses a 2D map, but incorporates video conferencing for groups to chat. *AlterSpaceVR* and *VRChat* are massively online VR communities, averaging over 10,000 users daily. In contrast, *Mozilla Hubs* and *Gather Town* support a maximum of 25 and 50 users respectively, although premium *Gather Town* rooms can host up to 500.

All these platforms have shown that social VR is a promising new medium for remote communication, which may better support social presence (e.g., intimacy and immediacy [7]), rich non-verbal communications (e.g., sign languages [8]), and immersive realistic interactions. However, the goal of social VR is not to completely replicate reality, but to facilitate and extend existing communication channels of the physical world. In this chapter, four user applications of social VR will be showcased, including a social VR clinic, a social VR cake co-design tool and birthday celebration, a social VR museum, and an immersive social VR movie. Apart from the useful and interesting applications, this chapter also discusses research methods of measuring user experiences in social VR applications.

This chapter introduces a few unique social VR applications, covering business areas, such as healthcare, food, cultural heritage, and entertainment. The social VR clinic (Section 22.2) is a remote consultation tool that enables patients who experience mobility difficulties to have fewer visits to hospitals, but still receive good surgery preparation guidance from doctors. Both doctors and patients are represented as upper-body human avatars. In CakeVR (Section 22.3), both pastry chefs and clients are represented as full-body human avatars, who can collaboratively make a 3D virtual cake together. The co-designed virtual cake will be used as a reference for the chef to make the real cake. The social VR birthday celebration steps further by live capturing the 3D videos of two remote users and a cake, and transmitting the 3D videos as photorealistic representations to a virtual café. So, the two users who were separated physically met each other in the virtual café and celebrated the birthday together. Using the same 3D video live capturing technology [9], the social VR museum (MediaScape XR) brings two remote users to experience a historical costume together in a nostalgic concert setup (Section 22.4). Last but not least, the social VR immersive movie enabled two to five photo-realistically represented users to "walk" into a 3D immersive mysterious murder movie (Section 22.5). The users can co-present in the movie scene with the movie characters, and participate in solving the crime together. Table 22.1 exhibits the main

---

[6] *Mozilla Hubs* (https://hubs.mozilla.com) offers private 3D virtual spaces that enable users to meet, share, and collaborate together.
[7] *Gather Town* (https://gather.town) is a remote gathering tool that combines 2D maps with video conferencing.

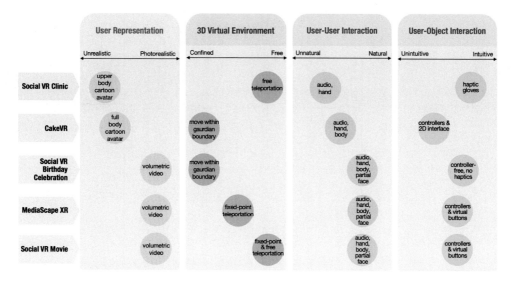

Figure 22.1 Mapping the social VR applications in terms of user representation, 3D virtual environment, user-user interaction, and user-object interaction.

characteristics of the social VR applications. Fig. 22.1 compares the realism of user representations, the 3D virtual environment, and the levels of user-user and user-object interactions. Apart from demonstrating the design and implementation process of the applications, Section 22.6 discusses methods and protocols for evaluating user experience in social VR.

22.2. The social VR clinic

A video demonstration of the social VR clinic is available at https://youtu.be/c89E98SQRqk, under the channel named "Distributed and Interactive Systems Group, CWI," with the title of "IMX2020 (demo): A Social VR Clinic for Knee Arthritis Patients with Haptics."

VR in healthcare has long been envisioned as a promising technology that can potentially approximate, or even optimize the face-to-face communication between patients and medical professionals (e.g., doctors and nurses) [10,11]. One of the pioneer VR applications in healthcare started in the 1990s, with the main purpose of visualizing complex medical data for medical professionals to prepare for the surgery [12]. So far, many VR healthcare applications have been developed for medical training [13], psychological consultation [14], and remote (psycho)therapy [15]. According to a national survey (2006–2017) in the US [16], the time people spent traveling to healthcare services was the longest compared to other professional services, such as legal services, personal care, or government activities. The time spent traveling and waiting for healthcare ser-

Table 22.1 Characteristics of the social VR applications.

Application areas	Social VR applications	Number of users	User representation	Interaction with virtual objects and 3D environment	Interaction between users
Healthcare	Social VR Clinic	2	Upper body cartoon avatar with hands	Free teleportation and haptic interaction with virtual objects (e.g., haptic virtual syringes)	Audio and hand gestures
Food	CakeVR	2	Full body cartoon avatar	Move within guardian boundary and interact with virtual objects (e.g., cakes and ingredients)	Audio, hand gestures, and body movements
	Social VR Birthday Celebration	2	Photorealistic avatar (volumetric video)	Move within guardian boundary and interact with the virtual cake (e.g., blowing candles)	Audio, hand gestures, body movements, partially facial expressions
Cultural Heritage	MediaScape XR	2	Photorealistic avatar (volumetric video)	Fixed-point teleportation, interaction with virtual objects (e.g., wearing the costume, playing with the musical instruments)	Audio, hand gestures, body movements, partially facial expressions
Entertainment	Social VR Movie	2–5	Photorealistic avatar (volumetric video)	Fixed-point and free teleportation, interaction with virtual objects (e.g., switch on the light)	Audio, hand gestures, body movements, partially facial expressions

vices was over 50% of the time spent receiving care. Besides the time cost, healthcare traveling can be painful for patients who have disabilities or suffer from chronic disease.

The social VR clinic aims at supporting patients with limited physical mobility to travel fewer times to the hospital, but still, communicate well with doctors and nurses. Patients with knee osteoarthritis are the target group of this application [17,18]. The social VR clinic simulates the real consultation room and facilities in the hospital, in which, patients can interact with the doctors or nurses with visualized information, such as surgery preparation procedures, 3D anatomical models, and a tour in the surgery room.

22.2.1 User journey

The user research with doctors, nurses, and knee arthritis patients provided an overall picture of a typical patient treatment journey (PTJ), which typically has three medical consultations [17]. All patients start with the first consultation with the doctor, for examination, and making decisions about the treatment. When the patient needs to have the surgery, a second consultation for patient surgery preparation and a third consultation for final before-surgery examinations will be scheduled with the nurse (Fig. 22.2).

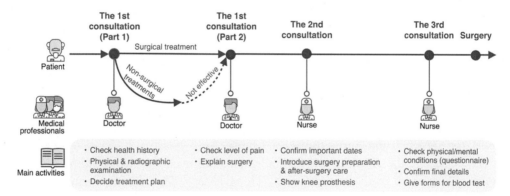

Figure 22.2 The knee arthritis patient treatment journey.

The user study also led us to focus on the second consultation of the PTJ to design the social VR clinic. The reason we choose the second consultation is that surgery preparations involve more active verbal communications and physical interactions between the nurse and the patient (e.g., showing the anatomical model) than the first and third consultation, but does not involve medical examinations that require professional equipment (e.g., X-ray). The second consultation has four main activities: (1) explain how patients should prepare for the surgery and stress the important information (e.g., dates, medications); (2) show a video about the surgery room; (3) explain the surgery process using the knee prosthesis and ask patients to feel its weight; and (4) train the patient to use an injection tool (a virtual syringe) to inject medicines to the knee.

22.2.2 Design and implementation

A combination of spoken and visual information is easier for patients to remember than only verbally explained information [19,20]. Therefore the social VR clinic maximizes information visualizations by (1) visualizing the preparation timeline and explaining the medical jargon; (2) allowing the patient to "walk into" a 3D virtual surgery room to "meet" the medical staff, and (3) enabling the patient to interact with an animated 3D knee anatomical model and a knee prosthesis to see what the differences are before and after the surgery. By wearing an *HTC Vive Pro Eye* HMD,[8] the patient can interact with the virtual nurse, teleport within the virtual rooms and operate the virtual artifacts. The nurse is represented by an avatar, which mirrors the real-time head, hands, mouth, and body movements of the nurse. The recorded social VR consultation can be replayed and shared with the patient.

In addition, the patient is equipped with mechanical VR gloves (*SenseGlove*[9]). *Sense-Glove* can position hands in VR using the HTC Vive Tracker,[10] and can accurately track the fingers, hand, and wrist of the patient's hand gestures, and provide force feedback on fingers. So, the patient can have the sensation of grasping objects. With *SenseGlove*, the patient can grab, hold, and press a virtual injection tool and practice injection with realistic haptic feedback, such as feeling the resistance when pressing the plunger of the virtual injection tool (Fig. 22.3).

The prototype is implemented in Unity (version 2018.4.1f1). The *HTC Vive* and the tracker are supported by *SteamVR* Plugin, and the *SenseGlove* is integrated into Unity by the free *SenseGlove* SDK.[11] The demo project runs on a 2.20 GHz Intel i7 Alienware laptop with an Nvidia RTX 2070 graphics card. Both the *HTC Vive* and *SenseGlove* are wired and connected to the laptop.

The knee and the prosthesis model implementations were adapted based on professionally 3D scanned medical models from Thingiverse.[12] We added the material layer and motion to the models in *Unity* and incorporated them into the prototype. The surgery room is based on an asset from the *Unity Store*,[13] including a set of realistic medical devices, furniture objects, and animations. Fig. 22.4 illustrates the implemented four surgery preparation activities in social VR compared to the real-world ones.

---

[8] *HTC Vive Pro Eye* HMD: https://www.vive.com/eu/product/vive-pro-eye/.

[9] *SenseGlove*: https://www.senseglove.com.

[10] *HTC Vive Tracker*: https://www.vive.com/ca/vive-tracker/.

[11] https://github.com/Adjuvo/SenseGlove-Unity.

[12] *Thingiverse*: https://www.thingiverse.com/thing:340254.

[13] A surgery room asset from the Unity Asset Store: https://assetstore.unity.com/packages/3d/props/interior/operating-room-18295.

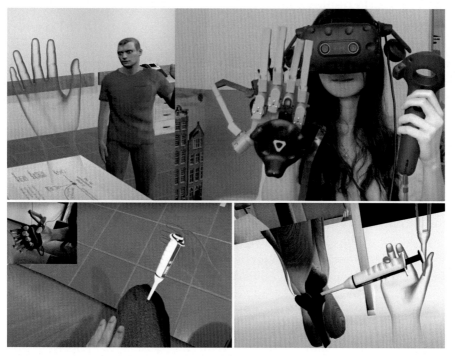

Figure 22.3 Use SenseGlove with HTC Vive tracker to position the hands in VR spaces and train the patient to use an injection tool. SenseGlove can track the fingers, hand, and wrist of user's hand gestures, and provides force feedback on fingers.

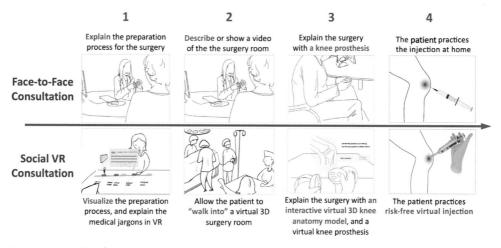

Figure 22.4 The four main activities related to a medical consultation: comparing the differences in the face-to-face consultation with the social VR clinic.

22.2.3 Real-world deployment

We set up the social VR clinic prototype in one usability lab of Delft University of Technology (TU Delft) and invited 22 user experience designers or design students from the faculty of Industry Design Engineering of TU Delft to experience both the face-to-face consultation and the social VR consultation. We made this decision due to the restrictions of visiting hospitals during the pandemic. The invited designers or design students were experienced in designing user journeys and user interfaces and can provide us with expert feedback in improving the experiences.

The results of design experts' evaluation showed the potential of social VR as a new medium to enable effective remote communications. The experts found the 3D visualizations of medical information and immersive "walk-in" experiences important. However, we noticed that, at the moment, social VR consultations cannot replace face-to-face ones, due to regulations that restrict performing medical examinations in a non-face-to-face setting [21]. Many design experts found face-to-face consultations less complicated and less distracting than social VR ones.

The social VR clinic aims at facilitating communication between two users (i.e., patient and nurse). However, in the end, we did not manage to obtain permission to set up the social VR clinic in the hospital. As an alternative, we recruited 22 non-patients for the evaluation. We as well considered the age factor when recruiting young participants. As we found in our user study [17] and literature [22], most of the elder patients are accompanied by their child or grandchild to the hospital. These young family members can be the target users of the social VR clinic, as they can attend and record the VR consultation for the patients. Our design is an initial exploration of social VR use cases in healthcare, aiming at facilitating immersive remote communication between two users. Further studies and design iterations are needed to allow elder patients to use the technology.

22.3. CakeVR and the birthday celebration

A video demonstration of the *CakeVR* application is available at https://youtu.be/HS8sN212toQ, under the channel named "Distributed and Interactive Systems Group," with the title of "CHI2021 - CakeVR: A Social Virtual Reality (VR) Tool for Co-designing Cakes."

Rarely is there a celebration without a cake. Apart from being an edible art, a customized cake is often a ceremonial symbol [23,24], which is special and personal, and closely associated with social relations and emotions [25]. Customized cake services enable clients to collaboratively personalize their cake in shape, color, and flavor with pastry chefs [26]. However, the customization process is not easy for both clients and chefs, which usually starts in a face-to-face meeting. Most of the follow-up communications are through text messages with the aid of reference cake pictures, which is

Figure 22.5 The difficulties in communicating the decoration and size of a customized cake: (*a*) design keywords from the clients, (*b*) a cake reference picture, (*c*) the final cake design in a 2D photo, and (*d*) the clients only saw the final cake at the celebration.

insufficient for them to fully communicate their creative thoughts and to have a clear image of the final design [27,28]. Cake customization requires professional skills. Based on 2D reference pictures and texts, it is not only difficult for clients to express the ideal decorations they want [28,29], but also challenging for pastry chefs to immediately visualize and show the size and decorations of the cake to the clients [27]. Fig. 22.5 illustrates such difficulties.

As a new remote communication medium [30], social VR is distinguished from video conferencing tools by their capacity to portray 3D spatial information [31], to exploit users' natural behaviors, and to immerse users in the virtual world [32,33]. In this application, we demonstrate that social VR is a promising medium to support clients to remotely co-design customized cakes with pastry chefs. Social VR allows pastry chefs and clients who are physically separated to co-present in a shared virtual space and to assist their cake co-design by providing intuitive virtual interaction techniques and real-time 3D visualizations of virtual cakes. Both clients and chefs can instantly see the real-size 3D cake visualizations as their co-design results.

22.3.1 User journey

Based on the interviews with pastry chefs and clients who had experiences of ordering customized cakes [34], we identified three main phases of the current communication process of cake customization, including (1) client input, (2) ideation and negotiation, and (3) agreement (Fig. 22.6).

At Phase 1, a client usually starts the conversation with a pastry chef by describing the cake he or she needs from three aspects: the main features of the cake, the context where the cake will be consumed, and the emotion that the cake should convey. The

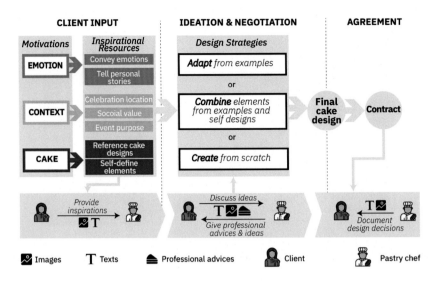

Figure 22.6 Three phases of current cake customization communication.

reference cake pictures and information obtained at Phase 1 help define the style, size, and high-level visual features (e.g., wood/forest elements) of the cake. At Phase 2, pastry chefs help clients turn the inspirations into tangible cake designs, with professional skills and equipment. We noticed that three design strategies were often applied, namely (1) adapting from examples (reference cake pictures), (2) combining elements from examples and self-designs, and (3) creating a new cake from scratch. At Phase 3, the clients and the pastry chefs agree upon the final design of the cake. The chefs precisely document all the design details into a formal contract, usually with a sketch or a collage of reference pictures.

To support Phase 1, it is essential to enable the pastry chef and the client to meet in the virtual space, and allow them to discuss with the aid of reference cake pictures, the celebration locations, and support the communication with natural hand gestures. To support Phase 2, social VR has its unique advantage in integrating different types of media to assist design activities and provide instant visualizations of the final design. It is important for *CakeVR* to support users to perform cake co-design activities in the virtual space, including making sketches, adding decorations, resizing the cakes, and instantly seeing the design outcomes. To support Phase 3, it is essential to assist in documenting the final cake with all the design details (e.g., exact colors, texture).

22.3.2 Design and implementation

We made a storyboard to describe the core functions and user scenarios of CakeVR, from preparation, initial idea discussion, ideation, and negotiation to confirmation (Fig. 22.7). The storyboard guided the implementation of CakeVR, which is a medium-

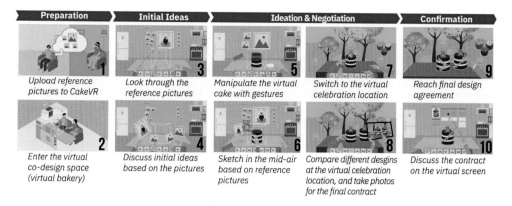

Figure 22.7 The storyboard of CakeVR, defining the core functions and user scenarios.

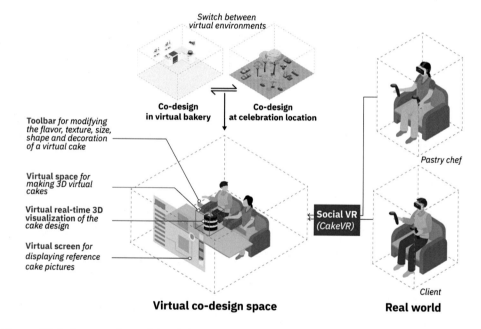

Figure 22.8 An overview of the CakeVR system.

fidelity social VR prototype for one client and one pastry chef to co-design a cake in a shared virtual space. Fig. 22.8 illustrates the system overview of CakeVR. The virtual co-design space can switch between a virtual bakery and a celebration location. Two users who are represented as cartoon-like avatars meet at the virtual space wearing HMDs. The virtual space has a graphical interface to guide them to build a 3D virtual cake together and visualizes the cake design in real-time.

The 3D cake models with textures and the pre-designed cake decoration components (e.g., different shapes of cakes, cream, fruits, flowers) were made in *Blender*,[14] and then exported into *Unity3D*[15] (version 2018.4.4f1). The virtual scenes, including the virtual café, the garden, and the two avatars were built based on selected assets from the *Unity Asset Store*.[16] How the users interact with the virtual interface and the gestural manipulations of the virtual cake were manually coded using C# in *Unity3D*. *Animation Rigging*, a plugin of *Unity3D* is applied for simulating the upper body motion of the avatars based on the spatial positions of the two hands and the head-tracked by the *Oculus Rifts* HMD. The *Oculus Rifts* HMD and the *Oculus Touch* controllers were supported by the *Oculus Integration plugin*. *PhotonPun*, a plugin *Unity 3D*, was utilized to connect two VR users and synchronize all the data (i.e., dynamic data of the 3D virtual objects, body movements of the avatars) via the Internet. Three basic gesture-based 3D manipulations were implemented in the prototype, namely moving, rotating, and scaling. By pressing the grip button of the *Oculus Touch* controller, users can virtually grab a 3D object, and change its position, orientation and size.

22.3.3 Real-world deployment

We invited six clients and four pastry chefs to use and evaluate the *CakeVR* prototype and found that CakeVR has improved the efficiency in the cake customization communication, and enhanced the shared understanding in the co-design process by allowing natural gestural interactions, intuitive manipulations of 3D objects, and instant 3D visualizations [34]. The findings also highlight *CakeVR*'s potential to transform product design communication through remote interactive and immersive co-design and to recreate (food-related) senses in social VR.

The Dutch National Research Institute of Mathematics and Computer Science (Centrum voor Wiskunde en Informatica (CWI))[17] celebrated its 75th birthday virtually, since the pandemic did not allow physical gatherings. As an extension of the *CakeVR* application, the virtual celebration brought two people to get immersed in a virtual world by wearing VR glasses and blowing candles on a virtual birthday cake together. The celebration demonstrated the state of the art of what is possible with volumetric video [9]. Each person and the birthday cake were recorded in separate locations using three *Microsoft Azure Kinect DK* depth cameras (hereinafter referred to as *Kinect* camera).[18] The volumetric videos were combined and transmitted into a virtual café in real-time so that the two people got the feeling that they were celebrating their birthday

---

[14] *Blender*: https://www.blender.org.

[15] *Unity 3D*: https://unity3d.com/get–unity/download.

[16] Unity Asset Store: https://assetstore.unity.com.

[17] Centrum voor Wiskunde en Informatica (CWI): https://www.cwi.nl.

[18] *Microsoft Azure Kinect DK* developer kit: https://azure.microsoft.com/en-us/services/kinect-dk/#industries.

Figure 22.9 Two persons and a cake were recorded in separate locations using three Kinect depth cameras. Their real-time volumetric videos were transmitted into a virtual café so that the two people felt that they were celebrating together.

together with a cake in front of them (Fig. 22.9). This demonstration is available online: https://youtu.be/KcRpp0s50RQ.

22.4. MediaScape XR: the social VR museum experience

The video demonstration of the *MediaScape XR* available at https://youtu.be/I7kY1cMZyD0, under the channel named "Distributed and Interactive Systems Group, CWI," with the title of "MediaScape XR | OBA – VRDays2021 | Short."

Today, a trip to museums often involves looking at precious objects through a protective glass screen. The artifacts cannot be touched or approached too closely, and there is only a limited amount of information about them, usually on a small white card next to the objects [35]. No wonder for some audiences, particularly the younger generation, who have grown up in a digital world, museum-going can feel passive, lacking in interactivity, and not very exciting.

Our society is proficient at studying culture from a historical perspective and possesses impressive longitudinal datasets on arts, media culture, and audio-visual archives. These datasets or artifacts have been digitized and made available online in recent years, such as Rijks studio of the Rijksmuseum [36]. Still, the ongoing effort has mainly focused on the creation of digital surrogates, and not so much on the provision of novel manners to enjoy the artifacts or interact with them in meaningful and socially engaging ways. Museums are exploring how to make their collection accessible remotely, but in most cases, this is limited to traditional web technology, such as websites, online catalogs, social media posts, videos, with little interaction and no immersion [37]. Museum curators also lack tools to present the full story behind the artifacts to remote visitors in an immersive manner [38]. The *MediaScape XR* application aims at changing this kind of passive museum visiting to interactive and immersive experiences by enabling visitors to enjoy a remote VR museum experience with photo-realistic user representations;

The *MediaScape XR* application integrates a 3D replica of a heritage object from the Netherlands Institute for Sound and Vision (NISV)[19] in an immersive virtual museum. Museum visitors, who are in realistic representations, will wear HMDs to get immersed and interact with the virtual object, such as dressing up in a historical costume, which will enable visitors to cherish the historical accomplishments through an immersive and engaging experience.

22.4.1 User journey

The focus group sessions with the curators at the NISV directed us to focus on one cultural artifact: the costume that Jerney Kaagman, lead singer of the rock band Earth and Fire, wore in the music program TopPop in 1979. In addition, a co-design session was conducted with a group of user experience designers that helped us specify a list of design requirements that indicate what interactions and activities could be implemented in this social VR application. The storyboard describes the main activities defined at the co-design session (Fig. 22.10). The requirements are the following: (1) The *MediaScape* application allows more than two remote visitors to co-present in a shared virtual environment with photo-realistic representations. (2) It allows visitors to freely explore the 3D virtual museum (six-degree-of-freedom). (3) It offers a user interface within the virtual museum to offer multimedia content about artifact-related knowledge. (4) It allows visitors to revisit the historical scene. In this case, it is the music hall where the costume was worn by Jerney Kaagman in the TopPop music program in 1979. (5) It allows haptic interaction with the museum artifact, which is impossible in the real world. In this case, the visitors can wear the costume virtually. (6) It guides visitors to collaboratively recreate the musical performance of Jerney Kaagman's "Weekend" in 1979. (7) Visitors can take the experience home by taking virtual photos or recording the videos.

22.4.2 Design and implementation

Based on the design requirements, the implementation of the *MediaScape* experience started with creating a 3D virtual museum. To make a more realistic museum experience for NISV, we integrated the 3D model of the NISV museum building into *Unity3D*

---

[19] The Netherlands Institute for Sound and Vision: https://www.beeldengeluid.nl/en.

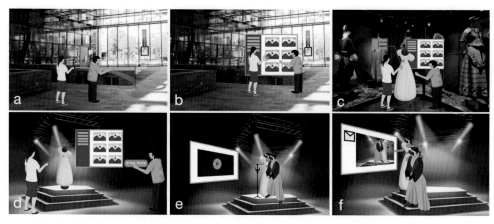

Figure 22.10 (*a*) Two remote users, captured as volumetric videos, were transmitted into the virtual museum; (*b&c*) they search for Jerney Kaagman's costume, which is shown as a placeholder costume in this storyboard, and closely "touch," examine, and rotate it; (*d*) the curated tour guide the users to a virtual stage; (*e*) they wear the costume and recreate the TopPop performance of Jerney Kaagman's Weekend; (*f*) they take home a photo of their virtual museum experience.

(Fig. 22.11). It was an open exhibit space, displaying a collection of archives representing the historical evolution of Dutch media (i.e., television, radio, costume), and letting visitors walk through among the collections. The 3D models of the NISV building and other props were built in *Cinema 4D*[20] and in *Blender*, and then imported into *Unity3D*. After that, we implemented the texture and lighting for the 3D model in *Unity3D*. Finally, we worked on the optimization of the VR viewing experience and improved the rendering efficiency by (1) baking light maps,[21] (2) activating occlusion culling,[22] (3) using the single-path rendering setting, (4) and switching the rendering quality to "VR" level. In this way, we were able to keep the frame per second (FPS) higher than 50, and significantly improve the rendering performance (Fig. 22.12).

Next, we replicated the historical scene, which is the TopPop music hall of the Weekend show in 1979. The videos of the Weekend show were used as a guideline for the spatial layout and decorations of the stage. Then, we built the 3D assets in *Blender*, and then loaded them into *Unity3D*. After that, we set the texture, lighting, and special effects (i.e., smoke) to the scene in *Unity3D* (Fig. 22.13).

---

[20] Cinema4D is a 3D modeling software https://www.maxon.net/en/cinema-4d/.

[21] Baking lighting is when Unity performs lighting calculations in advance and saves the results as lighting data, which is then applied at runtime.

[22] Occlusion culling is a process that prevents Unity from performing rendering calculations for game objects that are completely hidden from view (occluded) by other game objects.

Figure 22.11 The 3D architecture model in MediaScape application (*Left*); the physical space of NISV museum which is now under construction (*Right*).

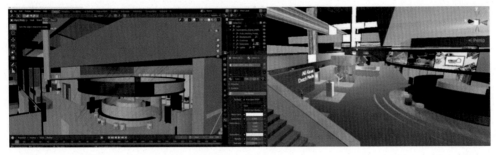

Figure 22.12 The 3D architecture model in Blender (*Left*); The 3D architecture model in Unity3D with texture and lighting (*Right*).

Figure 22.13 The replicated 1979 TopPop music hall in Unity3D.

Besides the creation of the virtual scenes, a realistic 3D model of the costume (Fig. 22.14) was built by transforming the 3D structure of the costume into 2D patterns by hand sketching. After that, we drew all the 2D textile patterns digitally, and trans-

Figure 22.14 A photo collage of the real costume.

form them into a 3D suit using *Marvelous Designer*.[23] We refined the mesh to achieve a decent textile feeling. To make it look more vivid, the texture of blue shining leather was painted on the garment digitally (Fig. 22.15).

To enable visitors to wear the costume virtually, we developed a mechanism to fuse the 3D model of the costume and the head part of the user photorealistic representation so that the virtual costume can be controlled in real time by the gestures and movement of the user. This is possible, because we bound the skeleton to the costume mesh in *Blender*, and loaded this rigged costume model into *Unity3D*. In *Unity3D*, the location and orientation of the three main joints (head, left hand, right hand) of the skeleton are controlled in real time by the joint position, captured by the HMD and the VR controllers. The rest of the joints (i.e., elbow, shoulder) are simulated using the animation rig plugin in *Unity3D*. This way, users can virtually wear the costume (Fig. 22.16).

22.4.3 Real-world deployment

Through capturing each visitor through three Kinect cameras in real time, the visitors with photorealistic representations met each other in the *MediaScape* virtual museum (Fig. 22.17). The experience is tailor-made for the costume worn by Jerney Kaagman in the *TopPop* show. In the virtual environment, visitors can freely explore the 3D virtual museum and closely examine the 3D model of the costume. They can also relive its history by watching the performance of Jerney Kaagman on the virtual screen and

---

[23] *Marvelous Designer* is a garment-making software with textile simulation function https://www.marvelousdesigner.com/.

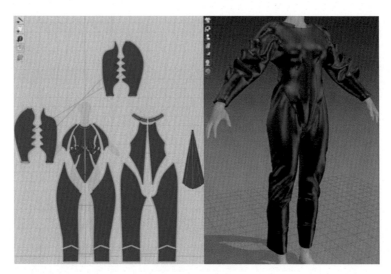

Figure 22.15 The 2D hand-sketched patterns of the costume (*Left*) and the 3D model of the costume (*Right*).

Figure 22.16 The skeleton controls the motion of the costume 3D model (*Left*); two users were wearing the costume in the virtual music hall (*Right*).

performing as the artist using the virtual music instruments. Both visitors can enjoy a curated tour of the virtual TopPop show and recreate Jerney Kaagman's *Weekend* music show with each other. The *MediaScape* application illustrates how the traditional model of a museum experience as a passive observation is shifting to active, interpretive

Figure 22.17 Two remote visitors greeting each other in the MediaScape XR virtual museum.

engagement. It facilitates novel manners to enjoy and experience the artifacts or interact with them in meaningful and socially engaging ways.

MediaScape XR was chosen to be exhibited on the main stage of the 2021 VR-Days,[24] which was held at the Amsterdam Public Library (OBA) in November 2021 (Fig. 22.18). Around 150 event visitors experienced and evaluated *MediaScape XR*. Through this event, we demonstrated that the application is robust and steady to run in an exhibit setting. We brought the application to the event visitors with diverse backgrounds and introduced the novel technology to the general public. In addition, we found that it achieved decent system usability and user experience. On the system usability scale [39,40], 6% of the visitors rated the application "best imaginable," 12% rated "excellent," 48% rated "good," 29% rated "ok," and only 5% found it "under ok." *MediaScape XR* has envisioned a future heritage experience that can be accessed remotely and socially. Through the deployment, we validated the added value that social VR can bring to the cultural heritage domain.

22.5. The social VR movie

Hunkering down on the couch and watching a movie together with friends or family is not only a nice cozy thing to do, but also enables us to share emotions, increase engagement, and social bonds with people we love [41]. However, this is not always possible if we live apart. Although people at a distance can text each other, video call,

---

[24] *VRDays* is an annual event in Amsterdam for exhibiting the emerging XR technologies: https://vrdays.co.

Figure 22.18 MediaScape XR was demonstrated to the public at the VRDays.

and share their screens, or even use video stream synchronization applications (e.g., Teleparty[25]), it is still far from the feeling of being together. As an emerging immersive remote communication tool, social VR has the potential to afford face-to-face-like social interactions than video calls, enabling users to feel co-present and interact with virtual objects [6,17,32,34]. The virtual space can be a computer-generated 3D scene or a 360° scene captured by an omnidirectional camera. Each user can be represented as a computer-generated avatar [42–44] or, in recently proposed systems, a user's virtual representation was live captured by depth cameras [9,45].

Recently, VR films are becoming popular, thanks to the market available and affordable HMDs. The Oculus platform offers a vast variety of immersive content, from 360° videos, immersive 3D wonderlands to interactive replicas of historical monuments. The 360° video documentary Rebuilding Notre Dame[26] immerses VR viewers with the footage from before and after the April 2019 blaze at the same locations, capturing the majestic architecture from angles that visitors usually cannot see. The Under Presents[27]

---

[25] *Teleparty* (https://www.netflixparty.com) is an application that synchronizes video playback and adds group chat to multiple over-the-top movie/TV content platforms, such as Netflix, Disney, Hulu.

[26] *Rebuild Notre Dame* is available at https://www.oculus.com/experiences/media/1353452644677196/210792686621494.

[27] *The Uder Presents* is available at https://www.oculus.com/deeplink/?action=view&path=app/1917371471713228&ref=oculus_desktop.

takes users to a new virtual world, where they enjoy live immersive theaters and explore novel interface-free interactions, such as the "scrunch" technique, in which users move forward by reaching out their virtual arms and pulling the destination towards them. The Anne Frank House VR[28] reconstructed the "Secret Annex," where Anne spent two years of her life hiding in. The experience invites users to wander through the rooms, immerse themselves in Anne's thoughts, and interact with Anne's belongings.

VR has increasingly become a sophisticated tool for storytelling, which guides viewers through the narrative in a novel way and invites viewers to participate [46]. Imagine a near-future scenario, where you and your friends or family who live apart can walk into the same virtual movie together and see each other as holograms. You co-present with the movie characters, interact with them, and influence the movie storylines without interrupting the watching experiences. This new type of interactive movie that supports immersive social interaction brings the co-watching experience to the next level. The conversations between us would no longer be "The detective found three fingerprints," but be "My mother and I saw the forensic report held by the detective, saying 'three finger prints'."

The social VR movie engages multiple users in such an immersive and interactive experience. Each user is captured in real-time by three Kinect cameras. The volumetric videos of users were transmitted into the virtual movie scene, so that they felt like walking into the movie and being together with each other.

22.5.1 The virtual movie production

The video demonstration of the social VR movie is available at https://youtu.be/t30ECMnocWk, under the channel named "VRTogether," with the title of "VRTogether Pilot 3: Interactive Scenario (Visit at the Crime Location)."

The 10-minute virtual movie is about the investigation of the murder of Ms. Armova, which was professionally produced by The Modern Cultural Productions (Madrid, Spain) [47]. The virtual movie invites four users to join in simultaneously, who form the Civilian Oversight Committee as the witnesses of the crime-solving process and allow interaction with the movie characters to help with the process. There are six movie characters: Sarge Hoffsteler (detective), Elena Armova (victim), Rachel Tyrell (policewoman), Evans Young (forensic technician), Christine Gerard (Elena's assistant), and Ryan Zeller (Elena's ex-boyfriend). The last two of the above characters are the two suspects. The movie characters were generated in three steps (Fig. 22.19): (1) record the full-body acting of the real actors and actresses; (2) capture movements of their faces using an iPhone and Reallusion's live face application and Character Creator[29]; (3) perform a body MoCap (full-body motion capture animation) during post-production.

---

[28] *The Anne Frank House VR* is available at https://www.oculus.com/deeplink/?action=view&path=app/1596151970428159&ref=oculus_desktop.

[29] Reallusion's character creator: https://www.reallusion.com/character-creator.

Figure 22.19 The generation of the virtual movie characters: (*a&b*) capture the movements of the actor's or actress's face using the Reallusion's live face application on an iPhone that is attached to a specially designed helmet; (*c*) perform a full-body motion capture animation (*MoCap*) of the actor or actress; (*d*) the generated virtual movie character based on the face and full-body capture.

Figure 22.20 The user-movie character interaction in the movie: (*a*) detective, Sarge, instructed one user to look for the phone finder and switch it off; (*b*) one HMD user found the phone finder on a lower table next to the window; (*c*) she switched it off.

Users can access the virtual movie either by using an HMD or using a screen with a game controller. HMD and screen users can use voice to answer the questions raised by the movie characters. However, the HMD users can only teleport between blue circles inside the virtual apartment, but can interact with the environment, such as switching on the light and clicking on buttons (Fig. 22.20). The screen users can use the game controller to freely navigate inside the apartment, but cannot interact with the environment. These differences were pre-defined by the movie production company, aiming at (1) reducing the motion sickness of the HMD users by limiting their movement to teleportation (e.g., joystick walking in VR may largely increase motion sickness [48]), and (2) increasing the collaboration opportunities between HMD and screen users, because they have to find out who can interact with the environment or talk to the movie characters to move on in the story.

The virtual movie takes place in the luxury apartment of the victim Elena. The first part of the movie happens in the living room (Fig. 22.21*a*), where four users are observing the crime-solving and interacting with the movie characters (e.g., help switch on the light or click on the phone finder). In the second part, the four users are separated into

Figure 22.21 The luxury apartment of the victim Elena Armova: (*a*) the living room with four users represented as point clouds and three virtual characters: (*from left to right*) Rachel, Sarge, and the hologram of Elena; (*b*) the kitchen with two users, Sarge and Evans; (*c*) the bedroom with Rachel and Elena.

two groups. Two users follow Sarge to the kitchen, where technician Evans is checking the evidence (Fig. 22.21*b*). The other two users follow Rachel to the bedroom, where the hologram of Elena confesses some secrets (Fig. 22.21*c*). The users are represented as hologram-like point clouds (Fig. 22.21*a*).

22.5.2 Real-world deployment

We set up four separate rooms, Room A, B, C, and D, located on the 3rd floor of the CWI building (Science Park, Amsterdam). Room A and B had an Oculus Rifts HMD. Room C and D had a desktop computer, a 50-inch monitor, and a game controller. Each Room had three *Kinect* depth cameras to capture users' volumetric representations and deliver them to the virtual movie as point clouds (Fig. 22.22). For each social VR movie session, we invited four users. The two HMD users were in Room A and B, and the two screen users were in Room C and D. There are two interactive objects in the virtual movie: a light switch and a phone finder. HMD users must interact with them as instructed by the detective to move forward with the story.

We recruited 48 participants (23 males, 25 females), with age range of 21–56 years (M = 34.9, SD = 10.3). 12 females and 12 males were HMD users; 13 females and 11 males were screen users. Thirteen (13) of them had never used VR, 33 had used it 1 to 3 times, and two were experienced VR users. They came to the social VR movie session in groups of four persons. In addition, 14 VR experts, from 9 companies/institutes[30] were invited to evaluate the photorealistic social VR movie. We set up two rooms equipped with an HMD and one room with a screen. The 14 experts came in two groups: Group 1 had 8 experts, and Group 2 had 6 experts. After all the experts rotated and experienced both the HMD and the screen version of the virtual movie, they were gathered in a spacious meeting room for a 30-minute focus group discussion (audio-

---

[30] The 9 companies/institutes are The Netherlands Institute of Sound and Vision, Medical VR, The Virtual Dutch Men, NEMO Science Museum, Erasmus University Medical Center, Sensiks, PostNL, Buitenboord Motor, and Interface.

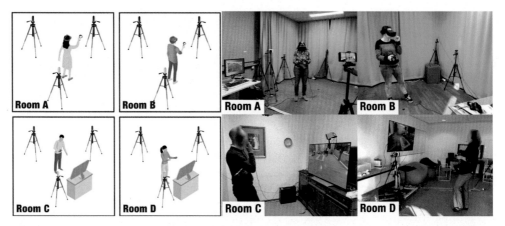

Figure 22.22 The (*left*) illustrations and (*right*) photos of the 4 rooms. Room A and B had an Oculus Rifts HMD. Room C and D had a screen computer, a 50-inch monitor, and a game controller. Each room had three Kinect depth cameras to capture users' volumetric representations.

recorded) about the potentials and challenges of the photorealistic social VR experiences [49].

The results showed that whereas HMD users reported a higher sense of presence and immersion, screen users reported a lower workload and could more easily explore the virtual environment. Both HMD and screen users did not report any difference in cybersickness. In addition, we found that males rated the "possibility to act" higher than females, indicating that they could more easily and more actively control and interact with the virtual environment. For the evaluation of the volumetric representations, we found that, within the HMD group, the ratings for self-representations were worse than the ratings for others' representations. However, no differences were found within the screen users between the ratings for self and others' representations.

All 14 experts (E1–E14) were impressed by the simple setup of the "hologram" capturing system and were excited to see the photorealistic representations, which enabled them to feel co-present in the same space. As we observed, they were waving at each other in the virtual space and talking about the texture of their clothes, and the possible scenarios for applying the social VR system. The virtual movie was short (about 10 minutes), but all the experts spent a much longer time exploring all the details. They saw the full potential of our social VR system in many market sectors, such as medical care, education, immersive meetings, family reunion, virtual dating. As E8 commented, "It doesn't feel like an avatar, but the real person. Despite the quality, it still needs a lot of improvement, but you go beyond the uncanny valley, and it's the person there. That's amazing. That's more than I expected. I expected it to be a nice virtual environment with a Skype-like interface, but you go way beyond that." The experts also pointed out challenges that we need to consider in our future work. E6 is a physician, she mentioned, "The realism level of the virtual objects needs to be much higher in a clinical context. Suppose we are going to reconstruct the breast of a cancer patient, not only the visual quality needs to be fully realistic, but the haptic feelings of the 3D reconstruction also need to be realistic. In this way, patients can have a correct expectation towards the surgery." E11 suggested, based on the comparison of the two devices, "The HMD was very immersive, but on the other hand, the screen with a game controller was more practical, perhaps also more addictive. I am curious to see the effects on 3D screens."

Overall, both users and VR experts found that photorealistic volumetric representations enhanced co-presence. We additionally found that gender influenced interactions with the movie.

22.6. Measuring user experiences in social VR

Instead of watching a film together on a screen, social VR can be experienced as if viewers are co-present in the same space. Although research interests in understanding social VR experiences are growing, there is no theoretical frameworks or experimental protocols to depict what factors influence social VR experiences and how to measure them. Many studies identified the importance of user representations for providing immersive experiences. Latoschik et al. [50] found that realistic avatars were rated significantly more human-like and evoked a stronger acceptance of the virtual body. Similarly, Waltemate et al. [51] concluded that personalized avatars significantly increase the sense of body ownership, presence, and dominance. Cho et al. [52] compared the actor captured by volumetric videos with the actor captured in 2D videos, and another 3D avatar obtained by pre-scanning the actor. The results show that users have the highest sense of social presence with the volumetric actor when performing dynamic tasks.

Apart from user representations, there are metrics (e.g., surveys, questionnaires) and experimental protocols that can be adapted to understand social VR experiences. Metrics for evaluating presence and immersion have been developed and widely validated, such as the presence questionnaire by Witmer and Singer [53] and the Slater-Usoh-Steed questionnaire [54]. Jennett et al. [55] suggested in their immersion questionnaire to include factors such as lack of awareness of time and involvement. Some other studies have explored user experiences in VR using different devices (e.g., 2D screens, HMDs). Srivastava et al. [56] examined how HMD and desktop would affect spatial learning when the ambulatory locomotion in HMD was restricted. They found that users spent more time and perceived less motion sickness and task effort using desktop than HMD. In their virtual earthquake training, Shu et al. [57] found that users reported a higher sense of spatial presence and immersion while using HMD than using a desktop.

Quality of experience (QoE) assesses the degree of delight or annoyance of the user of a system [58] and takes into consideration of a wide range of factors that contribute to a user's perceived quality of a system, including human, system, and context factors [59]. User experience (UX) research aims at investigating a user's perceptions and responses that result from the use and/or anticipated use of a system (ISO 9241-210:2019 [60]). UX includes both subjective evaluation of hedonic and/or meaningful experiences and emotions, and objective evaluation of the user-system interactions, such as task execution time and the number of clicks or errors. Users' expectations and motivations are important factors in UX evaluation [61]. A growing research effort is to combine the QoE and UX measurements to have a comprehensive understanding of the perceptual and experiential quality of user-system interactions in an immersive virtual environment [62]. Chessa et al. [63] combined objective measurements (i.e., heart rate and head movement) and subjective self-reports to assess how users perceived and experienced an immersive VR system, and found positive correlations between the two measurements. Chamilothori et al. [64] evaluated the adequacy of a virtual space as an alternative environment for subjective experiments by combining three metrics, namely the subjective evaluations of perceptual accuracy, the users' physiological reactions, and the presence questionnaire. Egan et al. [65] presented an evaluation study comparing immersive VR and non-VR environments, using objective metrics, including heart rate (HR) and electrodermal activity (EDA), and a subjective post-test questionnaire for evaluating immersion and usability. They found correlations between objective metrics and self-reported QoE. Further research is needed to develop a social VR experience model that combines objective and subjective metrics for measuring and predicting social VR experiences.

Though many works have attempted to measure interaction experience, presence, and immersion across real [55,66] and virtual interactions [53,67,69,70], only recently has some work address the social VR medium in general [68,71]. And though social presence measurement tools can vary (e.g., subjective self-report measures [72] or non-verbal signals such as gestures [43]), we do not yet have a validated questionnaire that can capture the richness and social interaction nuances of activities in social VR. It can get tedious to use many existing questionnaires in one single experiment. Therefore the challenge is how to combine the measurement metrics into one single questionnaire that is intended for social VR experiences. The challenge leads to two goals of the study: (1) develop a questionnaire to measure social VR (photo sharing) experiences; and (2) validate the social VR questionnaire by a (photo sharing) comparative study social VR, Skype, and Face-to-Face (F2F).

22.6.1 Developing a social VR questionnaire

We adopted a mixed-methods approach (Fig. 22.23) that combines a user-centric approach [73] and statistical techniques to develop an accurate and consistent questionnaire instrument (i.e., ensures test validity and reliability) for measuring social VR photo sharing [33].

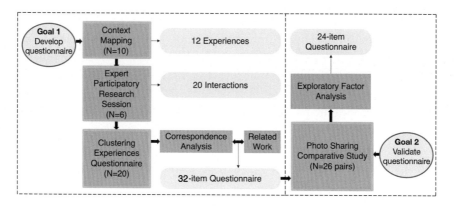

Figure 22.23 Methodological approach for constructing the social VR questionnaire.

We started with a series of user–centered studies with photo-sharing users, VR experts, and UX researchers. First, we conducted context mapping, which is a research method that involves users as "experts of their experience" [74]. With techniques such as workbooks and generative sessions, participants are facilitated to observe and reflect on the experiences of use. In the context mapping sessions, users mapped 12 typical experiences of F2F photo sharing. Based on the results of context mapping, the expert participatory session mapped 20 categories of relevant social interactions that can happen during F2F photo sharing in both the real world and in VR. Next, we designed an online questionnaire for clustering the 12 experiences based on 20 interactions, and we invited 20 UX researchers to participate [33]. Correspondence analysis of the clustering questionnaire resulted in three components of experience that are relevant to social VR, namely quality of interaction (QoI), presence and immersion (PI), and social meaning (SM).

Using the three components as guidance, we composed a 32-item social VR questionnaire.[31] The questions use a 5-point Likert scale. The question items are either derived from the well-validated questionnaires or composed based on the typical experiences mapped in the context mapping sessions.

Questions 1–11 are about QoI in social VR, which is defined as the ability of the user to interact with the virtual world and to interact with other users in that virtual world [75,76]. It assesses the quality of communication, mutual sensing of emotions, and naturalness between virtually represented users. Items 1, 2, 8, 9 were developed based on two experiences identified in the QoI cluster (i.e., feeling understood, feeling others' emotions). Items 3–7 were adapted from [67], and items 10–11 were from [77].

---

[31] The 32-item social VR questionnaire is available at https://www.dropbox.com/s/xhcb3zrt4fdjpkn/chi2019_32i_questionnaire.pdf?dl=0.

Questions 12–22 measure SM in social VR, which is defined as the experience of "being together," both mentally and physically. Items 12–16 were adapted from [78]; items 19–21 were from [79], and item 22 was from [76]. Items 17–18 were developed based on two experiences identified in the SM cluster (i.e., recall and recreate memories; and create stronger bonds).

Questions 23–32 measure presence and immersion. Witmer and Singer [53] defined immersion as a subjective and psychological state characterized by perceiving oneself to be involved in and interacting within a virtual environment. Item 23 was adapted from [69]. Items 24–25 were from [70]; item 26 was from [53], and items 27–32 were from [55].

22.6.2 Validating the social VR questionnaire

A within-subject controlled user study was conducted to compare photo-sharing experiences in three conditions: Face-to-Face (F2F), Facebook Spaces (FBS), and Skype (SKP). The resulting data is (a) used in the exploratory factor analysis (EFA) [80] to validate whether the three factors (i.e., QoI, PI, and SM) are indeed important to construct our social VR questionnaire, (b) provide empirical findings comparing photo sharing across study conditions using our social VR questionnaire [33].

We recruited 26 pairs of participants ($N = 52$, 23 females, $M_{age} = 27.6$, $SD_{age} = 7.9$), who are friends or colleagues. In the F2F condition, two participants were sitting together and showing each other photos on their smartphones. In the SKP condition, two participants were sitting in different rooms, and sharing photos on their smartphones through SKP. In the FBS condition, the photos were uploaded to the FBS. Two participants were sitting in different rooms, but they entered the same virtual space to share their photos represented in a smartphone display manner. After each condition, every participant filled in a social VR questionnaire.

We ran an exploratory factor analysis (EFA) [80] to better understand the important factors in our questionnaire. EFA is a statistical technique within factor analysis commonly used for scale development involving categorical and ordinal data and serves to identify a set of latent constructs underlying a battery of measured variables [81,82]. Given that our focus was to evaluate a complete list of questions, we ran our analysis only on data from the SKP and FBS evaluations (i.e., questions 24–33 for evaluating PI were removed for the F2F condition). Bartlett's sphericity test was significant ($\chi^2(2, 496) = 2207.187$, $p < 0.001$) and Kaiser–Meyer–Olkin was greater than 0.5 (KMO $= 0.85$); our data allowed for EFA. Given our earlier correspondence analysis that showed a grouping of three factors, we tested our model fit based on three factors corresponding to each set of questionnaire items. Furthermore, since we assumed that factors would be related, we used oblique rotation "oblimin" along with standard principal axes factoring. Standardized loadings are shown in Table 22.2.

Table 22.2 Exploratory factor analysis (EFA) was applied to our 32 questionnaire items. Questions in bold were kept for the 24-item social VR questionnaire.

No.		Factor 1 (PI)	Factor 2 (SM)	Factor 3 (QoI)
1	**"I was able to feel my partner's emotion during the photo sharing."**			**0.61**
2	**"I was sure that my partner often felt my emotion."**			**0.67**
3	"It was easy for me to contribute to the conversation."	0.17	0.44	0.37
4	"The conversation seemed highly interactive."	0.36	0.26	0.33
5	**"I could readily tell when my partner was listening to me."**			**0.60**
6	"I found it difficult to keep track of the conversation."	-0.12	0.45	0.36
7	"I felt completely absorbed in the conversation."	0.33	0.44	0.18
8	**"I could fully understand what my partner was talking about."**		0.18	**0.71**
9	**"I was sure that my partner understood what I was talking about."**			**0.73**
10	"The experience of photo sharing seemed natural."	0.51		0.41
11	**"The actions used to interact with my partner were natural."**	**0.36**		0.24
12	**"I often felt as if I was all alone during the photo sharing."**		**0.62**	0.20
13	**"I think my partner often felt alone during the photo sharing."**		**0.62**	0.20
14	**"I often felt that my partner and I were sitting together in the same space."**	0.82		0.16
15	**"I paid close attention to my partner."**	0.14	0.12	**0.38**
16	**"My partner was easily distracted when other things were going on around us."**	-0.20	0.32	0.26
17	**"I felt that the photo-sharing enhanced our closeness."**	**0.42**	0.21	
18	"Through the photo-sharing, I managed to share my memories with my partner."	0.11	0.41	0.37
19	**"I derived little satisfaction from photo sharing with my partner."**	0.12	**0.56**	
20	**"The photo-sharing experience with my partner felt superficial."**		**0.54**	0.18
21	**"I really enjoyed the time spent with my partner."**	0.18	**0.43**	0.29
22	"How emotionally close to your partner do you feel now?"	0.13	0.23	0.25

continued on next page

Table 22.2 (*continued*)

No.		Factor 1 (PI)	Factor 2 (SM)	Factor 3 (QoI)
23	"I had a sense of being in the same space with my partner."	**0.92**		
24	"Somehow I felt that the same space was surrounding me and my partner."	**0.87**	0.12	–0.15
25	"I had a sense of interacting with my partner in the same space, rather than doing it through a system."	**0.88**		
26	"My photo sharing experience seemed as if it was a face-to-face sharing."	**0.80**	–0.22	0.27
27	"I did not notice what was happening around me during the photo sharing." ⋆	**0.52**	0.30	–0.12
28	"I felt detached from the world around me during the photo sharing." ⋆	**0.71**	0.20	–0.20
29	"At the time, I was totally focusing on photo sharing."	0.36	0.38	
30	"Everyday thoughts and concerns were still very much on my mind."		**0.69**	–0.16
31	"It felt like the photo-sharing took shorter time than it really was."	0.25	**0.31**	
32	"When sharing the photos, time appeared to go by very slowly."	–0.10	**0.54**	
	SS loadings	5.67	3.83	3.65
	Proportion Variance	0.18	0.12	0.11
	Cumulative Variance	0.18	0.29	0.41

To ensure the factors are meaningful and redundancies eliminated (removing collinearity effects), we only took items with factor loadings of 0.3 and above, and with cross-loadings not less than 0.2 across factors. The cumulative explained variance of the three factors is 41%. The 24 questionnaire items[32] in bold were used for the evaluation of the three conditions (F2F, FBS, and SKP) along with the identified concepts: quality of interaction (QoI), social meaning (SM), and presence/immersion (PI). We furthermore tested each set of items for internal reliability by measuring Cronbach's alpha, and our final item sets show high reliability coefficients: F2F QoI ($\alpha = 0.8$), F2F SM ($\alpha = 0.89$), F2F PI ($\alpha = 0.74$), FBS QoI ($\alpha = 0.79$), FBS SM ($\alpha = 0.83$), FBS PI ($\alpha = 0.76$), SKP QoI ($\alpha = 0.78$), SKP SM ($\alpha = 0.79$), SKP PI ($\alpha = 0.75$).

As a first step towards external validity, we ran a controlled user study to compare photo-sharing experiences under F2F, SKP, and FBS. The detailed data analysis and results were presented in [17]. Based on our developed social VR questionnaire, we found

---

[32] The 24-item social VR questionnaire is available at https://www.dropbox.com/s/xnnn6b6i3kyl45r/chi2019_24i_questionnaire.pdf?dl=0.

that social VR is capable of closely approximating F2F sharing. Our questionnaire contribution and our empirical findings concerning photo-sharing experiences can provide researchers and designers with a tool to measure such reality-grounded activities.

Factor loadings of 0.3 and above and without cross-loadings of >0.3 are marked in bold.

22.7. Discussion

This chapter introduces the design, implementation, and evaluation of a series of social VR applications, covering healthcare, celebration, cultural heritage, and entertainment domains. We also presented a user-centered process of developing a social VR questionnaire and conducting a user experiment in a social VR environment (i.e., Facebook Spaces) to validate the questionnaire. This section discusses the lessons learned and provides several design recommendations.

22.7.1 Lessons learned and opportunities of social VR

22.7.1.1 Controlled experiments versus real-world products

The design and implementation of the applications focus on optimizing the user experiences, but are not all intended for laboratory experiments. Therefore not all aspects were fully controlled during the evaluation experiments. For example, the novel virtual movie was professionally produced by cinematography experts, which was not designed for laboratory experiments. The locomotion and interaction techniques used by HMD and screen users are not the same. To minimize the cybersickness, HMD users can only teleport among fixed locations in the virtual apartment, but screen users can move freely using the joystick on the controller. However, the goal of our evaluation studies is to exploratively evaluate possible user experiences in these novel immersive applications. We had to find the right balance between the "controlled experiments" and the "real products or applications." These real products or applications are not only operable in the laboratory, but also deployable to the real environment. We primed the aesthetics and user experience aspects over the perfectly controlled aspects. We find this important since we can derive important insights about user experiences in real-world setups.

22.7.1.2 Virtual representation and privacy

Privacy as a topic emerged during most user interviews. For example, in the social VR clinic evaluation, many users mentioned that they felt more relaxed and private in the social VR clinic than the F2F consultation, because their faces were hidden from the nurse. They do not need to pay attention to whether they look decent or whether their homes are tidy as they usually care during a video consultation [83]. However, the nurses or doctors stress, during remote consultations that it is necessary to see the patients' faces, to better understand their physical and mental conditions

[83]. The growing prevalence of real-time photorealistic human representations in VR (e.g., [9,84]) and research works on HMD removal [85] are all trying to make the user face visible to enhance the presence and immersive experience. However, the trade-off between the realism of the user representations and the privacy protections should be considered in future work.

22.7.1.3 Social VR as an extension of 2D video conferencing

As an extension to technology-mediated communication technologies, such as 2D video conferencing, social VR provides many benefits. First, social VR immerses the users in the same virtual world, providing a more realistic experience [86]. Li et al. [17] commented that the screen in video conferencing is like a "curtain" between two users, cutting off the sense of co-presence. Second, social VR uses virtual representations to offer embodiment experiences to users, and abilities to interact with the virtual environment and 3D virtual artifacts [87]. As we observed in the user evaluation of the social VR clinic, the guided "walk-in" experience, and 3D interactive anatomical models are more appreciated than watching the same content on a TV screen. Not only co-presence, but social VR also brings social connectedness and empathy to the experience, allowing people to see and feel from other persons' perspective. For instance, social VR can be used to train young physicians by simulating the circumstances the patients are going through, increasing their empathy and bonding towards the patients. Further use cases are needed to explore the potential of social VR.

22.7.1.4 Opportunities for controlled experiments

We identified many potential factors that require further investigation in a controlled manner, such as the influence of locomotion methods on users' cybersickness, (social) presence, and quality of interaction. In the social VR movie application, many users mentioned that they would have more interaction possibilities with the movie characters, the other users, and the virtual environment, indicating another research opportunity to investigate the influence of interactions on users' experiences. In addition, we also observed that there were differences in users' movement trajectories and differences in users' experiences using the devices. For instance, we noticed that male screen users moved more quickly and more frequently than female screen users, and their trajectories covered the whole virtual apartment. It also seemed that experienced VR game users finished the tasks faster than inexperienced users (e.g., find and switch on the light). We would like to further collect and analyze objective data from the users, such as movements, trajectories, gaze directions, operation errors, completion time, and audio sentiments to understand users' proxemics, social interactions, and emotions in virtual spaces. To do so, we need new production workflows that can create virtual movies that allow more interactions and can be instrumented to run controlled experiments.

22.7.1.5 Production opportunities for immersive narrative experiences

Recently, many novel media-watching experiences have been developed, such as interactive narratives that invite viewers to choose paths for lead characters (e.g., Black Mirror: Bandersnatch [88]); social TV or multiscreen TV that enable viewers to customize their viewing content and to comment during a show [89]; and cinematic VR with 360° videos that allow users to choose viewports [90]. However, these experiences were either limited at the interaction level or lacked narrativity. We expect that immersive and interactive movies with volumetric user representations will be the next innovation of media watching, where viewers are represented realistically and have the opportunity to sing along with the artists, re-watching a movie "inside," or even become a character in it. Schreer et al. [91] concluded the production challenges after one year of commercial volumetric video production, such as recording fast movements (e.g., basketball players); enabling a convincing integration of an actor into a virtual scene; recording extensive movements (e.g., walking along a road). Apart from volumetric videos, we are facing challenges in many other aspects of cinematic productions, including spatial audio design [92], attracting and directing viewers' attention [93], and creating interactable virtual objects and environments [94]. Crafting such new experiences requires incorporating interactive narratives, viewers' co-presence, interactive virtual environments, and social communications into production workflows.

22.7.2 Design recommendations for social VR
22.7.2.1 Conveying emotions in social VR

In many real-world deployments of our social VR applications, we found that the lack of facial expressions reduced the emotional connection between users, which negatively influenced the engagement of some participants. We recommend that it is important to enable the virtual human representations to show facial expressions or to implement a virtual interface for users to express visually their emotions. There is an increasing number of researchers working on removing the HMD to show the user's whole face in these volumetric representations [85], and training machine learning models to estimate emotions from the images of human faces wearing an HMD [95]. Another direction is to include visual cues of emotions in social VR. For example, emoticons and emojis are effective in conveying emotions in text messages [96]. We foresee the opportunities for designing new emoticons and emojis specifically for the virtual world, where users can experience new ways to use and interact with emoticons and emojis (e.g., throw an emoji to the air). Obrist et al. [97] investigated innovative mid-air haptic descriptions of specific emotions (e.g., happy, sad, excited, afraid), which inspires us to think about including these haptic descriptions in the next generation of virtual input devices (e.g., hand controllers).

22.7.2.2 Creative virtual environment

Users often comment that even the virtual environment looks realistic; it offers limited interaction resources, and there is a lack of serendipity to inspire them. We recommend that future social VR applications should, on one hand, provide sufficient resources (e.g., including an Internet search engine or various datasets for 3D models), and on the other hand, facilitate users to self-create virtual objects. For example, enable real-size 3D modeling or facilitate the interaction through brain-computer interfaces (BCIs) [98,99]. We see the potential of BCIs in automatically navigating users through the virtual space, enabling them to interact with virtual objects through mind-controlling, or in a more advanced manner, generating virtual visualizations based on users' thoughts.

22.7.2.3 Recreating the senses in social VR

In the *CakeVR* application, the users agreed that the 3D real-size virtual cake visualizations provide an instant overview of the co-design outcome. However, the fidelity of the virtual cake is not sufficient for them to imagine the flavor and texture of the cake. We would like to research recreating food-related senses in social VR, such as feeling the texture of a soft chiffon cake and a fluffy velvet cake, or even simulating the taste of the flavors. With incorporating haptic devices [100], the simulation of grasping, squeezing, pressing, lifting, and stroking in VR is getting promising. The handheld controllers developed by Benko et al. [101] enable users to feel 3D surfaces, textures, and forces that match the visual rendering. Apart from the multi-sensory experiences interacting with virtual objects, recreating the senses in the virtual environment is also an interesting direction to enhance the presence of social VR users. For example, the HMD accessories developed by Ranasinghe et al. [102] provide thermal and wind stimuli to simulate real-world environmental conditions, such as ambient temperatures and wind conditions.

22.7.2.4 Depth of interaction and fatigue

Many of our social VR applications aimed to cover the breadth of interaction to ensure users can have a complete virtual cake co-design, virtual clinic, or virtual museum experience. However, it is interesting to consider each sub-aspect of this experience. For example, what is the impact of creating impossible cakes or creating beyond-reality experiences, and how does that push designers to think more imaginatively inside the HMD? How can specific interactions (e.g., object snapping or finalizing a scale, and by whom) create more seamless interactions? In all the deployments, no users reported fatigue in using our applications. However, this needs further study for longer interaction periods, which may affect some users (e.g., older adults) [103].

22.7.2.5 Beyond reality experiences in social VR

During interviews of the social VR questionnaire validation study, a quarter of users stated they would like to perform activities in social VR that are not possible in the real world. Though exploring imaginary activities was not in our scope, it raises an important question about the role of social VR: are we more concerned with adapting our real-world social activities to social VR as is, or do we want to infuse our social environment with imaginary elements (e.g., do activities together on a virtual mountain)? Relatedly, should we relive the actual photo content, and will that exceed our experiences of collocated photo sharing? Though such questions may seem far away from current social VR technology, it highlights not only the role of embodiment in activities, such as photo sharing, but also what type of embodiment we assume [51]. For example, Schwind et al. [104] showed that women perceive lower levels of presence while using male avatar hands. Within our context, if a person shares a photograph of a time he was in the hospital with his friend, should the friend relive this memory by also being in the hospital, or from a 3rd person's point of view? Whose perspective do we take, the person as a patient or that of a supporting friend, and how does this affect the sense of presence? We can speculate whether our future communication tools (e.g., 3D video conferencing) should simulate physical F2F interactions as realistically as possible, or instead push activities only possible in the virtual world. For our social VR questionnaire, though it can be adapted to other social activities (e.g., collaborative tasks, gaming), these adaptations are assumed to be grounded in social interactions we draw from experience. The foregoing brings to question the underlying assumption that our current "gold standard" of comparing against F2F interactions will be the baseline of the future.

22.8. Conclusion

To achieve a more sustainable way of living, we are facing increasing pressure to reduce travel. Still, as a society, we need to efficiently and effectively, remotely and naturally, access healthcare and educational resources and collaborate. This first part of the chapter provides an overview of the design, implementation, and real-world deployment of social VR applications of multiple domains, supporting the remote communication of personalized healthcare, celebration, interactive access to cultural heritage, and immersive entertainment. The second part presents two experimental protocols: one is for developing and validating a social VR questionnaire based on a user-centered process; the other is for evaluating the visual quality of photorealistic digital humans in 3DoF and 6DoF conditions. As an emerging technology, social VR requires (1) the development of a standard protocol, including a set of qualitative and quantitative metrics for evaluating user experiences, and (2) a standard procedure of deploying social VR applications in the real world (e.g., hospitals and museums).

References

[1] M. Cai, J. Tanaka, Go together: providing nonverbal awareness cues to enhance co-located sensation in remote communication, Human-Centric Computing and Information Sciences 9 (1) (2019) 19.

[2] K. Inkpen, B. Taylor, S. Junuzovic, J. Tang, G. Venolia, Experiences2Go: sharing kids' activities outside the home with remote family members, in: Proceedings of the 2013 CSCW, 2013, pp. 1329–1340.

[3] J.G. Apostolopoulos, P.A. Chou, B. Culbertson, T. Kalker, M.D. Trott, S. Wee, The road to immersive communication, Proceedings of the IEEE 100 (4) (2012) 974–990.

[4] T. Szigeti, K. McMenamy, R. Saville, A. Glowacki, Cisco Telepresence Fundamentals, Cisco Press, 2009.

[5] J.R. Brubaker, G. Venolia, J.C. Tang, Focusing on shared experiences: moving beyond the camera in video communication, in: Proceedings of the Designing Interactive Systems Conference, 2012, pp. 96–105.

[6] C. Pidel, P. Ackermann, Collaboration in Virtual and Augmented Reality: A Systematic Overview, Springer, Cham, 2020, pp. 141–156, https://doi.org/10.1007/978-3-030-58465-8_10.

[7] J. Mütterlein, S. Jelsch, T. Hess, Specifics of collaboration in virtual reality: how immersion drives the intention to collaborate, in: PACIS, 2018, p. 318.

[8] V. Vinayagamoorthy, M. Glancy, C. Ziegler, R. Schäffer, Personalising the TV experience using augmented reality: an exploratory study on delivering synchronised sign language interpretation, in: Proceedings of the ACM CHI 2019, 2019, p. 532.

[9] J. Jansen, et al., A pipeline for multiparty volumetric video conferencing: transmission of point clouds over low latency DASH, in: Proceedings of the 11th ACM Multimedia Systems Conference, 2020, pp. 341–344, https://doi.org/10.1145/3339825.3393578.

[10] K.-F. Kaltenborn, O. Rienhoff, Virtual reality in medicine, Methods of Information in Medicine 32 (05) (1993) 407–417.

[11] D.G. McDonald, M.A. Shapiro, I'm not a real doctor, but I play one in virtual reality: implications of virtual reality for judgments about reality, Journal Of Communication 42 (4) (1992).

[12] R.M. Satava, Emerging medical applications of virtual reality: A surgeon's perspective, Artificial Intelligence in Medicine 6 (4) (1994) 281–288.

[13] G. Riva, Medical clinical uses of virtual worlds, in: The Oxford Handbook of Virtuality, Oxford University Press, New York, 2014, pp. 649–665.

[14] G. Riva, A. Dakanalis, F. Mantovani, Leveraging psychology of virtual body for health and wellness, in: The Handbook of the Psychology of Communication Technology, John Wiley & Sons, Ltd, Chichester, UK, 2015, pp. 528–547.

[15] P.E. Bee, et al., Psychotherapy mediated by remote communication technologies: a meta-analytic review, BMC Psychiatry 8 (1) (2008) 60.

[16] C.N. Rhyan, Travel and wait times are longest for health care services, https://altarum.org/travel-and-wait, 2019.

[17] J. Li, G. Chen, H. de Ridder, P. Cesar, Designing a social VR clinic for medical consultations, in: Extended Abstracts of the 2020 CHI Conference on Human Factors in Computing Systems, 2020, pp. 1–9.

[18] T. Xue, J. Li, G. Chen, P. Cesar, A social VR clinic for knee arthritis patients with haptics, in: Extended Abstracts of the 2020 ACM International Conference on Interactive Media Experience, 2020, pp. 1–5.

[19] R.P.C. Kessels, Patients' memory for medical information, Journal of the Royal Society of Medicine 96 (5) (2003) 219–222.

[20] A.M. Thomson, S.J. Cunningham, N.P. Hunt, A comparison of information retention at an initial orthodontic consultation, European Journal of Orthodontics 23 (2) (2001) 169–178.

[21] F. Gishen, N. Gostelow, Electronic consultations: a new art in clinical communication?, BMJ Innovations 4 (1) (2018) 1–4.

[22] M. Andrades, S. Kausar, A. Ambreen, Role and influence of the patient's companion in family medicine consultations: the patient's perspective, Journal of Family Medicine and Primary Care 2 (3) (2013) 283.

[23] S.R. Charsley, Wedding Cakes and Cultural History, Taylor & Francis, 1992.

[24] M. Douglas, Food in the Social Order, Routledge, 2014.

[25] E. Johansson, D. Berthelsen, The birthday cake: Social relations and professional practices around mealtimes with toddlers in child care, in: Lived Spaces of Infant-Toddler Education and Care, Springer, 2014, pp. 75–88.

[26] J. Sun, Z. Peng, W. Zhou, J.Y.H. Fuh, G.S. Hong, A. Chiu, A review on 3D printing for customized food fabrication, Procedia Manufacturing 1 (2015) 308–319.

[27] B. Sachdeva, How to prepare and conduct cake consultation, https://blog.bakingit.com/how-to-prepare-and-conduct-cake-consultation, Nov. 2015.

[28] P. Zipkin, The limits of mass customization, MIT Sloan Management Review 42 (3) (2001) 81.

[29] M. Miyatake, A. Watanabe, Y. Kawahara, Interactive cake decoration with whipped cream, in: Proceedings of the 2020 Multimedia on Cooking and Eating Activities Workshop, 2020, pp. 7–11.

[30] C. Anthes, R.J. García-Hernández, M. Wiedemann, D. Kranzlmüller, State of the art of virtual reality technology, in: 2016 IEEE Aerospace Conference, 2016, pp. 1–19.

[31] J.E. Venson, J. Berni, C.S. Maia, A.M. da Silva, M. d'Ornelas, A. Maciel, Medical imaging VR: can immersive 3D aid in diagnosis?, in: Proceedings of the 22nd ACM VRST, 2016, pp. 349–350.

[32] E.F. Churchill, D.N. Snowdon, A.J. Munro, Collaborative Virtual Environments: Digital Places and Spaces for Interaction, Springer Science & Business Media, 2012.

[33] J. Li, et al., Measuring and understanding photo sharing experiences in social virtual reality, in: Proceedings of the 2019 CHI Conference on Human Factors in Computing Systems, 2019, p. 667.

[34] Y. Mei, J. Li, H. de Ridder, P. Cesar, CakeVR: a social virtual reality (VR) tool for co-designing cakes, in: Proceedings of the 2021 CHI Conference on Human Factors in Computing Systems, 2021, pp. 1–14.

[35] J.H. Falk, L.D. Dierking, The Museum Experience, https://doi.org/10.4324/9781315417899, Jan. 2016, pp. 1–224.

[36] V. Rühse, The digital collection of the Rijksmuseum, in: Museum and Archive on the Move, Sep. 2017, pp. 37–56, https://doi.org/10.1515/9783110529630-003, Jan. 2016.

[37] P.F. Marty, Museum Management and Curatorship Museum websites and museum visitors: digital museum resources and their use, https://doi.org/10.1080/09647770701865410, 2008.

[38] B.J. Soren, N. Lemelin, 'Cyberpals!/Les Cybercopains!': A look at online museum visitor experiences, Curator: The Museum Journal 47 (1) (Jan. 2004) 55–83, https://doi.org/10.1111/J.2151-6952.2004.TB00366.X.

[39] J. Brooke, System Usability Scale (SUS): A Quick-and-Dirty Method of System Evaluation User Information, Digital Equipment Co Ltd, Reading, UK, 1986, vol. 43.

[40] J. Rieman, M. Franzke, D. Redmiles, Usability evaluation with the cognitive walkthrough, in: Conference Companion on Human Factors in Computing Systems, 1995, pp. 387–388.

[41] S. Gomillion, S. Gabriel, K. Kawakami, A.F. Young, Let's stay home and watch TV: The benefits of shared media use for close relationships, Journal of Social and Personal Relationships 34 (6) (2017) 855–874.

[42] D. Roth, et al., Avatar realism and social interaction quality in virtual reality, in: Proceedings - IEEE Virtual Reality 2016, Nov. 2016, pp. 277–278, https://doi.org/10.1109/VR.2016.7504761.

[43] H.J. Smith, M. Neff, Communication behavior in embodied virtual reality, in: Conference on Human Factors in Computing Systems - Proceedings, 2018, Nov. 2018, pp. 1–12, https://doi.org/10.1145/3173574.3173863.

[44] J. Williamson, J. Li, V. Vinayagamoorthy, D.A. Shamma, P. Cesar, Proxemics and social interactions in an instrumented virtual reality workshop, in: Proceedings of the 2021 CHI Conference on Human Factors in Computing Systems, 2021, pp. 1–13.

[45] F. de Simone, J. Li, H.G. Debarba, A. el Ali, S.N.B. Gunkel, P. Cesar, Watching videos together in social virtual reality: an experimental study on user's QoE, in: 2019 IEEE Conference on Virtual Reality and 3D User Interfaces (VR), 2019, pp. 890–891.

[46] J. Bucher, Storytelling for Virtual Reality: Methods and Principles for Crafting Immersive Narratives, Taylor & Francis, 2017.

[47] A. Revilla, et al., A collaborative VR murder mystery using photorealistic user representations, in: 2021 IEEE Conference on Virtual Reality and 3D User Interfaces Abstracts and Workshops (VRW), 2021, p. 766.

[48] E. Langbehn, P. Lubos, F. Steinicke, Evaluation of locomotion techniques for room-scale VR: Joystick, teleportation, and redirected walking, in: Proceedings of the Virtual Reality International Conference-Laval Virtual, 2018, pp. 1–9.

[49] J. Li, et al., Evaluating the user experience of a photorealistic social VR movie, https://doi.org/10.1109/ISMAR52148.2021.00044, Nov. 2021, pp. 284–293.

[50] M.E. Latoschik, D. Roth, D. Gall, J. Achenbach, T. Waltemate, M. Botsch, The effect of avatar realism in immersive social virtual realities, in: Proceedings of the 23rd ACM Symposium on Virtual Reality Software and Technology, 2017, p. 39.

[51] T. Waltemate, D. Gall, D. Roth, M. Botsch, M.E. Latoschik, The impact of avatar personalization and immersion on virtual body ownership, presence, and emotional response, IEEE Transactions on Visualization and Computer Graphics 24 (4) (2018) 1643–1652.

[52] S. Cho, S. Kim, J. Lee, J. Ahn, J. Han, Effects of volumetric capture avatars on social presence in immersive virtual environments, in: 2020 IEEE Conference on Virtual Reality and 3D User Interfaces (VR), 2020, pp. 26–34.

[53] B.G. Witmer, M.J. Singer, Measuring presence in virtual environments: A presence questionnaire, Presence: Teleoperators & Virtual Environments 7 (3) (1998) 225–240, https://doi.org/10.1162/105474698565686.

[54] M. Slater, M. Usoh, A. Steed, Depth of presence in virtual environments, Presence: Teleoperators & Virtual Environments 3 (2) (1994) 130–144, https://doi.org/10.1007/s13398-014-0173-7.2.

[55] C. Jennett, et al., Measuring and defining the experience of immersion in games, International Journal of Human-Computer Studies 66 (9) (Nov. 2008) 641–661, https://doi.org/10.1016/J.IJHCS.2008.04.004.

[56] P. Srivastava, A. Rimzhim, P. Vijay, S. Singh, S. Chandra, Desktop VR is better than non-ambulatory HMD VR for spatial learning, Frontiers in Robotics and AI 6 (2019) 50.

[57] Y. Shu, Y.-Z. Huang, S.-H. Chang, M.-Y. Chen, Do virtual reality head-mounted displays make a difference? A comparison of presence and self-efficacy between head-mounted displays and desktop computer-facilitated virtual environments, Virtual Reality 23 (4) (2019) 437–446.

[58] K. Brunnström, et al., Qualinet white paper on definitions of quality of experience, https://hal.archives-ouvertes.fr/hal-00977812, 2013. (Accessed 22 December 2021).

[59] U. Reiter, et al., Factors influencing quality of experience, in: T-Labs Series in Telecommunication Services, 2014, pp. 55–72, https://doi.org/10.1007/978-3-319-02681-7_4.

[60] ISO - ISO 9241-210:2019 - Ergonomics of human-system interaction — Part 210: Human-centred design for interactive systems, https://www.iso.org/standard/77520.html, 2019. (Accessed 22 December 2021).

[61] A.P.O.S. Vermeeren, E.L.-C. Law, V. Roto, M. Obrist, J. Hoonhout, K. Väänänen-Vainio-Mattila, User experience evaluation methods: current state and development needs, in: Proceedings of the 6th Nordic Conference on Human-Computer Interaction: Extending Boundaries, 2010, pp. 521–530, https://doi.org/10.1145/1868914.1868973.

[62] E. Siahaan, et al., Visual Quality of Experience: A Metric-Driven Perspective, PhD Thesis, Delft University of Technology, 2018, https://doi.org/10.4233/uuid:d0a8f1b0-d829-4a34-be5a-1ff7aa8679ca.

[63] M. Chessa, G. Maiello, A. Borsari, P.J. Bex, The perceptual quality of the Oculus Rift for immersive virtual reality, Human-Computer Interaction 34 (1) (Jan. 2016) 51–82, https://doi.org/10.1080/07370024.2016.1243478.

[64] K. Chamilothori, J. Wienold, M. Andersen, Adequacy of immersive virtual reality for the perception of daylit spaces: comparison of real and virtual environments, Leukos 15 (2–3) (Jul. 2018) 203–226, https://doi.org/10.1080/15502724.2017.1404918.

[65] D. Egan, S. Brennan, J. Barrett, Y. Qiao, C. Timmerer, N. Murray, An evaluation of Heart Rate and ElectroDermal Activity as an objective QoE evaluation method for immersive virtual reality environments, in: 2016 8th International Conference on Quality of Multimedia Experience, QoMEX 2016, Jun. 2016, https://doi.org/10.1109/QOMEX.2016.7498964.

[66] M. Usoh, E. Catena, S. Arman, M. Slater, Using presence questionnaires in reality, Presence: Teleoperators & Virtual Environments 9 (5) (Oct. 2000) 497–503, https://doi.org/10.1162/105474600566989.

[67] M. Garau, M. Slater, V. Vinayagamoorthy, A. Brogni, A. Steed, M.A. Sasse, The impact of avatar realism and eye gaze control on perceived quality of communication in a shared immersive virtual environment, in: Proceedings of the SIGCHI Conference on Human Factors in Computing Systems, 2003, pp. 529–536.

[68] P. Heidicker, E. Langbehn, F. Steinicke, Influence of avatar appearance on presence in social VR, in: 2017 IEEE Symposium on 3D User Interfaces (3DUI), 2017, pp. 233–234.

[69] M. Slater, Measuring presence: a response to the Witmer and Singer presence questionnaire, Presence: Teleoperators & Virtual Environments 8 (5) (Nov. 1999) 560–565, https://doi.org/10.1162/105474699566477.

[70] T. Schubert, F. Friedmann, H. Regenbrecht, The experience of presence: Factor analytic insights, Presence: Teleoperators & Virtual Environments 10 (3) (2001) 266–281.

[71] D. Maloney, G. Freeman, D.Y. Wohn, Talking without a voice: understanding non-verbal communication in social virtual reality, in: Proceedings of the ACM on Human-Computer Interaction (CSCW2), 2020, pp. 1–25.

[72] W. Albert, T. Tullis, Measuring the User Experience: Collecting, Analyzing, and Presenting Usability Metrics, Newnes, 2013.

[73] D.A. Norman, S.W. Draper, User Centered System Design; New Perspectives on Human-Computer Interaction, L. Erlbaum Associates Inc., 1986.

[74] F.S. Visser, P.J. Stappers, R. der Lugt, E.B.N. Sanders, Contextmapping: experiences from practice, CoDesign 1 (2) (2005) 119–149.

[75] J. Steuer, Defining virtual reality: Dimensions determining telepresence, Journal of Communication 42 (4) (1992) 73–93.

[76] M. Steen, M. Eriksson, J. Kort, P. Ljungstrand, (PDF) D8.8 user evaluations of TA2 concepts, https://www.researchgate.net/publication/291351579_D88_User_Evaluations_of_TA2_Concepts, 2012.

[77] N.C. Nilsson, S. Serafin, R. Nordahl, The perceived naturalness of virtual locomotion methods devoid of explicit leg movements, in: Proceedings of Motion on Games, 2013, pp. 155–164.

[78] F. Biocca, C. Harms, J. Gregg, The networked minds measure of social presence: Pilot test of the factor structure and concurrent validity, in: 4th Annual International Workshop on Presence, Philadelphia, PA, 2001, pp. 1–9.

[79] D.T. Van Bel, K.C. Smolders, W.A. IJsselsteijn, Y.A.W. De Kort, Social connectedness: concept and measurement, in: The Proceedings of 5th International Conference on Intelligent Environments (IE '09), July 20-21, 2009, Barcelona, Spain, 2009, pp. 67–74.

[80] A.B. Costello, J.W. Osborne, Best practices in exploratory factor analysis, Practical Assessment, Research & Evaluation 10 (7) (2005) 1–9.

[81] L.R. Fabrigar, D.T. Wegener, R.C. MacCallum, E.J. Strahan, Evaluating the use of exploratory factor analysis in psychological research, Psychological Methods 4 (3) (1999) 272.

[82] M. Norris, L. Lecavalier, Evaluating the use of exploratory factor analysis in developmental disability psychological research, Journal of Autism and Developmental Disorders 40 (1) (Nov. 2010) 8–20, https://doi.org/10.1007/s10803-009-0816-2.

[83] A.S. Islind, U.L. Snis, T. Lindroth, J. Lundin, K. Cerna, G. Steineck, The virtual clinic: two-sided affordances in consultation practice, Computer Supported Cooperative Work (CSCW) (2019) 1–34.

[84] S. Orts-Escolano, et al., Holoportation: Virtual 3D teleportation in real-time, in: Proceedings of the 29th Annual Symposium on User Interface Software and Technology, 2016, pp. 741–754.

[85] Y. Zhao, et al., Mask-off: Synthesizing face images in the presence of head-mounted displays, in: 2019 IEEE Conference on Virtual Reality and 3D User Interfaces (VR), 2019, pp. 267–276.

[86] C.N. van der Wal, A. Hermans, T. Bosse, Inducing fear: Cardboard virtual reality and 2D video, in: International Conference on Human-Computer Interaction, 2017, pp. 711–720.

[87] T. Jamieson, et al., Virtual Care: A Framework for a Patient-Centric System, Women's College Hospital Institute for Health Systems Solutions and Virtual Care, Toronto, 2015.

[88] C. Roth, H. Koenitz, Bandersnatch, yea or nay? Reception and user experience of an interactive digital narrative video, in: Proceedings of the 2019 ACM International Conference on Interactive Experiences for TV and Online Video, 2019, pp. 247–254.

[89] J. Li, T. Röggla, M. Glancy, J. Jansen, P. Cesar, A new production platform for authoring object-based multiscreen TV viewing experiences, in: Proceedings of the 2018 ACM International Conference on Interactive Experiences for TV and Online Video, 2018, pp. 115–126, https://doi.org/10.1145/3210825.3210834.

[90] J. Mateer, Directing for Cinematic Virtual Reality: how the traditional film director's craft applies to immersive environments and notions of presence, Journal of Media Practice 18 (1) (2017) 14–25.

[91] O. Schreer, et al., Lessons learned during one year of commercial volumetric video production, SMPTE Motion Imaging Journal 129 (9) (2020) 31–37.

[92] L. Reed, P. Phelps, Audio reproduction in virtual reality cinemas—position paper, in: 2019 IEEE Conference on Virtual Reality and 3D User Interfaces (VR), 2019, pp. 1513–1516.

[93] K. Dooley, Storytelling with virtual reality in 360-degrees: a new screen grammar, Studies in Australasian Cinema 11 (3) (2017) 161–171.

[94] M. Moehring, B. Froehlich, Effective manipulation of virtual objects within arm's reach, in: 2011 IEEE Virtual Reality Conference, 2011, pp. 131–138.

[95] H. Yong, J. Lee, J. Choi, Emotion recognition in gamers wearing head-mounted display, in: 2019 IEEE Conference on Virtual Reality and 3D User Interfaces (VR), 2019, pp. 1251–1252.

[96] D. Thompson, R. Filik, Sarcasm in written communication: Emoticons are efficient markers of intention, Journal of Computer-Mediated Communication 21 (2) (2016) 105–120.

[97] M. Obrist, S. Subramanian, E. Gatti, B. Long, T. Carter, Emotions mediated through mid-air haptics, in: Proceedings of the 33rd Annual ACM Conference on Human Factors in Computing Systems, 2015, pp. 2053–2062.

[98] F. Lotte, et al., Exploring large virtual environments by thoughts using a brain–computer interface based on motor imagery and high-level commands, Presence: Teleoperators & Virtual Environments 19 (1) (2010) 54–70.

[99] J. Jankowski, M. Hachet, A survey of interaction techniques for interactive 3D environments, in: Eurographics 2013 - STAR, May 2013, Girona, Spain, 2013.

[100] S.B. Schorr, A.M. Okamura, Fingertip tactile devices for virtual object manipulation and exploration, in: Proceedings of the 2017 CHI Conference on Human Factors in Computing Systems, 2017, pp. 3115–3119.

[101] H. Benko, C. Holz, M. Sinclair, E. Ofek, NormalTouch and TextureTouch: High-fidelity 3D haptic shape rendering on handheld virtual reality controllers, in: Proceedings of the 29th Annual Symposium on User Interface Software and Technology, 2016, pp. 717–728.

[102] N. Ranasinghe, P. Jain, S. Karwita, D. Tolley, E.Y.-L. Do, Ambiotherm: enhancing sense of presence in virtual reality by simulating real-world environmental conditions, in: Proceedings of the 2017 CHI Conference on Human Factors in Computing Systems, 2017, pp. 1731–1742.

[103] M. Hirota, et al., Comparison of visual fatigue caused by head-mounted display for virtual reality and two-dimensional display using objective and subjective evaluation, Ergonomics 62 (6) (2019) 759–766.

[104] V. Schwind, P. Knierim, C. Tasci, P. Franczak, N. Haas, N. Henze, 'These are not my hands!': Effect of gender on the perception of avatar hands in virtual reality, in: Proceedings of the 2017 CHI Conference on Human Factors in Computing Systems, 2017, pp. 1577–1582, https://doi.org/10.1145/3025453.3025602.

Index

Symbols

2D
  codec, 327, 329, 331, 338, 343, 353
  convolutional layers, 106, 219
  quality metrics, 543
  video coding conventional, 411, 412

3D
  color look-up tables, 293
  computer graphics, 491
  convolutional layers, 106, 219
  depth cues, 475
  liver modeling, 562
  video live capturing technology, 610

3D extension of HEVC (3D-HEVC), 212
4D prediction mode (4DPM), 215
4D transform mode (4DTM), 215
6DoF rendering, 10, 13

A

Absolute category rating (ACR), 19, 85, 88, 89,
    127, 271, 509

Acquisition
  constraints, 370
  data, 575
  devices, 13, 30
  general principles, 29
  geometry, 290
  LF video, 267
  method, 358
  model, 364
  process, 8, 32, 359, 364
  protocols, 561
  sparse, 369
  systems, 21, 36
  time, 559

Adaptation
  service, 428
  set, 429, 431, 432

Adaptive bitrate (ABR) streaming, 16
Adaptive feature adjustment (AFA), 460
Adaptive streaming, 21, 126, 150, 310, 429, 431,
    435
  algorithms, 431
  framework, 16, 310, 431

  mechanism, 433
  scene, 310
  strategies, 17
  systems, 100
  viewport, 97

Advanced coding tools, 364
Advanced video coding (AVC), 207, 210, 211
Adversarial texture loss, 307
Alternate representation, 193
Alternating DSIS, 521

Anchor
  codec, 514
  frames, 364
  HEVC, 219
  MPEG, 514
  views, 188, 196

Animatable volumetric videos, 313, 316

Animated mesh (AM), 389, 402, 404, 405
  compression, 402–404, 408, 409
  sequences, 406, 416
  sequences color, 408

Animation
  baked mocap, 586
  capabilities, 300
  compression tools, 410
  control, 586
  facial expressions, 305
  flexibility, 306
  generic, 410
  mesh, 303
  method, 303
  network, 308
  objects, 316
  parameter, 308
  process, 290
  rigid body, 584
  synthesis, 300
  systems, 584
  template mesh, 300
  virtual characters, 321
  virtual human characters, 299

Animation framework extension (AFX), 401

Printed in the United States
by Baker & Taylor Publisher Services